MODERN
TIMES

—— *Man & Music* ——

MODERN
TIMES

From World War I to the present

EDITED BY ROBERT P. MORGAN

First published in the United Kingdom 1993 by
The Macmillan Press Limited
Houndmills, Basingstoke, Hampshire RG21 2XS
and London

Associated companies in Auckland, Delhi, Dublin, Gaborone,
Hamburg, Harare, Hong Kong, Johannesburg, Kuala Lumpur,
Lagos, Manzini, Melbourne, Mexico City, Nairobi, New York,
Singapore, Tokyo

ISBN 0-333-51599-4 (hardback)

British Library Cataloguing in Publication Data
Modern Times: From World War I to the Present. –
(Man & Music Series; Vol. 8)
    I. Morgan, Robert P. II. Series
    780.9

Typeset by The Spartan Press Ltd, Lymington, Hants
Printed in Hong Kong

Contents

Modern Times

Abbreviations

Grove6	*The New Grove Dictionary of Music and Musicians*
GroveA	*The New Grove Dictionary of American Music*
IRCAM	*Institut de Recherche et de Coordination Acoustique/Musique*
JAMS	*Journal of the American Musicological Society*
JMT	*Journal of Music Theory*
ML	*Music and Letters*
MQ	*The Musical Quarterly*
NZM	*Neue Zeitschrift für Musik*
PNM	*Perspectives of New Music*

Illustration
Acknowledgments

The publisher would like to thank the following institutions and individuals who have kindly supplied and given permission to reproduce copyright illustrative material. Every effort has been made to contact copyright holders; we apologize to anyone who may have been omitted.

Archives de la Fondation Erik Satie, Paris: p.44; Musée des Beaux-Arts, Rouen: p.45; Dansmuseet, Stockholm: p.48; Editions Salabert, Paris/United Music Publishers Ltd.: p.57; Österreichische Nationalbibliothek (Bildarchiv), Vienna: pp.69, 78; Österreichisches Institut für Zeitgeschichte, Vienna: p.76; © Deutscher Verlag für Musik, Leipzig (music) and © Suhrkamp Verlag, Frankfurt am Main 1967 from *Gesammelte Werke* (text): p.86; Tate Gallery, London: p.93; Universal Edition, Vienna: p.96; Weill-Lenya Research Center, Kurt Weill Foundation for Music, New York: p.99; British Library (Newspaper Library), London: p.113; Private Collection/Fondazione Giorgio Cini, Venice: p.115; Signora Giulietta Malipiero: p.117; Moravské Muzeum, Brno: p.134; Néprajzi Múzeum, Budapest / photo Sándor Gönyei Ébner: p.135; Society for Cooperation in Russian and Soviet Studies, London: pp.143, 149, 156, 159, 295; Thomas L. Rhea, Buffalo, NY: p.146; Kongelige Bibliotek, Copenhagen: pp.165, 176; The Hulton-Deutsch Collection, London: pp.182, 202; The Bunyan Church and Museum Appeal, Bedford: p.189; From E. Salter, *Edith Sitwell*, reprinted by Bloomsbury Books (1988): p.191; Architectural Association, London: p.209; Music Division, Library of Congress, Washington, DC/Associated Music Publishers, Inc., New York: p.212; © 1931, Mills Music Inc., USA, reproduced by permission of EMI Music Publishing Ltd., London: p.217; Library of Congress (Irving Lowens Collection), Washington, DC: p.220; British Library, London: p.233; Board of Trustees of the Victoria and Albert Museum, London: p.252; © Lipnitzki-Viollet, Paris: p.258; Photo Philips, Eindhoven: p.266; Josef Svoboda, Prague: p.283; Staatsoper, Hamburg / photo Fritz Peyer: p.284; Camilla Jessel Panufnik, London: pp.298, 301; Musée National d'Art Moderne, Centre Georges Pompidou, Paris: p.303; Columbia-Princeton Electronic Music Center, Princeton, NJ: p.319; Terry Riley, California: p.320; Val Wilmer/Format, London: p.324; Cunningham Dance Foundation Inc., New York / photo Hervé Gloaguen: p.331; From M. Nyman, *Experimental Music: Cage and Beyond* (1974): p.336; Saatchi Collection, London: p.343; © Centre Georges Pompidou, Paris: p.355; Staatsgalerie, Stuttgart: p.362; Stella Cardew, London: p.366; © 1979 by Zen-On Music Co., Ltd., Tokyo: p.370; Universal Edition (London) Ltd / photo Nigel Luckhurst: p.380; Photo Richard A. Matthews: p.393; Color & Light, Berkeley, CA/photo Richard Blair: p.406.

Preface

The *Man and Music* series of books – eight in number, chronologically organized – were originally conceived in conjunction with the television programmes of the same name, of which the first was shown by Granada Television International and Channel 4 in 1986. These programmes were designed to examine the development of music in particular places during particular periods in the history of Western civilization.

The books have the same objective. Each is designed to cover a segment of Western musical history; the breaks between them are planned to correspond with significant historical junctures. Since historical junctures, or indeed junctures in stylistic change, rarely happen with the neat simultaneity that the historian's or the editor's orderly mind might wish for, most volumes have 'ragged' ends and beginnings: for example, the Renaissance volume terminates, in Italy, in the 1570s and 80s, but continues well into the 17th century in parts of northern Europe.

These books do not, however, make up a history of music in the traditional sense. The reader will not find technical, stylistic discussion in them; anyone wanting to trace the detailed development of the texture of the madrigal or the rise and fall of sonata form will need to look elsewhere. Rather, it is the intention in these volumes to show in what context, and as a result of what forces – social, cultural, intellectual – the madrigal or sonata form came into being and took its particular shape. The intention is to view musical history not as a series of developments in some hermetic world of its own but rather as a series of responses to social, economic and political circumstances and to religious and intellectual stimuli. We want to explain not simply *what* happened, but *why* it happened, and why it happened when and where it did.

We have chosen to follow what might be called a geographical, or perhaps a topographical, approach: to focus, in each chapter, on a particular place and to examine its music in the light of its particular situation. Thus, in most of these volumes, the chapters – once past the introductory one, contributed by the volume editor – are each devoted to a city or a region. This system has inevitably needed some modification when dealing with very early or very recent times, for reasons (opposite ones, of course) to do with communication and cultural spread.

These books do not attempt to treat musical history comprehensively. Their editors have chosen for discussion the musical centres that they see as the most significant and the most interesting; many lesser ones inevitably escape individual discussion, though the patterns of their musical life may be discernible by analogy with others or may be separately referred to in the opening, editorial chapter. We hope, however, that a new kind of picture of musical history may begin to emerge from these volumes, and that this picture may be more accessible to the general reader, responsive to music but untrained in its techniques, than others arising from more traditional approaches. In spite of the large numbers of lovers of music, musical histories have never enjoyed the appeal to a broad, intelligent general readership in the way that histories of art, architecture or literature have done: these books represent an attempt to reach such a readership and explain music in terms that may quicken their interest.

★

The television programmes and books were initially planned in close collaboration with Sir Denis Forman, then Chairman of Granada Television International. The approach was worked out in more detail with several of the volume editors, among whom I am particularly grateful to Iain Fenlon for the time he has generously given to discussion of the problems raised by this approach to musical history, and also to Alexander Ringer and James McKinnon for their valuable advice and support. Discussion with Bamber Gascoigne and Tony Cash, in the course of the making of the initial television programmes, also proved of value. I am grateful to Celia Thomson for drafting the non-musical part of the chronologies that appear in each volume and to Elisabeth Agate and her colleagues for their invaluable work as picture editors in bringing the volumes to visual life.

London, 1993   STANLEY SADIE

Chapter I

The Modern Age

ROBERT P. MORGAN

This volume, covering music from 1918 to the present, deals with a period that we feel to be, even when viewed as a whole, in some sense distinctly our own. Thus we continue to refer to the music of the entire period as 'contemporary', or 'modern', adjectives whose meaning appears to be seriously stretched when one considers that the earliest works encompassed date back almost three-quarters of a century. In spite of its unprecedented technical, stylistic and expressive variety, however, the music of this turbulent epoch is in some significant measure all of a piece. It is this common ground, then, that this introduction attempts to survey. The individual chapters that follow, directed towards the peculiarities of distinct geographical regions and more limited time-spans, mostly stress differences in musical developments; whereas their focus is on musical life and practice as a whole, in this chapter we shall concentrate on the compositional ideas embodied in twentieth-century music itself and the relationship between these ideas and the intellectual and cultural climate of the time.

THE END OF AN ERA

The choice of 1918 as a starting-point raises the question: why not include the whole century? Our almost constant use of the term 'twentieth-century music' suggests that the entire period has some larger coherence; and a strong case can be made for treating it as a whole. Yet in many respects the end of World War I provided a more fundamental historical division than the turn of the century. As a cataclysmic event of unprecedented proportion, the war marked a decisive break, evident not only externally, in the altered shape of the map of the world (which had to be radically redrawn according to the conditions of the peace treaties that brought the war to an end), but internally, in the transformation of basic beliefs concerning human nature and the nature of civilization.

Older political entities, such as tsarist Russia and the Austro-Hungarian Empire, disappeared after the war. The New World, taking its lead from the growing prominence of the USA, became a major new

1

participant in international affairs. The sheer destructive power of the confrontation left deep scars. Countless citizens suffered from its effects through loss of family and friends, of homes and property, and of economic and political stability. The brutal impersonality of modern machine warfare, here experienced for the first time on a global scale, shattered the world, leaving it irrevocably altered.

Perhaps even more far-reaching than these physical and geographical transformations, however, was the war's impact on attitudes. The confrontation created a cultural divide separating an old world view from a new one, bringing to an end the extended tradition of optimistic rationalism that had dominated European thought since the Renaissance. This tradition, based on an unshakable belief in human achievement and the steady progress of civilization, had been reflected before World War I in a series of remarkable scientific discoveries which seemed to foretell a future where all material needs would be overcome. Such inventions as the railway, electric light, the motor car and the aeroplane, along with improvements in hygiene, plumbing, engineering and communications, had transformed the material conditions of life with startling rapidity. An extended period of relative international peace added to a sense of increased prosperity and well-being. As the twentieth century dawned, the world appeared to be entering a new age of personal comfort and international harmony, when its inhabitants would be free to develop their potential in an atmosphere of security and growth. Even as signs of war began to appear, the view prevailed that, given the high state of civilization and the pervasive atmosphere of international cooperation and good will, a major conflagration was not only avoidable but unthinkable.

World War I put an end to these illusions, demonstrating that all the recently acquired scientific and technical achievements, touted for their ability to reduce the burdens of mankind, could just as readily be used to bring about human destruction. By the time the armistice was signed in 1919 there had been an almost universal reaction against the progressive mentality of the pre-war years. A new mood developed, favouring a more modest, sober and scaled-down approach to human activities, with the emphasis on present concerns rather than utopian possibilities. The change in ideology was dramatic, and so fundamental that it could be said to mark the real beginnings of the twentieth century as a cultural entity.

FIN-DE-SIÈCLE DISSOLUTIONS

The fact that the world war did take place indicates that conditions during the years before it were by no means as positive as many felt them to be. Signs of discontent and change were in evidence long before the confrontation broke out. Viewed in this light, the war can be seen not so much as a sudden catastrophe that brought an old way of life to an end but as the culminating blow in a series of profound shifts in attitude that gradually undermined stability and well-being. Since the course of twentieth-century art was deeply affected by these earlier developments, we will consider them before examining the new artistic climate that coalesced in the postwar period.

Paradoxically, the developments in question were partly brought about by the mentality of scientific rationalism that was responsible for the aura of pre-war optimism, the ultimate consequence of which was to erode the very belief in stability and progress upon which the previous age had grounded its faith. Late nineteenth-century discoveries in physics called into question the Newtonian concept of a stable universe controlled by predictable mechanistic processes, consisting of solid atoms moving in absolute time and space. The field of quantum mechanics produced unexpected revelations indicating that energy, rather than being consistent and continuous, was released through a series of discrete quantities whose behaviour was in significant measure unforeseeable. 'Natural' laws thereby lost their deterministic character, assuming instead an essentially statistical flavour. More generally, many of the leading scientific figures of the day, including Ernst Mach, Henri Poincaré and Hans Vaihinger, came to discard the traditional view of science as the neutral description of a fixed and objectively knowable external reality. They saw it rather as a set of subjective hypotheses, inevitably distorted by the particular place and disposition of the observer. These developments culminated in the revolutionary theories of Albert Einstein, who in the first decade of the new century postulated that all aspects of reality, including time, space and the scientific observer, were dependent on and affected by one another. Reality was redefined as 'relative'.

These scientific tendencies were closely paralleled by developments in other areas of thought. In philosophy, Nietzsche questioned all objective bases for truth and viewed reason as an illusion. Each age and culture shaped its own beliefs according to its own particular needs. Indeed, it was the responsibility of each individual to develop a personal view of the world. (Nietzsche especially attacked his contemporaries for their deep-seated commitment to the superiority of the Western scientific view.) Correspondingly, the eminent historian Wilhelm Dilthy interpreted knowledge of history not as an objective portrayal of a determinate set of events but as an empathetic and intuitive interaction between the historian and the past.

Perhaps the most profound mental revolution was evident in psychology, in Sigmund Freud's belief that the rational and civilized aspects of human behaviour, so praised by his contemporaries, were but the outer shell of a volatile, multi-levelled psyche. Human actions and attitudes, according to Freud, were controlled by deeply buried instincts, primary natural urges about which one had very little conscious knowledge and over which very limited control. Men and women, far from being rational and in charge of their own destinies, were driven by irrational impulses and hidden desires. In Freud's psychology, the much-revered civilized core was reinterpreted as only a superficial veneer.

These transformations in assumptions about human nature and the external world, and the degree to which that world can be grasped by rational processes, found precise equivalents in the arts. The correlations are perhaps most immediately evident in the visual arts: during the nineteenth century the time-honoured, deeply ingrained tradition of painting and sculpture as an objective and faithful reflection of the surrounding world – as a 'mirror of Nature' – began giving way to a more subjective view of art as an expression of individual emotion or an evocation of momentary effect. This tendency towards a more personal and idiosyncratic depiction of reality found expression, for example, in the French impressionists' commitment to the more accidental and impermanent aspects of visual experience. Their paintings presented only fleeting images, glimpses of objects whose solidity was compromised by changing conditions of light and shadow, or by the atmospheric effects of fog, smoke and rain.

If the impressionists offered a more subjective and fragile vision of reality, the post-impressionists like Paul Cézanne increasingly reduced it to a set of complex formal relationships. Cézanne remarked in a letter to a friend (the artist Emile Bernard) that he wished to reduce Nature to its most basic components: cylinders, spheres and cones. Maurice Denis, a follower of Cézanne and a leading theorist of turn-of-the-century art, defined painting as 'essentially a plane surface covered with colors assembled in a certain order'.[1] Such ideas culminated in the cubist revolution of the first decade of the new century. Pablo Picasso and Georges Braque broke objects up into their constituent parts and rearranged them in patterns dictated solely by imagination, producing a 'relative' visual universe echoing the physical one proposed by Einstein at almost exactly the same time.

Other painters, notably Van Gogh and Kandinsky, distorted objects to project them in terms of their own subjective, emotional responses rather than as independent entities separable from personal experience. In Kandinsky this led to the creation of abstract, 'non-representational' paintings, abjuring all pretence of intersubjective, external reality. The only subject matter was an interior truth, uniquely communicated by the personal vision of the artist.

THE PRE-WAR MUSICAL REVOLUTION

It might seem that music, as an art largely dissociated from everyday events, would be immune from these tendencies shaped by a more subjective, contingent and unstable conception of the outer world. Yet composers were as deeply affected by these developments as were other artists. Music's apparent lack of connection with external reality conferred upon it the unique status of 'absolute' art, leading it to be ranked first among all the arts during the nineteenth century. Yet music, as much as the other arts, was tied to objective conventions that transcended the individual composer, linking musical expression to a common core of widely accepted technical practices. Indeed, Western music of the eighteenth and nineteenth centuries was grounded in a sort of common language, a system of relationships based on well-defined assumptions regulating tonal centricity, harmonic stability (defined exclusively with reference to a single type of harmony, the triad) and goal-directed chordal progression. With its commitment to a single pitch centre, in relation to which all other pitches acquired a position of hierarchical subordination (and from which they derived their entire meaning), this traditional tonal system formed an ideal model for the classical beliefs in fixed truth, permanence and order.

Although virtually every Western composer conformed to this musical system to some degree even into the final years of the nineteenth century, its hegemony as a centralized musical language began to give way as more composers began undermining its structural foundations. Nor was it coincidence that developments towards a more subjective and personalized conception of reality were accompanied by this corresponding erosion of the conventions of traditional tonality during the waning years of the century. Composers, mirroring the broader tendency, became increasingly interested in expressing musical ambiguity, instability, even disorder. As they sought a uniquely personal vision, as unlike that of other composers as possible, the common language of tonality became a drawback.

To achieve such a vision, tonal relationships had to be treated in an ever more idiosyncratic manner. In the Germanic world this led to increased chromaticism (in Reger and Strauss, for example) – that is, the use of pitches more distantly related to a piece's tonal centre, producing the kind of strong tensions and expressivity associated with tonal conflict and ambiguity. In other parts of Europe there was widespread incorporation of materials from the folk and popular traditions of outlying countries (in Musorgsky, Smetana and Mahler, for example) or from the musical traditions of distant cultures or the distant past (Debussy and Satie).

The more progressive strains of European composition in the latter nineteenth century thus sacrificed what was shared and conventional in favour of what was personal, idiosyncratic and exotic. The common, unified language of European musical classicism, which only a hundred years previously could be referred to with only minor exaggeration as a 'universal language' (at least within the context of the

Western world), gave way to a range of personal and regional musical dialects, each with its own expressive nuances and technical vocabulary. The new stage was particularly reflected in the music of Mahler, whose earliest works began appearing well before the turn of the century. Here the flagrant juxtaposition of many types and levels of music, joined in a motley mixture that seemed to emphasize the contrasting characters as much as possible (even while also attempting to mediate among them), gave notice that music was moving into a new and different era. The twentieth century thus inherited a musical tradition already showing extreme signs of wear and tear, splintered into a number of diverse tendencies all apparently heading in different directions. The first decade or so of the new century, the years immediately preceding World War I, brought this tradition to its ultimate collapse.

Although the final dissolution can be traced in any number of different developments that took place during this brief period of less than fifteen years (which proved to be among the most turbulent – if not indeed the most turbulent – in the entire history of European music), it achieved its most emphatic form in the music of the Austrian composer Arnold Schoenberg. As the new century began, Schoenberg was working on an enormous vocal-orchestral composition, his *Gurrelieder*. Though chromatic, this work was still tonal, and its musical and dramatic conception remained comfortably within the mainstream, post-Wagnerian Germanic tradition. Yet by the end of the first decade Schoenberg had abandoned traditional tonality. Firmly espousing a belief in musical 'progress' (the continuing evolution towards more complex musical structures, a corollary to the more general view of progress discussed above) and a commitment to highly individualized personal expression, Schoenberg pushed his work ever closer to the limits until, as he wrote in 1908, he 'broke all barriers of a past aesthetic', completely renouncing the essential constraints associated with traditional tonality.

Schoenberg abandoned the triad as the sole basis for harmonic structure (avoiding triads altogether at this stage) and no longer treated one pitch as a privileged tonal centre. Instead he adopted an 'atonal' musical universe within which all pitches, at least in principle, were equally related, proclaiming what he called 'the emancipation of the dissonance': the right of all notes to exist on their own terms, without reference to some higher tonal authority. In so doing he negated a compositional principle that had governed Western music since its beginnings.

Schoenberg's 'revolution', though particularly drastic, was but one among many. Stravinsky's development during the pre-war years was almost equally consequential in transforming the nature of the art. While avoiding Schoenberg's total chromaticism, Stravinsky also adopted an essentially relativistic conception of tonal hierarchy, based partly on symmetrical polarities. Largely eschewing traditional notions of harmonic progression, he treated pitch complexes as static entities, as blocks of sound with little inclination to move to other sonorities. This enabled him to focus on the rhythmic dimension – on intricate repetitions, combinations and transformations of purely durational patterns – in a manner unprecedented in Western music. The famous riot that took place in Paris at the première of *The Rite of Spring* in 1913 reminds us of how radically new this music sounded at the time, as revolutionary in its own way as Schoenberg's atonality. Indeed music, one might argue, had been transformed almost as much between 1907 and 1913 – that is, between the appearance of Schoenberg's first post-tonal works and the première of Stravinsky's *Rite* – as it had been in the entire preceding 300 years.

Perhaps the most pointed indication that composition had entered a radically new phase when it passed beyond traditional tonality is found not in Schoenberg and Stravinsky, however, but in a series of manifestos issued by the futurists, a group of Italian artists, writers and musicians who formed an avant-garde movement during these same years. As if recognizing the possible implication of the musical situation created by the loss of tonality, the most progressive of the futurists seized on more drastic consequences than either Schoenberg or Stravinsky, rejecting not only the traditional tonal system but the very sound materials associated with it. It was no longer necessary to limit oneself to the small fund of pitches to which Western music had previously been tied. All imaginable sounds could now be accepted into the compositional vocabulary, with those most closely associated with modern life – industrial noises, the sounds of motor cars and aeroplanes, city streets and crowds – being especially preferred.

The leading theorist of futurist music, Luigi Russolo, even invented a set of mechanical 'noise makers' designed to broaden the limited range of available sound sources. (Though certain inventors, notably the American Thaddeus Cahill, were experimenting with electronic sound production, that field was to remain in its infancy for another half-century.) The extremity of Russolo's position is evident in even a brief extract from his manifesto *The Art of Noises* (1913):

> We must break out of this narrow circle of pure musical sounds and conquer the infinite variety of noise-sounds . . . We futurists have all deeply loved the music of the great composers. Beethoven and Wagner for many years wrung our hearts. But now we are satiated with them and derive much greater pleasure from ideally combining the noises of street-cars, internal-combustion engines, automobiles, and busy crowds than from re-hearing, for example, the 'Eroica' or the 'Pastoral'.[2]

Although the futurists' music proved to have little influence on other composers, the movement mirrored the state of profound crisis in which music found itself on the eve of World War I, a crisis in turn faithfully reflecting the larger one that was to bring on the war.

THE POSTWAR MOOD

The musical developments traced above, which reached their climax and fulfilment in the early years of the twentieth century, are inseparably linked by a process of evolution to subsequent ones. Yet even the most extreme compositional manifestations of the pre-war period are best understood as forming the final stage of musical Romanticism: Schoenberg's atonality, for example, as the ultimate consequence of extreme personal expression and visionary subjectivism; Stravinsky's neo-primitivism as the culmination of Romantic nationalism and folklorism. To that extent these developments can be viewed as the latterday products of the progressive, expansionist view characteristic of Western thought during the years preceding the war.

However, as we have seen, the war dealt a death-blow to these artistic developments and to the environment of progressive optimism with which they were associated. In the aftermath of the confrontation, new attitudes began to be adopted. Many had come to believe that a more modest conception of the arts was required, one that was more down-to-earth and closer to everyday experience. This view was in direct opposition to attitudes that had prevailed during the nineteenth century and the early years of the twentieth: the Romantic cult of personality, the preference for extreme subjective expression and emotional effusion, and the idea of art as a sort of substitute religion. Only after war broke out could a new and unmistakably twentieth-century aesthetic begin to form.

An early and extreme manifestation of this reaction against the past occurred in the anarchist, anti-art movement known as dada, which appeared in neutral Switzerland during the war years. The dadaists saw the war as the inevitable consequence of modern industrial society and placed the blame on Western civilization itself, turning against its most sacred and valued cultural achievements. For the dadaists, all art, including music, became an essentially negative force, a tool for protest and caricature, for deflating the pretensions and ambitions of the 'masterpieces' of the Western artistic tradition. Tristan Tzara, a leading figure in the movement, wrote in one of his manifestos of the need to 'sweep and clean': 'Art is a PRETENTION . . . MUSICIANS SMASH YOUR INSTRUMENTS'.

Less extreme, and more typical of the mood of the war years (for the nihilism of dada retained an unmistakably Romantic tinge), were several movements that emphasized the need for a new objectivity in the arts, stressing the function of art as one among many factors contributing within an encompassing political, social and artistic framework. A group of Dutch artists, including the prominent painter Piet Mondrian, in 1917 formed a confederation known as De Stijl, which promoted an art of mathematical purity based on simple geometrical designs. Romantic emotionalism and mystification were shunned in favour of clarity and logic. Two years later the German architect Walter Gropius founded the Bauhaus, a school of art dedicated to a craftsmanlike approach to creation based on rationalized construction, economy of means and undisguised use of modern industrial materials. In France a group known as the 'Purists', led by the architect Le Corbusier, espoused a similar aesthetic of clarity and simplicity and the consideration of the properties of modern materials in determining design.

An idea underlying all these groups was a belief in the efficacy of art as an instrument for social improvement. In place of the Romantic conception of 'art for art's sake', of art as a vehicle for personal expression and transcendent truths, they viewed art as a functional tool. (This attitude was projected with special force in Le Corbusier's description of a house as a 'machine to live in', 'a tool as the motor-car is becoming a tool'.[3]) Equally characteristic was the collective nature of these movements, reflecting a conviction that art should be a communal rather than an individual expression. Thus the Bauhaus, with a faculty including some of the leading artistic figures of the day (among them Mies van der Rohe, Paul Klee and Wassily Kandinsky), was committed to a notion of 'total art' where form followed function and where artists and craftsmen worked together on all aspects of design, contributing equally in a collaborative conception. Gropius wrote:

> The art of building is contingent on the coordinated team-work of a band of active collaborators whose orchestral cooperation symbolizes the cooperative organism we call society . . . There is a widespread misconception that art is just a useless luxury. This is one of our fatal legacies from a generation which arbitrarily elevated some of its branches above the rest as the 'Fine Arts', and in so doing robbed all of their basic identity and common life.[4]

This collaborative spirit had its counterpart in music and was anticipated in the productions of Stravinsky's three famous pre-war ballets – *The Firebird*, *Petrushka* and *The Rite of Spring* – composed for Sergey Dyagilev's Ballets Russes, which to a significant degree were the combined creations of several artists working in close association, including composer, choreographer, set designer and writer. It was a later Dyagilev collaboration, however, that defined the spirit of the postwar years: the ballet *Parade* (1917), with music by Erik Satie, sets by Pablo Picasso, choreography by Leonid Massin and a scenario by Jean Cocteau. The presence of Satie in this undertaking was in itself an indication of change. Satie's quest for a simpler, more objective and less pretentious kind of music dated back to the final years of the nineteenth century; but, consistent with the accepted cultural attitudes of that period, his compositions had been universally considered as little more than the naive musings of an eccentric dilettante. In the later war years, however, after opinions concerning the nature of art began to shift, Satie was suddenly treated seriously, both by a new generation of young composers and by some of the leading French intellectuals of the day.

Parade was immediately perceived as marking an important milestone in the arts. In praising the work's 'new spirit' in the programme book for the first production, the poet Guillaume Apollinaire provided a phrase that became a sort of official slogan for the arts in the postwar years (no less a figure than Le Corbusier adopted it for the title of his Purist journal *L'esprit nouveau*). Based on Cocteau's rough outline for a plot that combined features of the circus and music hall, *Parade* united music, dance, costumes, sets and action in an irreverent divertissement characterized by lightness, humour and absence of pretence. Satie's music was outlandish and shocking. It borrowed liberally from café music and ragtime and used revolver shots and clicking typewriters as essential components of the score. Equally shunned were the high-flown expressive intensities of Wagnerian music drama and the subtle shadings of Debussyan impressionism: this was music that made no effort to hide its clearcut segmentations and rough edges or its indebtedness to popular sources.

Perhaps more than any other artistic product of the time, *Parade* set the fashion for the postwar years. Cocteau, deeply affected by his collaboration with Satie, wrote an essay published the following year enjoining his contemporaries to adopt a new kind of 'everyday' art inspired by the composer's example: 'Satie teaches what, in our age, is the greatest audacity, simplicity . . . Enough of clouds, waves, aquariums, waterspirits and nocturnal scents; what we need is a music of the earth, every-day music'.[5]

Cocteau's 'Call to Order' (as he named the book in which his Satie-inspired essay was published) found immediate musical resonance in a group of six young composers living in Paris, most of whom had met while they were students at the Paris Conservatoire. With Satie as spiritual godfather and Cocteau as artistic counsellor and aesthetic spokesman, they joined in an informal confederation during the late war years. The membership included such notables as Darius Milhaud, Francis Poulenc and Arthur Honegger, composers who harboured significant differences in artistic outlook; these differences increased, so the group soon disbanded. But for a brief period Les Six, as they came to be known, espoused a common aesthetic that epitomized the postwar climate, summing up all that had come to be viewed as modern. Their music was clear in structure, direct in appeal, light in tone and free of the trappings of the concert hall; and it was not afraid to draw inspiration from various types of vernacular music.

NEO-CLASSICISM AND THE NEW SOBRIETY

Although the developments in France associated with Les Six had a unique flavour, they embodied many of the musical characteristics that typified the postwar years in general. The most pervasive compositional approach of the 1920s was that of the movement known as neoclassicism; not coincidentally, it had its origins in France, though not so much because of the example of Les Six as of that of Igor Stravinsky. Stravinsky took up residence in France in 1920 after having lived in Switzerland during the war; his move to the French capital seems symbolic – at least in retrospect – of a significant stylistic turn in his work, which he himself attributed in part to French influences. Looking back some years later, he remarked: 'My feeling for clarity, my fanaticism for precision was waked through France, and my distaste for hollow twaddle and bombast, false pathos, lack of discretion in creative effusions – that was all at least strongly encouraged through my stay in Paris'.[6]

Stravinsky's music had taken a new course long before, following the completion of *The Rite of Spring* in 1913. Works composed during the war years, such as *Renard* and *Histoire du soldat*, used much more modest forces than the pre-war ballets; and their music, though far removed from the simplicities of Les Six, was similar in being indebted to popular sources. *Renard* and *Histoire du soldat*, as well as *Les noces* (another major conception of the war years), were all based on folktales, handled with irony, humour and childlike directness, suggesting further parallels. The last piece Stravinsky completed before moving to Paris was *Pulcinella*, a stylized reworking of several eighteenth-century keyboard compositions. His re-use of borrowed material as a basis for a new composition, though by no means unprecedented (an almost contemporary instance, written in 1917, was Satie's *Sonatine bureaucratique*), proved to be critically important for his subsequent development. He became fascinated with the idea of reviving certain stylistic characteristics and compositional procedures of eighteenth-century music and transforming them through the harmonic and rhythmic vocabulary of contemporary musical language. As he later remarked, *Pulcinella* 'was my discovery of the past, the epiphany through which the whole of my later work became possible'.[7]

The earliest composition in which Stravinsky's neo-classical style appeared fully formed was the Octet for wind instruments, completed in 1923, a watershed work of the interwar years. Its emphasis on clarity, objectivity and economy followed characteristics evident in the music of Satie and Les Six as well as in Stravinsky's own music of the immediately preceding years. But while that music tended to mimic the expressive flavour, and even adopted certain technical features, of popular music, the Octet took its inspiration from the music of the past, especially J. S. Bach. With its renunciation of the 'primitivism' and folk-derived Russian flavour of the earlier music, which it replaced with subtle and elegantly restrained stylistic allusions, the Octet was as ground-breaking in its way as *The Rite of Spring*.

Stravinsky's belief in the special significance of the Octet was evident when, the year after its première, he published an article on it amounting to a kind of aesthetic manifesto. Characterizing the work as 'a musical object', he asserted that it was 'not an "emotive" work but a musical composition based on objective elements which are sufficient in themselves . . . [A] play of movements and volumes that puts into action the musical text, constitutes the impelling force of the composition and determines its form'.[8] There could be no statement more at odds with the bygone aesthetic of musical Romanticism – an aesthetic still fully embodied, it should be emphasized, in Schoenberg's conception of his pre-war atonal compositions as 'organic' in form, 'spiritual' in content and the fruit of a subjective, spontaneous and intuitive approach to creation.

In spite of neo-classicism's special associations with France, it was by no means confined to that country. Indeed, taken in its broadest sense as a stylistic tendency independent of a particular set of technical procedures, neo-classicism proved to be the dominant musical aesthetic of the interwar years throughout the Western world. It even flourished in Germany, where, given the country's central role in the Romantic heritage, one might have thought the new currents would have been slow to take hold. Yet Germany was especially ripe for a change in artistic focus following its defeat in the Great War. The dissolution of the old monarchy and the foundation of the 'Weimar' (or First German) Republic encouraged reaction against the past. The general mood promoted what was new and up-to-date, unencumbered by associations with the old way of life, releasing a burst of new energy in the arts. As in France, the Romantic aesthetic of personal expression was rejected in favour of a simpler and more streamlined approach better suited to the character of modern life.

The neo-classicism of Stravinsky and the cult of popular music advocated by Les Six found their German equivalents in the music of the two leading composers of the first Weimar generation: Paul Hindemith and Kurt Weill. While still in his mid-twenties, Hindemith gained notoriety as an *enfant terrible* with three scandalous one-act operas in 1920–21, two of which, *Mörder, Hoffnung der Frauen* ('Murder, the Hope of Women') and *Sancta Susanna*, dealt with topics of a controversial sexual nature (the second involving a nun), while the third, the puppet opera *Das Nusch-Nuschi*, parodied Wagner's *Tristan und Isolde*. During the early 1920s Hindemith also experimented with evocations of operetta, jazz bands, military music, café society and the like. But in the mid-1920s, following Stravinsky's lead, he shed these youthful impertinences and began looking to the more distant past for new stylistic moorings. With Bach as his primary model, Hindemith envisaged a type of music able to fulfil practical functions, produced in the same spirit as a skilled craftsman or artisan might ply a trade. (This caused the word 'Gebrauchsmusik' – literally 'music for use' – to be applied to his work, a term that stuck, though the composer himself strongly objected to it.) His music took on a lean, rhythmically propulsive quality derived from the linear textures of Baroque music. Typical of Hindemith's work at this time are the seven compositions, written between 1922 and 1927, known as *Kammermusik*, a title whose very neutrality already reflected the new aesthetic stance. With one exception, each piece features a solo instrument in combination with a chamber ensemble of ten or more players, with the two forces working together in quiet and efficient cooperation, abjuring all outward display. (This was a conception far removed from the nineteenth-century virtuoso concerto in which soloist and large orchestra competed against one another in 'heroic' confrontation.)

Weill too was drawn to neo-classicism during the 1920s; but later in the decade his music took a different, if not altogether unrelated, turn. Increasingly concerned with the political potential of music to foster social change, he embraced opera as the most powerful medium for this purpose – not traditional opera, which he considered 'socially exclusive', but a new kind conceived as a 'community-forming or community-advancing art'. Working in close collaboration with the playwright Bertold Brecht, Weill fashioned an 'epic' form of depersonalized and non-illusionist theatre with political ambitions. A series of remarkable joint creations appeared between 1927 and 1933, the best known being *Die Dreigroschenoper* and *Mahagonny*. Weill's undisguised evocations of popular music and jazz in these works recall Les Six; but whereas the latter sought a lighthearted, even frivolous, effect, his intent was uncompromisingly serious. He 'distanced' the vernacular aspect through parody and distortion, removing all hints of commercialism and cliché. From the theatre-orchestra scoring to the choice of harmonies and the shapes of melodic lines, everything seems slightly askew. The music's peculiar charm is that, while sounding strangely familiar, even banal, it is always unpredictable.

The hallmarks of neo-classicism – the evocation of earlier (especially eighteenth-century) music, the reduction of instrumental forces (with wind rather than strings especially favoured) and the use of a cooler, more detached and hard-edged expressive language – appeared in the music of virtually every leading postwar composer, regardless of nationality. In Italy Alfredo Casella turned away from the deeply ingrained operatic tradition of his country to foster a style that drew on the older Italian instrumental music of such figures as Scarlatti and Vivaldi. Gian Francesco Malipiero, though (unlike Casella) strongly committed to dramatic music, similarly turned to earlier Italian operatic traditions for inspiration in staking out a new stylistic direction. In his case it was a seventeenth-century composer, Monteverdi (whose works he also edited and published in a modern edition), who provided the principal source. Similarly, in Spain Manuel de Falla rejected the colouristic, folk-dominated nationalism of his predecessors Albéniz and Granados, as well as his own pre-war music, adopting a more severe, pared-down manner in which the nationalistic flavourings, though still evident, assumed a much more stylized character. England, like Italy and Spain, was largely exempt from the central European stylistic extremes of the pre-war years; but the appearance of William Walton's *Façade* (1922), a work close in spirit to Les Six, and of his later, more neo-classically orientated compositions, such as the Viola Concerto (1929) and First Symphony (1934), brought that country's music comfortably within the new stylistic orbit.

The postwar spirit even affected Bartók, perhaps the most important figure of the period to remain closely associated with the folk music of his native country. (Neo-classicism was above all an 'internationalist' movement, so much so that Stravinsky, its leading figure, not only avoided folk material in his post-Octet music but even began denying its significance for his earlier work.) From his first encounter with native Hungarian music, dating back to 1905, Bartók had set himself off from the nineteenth-century nationalists by approaching the music from an essentially 'scientific' point of view (thereby helping to establish, with his colleague and fellow countryman Zoltán Kodály, the modern discipline of ethnomusicology). As his use of folk material progressed, moreover, he increasingly tried to incorporate folk elements as an unexceptional, completely integral component of a consistent, total musical language. For Bartók the idea was never so much to reproduce the colour or atmosphere of such music but to draw on its structural principles in order to develop new approaches to rhythm, harmony and tonal organization. This tendency to focus on formal matters was already well established in Bartók's music before the war, making his adoption of neo-classicism far less disruptive than was the case with Stravinsky, even when Bartók was drawn – as in the First Piano Concerto of 1926 – to the 'back-to-Bach' movement (a phrase that had become a kind of rallying cry following the appearance of Stravinsky's Octet). In many of his compositions of the interwar years – the Third, Fourth and Fifth string quartets, among others – Bartók used complex formal structures of a symmetrical nature based on classical models.

Neo-classical styles also caught hold in more distant areas, such as the USSR and the USA. Almost every leading American composer of the first postwar generation went to Paris to study with Nadia Boulanger, who was deeply committed to the stylistic direction set out by the new, 'Parisian' Stravinsky. Boulanger, with Schoenberg perhaps the most important composition teacher of the interwar period, instilled in these young composers a concern for craftsmanship, formal clarity and expressive reserve. She believed, unlike the great majority of Europeans at the time, that it was advantageous for the modern composer to be non-European and thus free of the weight of an aging musical tradition, and this gave her special significance to American composers. Boulanger encouraged her American protégés to incorporate native elements into their work; and one finds, for example, jazz influences in Aaron Copland, hymn tunes in Virgil Thomson and evocations of folk music in Roy Harris. As in Bartók's music, however, these local echoes are usually treated as integral components of what is basically a 'geographically neutral' musical language.

In the USA there was also a more experimental strain that flourished during the 1920s in the work of such composers as Henry Cowell, Carl Ruggles and Ruth Crawford Seeger. Influenced in part by Charles Ives, these composers developed radical new techniques of tonal, rhythmic and textural construction. The best known was Edgard Varèse, a European by birth, who envisaged a music fully representative of the machine age, produced by electronic instruments capable of providing a range of sounds consistent with those of modern life. To some extent his views recalled those of the futurists. Yet the aggressively iconoclastic slant of the Italian movement was largely missing in Varèse, who thought of himself as a sort of artist-scientist (he was trained as an engineer) who explored new worlds of sound from a perspective of detached curiosity. Indeed the entire American experimental fringe, including the young John Cage (whose first compositions began to appear in the 1930s), worked within an objective and constructionist context that was consistent with the most essential features of neo-classicism. The focus was on innovations in form, rhythm and sonority, not with unbridled personal expression or even with sheer novelty of sound.

The situation in the USSR, which entered the postwar period after the most profound political revolution in history, was complicated by initial uncertainties about the role that music, and the other arts, would assume within the new Soviet system. Throughout most of the 1920s those in power fostered the idea that a new kind of society required a new kind of artistic expression unburdened by tradition. Thus modernist leanings and the international exchange of ideas were encouraged in the arts. One of the more extreme musical manifestations of this open atmosphere was Alexander Mosolov's latter-day futurist essay *The Iron Foundry*, part of his ballet *Steel* (1928). Combining dissonantly clashing layers of repeated figures, the work was a primitive effort to re-create with modern orchestral instruments the sonic atmosphere of a modern factory. (Less radical, if more musically differentiated, examples of 'machine' music were common in the early postwar years: Honegger's *Pacific 231* and George Antheil's *Ballet mécanique* are two among many.) Further indication of the liberal tenor of early Soviet music can be found in the works of Prokofiev, who, though living primarily in Paris during the 1920s, maintained close ties with his native country. His Second and Third symphonies of 1925 and 1928 are conceived in a progressive and 'international' style that places their composer comfortably within the Stravinsky orbit.

Paradoxically, perhaps the most representative indication of the new temperament in postwar music is found not in the Stravinsky camp but in the so-called Second Viennese School, consisting of Schoenberg and his two former pupils Alban Berg and Anton Webern. Schoenberg's compositional evolution illustrates with particular clarity the sense of disruption – and the necessity of finding a fresh direction – following the profound artistic crises preceding World War I. His journey was not easy. Well before the beginning of the war he had begun questioning the intuitive approach he adopted in his earliest post-tonal music, concerned that such a free-wheeling manner did not lend itself to the creation of large-scale, developmental works possessing the logic and coherence found in masterpieces of the past. Thus, like the neo-classicists, Schoenberg set about attempting to re-establish the qualities of order and clarity; unlike them, however, he did not believe that could be achieved by reviving compositional techniques and manners associated with older music. Instead, he set out to discover an entirely new compositional method that, though in some respects analogous to traditional tonality, would replace it.

The difficulty of this project is demonstrated by Schoenberg's failure to publish any new music between 1916 and 1923, years during which he struggled to find his new compositional principle. After many efforts along different lines, he eventually worked out the details of what is now called the 'twelve-note system'. Unlike the seven-note major and minor systems of tonality, the twelve-note system takes all twelve notes of the chromatic scale as its point of departure; these are arranged in a particular order, creating a 'row' or 'series' which forms the basis of a composition, assuming something of the function of a key in tonal music. In spite of its many revolutionary aspects (and, misleadingly, it is usually only these that are stressed), Schoenberg's 'serial' method grew out of an ideal of systematic order that was essentially conservative. Consistent with this ideal, almost all his twelve-note compositions are based on forms and genres from the eighteenth century: dance suite, sonata, rondo, theme and variations etc. Schoenberg's move from an intuitive to a 'constructivist' approach, and from a quasi-improvisatory formal conception to one based on classical models, was thus in direct line with the compositional orientation of the time.

THE COMING OF WORLD WAR II

All the most important innovations in music of the interwar years appeared during the late teens and twenties, a period of remarkable excitement characterized by progressivism and a spirit of freedom and experiment. It was a time of optimism, when life seemed full of the possibilities of rebirth and renewal after the catastrophic disruptions of the Great War – which, it was widely believed, was to put an end to all wars. While the pre-war years had given off the particular energy of a world in collapse, burning up from the intensity of its own heat, the postwar years radiated the energy of a new world in formation, full of hope and promise.

How quickly this passed. The flawed peace treaties that terminated the war produced unresolvable conflicts and tensions. It soon became evident that the new League of Nations, created in response to the increasingly international character of human affairs, would be unable to achieve lasting stability. Economic factors added to the tensions. Germany was gripped with rampant inflation in the 1920s, and during the following decade much of the world sank into a severe depression. As economic conditions in Europe deteriorated, producing widespread discontent, the shadow of totalitarianism fell over a significant portion of the continent, suppressing the free flow of ideas and stifling creative innovation in the arts. In Russia the earlier liberalism of the Soviet régime gave way to the repressive, anti-intellectual and anti-artistic reign of Joseph Stalin, who assumed dictatorial control by the early 1930s. Italy succumbed to Mussolini in 1926, Germany to Hitler in 1933. Under these new political conditions innovatory musical ideas had little opportunity to flourish.

At the same time that the politics of totalitarian régimes were forcing music to take a more conservative course, non-political factors conspired elsewhere to cause reaction against the heady musical atmosphere of the early postwar years. The hardships imposed by the Depression, which affected large numbers, encouraged composers to think of their work in more populist terms, to frame their musical ideas in a more straightforward manner directed towards a larger and less specialized audience. The problem of audience reception was felt acutely by many composers and reflected a growing conviction that modernism, whatever its attributes, had failed to become central to musical life as a whole. Although the major performing institutions, both opera companies and symphony orchestras, survived the cultural revolutions of the early twentieth century with remarkably little loss in importance, they were able to retain their central role, paradoxically, only by turning their backs on contemporary music.

Throughout the nineteenth century, symphony orchestras and opera companies had devoted a sizable portion of their repertories to new works. As the twentieth century progressed, however, this became less and less the case, and these institutions began to take on the character of museums, devoted mainly to the preservation of the musical past. Although new compositions were occasionally performed, programmes were overwhelmingly dominated by the masterpieces of the European tradition, mainly from the late eighteenth and nineteenth centuries. (Virgil Thomson complained, as he began working as a music critic in New York shortly before World War II, that the major orchestras relied heavily on a core repertory of '50 famous pieces'.) New music had become significantly isolated from the general music-listening public.

This isolation was reflected in one of the most striking novelties in twentieth-century musical life: the establishment of performing organizations devoted exclusively to contemporary music. Schoenberg's Society for Private Musical Performance, founded in Vienna in 1918, set the tone. The word 'private' in the title gave notice that admission was restricted to a membership; and a set of detailed rules underlined the highly specialized nature of the undertaking: each work was to be performed twice, all applause and all signs of disapproval were forbidden, and critics were not allowed to attend. Contemporary music, deprived of the central social role it had enjoyed in the past (so much so that there was no need even to designate it as 'contemporary'), became the province of a small and, for the most part, professionally trained élite.

It is thus not hard to understand that the social, political and economic problems of the 1930s fell heavily on the conscience of many composers working at the forefront of musical developments. Whether or not in conscious response to the increasingly difficult material conditions affecting the lives of so many people (and in many cases it is evident that it was conscious), composers everywhere began writing music addressed to a broader, more democratically representative audience. The 1930s, viewed from this perspective, were a period of musical retrenchment, a fact reflected in varying degrees in the work of virtually every leading figure of the time: in the significant simplification of rhythmic and harmonic elements in Bartók's later music; in Schoenberg's more liberal and flexible treatment of the twelve-note system and in his occasional returns to traditional tonality; in Copland's adoption of an openly populist style in works like *Rodeo* and

Billy the Kid. Or negatively: in the almost complete silence that overtook such experimentally inclined composers as Varèse and Crawford Seeger.

By the final years of the 1930s Europe was approaching a state of war. With Hitler first repossessing the Rhineland, then successively occupying Austria, Czechoslovakia and Poland, and with Franco's forces triumphant in Spain, the continent was thrown into a state of imminent collapse. The toll exacted in terms of cultural disruption can be effectively demonstrated solely by referring to the extraordinarily large number of European composers who by 1940 were living in political exile in the USA, a group that included Schoenberg, Stravinsky, Bartók, Milhaud, Hindemith and Weill. These displaced figures continued to compose, of course, as did those who remained in Europe. But as the world braced itself for the second widespread confrontation in less than a quarter of a century, their music lost something of the adventurousness and fervour it displayed so conspicuously during the previous decade.

THE AFTERMATH OF WORLD WAR II

The human and physical destruction caused by World War II was even greater than that of the previous war. Most of Europe and much of Asia was in ruins. The introduction of the atomic bomb in the final days of the confrontation virtually obliterated the Japanese cities of Hiroshima and Nagasaki. The total number of fatalities has been estimated at 15 million among the military and 25 million among civilians. Countless homes were levelled, producing numerous refugees. The destructive potential of modern strategic warfare, partly revealed in World War I, was now made fully evident. The birth of the atomic age, though it helped bring hostilities to a close, pointed to the likelihood that a third such confrontation would eradicate human civilization.

In spite of certain similarities in the postwar reactions, the impact of World War II on Western culture was even more fundamental than that of the previous war. Both were followed by a period of renewal in the arts, characterized by strong reconstructionist elements and the free exchange of ideas on an international scale. Yet the underlying atmosphere was quite different. The so-called Cold War, which the world faced immediately following the treaties of 1945, exacerbated by the unprecedented wartime devastation and the threat of future atomic conflict, produced a more pessimistic and subdued tone. The 1920s had given birth to attempts to renew contacts with an older heritage, as if the excesses of the more immediate past, of late nineteenth- and early twentieth-century Romanticism could be countered by reviving the simpler and more direct order of an earlier age. Following World War II, however, the tendency was to distrust the past. With the world in physical and cultural ruin, the best hope seemed to be to make a radical break with what had gone before, to make a new start. Thus many members of the younger generation of composers envisaged a new kind of music, as independent of previous Western models as possible. Especially distrusted was the neo-classicism of the interwar years, which had come to be viewed as a desperate attempt to escape musical reality in nostalgic pursuit of a falsely idealized image of a more innocent historical epoch.

The two most characteristic musical developments of the early postwar years gave expression to this attitude: integral serialism and indeterminacy. They both coalesced about 1950; and in spite of the relatively brief period of their ascendancy, they formed the most influential compositional directions of the time. On the face of it, the two seemed to represent diametrically opposed compositional philosophies. Integral serialism was founded on a highly rational, quasi-scientific approach in which mathematical determinations played a significant role, while indeterminacy advocated a largely irrational and intuitive mode of composition. Yet they also had much in common, not least a rejection of some of the most fundamental technical and aesthetic assumptions of previous Western music. And, in spite of their stated differences in technical approach, both incorporated a significant degree of abstract calculation and of unpredictability.

Integral serialism represented an extension of Schoenberg's technique of the serial control of pitch, developed during the 1920s in his early twelve-note compositions, now generalized to include all other elements of the musical structure: rhythm, dynamics, articulation, registration, instrumentation and even form. But the differences were much more fundamental than the mention of a mere technical extension might suggest. Schoenberg had introduced serialism as a way of establishing a degree of musical control over the chromatic pitch framework analogous to that supplied by tonality over the diatonic framework; and he used the method to create large-scale musical forms that retained characteristics of motivic development, phrase rhythm, sectional contrast and reprise that were closely related to, and clearly derived from, those of tonal music.

The integral serialists, on the other hand, viewed the serial method as a means of producing an entirely new kind of music. They believed that composition could become a completely rational and consistent process, producing an 'integrated' structure whose various components would all be shaped by a common structural source, the series, conceived not in Schoenbergian terms as a succession of pitches but as a sequence of abstract numerical proportions equally applicable to all facets of the music. In the more extreme forms of serialism, the creation of music became largely a 'pre-compositional' matter: the construction and disposition of abstract systems of numerical proportions worked out in advance of putting notes on paper. The compositional process itself – the determination of the notes – thus assumed an almost 'automatic' quality, limited to fleshing out the abstract system with the rhythms, dynamics, registers and timbres that it dictated. As described by Karlheinz Stockhausen, who with Pierre Boulez and Milton Babbitt was the leading figure in the movement, composing became 'the ordering of notes under a unifying principle', the final result being 'the combined effect of all the components, similar to vectorial values in multi-dimensional fields'.[9]

Since in their view Schoenberg had 'misused' serialism to maintain traditional formal values, most serialists considered Schoenberg's student Anton Webern to be their most significant predecessor. They believed he had come closest to realizing the full implications of his teacher's new compositional technique, seeing it not as a way of preserving the past but as a doorway opening up entirely new terrain. Webern had come closest to eliminating such traditional distinctions as those between melody and accompaniment, line and harmony, distinctions the younger generation felt were no longer valid. In Stockhausen's words, the new music should contain 'no repetition, no variation, no development, no contrast. All these presuppose "figures" . . . themes, motifs, objects – which are repeated, varied, developed and contrasted . . . All that has been given up'. Now, instead of 'the same figures in a changing light', as in tonal music, we have 'different figures in the same, all-penetrating light'.[10]

While the serialists broke with the past by creating a radical new type of musical structure, the indeterminists did so by rejecting the entire idea of a fixed and unchangeable musical structure. Before the war, John Cage, the leading figure in the movement, drawing on a tradition dating back through Varèse to the Italian futurists, had sought to broaden the scope of music to include every imaginable kind of sound, experimenting with such novel sound sources as brake drums, thunder sheets and the 'prepared piano' (a piano modified through the attachment of various objects, such as metal screws and rubber wedges, to its strings). During this period Cage was also preoccupied with mathematically derived proportional systems, by means of which he constructed 'empty' formal frames to contain the sounds he was using. The idea was to supply a structure within which the sonic materials could be presented 'neutrally', as passive objects that did not interact with – and thus did not shape – their environment.

In the early 1950s Cage took the more consequential step that brought him to indeterminacy. He had come to believe that musical sounds should be allowed to exist purely for their own sake and that any attempt to impose an external order or structure on them would deprive them of their own inherent beauty. In his words, we should 'set about discovering means to let sounds be themselves rather than vehicles for man-made theories or expressions of human sentiments'.[11] To achieve this, Cage decided that significant aspects of both the composition and performance of a work should be left to chance rather than being predetermined. He began constructing pieces in which critical aspects of the music, including pitches and their durations, were decided by such procedures as tossing dice or coins, consulting the *I Ching* (a Chinese book of oracles), tracing imperfections on the paper used, or reading astronomical maps. Similarly, performers were allowed to make decisions as to precisely what should be played, and how it should be played. In certain cases this meant that performers constructed the piece essentially from scratch, aided only by a set of general instructions provided by the composer.

The most radical of all indeterminate compositions was Cage's *4'33"*, which appeared in 1952. The score consists only of three Roman numerals, each followed by a duration (the total adding up to the four minutes and 33 seconds of the title), and the word 'tacit', indicating that nothing is to be played. Thus the only thing specified is the work's 'silence', with its temporal dimensions. Whatever sounds occur do so at the whim of the performers (the piece can be 'played' by any number) and the members of the audience, or they result from ambient sonic conditions in the physical environment (for example, air-conditioning hum or traffic noise). With this drastic gesture Cage removed the composer entirely from all decisions concerning the actual 'music' to be heard.

In spite of their obvious philosophical differences, serialists and indeterminists shared a tendency to 'objectify' the compositional act, to create a significant psychological distance between composer and composition. Thus both relied on elaborate systems to act as inter-mediaries between the two. Although the nature of these systems was quite different, one highly rational and the other essentially irrational, in both the composition lost much of its traditional role as an expression of human volition. Given this common conceptual background, it is not surprising that integral serialism and indeterminacy also turned out to sound somewhat similar. The serialists soon discovered that the more they predetermined certain aspects of their compositions, the more they were forced to surrender control over others. Moreover, the more precise and complex the controlling system, the more difficult it was for listeners to perceive its influence on what was actually heard; and thus the more random and arbitrary the result appeared to sound. The elaborate structural logic failed to produce a corresponding aural logic.

As a consequence composers began to reconsider the relationship between the two orthodoxies of the early 1950s, viewing serialism and indeterminacy as simply the opposite extremes of an unbroken continuum of compositional possibilities, all equally available. A shift towards the 'middle' was evident by the later 1950s, opening up rich new areas previously unexplored by composers on both sides of the serial-indeterminacy divide. The most immediate sign of change was the adoption of limited aspects of indeterminacy by many of the leading European serialists. Both Stockhausen and Boulez went through an extended period in which they devised indeterminate frameworks (often as complex in conception as the serial frameworks with which they were combined) that allowed performers to choose among a limited number of options without forfeiting control over the musical progress. Others adopted indeterminate procedures as a way of achieving unusual textural effects, usually involving intricate rhythmic interactions among several independent parts, creating passages that would have been extremely difficult to perform using traditional notation. Here the idea was not so much to achieve uncertainty, or even spontaneity, as to produce a type of complex composite rhythm in which what mattered was the total effect rather than the precise individual detail.

This use of indeterminacy points to a characteristic feature of both serial and indeterminate music: the tendency to focus attention on the surface of the music – on the way the textural components fit together in different configurations to produce a simultaneous effect. The very complexity of the individual details shifts the emphasis away from the particular event to the whole sonorous result. This triggered another musical development of the later 1950s that marked the end of the serial-indeterminate dichotomy: composition with large masses of aggregate sound, creating an aural fabric that depended not so much on the perception of individual components as on the generalized impression of the total combination. (In some cases the textures reached such density and opacity that the individual elements were not perceptible at all.)

The Paris-based Greek composer Iannis Xenakis had begun to explore this compositional avenue during the early 1950s, supporting his efforts with theoretical writings that criticized both strict determinacy and strict indeterminacy as equally contrary to nature. Xenakis's own compositional system, derived from the laws of probability and statistical approximation, mediated between the extremes of total determinacy and total indeterminacy, spawning works based on large-scale textural transformations that, though extremely complex in detail, were clearly perceptible in shape.

The two works most responsible for bringing this type of 'textural music' to public consciousness were written by two composers solidly grounded in serial techniques: Krzysztof Penderecki's *Threnody, To the Victims of Hiroshima* (1959) and György Ligeti's *Atmosphères* (1960). Both feature solid blocks of sound, massive and seemingly impenetrable clusters of notes placed so closely together that they appear to form unbroken bands. Like serial music, these works rejected such distinctions as those between melody and accompaniment; but the sheer sonic sensuality produced by their rich textural fabrics made them sound quite new – and much more accessible to the average listener. Both *Threnody* and *Atmosphères* were remarkably popular with audiences and widely performed in the years immediately following their first appearance, suggesting that, with strict serialism having apparently run its course, composers were ready to start investigating more varied possibilities.

THE REVOLUTIONS OF THE 1960s

In spite of the relatively short period in which it flourished, serialism was a remarkably dominant compositional movement (much more so than indeterminacy, its alter ego). Virtually every leading composer of the first postwar generation felt its influence. Even Stravinsky, the only one of the principal architects of the earliest twentieth-century musical revolution surviving to participate in developments of the second half-century, was profoundly affected by serialism. Olivier Messiaen, Witold Lutosławski and Elliott Carter, middle-generation composers who had established their compositional personalities before World War II, felt the influence of the postwar musical climate deeply, though none was strictly speaking a serialist. Messiaen, however, played a critical role in the movement's development, both through his compositions, which acquired a highly constructionist quality during the later 1940s, and as the most influential European composition teacher of the postwar years (Boulez, Stockhausen and Xenakis were among his many students).

In certain respects serialism was reminiscent of neo-classicism. It was international in orientation, reflected a detached and objective view of composition and was widely adopted, enjoying an equally central position in the postwar 1950s as neo-classicism held in the postwar 1920s. Indeed, in retrospect serialism might be said to have had the more profound influence on the subsequent course of music. In creating a type of music that almost totally negated traditional compositional values, it exposed for the first time – at least on a broad scale – the full implications of the abandonment of traditional tonality during the early years of the century: the loss of a 'natural' compositional system and the failure of a new one to assume its place had put composers in the unenviable position of having to make fundamental choices about even the most basic aspects of their work. Confirming a possibility already put forward by the futurists and, more consequentially, by Cage and his followers, it suggested that essentially anything and everything was musically possible.

Though serialism had been spawned in a desperate attempt to re-establish control (with what may now seem like immoderate force) over a compositional situation in disarray, it ended by showing that in the post-tonal period all such absolute control was ultimately arbitrary and dictatorial. The break-up of serialism came quickly, but the movement's repercussions were profound; and they are still with us (as is apparent from the fact that the description 'post-serial' continues to be applied to even the most current music).

The passing of serialism as a central movement by the end of the 1950s led to a period of extraordinary experimentation and expansion during the following decade. It was as if the compositional field had been cleared, opening up limitless new terrain for exploration. The resulting somewhat anarchic musical situation reflected the general political and social turmoil evident throughout the world in the 1960s. Many factors joined to produce a period of extraordinary volatility: paranoia associated with the Cold War, social agitation by minorities and the poor, and increasingly vocal demands from the Third World. A major revolt of the young, triggered in the USA especially by an extremely unpopular war in Vietnam, produced violent reactions against the norms of the older generation, creating additional domestic and international tensions. Students everywhere attacked the 'establishment'. The rights of the underprivileged were more vigorously advocated than perhaps at any previous moment in history. Centralized conventions of all kinds – political, social and artistic – were rejected and new ways of life advocated.

In this climate such traditional distinctions as those separating high art from popular and folk art were vigorously contested. The isolation of concert music as a separate and fragmented institution, dominated by highly trained specialists (more and more composers and performers were assuming positions in academia), was decried in favour of simpler and more integrated music-making. Guitars were suddenly in evidence everywhere. The individual was lauded in artistic matters as in others. The admonishment to 'do your own thing' became a kind of official proclamation for the self-described 'age of Aquarius'. Musical life, which had been so tightly prescribed during the preceding decade, responded with an explosion of new activity. A radical shift in orientation was evident in the sudden flourishing of various new forms of music theatre. Compositions appeared in which instrumentalists were required to wear masks (for example George Crumb's *Vox balaenae*) or full costume (Peter Maxwell Davies's *Eight Songs for a Mad King*); in others the performance itself was treated as a staged dramatic event (Luciano Berio's *Recital I*). New technology was incorporated within spectacular multi-media presentations that joined music with dramatic action, dance, film, slides and light shows (Cage's *HPSCHD*). (Synthesizers made their first appearance during the decade, offering a wealth of entirely new purely electronic sound possibilities as well as novel transformations of music played by live performers on acoustic instruments.)

Two developments that had an especially important impact were quotation music and minimal music. The former, which involved the use of earlier music as material for new compositions, represented an idea with a long tradition in Western music. Quotation had been a standard procedure during the medieval and Renaissance eras and it persisted in occasional use throughout the common-practice period. In the earlier twentieth century it became more prevalent again, no doubt partly in response to the tonal crisis. A typical feature of Ives's music, dating from the early years of the century, was the quotation of popular tunes, ragtime, hymns, marches and so on. And during the 1920s the simulation of jazz and light music became almost a cliché. Indeed, the neo-classical movement as a whole tended towards pastiche (most obviously in those cases, such as Stravinsky's *Pulcinella* and *The Fairy's Kiss* or Casella's *Scarlattiana*, where the scores were literally derived from earlier music).

Quotation music of the 1960s was set apart, then, not so much by how pervasive it was (though it was certainly that) but by the fact that the borrowed material consumed such a large portion of the musical structure and that its 'foreign' nature was emphasized to such a marked degree. The range of composers who began using quotation was extraordinary, including such diverse figures as Hans Werner Henze, Luigi Nono, Michael Tippett and George Rochberg, as well as almost all the postwar composers already mentioned. Not uncommonly, entire compositions were made up of quotations. In some instances the material was drawn from many different works, as in the third movement of Berio's *Sinfonia* (dating from 1965, one of the earliest and most influential pieces of the type), which, though based largely on a single movement from a Mahler symphony, incorporated additional quotations extending from Monteverdi to Stockhausen. In other instances the material came from only one source, as in Lukas Foss's three *Baroque Variations*, each derived from a single early eighteenth-century work. Foss described the first of his variations, based on a Larghetto from a Handel concerto grosso, as being like a 'dream' about Handel: 'Groups of instruments play the Larghetto but keep submerging into inaudibility (rather than pausing). Handel's notes are always present but often inaudible'.[12] The idea was to 'compose holes' into the original, creating a sort of 'perforated Handel' equipped with an unmistakably contemporary voice.

There was a marked element of nostalgia in the quotation movement, reflected in the fact that by far the most frequently quoted type of music was tonal music of the common-practice period. Foss's recomposition of Handel might even be understood as a symbolic lament for the loss of traditional tonality. The distortions and dislocations of his piece eloquently project the fragmented features of contemporary musical life, the sense of discontinuity produced by so radical a break with the musical past. But it is also notable that music using quotation, in spite of its very different aesthetic presuppositions, shared an important technical feature with serialism. Here too composition begins with material that to some extent exists before the piece in which it is used. Moreover, the tendency to break up material into fragments, rearranging them in new assemblages, was consistent with one of the most significant technical procedures found in twentieth-century art in general – that of collage.

Although quotation continues to play a role in current music, it has lost the pervasiveness it had in the later 1960s and 70s. Minimalism, on the other hand, continues to flourish – though significantly transformed – as an important compositional trend. Like quotation music, it grew out of a reaction against the prevailing climate of the 1950s; but whereas quotation was in large measure developed by composers who had themselves been serialists during the 1950s (a revolution from within, so to speak), minimalism was almost exclusively the creation of a group of independent young Americans who reached musical maturity only during the early 1960s. The earliest initiative came from LaMonte Young and Terry Riley. (The latter's *In C*, a seminal work in defining the school, also fell at least partly within the quotation camp as it was based entirely on melodic fragments drawn from the eighteenth-century musical vocabulary.) The two composers who eventually assumed the movement's leadership, however, were Steve Reich and Philip Glass.

One typical feature of 1950s music, serial or other, was its extreme complexity, making it difficult for performers to play and listeners to grasp. The minimalists believed that this was a principal reason for the isolation of serial music, which in their eyes epitomized the tendency towards specialization characteristic of modern music in general. It was conceived by highly educated, intellectually orientated composers, played by musicians specially trained in the rhythmic and ensemble intricacies of new music, and listened to by a small, quasi-professional élite (largely made up of composers). By contrast they advocated a simpler type of music that grew out of the particular performing skills of the composers themselves, that was conceived for a small group of performers working in close collaboration throughout the composition-al process, and that was structured in a sufficiently straightforward manner to be understood immediately by untrained listeners.

The minimalists thus began with the simplest possible musical materials – usually brief, diatonic scalic passages, not unlike traditional finger exercises – and subjected them to processes combining constant repetition with very gradual transformation. Typical was the technique known as 'phase shifting', explored by Reich in his early compositions.

In Reich's *Piano Phase* (1967), two pianists start by playing the same brief melodic figure simultaneously. After a number of repetitions in unison, one pianist begins playing the figure slightly faster, thus gradually 'pulling away' from the other so that the two move out of phase. As the piece progresses, the two parts separate more and more, producing slowly evolving rhythmic and melodic variations, until they eventually lock back into phase again.

Although minimalism represented a marked departure from the musical mainstream, it was not entirely unrelated to earlier twentieth-century compositional techniques. All the minimalists had to some degree felt the influence of Cage, especially the pre-chance Cage of the 1940s, whose prepared piano compositions incorporated similarly reiterative presentations of a limited number of musical elements. And they shared with the serialists a preference for systematic transformation, though the minimalists' processes were infinitely simpler and more readily discerned by listeners. Minimalism nevertheless represented a distinctly new compositional manner. The sound of the music often approached that of pop and rock music, a connection emphasized (in these early stages) by its conception for small groups led by the composer. Glass's ensemble included electronic instruments playing at extremely high levels of amplification, and was thus especially close to the pop/rock orbit (his recordings were even occasionally distributed on pop labels). Also characteristic was the rhythmic-percussive orientation of minimalism, which reflected yet another important influence: the music of non-Western cultures, especially those of Africa, India and Bali.

POSTMODERNISM AND THE PRESENT

The appearance during the 1960s of quotation music, minimalism and new forms of music theatre, along with a host of other compositional innovations (including such novelties as 'brainwave', 'environmental', 'scratch' and 'political' music), had a profound effect. By the end of the decade attitudes to composition had undergone a thorough transformation. In place of the two principal 'orthodoxies' of the 1950s – serialism and indeterminacy – there were diverse and competing tendencies. The relatively 'pure', historically neutral musical language of the earlier movements, favouring vocabularies with as few ties to traditional music as possible, gave way to a more inclusive mix that juxtaposed traditional and non-traditional elements with little concern for stylistic consistency or historical fidelity.

Quotation played an especially critical role in this connection, as it served to reintroduce triadic sonorities and traditional harmonic progressions that had for the most part been excluded from the modern canon. Their reappearance paved the way for a much-heralded 'return to tonality.' The odyssey of the American composer George Rochberg provides an instructive illustration: after passing through a serialist phase during the later 1950s and early 60s, Rochberg started introducing borrowed tonal music into his compositions in 1963 and shortly thereafter began producing 'simulated' tonal music of his own creation, combining it freely with more contemporary elements.

Given the previous history of twentieth-century music, this return to tonality was a particularly dramatic indication that something new, or at least different, was in the air. It was moreover but one of many manifestations of a trend to open up composition to a wider range of technical and stylistic possibilities. Especially characteristic was the cross-fertilization of concert music with infusions from other musical cultures and genres. Pop and jazz influences became pervasive during the 1970s, to the point that the borderline between concert and popular music often seemed extremely vague. Borrowings from distant cultures were increasingly prevalent and played a major role in reshaping musical content. Numerous composers expanded their stylistic base through musical ideas from the Far East, India, Africa and other regions, often making extended visits to these lands to study their art and culture.

These developments reflected a fundamental reinterpretation of the nature of musical style and culture that, though implicit in many aspects of earlier twentieth-century music, was only then becoming fully evident. The very psychology of composition seemed to change as composers found themselves confronted with an apparently limitless field of possibilities. No longer working with a well-defined set of conventions, sanctioned as part of a larger framework of widely accepted cultural norms, they were free to choose at will from an inexhaustible list of offerings. For younger composers like Alfred Shnitke, William Bolcom, Wolfgang Rihm, John Zorn and Robin Holloway (an appropriately eclectic list), composition became a matter of combining separate and often apparently unrelated entities in a new synthesis – a musical collage. They selected from an immense stockpile of items and recombined what was chosen in an eclectic amalgamation, more often than not emphasizing the fragmented nature of the individual components and the contradictions and ambiguities arising from their juxtaposition.

The open compositional atmosphere that grew out of the turbulent 1960s has continued to flourish. Current music is thus characterized above all by its pluralism, by the range of possibilities – technical, expressive and generic – available to it, and the spirit of freedom and eclecticism with which all of these are used. Such music can be taken as the ultimate consequence and expression of the post-tonal condition, its radical diversity giving voice to the rootlessness brought on by the loss of a common musical language, which achieves perhaps its most adequate representation in this pluralistic mix. The implications of post-tonality were of course to some extent evident from the start – in Ives and the futurists, and even in the 'defensive' nature of Stravinskian neo-classicism or Schoenbergian dodecaphony. The latter system, which attempted to shore up a dying tradition through the invention of the 'artificial' language of twelve-note music, offered a particularly poignant reflection of the crisis: a sort of Esperanto for twentieth-century music. But widespread acknowledgment of the new condition and realization of its implications for a fundamentally pluralistic musical universe did not take root until the recent past.

The failure of Schoenberg's twelve-note system, or any other musical system, to achieve the status of a common basis for twentieth-century compositional practice reflects a characteristic of the modern age which, transcending music and the other arts, colours the entire cultural fabric. The rootless and fragmented nature of current music is ultimately inseparable from the rootlessness and fragmentation of contemporary life. 'Postmodernism', the name that has been applied to recent art that revels in inconsistency, discontinuity and pluralistic mixing and matching, is from this perspective simply the final fallout of the modern condition itself.

Here one can recognize an important difference between postmodernism and 'classical' modernism: the latter remained largely committed to preserving at least the appearance of stylistic coherence, and thus to the projection of a consistent voice from composers, writers or painters. (In music, for example, one finds throughout the first half of the century an almost obsessive attempt to maintain traditional values of coherence and consistency, in spite of major disruptions in compositional language.) Postmodern art, on the other hand, not only gives up the attempt to create coherence and consistency but, as often as not, makes fun of the very pretence of doing so. And whereas modernism was ideologically tied to a search for the new, postmodernism tends to accept the fact that everything has already been done and that consequently nothing really new can be achieved. Since everything is already available, creation is basically a matter of recombination. The tone is detached and ironic or, if serious, so exaggeratedly so as to suggest caricature.

One of the strongest and earliest manifestations of this attitude was the pop art movement of the 1960s, which aggressively attacked the notion of distinct levels of artistic expression – of high as against low art, or of serious as opposed to commercial art. The paintings of Andy Warhol repeated images endlessly, trivializing them by sheer multiplication, or focussed on such mundane objects as Campbell soup cans and movie stars. Architecture, which provided the movement with its name, lent postmodernism perhaps its most forceful expression. In a ground-breaking book, *Complexity and Contradiction in Architecture* (1966), the architect Robert Venturi articulated the new philosophy: 'I like elements that are hybrid rather than "pure", compromising rather than "clear", distorted rather than "straightforward", ambiguous rather than "articulated", perverse as well as impersonal, boring as well as "interesting" . . . I am for messy vitality over obvious unity'.[13] In response to Mies van der Rohe's famous principle 'Less is more', which assumed the status of a credo for architectural modernism, Venturi countered with 'Less is a bore'.

Like their composer colleagues, Venturi and such other postmodernist architects as Michael Graves and James Stirling are fascinated with historical allusion and eclectic combination. Instead of integrating the historical elements into a consistent whole, they juxtapose them to stress their separateness, treating them as fragments joined together, along with elements from various vernacular and commercial traditions, underscoring the disequilibrium produced by their combination.

Postmodern art and music has also been shaped by a world increasingly dominated by electronic communications. International telephone, television and computer connections make possible the instantaneous transfer of an unprecedented range and variety of information, changing the way we think and see ourselves in relation to others. Those living in remote corners of the earth are now in some respects more our neighbours than those who lived even relatively nearby less than a century ago. We see images of their faces, hear recordings of their voices, enjoy their cultural products and feel the effects of their political decisions with remarkable immediacy. We are indeed close to living in what the media critic Marshall McLuhan referred to as 'a global village'; and this has had significant repercussions, not only on the nature of our cultural products but on the way we understand the very concept of culture.

One can see this in the spectacular growth both in the quantity and the variety of music available to us. Recordings, disseminated through radio and other media, now provide a wealth of material from all parts of the world and from many centuries. The music of the non-Western world has become almost as accessible as that of the West, the music of the distant past as accessible as that of our own day (indeed, in the case of 'art music', that of the past is probably more readily available than that of the present). All this music, drawn from different popular, folk, ethnic and historical traditions, becomes part of a vast electronic network within which any given item necessarily loses something of its uniqueness and particularity. As a fragment within a larger eclectic mix, it no longer has its own well-defined place or cultural function: it becomes just another component in the ubiquitous amalgam now commonly referred to as 'world music'. Since one can choose from this mix whatever one wishes, the choice varies markedly from one composer to the next, and often even from one piece to the next within the output of a single composer. With so much music available, musical culture loses its traditional focus, becoming an eclectic synthesis, a recycling of material drawn from a storehouse that is so large and flexible as to have no real shape of its own.

Whatever one may think about postmodern music, however, or about postmodern art in general, it reflects the world in which we live with striking fidelity. Its inconstancy mirrors a way of life largely based on the principle of disposability. Transformations of style and means, emphasis on surface at the expense of structure, on packaging as opposed to substance: these all speak of a society that treats its goods – cultural artefacts included – as so many exchangeable commodities. Still more basically, the pluralism of contemporary music mirrors the lack of consensus in the political, social and religious attitudes that govern how we live, act and interact. Current music, in spite of its many features of isolation, is, in the final analysis, not isolated at all, but an inseparable part of a more encompassing picture.

NOTES

[1] M. Denis, 'Definition of Neotraditionism' (1890), repr. in *Theories of Modern Art*, ed. H. B. Chipp (Berkeley, 1968), 94.

[2] Repr. in N. Slonimsky, *Music Since 1900* (New York, 4/1971), 1299.

[3] Le Corbusier, *Vers un architecture* (1923), repr. in Le Corbusier, *Towards a New Architecture*, trans. F. Etchells (New York, 1960), 219.

[4] W. Gropius, *The New Architecture and the Bauhaus* (1935), repr. in *Readings in Western Civilization*, ed. J. W. Boyer and J. Goldstein, ix: *Twentieth-Century Europe* (Chicago, 1988), 408.

[5] J. Cocteau, *A Call to Order*, trans. R. H. Myers (London, 1926), 18–19.

[6] Quoted in C. Oulmont, 'Besuch bei Stravinsky', *Melos*, xiv/4 (1946), 107–8.

[7] I. Stravinsky and R. Craft, *Expositions and Developments* (New York, 1962), 128–9.

[8] From 'Some Ideas about my Octuor' (1924), repr. in E. W. White, *Stravinsky: the Composer and his Works* (Berkeley, 1966), 575.

[9] K. Stockhausen, *Texte*, i (Cologne, 1963), 26.

[10] Ibid, 39.

[11] J. Cage, *Silence: Lecture and Writings* (Middletown, Conn., 1961), 4.

[12] Quoted in the notes for the recording by the Buffalo Philharmonic Orchestra, conducted by Lukas Foss (Nonesuch H-71202).

[13] R. Venturi, *Complexity and Contradiction in Architecture* (New York, 1966), 16.

Chapter II

Paris, 1918–45

MARK DEVOTO

21 March 1918 was the first day of spring. To celebrate it, the German army, hoping to break a stalemate that had lasted more than three years, attacked along the western front in Flanders, pushing back the allied armies within a few days to a point where Paris was within reach of long-range cannon. When Claude Debussy, who died on 25 March, was buried three days later in the Père-Lachaise Cemetery in Paris, nobody lingered for eulogies. The critic Louis Laloy wrote some years later:

> The sky was overcast. There was a rumbling in the distance. Was it a storm, the explosion of a shell, or the guns at the front? Along the wide avenues the only traffic consisted of military trucks; people on the pavements pressed ahead hurriedly . . . The shopkeepers questioned each other at their doors and glanced at the streamers on the wreaths. 'Il paraît que c'était un musicien,' they said.[1]

Fortified by the surrender of the Russians on the eastern front, the spring offensive of 1918 in France was the last and most desperate gamble of the German empire – and it almost succeeded. But its failure was decisive by late summer, and the greatest war in history was over by November, leaving in its wake a continent transformed by social convulsion, economic ruin and a devastation of human spirit. The four-year struggle had exhausted not only armies but whole civilizations. In the West, no country had suffered more than France, who had sacrificed one and a half million lives to preserve the republic. As the map of Europe came to be redrawn during the two decades after the war, it was the security of France against a resurgent Germany which dominated all other national issues. Yet by May 1919, when the Treaty of Versailles was concluded between Germany and the allies, the radiance of victory had already given way to disillusionment, for it was apparent to most observers that the war had failed to decide the paramount questions, that hatred and revenge would be the order of the foreseeable future and that there was no credible foundation for a lasting European peace. Marshal Ferdinand Foch, who had led the allied armies in 1918, said of the Treaty of Versailles with perfect prescience: 'This is not peace; it is an armistice for twenty years'.

THE ARTISTIC LEGACY

If the years of cautious experiment with the new French republic after 1871 had been punctuated by the severest kinds of social and political ordeal, they were also marked by the most extraordinary explosion of creative vigour in the arts. The artistic momentum of *la belle époque*, as the Parisian period of 1871 to 1914 is usually called, was transformed but not ended by the Great War, and those who lived through it propagated and led the major directions of the arts for another quarter-century. In music, Paris had created and sustained a large and extraordinarily successful society of professionals and institutions equalled only by those of Vienna. In both cities, but particularly in Paris, unparalleled opportunities existed and were continually created for acquiring training, for obtaining performances, for reaching intelligent audiences – and there were even appropriate bastions of corrupt artistic tradition against which the young and impetuous might rebel.

The largest and most famous of the conservatories was of course the Paris Conservatoire, but the Ecole Niedermeyer, the Ecole Normale de Musique and the Schola Cantorum attracted many students, as did somewhat later the conservatory at Fontainebleau. Among the established performing institutions, there were the very conservative Opéra and the more adventurous Opéra-Comique; Dyagilev's incomparable Ballets Russes which began performing in Paris in 1909; the venerable orchestras established in the names of Lamoureux, Colonne and Pasdeloup, to which would be added the Orchestre Symphonique de Paris, the Concerts Straram, the Concerts Koussevitzky and the Concerts Golschmann among many others; chamber music and recital series almost without number; and from the mid-1920s regular performances from a number of jazz ensembles, both home-grown and imported. Composers had their own organizations, such as the Société Nationale de Musique Française and its chief rival, the Société Musicale Indépendante. And beginning in November 1920 there was the monthly *Revue musicale* which, under the able editorship of Henri Prunières and with a staff of astute and forward-looking writers, reported in detail on this whole musical scene and on many other musical matters in Europe and America.

The end of the *belle époque* coincided with the end of a brilliant and versatile older generation of French composers and the rise of a hardly less brilliant younger one, with a middle generation led by Maurice Ravel and the Russian Igor Stravinsky (43 and 36 years old in 1918). The death of Debussy (1862–1918) in the darkest hours of the war was a reminder that no living composer in western Europe had achieved as much as he – no other French composer had ever done so – and the impressionist aesthetic in music, which Debussy himself had ignored but which his works had done so much to nurture, would exert an influence on every succeeding generation. It remained to be seen what direction the next generation would choose, for by 1918 the momentum of impressionism in music was past its peak; its greatest vigour had been reached in the six years before the war, culminating in two ballets given their premières in Paris by the Ballets Russes: Ravel's *Daphnis et Chloé* (1912), his largest piece, and Debussy's *Jeux* (1913), his most colouristically complex score. It was hard to imagine anything more resplendent than works like these; and yet in the same year as *Jeux*, the explosive ecstasy of Stravinsky's *Rite of Spring* offered the starkest possible challenge to the impressionist aesthetic, as well as a striking foreshadowing of the violence about to be let loose on European civilization. The outbreak of war was a signal for a decisive change in the direction of all three composers. Debussy, the arch-anti-classicist, would rediscover sonata form; Ravel and Stravinsky would both become leaders in the youthful neo-classicism that became the strongest and most cohesive aesthetic movement in European and American music up to World War II.

CLASSICAL SURVIVORS

The classical tradition in French music was still proudly represented by a generation of grand old men, of whom the oldest was Camille Saint-Saëns (1835–1921). Saint-Saëns had had a long and successful career as a concert pianist and continued to play and conduct even in the last year of his life. In his many popular works he re-created Mendelssohn's untroubled elegance, and much of the same flavour, in a distinctive Gallic manner. As one of the founding members of the Société Nationale, Saint-Saëns had done more than anybody to assure the revival of concert music in France after 1871. His most illustrious pupil, Gabriel Fauré (1845–1924), had been one of the most forward-looking composers of the 1880s and 90s, with a large body of piano pieces, songs and chamber music in an original and very personal harmonic idiom. Fauré in turn had been the beloved teacher of a generation of composers beginning with Ravel, and had served as director of the Paris Conservatoire; suffering from deafness in his last years, he retreated into an isolation somewhat like Beethoven's, writing a series of chamber works of great concentration and harmonic originality, including his only string quartet, completed shortly before his death.

The principal legacy of the Belgian César Franck (1822–90) was the continuation of a genuinely French school of symphonists. Many of these composers were influenced by Wagner's chromaticism and orchestral style, though Bruckner and Mahler had as little effect on them as Debussy's anti-classicism. The oldest and best-known was Vincent d'Indy (1851–1931), whose reverence for Franck's teaching was matched by his absorption in Wagnerian music drama; d'Indy's orchestral music is saturated with Wagnerian harmony and motivic development, and his opera *La légende de St Christophe*, performed in 1920, is one of his most significant late works. A more important composer of symphonies was d'Indy's pupil Albéric Magnard (1865–1914), killed in the war, whose impressive works had only an underground following but are now being rediscovered. D'Indy's idiom was inherited in part by his pupil Joseph Canteloube (1879–1957), composer of the opera *Vercingétorix* (Paris Opéra, 1933) but best known for his tastefully arranged and beautifully orchestrated *Chants d'Auvergne* (1923–30), still widely performed.

Franck's symphonic aesthetic, most familiar from his orchestral and chamber music, is demonstrated equally in his organ works, which together with Liszt's are the most important examples of their genre in the nineteenth century. But their influence on succeeding generations was even more impressive, and the works of the 'modern' French school became and remained the most widely played music for the 'king of instruments' after the works of J. S. Bach. Their natural vehicle was the 'symphonic' French organ of multiple divisions with vastly extended registers and an enormous variety of reed pipes. With such instruments, whose great size could be controlled for the first time by electric action, it was possible – for better or worse – to emulate the orchestra's resources. One of the most versatile of these organ composers was Charles-Marie Widor (1844–1937), the teacher of many composers of the youngest generation (including Varèse). His eight symphonies for organ, still widely performed, are in an idiom comparable to that of his contemporary Saint-Saëns. No less enduring is his modern edition, in collaboration with Albert Schweitzer, of Bach's complete organ works.

Louis Vierne (1870–1937), a blind pupil of both Franck and Widor and himself a composer of six symphonies for the organ, adopted the harmonic vocabulary of Debussy and Ravel in a well-crafted, personal manner; his *Pièces de fantaisie* and *Pièces en style libre* are still staples of the modern repertory. Vierne's pupil Marcel Dupré (1886–1971) was especially known for his skill in improvisation, which helped to sustain an interest in this art that had flagged for a century. Another Vierne pupil, Maurice Duruflé (1902–86), who also studied with Dukas, had a distinguished career as an organist and professor of harmony at the Conservatoire; as a composer he is known today especially for his Requiem (1947), an expertly crafted work in an original post-Fauré manner, which remains one of the most widely performed pieces of twentieth-century sacred music. The tradition continued with Dupré's pupil Olivier Messiaen, one of the most important French composers to emerge after World War II.

THE ACHIEVEMENT OF RAVEL

At the time of Debussy's death, the only other living French composer with a record of achievement comparable to his was Ravel (1875–1937), and he too had been permanently affected by the war. After a year of service at the front as a truck driver, transporting munitions during the agony of Verdun, he suffered a breakdown and was discharged. He never regained his remarkable earlier productivity. Ravel's salute to the end of the war was *La valse*, a 'choreographic poem for orchestra', completed in 1920; his original title had been *Wien*, but even with the new one the satirical intent is plain enough.

Ravel's second opera, the 'lyric fantasy' *L'enfant et les sortilèges*, to a libretto by Colette, was begun soon after the war but not completed until 1925. In this delightful work, a naughty child, impatient with his lessons, throws a tantrum and smashes his favourite possessions, which come to life and haunt him into repentance. In a way that a decade later would have done credit to Walt Disney, the stage is populated with a personified armchair, a teapot, a fire, a magic princess, an arithmetic book and a fine collection of animals, including a memorable duo of cats. Parts of this opera, especially the end, show a sentimental side of Ravel as does no other work. In striking contrast are the *Chansons madécasses*, composed in 1926. Here Ravel's harmony is the most complex in any of his music, from a carefully controlled mixture of diatonic and polytonal harmony in the first song to strident atonality in the second and third.

Ravel wrote few works after this, but his *Boléro* (1928), a ballet commission from Ida Rubinstein, became his most universally popular piece. Few of those who complained of *Boléro*'s obsessive repetition took pains to ascertain that the complete melody appears only four and a half times. 'Once the idea of using only a single theme was in mind', Ravel apparently said with modesty, 'any conservatory student could have done as well'. But it required a composer of his ability to create that extraordinarily long and intense theme with such consummate craft and refinement.

THE IMPACT OF STRAVINSKY

Only 28 years old in 1910, when the première by the Ballets Russes of his dazzling *Firebird* established him immediately as the most brilliant composer of his generation, Stravinsky (1882–1971) continued to dominate musical life in pre-war Paris. After Beethoven, the history of music offers no other example of a composer who could produce as many pathbreaking masterpieces in so short a time as did Stravinsky with the ballets *Petrushka* (1911) and *The Rite of Spring* (1912–13) and the opera *The Nightingale* (1908–9, 1913–14), not to mention a number of excellent smaller works. Stravinsky spent the war years in Switzerland; his isolation caused his musical language to undergo marked changes, leading eventually to his 'reinvention' of eighteenth-century diatonic melody and rhythm.

When the war ended, Stravinsky returned to Paris with an assortment of new works revealing unsuspected sides of his developing musical personality. *The Soldier's Tale*, 'to be read, played, and danced', composed in 1918 to a libretto by C. F. Ramuz, was the musical antithesis of his large-scale productions of the pre-war years; with only three characters and a narrator, accompanied by a miniature orchestra of clarinet, bassoon, cornet, trombone, violin, double bass and percussion, it could be produced on a stage not much bigger than the flatbed of a truck. The 'Great Chorale' in this work is a harbinger of Stravinsky's later neo-classical harmony; it sounds like *Ein' feste Burg* with wrong-key cadences and pungent dissonances, but it retains a strong and obvious tonality. Other parts develop a sense of bitonality, while the chromatic dissonance of the 'Triumphal March of the Devil' verges on atonality, though no more so, probably, than some parts of *The Rite of Spring* and *The Nightingale*. Another deeply personal side of Stravinsky's protean harmonic language was revealed in the *Symphonies of Wind Instruments*, written in 1920 in memory of Debussy. At a distance of 70 years, this 'austere ritual which is unfolded in terms of short litanies between different groups of homogeneous instruments',[2] as he described it, still stands as a notable example of a complex bitonal harmony which he did not explore further.

The characteristic rhythmic and harmonic language of *The Rite of Spring* appeared with new vigour in *The Wedding* (often known by its French title, *Les noces*), produced by Dyagilev in 1923 after Stravinsky had worked on it sporadically for nine years. The attempt to re-create a nineteenth-century Russian peasant wedding through a series of stylized dialogues and gestures, in twenty minutes of uninterrupted singing, wailing and shouting of six solo singers and a chorus accompanied by four pianos and sixteen percussion instruments, is as refreshing as anything in our century.

NEO-CLASSICISM

The aesthetic movement known as neo-classicism reached its fullest flowering in the 1920s and 30s, led by composers like Prokofiev, Hindemith and, especially, Stravinsky; but its roots go back a century or more. Even in the eighteenth century there was a tendency towards preserving the spirit of the elaborately contrapuntal styles of Baroque sacred music, and Mendelssohn and Schumann would look 'back to Bach' in some of their works. By the end of the nineteenth century, when counterpoint was revitalized in the symphonic domain through the increasingly complex chromatic harmony of Bruckner, Mahler and Franck, there were still pieces by Brahms that recaptured the forms of the sarabande, the minuet and the chorale prelude for organ. In France the establishment of the Société Nationale (1871) ensured the preservation of classical values in orchestral music and especially chamber music, upheld by the conservative Saint-Saëns as well as by the more 'chromatic' generation of Franck and his disciples.

By the second decade of the twentieth century, neo-classicism, even if not articulated as an aesthetic doctrine, represented the strongest counter-current to impressionism in the music of Debussy and Ravel. Throughout his career, Ravel was the more classically minded. His *Menuet antique*, inspired by Chabrier's *Menuet pompeux*, was written in 1895 when he was twenty, while *Le tombeau de Couperin*, six movements for piano modelled after the French Baroque suite (including an ingenious 'school fugue' of haunting beauty), appeared in the last year of the war. And Debussy, the star pupil of the Conservatoire, whose entire career had been a testimony of rebellion against textbook forms, set himself a final project of 'Six sonates pour divers instruments, par Claude Debussy, musicien français'. He lived to complete only three of them, but in his last work, the Violin Sonata, he made no effort to conceal his mastery of sonata form. Even such an unconventional character as Satie contributed to the Parisian neo-classical movement with his *Sonatine bureaucratique* of 1917, an unabashed parody of Clementi's Sonatina in C major op.36 no.1.

Stravinsky's gradual stylistic change from the expressionist harmony and percussive textures of his Russian works to the fully developed neo-classicism of the 1920s was widely regarded as a *volte-face*, as an unnatural tendency in his musical evolution; and his adoption of eighteenth-century stylistic mannerisms alienated many of those who preferred what they considered the more exotically authentic style of works like the *Symphonies of Wind Instruments* and *The Wedding*. In *Pulcinella* (1919), a ballet for Dyagilev with décors and costumes by Picasso, Stravinsky adapted excerpts from operas and chamber music by Pergolesi and other eighteenth-century Italians in a way that retains all that century's melos and feeling but marks the music indelibly with his own harmonic language. It is not too hard to imagine that Stravinsky perceived in Pergolesi's rhythms and catchy tunes an obvious vehicle for a set of dance pieces, and today we can enjoy the marriage of eighteenth and twentieth centuries in *Pulcinella* as easily as in Respighi's *Antiche arie e danze* written a few years earlier. Critical opinion at the time, indignant over the alleged disrespect to Pergolesi, received Stravinsky's rejoinder: 'You "respect", but I love'.[3]

No work by Stravinsky is more appealing than the Octet for wind instruments, a perfect realization of his neo-classical ideal: 'Composition, structure, form, here all are in the line of the 18th-century masters'.[4] He composed it quickly in 1922 for the painter Vera de Bosset, whom eighteen years later he married, after the death of his first wife. By contrast, the Concerto for piano and wind instruments of 1924 is on a larger scale, with a curious mixture of Bach-inspired counterpoint and cantilena, dissonant triadic harmony and a percussive, rhythmically complex pianism. The spirit of Bach also looms large in two works for solo piano from 1924 and 1925, the Sonata and the Serenade in A, and Stravinsky's new style seemed to be consolidated. Stravinsky's largest stage work of this period was the opera-oratorio *Oedipus rex*, with a Latin text translated from a libretto by Jean Cocteau, produced by Dyagilev in Paris in 1927.

At a tangent from these are two major works inspired by Tchaikovsky. *Mavra*, a short comic opera in one act with a libretto adapted from Pushkin by Boris Kochno, consciously attempts to recapture the Italianate *bel canto* style of Tchaikovsky's songs and operas. On the other hand, *Le baiser de la fée*, a ballet on Stravinsky's own scenario based on Hans Christian Andersen's story *The Ice Maiden*, adapts directly a number of Tchaikovsky's own melodies and even whole passages from his songs and piano pieces, for which Stravinsky provided about half the additional connective material and a rich, subtle orchestration. *Le baiser de la fée* was commissioned in 1927 by Ida Rubinstein, a former dancer with Dyagilev's Ballets Russes who had recently formed her own company, and was choreographed by Bronislava Nijinska. Dyagilev broke with Stravinsky over this, deeply offended that he should have undertaken the project with a rival company; 'Our famous Igor, my first son, has given himself up entirely to the love of God and cash', he wrote to his choreographer Serge Lifar.[5]

The climax of this decade of Stravinsky's continually evolving activity was one of the prime masterpieces of neo-classicism and the most important single achievement in twentieth-century sacred music: the *Symphony of Psalms* for chorus and orchestra. Stravinsky's orchestra here does without the 'expressive' clarinets, violins and violas, instead increasing the volume of wind tone with extra flutes, oboes and trumpets and adding two pianos to the percussive resources. The result, 'composed to the glory of God', is a proclamation of faith through the unadorned expression of triadic or unison choral writing, diatonic counterpoint (the second movement is a fine double fugue) and the spirit of King David's orchestra of the 150th Psalm, which forms the text of the final movement; much of the characteristic sound of the Piano Concerto and the *Symphonies of Wind Instruments*, but little of the austerity, survives in the *Symphony of Psalms*, which after the early ballets remains the best loved of all Stravinsky's works.

SATIE AND LES SIX

At the outbreak of the war, Erik Satie (1866–1925) had for years been well known to his fellow Parisian composers as a gentle eccentric who wrote absurdist piano pieces with fantastic titles like *Embryons desséchés* and *Obstacles vénimeux* and who even in his earliest works of the late 1880s had shown an original harmonic imagination, with a fondness for non-functional harmony and unresolved dissonances. His music had a distinct influence on Debussy and Ravel, with whom he maintained a self-effacing but enduring friendship; after 1910 he made friends with the newcomer Stravinsky, who later wrote about him: 'He was certainly the oddest person I have ever known, but the most rare and consistently witty too . . . With his pince-nez, umbrella, and galoshes he looked like a perfect schoolmaster, but he looked just as much like one without these accouterments'.[6] To the larger Parisian public Satie was unknown, and he had never had even a modest popular success; it was characteristic of his wit that he three times offered himself as a candidate for the Institut de France.

In 1915 Satie was discovered by Jean Cocteau (1889–1963), the *enfant terrible* poet and tireless organizer who had been part of Dyagilev's circle. Unable to work out a collaboration with Stravinsky (who was spending the war years in Switzerland), Cocteau, with Dyagilev's encouragement, had written a bizarre scenario for a ballet called *Parade*; Satie composed for it the most complex orchestral score he ever wrote, including at Cocteau's suggestion such special instruments as a lottery wheel, a pistol, a typewriter, two sirens, a 'bouteillophone' and something called 'flaques sonores' ('sonorous puddles'). Pablo Picasso, commissioned to design the décor and costumes, dressed the sideshow's manager in a costume ten feet tall which looks like nothing so much as an aerial view of New York. When *Parade* was produced by the Ballets Russes in 1917, the uproar was reminiscent of the one at Stravinsky's *Rite of Spring* four years before. The avant-garde poet and art critic Guillaume Apollinaire (1880–1918) saw in *Parade* a milestone not only for music but for the visual arts as well, as he wrote in a short piece for the programme book:

> [*Parade*] is a scenic poem transposed by the innovative musician Erik Satie into astonishingly expressive music, so clear and simple that it seems to reflect the marvelously lucid spirit of France.
>
> The cubist painter Picasso and the most daring of today's choreographers, Léonide Massine, have here consummately achieved, for the first time, that alliance between painting and the dance, between the plastic and mimetic arts, that is the herald of a more comprehensive art to come . . . This new alliance . . . has given rise, in *Parade*, to a kind of surrealism, which I consider to be the point of departure for a whole series of manifestations of the New Spirit that

is making itself felt today and that will certainly appeal to our best minds. We may expect it to bring about profound changes in our arts and manners through universal joyfulness, for it is only natural, after all, that they keep pace with scientific and industrial progress.[7]

Apollinaire was not a musician, but what he predicted as the musical legacy of *Parade* seems as tellingly accurate as what he foresaw in the other arts. Apollinaire's poetry had done much to free French literary art from traditions and inhibitions, and the *esprit nouveau* of his *Parade* critique (which gave the word 'surréalisme' to the world) would be echoed by many successors. Within a year, the 'new spirit' in music would have a manifesto, in the form of a lively booklet by Cocteau called *Le coq et l'arlequin*.[8] In words that would be echoed in the succeeding decades by those who wanted a new objectivity, a new proletarian music, or 'music for use', Cocteau called for uninhibited and direct music, stripped of intellectual refinement and artistic understatement:

TO BE DARING WITH TACT IS TO KNOW HOW FAR WE MAY GO TOO FAR.
Wagner, Stravinsky, and even Debussy are first-rate composers. Whoever goes near them is hard put to it to escape their tentacles; Satie leaves a clear road open upon which everyone is free to leave his own imprint.
. . . The music-hall, the circus, American Negro bands – all this is as fertilizing to an artist as life itself.

For the first time Satie found himself a famous composer, looked up to by a younger generation who were as eager to throw overboard the impressionist legacy as they were to scorn Wagner and all 'Boche' music. Though he may have enjoyed his new celebrity, he continued to live 'poor by conviction',[9] as Stravinsky put it, and to compose steadily in larger forms than he had worked in before *Parade*. Soon another commission came, from the Princess Edmond de Polignac, the American-born heiress of the Singer sewing-machine company fortune, who had commissioned Stravinsky's *Renard* during the war and would soon commission Manuel de Falla's marionette opera, *El retablo de Maese Pedro*. Satie's commission was for his 'symphonic drama' *Socrate*, a work that must be regarded as unique not only for its time but also in Satie's output. *Socrate* is not very symphonic and only subtly dramatic; it is more of a ceremonial cantata in three parts, for three sopranos and chamber orchestra, narrating the death of Socrates in a text from Plato's *Phaedo* in Victor Cousin's translation. The vocal style has more *bien chanté* than Debussy's *Pelléas*, but rocks in 6/8 or walks in 4/4 for lengths that must have been hypnotic in 1920, when *Socrate* was performed at the princess's salon and again at the famous Paris bookshop, Shakespeare & Co. Stravinsky was not convinced: 'Who can stand that much regularity? All the same, the music of Socrates' death is touching and dignifying in a unique way'.[10] The steady rhythm, which never seemed problematic in Satie's shorter pieces, is so persistent in *Socrate* that it seems a perfect harbinger of the minimalist music of the 1960s.

Shortly after the première of *Socrate*, in connection with a performance in the Galerie Barbazanges, Satie invented what he called 'musique d'ameublement' ('furniture music'), to serve as unobtrusive decoration to ordinary human activity. A note in the printed programme read:

> We present to you for the first time, thanks to M. Erik Satie and Darius Milhaud, and under the direction of M. Delgrange, 'musique d'ameublement' during the entr'actes of the play. We beg you earnestly to attach no importance to it and to behave during the entr'acte as if it did not exist. This music, specially written for Max Jacob's play (ruffian, always; vagrant, never), claims to contribute to everyday life just like a private conversation, a picture in the gallery, or the chair on which you may or may not be seated. You will try it out. Messrs. Erik Satie and Darius Milhaud remain at your disposal for all information and requests.[11]

Satie positioned five instrumentalists in various corners of the hall, and during the intermissions they repeatedly played melodic phrases from popular operas. The experiment failed, however; in spite of Satie's entreaty, people stopped talking and listened as soon as the music began. It was another 30 years before Satie's idea was reborn as the banal and ineradicable instrument of sonic climate control that we now call Muzak, found everywhere from offices to aeroplanes – exactly as Satie might have predicted when he composed his own *Carrelage phonique* ('sonic tilework'): four bars repeated ad infinitum.

Satie still had two important premières to come. *Mercure* (1924), sub-titled 'pictorial poses in three acts', was a collaboration with Picasso, whose scenery and costumes were cheered by the same group of surrealists that derided Satie's music. *Relâche*, 'instantaneist ballet in two acts, with a cinematographic entr'acte and "the tail of the dog"', was the brainchild of the dada artist Francis Picabia, who put together an absurdist scenario for which Satie provided a boisterous score full of heavy harmonizations of popular tunes. The 'cinematographic entr'acte' was provided by a ten-minute film by René Clair in which, among other things, Picabia and Satie appear firing a cannon from the roof of the Louvre, and a hearse is drawn by a camel around a five-foot-high miniature Eiffel Tower. Satie's score for this entr'acte is like his *Carrelage phonique* – short phrases repeated over and over again.

Erik Satie and the Dada artist Francis Picabia in René Clair's film 'Entr'acte' (1924), which was shown between the two acts of the ballet 'Relâche' (1924), with music by Satie, scenery by Picabia.

Performed in November 1924, *Relâche* was a considerable and uproarious success, but it was the last production of the Ballets Suédois, which disbanded soon afterwards.

It was also Satie's last work. Already ailing from cirrhosis of the liver, and without funds or family, he left his room in Arcueil and moved to a hotel in Paris, where his friends·cared for him. After his death in July 1925, Milhaud and a few others saw to the disposition of his possessions, including the dozen identical corduroy suits which Satie had never worn, several thousand miniature fantastical drawings and curious calligraphic inscriptions, and a number of music manuscripts, many of which were published in later years.

Darius Milhaud (1892–1974), who became in time the most famous of Satie's young enthusiasts, had begun his career only a few years before. From a distinguished Jewish family from Aix-en-Provence, and a product of the Conservatoire, he was 22 when the war began and had shared in the rich experiences of Parisian musical life with all the vigorous enthusiasm of one discovering an entire culture for the first time. His war service, as a civilian, did not stifle his remarkable productivity as a composer. In 1917 he went to Brazil as personal secretary to the writer Paul Claudel, who had been appointed to a ministerial position by the French government. After the armistice, Milhaud returned to Paris with a sheaf of new works – chamber music, piano pieces permeated with Brazilian rhythms, songs, several stage works with texts or scenarios by Claudel and a symphony for small orchestra. Soon he became *de facto* leader of what the critic Henri Collet called the 'Groupe des Six'. As Milhaud wrote later:

> Quite arbitrarily [Collet] had chosen six names: Auric, Durey, Honegger, Poulenc, Tailleferre, and my own, merely because we knew one another, were good friends, and had figured on the same programs; quite irrespective of our different temperaments and wholly dissimilar characters. Auric and Poulenc were partisans of Cocteau's ideas, Honegger derived from the German romantics, and I from Mediterranean lyricism. I fundamentally disapproved of joint declarations of aesthetic doctrines and felt them to be a drag, an unreasonable limitation on the imagination of the artist, who must for each new work find different, often contradictory means of expression; but it was useless to protest. Collet's article excited such world-wide interest that the 'Group of Six' was launched, and willy-nilly I formed part of it.[12]

In spite of the irrepressible Cocteau's animation, Les Six were active as a group only for a few years during the 1920s, producing concerts of their own works and those of their contemporaries. As individual composers they were too different to ensure successful collaborations,

'Les Six': group portrait of five members of Les Six by Jacques-Emile Blanche, with Jean Cocteau (top right), Marcelle Meyer, pianist (centre), and Jean Wiener, conductor (centre background). Les Six appear thus: Germaine Tailleferre (bottom left), Darius Milhaud (left, facing front), Arthur Honegger (left, facing right), Francis Poulenc (right, head inclined), Georges Auric (seated right); Louis Durey is absent.

and only once did they compose a work together (the *Album des Six* for piano, 1920), although they came close in Cocteau's ballet *Les mariés de la tour Eiffel*, written (without Durey) in 1921 for the Ballets Suédois. After their all too brief flowering as a semi-organized group, the six composers pursued their careers separately, though remaining friends. Louis Durey (1888– 1979) and Germaine Tailleferre (1892–1983) continued to write interesting music but within a decade had lapsed into undeserved obscurity. The music of Georges Auric (1899–1983) interested Dyagilev, who commissioned two successful ballets from him; but his most famous work today is the 'Song from the *Moulin Rouge*', from his film score of 1952. Of the remaining composers of Les Six, Milhaud and Honegger (1892–1955) became and remained the most distinguished native French composers of their time up to the beginning of World War II; Poulenc, slightly younger, achieved his fame later, particularly after 1945 with a number of highly regarded operas and choral works.

In many ways Milhaud's music perfectly illustrates the new ideals in French music that Cocteau had striven to articulate: a classicism inspired by Bach and Mozart rather than the later German 'heavies', usually serious but never solemn, direct and assertive with no trace of Debussy's understatement or perfumed subtlety, and sometimes lighthearted or even farcical. It is marked by a vigorous melodism deriving from international folksong, popular dance and American jazz, from the *bel canto* of Italian opera more often than the *bien chanté* of French art song, and even from the *nigun* of the Provençal synagogues' Sephardic rites. Milhaud's harmony is the most complex aspect of his style, varying from an unadorned Stravinskian pandiatonicism to a polytonality so dense as to be completely obscure. Bitonality had been used before Milhaud in isolated moments in Ravel's *Jeux d'eau* and earlier, and more extensively in Stravinsky's *Zvyezdoliki* and *The Rite of Spring* and some of Charles Ives's works; but the use of a layered and systematic bitonality became an outstanding feature of Milhaud's style as early as *Les Choëphores* (1915, to a text by Claudel after Sophocles), first performed in Paris in 1919.

Milhaud's populist tendencies are most apparent in his well-known ballet *Le boeuf sur le toit* (1920), for which Cocteau wrote a scenario that takes place in an American speakeasy, with décors by Raoul Dufy. *Le boeuf sur le toit* was 'assembled' out of popular tunes that Milhaud had picked up in Brazil, 'with a rondo-like theme recurring between each two of them'.[13] This uninhibitedly rowdy work, together with his ever-popular *Scaramouche* (1939), has given the impression outside France that Milhaud was a figure of fun, impeding his appreciation as a serious composer. Much more interesting is the ballet *L'homme et son désir*, written with Claudel during their years in Brazil and performed by the Ballets Suédois in 1921. Claudel's programme note describes the scenario 'born of the Brazilian forest': 'The action proper takes place on the intermediary platform between the sky and the waters below. And the principal character is Man, over whom the primitive forces have resumed their sway, and who has been robbed by Night and Sleep, of Name and Countenance'.[14] The 'primitivist' fascination that had inspired Picasso's *Les demoiselles d'Avignon*, with its shapes drawn from African sculpture, and Stravinsky's 'sacrificial virgin' in *The Rite of Spring*, now made its mark on this Franco-Brazilian ballet, for which Milhaud had assembled a wailing chorus and a large percussion ensemble in addition to the usual orchestra. (Two years later, in 1923, a native Brazilian, Heitor Villa-Lobos (1887–1959), would come to Paris with another 'jungle' piece, his Nonet with chorus, percussion and seven instruments.)

The climax of this stage of Milhaud's art is *La création du monde* (1923), still perhaps his most often performed work. Blaise Cendrars wrote a scenario, freely based on creation legends in African folklore, that gave Milhaud 'the opportunity I had been waiting for to use those elements of jazz to which I had devoted so much study. I adopted the same orchestra as used in Harlem, seventeen solo instruments, and I made wholesale use of the jazz style to convey a purely classical feeling'.[15] The orchestra consists of six woodwind, four brass, piano, a dozen percussion instruments and a solo string section in which an alto saxophone substitutes for the viola. The 'classical' feeling is provided by a gentle D minor lullaby, but the jazz style, in which the saxophone and bowed bass take leading roles, is Dixieland with overtones of a klezmer band. The production, with scary décors by Fernand Léger, was one of the triumphs of the Ballets Suédois.

Throughout the 1920s Milhaud composed and performed, appearing as a pianist and conductor in his own works and occasionally in others. In 1921, in one of the concert series organized by the pianist Jean Wiéner, Milhaud conducted the first performances in Paris of Schoenberg's *Pierrot lunaire*, with Marya Freund as the speaker, giving the Parisian public the opportunity to hear first-hand, in French, the work that had influenced Ravel's *Trois poèmes de Stéphane Mallarmé* and Stravinsky's *Trois poésies à la lyrique japonaise* (both 1913). In his own works Milhaud divided his attention between chamber music, orchestral music and the theatre and took a special interest in opera. His first, *La brebis égarée*, a 'musical novel' based on a play of Francis Jammes, was completed in 1915 and produced by the Opéra-Comique in 1923. Fortified by its success, Milhaud wrote a series of shorter operas, *Les malheurs d'Orphée* (1926, Brussels) on a libretto by his childhood friend Armand Lunel and, with Cocteau, *Le pauvre matelot* (Opéra-Comique, 1928) which became his most popular opera. Lunel also wrote the libretto for *Esther de Carpentras*, a two-act comic opera in the form of a Purim play. Not content with the relative brevity of these

Design by Fernand Léger for the first production of Milhaud's ballet 'La création du monde' by the Ballets Suédois in Paris, 1923.

pieces, Milhaud wrote a trilogy of 'opéras minutes', 27 minutes long in all. On a more impressive scale were the full-length operas *Christophe Colomb* (1928), to Claudel's libretto about Columbus, and *Maximilien* (1930), on Lunel's adaptation of Franz Werfel's play about the short-lived Emperor of Mexico.

Arthur Honegger, born in France of Swiss parentage, like Milhaud had studied at the Conservatoire with Widor, Gédalge and d'Indy. But while Milhaud's melodic style is Mediterranean, Honegger's is more Germanic, with a preference for thicker instrumental and vocal textures. Like Milhaud, Honegger was particularly interested in symphonic music and works for the stage. His *Antigone* (1927, Brussels) and his 'biblical drama' *Judith* (1926, Monte Carlo), were reasonably successful, as was his comic opera *Les aventures du roi Pausole* (1930), based on Pierre Louÿs's novel. In the field of dramatic composition, however, Honegger's reputation rests entirely on his popular choral oratorio *Le roi David*, with an extensive part for a narrator; the French libretto was adapted by René Morax from Old Testament texts. Honegger wrote this work in only a few months in 1921 for a chamber orchestra of wind, piano and percussion, revising it the same year for full orchestra. The style is heterogeneous, from neo-Handelian counterpoint to percussive chordal textures worthy of Stravinsky; but the lyric Alleluia chorus, as Honegger once amusingly suggested, points back to Massenet. On a much more lush and imposing scale – and less successful – is the opera-oratorio *Jeanne d'Arc au bûcher*, on a text by Claudel (1935). Among his numerous orchestral works, which include five symphonies, the most popular is still the 'train' piece *Pacific 231*, depicting a locomotive slowly achieving full speed. The Prelude, Fugue and Postlude, adapted from the melodrama *Amphion* (1929), is another good example of Honegger's mature orchestral style, in which colouristic polytonal harmony, with shimmering orchestra to match (including a saxophone), co-exists with episodes of dense contrapuntal development.

Francis Poulenc (1899–1963) had enjoyed modest early success immediately after the war with his Satiesque *Mouvements perpétuels* for piano and his whimsical song cycle *Le bestiaire* (to texts by Apollinaire); the works of the 1920s, however, show the vigour of his maturity. *Les biches*, his 1924 ballet for Dyagilev, became very popular, and in 1927 he was one of the composers who collaborated on a mini-ballet, *L'éventail de Jeanne*, written for the salon of Jeanne Dubost and performed in her home (the others were Ravel, Ferroud, Ibert, Roland-Manuel, Delannoy, Roussel, Milhaud, Auric and Schmitt). Poulenc's Concerto for two pianos and orchestra (1932) shows all the characteristics of his style: a clattering, percussive pianism reminiscent of the Javanese gamelan, a brash can-can from the music hall, an expressive lyricism couched in rich, Ravel-like appoggiatura chords and shameless parodies of Mozart's piano concertos are all juxtaposed, sometimes with deliberate crudeness, more usually with effortless elegance. The same eclecticism appears in greater or lesser degree in his numerous chamber works of the 1930s and later, especially the well-known Sextet for piano and wind (1932) and *Le bal masqué* (1932) for voice, oboe, clarinet, bassoon, violin, cello, percussion and piano, to a text by Max Jacob. In the mid-1930s Poulenc began to appear regularly as a pianist with the baritone Pierre Bernac, supplying part of the repertory with his own songs, which have since been recognized as among the finest of their time in any language.

Jacques Ibert (1890–1962) was not a member of Les Six, but the urbane and witty Parisian style of his very successful works is comparable to theirs. Of his operas, *Angélique* (1927) and *Le Roi d'Yvetot* (1930) were the most successful; *L'aiglon* (1937) was written in collaboration with Honegger. Two of his orchestral works, the impressionistic *Escales* (1924) and the Flute Concerto (1934), are still often heard.

Modern Times

During the last years of Satie's life yet another group of young Turks rallied to his cause, forming what was informally called the 'Ecole d'Arceuil': Roger Désormière (1898–1963) soon achieved international fame as a conductor; Henri Sauguet (1901–89), a pupil of Koechlin, became well known as a composer of comic operas, especially *La chartreuse de Parme* (1939), based on Stendhal's novel.

SOLITARY HEROES

Some older French composers who lived in the 1920s stand out for their individual achievements and are not usually associated with groups, artistic movements or 'schools'. One was Ravel's close contemporary Albert Roussel (1869–1937), a pupil of d'Indy who had initially chosen a career in the French navy. Roussel's work is marked to some extent by Debussy's impressionist harmonic vocabulary and orchestral style, by the classical forms of the Franck school and by an interest in oriental subjects (the opera *Padmâvatî*, based on an Indian legend, was one of the big events of the 1923 season); in his later works Stravinsky's influence is apparent. Yet Roussel's well-crafted and colourful style is distinctive: his four symphonies are the most impressive representatives of the French symphonic tradition in the 1920s and 30s, and the ballet *Bacchus et Ariane* (1931), having little in common with the stylized Hellenism of Ravel's *Daphnis et Chloé*, is still one of his most popular works.

The early fame achieved by Florent Schmitt (1870–1958) with his brilliant ballet *La tragédie de Salomé* (1907) and his setting of the 47th Psalm (1904) was sustained in the postwar years in several dramatic works, including incidental music to Shakespeare's *Antony and Cleopatra* (1920, Opéra) and an opera after Hans Christian Andersen, *Le petit elfe Ferme-l'oeil* (1924, Opéra-Comique), as well as a film score rewritten as an orchestral suite, *Salammbô*, after Flaubert (1925). Thereafter Schmitt composed prolifically in a variety of genres, but his popularity in France was increasingly eclipsed.

The strict Conservatoire tradition had been preserved by the venerable professor André Gédalge (1856–1926), teacher of a generation from Ravel to Milhaud and author of a standard textbook on the 'school fugue'. After he died the pedagogical mantle, but not the professorship, passed to his pupil Charles Koechlin (1867–1950), who had made his mark with his expert orchestrations of Fauré's *Pelléas et Mélisande* (1899) and Debussy's *Khamma* (1912). Living quietly in Paris and supporting himself by private teaching, by writing for the *Revue musicale* and in other enterprises, Koechlin did not aggressively promote his own compositions, and his achievement is only now beginning to be widely recognized. He adopted the neo-classical manner of his time in an extensive list of piano pieces and chamber works. A number of his fellow composers had visited the east coast of America, but Koechlin, almost alone among his countrymen, went to California as a visiting teacher and was enriched by the Hollywood experience; among the curious results is the *Seven Stars Symphony* op.132, a set of orchestral portraits of cinema personalities.

In the 1930s Koechlin was one of the few French composers to become interested in the techniques of the Second Viennese School. The influence can be seen in his largest and probably most remarkable work, *Les bandar-log (Scherzo des singes)* (op.176) completed in 1940 as the seventh and final symphonic poem in a series based on Kipling's *Jungle Book*. As descriptive music this 'monkey scherzo' is as brilliantly effective as any of the interwar years, with its luminous polytonal harmony, frantic orchestral virtuosity (the 'Entrance of the Monkeys') and broadly comic parodies of academic counterpoint and twelve-note orthodoxy.

Most of these composers gained reputations as teachers of composition, but their achievement was surpassed by Nadia Boulanger (1887–1979), a brilliant organist who studied with Vierne and Fauré. Following the early death of her superbly talented younger sister Lili (1893–1918; Grand Prix de Rome, 1913), she gave up composing, devoting herself to teaching and to obtaining performances and publication of Lili's works. Nadia Boulanger's classes at the American Conservatory at Fontainebleau (from 1921), and later in her own studio, soon attracted a large number of students, especially from the USA, including such diverse personalities as Aaron Copland, Walter Piston, Virgil Thomson, Roy Harris, Elliott Carter, Harold Shapero, Lennox Berkeley, Jean Françaix, Dinu Lipatti and Philip Glass. Stravinsky and Roussel were regular visitors to her gatherings and often gave her their new scores for study even before publication. A consummate master of sight-singing and score-reading, she was widely known as an analyst with an unerring ability to discern a score's essential qualities; she could go to the heart of the difficulties and uncertainties in a new piece, but at the same time could suggest improvements and fortify a young composer's self-confidence. Her 'Oh, you can do it!' was gratefully believed – and triumphantly vindicated – by composers for half a century.

RUSSIANS IN PARIS

Stravinsky had been as important in Parisian musical life as any Frenchman since 1910, and after 1914 he more or less established himself in the West, first in Switzerland and then, after the war, in France. Meanwhile he would be followed by a rich assortment of his musical countrymen. When the war ended in the West, it began again within Russia as Lenin's Bolsheviks consolidated their grip on the scattered and starving multitudes of the Russian republics. The first few years after 1918 witnessed the departure from Russia of thousands who could not accommodate to the new régime. Among the musicians who fled to Paris, one of the first was Serge Koussevitzky (1874–1951) who had begun a distinguished career in Russia as a conductor and music publisher (Edition Russe de Musique). By 1923 his series of summer orchestral concerts in Paris, which continued until 1928, were notable both for their high standards and for the frequent performances of new works, many commissioned by Koussevitzky: in the 1924 season alone, he conducted premières of Honegger's *Pacific 231*, Prokofiev's *Sept, ils sont sept*, Stravinsky's Piano Concerto and several other works.

Sergey Prokofiev (1891–1953), who had been an *enfant terrible* in pre-war Russia, spent the war years in his native country and then, after a world tour as a pianist, settled in Paris in 1920, renewing the brief association that he had begun just before the war with the Dyagilev ballet companies. Except for occasional periods on tour in Europe and the USA, he remained in Paris for the next twelve years, stimulated by the variety of music round him and writing, with great facility and intensity, what are considered his best works. Among them were three ballets for Dyagilev, *Chout* (*The Buffoon*, 1920), *Le pas d'acier* (1924) and *L'enfant prodigue* (1928); two operas, *The Fiery Angel* (1919) and *The Love for Three Oranges* (1920–21, after a fairy tale of Carlo Gozzi); two symphonies; the popular *Overture on Hebrew Themes* for clarinet, string quartet and piano; and his Piano Concerto no.3, the most popular of all modern works in this genre, which he performed with surpassing brilliance. Prokofiev continued to be profoundly influenced by Stravinsky, but his individual mature style was as influential as Stravinsky's on the developing neo- classicists in Paris, Poulenc especially.

Among the occasional features of Parisian concerts were the works of several Russian composers whose music seems to derive from the peculiar chromatic harmony and arcane aesthetics of the late works of Alexander Skryabin (1872–1915). A complex, atmospheric and almost atonal harmony characterizes the music of Arthur Lourié (1892–1966), who went to Paris in 1921 and for a while did editorial work for Stravinsky. Ivan Vyshnegradsky (1893–1979), who arrived in 1920, composed works for a microtonal piano of his own design and for two pianos tuned a quarter-tone apart. The strangest of these expatriate mystics was Nicolas Obukhov (1892–1954), who had studied with Ravel. Several fragments of his *Le livre de vie*, written in a complex musical-hieratic notation, were performed in Paris in the 1920s, but he continued to work at it long afterwards; the unpublished, 2000-page orchestral score is partly written in the composer's blood.

THE 1930s

The end of the 'Roaring Twenties' coincided with the beginning of the worldwide economic collapse that would soon be called the Great Depression. By 1933 this would propel Adolf Hitler and his National Socialists to political triumph in Germany. In France discontent brought old anti-republican elements out into the open, when aging monarchists, Boulangists from the 1880s and anti-Dreyfusards from the 1890s looked sympathetically on the gangster régimes rising in Germany and Italy. When a pro-fascist mob confronted the police in the Place de la Concorde in February 1934, a number of people were killed; the reaction brought together a coalition under the leadership of the Socialist Léon Blum. Blum's Popular Front, through effective social legislation, was able to address the principal complaints of the working class but could not carry out a rearmament programme to keep pace with Germany. In 1936 Hitler sent troops into the demilitarized Rhineland. The French forces, which could have opposed this strategic affront decisively and with vastly superior strength, decided to accept it rather than aggravate discontent at home. By 1938 the new government of Edouard Daladier was faced with continuing a defence policy of too little and too late, hoping to buy time with the course of appeasement urged on it by Neville Chamberlain's ministry in England. The tragedy of Munich followed, and within a year, in September 1939, France and Germany were at war.

Ravel composed his last work, *Don Quichotte à Dulcinée*, in 1931 and conducted his new Piano Concerto the following year. He lived five more years, hoping to write a large-scale ballet, *Morgiane*, on the subject of Ali Baba and the 40 thieves, but a still unexplained neurological condition left him incapacitated. After an unsuccessful brain operation, he died in 1937.

Milhaud, Honegger and Poulenc, their reputations secure and their production of new works vigorous as ever, were beginning their middle age; and some composers in their twenties were beginning to be heard. The twenty-year-old Jean Françaix performed his clever and witty Concertino for piano and orchestra in 1934. That year, Stravinsky, expatriate from Russia for twenty years (it would be another twenty-eight before he saw his native land again), became a French citizen, and his *Perséphone*, a ballet with singers, chorus and reciter on a perfumed libretto by André Gide, was produced at the Opéra. In 1935 Stravinsky and his son Sviatoslav Soulima gave the première of his Concerto for Two Pianos.

In 1936 Stravinsky sought election to Paul Dukas' seat in the Académie Française (it went to Florent Schmitt), and the second volume of his autobiography was published. One of the big events of the year was the première of *Oedipe*, the magnum opus of the Romanian violinist and composer Georges Enescu (1881–1955), who never composed a work that would capture public attention as had his early and too repetitive *Romanian Rhapsody no.1*. Also in 1936 a concert of works by members of a new group of four composers was accompanied by a manifesto: 'La Jeune France has for its goal the dissemination of youthful, free works as far removed from revolutionary as from academic formulae'. The works of Daniel Lesur and Yves Baudrier did not become widely known, but André Jolivet, the most prolific of the four, achieved a durable reputation in France and abroad, and Olivier Messiaen (1908–92) came to be regarded as the avatar of French music in the post-1945 generation.

Messiaen had studied the organ (with Dupré) and composition (with Dukas) during eleven years at the Conservatoire beginning in 1919; he later carried on independent studies of Hindu and ancient Greek music and of the songs of birds from round the world. These subjects, and a deeply personal Catholic philosophy, continued to be the dominant influences on Messiaen's music, which also shows an absorption in Ravel's harmonic and orchestral sound and, in the later works, a complex chromaticism resembling Schoenberg's serial music. An early orchestral work, *L'ascension* (1933), is remarkable for its tonal chromaticism freely indulging in frank sentimentality and for its strongly mystical flavour, reinforced by the abundance of descriptive expressions and tempo markings similar to those in Skryabin's sonatas; Messiaen, however, claimed that his music was theological, not mystical, in intent. His interest in Asian rhythms is reflected in the variable bar lengths of *Les offrandes oubliées* for orchestra (1931), in which regular rhythms are distorted by the addition of one or more short note-values. Other works followed in which an increasing complexity of harmonic texture and rhythm is apparent: *La nativité du Seigneur* (1935) for organ, *Poèmes pour Mi* (1936), *Chants de terre et de ciel* (1938), *Les corps glorieux* (1939) for organ. From 1936 Messiaen taught at the Ecole Normale and at the Schola Cantorum.

The threat of war increased as the decade drew to a close. In summer 1939 Stravinsky went to the USA to give lectures at Harvard, and he stayed mostly in California during the war, becoming an American citizen in 1946. His last music written in Europe was the first two movements of the Symphony in C which, as he later confided, bears the imprint of his own illness with tuberculosis and the deaths of his wife, daughter and mother within a few months of each other, as well as the development of the catastrophe about to break out in Europe.

WAR, OCCUPATION, LIBERATION, RENEWAL

The collapse of the Third Republic is still remembered with horror by those who lived through May and June 1940. The world watched in stupefied amazement as the mighty French nation, which had withstood four years of appalling destruction to achieve victory in 1914–18, was brought to her knees in a little more than a month by the armies of the Third Reich. The instrument of this conquest was the Blitzkrieg – 'lightning war' – the armoured vehicles of which simply ran round the northern end of France's fixed fortifications and broke through the line of infantry at every point; the world had never seen anything so swift and violent. After giving up a third of her younger generation in the previous war, France had no heart for further slaughter, and in sullen surrender would be spared much physical destruction. But the hated Vichy régime was a constant reminder (as Marcel Ophuls's 1969 documentary film *The Sorrow and the Pity* has shown so effectively) that the repression and deprivation wrought by the Nazis was not as dehumanizing as the acts that they forced the French to carry out on their own people and their own nation. For four years France would suffer this shame and despair, until the triumph of liberation brought forth again the republic that stands today.

It may seem surprising that during the occupation the arts continued to function in France with a vigour that seemed to contradict the repressions in everyday life and commerce that prevailed. Most composers were able to practise their art privately, and many of the official institutions continued to function as well. The national theatres, including the Opéra and the Opéra-Comique, reopened even in summer 1940 with *La damnation de Faust* and *Carmen*, and the favourite music halls, the Folies-Bergère, the Casino de Paris and many others, continued to operate; these institutions were especially popular with the occupying forces, and it was difficult to overlook the indignity of the best seats being turned over to Wehrmacht officers and Nazi bigwigs who were enjoying themselves in Paris. After a year of occupation, when there was severe rationing and widespread hunger, artistic activities became at once more difficult and more vital. As Georges Auric wrote after the liberation: 'As time passed, it became clear that music would be called on to take a far more important place than we had dared hope at first. Was it not, in the midst of our daily anguish, one of the best, the surest of refuges?'[16] After the war the world heard what the best French composers had expressed in their music of those years. Honegger's Symphony no.2 for strings (with trumpet added in the final bars) projected a feeling of despair concluding on a note of pride and hope. Poulenc's cantata *Figure humaine*, for twelve-part *a cappella* chorus on a text by Paul Eluard, struck a similar mood.

The Opéra functioned in what was called a 'state of hibernation', but *Tristan und Isolde* and *Die Entführung aus dem Serail* were part of the 1940–41 winter season, with Herbert von Karajan conducting; later productions included *Aida*, *Otello*, *Faust*, *Boris Godunov*, *Die Zauberflöte*, Rabaud's *Mârouf*, Lalo's *Le roi d'Ys*, Rameau's *Castor et Pollux* and, incredibly, Milhaud's *Medée*.[17] Some organizations were able to mount new works; Sauguet's operetta *La gageure imprévue* was successfully produced in 1944 by the Opéra-Comique and Jolivet's ballet *Guignol et Pandore*, with choreography and scenario by Serge Lifar, was performed the same year at the Académie Nationale.

Orchestral concerts flourished. The Association des Concerts du Conservatoire under Charles Münch performed 'every Sunday afternoon for four years' in the Palais du Chaillot. The Concerts Colonne, under the Vichy régime, were officially renamed the Concerts Gabriel Pierné because Colonne, who had founded the orchestra in 1874, was Jewish. In protest, Paul Paray refused to conduct the orchestra and spent the war years in retirement; he was cheered for his brave stand when he returned after the war.

Milhaud and his family had to flee for their lives, and with great difficulty got to Portugal and then to the USA. Before leaving, Milhaud hid all his manuscripts in a secure place, recovering them after the war. Poulenc and Bernac continued their 20th-century song recitals throughout the war years. Auric wrote of 'the fine courage they displayed in rejecting the least compromise, the least concession, the least hint of propaganda', and noted the risk they took in performing Poulenc's songs on texts by Louis Aragon, the communist writer whose works were banned by the Nazis.[18] One is the bittersweet song *C*, about the desperate flight across the Caesar bridges at Angers in 1940:

. . . *Et j'ai bu comme un lait glacé*	(And I have imbibed like iced milk
Le long lai des gloires faussées	The long song of falsified glories
Le Loire emporte mes pensées	The Loire carries away my thoughts
Avec les voitures versées	Along with the overturned cars
Et les armes désamorcées	And the defused weapons
Et les larmes mal effacées	And tears badly wiped away
O ma France, ô ma délaissée	O my France, my abandoned one
J'ai traversé les ponts de Cé.	I have crossed the bridges of Cé.)

The month of fierce combat had claimed a few musicians. The organist Jehan Alain, at 29 already a prolific composer of vividly imaginative organ works and even greater promise, was killed in action on 20 June. The 40-year-old Maurice Jaubert, composer of film scores and concert music, was killed on 19 June. Messiaen was captured and interned in a Stalag, where he composed a memorable chamber work, *Quatuor pour la fin du temps* for clarinet, violin, cello and piano, performing it there with fellow prisoners. Released in 1942 and brought back to Paris, he was appointed professor of harmony at the Conservatoire, where a number of young composers attended his classes. During the next two years he wrote several works on a larger scale than before, including *Sept visions de l'amen* for two pianos (1943), *Vingt regards sur l'enfant Jésus* (1944) for solo piano and *Trois petites liturgies de la présence*

The last section of Francis Poulenc's setting of 'C' by Louis Aragon, composed in 1943.

divine (1944) for eighteen sopranos, piano, ondes martenot and orchestra (1944). These works, which show an increasing density in Messiaen's harmony, oscillating between Ravel-like polychordal sonorities and a thick chromaticism which is often fully atonal, are among the earliest French works to demonstrate a sympathetic leaning toward Viennese atonality without actually adopting serial techniques; Koechlin's larger works were still unpublished, and the teachings of Webern's pupil René Leibowitz, resident in France since 1925, would not become widely known until after the war.

When Paris was liberated in summer 1944, the organized forces of the Free French marched at the head of the allied armies that entered the city. 1945 brought the end of the war and the beginning of recovery for an exhausted but jubilant nation. One familiar sign of the new vitality in French music was the riotous performance in April of Messiaen's *Trois petites liturgies*. Messiaen's star pupil, the twenty-year-old composer Pierre Boulez, graduated the same year from the Conservatoire and would within a decade be leader of his generation of French composers as well as a distinguished conductor.

Yet it was already evident to the rising generation that French music had been transformed by the war years to the point where it formed only one component of a new postwar European music, even without surrendering its Gallic individuality. Radio and the phonograph, and later television, became ever more powerful vehicles for musical communication between cultures. It was possible, even in the wake of social cataclysm, to look forward to the 1950s and 60s and an internationalization of music on a scale never before imagined. Stravinsky and Milhaud would come back to Paris and return to America again and again, proud citizens and masters of two cultures; Maurice Chevalier would sing the glories of Paris in English; Satie's *Gymnopédies* would enjoy worldwide renown as pop tunes. If the free world, in an era of instantaneous intercultural communication, was being transformed into the 'global village', Paris remained one of the capitals of the planet, confident of being in the forefront of another millennium of artistic and social progress.

NOTES

[1] L. Laloy, 'Debussy', *Revue des deux mondes* (15 July 1932); quoted in E. Lockspeiser, *Debussy: his Life and Mind*, ii (London, 1965), 225.

[2] I. Stravinsky, *Chroniques de ma vie* (Paris, 1935–6, 2/1962); Eng. trans. as *An Autobiography* (New York, 1936), 95.

[3] I. Stravinsky and R. Craft, *Expositions and Developments* (London and New York, 1962), 129.

[4] I. Stravinsky, programme note (1952); quoted by R. Craft in notes for a recording (Columbia ML 4694).

[5] S. Lifar, *Diaghilev* (London, 1940); quoted in E. W. White, *Stravinsky: the Composer and his Works* (London, 1966), 314.

[6] I. Stravinsky and R. Craft, *Conversations with Igor Stravinsky* (London and New York, 1959), 74.

[7] G. Apollinaire, 'Parade', in *The Documents of 20th-Century Art: Apollinaire on Art – Essays and Reviews 1902–1918* (New York, 1972), 452.

[8] J. Cocteau, *Le coq et l'arlequin* (Paris, 1918) (according to Cocteau, published by himself and Blaise Cendrars). The quotations here are from F. Steegmuller's *Cocteau: a Biography* (Boston, 1970), 206–7.

[9] Stravinsky, *Conversations*, 74.

[10] Ibid, 75.

[11] P.-D. Templier, *Erik Satie* (Paris, 1932), 43.

[12] D. Milhaud, *Notes sans musique* (Paris, 1949); *Notes without Music* (New York, 1953), 97.

[13] Ibid, 101.

[14] Quoted in Milhaud, *Notes*, 80.

[15] Milhaud, *Notes*, 148–9.

[16] G. Auric, 'Paris: the Survival of French Music', *Modern Music*, xxii/3 (1945), 157–60.

[17] J. Gourret, *Histoire de l'Opéra de Paris 1669–1971* (Paris, 1977).

[18] Auric, 'Paris: the Survival of French Music'.

BIBLIOGRAPHICAL NOTE

The historical and aesthetic background of the early part of the period is exhaustively surveyed in E. Lockspeiser's *Debussy: his Life and Mind*, 2 vols. (London, 1962–5), which is especially strong on the literary and visual arts of Debussy's time. A more recent book by E. Brody, *Paris: the Musical Kaleidoscope 1870–1925* (New York, 1987), is more general but richly detailed; neither book dwells on analysis of the music. E. B. Hill's *Modern French Music* (Boston, 1924) is full of historical detail and makes good reading; M. Cooper's *Modern French Music: from the Death of Berlioz to the Death of Fauré* (London, 1951) is more specialized but deals extensively with the music. Individual composers of the later part of the period are discussed in a long article by D. Drew, 'Modern French Music', in *European Music in the Twentieth Century*, ed. H. Hartog (London, 1957, 2/1961).

The later years of the Dyagilev Ballets Russes are well described in S. L. Grigoriev, *The Diaghilev Ballet: 1909–1929* (Harmondsworth, 1960); much about the personalities can be found in A. Gold and R. Fizdale, *Misia: the Life of Misia Sert* (New York, 1980), and in F. Steegmuller, *Cocteau: a Biography* (Boston, 1970).

The last years of Satie and flowering of Les Six are covered in R. H. Myers, *Erik Satie* (London, 1948), and especially in J. Harding, *The Ox on the Roof* (London, 1972). R. Shattuck's superb *The Banquet Years: the Origins of the Avant-Garde in France, 1885 to World War I* (New York, 1958), provides some musical coverage of the period but its main emphasis is on the *belle époque*. A. Orenstein, *Ravel: Man and Musician* (New York, 1975), is the best recent study of Ravel's life and works.

Stravinsky's memoirs and conversations with Robert Craft are full of intensely readable information about his French years, especially the first three volumes, *Conversations with Igor Stravinsky* (London and New York, 1959), *Memories and Commentaries* (London and New York, 1960), and *Expositions and Developments* (London and New York, 1962). Stravinsky's *Chroniques de ma vie* (Paris, 1935–6), in English as *An Autobiography* (New York, 1936), is chronologically ordered but not as detailed. No less interesting is Milhaud's autobiography, *Notes sans musique* (Paris, 1949, rev. and enlarged 2/1974 as *Ma vie heureuse*), in English as *Notes Without Music: an Autobiography* (New York, 1953).

The historical background to the catastrophe of 1940 and occupation is treated *in extenso* in W. L. Shirer, *The Collapse of the Third Republic* (London, 1970). M. Ophuls's poignant documentary film, *The Sorrow and the Pity* ('Le chagrin et la pitié'), produced in 1969, is also published as an illustrated screenplay (New York, 1972).

Chapter III

Vienna after the Empire

DOUGLAS JARMAN

When I attempt to find a simple formula for the period in which I grew up, prior to the First World War, I hope that I convey its fullness by calling it the Golden Age of Security. Everything in our almost thousand-year old Austrian monarchy seemed based on permanency . . . in this vast empire everything stood firmly and immovably in its appointed place, and at its head was the aged emperor; and were he to die, one knew (or believed) another would come to take his place and nothing would change in the well-regulated order.

These are the opening words of Stefan Zweig's autobiography.[1] By 1918 the security that Zweig and his fellow Austrians had regarded as one of the characteristics of the Habsburg Empire had disappeared. Following the assassination of the Archduke Franz Ferdinand at Sarajevo on 28 June 1914, Europe had been plunged into a war that had ended in the disappearance of all three of the great ruling families of central Europe – the Habsburgs in Austria, the Romanovs in Russia and the Hohenzollerns in Germany. The 86-year-old Emperor Franz Joseph of Austria, the one figure who had kept the diverse parts of the great Austro-Hungarian Empire together, had died in 1916, after a reign of 68 years, and had been succeeded by his grandnephew Karl I. On 11 November 1918 Karl abdicated and the following day Austria was proclaimed a republic.

It was, however, a republic that rested on insecure foundations. With the end of the war an inflationary spiral began that saw the Austrian krone drop from a parity of 110 to the pound sterling in May 1919 to 335,000 to the pound in June 1923, when inflation was at its height.[2] Racketeering was rife. Black-marketeers and specu-lators flourished while those who relied on their pensions and savings – including those patriotic citizens who had invested their money in war bonds – were reduced to genteel poverty. Foreigners, who could live in luxury for next to nothing, flocked to the city. As Zweig observed, 'even Germany, where the inflation started at a much slower pace, even if eventually to become a hundred thousand times greater than in Austria, exploited the shrinking krone to the advantage of her mark'.[3]

With the industrial and agricultural areas that had supported the empire returned to Hungary, Czechoslovakia, Poland and Italy, Austria was now also cut off from its previous sources of power and food. Food was scarce (there were hunger riots and lootings in Vienna in the hard winter of 1921) and of bad quality. Austrian bread, said Bruno Walter in his memoirs, 'could hardly be called food any longer. It caused intestinal and stomach trouble to even robust constitutions',[4] while Zweig remembered it as tasting 'like pitch and glue'.

From being the capital of a vast and powerful empire, Vienna found itself the centre of a small and impotent republic – a centre that was both absurdly large for the country's size (the two million people in Vienna formed a third of the total population of Austria) and, with its socialist city government, was politically out of step with the surrounding predominantly conservative catholic area.[5] Yet Vienna, unlike Munich and Berlin, saw relatively little unrest in the immediate postwar years and there were (at least at first) no serious attempts to overthrow the government and no political murders of the kind that were common in the Weimar Republic.

The left-wing Social Democrats were moderates (so much so that they defeated an attempt to turn Austria into a communist workers' republic of the kind that had been established in nearby Bavaria) while the right-wing Christian Socialists, though they used extreme language, were willing to arrive at some understanding with their opponents. And so, in spite of the underlying tensions within the country, Austria 'pillaged and desolate, managed to escape disintegration . . . in the critical hour the two largest parties, despite their fundamental differences, formed a coalition government. There were mutual concessions in order to prevent a catastrophe which might have swept all Europe with it and in due time life became ordered and integrated'.[6]

Life in Vienna carried on much as it had done before the war: Viennese intellectuals and artists continued to meet in the coffee houses, even if, now that a cup of coffee was made of roast barley and cost thousands of krone, they made a glass of water last a whole afternoon; fashionable men and women continued, even in their reduced circumstances, to take their stroll on the Ringstrasse, and the Viennese passion for the arts continued unabated. Zweig, who described a pre-war Vienna in which devotion to the arts amounted almost to fanaticism, in which a court actor or an opera singer was recognized by every shopgirl and cab driver, and in which the first thing that the average Viennese looked at in the morning paper was the theatre repertory, painted an equally vivid picture of the role played by the arts in Vienna in the postwar years:

I shall never forget what an opera performance meant in those days of direst need. For lack of coal the streets were only dimly lit and people had to grope their way through; gallery seats were paid for with a bundle of notes in such denominations as would once have been sufficient for a season's subscription to the best box. The theatre was not heated, thus the audiences kept their overcoats on and huddled together, and how melancholy and grey this house was that used to glitter with uniforms and costly gowns. There was never any certainty that the opera would last into the next week, what with the sinking value of money and the doubts about coal deliveries ... the Philharmonic players were grey like shadows in their shabby dress suits, undernourished and exhausted by many privations and the audience too seemed to be ghosts in a theatre which had become ghostly. Then, however, the conductor lifted his baton, the curtain parted and it was as glorious as ever. Every singer did his best, his utmost, for each had in mind that perhaps it might be the last time in this beloved house. And we strained and listened because perhaps it really was the last time. That was the spirit in which we lived, thousands of us, multitudes giving forth to the limit of our capacity in these weeks and months and years on the brink of destruction. Never have I experienced in a people and in myself so powerful a surge of life as at that period when our very existence and survival were at stake.[7]

In the five years immediately after World War I the Staatsoper was under the co-directorship of Franz Schalk and Richard Strauss (and subsequently, until 1929, under Schalk alone), but the great days of the Mahler period were over. Viennese tastes had always been conservative and the war had made even stronger the desire to return to the safe values of the past. 'Whatever had meant much to us in days gone by meant more than ever now', said Zweig. Now, with Vienna the capital of a country reduced to a shadow of its former greatness, torn apart by war, by food shortages and by inflation, the function of the Staatsoper and other representatives of the musical establishment was to reassure, to reassert, rather than to question tradition. It was a function that was to become more evident during the increasingly turbulent political climate of the 1920s and 30s.

The coalition between the two main political parties that had ensured the political stability of the young republic came to an end in October 1920, when the Christian Socialists became the government and the Social Democrats the opposition. The relationship between the right- and left-wing factions became increasingly bitter in the years that followed, with violent skirmishes breaking out between the private armies of the two parties – the Social Democrats' *Schutzbund* ('protection league') and Prince Starhemberg's *Heimwehr* ('home front'), which supported the Christian Socialists. Inevitably in a city in which the arts played so important and so symbolic a role, political differences were reflected in artistic allegiances, the progressives tending to sympathize with the left-wing faction while the conservatives and traditionalists became associated with the right. But the differences between artistic factions were not just political. Vienna remained, as it always had been, a deeply conservative city in which the music of Mahler and even of Wagner was still regarded with suspicion; Vienna was simply not ready to accept radical modern music and the admirers of the new music (the 'Neutöner') and the more conservative audiences and press were constantly involved in the most bitter and public disputes.

It is against this background that we must see the figures of Arnold Schoenberg, Alban Berg and Anton Webern – the three composers whom we now describe as members of the 'Second Viennese School' and whom we regard as the dominant figures in Austrian music before and after World War I but who, at the time, were only three of a large number of composers working in Vienna. The composers associated with Schoenberg's circle were not without influence or important supporters. In Universal Edition, under its director the great Emil Hertzka, they had a publishing house that had made its reputation promoting new music. They had the support of many artists, of a circle of fine musicians (including the pianist Eduard Steuermann, the violinist Rudolf Kolisch and the conductor Heinrich Jalowetz), of such influential figures as the composer Franz Schreker, the composer and conductor Alexander von Zemlinsky (Schoenberg's brother-in-law), Franz Buschbeck, the director of the progressive Academic Association for Music and Literature, and David Joseph Bach, head of the important arts section of the Social Democrats. They also had the friendship of the redoubtable Alma Mahler, who knew everyone of influence and was an invaluable source of contacts and, when required, of financial aid (it was Alma Mahler who paid for the first privately printed edition of *Wozzeck*).

Schoenberg's importance was recognized (a public opinion poll organized by a Viennese newspaper in the late 1920s named Schoenberg and Erich Korngold as the two greatest living composers) and was even officially acknowledged on such occasions as his 50th birthday, when the mayor of Vienna made a speech at a celebratory concert in his honour. But for much of the period Schoenberg and his circle were peripheral to musical life in the city and were regarded as a radical and fanatical (albeit a vociferous and argumentative) clique by the musical public, establishment and press.

The major musical institutions represented, on the whole, the more conservative elements. The Hochschule für Musik was under the direction of the composer Josef Marx and the Vienna Academy under Franz Schmidt for much of the period. The Lektor at the Institute for Musicology at the University of Vienna from 1919 to 1929 was Hans Gál, whose place (when he left to become director of the Mainz Conservatory) was taken by Karl Weigl, previously professor of theory and composition at the New Vienna Conservatory. Schalk, director of the Staatsoper, was also essentially a conservative, though he had appointed in Robert Heger an assistant able to take charge of the productions of new operas.

The press, in particular its senior representative, Julius Korngold, the most influential critic in Vienna and Hanslick's successor on the important *Neue freie Presse*, was similarly conservative. Korngold (who as father of the composer Erich Korngold was not completely objective in his critical stance) was a declared enemy of the Schoenberg circle. Since Schoenberg was sensitive to any slight, and since his pupils and admirers were always ready to take up their pens in their teacher's defence, they and Korngold (and to a lesser extent other critics including the composer Hans Pfitzner) carried on a heated exchange of opinions in the columns of the press. At one point the exchanges became so bitter that Korngold took Berg's pupil Willi Reich to court for libel.

Nor were the exchanges between the factions confined to words. Concerts were frequently disrupted by the booing, whistling and even fighting of the audience. The first performance in Vienna of *The Rite of Spring* in 1925, under Schalk, was stopped by disturbances that lasted for almost ten minutes. As one of the musicians who performed under Schoenberg remembered, 'We had sometimes to get Schoenberg out of the concert hall by a back entrance and had shielded him with our very bodies against all the things that were thrown at him'.[8] It was as a result of such press and public opposition that Schoenberg started the Verein für musikalisches Privataufführungen (Society for Private Musical Performances) in 1918, formed, according to its prospectus, to 'give artists and art-lovers a real and accurate knowledge of modern music'. The rehearsals and performances were open only to members (the society had about 320 in its heyday), the press banned and no applause allowed. The society existed from late 1918 until October 1922 and performed not only the works of the Schoenberg school (which it did only rarely) but of Debussy, Reger, Bartók, Ravel, Mahler and other still relatively unknown composers.

To most Viennese music-lovers the three most prominent composers living in Vienna or associated with the city would probably have been Richard Strauss, Franz Schreker and, from 1920, the young Erich Wolfgang Korngold. Schreker had established himself with the sensational première of his first opera *Der ferne Klang* in 1912. The enormous success of his two subsequent ones, *Die Gezeichneten* and *Der Schatzgräber*, which had their premières in Frankfurt in 1918 and 1920 respectively, confirmed his position as perhaps the most important living opera composer after Strauss. Both of the later operas were immediately taken up by the Vienna Staatsoper for productions the following season. Even more extraordinary was the case of the young

Korngold, whose first two one-act operas, *Violanta* and *Der Ring des Polykrates*, written at the age of 18, were given their premières under Bruno Walter in Munich in 1916 and were also immediately staged at the Staatsoper. So great was their success that Korngold's next opera, the full-length *Die tote Stadt*, written at the ripe old age of 23, had simultaneous premières at Hamburg and Cologne in December 1920, only four months after Korngold had finished it.

Die tote Stadt received its Vienna première at the Staatsoper under Schalk the following January with a cast that included the great Maria Jeritza (and would later include both Lotte Lehmann and Richard Tauber) and was so successful that Korngold was publicly congratulated by Strauss between each act. It is some indication of the relative popularity and importance of Schoenberg's circle that whereas, after its first performance in Berlin in 1925, Berg's *Wozzeck* was not performed in Vienna for five years, *Die tote Stadt* not only had its Vienna première a month after its first performance but also ran for 60 performances and was soon in the repertory of some 80 theatres.

It is equally significant that, whereas none of the Schoenberg circle held a teaching post at any academy or conservatory in Vienna, Korngold was appointed teacher of opera and composition at the Staatsakademie and while still in his twenties was awarded an honorary professorship by the Austrian president. The lush, eclectic and decorative (and also, it should be said, skilful and often very beautiful) *Jugendstil* music of such composers as Schreker and Korngold was the successful modern music of the period.

For the rest, Vienna, again in the words of Zweig, was 'cautious and non-committal to young men and daring experiments'.[9] Even Zemlinsky, another now unjustly neglected composer, found Schoenberg's music puzzling, though he none the less continued to be a staunch supporter. Zemlinsky's own creative allegiances were to the late Romantic world of Wagner, Strauss and Mahler; he recognized the importance of what Schoenberg had achieved, but the step from tonality to atonality was not one that he felt able to take. 'Mahler's works fill me with the most unlimited, boundless admiration', wrote Zemlinsky in 1913; 'Schoenberg's latest works have not always aroused in me the same love, although I feel enormous respect for them.'[10]

If Vienna remained conservative, Berlin, in contrast, thirsted for novelty. Berlin had long been an important outlet for the work of Viennese artists. 'Plays by Hofmannsthal, Beer-Hoffmann, Schnitzler have always been performed in Berlin first and not even at a later date in Vienna . . . Viennese writers only become famous thanks to their Berlin publishers and the Berlin theatres', wrote the critic Paul Stefan in 1913.[11] Before the war, Berlin had been one among many centres that shared the lead in artistic and intellectual matters. Now rapid economic growth, the arrival of large companies and wealthy families in its suburbs, led to an unprecedented artistic explosion. For a period of about fifteen years Berlin became the cultural and artistic centre not only of the German-speaking world but of the whole of Europe. Prague, where Zemlinsky, as director of the Deutsches Theatre and one of the conductors of the Prague Philharmonic Orchestra (1911–27) championed the cause of Mahler and the young Viennese composers, remained an important outpost, as did the other great German opera houses outside Berlin, especially Munich, Dresden, Stuttgart and Frankfurt. No country outside Germany had so extensive and so organized a network of opera houses; only by gaining acceptance into these could a new work be financially successful. Thus, for example, in spite of the fact that Strauss and Schalk wanted the première of *Die tote Stadt* for Vienna, Korngold gave it to German opera houses.

Berlin offered the greatest opportunities and remained the prize. As Stefan Zweig observed, 'The Viennese Max Reinhardt would have had to wait patiently for two decades to achieve the position in Vienna that he assumed in two years in Berlin'.[12] Viennese composers had to conquer Berlin if they were to be both artistically and financially successful: it was for the post of director of the Berlin Musik Hochschule that Schreker left Vienna in 1919; it was Berlin that recognized Schoenberg's stature as a composer and teacher by offering him a post teaching a composition master class at the Prussian Academy of the Arts (Schoenberg took up the post in January 1926 and visited Vienna only rarely between then and his emigration in 1933); it was to the Kroll Opera in Berlin that Zemlinsky moved in 1927; and it was the success of the première of *Wozzeck* in Berlin that elevated Berg, almost overnight, into a composer of international stature.

And yet Viennese composers remained, on the whole, curiously unaffected by those political and social elements that were among the most characteristic features of Weimar culture. To many of the most important German artists of the interwar years, expressionism, which had dominated all the arts in Germany before the war, seemed little more than a self-indulgence, an élitist and outmoded aesthetic which had no relevance to the conditions under which people lived. What was needed, argued these artists, was an art that spoke directly to and on behalf of the people, that took a political and moral stance and that replaced the subjective, hyper-emotional art of the late Romantics with one that was hard-edged, objective and unemotional.

The 1920s in Berlin, as we shall see in Chapter IV, was the period of the didactic *Lehrstück*, of the *Zeitstuck* and *Zeitoper* (pieces which attempted to capture the spirit of the times by using popular idioms and styles), of emotionally cool neo-classicism and of music intended to be functional and socially useful. It was a period characterized by the *Gebrauchsmusik* of Hindemith, by the highly successful *Die Dreigroschenoper* of Weill and by the overtly political music of Hans Eisler, who, having studied with Schoenberg in Vienna between 1919 and 1923, was eventually led to declare his disillusionment with the élitism of new music: 'I am bored by modern music, it is of no interest to me, much of it I hate and despise. If possible I avoid hearing or reading it (and, alas, I must include my own efforts of recent years in this)'.[13]

Viennese composers were out of sympathy with such trends. Indeed one of the reasons for the decline in popularity of Schreker (and to a lesser extent Korngold) during the mid- and late 1920s was that his music failed to reflect these fashions. Zemlinsky briefly toyed with jazz in some of his later songs and his opera *Kreidekreis* (written in Berlin in 1933, with a libretto by the great cabaret poet Klabund), but otherwise, of all Viennese composers, only the work of Berg (the most eclectic and most open to outside influence of the Schoenberg circle) showed even the slightest influence of the characteristic concerns of the Weimar artists. And even in Berg's music it was an influence that had little effect on his musical language. The dramatic method of *Lulu* may use devices reminiscent of the kind of alienation techniques popular in the German theatre at that time, but the musical language, compositional techniques and formal preoccupations remain unmistakably those of the Viennese School; the jazz elements are 'stage effects' used for a specific and momentary dramatic purpose rather than a sign of Berg's attempting to find a new, simpler and more popular musical style. While the Berlin success of Berg's *Wozzeck* undoubtedly owed something to the fact that its political concerns reflected those of many people in the Weimar Republic, the work's aesthetic attitude, as many critics remarked at the time, was that of Wagnerian music drama rather than of the 'new opera' of the time. To Berg's German contemporaries *Wozzeck*, as Kurt Weill perceptively remarked in his review of the première, was both a 'masterpiece of tremendous power' and 'the grandiose conclusion' to the Wagnerian tradition.[14]

Deeply conscious of their historical position as the heirs of Brahms, Beethoven and the Classical composers (perhaps ironically so in view of their reputation as radical iconoclasts), Schoenberg, Berg and Webern held themselves aloof from such fashionable trends and remained firm in their belief in high art unaffected by political or social concerns.

'What do you find of our great Middle-European tradition in such a composer?', asked Webern of Weill, 'that tradition that includes the names of Schubert, Brahms, Wolf, Mahler, Schoenberg, Berg and myself?'[15] To Schoenberg the socio-political orientation of the Berlin composers showed, at best, a misunderstanding of the pure aesthetic and technical matters that were the true concerns of art and, at worst, a cynical exploitation of a 'crass opportunity to make money the easy way'. 'It is self-evident', wrote Schoenberg in 1922, 'that art which treats deeper ideas can never address itself to the many. "Art for everyone": anyone regarding that as possible is unaware how "everyone" is constituted and how art is constituted.'[16] Although Vienna was not immune to the new musical fashions from abroad – Krenek's jazz opera *Jonny spielt auf* and Weill's *Die Dreigroschenoper* took Vienna, as they had taken Berlin, by storm – the members of the Second Viennese School remained distrustful of attempts to gain a popular following and suspicious of popular success when it occurred.

And yet, if Viennese composers were unaffected by the new fashion for *Neuesachlichkeit* – an art that was emotionally objective – they were none the less concerned during the 1920s and 30s with establishing a technically objective musical language. As in architecture, economics, philosophy, psychoanalysis, painting and many other disciplines, the most significant developments in music had taken place in the years immediately before World War I when (with the final movements of the Second String Quartet and in works such as *Erwartung*, the Orchestral Pieces op.16 and *Das Buch der hängenden Gärten* that followed) Schoenberg had made the decisive move from tonality to atonality. For Schoenberg, Berg and Webern the interwar period was one of consolidation and codification, when the achievements of the years of free atonality were assessed and formalized. The result of this process was the twelve-note system, intended to provide a permanent basis for the logical organization of post-diatonic music. Schoenberg first revealed the twelve-note system to his pupils at a famous meeting in 1923, and it was subsequently adopted by most of the composers in his circle. A similar process of objective theorization was underway in many of the arts (Kandinsky, Klee and Russian painters were formulating the principles of abstract art; Eisenstein and Pudovkin were laying down the principles of cinematic montage) and Schoenberg and his disciples were not alone among composers in feeling the need for some systematic method of organizing music in which tonality no longer played an important role. Skryabin, Bartók and Stravinsky had all developed (or were developing) their individual methods; and by the 1920s the Viennese composer Johann Mathias Hauer had already evolved a system, predating Schoenberg's, of handling the twelve notes of the chromatic scale.

Although vaguely Social Democrat in their allegiances, Schoenberg, Berg and Webern, unlike many of their friends and acquaintances who were deeply involved in left-wing politics, were essentially uncommitted politically; influenced by the ideas of Karl Kraus, they regarded politics as an ethical rather than a practical matter. Writing to his wife Helene in March 1934, Berg defined his political position through a reference to the memoirs of Gerhart Hauptmann: ' "Even though my position was near to socialism, I never felt myself to be a Social Democrat". How wonderfully simple an expression of his point of view, which would also do for me'.[17] Yet however politically uninvolved, and

Operntheater

Sonntag den 30. März 1930
Besondere Preise
Zum 1. Male:

WOZZECK

Oper in drei Akten (15 Szenen) nach Georg Büchners Drama von **Alban Berg**

Spielleitung: Hr. Dr. Wallerstein   Musikalische Leitung: Hr. Clemens Krauß

Wozzeck	Hr. Manowarda
Tambourmajor	Hr. Graarud
Andres	Hr. Gallos
Hauptmann	Hr. Maikl
Doktor	Hr. Wiedemann
Erster ⎫ Handwerksbursch	Hr. Norbert
Zweiter ⎭	Hr. Madin
Der Narr	Hr. Wernigk
Marie	Fr. Pauly
Margret	Fr. With
Mariens Knabe	Kl. Katz
Ein Soldat	Hr. Maiwald

Soldaten und Burschen, Mägde und Dirnen, Kinder

Ort der Handlung:

1. Akt: I. Zimmer des Hauptmannes   2. Akt: I. Mariens Stube
II. Freies Feld, die Stadt in der Ferne   II. Straße in der Stadt
III. Mariens Stube   III. Toreinfahrt bei Mariens Wohnung
IV. Studierstube des Doktors   IV. Wirtshausgarten
V. Toreinfahrt bei Mariens Wohnung   V. Wachstube der Kaserne

3. Akt: I. Mariens Stube
II. Waldweg am Teich
III. Schenke
IV. Waldweg am Teich
V. Toreinfahrt bei Mariens Wohnung

In Szene gesetzt von Dr. Lothar Wallerstein

Entwürfe der Dekorationen und Kostüme: Prof. Oskar Strnad

Das offizielle Programm nur bei den Billetteuren erhältlich. Preis 50 Groschen

---

Nach dem zweiten Akt (zehntes Bild) eine größere Pause

Der Beginn der Vorstellung sowie jedes Aktes wird durch ein Glockenzeichen bekanntgegeben

Kassen-Eröffnung nach 6½ Uhr   **Anfang 7½ Uhr**   **Ende nach 10 Uhr**

Während der Vorspiele und der Akte bleiben die Saaltüren zum Parkett, Parterre und den Galerien geschlossen. Zuspätkommende können daher nur während der Pausen Einlaß finden

Der Kartenverkauf findet heute statt für obige Vorstellung und für

Montag   ben 31. Der Evangelimann. Theatergemeinde Serie E, gelbe Mitgliedskarten. Beschränkter
     Kartenverkauf (Anfang 7 Uhr)
Dienstag   ben 1. April. Ariadne auf Naxos. Dirigent: Hr. Dr. Richard Strauß. Im Abonnement.
     Erhöhte Preise (Anfang 7½ Uhr)

Weiterer Spielplan:

Mittwoch ben 2. Die Bohème. Im Abonnement (Anfang 7½ Uhr)
Donnerstag ben 3. Carmen. Zu besonderen Preisen (Anfang 7 Uhr)

„Elbemühl", Wien IX.

Operntheater poster advertising the Vienna première of Berg's 'Wozzeck' in 1930. The Berlin première of 1925 had raised Berg to international stature overnight, but the 1930 première in Vienna was denounced before the performance.

however apolitical their artistic and personal stance, the three composers could hardly divorce themselves from the effects of the turbulent political events of the mid- and late 1920s. In spite of the collapse in the 1920s of the coalition government and the increasing bitterness of the war of words in the following years, there was still, until summer 1927, the possibility that the two opposing parties might reach some consensus and work together for the good of the country.

In July 1927 three members of the Heimwehr, the private army of the right-wing Christian Socialists, were tried and acquitted of the murder of a member of the left-wing Schutzbund and an eight-year-old boy. The announcement of the court's verdict brought thousands of people out on to the streets of Vienna on 15/16 July. There were violent scenes of protest during which the Palace of Justice was set ablaze and the armed police, attempting to control the situation, fired on the crowd. 80 people died. It was an event that was to seal the fate of Austria: no reconciliation between the two main parties was now possible. It was not long before the Austrian National Socialists began to profit from the division between the Christian Socialists and the Democratic Socialists. The increasing success of the German Nazi Party in the elections from 1930 onwards, coupled with an intensive propaganda campaign directed against Austria, gave new life to the Austrian National Socialist party. In three years, from 1930 to 1933, membership of the Vienna Nazi Party grew from 300 to 40,000.

Although the National Socialists did not come to power in Germany until January 1933, they were a major political force whose effects were felt in the arts as elsewhere from 1930. In March 1930, for example, the première of Weill's *Aufstieg und Fall der Stadt Mahagonny* in Leipzig was greeted by a Nazi-led riot, while the planned 1931 première of Schreker's new opera *Christophorus* in Freiburg was cancelled because of the threat of similar demonstrations.

Artistic life was not yet so difficult in Vienna. To be sure, the Austrian National Socialist Party both attempted to stop the 1928 Vienna production of Krenek's *Jonny spielt auf* ('this Jewish-negroid defilement of our state opera by a Czechoslovakian half-Jew', announced the posters with which the city was covered) and to create trouble at the 1930 Vienna première of Berg's *Wozzeck*. The day before the *Wozzeck* première the official newspaper of the Austrian Nazi Party published an article denouncing the opera as 'one of the most provocative agit-prop pieces ever written':

> the Social Democrats along with the rowdy U[niversal] E[dition] and Schoenberg circle will do everything possible on Sunday to ensure propaganda for this unspeakably botched work with which our opera will be disgraced. The sound sense of the Viennese public will give these compromising Austro-marxist activities of the State Theatre the answer they deserve.

Yet, in spite of these attempts to intimidate the Staatsoper, both works were successfully staged. At a time when the works of Kurt Weill and Bertold Brecht were disappearing from the German stage, it was still possible for Erwin Stein to conduct a performance of their *Der Jasager*, one of their most overtly political pieces, in Vienna in February 1932, and for Berg's pupil Gottfried Kassowitz and Hans Heinsheimer, the head of Universal Edition's opera list, to perform a version of *Mahagonny* two months later.

Only when the Nazis finally assumed power in Germany in January 1933 did the full ramifications of their racial and artistic policies become clear. Within three months of Hitler having become chancellor, Goebbels decreed that no Jewish artists were to perform in Germany, nor was the music of Jewish composers, or of any composers who could be regarded as having been influenced by such non-aryan cultures, to be performed. At the beginning of April 1933 when Furtwängler protested that these decrees would make it impossible for great artists like Bruno Walter, Otto Klemperer and Max Reinhardt to express themselves, he was told that it would have been more suitable had he protested 'when the whole world of German art was almost exclusively dominated by the love of experiments on the part of elements alien to the people and of the race who tainted and compromised the reputation of German art.'[18]

Furtwängler could easily have added the names of Schoenberg and Schreker to his list of those who would no longer be allowed to pursue their art. In February 1933 Berg, acting as juror at a meeting of the Allgemeine Deutsche Musikverein, the main forum for new music in Germany, had already observed that 'The Nazis have to be considered so much that Schoenberg drops out, and also non-German names like Pisk and Jellinek'.[19] By summer 1933 Schoenberg and Schreker had been dismissed from their posts in Berlin and given official 'leave of absence'. Schreker died, a broken man, the year after his dismissal. Schoenberg left Berlin for France and then for the USA. Like many Viennese Jews he had converted to Protestantism but he now returned to his original faith. Schoenberg never went back to Vienna.

Again, the situation was not yet as bad in Austria as in Germany. It was still possible even in 1935, for example, for Webern to put on a deliberately defiant concert with the Freier Typographia Chor (the choir of the printing unions), the programme of which juxtaposed, among other things, the Prisoners' Chorus from *Fidelio* and music by the banned Mendelssohn. Few composers resident in Vienna thought it necessary to emigrate; Austria, after all, was still an independent country unaffected by the laws passed by its neighbours and so, though some composers and musicians like Schoenberg, Eisler and Adorno left in 1933–4, many returned to Vienna for sanctuary from Berlin.

Neither Berg nor Webern was Jewish but their association with

Schoenberg and the very nature of their music were enough to place them on the list of composers whose works were prohibited in Germany and to debar them from official activities; in May 1933 Berg was asked to resign his position on the jury of the Allgemeine Deutsche Musikverein on the grounds that his own work represented music not permitted by the state. The banning of Berg's music had a drastic effect on his financial position since for the previous eight years, from the première of *Wozzeck* in 1925, he had been able to live on the royalties from performances of his music in Germany and on the small monthly stipend which Universal Edition were paying him as he worked on *Lulu*. But Universal were also in a precarious financial position since they themselves depended on the income from music that was now banned. Berg had been receiving a monthly stipend of 1000 schillings while working on *Lulu*, but this was reduced to 700 in June 1933 and stopped altogether in October. A stipend of 500 schillings (worth a little under £18) was finally agreed and Berg became dependent on royalties from performances abroad, on fees from commissions (both *Der Wein* and the Violin Concerto, for example, were written at this time) and on selling the manuscripts of his works to American libraries. Webern's livelihood depended mostly on private teaching and conducting, both of which continued unaffected, for a while, by political events abroad. He was, however, to feel the consequences of Austria's changing domestic affairs, which now began to move with frightening rapidity.

In March 1933 the Federal Chancellor Engelbert Dollfuss, unsure of his slender majority, had taken advantage of a procedural crisis to suspend parliamentary democracy and replace it by an authoritarian state. Feeling himself threatened by both the Nazi-inspired (and Nazi-funded) right-wing and by the left-wing Social Democrats, Dollfuss formed an alliance with the Austrian fascists, the Heimwehr and the Christian Socialists. In February 1934 civil war erupted on the streets of Vienna as Dollfuss's troops clashed with the left-wing Schutzbund. The combined army, police and Heimwehr militia surrounded and opened artillery fire on a block of workers' flats in which women and children as well as armed men were sheltering. At the end of four days' fighting, a thousand workers – men, women and children – had been killed and some three to four thousand wounded. The Schutzbund was dissolved, its leaders executed and the Social Democratic Party and its institutions declared illegal. Among those arrested and jailed were Karl Seitz, the mayor of Vienna who had given a speech in honour of Schoenberg's 50th birthday. But the real threat to Dollfuss came not from the left but from the right and, in particular, from the Austrian National Socialist Party which, having been banned since the previous summer, was (as the government knew) about to launch a Putsch. In May–July 1934 a wave of Nazi terror swept through the country, culminating on 25 July when the Austrian Nazis broke into the Vienna chancellery and assassinated Dollfuss. Kurt von Schussnig (an old friend of Alma Mahler) was appointed chancellor.

The Social Democrats had been the stimulus behind many artistic ventures in Vienna, and the banning of the party and its institutions had far-reaching artistic consequences, not least for Webern. Much of his conducting work was with Socialist music groups, his association with which undoubtedly hastened the end of his public career. The 1935 concert with the Freier Typographia was Webern's last appearance conducting a choir. It was soon followed by his last radio concert with the Wiener Philharmonik for RAVAG, the government-controlled radio station. Webern's income from royalties had never been high – they amounted to 2735 schillings (about £100) in 1933, and 1544 schillings (£54) in 1934 – and without his conducting posts and reduced to private teaching he could barely survive. As his biographer Hans Moldenhauer observed, 'The very basis of Webern's existence crumbled. His monthly salary of 200 schillings from the Singverein and his revenues from the periodic Workmen's Symphony concerts were eliminated overnight'.[20]

Some indication of the mood of the time, and of the Viennese musicians' response, is given by the periodical *23*, a polemical magazine modelled on Kraus's *Die Fackel*, which mounted a series of aggressive (and often witty) attacks on the musical establishment and on the extent to which the artistic doctrines of the National Socialists were beginning to influence Austrian cultural life. Edited by Ernst Krenek, Willi Reich and Rudolf Ploderer, all associated with the Schoenberg circle, *23: a Viennese Music Periodical* appeared from January 1932 until it was closed down at the end of 1937.

In November 1933 *23* published an article entitled 'Which Camp is Austria In?', protesting that the Viennese concert authorities were ignoring their obligations to those Viennese composers whose music was no longer played in Germany. The substance of the complaint is amply demonstrated by the programmes for tenth birthday celebrations of RAVAG the following year. The celebrations opened with a concert consisting of works by living Austrian composers but including no music by Schreker, Korngold, Schoenberg or any of his pupils. The composers with whose music RAVAG chose to celebrate its first decade were Otto Siegl, Fritz Schreiber, Hans Holein, Hans Gál, Egon Kornauth, Robert Wagner, Joseph Rinaldi, Julius Bittner and Friedrich Reidinger. 'I have heard from highest official offices that the performance of *Wozzeck* is considered to have been a desecration of the Vienna State Opera', remarked Berg bitterly in a letter to Malipiero in the wake of the celebrations, 'yet composers of whom one has never heard anything are now getting recognition and the smallest talents like Marx or Rinaldi receive the highest musical honorary positions.'[21]

A few months earlier *23* had bravely published a lengthy denunciation by Rudolf Ploderer of a newly published book on music and race by

Richard Eichnauer and a heroic attack by Ernst Krenek on the Nazi policy to the arts entitled 'On some Propositions of Dr Goebbels'. Inevitably, *23* soon acquired powerful enemies; following the publication of Krenek's article, the periodical was banned in Germany and the planned production of his opera *Karl V*, scheduled for the Vienna Staatsoper, was cancelled 'for political reasons'.

To coincide with the RAVAG festival the composer Friedrich Bayer, whose piano concerto was also performed during the celebrations, published a widely acclaimed statement on music in Vienna in which he discussed the 'living masters' of the Viennese school (Kienzl, Bittner, Schmidt and Marx), remarked on the existence of a distinguished school of young Viennese composers consisting of Caspar Hochstetter, Franz Ippsich, Adalbert Skocic, Leopold Welleba and Othmar Wetchy and attacked the 'apostles of atonal music whose music is rootless, ethnically foreign and divorced from the people. Such music stands in strong contrast to indigenous Austrian music with its melodic joyousness and its charming harmonies'. 'This is the language and the thought of the Third Reich', declared *23* in response to Bayer's attack on the atonalists, 'and it is intolerable that we in Austria should be required to tolerate it.' It was clear by then, however, that the artistic policies of the Austrian establishment would be more and more determined by the dictates of the German Reichsmusikkammer.

Although Berg had been instrumental in launching *23* (both the magazine and the title had been his suggestion), he and Webern continued to display a curious naivety about what was happening, as though in spite of having seen their music labelled as 'degenerate' and 'cultural bolshevism' they were unwilling to believe that such things could really affect them. Thus while attempting to find safe positions abroad for his Jewish friends and students (he wrote, for example, to Edward Dent at Cambridge to try to secure a post for T. W. Adorno), Berg continued to work on *Lulu* in the apparent belief that it would still be possible to stage the completed opera, though it must by then have been evident that a production in Germany (and indeed in Austria or Italy) was unthinkable. Only in May 1934, when Furtwängler told him that it would be impossible ever to stage the opera in Germany, did Berg seem to have accepted the reality of the situation. The circumstances surrounding the première of the *Lulu* Suite, which Kleiber, with characteristic bravery, performed for the first time in Berlin in November 1934, only confirmed Furtwängler's warning of six months earlier.

This performance came at a time when the relationships between musicians and the Reich had reached a crucial point. On 25 November 1934 Furtwängler had published a spirited defence of Hindemith and as a result had been greeted with an ovation at the performance of *Tristan* that he conducted the same evening. Kleiber's triumphant performance of the *Lulu* Suite, which, according to the *Prager Tagblatt*, was an undisputed success, took place only five days later. It was to be the last time for ten years that Berg's music was performed in Germany. Kleiber resigned immediately afterwards. A few days later, on 7 December at the Berlin Sportplatz, Goebbels mounted a public attack on Hindemith and the atonalists in a speech in which he denounced them as being a sign of 'how strong the Jewish intellectual infection has taken hold of our national body'. Commenting on the *Lulu* Suite première shortly after Goebbels's speech, *Die Musik* (the official organ of the Nazi Cultural Committee) observed that

> It is significant that one of the most degraded foreign yellow newspapers, the *Neues Wiener Journal*, was able to quote several Berlin reviews which seem favourably inclined towards the music of this émigré Jewish musician [*Musikjuden*] . . . such reviews are inadmissible in our age of directed public opinion for they befuddle the mind and hinder the rebuilding of our culture.

Performances of Berg, Webern and the music of other 'advanced' composers were still to be heard in Vienna in the two or three years before the Anschluss, but they were infrequent and were mainly mounted and attended by friends and well-wishers of the composers. Universal Edition and the Vienna section of the International Society for Contemporary Music put on a number of small concerts for Berg's 50th birthday in February 1935; in November 1935 the Vienna ISCM gave a concert that consisted of music by Krenek, Zenk, Webern, Hauer and Schoenberg; the Kolisch Quartet played Webern's op.5 and gave the première of Schoenberg's new Fourth Quartet on 4 May 1936; the newly completed Piano Variations op.27 of Webern had their première on 26 October 1936. The repeat performance of the op.27 Variations at the Verein für neue Musik a few days later was the last occasion on which Webern heard his music played in Vienna.

Louis Krasner, the American violinist who commissioned and first performed Berg's Violin Concerto, remembers members of the Vienna Philharmonic and government officials attempting to cancel the Viennese première of the work in 1936. The concert went ahead at the insistence of the conductor, Otto Klemperer, but the entire Vienna Philharmonic Orchestra walked off the stage at the end, leaving only Krasner, Klemperer and the veteran Arnold Rosé (who had returned to lead the orchestra as a mark of respect to Berg's memory) to acknowledge the applause.

On 12 February 1938 Kurt von Schussnig, the Federal Chancellor of Austria, and his Foreign Secretary met Hitler at Berchtesgaden and agreed to lift the ban on the Nazi Party in Austria. They also agreed that Seyss-Inquart, a Nazi sympathizer, be appointed Minister of the Interior with control of the police and security forces and that two other pro-Nazis be appointed to the other key posts of Minister of War and

Minister of Finance. As Austria erupted in pro-government and pro-Nazi demonstrations in the following weeks, Schussnig determined to strengthen his hand by holding a referendum of the Austrian people on 13 March. The referendum never took place. Hitler demanded the resignation of Schussnig and the appointment of Seyss-Inquart as chancellor. Miklas, the state president, eventually capitulated and, at daybreak on Saturday 12 March German troops crossed the frontier and Austria became a province of the German Reich. Thousands of Nazi opponents were arrested in the next weeks (76,000 in Vienna alone). In the election that followed, 99.75% of the electorate voted in favour of the new régime.

Antisemitism, which had always been a feature of Austrian public life, now became state policy, and the directives of the Reichsmusikkammer about the blacklisting of 'culturally bolshevik' composers, the ban on the music of Jewish composers and on performances by Jewish musicians became officially applicable to Austria. Many musicians, like Zemlinsky, had sought refuge in Vienna when the Nazis came to power in Germany and there now began, as

The Staatsoper, Vienna, May 1938, showing the Nazi occupation of Vienna, city of high art.

had already occurred in Germany, a great exodus which included many musicians, artists and intellectuals.

Some musicians were fortunate in being abroad when the Anschluss took place. Bruno Walter, who had given a concert consisting of Bruckner's Fourth Symphony and Egon Wellesz's *Prosperos Beschwör-ungen* in Vienna on 19 February, three weeks before the invasion, was with Wellesz in Amsterdam where they were preparing a further performance of the same programme when he heard what had happened. Korngold was in Hollywood (on the day that Schussnig met Hitler, Korngold had signed a contract with Warner Brothers to write the music for the Douglas Fairbanks film of *Robin Hood*) and stayed in the USA where he made a career as a most distinguished film composer. Over a hundred other musicians (composers, conductors, instrumentalists, musicologists and critics, including such names as Alexander von Zemlinsky, Karl Weigl, Ernst Toch, Karl Rankl, Norbert Brainin, Fritz Kreisler, Otto Erich Deutsch and Karl Geiringer) managed to escape, mainly to England or America. Not all musicians were so fortunate. The Schoenberg pupil Viktor Ullman, who had been one of the organizers of the Society for Private Musical Performances, was arrested and taken to Auschwitz where he died; his last work, the opera *Der Kaiser von Atlantis*, was written in the concentration camp town of Terezin.

In Austria, as earlier in Germany, all the leading musical institutions – the opera, the Musikverein, the universities and colleges – were now subjected to a process of 'Gleichstaltung' or Nazification. The mainly Jewish directors of Universal Edition were dismissed and replaced by those sympathetic to the Nazi cause; the names of Jewish composers were removed from the firm's lists (though, even then, Universal found itself in the uncomfortable position of having a catalogue of which the most important works were banned). The state theatres were placed under the control of Lothar Muttel, the General Intendant, and the opera companies were forced to accept a stream of second-rate directors and conductors; the principal conductors at the Staatsoper during this period, for example, were Wilhelm Loibner, Leopold Ludwig and Rudolf Moralt.

The racial and artistic directives of the Nazi government not only determined which musicians were to play or sing but also which composers could be performed. The Staatsoper could stage the works of Wagner, Mozart, Verdi, Strauss and Pfitzner (the last four being the subject of big retrospective festivals during this period) and new operas by composers (including Orff, Werner Egk and Franz Salmhofer) favoured by the Nazis; it could not stage the operas of Berg, Krenek, Schreker, Korngold or any of those composers whose music had been proscribed. The occasional curiosity managed to slip through the censor's net: Rudolf Wagner-Régeny's *Johanna Balk*, for example, produced at the Staatsoper in April 1941, based on a libretto by Brecht's former collaborator Caspar Neher and dealing with the subject of political tyranny, had already been rejected on political grounds by the Berlin authorities. Such slips, however, were uncommon. So thorough was the administration in pursuit of its artistic and racial policies that the city of Vienna even took over the estate and inheritance of Johann Strauss to ensure that they did not go to the rightful, but non-aryan, heir.

Berg died in December 1935 and with Schoenberg in America, only Webern of the three composers of the Second Viennese School – indeed of all the leading composers of his generation – remained in Vienna. Shortly after the Anschluss the notorious 'Exhibition of Degenerate Art', which the Nazis had already staged in Germany, was mounted in Vienna and included the music of Webern as well as that of Berg, Schoenberg, Schreker, Krenek and many others. Branded as a 'degenerate' artist, Webern was ignored by the official musical bodies. 'There is a music festival here in Vienna that I want to tell you about', wrote Webern's pupil Karl Amadeus Hartmann to his wife in autumn 1941:

> Just imagine a contemporary music festival in Vienna without Schoenberg, Berg and Webern, an event in which Webern goes about physically but like a ghost whom nobody sees or knows . . . Webern is invited neither to a performance nor to other festivities, let alone to the reception by the governor. In the opera none of the composers present recognized him, neither would they have found it worth the effort to seek his acquaintance. We – Webern, Hans Erich Apostel and I – walked about the theatre like strangers and could rightfully feel ourselves to be outcasts.[22]

Unable to conduct, Webern was reduced to teaching his few remaining students and working for Universal Edition which, though it no longer published any of his music, continued to employ him as arranger and adviser.

Before the Anschluss, Webern seems to have had some sympathy with some of the aims of the National Socialists, believing that Hitler would modify his policies and that such a régime in Austria would eventually acknowledge the stature of composers like Mahler and Schoenberg. Peter Stadlen has told how during preparations for the first performance of the op.27 Piano Variations Webern suddenly remarked, 'When the Nazis come I shall go to Goebbels and tell him that he has been wrongly advised and twelve-note music isn't cultural bolshevism'.[23] 'One must convince the Hitler régime of the rightness of the twelve-note system', he is reported to have remarked to another colleague.[24]

Anton Webern (1883–1945) in the year he was killed. He was the only major Austrian composer not to go into exile.

Even after the Anschluss, Webern is said to have argued that 'for the sake of good order *any* ruling body must be respected'.[25] By 1940, however, his naivety and optimism had been shattered. Many of his friends and pupils had been arrested on the Austrian 'Kristallnacht' of 10 November 1938, when thousands of Jewish homes, shops and synagogues were burnt and thousands of Jews arrested, brutally beaten and sent to concentration camps. Webern's loyalty during this dangerous period to his Jewish friends, like David Bach and Josef Polnauer, is well attested. Yet his son Peter was a member of the Nazi Party (even when membership was still illegal in Austria) and his daughter Christine (the dedicatee of the Symphony op.21), previously a member of the Hitler youth, was the wife of a Nazi stormtrooper. Torn apart by conflicting artistic, political and personal convictions, Webern gradually withdrew into his own private world.

In remaining enthusiastic about the progress of the war in its early years, Webern was no different from most of his fellow countrymen. Only after the battle for Stalingrad, with defeat on the eastern front inevitable and with the gradual realization that unless the Russian advance was stopped Vienna would soon be a front-line city, did the climate in Austria change; with the city under heavy air attack and much of it (including, in the final weeks of the war, the Staatsoper and the Burgtheater) damaged by bombing, Austrian nationalism begin to reassert itself. By 10 April the Red Army had entered the city and by the evening of 13 April the war was over as far as Vienna was concerned.

Seven years before the end of the war Webern, by implication, had declared his belief that art was independent of, and more important than, political events. 'I am totally immersed in my work and cannot be disturbed', he had written to friends on 12 March 1938, the day of the Anschluss. When he died, accidentally killed by an American soldier on 15 September 1945, the last entry in his diary was a quotation from Rilke: 'Survival is everything'.

NOTES

[1] S. Zweig, *The World of Yesterday* (London, 1943), 13.

[2] See J. Brand, C. Hailey and D. Harris, *The Berg–Schoenberg Correspondence* (New York, 1987), p.xxvii.

[3] Zweig, *The World of Yesterday*, 223.

[4] B. Walter, *Theme and Variations* (London, 1947), 256.

[5] See M. Esslin, 'Berg's Vienna', in *The Berg Companion*, ed. D. Jarman (London, 1988).

[6] Zweig, *The World of Yesterday*, 226.

[7] Ibid, 225–6.

[8] J. A. Smith, *Schoenberg and his Circle* (New York, 1986), 70.

[9] Zweig, *The World of Yesterday*, 222.

[10] Quoted in R. Stephan, *Kieler Vorträge zum Theater*, iv (Kiel, 1978), 19.

[11] Paul Stefan; quoted in R. Hilmar, *Austria Documentation: Alban Berg* (Vienna, 1984), 17.

[12] Zweig, *The World of Yesterday*, 93.

[13] Hans Eisler; quoted in A. Bress, *Hans Eisler, Political Musician* (Cambridge, 1981), 41.

[14] K. Weill, 'Alban Berg: "Wozzeck"', in D. Drew, *Kurt Weill: Ausgewahlte Schriften* (Frankfurt, 1975).

[15] L. Dallapiccola, *Incontri can Anton Webern*, in H. Moldenhauer, *Anton von Webern: a Chronicle of his Life and Works* (London, 1978), 537.

[16] A. Schoenberg, *Style and Idea* (London, 1975), 336.

[17] A. Berg, *Letters to his Wife* (London, 1971), 425.

[18] See J. Noakes and G. Pridham, *Documents on Nazism* (London, 1974), 342.

[19] Berg, *Letters to his Wife*, 400.

[20] H. Moldenhauer, *Anton von Webern*, 408.

[21] See A. M. Morazzoni, 'Berg and Italy in the Thirties', *Newsletter of the International Alban Berg Society* (spring/summer 1985), 19.

[22] Karl Amadeus Hartmann; quoted in Moldenhauer, *Anton von Webern*, 541.

[23] *Österreichische Musik Zeitschrift*, iv (1988), 195.

[24] Moldenhauer, *Anton von Webern*, 474.

[25] Ibid, 541.

BIBLIOGRAPHICAL NOTE

Among the general histories, K. Stadlen's *Austria* (London, 1971), which deals with the period from the end of the Habsburg Empire to the present day, and G. B. Shepherd's *Anschluss: the Rape of Austria* (London, 1963), which deals only with the Nazi takeover of the country, are recommended as the most approachable expositions of the complexities of Austria's political history during the period. K. von Schussnig's own account of the Anschluss in *The Brutal Takeover*, trans. R. Barry (London, 1971) has, of course, its own special interest. On a more individual level Stefan Zweig's autobiography *The World of Yesterday* (London, 1943) remains the most vivid account of what it was like to grow up during, and live through, the period before 1938, though George Clare's recent *Last Waltz in Vienna* (London, 1982) and the three volumes of Elias Canetti's autobiography (*The Tongue set Free*, *The Torch in my Ear* and *The Play of the Eyes*; London, 1990) also provide fascinating personal accounts of the years up to 1942 and 1938 respectively. J. A. Smith's *Schoenberg and his Circle* (New York, 1986) consists of transcriptions of interviews with many of those artists who lived in Vienna during the period.

Comprehensive and scholarly biographies of both Schoenberg and Berg remain to be written. H. H. Stuckenschmidt's *Arnold Schoenberg* (London, 1959) and W. Reich's *Schoenberg: a Critical Biography*, trans. L. Black (London, 1978), and Reich's partial and highly selective biography *Alban Berg* (London, 1963), are useful but H. Moldenhauer's biography *Anton von Webern: a Chronicle of his Life and Works* (London, 1978) remains the only adequate biography of any member of the Second Viennese School.

The other major figures of the period are even less well served. There is, for example, no book on Zemlinsky, though P. Heyworth's invaluable *Otto Klemperer: his Life and Times*, i (Cambridge, 1983), includes much information, and only books in German (most of them as part of the *Österreichische Komponisten den XX. Jahrhundert*) on Schreker, Bittner, Hauer and many other figures. Useful material on these composers, however, can be found in a number of short booklets, pamphlets and newsletters. Thus the Historisches Museum der Stadt Wien published a valuable booklet in 1963 to celebrate the centenary of J. M. Hauer's birth (Hauer's own theoretical writings are also published by Universal Edition, Vienna) while a flourishing Korngold Society produces a series of newsletters and booklets (the most substantial being B. G. Carroll's *Erich Wolfgang Korngold: his Life and Works*, Paisley, 1984).

While there are many books on *fin-de-siècle* Vienna, there are relatively few on Viennese culture in the interwar period and almost nothing on the period after 1933. Unlike German cultural historians, who have produced important books on music and art under the Third Reich, Austrian musicologists and cultural historians, as Walter Pass complained in the *Österreichische Musikzeitschrift*, have hardly begun to come to grips with detailing, let alone explaining, what happened during the Nazi occupation. Two editions of the *Österreichische Musikzeitschrift* (nos.3 and 4, 1988) on this topic were exceptional.

The most valuable sources of such general cultural as well as biographical information should be the letters and memoirs of the artists involved, but here, again, much work remains to be done. Of the letters of the three composers of the Second Viennese School only those between Berg and Schoenberg (which, of course, end with Berg's death in 1935) have been published in anything like their entirety in J. Brand, C. Hailey and D. Harris, *The Berg–Schoenberg Correspondence* (New York, 1987), an admirable book in which the editorial footnotes are as informative as the letters themselves (and indeed sometimes more so). A brief selection of 265 of Schoenberg's letters from the period 1910–51 has also been published (London, 1964), but the bulk of the important Schoenberg–Webern and Webern–Berg correspondence remains unpublished.

Modern Times

Finally, two important and highly recommended books that, covering a much larger period than that dealt with in the present chapter, attempt to weave together the cultural, political and social history of Vienna, are W. M. Johnston, *The Austrian Mind: an Intellectual and Social History 1848–1938* (Berkeley, 1972), and P. N. Hofmann, *The Viennese: Splendor, Twilight and Exile* (New York, 1988).

Chapter IV

Germany, 1918–45

STEPHEN HINTON

Historians, of whatever discipline, have little reason to view the period in German history from 1918 to 1945 as a self-contained unit other than that its boundary dates mark the ends of the two world wars. Rather, it is customary to divide it into two epochs: the years of the Weimar Republic (1919–33) and those of the Third Reich (1933–45). The division also makes sense in terms of music history. The social and political changes wrought by the two wars affected the cultural climate in Germany to a significant extent, just as the National Socialists' accession to power in 1933 had dramatic consequences for all artistic pursuits, not least in music. Yet there is a deeper reason for the historian to discuss the music of these epochs within a socio-political framework. Even the work of many so-called 'serious' composers is overtly 'of its time'; the impulses behind its creation are more intimately bound up with its immediate social context than was often the case in other periods. Whereas in the nineteenth century one may invoke the notion of music's (relative) autonomy and hence to a justifiable extent absolve it from extra-musical considerations, in both the Weimar Republic and the Third Reich it was precisely that autonomy that was called into question, in each case in different ways. This development is closely linked to the diverse fortunes attending the phenomenon of New or Modern Music.

THE WEIMAR REPUBLIC

The birth of the Weimar Republic, in January 1919, took place against the backdrop of the social and political turmoil that followed World War I. From the start, Germany's new parliamentary democracy was dogged by instability, both economic and political. And the fact that it survived a mere fourteen years under continual threat of collapse has prompted some commentators to see the republic's beginnings more in terms of a miscarriage. The Kaiser's abdication on 9 November 1918 none the less paved the way for sweeping reforms, among them the lifting of censorship and the extension of suffrage to women. To be sure, the reactionary backlash which eventually asserted itself with such devastating force in the early 1930s continually sought to undermine the republic's democratic foundations; but that of course was partly because the process of liberalization could itself boast substantial achievements, particularly in the cultural domain.

Although German expressionism was largely a pre-war phenomenon, it was only in the postwar period that it was allowed to flourish in the public sphere. There is a double irony here. Expressionism, whether in painting, theatre, poetry or music, was essentially the art of the outsider, a violent expression of protest against the very social restrictions that had now been relaxed. It had thrived on what Theodor W. Adorno termed a 'dialectic of loneliness', whereby 'the solitary discourse says more about social tendencies than the communicative one'.[1] Now, with the lifting of censorship and the advent of greater tolerance, it had become, in both senses of the word, presentable. However, expressionism was soon rejected precisely because it was seen as belonging to the old, pre-war world.

In 1919 the musicologist Arnold Schering discussed 'The expressionist movement in music', to quote the title of his article, which was probably the first publication to link the concept of expressionism specifically to music. Yet it is symptomatic that what Schering chiefly had in mind was not any postwar music, but the atonal works of Arnold Schoenberg (1874–1951) composed in the period 1908–13, such as the Piano Pieces op.11 and the monodrama *Erwartung*. Schering describes the expressionist qualities of this music in terms of 'unfathomable exaltations . . . ecstasies . . . angst, visionary torment', an intensity that owes its effect to the avoidance of 'all repeats and sequences' and to the fact that Schoenberg 'raises dissonance to the rule, the embodiment of music'.[2]

It is, above all, these qualities – the systematic dissolution of traditional tonality and musical gestures which are at once extremely economical and extremely expressive – that have given rise to the description of Schoenberg's compositions as 'New Music'. Yet there is an important sense in which the new music of Schoenberg can be seen less as departing from nineteenth-century practices than as continuing them. Moreover, the technical innovations were in many ways merely the extreme manifestation of an expressive ideal whose roots can be traced at least as far back as Wagner. Schoenberg may have been a revolutionary of musical material, but his philosophy of art – the aesthetic behind his innovatory creations – was essentially conservative.

Given that Schoenberg's tract 'Das Verhältnis zum Text' was published in the expressionist almanac *Der blaue Reiter* in 1912, at the time when he was producing the epoch-making freely atonal works, this discrepancy between style and aesthetics seems particularly striking. Schoenberg's philosophy of art as expressed in 'Das Verhältnis zum

Text' owes much to the thinking of Schopenhauer, as did that of most late nineteenth-century German composers. The passage he reproduces verbatim from Schopenhauer is the classic formulation of a metaphysics of absolute music: 'The composer reveals the innermost essence of the world and utters the profoundest truth in a language that his intellect does not understand'. To this central idea, Schoenberg adds others which are also demonstrations of unadulterated Romanticism: the notion of the inspired, creative genius who, 'in a frenzy of composition', produces self-contained works (each 'a perfect organism'), without any regard for material realities, 'because one only has to heed what the work of art has to offer and not its external motivation'. What counts above all is that 'the artist who has expressed himself here speaks to us'.

The technical, stylistic licences taken by atonal compositions serve an expressive purpose; they heed what the philospher Ernst Bloch, in his *Geist der Utopie* of 1918, termed 'the logic of expression'. Only by shunning traditional grammatical conventions can the composer achieve authentic, individual expression. In this sense, the difference between Schoenberg's music and that of his Romantic predecessors is only one of degree. The aesthetic postulates it realizes remain fundamentally the same, part of a well-established tradition.

The radicality with which musical expressionism represented the metaphysics of absolute music continually bordered on subversion. The logic of uncompromised expression appeared, to many, illogical. By enlisting to the full its expressive means, music paradoxically lost its capacity for communication. What was new appeared abstruse on account of its incomprehensibility; because of solipsistically exaggerated self-preoccupation, subjectivity teetered on the brink of neurosis; by eschewing common sense, autonomy turned into isolation. The new works existed almost exclusively as texts: they were seldom performed. Finding little resonance among the public, they awaited future addressees, which is why Adorno likened the radical New Music to 'messages in a bottle'.[3] Yet in spite of its virtual debarment from the public sphere, the New Music was conceived essentially for the concert hall. Its aesthetic premises, as Schoenberg's 'Verhältnis zum Text' demonstrates, remained largely those of the bourgeois age. Even the most marginal music, however potentially repellent to the average concert-goer, still laid claim to being understood as art music.

Seen in this way, as younger composers in the early 1920s began to see it, the New Music of the pre-war years was not new but rather an extreme, even decadent incarnation of older values, which no longer had a place in the cultural ambience of the new republic. The postwar generation of composers participated in a widespread condemnation of the radical, oppressive subjectivity and the resulting isolation of pre-war art. Both, they maintained, had led to a stylistic as well as an

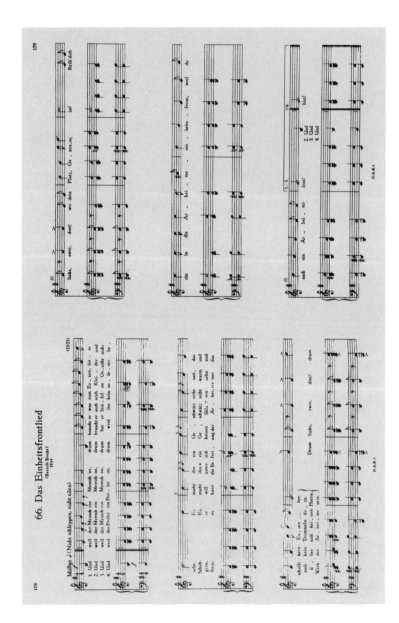

'Das Einheitsfrontlied' was written in London in 1934 (music by Eisler, text by Brecht) for the international anti-fascist movement. Like many other Eisler/Brecht songs it has remained familiar and retained its social relevance through decades of change, emphasizing the unchanging nature of the working-class role.

aesthetic impasse. One of the more vociferous was the Schoenberg pupil Hanns Eisler (1898–1962), who broke away from his teacher in the mid-1920s and aligned himself with the aims of the German Communist Party (KPD). Apart from serving the party cause with all kinds of 'applied music' (*angewandte Musik*), as he himself described it, meaning his proletarian choral music as well as compositions for agitational plays and films, Eisler worked as music critic for the party newspaper *Die rote Fahne*. In 1927 this carried an article by him which contained a diagnosis of its subject matter as characteristic of the author as it was symptomatic of Eisler's generation as a whole:

> Modern music has no audience; no-one wants it. The proletariat views it with indifference as the private concern of well-bred persons. The bourgeoisie seeks stronger stimulants and means of entertainment. Modern music, more than almost any other art, leads a phantom existence. The decline of bourgeois culture finds its strongest expression of all the arts in music. In spite of all its technical refinement, it is redundant, since it is devoid of ideas as well as a community. Art that loses its community loses itself. It is up to the proletariat, with the experience and artistic means of the bourgeoisie, to create its own new music.[4]

Where many of Eisler's contemporaries departed from his diagnosis was on the question of the appropriateness of Marxist categories; only a handful of composers took up the Communist cause wholeheartedly. Yet there was a common thread in the younger generation's thinking. Most were increasingly discontent with the values of the old, bourgeois culture and, like Eisler, sought instead a new public or 'community'. Their endeavours mirror political trends in the new republic, in particular the moves towards democratization and reform in cultural life, although the democratic concepts to which they subscribed were, by the same token, as numerous and diverse as the political parties and coalitions which represented and held together the new democracy. As will be seen, it was a diversity that ultimately proved to be the republic's undoing.

The reaction against the Wilhelminian culture was by no means synonymous with attempts to establish a new musical community. Initially, opposition to pre-war values tended to resemble adolescent rebellion against parental authority. Rather than seek out the new public, young composers appeared to scoff at the old one. For a while, music trespassed on the literary preserves of surrealism and dadaism. A notable example is Paul Hindemith (1895–1963), given in his earliest works to madcap experiments. Indeed his composing career was launched on a wave of *succès de scandales* which earned him the reputation of *musikantischer Bürgerschreck*, a prodigious but almost naive talent who indulged a puerile propensity for transgressing bourgeois conventions. Many aspects of his works from the early 1920s were wilfully conceived in an *épatant* spirit; for example he quoted a foxtrot and sounded a siren in the final movement of the *Kammermusik* no.1 (1922), he ironically invoked *Tristan und Isolde* in the one-act opera *Das Nusch-Nuschi* (1920), and he inserted in scores facetious, prankish remarks to performers.

Eisler wrenched himself away from the spiritual patronage of his teacher Schoenberg with similar displays of irreverence, for instance in the piano songs *Zeitungsausschnitte* op.11 (1925–7) composed at the time of the break with Schoenberg. Just as Hindemith had caused a collision between the world of the foxtrot and the loftier realms of chamber music, so here Eisler introduces banal newspaper cuttings, including 'lonely hearts' notices and other texts such as a children's song from Wedding (a proletarian district in Berlin), into the esoteric language of the late Romantic art song. The humorous parodistic effect clearly bespeaks a critical intention. By allowing traces of low life to infiltrate the territory of art (and vice versa) Eisler is not only blurring a traditional boundary but expressing his exasperation with it. In the second of the 'lonely hearts' notices, for example, he draws attention with a footnote to a rising chromatic figure in the piano accompaniment which he identifies as a quotation from *Tristan und Isolde*. The quotation is of course heavily ironic. In the final song, 'Frühlingsrede an einen Baum im Hinterhof', he uses a similar chromatic figure, this time at the mention of spring and dreams of the verdant forest. The tree in the rear courtyard, however, is not in bloom; it is 'on strike'. Whereupon the rhetorical question is put to the tree: 'Perhaps you think it superfluous to bloom in these times? What place have young, tender leaves on the barricades?' What place, in other words, do lyrical outpourings, epitomized by the musical language of Wagner's *Tristan*, have in the squalid surroundings of a Berlin tenement block? The harsh, gruff chords that conclude the *Zeitungsausschnitte* suggest a negative answer.

As Eisler's songs show, Wagner's musical language had become a symbol of a superannuated approach to musical expression, if not of the very source of expressionism. The same can be said of his conception of music drama, which served largely as a negative model in an age that was consciously post-Wagnerian. The musical theatre of Bertolt Brecht (1898–1956) and Kurt Weill (1900–1950), which remains perhaps the most endurable expression of Weimar's *Zeitgeist*, can be described as an almost systematic repudiation of Wagnerian precepts. It should be remembered, however, that important impulses came from Weill's teacher, Ferruccio Busoni, whose *Entwurf einer neuen Ästhetik der Tonkunst* (first published in 1907) anticipates much that his pupil was later to put into practice under the name of 'epic theatre'. Where, for example, Brecht calls in his theory for a 'separation of the elements', as opposed to their integration in a Gesamtkunstwerk, Busoni had already propagated the reinstatement of absolute musical forms in a dramatic context. Where Brecht developed the notion of 'alienation', according to which both actor and audience are supposed to be in no doubt as to the artificiality of the theatrical spectacle, Busoni had formulated a corresponding demand: 'The player "plays" – he does not experience. The spectator remains in disbelief and hence unhindered in his intellectual perception and appreciation'. And like Brecht, Busoni blamed the craving for intoxication in the theatre on the outside world: 'most people demand a powerful human experience from the stage because such an experience is missing from their everyday existence; and because they lack the courage for such conflicts as their longing demands'.[5]

If Busoni's influence remained largely theoretical, with his own stage works having little direct impact, then it was Stravinsky (1882–1971) who served as a practical example – or rather, one of his particular works: *The Soldier's Tale*. Just as the 20th-century phenomenon of music theatre can trace its beginnings to this work, so the first German performance of *The Soldier's Tale*, in June 1923, proved to be a formative experience for the young Weill. Writing to his teacher from Frankfurt, where the performance had taken place, he described the work as 'a kind of "folk play with song and dance", something in between pantomime, melodrama and farce. As far as this kind of theatre permits, it is masterfully structured, and even the glance towards the taste of the man in the street is bearable in the way it fits the subject matter'.[6] Five years later, Weill and Brecht were to produce something closely fitting this description with their own *Dreigroschenoper* which became the theatrical sensation of its time, thereby repeating the success enjoyed, exactly 200 years earlier, by John Gay's *Beggar's Opera*, of which it is a loose adaptation.

The phenomenal success of *Die Dreigroschenoper*, which received its première in Berlin at the Theater am Schiffbauerdamm on 31 August 1928, was such that the term 'Threepenny Fever' (*Dreigroschenfieber*) was coined to describe its clamorous early reception. Sheet music of its smash hits was widely available. There even opened a café called the 'Dreigroschen-Keller', which restricted its musical fare solely to gramophone recordings of selected numbers from the *Dreigroschenoper*, including various arrangements for jazz orchestra which the composer encouraged. The success itself became the subject of frequent critical debate. The press on the whole endorsed the public's response to the work. Yet a handful of influential commentators, most of them keen either to defend Weill's reputation as a 'serious' composer or to protect the credentials of Brecht as a political artist (or both), declared the work's popularity to be a misunderstanding. Others were more guarded and equivocal, such as the Schoenberg pupil Alban Berg

(1885–1935), who took the occasion of Schubert's 100th anniversary in November 1928, in the throes of 'Dreigroschenfieber', as an opportunity to reflect not only on the Viennese master's enormous popularity but on Weill's as well. Schubert's standing, he maintained, was to be put down to 'popular misunderstanding' which, in turn, arose from 'a lack of distance in artistic judgment', to which he added: 'But perhaps such a lack of distance in artistic judgment should come as no surprise in an age in which even the likes of us do not know whether to choose a Threepenny Opera or a Ten Thousand Dollar Symphony'.[7] Berg is none the less willing to concede a certain indecisiveness among 'the likes of us', that is, on the part of serious composers.

Weill's remarks on the Schubert celebrations, published in *Der deutsche Rundfunk*, the radio guide for which he acted as music correspondent, are equally telling in being quite contrary to Berg's. It is precisely Schubert's popularity that Weill finds so laudable: 'Schubert counts among the very few artists', he wrote, 'who have found direct contact with the public at large, even though their achievement in their chosen art is of the highest standard known to man. His melodies . . . have found their way into the hearts of the people because they are born of popular feeling'.[8]

Although ostensibly discussing Schubert, Berg and Weill are of course alluding to an aesthetic that has a direct bearing on their own creative pursuits. While Berg grudgingly acknowledges a change in attitude to which he himself does not subscribe, Weill appears to embrace it without reservation, both as composer and publicist. The melodies of *Die Dreigroschenoper* can be said to have found their way into the hearts of the people. By the same token, Weill's compositional development, from about 1927, offers clear evidence of 'Shifts in Musical Production', to quote the title of his own programmatic article published at the time. In it he observed that:

> A clear split is becoming apparent between, on the one hand, those musicians who, full of disdain for their audience, continue as it were by shutting out the public sphere to work on the solution to aesthetic problems and, on the other, those who enter into contact with some sort of audience, integrating their work into some sort of larger concern, because they see that above the artistic there is also a common human attitude that springs from some sense of communal belonging and which is decisive for the creation of a work of art.[9]

Weill summarizes this 'shift' as a 'withdrawal from the individualistic principle of art', a development which through the repetition (twice) of the determiner 'some' he defines as loosely and hence as all-embracingly as possible. Unlike Eisler, say, whose ideologically slanted criticism of his colleagues often bordered on the destructively sectarian, Weill is at pains to include in his programme the endeavours of as many composers as possible. His central demand is that 'music seeks . . . a rapprochement with the interests of a wider audience. It does this by utilizing the lightness and playfulness achieved in recent years in order to create a worthwhile "Gebrauchsmusik"'.

In defining his new musical ideal as *Gebrauchsmusik* (literally, 'use music'), Weill was taking up a word that had recently become currency in musicological circles and that had begun to serve as a slogan in musico-political quarrels. The fact that the concept had first become established a few years earlier by music historians is no coincidence: musicologists were participants in the discussion of contemporary cultural politics and their academic work bore a direct relation to the issues being debated. *Gebrauchsmusik* forms one half of a conceptual pair; the other half is 'self-sufficient' (*eigenständige*) or 'presentation' music (*Vortrags-* or *Darbietungsmusik*). It was used, then, to define all music that stands outside what is now commonly called 'autonomous music' and that, on account of its functionality, differs fundamentally from music of the Classical and Romantic tradition. Musicologists wanted to grasp the specific status of music before that tradition. The methods of musicology, they argued, were largely informed by the concept of music's autonomy, in particular the notion of the self-sufficient, organically conceived work – an approach which they saw as inappropriate, because anachronistic, when applied to pre-classical music. 'It requires no further comment that such works are not created for "aesthetic enjoyment", that they do not concern the "listener" in the usual sense of the word': the remark is Heinrich Besseler's, from his dissertation on motet composition in the 13th and 14th centuries (Freiburg, 1925), in which he demonstrated that such music should be treated not as an autonomous aesthetic object but as an integral part of everyday life, something that grows naturally out of the community.

In his early writings Besseler made a point of acknowledging an intellectual debt to the philosopher Martin Heidegger, with whom he had studied and whose existential phenomenology influenced his theory of two distinct approaches to music. Translated back into Heideggerian terminology *Gebrauchsmusik* belongs to the more immediate, primordial realm of *Zeug* ('equipment') as opposed to that of *Ding* ('thing'). It is *zuhanden* ('ready-to-hand'), an object of manipulation, in contrast to objects of bare perceptual cognition or reflection, which Heidegger describes as merely *vorhanden* ('present-at-hand'). Apart from being the central figure in the musicological discourse on the concept of *Gebrauchsmusik*, Besseler was also a forceful mediator between the past and the present. His reflections led him to evaluate the cultural importance of the concert hall, not only for his historical research but also with regard to developments in contemporary music, where his ideas took on normative implications. The connection becomes evident in his highly influential and, at the time, controversial essay 'Grundfragen des musikalischen Hörens' in which the paradigm change he proposes, in objectively musicological terms, from *eigenständige Musik* to *Gebrauchsmusik* can also be read – and indeed was read – as the basis of a cultural strategy.

> One would first of all presuppose fundamentally different approaches to music where the essentially concert-determined characteristics were missing. Perfection of reproduction would accordingly count as inessential, the listeners would not constitute a limitless crowd taking in what is performed in passive devotion, but would encounter the music as a genuine community of like-minded individuals with an active attitude and in active expectation. Such art would therefore always correspond to a concrete need, it would not have to find its public but would grow out it. Such an art is *Gebrauchsmusik*.[10]

If the early works of the younger generation had expressed an occasionally jejune reaction against the tradition of aesthetic autonomy and its institutional underpinnings (the concert hall and, to a certain extent, the opera house), then a plea for a return to the values of *Gebrauchsmusik* as outlined by Besseler revealed the more serious face of that protest. Rather than poke fun at tradition, one historicized it. Where, in other words, those with dadaist leanings seemed to be saying of the Romantic movement: 'This can't go on', the adherents of a new community music retorted: 'It hasn't always been like this'. The repudiation of the Romantic musical aesthetic can thus be seen as part of a pervasive historicism in the 1920s, which spawned a range of activities, from the research of historical musicologists into early music as well as organizing performances of such music, whether Netherlands polyphony or Handelian opera, to attempts to influence contemporary production along similar lines. The emphasis was less on the mere enrichment of the repertory with forgotten masterworks than on penetrating and propagating an entirely different conception of music. (It is in such historicist thinking that the seeds of the more recent preoccupation with 'authentic performance' can be discovered.)

The 'shift' of which Weill spoke also corresponds, in broad terms, to the concept of *Neue Sachlichkeit*. Although originally used in connection with painting, in the latter half of the 1920s *Neue Sachlichkeit* circulated as an umbrella term to describe trends in all the arts. Like many slogans, it subsequently became so overused that it was rendered virtually meaningless or, rather, so overladen with meanings that its original connotation became obscured. The director of the Mannheim art gallery, G. F. Hartlaub, coined the word as the title for an exhibition of contemporary paintings and drawings which opened under his auspices on 14 June 1925. Yet he had in mind less a certain style of

'Carnival' by Max Beckmann (1920), an example of Neue Sachlichkeit painting; the traditional German 'Fastnacht' recognizes the vanity, futility and transience of the world. (Beckmann includes a self-portrait as a clown in a monkey mask).

painting, which is how the *Neue Sachlichkeit* is frequently defined, than an aesthetic attitude common to the painters he was exhibiting, among them Max Beckmann, Otto Dix and, above all, George Grosz. It would be more accurate to describe that attitude as anti-aesthetic, particularly in the light of Hartlaub's own appraisal of the artists, whom he represented more out of a sense of professional duty than for reasons of personal attachment or approval. For Hartlaub, at least, the *Neue Sachlichkeit* had a pejorative connotation, something which readily becomes apparent in an article he published in 1924 under the title 'Zynismus als Kunstrichtung'. As he later remarked, 'the fact of mounting a renowned exhibition and the far-reaching coinage of its title . . . by no means excluded, even then, an inner distance felt by the organizer'. Why, according to Hartlaub, were the artists of the *Neue Sachlichkeit* cynical? Because 'they do not believe whole-heartedly anymore in *art*'. 'What [the modern realist] offers', he lamented, 'extends to utility [*Gebrauchszweck*], to tendentiousness'.[11]

In his review of the epoch, written in the early 1930s, Besseler similarly eschewed purely stylistic criteria in his definition of the *Neue Sachlichkeit*. Unlike Hartlaub's, however, his assessment of the movement was positive. 'What it contains by way of protest was directed less against the dramatic gestures and soulfulness of a style, which already no longer stood in the forefront, than against the abstractness and human isolation of expressionism'.[12] Besseler's distinction is crucial if the term 'Neue Sachlichkeit' is to possess any genuine significance for the aesthetics of the period. If one focussed solely on stylistic issues, then, as has often been done, Schoenberg's twelve-note compositions, which he began to produce in the early 1920s, might be subsumed under the label of *Neue Sachlichkeit*. Stravinsky, too, could qualify for inclusion, perhaps more so given his conscious rejection of *espressivo*. One might be tempted to equate *Neue Sachlichkeit* with neo-classicism. But that would be to operate within the confines of a musicological tradition which Besseler strove to break away from and the negation of which found a close correlation in his understanding of the *Neue Sachlichkeit*.

Young German composers availed themselves of neo-classical means, just as Stravinsky and Schoenberg did: the former in his use of pre-Classical and Baroque idioms (*Pulcinella*, 1919–20, and the Wind Octet, 1922–3), the latter in his reliance, in his twelve-note compositions, on largely pre-Classical dance forms (Suite for piano op.25, 1921, and the Suite op.29, 1924–6). (The models to which composers reverted were rarely from the Classical period nor always part of a classical canon, so 'neo-classicism' – in contrast to nineteenth-century classicism – is strictly speaking a misnomer. Stravinsky's creative borrowings from Pergolesi in *Pulcinella*, for example, fulfil neither of the above requirements. What remains salient is the use of a compositional model, irrespective of its historical provenance or its aesthetic quality. So Stravinsky's use of jazz also belongs to his neo-classical attitude.) Where the neo-classicism of such composers as Weill, Hindemith and Eisler departs from that of Stravinsky and Schoenberg is in the ends to which the compositional means are put.

The confusion of means and ends has been compounded in English by the translation of the essentially untranslatable term 'Neue Sachlichkeit' as 'new objectivity'. Schoenberg's application of given, 'objective' methods, whether formal paradigms or the twelve-note technique, yields structural, largely subcutaneous features of the individual musical work. Stravinsky, on the other hand, uses his models, including jazz idioms, in the spirit of Russian formalism, as mechanized material; he wanted to parody familiar musical language and hence, by re-organizing it, to defeat the listener's expectations. The German neo-classicists learnt much from this approach. Crucial differences remain, however. Hindemith's Baroque-influenced writing is less a sophisticated device of formalist 'alienation' than part of a programme of robust playfulness (*Spielfreudigkeit*). The last six of the seven *Kammermusiken*, for example, composed between 1924 and 1927, were conceived as a form of *Gebrauchsmusik* for the virtuoso soloist.

Weill's use of jazz idioms similarly serves different ends from Stravinsky's. Even when he takes a 'glance towards the taste of the man in the street' (to quote Weill's earlier comment on *The Soldier's Tale*), Stravinsky remains firmly within the bounds of artificial music, far removed from the popular world of hit tunes. Weill sought to break those bounds. For all his artistry and sophistication, it was Weill's aim not to content himself with a mere glance towards the street (as he had done with the quasi-surrealist intonations of his cantata for soprano, violin and orchestra, *Der neue Orpheus*, composed in 1925) but actually to inhabit it. For him, the rhythms of modern dance music and jazz harmonies, such as he used in *Die Dreigroschenoper* and *Happy End* (1929), constituted important ingredients of a truly popular style, not the mere temporal equivalent of *couleur locale* such as can be found in Ernst Krenek's opera *Jonny spielt auf*.

Given its première in 1927, *Jonny spielt auf* enjoyed a startling overnight success; but like other operas that strove for fashionable immediacy under the label 'Zeitoper' ('opera of the time', such as Max Brandt's *Maschinist Hopkins* and Hindemith's *Neues vom Tage*) it has proved a mere historical curiosity, one of the more ephemeral offshoots of the *Neue Sachlichkeit*. Precisely because they exude an aura of the mythical 'Golden Twenties', such modish works have been viewed by some commentators as central to that movement – a perspective that also informs negative images of the *Neue Sachlichkeit*. Indeed, there is an influential brand of cultural criticism, first advanced by Eisler in the latter half of the 1920s and subsequently taken up by leading exponents

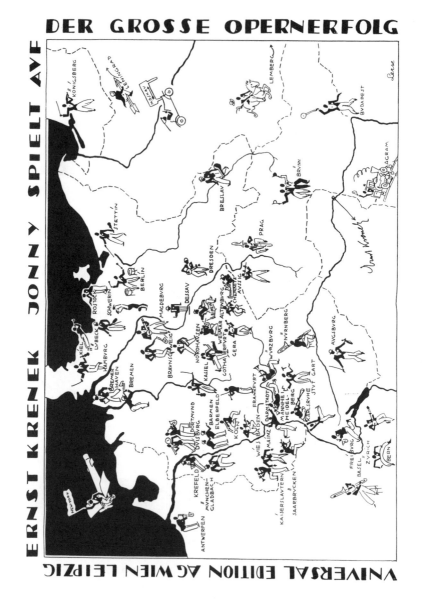

Poster by Universal Edition advertising 'Jonny spielt auf' (1927) signed by Ernst Krenek in Vienna.

of Marxist-orientated Critical Theory, in particular Adorno and Ernst Bloch, which interprets the *Neue Sachlichkeit* as representing a false objectivity on account of its apparent apoliticism. As a result, it is charged with tacitly complying with the ruling forces of reaction rather than confronting social contradictions. This line of interpretation, however, which operates within a dualistic ideological framework of progress and reaction, is especially precarious in a musical context. To cite an example: when Weill's music of the late 1920s first appeared, Adorno (in spite of certain technical reservations) passionately exempted it from the charge of false immediacy and hence from the *Neue Sachlichkeit* as he understood it; instead he accorded it a 'genuine socially polemical impact'. Yet in later writings he appeared to have partly revoked his original view. Such a definition of music, based on an assessment of its ideological impact (as opposed to its ideological intent), must remain highly subjective and hence an unreliable basis for distinguishing tendencies in Weimar aesthetics.

Whereas neo-classicism can be viewed as a kind of objectivity afforded by the dependence on compositional models, both formal and idiomatic, the 'objectivity' of the New Objectivity has a significance located less in aspects of language, style or, indeed, ideology than in distinctions drawn by contemporary phenomenology, which proceeded on the basis of a return to objective, intersubjective reality ('zu den Sachen selbst', as Heidegger wrote at the beginning of his epoch-making work *Sein und Zeit*, published in 1927). Of course style plays an important part, but only as a means, not as the end. This is why the idea of *Gebrauchsmusik* became so vital – a music that is an integral part of everyday life rather than occupying what became seen as the hermetic, autistic microcosm of late Romanticism and expressionism. The most lucid and representative exposition of this 'post-expressionist conviction' is to be found in a systematic study of contemporary cultural life by the phenomenologically inclined cultural philosopher Emil Utitz. He stresses the 'objective being of intrinsic values' which he translates into an artistic credo. 'The aesthetic dimension', he writes, 'cannot be the central value . . . because its essence is a value of expression and because it is aimed at the "appearance", not at full, whole being . . . In the end, what matters is not how we "express" ourselves but how we "are"'.[13] Such a de-emphasization of the 'aesthetic dimension' forms the fundamental precept of the movement Utitz describes as the *Neue Sachlichkeit*. The same perspective guides Weill's understanding of the cultural import he attached to New Music in the late 1920s. Responding to a series of questions from the editors of the music journal *Anbruch* concerning the 'sensational success of *Die Dreigroschenoper*', he stated that the work

> aligns itself with a movement that has taken over almost all young composers. The abandonment of the *l'art pour l'art* standpoint, the

turning away from an individualistic principle of art, the ideas on film music, the joining up with the youth music movement, the simplification of the musical means of expression connected with all these things – these are all steps along the same path.[14]

As a rule, the path chosen by the *neusachlich* composers was marked with pedagogic and reformist signposts. An obvious instance is the emphasis placed on amateur music, which led Hindemith (though not, incidentally, Weill) to join up with the youth music movement (*Jugendmusikbewegung*). This gradual shift away from 'the individualistic principle of art' can readily be discerned in the programmes of the annual contemporary chamber music festival in Germany, which began in 1921 in Donaueschingen, moved in 1927 to Baden-Baden and finally in 1930 to Berlin, where it was staged for the last time. At first the radical New Music commanded attention (Schoenberg, Webern, Stravinsky, Bartók), the last festival in Donaueschingen, however, in 1926, revealed the influence of Hindemith, who had been a member of the organizing committee since 1924. Music for mechanical instruments as well as 'entertainment' music featured prominently, including Hindemith's own Toccata op.40 no.1 (1926) for mechanical piano and his music for Oskar Schlemmer's *Das triadische Ballett*, conceived for mechanical organ. In 1927 the focal point became experimental forms of music theatre (*Kurzopern*, as they were called), such as Ernst Toch's *Prinzessin auf der Erbse*, Hindemith's palindromic *Hin und zurück* and Weill and Brecht's *Mahagonny Songspiel*. By 1929, however, the festival was devoted exclusively to diverse forms of *Gebrauchsmusik*. The four categories of New Music listed that year were films with sound-track, music for amateurs, specially composed music for radio and 'Lehrstück'. The underlying aim was to experiment with new channels for the performance as well as dissemination of music. Perhaps the most innovatory composition in this respect was one in the group of compositions for radio, *Der Lindberghflug*, with a text by Brecht and music by Hindemith and Weill; the idea behind the piece was that the listener should take part at home, performing the role of Charles Lindbergh crossing the Atlantic while the orchestral and choral accompaniment was broadcast.

The piece entitled *Lehrstück* (literally, 'didactic piece'), also by Brecht with music by Hindemith, soon lent its name to a whole genre of works with a didactic purpose. Brecht himself remains the leading practitioner as well as theoretician of the genre. His restless development in these years is reflected in repeated reworkings of the pieces as well as in extensive adjustments to the theory. In its original version, *Lehrstück* (first performed on 28 July 1929) was intended to realize an accompanying motto which was on display throughout the première: 'Musik machen ist besser als Musikhören'. Later, having accentuated

First performance of 'Der Lindberghflug' (music by Hindemith and Weill), at the Kurhaus, Baden-Baden, 27 July 1929, as part of the Deutsche Kammermusik festival: Frankfurt Radio Orchestra, vocal soloists and Hugo Holles Madrigal Society, conducted by Hermann Scherchen (Brecht is standing on the right).

the socially critical content in a revised version, Brecht distanced himself from the piece's original purpose. This had been a musical one, as much as anything, as Hindemith outlined in his preface to the published score:

> Since the Lehrstück has the purpose of engaging all those present in the execution of the work and does not, in the first instance, wish to create particular impressions as a musical and poetic utterance, the form of the piece is, as far as possible, to be adapted as required. The order given in the score is therefore more a suggestion than a set of instructions. Cuts, additions and reorderings are possible.

The orchestration is also left open: 'The intentionally rough division of the score into high, middle and low voices makes it possible for the conductor to distribute the parts according to the abilities and desires of the players'.

Of all Hindemith's compositions, *Lehrstück* marks the most radical departure from the notion of the discrete, organic work. Only when performed does the music become complete and thereby acquire its full significance. It represents the closest any 'serious' composer came in this period to an uncompromised realization of the postulates of *Gebrauchsmusik* as defined by Besseler – in other words, to producing as near as conceivable the musical equivalent of Heidegger's *Zeug*.

The staging of the festival of New Music in Berlin in 1930 further underlined the city's cultural preeminence in the Weimar Republic. Thanks to Germany's former division into dozens of petty principalities, the provinces retained strong cultural traditions, particularly in opera. Many new operas were given a trial run in a smaller town before making a bid for consideration in the metropolis. But Berlin remained the undisputed centre of attraction. In the early 1920s Busoni's master-class at the Akademie der Künste had enticed the young Weill to return to Berlin after an abortive start under the tutelage of Humperdinck. Busoni's successor was Schoenberg, who moved to the city from Vienna in 1925. Franz Schreker at the Hochschule nurtured such talents as Krenek, Alois Hába and Berthold Goldschmidt. Hindemith moved to the capital in 1927, following his appointment to a professorship at the Hochschule, where his duties included supervising a class in film music. In the same year Otto Klemperer became director of the newly constituted Kroll Opera, an artistically independent branch of the Staatsoper, which soon became a byword for innovatory productions, both in repertory and staging, as well as for attempts to reach a wider public.

The glory and prosperity were short-lived. A decisive turning-point came on 25 October 1929, the day of the Wall Street Crash, known as 'Black Friday'. Economic decline led not only to intolerable unemployment but also to a widespread sense of cultural pessimism. The internal wranglings at the New Music festival in 1930 over Brecht and Eisler's *Die Massnahme*, a political *Lehrstück*, suggest, in retrospect, an ominous portent of the ensuing squabbles on Germany's political Left: the Social Democrats and Communists deemed their respective ideological differences to be greater and more serious than the potential threat of the remorselessly rising National Socialists who, in effect, were handed a ready-made opportunity. As head of Germany's most powerful party, albeit without the requisite majority following the November elections, Hitler acceded to power on 30 January 1933.

THE THIRD REICH

The question that irksomely hangs over any discussion of German culture in the 1930s and 40s is that of continuity. To what extent was National Socialism presaged in German culture before 1933? Or, conversely, what was unique about it? Were the more abhorrent facets of its policies and ideology logical perversions of previous cultural property or were they new developments? In what ways, then, did German *Geist* already harbour the seeds of the ensuing *Ungeist*?

The National Socialist government, having consolidated its political hegemony with massive gains in the national elections in March 1933, swiftly set about reversing the process of liberalization that had characterized the Weimar years. By 7 April a law had been passed that was to transform the cultural scene in Germany beyond recognition. To quote the third section of the new statute 'for the re-establishment of [national] civil servants with tenure': 'civil servants who are not of Aryan descent are to be put into retirement'. In Germany it was (and still is) not only government administrators who were classified as civil servants but a whole range of employees in education and the arts. Two immediate and conspicuous victims of the policy were Franz Schreker, director of the Berlin Hochschule, and Arnold Schoenberg, professor at the Akademie der Künste, both of whom were released from their duties in May. Many other prominent figures accompanied them – Hermann Scherchen, Bruno Walter, Jascha Horenstein, Gustav Brecher and Berthold Goldschmidt among many others. There also began the odious process of investigating 'questionable' cases of racial extraction, so that all civil servants who failed to meet the stipulation 'aryan and free from traces of Jewish and coloured blood' were liable to dismissal.

At the same time, also on 7 April, a law was passed 'Zur Gleichschaltung der Länder', which meant that the various states (*Länder*) constituting Germany's federal system of government were 'brought into line' (*gleichgeschaltet*) as part of a unified Reich. It was an administrative measure that soon found a far-reaching and despotic parallel in cultural policy, whereby every conceivable facet of German culture was 'brought into line' with National Socialist ideals. The first public demonstration of this process came on 10 May, when thousands of publications considered unacceptable by the state were publicly burnt in front of the Berlin Staatsoper, among them the works of Thomas, Heinrich and Klaus Mann as well as scores by Schoenberg, Weill and others. Meanwhile steps were taken to institutionalize the *Gleichschaltung* of musical life with the setting-up of the *Reichsmusikkammer*, the Reich's 'Chamber of Music', which formed a branch of the *Kulturkammer* under the direction of the Minister for Public Enlightenment (*Volksaufklärung*) and Propaganda, Joseph Goebbels. Officially inaugurated on 15 November 1933, with Richard Strauss as president and Wilhelm Furtwängler as his deputy, the *Reichsmusikkammer* had the right to ban all musical performances it judged unworthy of its aims. Moreover, membership of the Chamber soon became obligatory for all composers seeking permission for the performance of their music. All independent music organizations came under the direct jurisdiction of the Chamber, in order, as one sympathizer put it, 'to eliminate troublesome competition as well as the fragmentation of forces'.[15]

One of the most common metaphors for the National Socialists' monolithic and authoritarian aims was *Reinigung* ('purification'), which affected not only Jewish artists but also anyone seen as contributing to the degeneration of German culture. The notion of 'degeneration' (*Entartung*) was not in itself new. Nietzsche, for example, had used the term; and it had first become an established category of art criticism as early as 1893, when the Jewish doctor and writer Max Nordau used it as the title for a book in which he drew a parallel between the 'curious manner of recent painters' and neurological disorders. Such a biological connotation also played a part in the Nazi's appropriation of the concept. Hanns Eisler suffered denunciation on no fewer than three counts: as a half-Jew, as a communist and as a composer of New Music which, along with jazz, was officially castigated as a manifestation of cultural bolshevism. Away from Germany in the early months of 1933, he was not to return until 1948. Schoenberg, Weill, Toch and other Jewish composers soon followed him, most of them eventually settling in the USA. It was only a matter of a few years before the National Socialist methods of terror and humiliation had ostracized most of the prime movers in the country's recent cultural history. Those same artists had to continue their work in the unfamiliar and not always congenial surroundings of enforced exile. Significant German musical activity in this period happened, for the most part, outside Germany.

The case of Hindemith was less straightforward, as is testified by the furore following the première of his Symphony *Mathis der Maler* on 12 March 1934. In many ways it became a test case for the shape of things to come. The symphony can be said to reflect a renewed interest, symptomatic of the early 1930s, in music of large-scale proportions. Hindemith himself had remarked on this change in March 1931 in a letter to his publisher in which, among other things, he described progress on his oratorium *Das Unaufhörliche*, for which Gottfried Benn wrote the lofty, in places mystical, text. With an eye as much on general trends as on his own work, he said: 'It would appear that a wave is gradually returning for serious and great music. (Stravinsky's [Symphony of] Psalms was a great success.)'[16] Hindemith's Philharmonic Concerto, composed for the Berlin Philharmonic Orchestra's golden jubilee in 1932, similarly signalled a return by his generation to the sphere of absolute music. The new 'monumentality' was not the exclusive aesthetic property of the National Socialists but part of the general *Zeitgeist*, which the Nazis happily usurped.

Hindemith originally conceived of the movements of the Symphony *Mathis der Maler* as instrumental preludes and interludes for the opera of the same name, which he completed in 1935. The idea of presenting them as a suite came from Furtwängler, the conductor of the première, who was keen to make propaganda for Hindemith in general and his new opera in particular. Such was the critical success of the first performance that Paul Zsorlich, one of the few critics who unequivocally condemned the work, saw fit to conclude his review (in the *Rostocker Anzeiger*) by pointing out the eccentricity of his own position. 'What effects this success, which could signify a re-evaluation of all values, will have on German musical life can by no means be foreseen at this moment. Nevertheless, the fact of this undisputed success is as important as it is surprising'.

Clearly much more was at stake than the reputation of one work or even one composer. The supporters of the year-old régime were in search of a new composer on whom they could confer representative status; and many thought – mistakenly – that in Hindemith, at least the Hindemith of the *Mathis* Symphony, they had found one. This involved casting him in the mould of bad boy made good; several even spoke in terms of a Pauline conversion. The supporters of the officially defamed New Music, on the other hand, considered the new work's success a triumph for their own cause. They were keen to stress that although Hindemith had in no way relinquished his modernist credentials he none the less showed the way forward for German music. Hans Heinz Stuckenschmidt's review in the *B. Z. am Mittag* thus dwelt on fairly advanced technical matters, the very features that other critics cited with a view to branding Hindemith a *Systemkomponist* or even as *Volksfremd* (alien to the people). In short, Hindemith was turned into a politico-cultural football, kicked around by many with an abandon inversely proportional to any informed understanding of his art – or politics.

Nor did the controversy die down after the première; it intensified, becoming the key topic of discussion in most music journals. The *Zeitschrift für Musik* persisted in championing Hindemith as a 'German artist in the best sense of the word' on the strength of his recent work. His music should not be damned, the journal contended, 'because its master once followed the path of Jewish-Marxist intellectualism. The artist speaks to us through his work'. It sought to present evidence for its position with an extended article on the *Mathis* Symphony, a tactic which the journal *Die Musikpflege* also used.[17] For others, such as the editors of *Die Musik*, which had become an official organ of the *NS-Kulturgemeinde* (the National Socialist Cultural Association), Hindemith's allegedly tainted past was irrevocable. And it was this view that eventually won the day. To underline its authority, *Die Musik* concluded its condemnation of Hindemith with a quotation from Hitler's speech to the party conference held in September 1933:

> It is . . . impossible that a man, having so belittled himself, could suddenly learn anew and create something better. He is valueless and shall remain valueless. To make one's mark with conscious absurdi-

ties and thereby to win public attention not only testifies to artistic
failure but also to a moral defect . . . Of one thing we are certain, that
under no circumstances may the representatives of the decline which
lies behind us suddenly become the standard-bearers of the future.

Although he named no names, Hitler had clearly established a
precedent for future denunciations.

The fatal blow came in November 1934. *Die Musik* published a
further defamatory article about Hindemith in which he was declared,
in cultural political terms, 'unacceptable', with the *NS-Kulturgemeinde*
imposing an official ban on performances of his music.[18] Furtwängler
reacted with an open letter 'Der Fall Hindemith' which appeared in the
Deutsche Allgemeine Zeitung on 25 November. Furthermore, if unsuccessful in his protest, he threatened to step down from his posts as vice-
president of the *Reichsmusikkammer*, chief conductor of the Berlin
Philharmonic Orchestra and director of the Staatsoper. In principle,
but with words of support for the music, Furtwängler conceded the
charge concerning Hindemith's 'sins of youth', especially the choice of
texts in his earlier works. By drawing on the example of the *Mathis*
Symphony, however, he was at pains to persuade his audience of
Hindemith's thorough Germanness. He concluded with the plea that,
'in view of the *unspeakable paucity* of truly productive musicians
throughout the world, we simply cannot afford to do without a man
such as Hindemith'. Whereas an overwhelming ovation for
Furtwängler at a performance of *Tristan und Isolde* given at the
Staatsoper on the day after his article's appearance indicated enormous
public support for the conductor, Goebbels and company remained
intransigent. Furtwängler carried out his threat, resigning all his posts
on 4 December. Two days later Goebbels gave a speech to the
Kulturkammer in which he alluded to formulations in Furtwängler's
defence of Hindemith, agreeing that 'we cannot afford to do without a
truly German artist'. 'But', Goebbels added, 'he should be a genuine
artist, not an atonal noise-maker.' Without naming the composer or the
work, he persisted in censuring atonal composers 'who have women
appear on the stage in the bath in the most obscene and vulgarly kitschy
scenes' – a reference to Hindemith's *Neues vom Tage* (1928–9). The
official verdict on Hindemith had been passed. Although Furtwängler
was later reinstated, Hindemith was less accommodating. On 30
September 1937 he gave up his professorship at the Hochschule,
leaving Berlin for good in August 1938. After a brief period in
Switzerland he eventually took up a professorship at Yale University in
February 1940.

The National Socialists' ideology of aryan racial superiority and
their totalitarian insistence on German values found expression and
support in the work of leading academics. In musicology, as in all the

humanities, a principal point of interest became the question of art's racial identity. 'The atonal movement' was rejected on the grounds of 'conflicting with the rhythm of the blood and soul of the German people'.[19] The major mode, on the other hand, was considered inherently German, as obeying a biological law. One of the most prominent figures to address such questions was Friedrich Blume who lectured widely on 'the problem of race in music', to quote the title of his book (*Das Rassenproblem in der Musik*), which appeared in 1939. A year before, in Düsseldorf, there had been a conference devoted to this subject at which he had given a key speech. A central part of it, published in *Die Musik*, analysed what Blume termed a 'racial experience' in listening to music:

> Every German who is capable of hearing and has acquired the facility of clarifying his musical experience at the deepest level will be confronted by something from the *Ring des Nibelungen* or the Ninth Symphony that goes beyond the mere aural and emotional experience and which can perhaps most directly be defined as a kind of *Heimatgefühl*: the self experiences a sense of security, of being 'at home'. It feels warmly embraced by something old and familiar, not because we are used to this 'type of music', but because something is alive in it from the blood and race of our own being.[20]

In other words, music, in particular that of Wagner and Beethoven, was usurped for specious ideological ends. The National Socialists' exploitation of the 'Bayreuth Master' to underwrite and celebrate their own master-race philosophy is well documented. To be sure, aspects of Wagner's oeuvre invited exploitation of this kind, especially the pamphlet *Das Judentum in der Musik* which was hailed by the Nazis as a prophetic model for their own musical antisemitism. The pamphlet's even more pernicious successor was *Das Lexikon der Juden in der Musik* (Berlin, 1940), which contained about 5000 names and 1600 titles; it represented the seemingly indefatigable efforts of the 'Institute of the NSDAP for Research into the Jewish Question' and was considered an important educational tool. As its preface proudly announced, 'The purification of our cultural and, consequently, our musical life of all Jewish elements has been accomplished'.

The dictionary's publication followed in the wake of other 'purification' rituals which, as mentioned, had started in 1933 with the burning of books in front of the Berlin Staatsoper. On 19 July 1937 one of the infamous collections of 'degenerate' modern art was put on display in Munich. It attracted an average of 20,000 visitors a day, incomparably more than the exhibition of officially sanctioned art that had opened in the city a day earlier. The exhibition's popularity is beyond question. Yet how should the social historian interpret such a phenomenon?

Were the majority of visitors really interested in the pictures themselves, were they defiantly expressing their approval of the artists represented, or were they gleefully lending support to the régime's imperious displays of *Schadenfreude*? Answers to these questions could contribute enormously to an understanding of the workings of National Socialism, but they remain frustratingly elusive. The exhibition's organizers, shrewd tacticians in matters of mass psychology, were in no doubt as to its effect. A year later, on 25 May 1938, they staged something similar in Düsseldorf, this time an exhibition of 'degenerate music'. To complement and illustrate the inventory of 'degenerate' musicians on display, jazz and non-tonal music could be heard, at the touch of a button, from specially constructed boxes. Among the exhibits was a poster paying defamatory tribute to the 'theorists of atonality': Schoenberg, the author of the *Harmonielehre* (1911), and Hindemith, whose *Unterweisung im Tonsatz* had appeared just a year before. Strictly speaking, the tribute is unmerited: Schoenberg's tract deals only briefly, in an appendix, with the dissolution of tonality, while Hindemith's composition treatise is anything but a theory of atonality. But such details were irrelevant to blanket denunciations of this kind. Indeed, the text of the poster provides a typical digest of musical opprobrium as practised by the Nazis:

> We possess in these pacemakers of the atonal movement, which displays parallel symptoms to the process of disintegration in the figurative arts and poetry, important spiritual fathers of intellectual constructivism and the most dangerous destroyers of our national and racial instinct to look for things that are clear, pure and organic and we oppose them from the highest standpoint of national traditions as international, rootless charlatans.

The cultural senator who organized the exhibition, Hans Severus Ziegler, compiled the accompanying catalogue. After outlining the phenomenon of 'degeneration' as an essentially Jewish product, he concluded his preface with a description of 'the aryan tonal order': 'the freedom of linear melody . . . within the bounds of the higher order of the triad as revealed to us by nature'. Of course there is nothing specifically aryan about tonal polyphony, just as all essentialist interpretations of artistic means are nothing if not arbitrary. What is at issue is not the validity of racial theories as applied to music – their absurdity and crudity is beyond the slightest doubt – but the fact that they could have found such widespread resonance and served such horrendous ends in a country whose cultural identity was partly rooted in the Enlightenment. To that extent, it would be to fall into the same ideological trap to suggest that there were any such thing as National Socialist music. National Socialism was a racist, totalitarian and jingoistic ideology, cobbled together from diverse sources, often recklessly improvised, which for twelve years became appalling political reality. The folksong idioms the Nazis appropriated were no more specifically National Socialist than the German classical music they usurped to promulgate master-race supremacy. By the same token, no music can be defined as 'fascist' *per se*, but only in the way it is drawn into a particular functional context – which admittedly often leaves indelible traces. But even here one has to exercise extreme caution.

In 1935 the German philosopher and man of letters Walter Benjamin attempted to draw a clear distinction between fascism and communism by suggesting that whereas the former aestheticized politics, the latter responded by politicizing art. The idea is neat and simple – seductively so. Yet Benjamin's distinction makes only limited sense unless one remembers that he was writing in 1935, and that his understanding of 'politicization' was essentially Marxist. 'Fascism', wrote Benjamin, 'attempts to organize the newly formed proletarian masses without disturbing the property relations which those masses work to abolish . . . The masses have a right to a change in property relations; fascism seeks to give expression to the masses in the conservation of those relations. Consequently, fascism leads to an aestheticization of political life.'[21] Benjamin illustrated his thesis by citing a manifesto by Marinetti in which the Italian futurist shamelessly espoused the beauty of war. He could equally well have invoked the choreography of the masses which the Nazis raised to an art form in, for example, the Nuremberg Rally of 1934. A vital factor in the organization of that rally was the plan that it should serve as the set for a propaganda film, *Triumph des Willens* (Leni Riefenstahl, 1935). Consequently the film is not a documentary account of reality; rather, reality was constructed so that it could be effectively reproduced.[22]

By asserting that communism responded by politicizing art, Benjamin doubtless had in mind the agitational songs and graphic art as well as the didactic plays that had proliferated towards the end of the Weimar Republic and which sought to enlighten and hence mobilize the proletariat in the face of economic exploitation. Yet, in retrospect, can the distinctions between the methods of communism and fascism really be so sharply drawn? If one includes in a definition of politics not just an analysis of the relations of production but also government policy in general, was the Nazi's philosophy of art on occasions not overtly political? And are not the political rituals of communist states themselves highly aestheticized? 'Features of fascist art proliferate in the official art of communist countries . . . The tastes for the monumental and for mass obeisance to the hero are common to both fascist and communist art, reflecting the view of all totalitarian regimes that art has the function of "immortalizing" its leaders and doctrines.'[23] The ideological and aesthetic boundaries, in reality, are a lot less clear than Benjamin's demarcation suggests, particularly if one considers the relative cultural freedom enjoyed in fascist Italy as compared with its putative counterpart, Nazi Germany.

The lack of artistic autonomy in Germany forced most important composers and performers, who were either unable or unwilling to put their music at the service of the totalitarian state, to emigrate. Some, notably the composer Karl Amadeus Hartmann (1905–63), were driven into 'inner emigration': they stayed in Germany without accommodating themselves to the dictates of official policy. Hartmann's uncompromisingly atonal works from this period, which include large-scale symphonic compositions, were a highly personal and necessarily silent protest, in certain ways comparable to the lonely outcry of the musical expressionists two or three decades earlier. Hartmann had to wait for the post-1945 era and the 'denazification' of Germany until his music could receive public exposure.

Just as in 1933 the National Socialists transformed the cultural scene in Germany virtually overnight, so there was in 1945 a widespread sense of, and desire for, a new start. In all walks of life, there was talk of 'the hour zero', a wishful need to turn the clock back by denying any historical continuity with the immediate past. The New Music that flourished in the rarefied climate of the festivals in Darmstadt in the late 1940s and early 1950s in many ways reflected that need. The principle of total serialism, which governed the compositions of Stockhausen and others in this postwar period, can be seen as an attempt to reinstate complete and utter artistic autonomy. Each work dictates its own terms, constructs its own set of rules, its own immanent language, all of which is accessible only to a very select group of initiated specialists. The ceaseless experimentation with abstract 'parameters', though justified at the time in terms of an adherence to the ineluctable historical tendency of musical material, invites an analogy with a scientific laboratory. It is difficult to imagine a more thorough negation of everything that, musically speaking, the Nazi period had stood for.

NOTES

[1] T. W. Adorno, *Philosophie der neuen Musik* (Frankfurt, 1949), 44.

[2] A. Schering, in *Einführung in die Kunst der Gegenwart*, ed. M. Deri (Leipzig, 1919), 139ff.

[3] Adorno, *Philosophie der neuen Musik*, 120.

[4] H. Eisler, 'Über moderne Musik', in *Musik und Politik: Schriften 1924–1948*, ed. G. Mayer (Leipzig, 1973), 32f.

[5] F. Busoni, *Entwurf einer neuen Ästhetik der Tonkunst*, repr. in *Von der Macht der Töne: Ausgewählte Schriften*, ed. S. Bimberg (Leipzig, 1983), 59.

[6] Unpublished letter from Weill to Busoni, dated 21 June 1923; the original is in the Berlin Staatsbibliothek.

[7] A. Berg, 'Zu Franz Schuberts 100. Todestag', *Vossische Zeitung* (18 Nov 1928), repr. in *Glaube,*

Hoffnung und Liebe: Schriften zur Musik, ed. F. Schneider (Leipzig, 1981), 308.

[8] K. Weill, 'Schubert-Feiern', *Der deutsche Rundfunk* (16 Nov 1928), repr. in *Ausgewählte Schriften*, ed. D. Drew (Frankfurt, 1975), 126.

[9] K. Weill, 'Verschiebungen in der musikalischen Produktion', *Berliner Tageblatt* (1 Oct 1927).

[10] H. Besseler, 'Grundfragen des musikalischen Hörens', *Jahrbuch der Musikbibliothek Peters*, xxxii (1925), 35–52; quoted from H. Besseler, *Aufsätze zur Musikästhetik und Musikgeschichte*, ed. P. Gülke (Leipzig, 1978), 29–53 (32f).

[11] G. F. Hartlaub, 'Zynismus als Kunstrichtung?', *Fragen an die Kunst: Studien zu Grenzproblemen* (Stuttgart, n.d.), 39.

[12] H. Besseler, *Die Musik des Mittelalters und der Renaissance*, Handbuch der Musikwissenschaft, ed. E. Bücken (Potsdam, 1931), 18ff.

[13] E. Utitz, *Die Überwindung des Expressionismus* (Stuttgart, 1927), 96, 115.

[14] K. Weill, 'Korrespondenz über *Dreigroschenoper*', *Musikblätter des Anbruch*, xi (1929), 24.

[15] F. Welter, *Musikgeschichte im Umriss* (Leipzig, 1939), 301.

[16] G. Benn, *Briefwechsel mit Paul Hindemith*, in *Briefe*, iii, ed. A. C. Fehn (Wiesbaden and Munich, 1978), 95.

[17] A. Brasch, 'Musik zum Isenheimer Altar: Paul Hindemiths Symphonie "Mathis der Maler"', *Zeitschrift für Musik*, ci (1934), 1203–7; H. Boettcher, 'Paul Hindemiths Symphonie Mathis der Maler', *Die Musikpflege*, v (1934), 247–54.

[18] 'P. Hindemith – kulturpolitisch nicht tragbar', *Die Musik*, xxvii (1934), 138–40.

[19] A. Rosenberg, *Gestaltung der Idee* (Munich, 1940), 337; quoted in J. Wulf, *Musik im Dritten Reich* (Gütersloh, 1963), 230.

[20] F. Blume, 'Musik und Rasse: Grundfragen einer musikalischen Rassenforschung', *Die Musik*, xxx (1938), 736–7.

[21] W. Benjamin, 'Das Kunstwerk im Zeitalter seiner technischen Reproduzierbarkeit', *Illuminationen* (Frankfurt, 1977; Eng. trans., 1973), 167f.

[22] S. Sontag, 'Fascinating Fascism', *New York Review of Books* (6 Feb 1975); repr. in S. Sontag, *Under the Sign of Saturn* (New York, 1980), 73–105.

[23] Ibid, 91.

BIBLIOGRAPHICAL NOTE

The nature of the musical culture of the period, as described in this chapter, militates against making any clear-cut distinction between 'historical background' and 'music'. The two are also closely linked in the literature, which is vast. Unlike the chapter itself, however, both the general and the specifically musical publications tend to deal either with the Weimar Republic or with National Socialism, seldom with both. Since many important figures in the arts became émigrés after 1933, the division quite rightly stresses the separateness of the two epochs. Yet it also ducks the issue of historical and cultural continuity. A comprehensive history of 20th-century German music that does not bracket off the 12 years of National Socialism has yet to be written. A rare attempt to traverse the two epochs can be found in the symposium 'Die Musik der 1930er Jahre', *Bericht über den Internationalen Musikwissenschaftlichen Kongress Bayreuth*, ed. C.-H. Mahling and S. Wiesmann (Kassel, 1983).

One of the best short introductions to the period 1918–33 is still P. Gay's *Weimar Culture* (London, 1969). J. Willett's *The New Sobriety: Art and Politics in the Weimar Period 1917–33* (London, 1978) complements Gay's book with a wealth of information (belying the sobriety of the title) on the various artistic media, especially theatre. There is nothing comparable in English for the Nazi years. However, the collection of essays *The Nazification of Art: Art, Design, Music, Architecture and Film in the Third Reich*, ed. B. Taylor and W. van der Will (Winchester, 1990), covers much important ground. Both this volume and *Culture and Society in the Weimar Republic*, ed. K. Bullivant (Manchester, 1977), offer a representative conspectus of British scholarship on the period as a whole.

Modern Times

Of the vast number of German books available, H. Köhler's *Geschichte der Weimarer Republik* (Berlin, 2/1982) presents an admirably succinct account of that era's perplexing political history. Three standard volumes on the Nazi period, with particular reference to music, are: F. K. Prieberg's *Musik im NS-Staat* (Frankfurt, 1982), which tends to pass severe judgment on those musicians who stayed after 1933; the essay collection *Musik und Musikpolitik im faschistischen Deutschland*, ed. H.-W. Heister and H.-G. Klein (Frankfurt, 1984), which begs the question of whether the term 'fascism' can apply to German as well as to Italian demagogy; and the useful collection of documentary material *Musik im Dritten Reich: eine Dokumentation* by J. Wulf (Gütersloh, 1963).

For detailed information on *Gebrauchsmusik* and *Neue Sachlichkeit*, see the present author's monographs on these terms in the *Handwörterbuch der musikalischen Terminologie* (Wiesbaden, 1988, 1990). T. W. Adorno's highly influential *Philosophie der neuen Musik* (Tübingen, 1949; Eng. trans. A. Mitchell and V. Blomster, 1973) is the best account of the German modernist's perspective on New Music. C. Dahlhaus's *Schoenberg and the New Music*, trans. D. Puffett and A. Clayton (Cambridge, 1987), is specifically illuminating on the relationship between sociology and aesthetics.

Studies either by or on key composers of the period abound. F. Busoni's own 'Sketch of a new aesthetic of music', in *Three Classics in the Aesthetics of Music* (New York, 1962), is seminal for the reasons outlined in the chapter. The selection of writings by H. Eisler, *A Rebel in Music*, ed. M. Grabs (Berlin, 1978), provides an excellent introduction not only to this composer's Marxist dialectics but also to his times. Another highly enjoyable portrait of the Weimar Republic's musical life, seen through the life of the conductor and composer Otto Klemperer, is provided by the late P. Heyworth's excellent biography *Otto Klemperer: his Life and Times*, i: 1885–1933 (Cambridge, 1983). *A New Orpheus: Essays on Kurt Weill*, edited by K. H. Kowalke (New Haven, 1986), covers the entire career of this major reformer of musical theatre, as does D. Drew's splendid *Kurt Weill: a Handbook* (London, 1987). The fates of other émigré composers are related in *Verdrängte Musik: Berliner Komponisten im Exil*, ed. H. Traber and E. Weingarten (Berlin, 1987).

Chapter V

Italy from the First World War to the Second

JOHN C. G. WATERHOUSE

In the history of Italian musical life, as of so much else, the World War I period was something of a watershed. Before the war the long-standing predominance of opera was already beginning to be challenged by a gradual revival in the fortunes of non-operatic music, after the low ebb that it had reached in Italy in the third quarter of the nineteenth century. Nevertheless, in the first few years of the twentieth century, opera remained the one relatively complex musical genre that enjoyed the enthusiastic support of a large and miscellaneous section of the Italian public. It is hardly surprising, therefore, that almost all the really successful Italian composers whose careers were at their heights in the two decades on either side of 1900 were largely (in some instances almost exclusively) opera specialists: that was obviously the case with Giacomo Puccini (1858–1924), Pietro Mascagni (1863–1945), Ruggero Leoncavallo (1857–1919), Umberto Giordano (1867–1948) and Francesco Cilea (1866–1950).

These composers' overwhelming preference for opera composition was fostered not only by the continued receptivity of the large Italian public to new operas (a receptivity that was only just beginning to wane at the turn of the century as a growing proportion of the repertory was taken up with well-established nineteenth-century favourites): it was also encouraged by fierce commercial rivalry between Ricordi and Sonzogno, the two most powerful Italian music-publishing houses of the time, for whom popular new operas were big – and aggressively publicized – business in the international market. Ricordi was making a huge fortune out of the operas of Puccini (as already out of those of Verdi), which Sonzogno sought to emulate, with some considerable success, by backing all four of the other above-mentioned composers. Meanwhile, the very few established figures who swam against the current by preferring to write instrumental music (Giuseppe Martucci, 1856–1909, was much the most distinguished) enjoyed only a relatively modest *succès d'estime* for the simple reason that their support from public and publishers alike was limited and the opportunities to have their music performed were comparatively few and inconspicuous.

By the second decade of the twentieth century, however, all this was changing, and the rate of change was accelerated by the war itself. The founding of the Augusteo concert hall in Rome in 1908 was the most famous of several crucial steps forward in bringing orchestral music before a wider public; and a new generation of musicians, increasingly aware both of innovatory developments abroad and of the much greater versatility of Italy's own music in the remoter past, were rebelling – in varying degrees and ways – against the opera-dominated status quo, thus preparing the ground for the very different Italian musical world of the inter-war period. Meanwhile the less firmly committed members of the opera public were beginning to be inveigled away by the new-fangled attractions of the cinema;[1] and those who did remain faithful were becoming more and more hidebound in their preference for the 'standard repertory' (a concept that had hardly existed in Italian opera 70 years earlier). The new concert-going public, though it still remained smaller than the audience for opera, was on average more intelligent and more receptive (up to a point) to new ideas. It was natural, therefore, that young Italian composers with something new to say tended increasingly to give of their best in music for the concert hall, even if most of them did not altogether cease composing operas.

Among the symptoms of the new, rebellious spirit that was emerging in the immediately pre-war period was the appearance of polemical books such as Fausto Torrefranca's vitriolic diatribe *Giacomo Puccini e l'opera internazionale*[2] and Giannotto Bastianelli's far more broad-visioned and richly thought-provoking *La crisi musicale europea*.[3] The lasting significance of Torrefranca (1883–1955) lay more in his energetic, fiercely nationalistic contributions to the rediscovery of early Italian music, a trend in which some of his composer contemporaries were also already involved before 1914. Bastianelli (1883–1927) was an enterprising minor composer himself, who for a short while in 1911 became the ideological spokesman of an innovatory pressure group calling itself 'la lega dei Cinque' or 'i "Cinque" italiani', clearly following the well-known Russian precedent: the other members were Ildebrando Pizzetti (1880–1968), Ottorino Respighi (1879–1936), Gian Francesco Malipiero (1882–1973) and the relatively unimportant Renzo Bossi (1883–1965).[4] Bastianelli and Pizzetti also played a significant part in that earnest search for new ideas in all the arts whose main mouthpiece was the famous Florentine cultural periodical *La voce* (1908–16).

The innovations of the futurist movement, aggressively launched in 1909 by the poet Filippo Tommaso Marinetti (1876–1942), were more flamboyantly iconoclastic in tone than those associated with *La voce*.

NOISE - MAKERS FOR THE FUTURIST CONCERT OF NOISES.

1. THE CRÉPITATEUR; FOR PRODUCING THE SOUND OF WOOD BEING SAWN.
2. THE RONFLEUR; FOR PRODUCING THE SOUND OF SNORING.
3. INSTRUMENTS USED IN THE "GRAND FUTURIST CONCERT OF NOISES," AT THE LONDON COLISEUM: "NOISE - TUNERS" REHEARSING.
4. M. PIATTI, CO-INVENTOR, WITH M. RUSSOLO, OF THE ART OF NOISES, WITH THE INSTRUMENT FOR PRODUCING THE SOUND OF WHISTLING.
5. THE FROISSEUR; FOR PRODUCING THE SOUND OF CRACKLING PAPER.
6. M. RUSSOLO, CO-INVENTOR, WITH M. PIATTI, OF THE ART OF NOISES, WITH AN INSTRUMENT FOR PRODUCING THE SOUND OF A LION'S ROAR.

In the Bill at the London Coliseum this week, No. 12 is "Marinetti . . . The Art of Noises." The Marinetti is, of course, Signor Marinetti, leader of the Futurists; "The Art of Noises" is his lecture on that subject, which will be part of "A Grand Futurist Concert of Noises." The special Futurist instruments used are played by selected members of the Coliseum Orchestra, called "noise-tuners" for the time being.—[*Photographs by Sport and General.*]

A demonstration on 15 June 1914 of futurist 'noise-intoners', played by members of the London Coliseum Orchestra under the direction of Luigi Russolo and his assistant, Ugo Piatti ('The Sketch', 17 June 1914).

Best remembered now for its powerful achievements in the visual arts, futurism also made a limited yet prophetic contribution to music: the ideas and inventions of Luigi Russolo (1885–1947) have a notable place in the prehistory of *musique concrète*, even if his once notorious *intonarumori* ('noise-intoners'), first demonstrated in 1913–14, inevitably seem primitive when measured against the technological advances of the later twentieth century. Meanwhile Gabriele D'Annunzio (1867–1938), the most celebrated and provocatively colourful Italian writer of the time, was influencing the musical world in a number of ways. Highly musical himself, he did much to encourage both the revival of old music and the exploratory development of new styles. However, the opulently decadent, *fin de siècle* qualities in his own work appealed most naturally to the more conservative (or only moderately innovatory) younger composers of the time, from Riccardo Zandonai (1883–1944) to Respighi and the young Pizzetti. Zandonai, regarded by Ricordi as Puccini's natural successor, won worldwide fame with his D'Annunzio opera *Francesca da Rimini* (1914); Respighi's richly decorative orchestral tone poems, from the well-known *Fontane di Roma* (1914–16) onwards, have many D'Annunzio-like qualities; while Pizzetti's highly personal, nobly expressive first published opera *Fedra* (1909–12) was written in close collaboration with the poet.

A major turning-point in the modernization of Italian music and musical life was reached when Alfredo Casella (1883–1947) returned to Italy in 1915, after nineteen years in France. While there, he had been in close contact with some of the most crucial new musical developments of the age (from Debussy to Stravinsky) and had been fruitfully influenced by them in his own works. In addition to being a talented if eclectic composer, Casella was a born leader and organizer, and he quickly established himself as the central figure in Italy's musical avant garde, retaining that position for over two decades. His Società Italiana di Musica Moderna (1917–19) provided a platform for nearly all the more adventurous young Italian composers; while his slightly later Corporazione delle Nuove Musiche (1923–8; founded with enthusiastic support from D'Annunzio) was more concerned with bringing major modern foreign works to Italy – including Schoenberg's *Pierrot lunaire* and Stravinsky's *The Wedding*, both of which were presented on tour in many Italian cities. Before long the Corporazione became closely (and appropriately) bound up with the International Society for Contemporary Music.[5]

Casella's own works from the period of World War I (composed in what is commonly called his 'seconda maniera') at first provoked violent hostility, with their complex dissonances and their characteristic alternations between sardonic humour and an ominous stillness in which some have sensed a kinship with the 'metaphysical' paintings of Giorgio de Chirico (1888–1978). Nor was this the last time that

Alfredo Casella: portrait (?1926) by Felice Casorati, a painter Casella regarded as an important influence on his musical development.

Casella's stylistic orientation could be paralleled in the visual arts: he considered that his conversion, in the early 1920s, to the more neo-classical approach of his 'terza maniera' had as much to do with his friendship with the painter Felice Casorati (1886–1962) as with his awareness of recent developments in the music of Stravinsky.

The other relatively radical major figure in Casella's generation of Italian composers (the 'generazione dell'Ottanta', as it is known in Italy) was Gian Francesco Malipiero, whose exceedingly unconventional theatre works similarly provoked fierce controversy. Many had their premières abroad, as the Italian opera world was totally unprepared for such eccentricities. Compositions like *Pantea* (1917–19), for solo dancer, offstage voices (mostly wordless) and orchestra, and *Sette canzoni* (1918–19), which consists of seven tiny, self-contained musico-dramatic vignettes lasting 45 minutes in all, represent an uncompromising rebellion against the established operatic tradition: in their distinctive way they reflect the same sort of restlessly experimental ethos as can be seen in the Italian spoken theatre of the time, for example the 'grotteschi' of Luigi Chiarelli (1884–1947) and others, or the famous 'paradoxical' plays of Luigi Pirandello (1867–1936). It was appropriate that in due course Pirandello and Malipiero collaborated, as librettist and composer of the somewhat more normally conceived opera *La favola del figlio cambiato* (1932–3).

The other leading members of the 'generazione dell'Ottanta' soon settled, by and large, for more traditional styles and attitudes: on 17 December 1932 several of them (including Pizzetti, Respighi and Zandonai) signed a notorious, rather muddle-headed manifesto, published in several Italian newspapers, attacking the more progressive trends of the time, without, however, mentioning Casella and Malipiero by name[6]. Yet the ferment of new ideas in the immediately postwar period was not lost on the one established composer of the older generation who was still genuinely capable of renewing himself: Puccini not only listened with open-minded interest to one of the Corporazione delle Nuove Musiche's performances of *Pierrot lunaire*, but his last opera *Turandot* (1921–4) contains boldly dissonant elements that are demonstrably akin to those in the 'seconda maniera' of Casella.[7]

Meanwhile the rediscovery of the music of the remoter Italian past was going on apace: by the mid-1920s almost all the main members of the 'generazione dell'Ottanta' – radicals and moderates alike – had been affected by it. Pizzetti's responsiveness to the influence of early Italian music (especially Gregorian chant and Renaissance polyphony) is evident, above all, in his choral pieces, from those he wrote as early as 1905–7 for use in D'Annunzio's play *La nave* to the radiantly beautiful unaccompanied Requiem Mass (1922–3) and beyond. Respighi, too, became increasingly interested in adapting archaic idioms

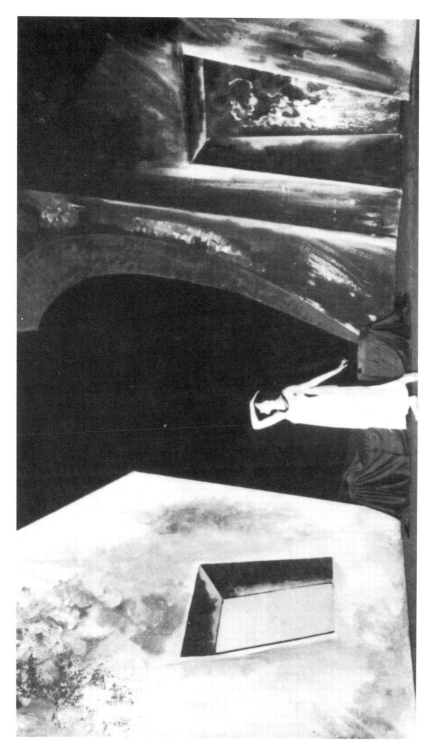

Scene from the first production of Malipiero's 'Pantea' for solo dancer, offstage voices and orchestra, which took place at the Teatro Goldoni, Venice, in September 1932.

to his needs: the *Lauda per la natività del Signore* (1928–30) exemplifies this side of his art at its frankly picturesque yet far from despicable best. Even Casella, who before 1920 had sometimes written scathingly about other composers' interest in early music as a source of inspiration,[8] now changed his attitude drastically. His ideal now, as expressed in a collection of lucidly argued essays published under the laconic title *21+26*,[9] was to seek an 'equilibrium between the immense national past and the constructive dynamism of this fevered century'. The dense harmonies of his 'seconda maniera' gave place, in his 'terza maniera', to clearcut linear textures, whose links with the Italian past are typified (in, it is true, an unusually explicit form) by *Scarlattiana* (1926): this nimble divertimento for piano and orchestra includes about 80 deftly handled quotations from Domenico Scarlatti's sonatas.

None of these composers, however, threw themselves more obsessively into the renewal of contact with earlier phases of Italian civilization than Malipiero did. Already in *Sette canzoni* the sung texts consist almost entirely of early Italian poetry; and in *San Francesco d'Assisi* (1920–21) authentic medieval words are set to music whose antique, Giottoesque calm is worlds away (for most of the time) from the dissonant turbulence of *Pantea*. In 1926 Malipiero's involvement with the music of Monteverdi in particular (which had begun as long ago as 1902) bore fruit when he started work on his pioneering edition of that composer's entire extant output. This monumental task, not completed until 1942, had a considerable impact on Malipiero's own style. Yet there is seldom any question, in his music, of mere pastiche of ancient idioms: one has the impression, rather, of an ambivalent, very personal and at bottom profoundly pessimistic relationship with the past glories of Italian civilization, seen as an ultimately irrecoverable golden age.[10]

There can be no doubt that all these composers' renewals of contact with the Italian past were encouraged, after 1922, by some of the cultural policies of fascism, which sought to affirm the Italian people's continued creative potential by atavistically highlighting their great achievements in earlier centuries. Italian fascism's effect on the arts was, however, changeable and full of contradictions. Mussolini clearly wanted the world to believe that he was a refined connoisseur of music as of most other things, and he seems, indeed, not to have been wholly ignorant of the subject.[11] Yet it is hard to find any consistent stance or aim in his known musical pronouncements. Sometimes he made a show of encouraging innovation – appearing, for instance, to disapprove of the reactionary 1932 manifesto (just as he defended the modern architecture of Florence's new railway station at about the same time).[12] At other times, however – for example, when he banned *La favola del figlio cambiato* in 1934, after just one Italian performance[13] – he acted in an arbitrarily repressive manner that calls to mind the other two leading dictators of the day.

These contradictory attitudes co-existed also among Mussolini's immediate subordinates. On the one hand the deplorable Roberto Farinacci (1892–1945) was the principal advocate, in the late 1930s, of artistic censorship on frankly Nazi lines. On the other, Giuseppe Bottai (1895–1959; minister of education from 1936 to 1943) firmly insisted on allowing complete creative freedom in music as in the other arts. Bottai was a friend of Casella, and had himself once been involved in the futurist movement. Although his career, too, had murkier moments and perplexing contradictions, he seems to have done as much as anybody to fend off the danger of wholesale alignment with Hitler's cultural policies.[14]

Further down the hierarchy, in the parts of the fascist bureaucracy that specifically affected music, the same dichotomies can be seen yet again. A key figure here was the influential arts bureaucrat Nicola de Pirro (1898–1979), whose enlightened activities in various crucial posts did much to keep the door open for novel creative ideas. It seems, for instance, to have been he who made it possible for Berg's *Wozzeck*, which had long been banned in the countries under direct Nazi rule, to have its Italian stage première (almost incredibly) in Rome in autumn 1942.[15] The composers in key positions within the hierarchy were mostly minor figures, of widely varying outlook. Mario Labroca (1896–1973), who had been a close ally of Casella in founding the Corporazione delle Nuove Musiche, played an admirably open-minded role in interpreting and implementing the policies of the Bottai-De Pirro faction.[16] Meanwhile the far more conservative, vociferously xenophobic Adriano Lualdi (1885–1971) and Alceo Toni (1884–1969) were the most domineering leaders of the 'official' musical world's more reactionary wing: it was in fact Toni who originally drafted the 1932 manifesto and assembled its distinguished band of signatories.

The responses of the major composers to this complex, confused situation were variable and (it has to be said) seldom wholly untainted by opportunism. No composers whatsoever made firm and consistent stands against the régime, such as were conspicuously made by Arturo Toscanini (1867–1957) and by the leading music critic Massimo Mila (1910–88): the latter was imprisoned from 1935 to 1940 for his political activities.[17] The full extent of composers' involvements with fascism, and of their sometimes voluminous correspondences with the upper echelons of the hierarchy, has only recently been systematically revealed.[18] It would appear from the documentation that very few of them were motivated by fully comprehending sympathy with fascist ideology (such as it was): more important to most of them was the simple need to advance their careers, or to realize their plans for improving the musical world. The lucrative and flattering privilege of becoming a member of the Reale Accademia d'Italia (founded by

Mussolini in 1929) was an additional inducement to several of them: Mascagni, Giordano, Cilea, Respighi and Pizzetti all became members of that pompous organization, alongside such notable figures in non-musical spheres as D'Annunzio, Pirandello and Marconi. Moreover, other composers – including both Casella and Malipiero – are known to have had unfulfilled aspirations in the same direction.

A further factor underlying many musicians' passive or active support for the régime was, quite simply, that plausible appearance of orderliness which fascism for a time brought to many aspects of Italian life, after the unnerving instability of the immediately postwar years. It was probably this, as much as anything else, that convinced Casella and led him to see the neo-classical tendencies in his own recent works (and those of others) as a musical counterpart to that orderliness.[19] It may be no coincidence that by the 1930s Mussolini's illustrious foreign admirers included no less a person than Stravinsky, who was then in the midst of his own neo-classical period, and who had, it has been said, 'an obsessive, almost pathological need for order' which led him to 'feel comfortable with oligarchies and autocracies'.[20]

The extent to which Italian musical styles directly mirrored the fascist ethos is hard to assess in view of music's abstract nature. The subject matter and colourful grandiloquence of parts of Respighi's *Pini di Roma* (1923–4) and *Feste romane* (1928) suggest obvious parallels with fascism's cult of ancient Rome; and Casella's more 'monumentally' neo-Baroque works of the time – the *Concerto romano* (1926), for instance – may perhaps be compared with certain aspects of fascist architecture, still visible (for example) in the E.U.R. district just outside Rome. Fascism's part in more generally encouraging composers to 'return to the Italian past' has already been mentioned. Nevertheless a great deal of the music written by composers who seemingly supported the régime (however naively or superficially) shows no readily identifiable fascist characteristics. One should therefore be wary of accepting at its face value the tendency, in recent decades, of influential left-wing Italian critics to dismiss most of the music of the fascist period *a priori*.[21] Many works composed under fascism were certainly third rate or worse by world standards and won more approval at home when new than they deserved. But the same can be said of the music of most periods in most countries, whatever the current political situation; and to claim (as some have come near to doing) that a composer's support for fascism *ipso facto* puts his music beyond the pale of respectability is rendered obviously absurd by the embarrassing case of Stravinsky.

During the fascist years new musical organizations continued to be created to promote modern works and revive early music in perform-ance. Notable were the Teatro di Torino (1925–31; established by the influential music critic Guido M. Gatti, 1892–1973), the Venice International Festival of [Contemporary] Music (founded in 1930 as an offshoot of the famous Biennale art festival); and the Maggio Musicale Fiorentino (founded in 1933).[22] The Venice Festival, in its early years, was run by Lualdi and Casella in a rather uneasy collaboration which epitomized the basic ambiguity in fascism's attitude to modern music. Yet the first festival featured works by relatively 'advanced' foreign composers, such as Bartók, Hindemith, Milhaud and Szymanowski, in addition to Italians of most shades of opinion. As late as 1937 (when the festival was directed by Casella on his own) it was still possible to include Schoenberg's dodecaphonic Suite op.29, even though quasi-Nazi attitudes were gaining ground in Italy and the antisemitic campaign (launched by Mussolini in 1938) was just round the corner.

Other new opportunities for composers arose with the growing importance of the radio as an outlet for music of all kinds; and relatively new publishing houses like Carisch and (especially) Suvini Zerboni became increasingly associated with modern music. Meanwhile Ricordi's former overriding preoccupation with popular operatic success had by the 1930s given place to a more flexible policy, which helped to maintain the firm's dominant position in a changing musical environment.[23] Another notable bastion of open-mindedness in Italian musical life was the periodical that G. M. Gatti had founded in 1920 as *Il pianoforte*, which in 1928 changed its name to *La rassegna musicale*.[24] Throughout its existence (it lasted into the 1960s) this important forum of intelligent musical opinion acted as a valuable antidote to the narrow cultural provincialism that was all too prevalent in the daily press, especially (but not only) in the later fascist years.

These various institutions (all of which could be said to reflect the more enlightened, 'Bottai-De Pirro' side of fascist cultural policy) together helped to keep Italian musical creativity alive and vigorous throughout the 1930s, in spite of the more negative forces that increasingly threatened to destroy it. Some of the leading members of the 'generazione dell'Ottanta' (including even Casella) were by then showing signs of merely repeating themselves; but a new generation of composers was coming forward, reaping richly fruitful benefits from the creative and practical achievements of their predecessors. Much the most important of these newcomers were Luigi Dallapiccola (1904–75) and Goffredo Petrassi (*b* 1904), though Giovanni Salviucci (1907–37) might have risen to comparable eminence but for his early death, and the rather older Giorgio Federico Ghedini (1892–1965) reached a belated, highly individual maturity in his best works of the 1940s.

Dallapiccola's early music (like his choice of texts) shows clear affinities with the 'archaizing' side of Pizzetti and Malipiero while also reflecting his responsiveness to major foreign composers of the turn of the century, from Debussy to Mahler. However, he had been present at one of the Corporazione delle Nuove Musiche's performances of *Pierrot lunaire*, and a seed was sown then which in due course bore fruit in a gradual adoption of Schoenbergian twelve-note technique. The fact that Dallapiccola's first truly (if still not quite strictly) dodecaphonic pieces date from the early 1940s provides yet another instance of how 'advanced' musical idioms still stood a chance in Italy even in those terrible times. The most intense and 'committed' Dallapiccola work of these years, the only partly dodecaphonic *Canti di prigionia* (1938–41), was a direct response to the current holocaust: the urge to write it was triggered off in the first place by the antisemitic campaign, which came as a direct threat to the composer's Jewish wife. The human drama underlying this justly famous piece of 'protest music' takes on an additional dimension when one knows that Dallapiccola had himself naively supported the régime until hostile circumstances abruptly tore the scales from his eyes.[25]

Petrassi, too, started as an heir to the 'generazione dell'Ottanta' and as an ingenuously believing fascist. His main mentor in the older generation was Casella, whose neo-classical style interacted, in the younger man's work, with strong influences first from Hindemith and then from Stravinsky. *Salmo IX* (1934–6) is a vigorous Italian response to the impact of the Russian composer's *Oedipus rex* and *Symphony of Psalms*, setting words whose penultimate line 'Costitue, Domine, legislatorem super eos' were linked in Petrassi's mind (as he still freely admits) with the image of the Duce.[26] However, by the beginning of the 1940s a very different spirit was entering Petrassi's work – impressively embodied in the darkly stoical *Coro di morti* (1940–41), a choral setting of one of Leopardi's most famous and most pessimistic poems.

The achievements of Dallapiccola and Petrassi (like those of Ghedini and several others) together indicate the extent to which musical creativity could remain unfettered by current political circumstances. (Even the *Canti di prigionia* were performed in Rome in 1941.) Nevertheless the insidious activities of the Nazi-like factions associated with Farinacci were making increasing inroads into other aspects of the musical world. It became common for adventurous composers to be attacked in the daily press for being 'internazionale' – a gibe that echoed the chauvinistic stance of the 1932 manifesto and was sometimes reinforced by antisemitic insinuations.[27] After sanctions had been imposed against Italy in 1935 as a result of the Ethiopian war, the answering 'counter-sanctions' launched within Italy included a not very effective ban on performances of music from the countries considered most hostile.[28]

As an extension of this process, pressures built up to introduce the principle of autarky into the musical field, with results whose absurdity must have been obvious even to many of those involved. For example, in 1941 Bottai (of all people), in his capacity as minister of education, convened a committee to consider a drastic overhaul of conservatory curricula, the aim being that, in future, students would study only Italian music, apart from a small handful of recognized 'immortal classics'. Pizzetti, Casella, Malipiero, Zandonai, Dallapiccola and Petrassi were all caught up (albeit briefly) in this ridiculous exercise, which, needless to say, bore no practical fruit even in the short run.[29] A slightly more effective aspect of autarky, at least for a time, was the attempt to ban non-Italian types of popular music, especially jazz and kindred styles emanating from across the Atlantic, which were considered to be alien to the race. However, even a more efficient totalitarian state would have had difficulty in suppressing a phenomenon so closely woven into the fabric of modern civilization.

The idea of autarky sometimes went hand in hand with resolute populism, epitomized in Mussolini's widely quoted directive to 'andare verso il popolo'. While this attitude had no perceptible effect on more serious concert life, it did make headway, during the later fascist years, in opera (where it had positive aspects, seen in determined efforts to attract ordinary working people back into audiences).[30] However, the approach here remained ambiguous. By the mid-1930s Italian opera houses had all been weaned away from the old impresario system and had become centrally organized, generously subsidized and consequently highly politicized – as they have continued to be to the present day.[31] In the late 1930s the Ministry of Popular Culture imposed a rule that in order to qualify for their subsidies, opera houses that were *enti autonomi* should devote at least a quarter of their repertories each season to works composed during the past twenty years (and a further quarter to works written this century). The effectiveness of this potentially highly beneficial regulation was somewhat blunted, however, by a strong bias in favour of Italian composers of relatively conservative outlook, and sometimes of mediocre talent.[32] More adventurous operas tended to be relegated to the major festivals or to special 'ghetto institutions' such as the Teatro delle Novità in Bergamo, founded in 1937 specifically for staging new Italian works. The dearth of performances of major foreign operas tended to encourage stylistic provincialism; yet the aforementioned 1942 performance of *Wozzeck* proves how inconsistent the situation remained right to the end of the régime.

As fascism entered its degenerate final phase, many who had previously acquiesced began at last to perceive the grimmer realities which lay behind the régime's deceptively glittering surface. Potential victims of the racial campaign included Casella's wife as well as Dallapiccola's, though the worst threats did not arrive until the direct German occupation of 1943–5 (by which time many ex-fascists, including De Pirro,[33] had become partisans). Jewish composers who emigrated permanently included Mario Castelnuovo-Tedesco

(1895–1968) and Vittorio Rieti (*b* 1898), both of whom settled (in 1939–40) in the USA.[34] By the end of the war many aspects of the musical establishment, as of so much else, were metaphorically or literally in ruins; and after the war, although older musicians often showed remarkable abilities to adapt to new circumstances (putting their various involvements with fascism discreetly behind them), the scene was naturally set for a transfer of power and prestige to a generation young enough to be able to blame their parents, rather than themselves, for what had happened.

The work of this younger generation – cosmopolitan and often radically innovatory in their creative outlook, predominantly (sometimes fanatically) left wing in their political convictions – lies beyond the scope of this chapter. We have seen, however, that their understandable but sometimes simplistic revulsion against the overthrown political order, which their seniors had helped to create and maintain over a twenty-year period, has led to specifically musical prejudices, some of which are based more on gut reactions than on balanced judgment. If the musical world outside Italy is now ill-informed about Italian music between the heydays of Puccini and of Luciano Berio (*b* 1925), prejudices within Italy are considerably to blame. Only now, thanks partly to the efforts of a still younger generation of Italians, born after fascism and all its works had begun to recede into history, is a more objective assessment of the period beginning to be achieved.

NOTES

[1] See H. Sachs, *Music in Fascist Italy* (London, 1987), 63–4.

[2] F. Torrefranca, *Giacomo Puccini e l'opera internazionale* (Turin, 1912).

[3] G. Bastianelli, *La crisi musicale europea* (Pistoia, 1912); repubd (Florence, 1976) with an excellent introduction by G. Gavazzeni.

[4] Concerning this short-lived and little-known group, see especially F. Nicolodi, *Musica e musicisti nel ventennio fascista* (Fiesole, 1984), 126–8; it includes a substantial quotation from Bastianelli's manifesto of 2 July 1911.

[5] Casella's most detailed, somewhat self-congratulatory account of his numerous important contributions to Italian musical life is in his autobiography, *I segreti della giara* (Florence, 1941); S. Norton's English translation (as *Music in my Time*, Norman, OK, 1955) is a shortened version, tactfully omitting most of the politically compromising passages.

[6] The best discussion of this manifesto (quoted in full) and of the controversy it unleashed, is in Nicolodi, *Musica e musicisti*, 140–49; see also Sachs, *Music in Fascist Italy*, 23–7. For Casella's reaction, see *I segreti della giara*, 258–9 (= *Music in my Time*, 193–4).

[7] J. C. G. Waterhouse, 'Puccini's Debt to Casella', *Music and Musicians*, xiii/6 (1965), 18–19, 44.

[8] In *Ars nova*, the journal of the Società Italiana di Musica Moderna (which Casella edited, 1917–19), for example, Verdi's famous dictum 'Torniamo all'antico' is repeatedly held up to ridicule under the general heading 'Sciocchezze, spropositi, enormità, ecc. ecc.'.

[9] A. Casella, *21+26* (Rome and Milan, 1931); the quoted passage appears on pp. 46–7.

[10] This widely held view of Malipiero's relationship with the Italian past was first proposed by F. d'Amico in 'Ragioni umane del primo Malipiero', *La rassegna musicale*, xv (1942), 45–55; rev. in *L'opera di Gian Francesco Malipiero: saggi di scrittori italiani e stranieri con una introduzione di Guido M. Gatti . . .* [but ed. Gino Scarpa] (Treviso, 1952), 110–26. For a magnificently full and thought-

provoking discussion of many aspects of Malipiero's involvement with early Italian music, see F. Degrada, 'Gian Francesco Malipiero e la tradizione musicale italiana', in *Omaggio a Malipiero*, ed. M. Messinis, Studi di Musica Veneta, iv (Florence, 1977), 131–52.

[11] A typically sycophantic fascist eulogy of Mussolini's supposed musicality is R. de Rensis, *Mussolini musicista* (Mantua, 1927); for a more balanced, sceptical view, see Sachs, *Music in Fascist Italy*, 11–17.

[12] Nicolodi, *Musica e musicisti*, 147.

[13] Ibid, 223–9; for a slightly different account of what happened, see F. d'Amico, 'La farsa degli equivoci nella *Favola del figlio cambiato*', *Vie nuove*, viii/33 (17 Aug 1952), 19; enlarged version in *Cinquant'anni del Teatro dell'Opera 1928 Roma 1978*, ed. J. Tognelli (Rome, 1979), 207–9.

[14] For a clear, succinct survey of Mussolini's subordinates who had some impact on the musical world, and of the musicians in key posts in the hierarchy, see Sachs, *Music in Fascist Italy*, 17–23. For a balanced and objective biography of Bottai in particular, see G. B. Guerri, *Giuseppe Bottai: un fascista critico* (Milan, 1976).

[15] See Sachs, *Music in Fascist Italy*, 198; and Nicolodi, *Musica e musicisti*, 25–6.

[16] Labroca's own valuable account of his experiences and organizing activities before, during and after the fascist period, is in his *L'usignolo di Boboli (cinquant'anni di vita musicale italiana)* (Venice, 1959).

[17] For Toscanini's anti-fascism, see especially Sachs, *Music in Fascist Italy*, 207–40 (chapter: 'The Toscanini Case'); for Mila's, see ibid, 47–55 (interview with Mila), and Nicolodi, *Musica e musicisti*, 302–3.

[18] These correspondences have now been mercilessly displayed in print in Nicolodi, *Musica e musicisti*, 306–472 (appendix: 'Documenti, testimonianze, carteggi dagli archivi storici del regime').

[19] See, for example, p.170 in his article 'Problemi della musica contemporanea italiana', *La rassegna musicale*, viii (1935), 161–73.

[20] See especially Sachs, *Music in Fascist Italy*, 167–9. The quoted words are from V. Stravinsky and R. Craft, *Stravinsky in Pictures and Documents* (New York, 1978), 551.

[21] The most substantial and widely influential expression of this attitude (while nevertheless making a tendentiously whitewashed exception for Malipiero, not borne out by the now-available documents) is L. Pestalozza's famous polemical introduction to his *La rassegna musicale: antologia* (Milan, 1966), pp. IX–CLXXVIII [*sic*].

[22] For the complicated and often fraught early histories of these festivals (and of others), see especially F. Nicolodi, 'Su alcuni aspetti dei festivals tra le due guerre', in *Musica italiana del primo Novecento: la generazione dell'80*, ed. F. Nicolodi (Florence, 1981), 141–203.

[23] An informative account of the changing face of the Ricordi publishing house, during its long history, is in C. Sartori, *Casa Ricordi* (Milan, 1958).

[24] A 679-page selection of articles and reviews from *La rassegna musicale* (plus a few from *Il pianoforte*) has been gathered together in Pestalozza, *La rassegna musicale: antologia*.

[25] See especially Nicolodi, *Musica e musicisti*, 289–90.

[26] See, for example, p.146 of Sachs, *Music in Fascist Italy* (in his interview with Petrassi, 139–47); and p.108 of L. Lombardi, *Conversazioni con Petrassi* (Milan, 1980).

[27] See especially F. Santoliquido's notorious article 'La piovra musicale ebraica', pubd in the newspaper *Il Tevere* (15 Dec 1937), extensively quoted in Nicolodi, *Musica e musicisti*, 263–4, and summarized in Sachs, *Music in Fascist Italy*, 181–2.

[28] Nicolodi, *Musica e musicisti*, 26–30.

[29] Ibid, 198–9.

[30] Ibid, 18; and Sachs, *Music in Fascist Italy*, 63–4.

[31] For a detailed account of this wholesale transformation of the way opera houses were organized, see Sachs, *Music in Fascist Italy*, 55–86; see also his wry comments on the continuing after-effects, ibid, 242.

[32] Ibid, 69–70; and especially Nicolodi, *Musica e musicisti*, 17–25.

[33] Nicolodi, *Musica e musicisti*, 31.

[34] The effect on the Italian musical world of the antisemitic campaign and of racism in general (with a detailed account of Castelnuovo-Tedesco's experience) is discussed in Sachs, *Music in Fascist Italy*, 175–93.

Modern Times

BIBLIOGRAPHICAL NOTE

General background

Books on the political and social history of early twentieth-century Italy are now quite numerous, even in English (and the literature in Italian is immense): D. Mack Smith, *Italy: a Modern History* (Ann Arbor, 1959, rev.), still makes an excellent, compulsively readable starting-point. Far less has been written, in English or indeed in Italian, on the music of the period and on its relationship to its political, social and cultural background. The most comprehensive survey of the music itself (with relatively brief accounts of background influences) remains J. C. G. Waterhouse, *The Emergence of Modern Italian Music (up to 1940)* (diss., U. of Oxford, 1968). It is immature in a number of respects; nevertheless it has not yet been wholly superseded and therefore probably continues to have its uses.

Two very different books in English can be recommended as significant contributions (each within its chosen limits) to an understanding of Italian musical life between the wars. Casella's autobiography, *I segreti della giara* (Florence, 1941; Eng. version as *Music in my Time*, trans. S. Norton, Norman, ok, 1955), provides a clear, straightforward if inevitably somewhat biased account of the musical world as experienced by the most variously active innovator in the 'generazione dell'Ottanta'. H. Sachs, *Music in Fascist Italy* (London, 1987), is an illuminating if relatively simple introduction to the complexities (and absurdities) of musical life under fascism; it does not, however, attempt to discuss the music itself.

In Italian the relevant literature is naturally larger, though still not nearly as extensive as it ought to be. D. de' Paoli, *La crisi musicale italiana (1900–1930)* (Milan, 1939), is essentially a survey of the 'generazione dell'Ottanta'; though rather improvised and somewhat dated, it is frequently perceptive and very easy to read. F. Nicolodi, *Musica e musicisti nel ventennio fascista* (Fiesole, 1984), is a much tougher proposition for non-Italian readers. However, for anyone wanting to delve more deeply into the intricacies of musical life under fascism (and in the immediately pre-fascist period too), it has a great deal to offer which Sachs's book hardly touches. Moreover it contains some comment on the music, as well as a substantial documentary appendix. Nicolodi is also editor of *Musica italiana del primo Novecento: la 'generazione dell'80'* (Florence, 1981), the proceedings of an important conference.

Three interestingly personal books, by musicians who, in their different ways, played influential parts in Italian musical life are G. Bastianelli, *La crisi musicale europea* (Pistoia, 1912, R1976); M. Labroca, *L'usignolo di Boboli (cinquant'anni di vita musicale Italiana)* (Venice, 1959); and A. Lualdi, *Viaggio musicale in Italia* (Milan, 1927). L. Parigi, *Il momento musicale italiano* (Florence, 1921), is another intelligent, though again rather 'improvised', commentary on aspects of the musical scene just after World War I. A very different, intensely polemical retrospective view of Italian music between the wars is provided by L. Pestalozza's long introduction to his *La rassegna musicale: antologia* (Milan, 1966), a passionate, even violent anti-fascist diatribe which had an overwhelming influence on left-wing Italian critical opinion in the late 1960s and 70s.

Among the direct connections between music and the other arts, the most thoroughly studied has been D'Annunzio's many-sided involvement with music and musicians: see, for example, D. de' Paoli, 'Gabriele d'Annunzio, la musica e i musicisti', in the anonymously edited symposium *Nel centenario di Gabriele d'Annunzio* (Turin and Rome, 1963), 41–125; and especially R. Tedeschi, *D'Annunzio e la musica* (Scandicci [Florence], 1988).

Individual composers

There are books in English on only two composers in the 'generazione dell'Ottanta'. G. M. Gatti, *Ildebrando Pizzetti* (Turin, 1934, rev. 2/1954; expanded Eng. trans. London,

1951), is a partisan and now dated critical study – still, however, useful as far as it goes. E. Respighi, *Ottorino Respighi: dati biografici ordinati* (Milan, 1954; abridged Eng. trans., London, 1962), is a very informative (if biased) biography, with only rudimentary comments on the music. Serious readers will need the Italian edition, which is fully twice as long and detailed. Much the most substantial book on Pizzetti in Italian (in spite of its deceptively unassuming title) is *Ildebrando Pizzetti: cronologia e bibliografia*, ed. B. Pizzetti (Parma, 1980); it, too, is a documentary biography – in this case mercilessly objective and strikingly free from family bias. The biggest book yet available on Respighi is *Ottorino Respighi*, ed. G. Rostirolla (Turin and Rome, 1985), which, like most symposia, is of uneven quality; but it contains many useful things.

The best book on Casella remains the symposium *Alfredo Casella*, ed. G. M. Gatti and F. d'Amico (Milan, 1958). Among Casella's own writings (other than the above mentioned autobiography) the most important is the collection of essays *21+26* (Rome and Milan, 1931), an essential document of the ideals and aims of Italian neo-classicism. Malipiero's far more subjective and idiosyncratic writings on music are well represented by his *Il filo d'Arianna: saggi e fantasie* (Turin, 1966). Notable books about him include the indispensable *L'opera di Gian Francesco Malipiero: saggi di scrittori italiani e stranieri con una introduzione di Guido M. Gatti, seguito dal catalogo delle opere con annotazioni dell'autore e da ricordi e pensieri dello stesso* (Treviso, 1952: ed. G. Scarpa, whose name does not appear, however, on the cover or title-page); and *Omaggio a Malipiero*, ed. M. Messinis (= Studi di musica veneta, iv; Florence, 1977 [conference proceedings]). The first unified, comprehensive study of the whole of Malipiero's musical output is J. C. G. Waterhouse, *La musica di Gian Francesco Malipiero* (Turin and Rome, 1990; English version in preparation).

A highly informative (though amateurishly written and produced) book on Luigi Russolo's futurist experiments is G. F. Maffina, *Luigi Russolo e l'arte dei rumori* (Turin, 1978). For books relating to composers of the generation older than the 'generazione dell'Ottanta', see the bibliography at the end of Chapter V in *The Late Romantic Era*. It should here be mentioned that L. Lombardi, *Conversazione con Petrassi* (Milan, 1980), and *Petrassi*, ed. E. Restagno (Turin, 1986), both contain revealing material about the composer's early experience and attitudes while working within the fascist musical hierarchy in the 1930s.

Chapter VI

Eastern Europe, 1918–45

MICHAEL BECKERMAN, JIM SAMSON

During the period of Communist rule in eastern Europe it was easy to consider the region as a coherent though diverse area where rather domesticated groups of Slavs, Magyars and gypsies lived together in some semblance of harmony. Recent events, though, have reminded us of the tumultuous differences in history, religion and culture which exist between the various nation states and the ethnic groups which inhabit them. Yugoslavia is in the midst of one of the worst bloodbaths of human history, while the Czech lands are independent for the first time since 1621, and seem well on the way to peace and prosperity. Romania may be worse off now than it was under Ceaucescu and the ethnic hostility between Hungarians and Slovaks has never been worse. The Polish economy is a shambles and over a million gypsies are treated as scapegoats. Gone is any lingering sense that eastern European nationalism is something arcane to be studied in a musty textbook. In the last three years the continuing drama of the region has often been horrifyingly re-enacted before our very eyes as the unresolved conflicts of the past have tainted the present with blood and confusion.

How different things appeared in 1918, when it seemed that eastern Europe might enjoy a vital and prosperous renascence! In November of that year the Moravian composer Leoš Janáček wrote a work for male voices called *The Czech Legion*. Based on a popular and exuberant poem by Antonín Horák, it evolves from a dissonant texture, representing the struggles of war, to a sentimental and consonant reference to the Czech national anthem. Though not as monumental as Janáček's patriotic *Taras Bulba*, completed seven months earlier, or the *Sinfonietta* of 1926, *The Czech Legion* shows how the sense of national pride and rejuvenation which came to much of eastern Europe at the close of World War I had immediate repercussions in music. To understand how and why the end of World War I marked a new beginning in the musical life of eastern Europe, we must consider the political and cultural situation in the region.

A map of eastern Europe shows a duck-shaped land mass (with Bohemia as the beak) about the size of France, Spain and Portugal combined, which includes Poland, Czechoslovakia, Hungary, Romania, Yugoslavia and Bulgaria. Several of these territories had been independent medieval kingdoms (including Poland, Hungary, Serbia and Bulgaria) and invoked 'historic rights' to validate their claims to national independence in the late nineteenth century. But this was not a crucial factor in the struggle for self-determination. That struggle was equally committed and equally fierce in regions which had no such political roots but whose sense of ethnic identity, sustained by language and culture, was strong enough for all that. In the end the political settlements of 1918, however crude, represented a triumph of nationalism over the dynastic principle. The most significant change in eastern Europe after the war was 'the gradual disappearance, step by step, of multinational states and their replacement by national ones'.[1] Thus, although European nationalism had been an active force for over a century, the newness of the political frameworks of eastern European countries led to a replication of nationalist sentiment after 1918. This notion of a new nationalism, however, should not imply any approach to regional unity. The new Hungary formed something close to a politically and culturally unified entity, but the emerging Czechoslovak state represented the joining of the Czech lands of Bohemia and Moravia to Slovakia. This was bound to create tensions since the former had firm historical ties with Austria and a strong German-speaking minority, while Slovakia, long a part of the Hungarian orbit, had a considerable Magyar population. Yugoslavia's situation was even more ambiguous since the new nation was a coalition of Serbs, Croats, Slovenes, Montenegrans, Macedonians and Albanians, with a mixture of Orthodox, Catholic and Muslim religions.

Bulgaria, which became independent in 1878, was a backward remnant of the Ottoman Empire, while Romania was carved out of the Russian and Ottoman empires after the Congress of Berlin in 1881. Poland was formally constituted in 1918 following a series of disastrous partitions by Prussia, Germany and Russia. Thus when we consider this motley collection of nation states known as eastern Europe we cannot apply any single theory; we must acknowledge that modern western Europe is no model with which to approach the East, with its uneasy relations between Slavs, Magyars, Bulgars and Germans. Rather we might draw an analogy with ancient England, with its competing forces of Angles, Saxons and Jutes.

Given the diversity of cultural influences at work in the region (four competing dynasties held sway in the nineteenth century) it is hardly surprising that the institutions of formal culture, including those of organized music-making, were at very different stages of development in 1918. At one extreme there was the thoroughly professional middle-class musical life of Prague and Budapest. As major capitals of the Habsburg Empire, these cities had flourishing opera companies, national theatres, philharmonic societies and conservatories, with adventurous and catholic repertories not so different from those of major west European capitals. Here the dynastic presence played an enabling role in the eighteenth and early nineteenth centuries and only later came to be viewed as a focus for ethnic and nationalist discontent.

At the other extreme were those territories which had been under Ottoman rule until the late nineteenth century. In Bulgaria, for instance, the establishment of an institutional framework for art music was delayed until the present century, with the Sofia National Opera and the State Music Academy both founded in 1921 and the National Philharmonic Society in 1924. Much the same was true of parts of modern Yugoslavia, notably Bosnia and Hercegovina, Montenegro and Macedonia. Even Serbia, which gained its independence from the Turk in the early nineteenth century, was slow to organize a professional musical life. The National Theatre in Belgrade housed opera intermittently in the late nineteenth century, but it was only in the aftermath of 1918 that the Belgrade Opera Company and the Belgrade Philharmonic Society were established.

The musical awakening in war-torn Belgrade was part of a more general reorganization of formal culture in the wake of the political settlement of 1918. New institutions were established elsewhere in postwar Yugoslavia – the Zagreb Philharmonic and Croatian State Conservatory in the early 1920s; a new Slovenian Conservatory in Ljubljana in 1919; a National Theatre in Sarajevo in 1919. But as capital of the new state, Belgrade had special responsibilities, and its promotion (in 1926) of a major concert and exhibition of music from Yugoslavia as a whole was of immense symbolic significance. There were similar developments in Romania, where the establishment of a Union of Romanian Composers in 1920 was an obvious attempt to bind together the culturally distinct provinces of Moldavia, Wallachia and Transylvania. And also in Poland, where the rebirth of the state after more than a century of tripartition resulted not only in a wave of celebratory nationalism, but in the gradual disappearance of longstanding divisions and rivalries between native and foreign companies and venues. In cities such as Poznań and L'vóv, just as in Zagreb, Prague and Budapest, the segregation of cultural communities (native and German) could not be sustained indefinitely in the face of new political realities.

Given the nature of those political realities, it is not surprising that nineteenth-century concepts of nationalism continued to influence the stylistic history of music in the region as a whole. It is worth examining those concepts briefly at this stage. In addition to traditional notions stressing loyalty to a particular nation state, the Romantic nationalist saw the nation as a philosophical entity and a metaphysical reality. At the core of this approach was the almost religious belief that the nation had a kind of ineffable essence, which could be described only as a Germanness, Russianness, Czechness or Hungarianness, to distinguish it from all other nations. The nationalist statesman's task was to articulate this essence and fight for a future where it might be realized as the basis of a political entity; the artist's goal was to express the peoples' metaphysical identity in poetry, painting, drama, and song. Since the combination of all these art forms was thought to be especially powerful, opera became the most palpable way of communicating nationalism to a wide public. Thus in the mid- to late nineteenth century, national opera flourished, and such works as Glinka's *A Life for the Tsar*, Smetana's *Libuše* and *The Bartered Bride*, Musorgsky's *Boris Godunov* and Wagner's *Der Ring des Nibelungen* and *Der Meistersinger* became, in effect, national pageants, blending history, myth and folklore in a mighty collage.

Music, which in the canon of Romantic arts was thought most capable of expressing the ineffable, became the paramount artistic embodiment of the subtle nuances of the nation's essence. Though the struggle for national cultural identity implied a certain degree of tension, which could be associated with the most dissonant and innovatory aspects of the musical language, there was another quite different vision which became critically important: the image of the naive and pure folk 'on location', whose simple virtues and intuitive understanding became a source of national spirit. Obviously, this aspect of national culture was to be represented by folk music, either through literal citation, or more frequently, through the creation of a kind of stylized folk language. Much of the vitality then of music which sought to enter the national arena lay in the contrast between the richly cosmopolitan and the conspicuously national.

Although the various eastern European national schools have common features, their chronologies are not the same. In the Czech lands, Hungary and, to a certain extent, Poland the national movement, with its accompanying schools, conservatories, composers of national opera and of works incorporating folk music, began as early as the 1840s and lasted well into the first decades of the twentieth century, while in Romania, Bulgaria and parts of Yugoslavia the same sequence of events (in a much accelerated form) only began after 1918. The Czech school is perhaps the most coherent, with Smetana as its founding-father, followed by Dvořák, Janáček and Martinů. In Poland and Hungary the situation was a little more ambiguous because the revisionist 'fathers' – Chopin and Liszt – had ambivalent attitudes both towards their homelands and national music in general.

Many composers in eastern Europe between the wars retained an allegiance to this essentially nineteenth-century concept of national music, remaining convinced that the greatest and truest art must be national art – that individuality is paramount, but that the proper voice of the individual is through the national. This commitment informed much of the music written in Yugoslavia, for instance, as a brief glimpse at its three most culturally developed provinces suggests. The level of creativity was perhaps highest in Slovenia. Here the nationalist ideals of the Cecilian movement persisted well into the interwar period, notably in the music of Risto Savin (1859–1948), whose operas and symphonic works absorbed folkloristic materials into a musical style rather akin to Dvořák's. This was indeed the most characteristic idiom of Slovenian music during the period. But there were more progressive trends, too, especially in the music of the Schoenberg pupil Marij Kogoj (1895–1956), whose *Črne maske* ('Black Masks') of 1921 was the closest Yugoslavian music came to a thoroughgoing expressionism, and in several works by Slavko Osterc (1895–1945), who experimented with twelve-note writing as well as a neo-classicism owing something to Stravinsky and Prokofiev.

Such modernist tendencies were less conspicuous in Croatia and Serbia. Following a lengthy period dominated by the prolific but anachronistic output of Ivan Zajc, Croatian music was symbolically reborn with a celebratory concert in Zagreb in 1916. The Zagreb newspaper *Jutarnji list* called the event 'the birth of a new era in the life of our Croatian fatherland'. Such composers as Antun Dobronić and Jakov Gotavac instigated a major revival of the Illyrian movement in Croatian music, turning once more to folksong as the basis for a nationalist idiom, albeit one which remained unadventurous in relation to contemporary European trends. More crucially, Josip Slavenski (1896–1955) – one of the most powerful creative forces in Yugoslavian music of the interwar period – integrated Croatian folk elements into a thoroughly modernist musical language in a manner that inevitably suggests parallels with Bartók and Enescu.

Serbian music at this time could claim greater continuity with nineteenth-century national traditions since these were already firmly in place from the last third of the century. Stevan St Mokranjac (1856–1914) is considered the founder of Serbian national style, a kind of counterpart to Glinka, Smetana and Erkel, and his collections of choral music, based on national songs, were to have a profound impact on subsequent composers. We also find a close connection between Belgrade and Prague, where such composers as Jovan Bandur (1889–1956), Ljubica Marić (*b* 1909), Milan Ristić (*b* 1908), Predrag Milošević (*b* 1904) and Mihailo Vukdragovic (*b* 1900), studied with Krička, Suk, Novak and Hába. Among the major achievements of interwar Serbian national music are Bandur's massive cycle of madrigals for male- and mixed-voice choirs based on folk texts, and Vukdragovic's Nocturne for Orchestra (1927) and Symphonic Meditations (1939).

Slavenski apart, much of the nationalist music composed in

Yugoslavia remained anachronistic. Yet elsewhere in eastern Europe composers succeeded in reconciling a continuing commitment to nationalism with a more contemporary musical idiom. At this stage it may be helpful to look at some concrete examples.

Two of the clearest statements of a type of ultimate national myth can be seen in a pair of operas written almost simultaneously: Zoltán Kodály's *Háry János* (1926) and Jaromir Weinberger's *Švanda the Bagpiper* (1927). Both enjoyed enormous popularity and are still known to wider audiences through the suites extracted from them. At first glance they have little in common; *Švanda* is a conventional comic opera in traditional form which uses almost no original folk material. Kodály's work, however, is based almost entirely on original Hungarian folksongs; indeed, one of its avowed purposes was to bring these folksongs to public attention.

Yet only slightly beneath the surface we find intriguing similarities. Both operas deal with a folk hero (Weinberger calls his work a 'folk opera') who is gifted yet also a kind of n'er-do-well, and both feature monomythic journeys into a kind of sophisticated urban underworld (the kingdom of the Ice Queen and the court of Vienna) where the hero loses his heart to a cold, sophisticated woman. Finally, both heroes are returned to their villages through the interventions of their innocent yet determined sweethearts, who stand out as angelic figures in stark contrast to the spoilt, manipulative 'urban' women who seduce them. Thus the nation itself is represented both by an imaginative and virile yet slightly irresponsible masculine element and a reliable and stolid yet sweet and naive feminine side.

In both these works audibly national music is used as a recurring symbol of virtue. For example, when Švanda speaks for the first time it is in a musical language immediately recognizable to the Czech audience – a sort of 'high national style' combining elements of Smetana's *Má vlast* and Dvořák's Slavonic Dances; Kodály's Romantic-nationalist tendencies are neatly summed up in the duet between Háry and Örsze in Act 1 (no. 4 in the suite), with its folk modality harmonized in a manner more reminiscent of Debussy than any Hungarian peasant. Conspicuously 'modernist' cosmopolitan idioms are reserved for the courts of high society, where dissonance is usually equated with decadence.

Finally, both operas conclude with massive choral tableaux and a conspicuous return to folklike textures, suggesting unequivocal glorifications of the nation. It was through using stylized or arranged folk music as a symbol for the ideal nation and more contemporary idioms for the real world that these composers (and many others) sought to establish links between the tradition of folk opera and western European modernism. In such works as *Háry János* and *Švanda* composers spoke to a large public in a language at once new and

Modern Times

Autograph sketches of Janáček's 'Příhody Lišky Bystroušky' ('The Cunning Little Vixen'), composed 1921–3.

familiar, and it is initially surprising to find such a perfect crystallization of national art at a time when substantial areas of western Europe viewed such expressions as appallingly outdated. But it was precisely the fluctuating political and cultural situation in eastern Europe that demanded expressions of national identity – and would continue to do so even after World War II.

For all that, the most innovatory achievements of east European music during this period cannot easily be confined within a nationalist aesthetic. The musical 'awakening' in the region is perhaps epitomized in the achievements of four composers: Janáček, Bartók, Enescu and Szymanowski. It would be inadequate to consider their music exclusively in nationalist terms, though for all four a nationalist commitment was the trigger for a more radical, authentically modernist musical language. 'I hold on to the roots of our people's life – therefore I grow and do not succumb', said Janáček. This might be read superficially as a nationalist credo. But it was a much larger statement, proclaiming an allegiance rather to Russian-inspired concepts of realism and populism. Janáček was a passionate Russophile from the 1890s and was a founding member of the Russian Circle in Brno. Several of his works (*Taras Bulba*, the 'Kreutzer Sonata' String Quartet, and the operas *Kát'a Kabanová* (after Ostrovsky's *The Storm*) and *From the House of the Dead* (after Dostoevsky) are based on Russian sources. Furthermore, theories of

Russian realism stressing the opposition between the world of everyday life and the mysterious forces beyond played a significant role in his compositional and dramatic development. Throughout Janáček's writings, and triumphantly manifest in his music, is a single – profoundly anti-aestheticist belief – that art is a component of life and must remain 'anchored' by it, so that even the minutest technical detail may be validated by experience.

This is especially clear in the operas written during this period. *The Cunning Little Vixen*, *The Makropoulos Affair*, *Kát'a Kabanová* and *From the House of the Dead* deal grippingly with questions of death and rebirth, reflecting both the most contemporary trends and the realist concerns of the 1900s, while compositions like the *Glagolitic Mass*, the string quartets and the Sinfonietta deal quasi-programmatically with both national and personal subjects. There is also a strong Pan-Slavic tendency, exemplified by such works as *Taras Bulba*, after Gogol, the *Glagolitic Mass*, based on the Old Slavonic Mass, the incomplete symphonic work *Dunaj* ('The Danube'), depicting a river which (as the composer pointed out) flows through four Slav countries. Finally, in such works as *The Diary of One who Disappeared* he concerned himself with the mysterious gypsies, who, for the Czechs, were a clear symbol of both the exotic and the erotic.[2]

Hungarian gypsy band with typical Central Transylvanian instrumentation (clarinet, violins, flat-bridged viola, cimbalom and bass): Cserépváralja, County Borsod, 1929.

Janáček's musical language, ostensibly derived from the rhythmic patterns of everyday speech coupled with the scale patterns of Moravian folksong, is tonal but rich in modal inflection and marked by the idiosyncratic repetition of small motifs. Motifs and sections are strung together by a process Janáček called 'layering', in which they are placed in a series of overlapping sequences; this sometimes gives his works a jagged and terse quality. Although he kept up with developments in western European music (he was familiar with such works as *Madama Butterfly*, *Elektra* and *Wozzeck*), he remained, as he put it, 'close to the soil', and 'the humble Czech man', exuberantly productive until his death at 74.

Like Balakirev before him, Janáček was a composer-ethnographer. He began his fieldwork in the 1890s and by 1900 he had collected and transcribed more than a thousand songs. In this regard he foreshadowed Kodály and above all Bartók, who more than any other composer tried to understand folk music on its own terms, both musical and contextual, and to find an appropriate way of introducing it to the world. In his essay 'The Influence of Peasant Music on Modern Music' Bartók distinguished several ways in which composers might respond creatively to folk music. Of these, the most important is described as follows:

> Neither peasant melodies nor imitations of peasant melodies can be found in his music, but it is pervaded by the atmosphere of peasant music. In this case we may say, he has completely absorbed the idiom of peasant music which has become his musical mother tongue. He masters it as completely as a poet masters his mother tongue.[3]

Here the absorption of folk music satisfies the demands of both the 'national' and the 'modern'.

This approach to folksong – found in Janáček and in the major works of Bartók's stylistic maturity (from the Second String Quartet of 1917 onwards) – represents a significant departure from nineteenth-century tradition. Above all, there is an enhanced respect for peasant music and a new realism in its interpretation and analysis. Unlike the rationalized folk and popular musics of Romantic nationalism, these peasant traditions were valued precisely because they had fallen largely outside the dominant Western process of rationalization and could therefore be used critically for radical, progressive ends. Something of the symbolic values associated with folk music remained, in particular its identification with a collective 'natural' community. But it was no longer a national community that was evoked. Far from using peasant music to publicize Hungarian nationalism, Bartók promoted the music of the Slovakian and Romanian ethnic minorities within Greater Hungary. The project was in brief less a nationalist than an authentically modernist one – to span the gulf between an ahistorical epic natural community and the contemporary world of Western modernity.

In stylistic terms this amounted to an interpenetration of east European peasant idioms and the handed-down genres, formal types and tonal schemata of a Western high-art tradition, and much of Bartók's music of the 1920s and 30s can indeed be understood in these terms. Folk music was not here an agent of Romantic nostalgia, as in the early nineteenth century, nor of national heritage-gathering, as later in the century. Rather it was a means of confronting what Adorno described as the 'rupture between the self and the forms' which characterized modernity. Adorno's analysis of Bartók's significance for our music is indeed challenging. He argues that the folk material, and the 'natural community' it signifies, are brought into confrontation with the 'dead forms', so to speak, of an increasingly fragmented Western art music. The resulting fusion does not conceal alienation under the mask of a false reconciliation of the epic and the modern. Rather, in using the folk material as a critique of the used-up forms of Western art music, it throws alienation into relief. It may forge a new and integrated musical language, but in doing so it does not hide the fractured character of its components. In short, its modernist credentials are never in doubt.

There are parallels here with Enescu in Romania and Szymanowski in Poland. Indeed, the formative developments of all three composers were strikingly similar. Their efforts to throw off prevailing late Romantic influences turned them first to modern French and Russian music and then to their native folk music. It was only at the end of the second decade of the century that all three achieved a fully mature, self-consistent musical language in which folk elements are integrated (at a level of considerable abstraction) with contemporary techniques. For Enescu, as for Bartók, nationalism was in the end subsumed by a larger aesthetic project – a kind of East–West synthesis which penetrated to the core of his musical language in such works as the Piano Sonata op.24, the Second String Quartet and the opera *Oedipe*. Similarly, for Szymanowski an involvement with Tatra folk music in the op.50 mazurkas, the ballet *Harnasie* and the late instrumental works (Second String Quartet, Second Violin Concerto, *Symphonie concertante*) was only in part a response to the nationalist imperative. No less important was the potential of this music as an exoticism – a world of presumed innocence and vitality which could stand muster as an alternative reality, suggestive both of ancient roots and of Dyonisian escape.

By couching folkloristic materials in lucid, tonally rooted structures, Szymanowski's later works foreshadowed to some extent Polish music of the 1930s and 40s. But the younger generation of Polish composers looked more towards Paris, to the clearcut forms and mannered charm of neo-classical styles influenced by Stravinsky, Prokofiev, Milhaud and Poulenc and owing much to the teaching of Nadia Boulanger. The Association des Jeunes Musiciens Polonais à Paris was established in 1926, with Szymanowski's pupil Piotr Perkowski as its first chairman; the music composed by its members tended to adopt a moderately toned neo-classical idiom, occasionally spiced by elements of Polish folk music. This is broadly true of Perkowski's own Sinfonietta, as well as the early music of Stanisław Wiechowicz (*Chmiel* – 'Hop Wine'), Michal Kondracki (Partita and Concerto for Orchestra), Antoni Szalowski (Overture) and Michał Spisak (Serenade for orchestra). Neo-classical sympathies are also apparent in the Symphonic Variations by Witold Lutosławski (*b* 1913) and even in the surviving twelve-note works by Józef Koffler, the only Polish composer at that time to take Schoenberg's path.

Parisian neo-classicism is also an appropriate context in which to view the early achievements of Bohuslav Martinů, one of the few Czech composers following Janáček to achieve international standing. He moved to Paris in 1923 (studying there with Roussel) and responded to both Stravinsky and Les Six with a group of pastiche theatre works (*Tri prani* – 'The Three Wishes'; *Kuchynska revue* – 'Kitchen Review') and an extended series of neo-classical instrumental works owing much to the concerti grossi of Corelli and Vivaldi. He effectively commuted between Czechoslovakia and Paris until the late 1930s when the growing dangers of war made it impossible. Martinů barely escaped Paris before the German invasion. He had been blacklisted by the Nazis for his support of the Czech National Council in Paris and was in danger. After a few frenetic months, the efforts of such figures as Ernest Ansermet and Rudolf Fírkušný made it possible for him to go to the USA in 1941.

It is difficult to tell what the effect of such a jarring move is on the creative life of a composer. It is tempting to draw a parallel here with Bartók, also exiled in America in his last years. Politically progressive figures like Martinů and Bartók, who were deeply concerned about the destruction of their homelands under fascism, experienced a kind of final wave of national feeling. Thus it was perhaps the combination of a new beginning with homesickness and anxiety that led to a stylistic clarification, not unlike that in Dvořák's American Music. Many of Bartók's late works, including the Third Piano Concerto, the Concerto for Orchestra and the Viola Concerto, show a kind of popular national synthesis. This is also the kind of change found in the later works of Martinů. Gone are many of the Parisian gestures, and we find gems like the *Songs on One Page* (1943), *Memorial to Lidice*, the Second Violin Concerto (1943) and the String Quartet no.7 (1947) which eschew gratuitous modernist gestures and clichés and strive towards a more concentrated and transparent lyricism. Wandering from province to city, from the cities of one country to another, through war and upheaval, has been the lot of most successful eastern European composers. Bartók and Martinů were lucky, unlike such composers as the Czech student of Janáček, Pavel Haas, the Bartók student JenoDeutsch and the Yugoslav student of Berg, Rikard Szvarc, who perished with millions of others in concentration camps.[4]

It is perhaps in such a place though that this discussion should end, since it provides in a literal and quite striking manner a metaphor for the way east European musical culture was destroyed during World War II. Much is made in general European histories of the way the old régime was dismantled as a result of World War I, but one could argue that the 1920s and 30s were a time when, at least in eastern Europe, many of the tendencies and aspirations of the late nineteenth century were fully realized. Thus this period, in spite of astonishing growth and change, was marked by continuity with the past. Many of the countries in the region, as we have seen, became independent directly after the war, and the spirit of ambition and of a fresh beginning permeated musical culture. It was World War II, though, that destroyed the identity and vitality of east European cultural and intellectual life.

NOTES

[1] See 'Assimilation and nationalism in East Central Europe during the last century of Hapsburg rule' in *The Carl Beck Papers in Russian and East European Studies*, paper no.202.

[2] Of all the groups in eastern Europe, the gypsies have been given least attention in scholarly studies of music. It could easily be argued that the vitality of various eastern European folk musics was largely preserved through itinerant gypsies, who had a kind of 'cross-fertilizing' effect on widely divergent cultures. The literature, however, taking its cue from Bartók (citing Liszt as the villain) considers the gypsies mere popularizers and vulgarizers.

[3] This essay can be found in the excellent collection *Béla Bartók Essays*, ed. B. Suchoff (New York, 1976). No composer wrote more articulately or compellingly about his work and the pressing artistic questions of his time.

[4] Musical life in concentration camps is a subject in itself; there is a poignant study of the Terezin camp, with its many musicians and chorus, and its performances through the years: see J. Karaś, *Music in Terezin 1941–45* (New York, 1985). A record ('Hudba psánáv Terezíně ['Music written at Terezin']) is available on the Panton label.

BIBLIOGRAPHICAL NOTE

Historical background

Since the completion of this chapter there have been monumental changes in the politics of eastern and central Europe. The collapse of communism in the territories which formed part of Soviet-dominated 'Eastern Europe' was indeed a liberation. But it has inevitably created new problems, both social and socio-economic, and there is already an extensive bibliography documenting the progress of the new democracies. These recent events do not bear directly on the period investigated by this chapter, but they do influence our reading of earlier literature on the pre-communist and communist eras. Above all they bring home to us the need to balance interpretative positions which are often ideologically informed.

There is of course a substantial literature on individual countries. But it seems more appropriate to concentrate here on general accounts of the region. The following are recommendable: O. Halecki, *The Limits and Divisions of European History* (New York, 1950) and *Borderlands of Western Civilisation* (New York, 1952); R. Portal, *The Slavs*, trans. P. Evans (London, 1965); F. Dvornik, *The Making of Central Europe* (London, 1949) and *The Slavs in European History and Civilisation* (New Brunswick, 1962); *Nationalism in Eastern Europe*, ed. P.F. Sugar and I. Lederer (Seattle and London, 1969).

For more detailed studies of the interwar period it is best to turn to specialist journals, notably *Slavonic and East European Review* (London); *Slavic Review* (Michigan); *Balkan Studies* (Thesaloniki) and *Co-existence* (Glasgow). Of special relevance to this chapter is *Cross-Currents: a Yearbook of Central European Culture* (Michigan), where the effects of Nazism and World War II and the roles of competing religious and ethnic groups are explored in numerous articles.

Music

General studies in English include G. Abraham, *Slavonic and Romantic Music* (London, 1968) and *Essays on Russian and East European Music* (Oxford, 1985); R. Newmarch, *The Music of Czechoslovakia* (London, New York and Toronto, 1942); V. Štěpánek and B. Karásek, *An Outline of Czech and Slovak Music* (Prague, 1964); B. Szabolski, *A Concise History of Hungarian Music* (Budapest and London, 1964); *Polish Music*, ed. S. Jarociński (Warsaw, 1965); Ludwik Erhardt, *Music in Poland* (Warsaw, 1975); V. Cosma, *A Concise History of Romanian Music* (Bucharest, 1982); V. Krustev, *Bulgarian Music* (Sofia, 1978); J. Andreis, *Music in Coatia* (Zagreb, 1974); I. Županović, *Centuries of Croatian Music* (Zagreb, 1984); S. Djurić-Klajn, *A Survey of Serbian Music through the Ages* (Belgrade, 1972).

There are two general books on Janáček in English: J. Vogel's *Leoš Janáček* (London, 1962), and H. Hollander, *Janáček* (London, 1963). Janáček's own writings can be read in translation in *Janáček's Collected Essays*, ed. M. Zemanova (London, 1989). Bartók is best approached through H. Stevens, *The Life and Music of Béla Bartók* (New York, 1953), and P. Griffiths, *Bartók* (London, 1984). Two studies of Kodaly in English are L. Eösze, *Zoltán Kodály: his Life and Work* (London, 1962), and P. M. Young, *Zoltán Kodály: a Hungarian Musician* (London, 1964). Szymanowski is best served by J. Samson, *The Music of Szymanowski* (London and New York, 1980), and Enescu by N. Malcolm, *George Enescu* (London, 1990). The major studies of Martinů in English are M. Šafránek, *Bohuslav Martinů: his Life and Works* (London, 1962), and B. Large, *Martinů* (London, 1975).

Chapter VII

The USSR, 1918–45

LAUREL E. FAY

An aesthetic reaction against the carnage of World War I was a common phenomenon in much of postwar Europe. In Russia it was not so much the war itself that came to capture the imagination of postwar artists, but the revolutionary toppling of the autocratic government in February 1917 and, most significantly, the unexpected seizure of power, in October that year, by Lenin and his Bolshevik Party in the name of the working class.[1] Beyond the broad notion that 'art belongs to the people'[2] and the conviction that artistic culture could and should play an important role in the building of the first socialist state, the revolutionaries had no firm understanding of what that might entail. That 'Soviet' art would somehow be as new and unprecedented as the socialist workers' paradise was a matter of faith. Whether the workers should be creators of the new art or its consumers, whether art should build on the traditions of the bourgeois past or jettison them to begin from scratch, and what forms that art should take, were questions that animated debate for a long time. In many respects, the first twenty years or so of the revolution can be seen as a period of restless struggle to find answers, to define art anew. The resolution to the search would eventually come in the form of a mandate from above.

The political upheavals in Russia coincided with a natural watershed in musical generations. The death of Nikolay Rimsky-Korsakov in 1908 was followed by that of Anatoly Lyadov in 1914, Sergey Taneyev in 1915 and César Cui, the last of the 'Mighty Handful', in 1918. The premature death of Alexander Skryabin in 1915 proved a particular disappointment to the revolutionaries, who heard in his late works a reflection of the era's social upheaval. Alexander Glazunov and Mikhail Ippolitov-Ivanov, two revered composers of the older generation who bridged the gap, helped ensure the high standards and continuity of the pedagogical traditions of the Petrograd[3] and Moscow conservatories, respectively, but their activity and influence as composers had already passed its peak.

The devastation of the world war and the instability, famine and incredible hardships of the civil war period from 1917 to 1920 – above and beyond the political upheavals of 1917 – also contributed to a widespread exodus of artists who might have played a role as cultural standard-bearers in the fledgling Soviet state. The list of emigrés would eventually grow to include the composers Igor Stravinsky, Sergey Rakhmaninov, Nikolay Medtner, Nikolay Tcherepnin and Alexander Grechaninov, the conductor Sergey Koussevitsky, the bass Fyodor Shalyapin, the violinists Jascha Heifetz and Nathan Milstein and the pianist Vladimir Horowitz. Sergey Prokofiev was a special case. Like so many musicians indifferent to politics, the *enfant terrible* of pre-revolutionary music sought permission by the new government to try his fortunes abroad, which in 1918 he was reluctantly granted. After an extended sojourn in the West, he chose to return permanently to his homeland in the 1930s.

The burden of restructuring the educational system and overseeing cultural development for the new government rested on the shoulders of Anatoly Lunacharsky, Lenin's appointee as head of Narkompros (People's Commissariat of Enlightenment). Lunacharsky was a Bolshevik intellectual, a critic and sometime playwright whose passionate involvement in the arts helped promote their vital role in the new society. While, like Lenin, he defended the pre-revolutionary cultural heritage as a legitimate birthright of the working class, Lunacharsky encouraged the broad-based exploration of new forms of artistic expression uniquely suited to the revolutionary moment. His tolerance of sometimes radically differing approaches and his policy of inclusion rather than exclusion helped foster, in the 1920s, an exhilarating if sometimes clamorous period of artistic experimentation.

On the surface, musical life after the October Revolution continued to function much as before. The music performed in the years that immediately followed – the operas of Verdi, Puccini, Bizet and Wagner balanced by the Russian classics including works by Musorgsky, Tchaikovsky and Rimsky-Korsakov, the symphonic and chamber repertory ranging from Mozart, Beethoven and Schumann to Skryabin – was almost indistinguishable from that which preceded it. What did change significantly was the audiences. Workers, students and soldiers, to whom tickets were distributed free or at nominal charge, replaced the élite, bourgeois public of the tsarist era. The new public, largely untutored in the substance or etiquette of the high arts, none the less impressed observers by its reverent attitude and thirst for the culture which had previously been inaccessible.

In music, more so than in the other arts, professionals were slow to see the possibilities of the situation and seize the initiative for developing new art forms to correspond with social reality. Avant-garde activists such as the artist Alexander Rodchenko, the poet Vladimir Mayakovsky and the theatre director Vsevolod Meyerhold took their art into the streets and infused their work with the spirit of daily life, producing poster art, decorating railway carriages with

The Red Army Ensemble, conducted by Alexander Alexandrov.

festive. 'agitprop' (agitational propaganda) or staging participatory mass spectacles designed to entertain, educate and inspire.

Music played a part in this revolutionary ferment. Concert 'brigades' performed in factories and for the troops. Military bands and choruses were a fixture at the public celebrations of May Day and the anniversary of the revolution. The singing of the 'Internationale' and other popular revolutionary songs capped every public gathering, large or small. As an offshoot of the notion that the people must evolve their own culture – a basic tenet of the proletarian cultural organizations (Proletkult) in the civil war years – amateur choruses and bands proliferated as well as more unusual forms of mass participation. The performance of choral recitation, the sometimes elaborately 'composed' declamation of texts, and of 'noise orchestras' which exploited the sound-making potential of the most utilitarian objects, became widespread. Among the most extraordinary experiments in mass music-making was the *Symphony of Hooters* by Arseny Avraamov,[4] produced first in Baku on the anniversary of the Revolution in 1922 and re-created a year later for the same anniversary in Moscow; in it the composer used factory and train whistles, sirens, cannon volleys and the clatter of machine-guns, coordinated with fanfares, and both choral and instrumental renditions of the 'Internationale', in an attempt to create a meaningful musical work out of the vast sound and spatial potential of cities during their festive celebrations.

Either through inertia or because many musicians were at best suspicious if not openly hostile to the goals of the Bolshevik government, it took some time for new ideas and spirit to seep into the repertories of the opera houses and concert halls. When Nikolay Miaskovsky's Fifth Symphony (1918) was first performed in Moscow in 1920, it was hailed as the first specifically Soviet symphony, though its genesis dated back to his service on the Austrian front during World War I and its style testified more to the continuity of symphonic traditions than to new beginnings. As late as 1924, Boris Asafyev, the versatile musician who became best known for his considerable accomplishments as critic, theorist and scholar, pointed to the 'crisis in individual creativity', cajoling composers to discard their 'aristocratic' aesthetic attitudes and respond to the realities of life around them.[5]

The situation in opera was particularly acute. Even before the revolution, critics had lamented the atmosphere of stagnation which had set in since the death of Rimsky-Korsakov, the last great Russian exponent of the genre. After the revolution, there was significant pressure, principally from the radical left, to terminate this expensive and outmoded form of bourgeois entertainment. The nation's two major opera houses, the Maryinsky in Petrograd and the Bolshoy in Moscow, were granted the designation 'Academic' in 1919, guaranteeing them state subsidies, but under renewed pressure in 1921 Lunacharsky was barely able to avert the closing of the Bolshoy.

In opera there was no ready-made 'revolutionary' repertory to supplant the classics, Russian and Western, of the pre-revolutionary past. Crude attempts to get the genre 'in tune with the revolution' by grafting new librettos on to the music of popular works – *The Battle for the Commune*, for instance, a reworking of Puccini's *Tosca* which transferred the action to the Paris Commune (staged in Leningrad in 1924), or *Hammer and Sickle*, two separate adaptations of Glinka's *A Life for the Tsar* set in Soviet Russia at the time of the Polish intervention (staged, respectively, in Odessa and Sverdlovsk in 1924 and 1925) – met with little enthusiasm. Glinka's first opera, regarded as the cornerstone of the Russian operatic tradition, posed a particularly thorny problem because of its implicit glorification of tsarist autocracy. In spite of early attempts to shift its focus, the work disappeared from the stage until 1939, when it returned with a refurbished libretto under its original title *Ivan Susanin*.

The end of the civil war in 1920, the return to a stable peacetime environment and an improvement in economic conditions facilitated by the institution of Lenin's New Economic Policy (NEP) in 1921, brought a burst of new activity to the country's musical life. Having abolished the increasingly troublesome and dogmatic Proletkult organizations in 1920, Lenin advocated a patient approach to the development of the arts: 'Cultural problems cannot be solved as quickly as political and military problems . . . 'we must adapt ourselves to this longer period, calculate our work accordingly, and display a maximum of perseverence, persistence, and system'.[6]

With the threat of foreign military intervention removed, stimulating creative contacts with the West, interrupted since the beginning of World War I, were resumed. Touring Western performers brought new interpretations and visiting Western composers, including Darius Milhaud, Paul Hindemith, Franz Schreker, Alban Berg and Alfredo Casella, brought modern repertory to invigorate Soviet musical life. They, in turn, helped promote performances of the most interesting new Soviet music abroad. Productions of modern Western operas – Prokofiev's *Love for Three Oranges* (1926), Berg's *Wozzeck* (1927), Ernst Krenek's *Jonny spielt auf* (1928) – brought fresh perspectives to the opera theatre. Jazz, that quintessentially American brand of mass culture, flourished in reopened nightclubs and dance halls, offering potent competition to the officially nurtured mass culture of folk and patriotic songs.

In 1924 the Association for Contemporary Music (ASM) was formed in Moscow as an offshoot of the International Society for Contemporary Music. With the broad goal of promoting the works of contemporary Soviet composers, balanced by the exposure of modern Western works, the ASM attracted the most progressive Soviet musicians, irrespective of stylistic inclination. It sponsored a series of chamber, and later orchestral, concerts and lectures and issued publications and a journal that featured music by a wide spectrum of composers including Bartók, Hindemith, Schoenberg, Stravinsky, Prokofiev, Satie and Les Six. Although the organization numbered among its advocates such highly respected musicians as Myaskovsky in Moscow and Asafyev and Vladimir Shcherbachev in Leningrad, its activities also served as a catalyst for a new generation of Soviet composers, including Vladimir Deshevov (1889–1955), Lev Knipper (1898–1974), Alexander Mosolov (1900–73), Leonid Polovinkin (1894–1949), Gavriil Popov (1904–72), Vissarion Shebalin (1902–63) and Dmitry Shostakovich (1906–75).

The adventurous spirit and optimism that had stimulated developments in the visual arts and the theatre infused the world of music. Nikolay Roslavets (1881–1944), who, even before the revolution, was pioneering a new harmonic vocabulary which embraced a twelve-note system similar in concept to the better-known technique later developed by Schoenberg, became a leading figure in avant-garde musical circles. Experiments in microtonal music had also predated the revolution, but under the auspices of the Society for Quarter-Tone Music founded in Petrograd in 1923 by Georgy Rimsky-Korsakov (a nephew of Nikolay Rimsky-Korsakov), the exploration of new tonal systems and new instruments became vigorous. In April 1922 the

Lev Termin playing the electronic instrument he first demonstrated at an industrial trade fair in Moscow (1922). Lenin met Termin and declared the invention worthy of the new state; he ordered 600 instruments to be made and offered Termin a concert tour of the USSR, but died before the promotion could be implemented.

engineer Lev Termin (*b* 1896) demonstrated to Lenin the prototype of an electronic musical instrument, the 'terminvoks' (known in the West as 'theremin'): using radio oscillators, pitch frequency was controlled by the distance of the performer's right hand from the instrument's antenna while the left hand regulated the volume. A number of Soviet composers wrote works for the instrument and it also drew the attention of Western musicians, including Edgard Varèse who included two theremins in the original score of *Equatorial* (1934).

Fascination with the image of a utopian, futuristic socialist society was fuelled by the compositions of Alexander Mosolov, especially by the raw energy and dynamism of *The Iron Foundry: Machine Music* (1926–8), a three-minute orchestral episode from the music to the ballet *Steel*, which was never staged. *The Iron Foundry* remained a popular concert piece at home and abroad until the mid-1930s. Mosolov's reputation as a musical 'constructivist' was symptomatic of the interest of many young Soviet composers in the expressive potential of motoric rhythms, ostinatos, jagged melodic lines, percussive techniques and harsh dissonance, which closely paralleled the interests of their European counterparts. It contrasted sharply with the enthusiasm for Skryabin's aesthetic prevalent ten years earlier. As Shostakovich told an interviewer in 1930: 'we regard Scriabine as our bitterest musical enemy. Why? Because Scriabine's music tends to an unhealthy eroticism. Also to mysticism and passivity and escape from the realities of life'.[7]

One of the most unusual responses to socialist democracy was the foundation of a conductorless orchestra, the First Symphonic Ensemble (in Russian abbreviated as Persimfans), in Moscow in 1922. An artistic council of players replaced the tyrannical authority of conductor; questions of repertory and the myriad details of interpretation, technique and style were painstakingly worked out in rehearsal. Persimfans impressed critics with its polished performances of the most difficult and challenging contemporary scores. It led a successful existence for a decade. Following its model, ensembles were formed in other cities though most of these proved short-lived. Among other factors contributing to the demise of the experiment in 1932 was the inefficiency of the democratic process, which required inordinate amounts of rehearsal time to produce results much more quickly achieved by a conductor.

The Russian Association of Proletarian Musicians (RAPM), another musical organization founded in 1923, was equally idealistic but pursued a different creative agenda from that of the ASM. With a heightened sense of political and civic consciousness, members of RAPM rejected Western influence, modernism and the élitist pretensions of 'high' art. They focussed their activities on simple, directly accessible and ideologically proven forms of mass culture – chiefly on mass songs and choral genres. Ideological virtue, however, was no guarantee of musical quality, and few of the composers made a lasting impact. A noteworthy exception to the low professional standards of RAPM composers was achieved by members of the Production Collective of Student-Composers of the Moscow Conservatory (Prokoll), a group organized in 1925. While they shared the proletarian agenda, they rejected the notion of over-simplification of musical language and style in mass music, seeking to create music both widely accessible and of high artistic merit.

The most talented figure in Prokoll was Alexander Davidenko (1899–1934), author of choral works and songs, including *Budyonny's Cavalry* (1925), of enduring popularity. For the tenth anniversary of the revolution, eight members of the collective produced a collaborative oratorio, *The Path of October* (1927): the musical contributions were uneven and only the two choruses by Davidenko rose above the mediocre, but the stirring, heroic treatment of revolutionary events, performed by soloists, chorus and orchestra, became the prototype of a genre widespread in the later Soviet period.

Shostakovich was unquestionably the most gifted Soviet composer to come forward in the 1920s. His First Symphony, composed in 1924–5 as his graduation piece from the composition faculty of the Leningrad Conservatory, brought the nineteen-year-old rapidly to international attention after its première conducted by Nikolay Malko in Leningrad in 1926. There was little innovation in its structure, and the influence of early Stravinsky, Prokofiev and other composers is evident, but there was something compellingly fresh and assured in the thematic writing and a mastery of the orchestra that signalled a distinctive musical individuality.

Nourished in the cultural milieu of Leningrad, which in the 1920s was more aggressively 'modern' than Moscow's, Shostakovich was an extremely versatile composer. He participated in the activities of the ASM and absorbed the latest trends in Western composition. Compositions like the Piano Sonata no.1 (1926) and the *Aphorisms* (1927) for piano were uncompromising in their adherence to modernistic idioms, complex textures and astringent harmonies. On the other hand, Shostakovich was equally attracted to utilitarian music and wrote for film and the dramatic theatre. Here the aesthetic of the music hall, circus and carnival, jazz and street ditties, was irresistible. In collaborating with Meyerhold on the production of Myakovsky's play *The Bedbug* in 1930, Shostakovich obliged the poet's whim for 'firemen's' music.

The extremes of Shostakovich's interests were juxtaposed in his Second Symphony, 'To October', his contribution to the revolutionary anniversary in 1927. The episodic, non-thematic nature of the lengthy orchestral prologue in this one-movement work, complete with com-

Scene from a performance at the Meyerhold Theatre, Moscow, of 'The Bedbug' (play by Mayakovsky, music by Shostakovich, directed by Meyerhold, with scenery by Rodchenko).

plex 'constructivist' layering of contrapuntal strands, sharply contrasts with the transparent tonal clarity at the climax and in the concluding choral section, on a patriotic text by Alexander Bezymensky, which in substance and spirit stands much closer to the ideals of Prokoll.

Having gradually consolidated political power after the death of Lenin in 1924, Joseph Stalin abandoned the modest economic advances of NEP and embarked on a rapid industrialization drive of massive proportions. To galvanize the population and channel all its energy into the successful completion of the First Five-Year Plan (1928–32), the country was put on a warlike footing. The atmosphere of imminent crisis was fuelled by threats of foreign intervention, conspiracy and counter-revolution. Campaigns against 'class enemies' took on a new urgency. The collectivization of agriculture was fundamental to Stalin's plan; it dictated the 'liquidation of the kulak class' – those peasants deemed to be prosperous – by expropriation, arrest and exile.

The militant rhetoric of vigilance filtered into the world of culture. The communist membership of the proletarian arts organizations, self-appointed ideological watchdogs, mounted increasingly strident attacks on those art forms which deviated from their narrow definition of genuine 'proletarian' art. The range of acceptable music essentially subsumed mass songs and choral genres imbued with suitable propaganda value and moral virtue. Any music not immediately accessible to all listeners on first hearing signalled the influence of 'bourgeois' social elements. Jazz was an obvious target. This licentious, degenerate musical form, clearly a subversive weapon of the capitalist conspiracy, was ruthlessly suppressed. Artistic experiments which, until recently, had been seen as compatible with the building of communism were now branded by the RAPM as a pernicious threat to the very fabric of socialist society.

The artistic vitality and diversity that had characterized the NEP period gradually succumbed to the zealous proletarian forces' campaign. In conflict with Stalin over his economic and educational programme, the broad-minded Lunacharsky resigned from the government in 1929. By the early 1930s the ASM and related organizations had ceased activity and, if only as a means of self-preservation, many former members gave lukewarm support to the RAPM platform. In spite of programmes to increase the number of workers and peasants in the artistic ranks, by 1930 few professional musicians could legitimately claim a proletarian background. Works by contemporary Western composers disappeared from concerts and 'bourgeois' professors in the conservatories were subjected to harrassment and even dismissal. Young composers who had been enthusiastic leaders of the experimental avant garde fell silent; most did not survive the repression with their creative individuality intact. Mosolov, for instance, continued to compose until his death in 1970 but shifted to conventional forms and a resolutely tonal style; his 'constructivist' music was replaced by patriotic songs and choral music and his pioneering instincts were channelled into exploring the folk music of distant regions. His fate was by no means unique.

Shostakovich's versatility and broad interests stood him in good stead. The proletarian critics had found admirable qualities in his Second and Third ('First of May') symphonies (1929), as well as in his music for theatre and film. Although they savaged his first opera, *The Nose* (1927–8; based on Gogol's grotesque short story and staged by Leningrad's Maly Theatre in 1930), for its atonal, experimental idiom, its avoidance of a Soviet topic and its lack of social and ideological relevance to the working masses, they attributed this failure to a youthful aberration and pointed with evident relief to subsequent works by Shostakovich that appeared to reject the Western-influenced, avant-garde aesthetic. The cheerful 'Song of the Counterplan' from his music to the film *Counterplan* (1932) became an instant hit.

In April 1932, by a resolution of the Central Committee of the Communist Party, the proletarian organizations in literature, art and music were abolished. Indicating that the framework of these organizations had become too narrow, inhibiting the serious scope of artistic creation, and warning of the dangers of sectarianism, the party promised to replace the dissolved organizations with separate creative unions, each containing a communist faction, uniting all artists 'who uphold the platform of the Soviet régime and who strive to participate in socialist construction.'[8] Most musicians were encouraged by the resolution; they were relieved to see RAPM's tyrannical stranglehold on cultural life broken and optimistic about the prospect of a broader-based and more constructive forum for composers. They could not foresee that the new Union of Soviet Composers (in 1957 its name was changed to Composers' Union of the USSR) would quickly become the tool for the absolute dictatorship of aesthetic policy by the state.

As all this turmoil was taking place in the country's cultural life, Prokofiev was contemplating the radical step of returning permanently to the USSR, prompted by dissatisfaction with his career in the West and increasing nostalgia for his homeland. Throughout the 1920s he had maintained contact with Soviet musical circles and followed the reception of his works there. In 1927 he made a concert tour to the USSR and was gratified by the warm reception given him and his music. The success of a second trip, in 1929, was more qualified: the composer who was regarded with curiosity in the West as a representative of 'Soviet' culture, notably in such works as the ballet *Le pas d'acier* (1925–6), for instance, was politically suspect at home for his long tenure abroad and lack of commitment to the revolutionary cause. Prokofiev was aware of the changing cultural climate in the USSR but, never politically astute, he disregarded the ominous signs. Moreover, his own aesthetic interests were coming closer to those influencing the development of Soviet music. Reacting against the formidable complexity and dissonance of earlier works like his Second Symphony (1924–5), Prokofiev was becoming interested in writing more accessible music: 'We want a simpler and more melodic style for music, a simpler, less complicated emotional state, and dissonance again relegated to its proper place as one element of music'.[9]

Prokofiev's repatriation was not sudden. From November 1932 he made frequent extended visits to Moscow, collaborating on the Soviet film *Lieutenant Kijé* (1933), from which the popular suite was drawn, and writing other works to Soviet commissions, including the symphonic fairy tale *Peter and the Wolf* (1936) and the ballet *Romeo and Juliet* (1935–6), which would support his claim to a simpler, more melodic and more accessible idiom. His move was complete only in spring 1936 when he and his family settled permanently in Moscow.

The dissolution of the proletarian arts organizations, though it contributed at least temporarily to a more settled and constructive creative atmosphere, did not mark a return to the extremist experiments and lively debate of the NEP period. Firmly in control, Stalin repudiated the aggressive tactics of the First Five-Year Plan and steered the country towards more conservative moral values, discipline and respectability. Uniting in creative unions under the supervision of party ideologues, artists groped towards an understanding of the role art should play in socialist construction, and the catch-phrase Socialist Realism, succinctly characterized as 'a creative method based on the truthful, historically concrete representation of reality in its revolutionary development', became a convenient concept. In music, the most abstract of the arts, few disputed the lofty idealism of Socialist Realism but its practical implications were too vague to be perceived as a proscriptive dogma.

The almost simultaneous premières – in Leningrad on 22 January 1934 and in Moscow two days later (under the title *Katerina Izmaylova*) – of Shostakovich's second opera, *Lady Macbeth of the Mtsensk District* (1930–32), proved a milestone: the Soviet musical world had waited long and patiently for an opera which, in its quality and originality, could forge the continuation of the distinguished traditions of pre-revolutionary Russian opera. Having experienced numerous attempts and failures, critics were quick to hail Shostakovich's new opera as a major event; the critical success was matched by a sensational popular one. In the two years following its première, *Lady Macbeth* played nearly 200 times in Leningrad and Moscow, was staged in other Soviet cities and was exported to Europe and the USA.

Shostakovich did not choose a Soviet subject for his opera. By skilfully adapting Nikolay Leskov's 1865 tale of the same name about uncontrollable lust and murder in provincial Russia, Shostakovich aimed to create a 'tragedy-satire', a searing indictment of the conditions of women in pre-revolutionary society. To do so he used musical means to portray his heroine – a merchant's wife who deceives her husband and commits murders to protect her relationship with her lover – as a figure deserving of sympathy, while all those around her are exposed as morally corrupt. The action is fast-paced and packed with violence of all types, including verbal abuse, torture and rape in addition to murder and suicide. The music satirizing stock authority figures – the police, the priest, the feeble husband and tyrannical father-in-law, as well as the opportunistic lover – makes extensive use of the parodied idioms of operetta, circus and dance hall styles; only the heroine, Katerina, has music of memorable lyrical and emotional warmth. It is a volatile combination of musical and dramatic effect that was almost guaranteed to give the opera 'mass' appeal.

On 17 January 1936 Stalin, accompanied by high government officials, attended a performance of a new Soviet opera, *The Quiet Don* by Ivan Dzerzhinsky (1909–78). Loosely based on Mikhail Sholokhov's novel of the same name, it tells of the suffering and heroism of Don cossacks during the civil war. The music, extensively revised and greatly improved with Shostakovich's help, is tuneful and unpretentious and the dramatic development of its patriotic theme is conventional. During the final interval in the performance, Dzerzhinsky and others connected with the production were summoned for a conversation with Stalin. In comments which were well publicized, Stalin stressed the need for Soviet operatic classics and gave his seal of approval to the aesthetic and ideological character of the production.

On 26 January 1936 Stalin and his colleagues went to the opera again, this time to see Shostakovich's popular *Lady Macbeth of the Mtsensk District*. They left before the end. Two days later the government newspaper *Pravda* published an unsigned editorial, 'Muddle instead of Music',[10] an uncompromising condemnation of Shostakovich's opera which sent shock-waves through the artistic community: 'From the very first moment, listeners are stunned by the deliberately dissonant and confused stream of sounds . . . singing is replaced by screaming . . . the music quacks, hoots, pants and gasps in order to express the love scenes as naturally as possible'. The editorial censured the opera's pretensions as social satire and its utter rejection of the principles of classical opera and of 'a simple, accessible musical language'. Equating its flaws with petty-bourgeois, leftist distortions in the theatre, literature and other fields (the opera's popularity in the West was adduced as proof), the editorial contrasted this with the realistic, wholesome character of the 'true' art demanded by the people, and threatened that 'this game . . . may end very badly'.

The warning did not go unheeded. The timing and context of the editorial – its proximity, for instance, to the positive evaluation of Dzerzhinsky's *The Quiet Don* – left no doubt that this was a strategically planned official assault whose ramifications extended well beyond the fate of this particular opera and the boundaries of music. This was confirmed by additional editorials, including the devastating critique of Shostakovich's ballet *The Limpid Stream* published on 6 February 1936[11] and the creative 'debates' staged and directed in the next few months in most of the artistic unions. It represented the explicit subjugation of the individual creative freedom of Soviet artists to the repressive control of the Communist Party and state. Adherence to the aesthetic doctrine of Socialist Realism became not merely a desirable goal but the obligatory condition for all Soviet art. The consequences of succumbing to its opposite, formalism, frequently characterized as an anti-Soviet sickness, could be catastrophic if left undiagnosed and uncured. Musicians, artists, poets and critics were among the uncounted victims of Stalin's purges, which rose to a peak in 1937. And the perceived failure of Soviet composers to respond adequately to the challenge would be at the root of a subsequent cultural crackdown in 1948.

The ideal of creating serious and significant musical works expressing the uniquely Soviet experience in images 'full of beauty and strength' – monumental symphonies, for instance, which would rival the emotional and psychological impact of Beethoven's Ninth – was easier to conceive in theory than in practice, particularly when epigonism was viewed with as much disgust as the decadent, formalist techniques associated with Western modernism. To be safe, many composers steered away from abstract music and composed works with patriotic texts or extra-musical programmes. At its most mediocre, the conservative lexicon of musical Socialist Realism came to resemble a collection of stock expressive formulae: fanfares of trumpets and drums, major tonalities, simply harmonized folk melodies, uplifting choral finales, and so on. A peculiar hybrid of abstract and illustrative genres, the 'song symphony', which attempted to integrate simple settings for voice or chorus of ideologically persuasive texts into the traditional framework of developmental symphonic structure, attracted interest but failed to become established.

Indigenous folk music, both Russian and that of other ethnic regions, was a great source of inspiration. From 1936 festivals of national culture, each devoted to the art of one constituent republic, were held regularly. One of the most successful composers to come forward in the 1930s was Aram Khachaturian (1903–78), born in Soviet Georgia of Armenian extraction and educated at the Moscow Conservatory; he achieved striking results in synthesizing the 'exotic' oriental melodic and rhythmic qualities of Armenian folk music with traditional Western forms. His most effective works include a Violin Concerto (1940) and the ballet *Gayaneh* (1941–2), from which the popular 'Sabre Dance' is drawn. Like most of his contemporaries, he also underscored his political loyalty by composing such works as *Poem about Stalin* (1937–8) for orchestra and mixed chorus, the orchestral *Ode in Memory of Vladimir Ilich Lenin* (1948) and many patriotic songs.

In opera it was Dzerzhinsky's *The Quiet Don* rather than Shostakovich's work which was destined to be the model for future development. The 'song opera', an unsophisticated compilation of folksongs, tuneful choruses and dances, avoiding dramatic ambiguities and based on subjects extolling revolutionary bravery and sacrifice or glorifying the heroic exploits of Russia's past, became a formulaic prototype for opera in the Stalinist period. Tikhon Khrennikov's *Into the Storm* (1936–9, revised 1952) was the most notable achievement in the genre; it also marked the first appearance of Lenin, albeit in a spoken cameo, in Soviet opera. Dzerzhinsky, who composed eight more operas, was never able to repeat the success of his first.

Prokofiev was opportunely abroad on tour when the *Pravda* editorial appeared and was spared the worst excesses of recrimination and recantation that followed it. As he had once been a composer of demonstrably 'formalist' tendencies, his works were subject to particular scrutiny. In a lucky inspiration apparently unrelated to the turbulence around him, in spring 1936 Prokofiev composed one of his most popular works for children, *Peter and the Wolf*, a unique synthesis of musical fable and pedagogical guide to instruments; it quickly found a permanent niche in the world's concert repertory. When Prokofiev set out to respond consciously to political pressures, however, as in the *Cantata for the Twentieth Anniversary of the October Revolution* (1936–7), a vivid illustrative tract for enormous forces set to texts by Marx, Lenin and Stalin, the attempt backfired and he was accused of vulgarity. The work remained unperformed until 1966. Similarly, Prokofiev chose the apparently unexceptionable tale of a young Ukrainian civil war partisan as the subject of his first Soviet opera, *Semyon Kotko* (1939), but his pervasive use of melodic recitative to draw strong musical characterizations and motivate the dramatic development, and the corresponding avoidance of the self-contained arias, folksongs and dances characteristic of the officially approved 'song opera', were significant factors in the opera's failure.

Like many Soviet composers, Prokofiev found productive employment writing film music. Unlike most, he was privileged to work with one of the most original directors of the era, Sergey Eisenstein. In 1938 Eisenstein invited Prokofiev to collaborate in the making of his first completed sound film, *Alexander Nevsky*, a historical epic depicting the thirteenth-century victory of Russian forces over the invading Teutonic knights, a subject that had contemporary relevance both from the standpoint of the gathering Nazi menace and from Stalin's well-known penchant for historical parallels with heroic leaders. Eisenstein and Prokofiev worked together closely; music and visual imagery were tightly integrated in the dramatic concept. At its première in December 1938 the film was an immediate hit. From its score Prokofiev arranged an equally successful concert piece, a model example of the patriotic cantata. It is an ironic commentary on the fate of politically induced art that both film and cantata became ideologically inconvenient after the Soviet-German non-aggression pact had been signed in August 1939. Once Hitler invaded Russia in 1941, however, the works returned to prominence.

After the humiliating disgrace of the *Lady Macbeth* episode, Shostakovich, who at 29 already attracted widespread international interest, prudently dropped out of the limelight. He continued composing, completing his Mahlerian Fourth Symphony (1936), though after it had gone into rehearsal he withdrew it, citing dissatisfaction with the score. The anxiously awaited public test of his aesthetic and political rehabilitation came with the première of his Fifth Symphony in November 1937. It proved a resounding success and a critical step towards the restoration of Shostakovich's professional status. One misconception about that work lingers: that Shostakovich sub-titled it 'an artist's reply to just criticism'. Shostakovich made no

Still from Eisenstein's film 'Alexander Nevsky' (1938), for which Prokofiev wrote the music.

hasty claims for his symphony and gave it no sub-title; waiting until after it had been extensively discussed and vetted by the Communist Party, music professionals and the public, and it was clear that there was an overwhelming consensus that the Fifth Symphony marked a triumphal affirmation of Socialist Realism, Shostakovich passively reviewed the press: 'Among the reviews ... one gave me special pleasure, where it said that the Fifth Symphony is the creative answer of a Soviet artist to just criticism'.[12]

What Shostakovich's Fifth Symphony accomplished was all the more remarkable because it was not a programmatic work or a patriotic cantata but an abstract composition in traditional symphonic form. It differed in significant ways from much of his earlier music. Principally it revealed an emotional depth and scope and a natural feel for the powerful dramatic potential of symphonic form which had not so far been prominent in his music. While the Fifth Symphony was clearly an extension of the continuum from Beethoven to Tchaikovsky and Mahler, the originality of Shostakovich's language and his remarkable command of the orchestra made a strong case for the viability of the genre in the twentieth century. If the finale was weakened slightly by unconvincing heroic posturing, that did not detract from the emotional conviction of the work as a whole. Its continued popularity in the world's symphonic repertory also helped to demonstrate that, in the hands of a supremely talented composer, Socialist Realism was not inherently inimical to the creation of enduring works of art.

When the Nazi troops invaded Russia in June 1941, Soviet musicians needed no prodding to react vigorously to the attack. The policing of creative activity against the suspicion of formalism was trivial in the face of the overwhelming and patently evil threat of national annihilation. In a country so ill prepared physically for the challenge of war – the situation was not improved by the fact that Stalin had purged the top ranks of the military in 1937 – the concept of art as a powerful weapon of propaganda was already well developed. The wholesale production of war songs, a genre with clearcut emotional and psychological functions, was a natural outlet for many composers. Some of the songs, Alexander Alexandrov's solemn *Sacred War* (1941), for instance, rose above the merely functional to become ubiquitous symbols of patriotic commitment and staunch resolve; others, such as Moisey Blanter's *Katiusha* (1938), which predated the war but gained popular significance during it, entered the sphere of timeless folklore.

Musical activity was by no means restricted to popular genres. While many musicians took up arms and went to the front (their losses were a proportionate share of the staggering total) others endeavoured to sustain the much-needed semblance of civilized existence in the cities or in evacuation. The leading musical institutions of Moscow and Leningrad – the Bolshoy and Kirov ballets, the conservatories, the philharmonic orchestras – were evacuated to remote cities in Siberia, the Caucasus and the Far East, safely out of the path of advancing Nazi troops. So too were the most prominent Soviet composers including Myaskovsky, Khachaturian, Prokofiev and Shostakovich. At a time when basic issues of physical survival were necessarily uppermost in everyone's mind, the priority given to the preservation of cultural values was not questioned.

Shostakovich's immediate response to the war produced an unprecedented worldwide resonance. Remaining in his native Leningrad as the Germans moved to capture the city quickly, and frustrated by his rejection from the armed services, Shostakovich dug ditches, served in the cons started a major composition dedicated to his native city. (Striking portraits of him in his fireman's helmet and on the roof of the conservatory made the international press, but he never actually put out a fire.) His progress on the new work was avidly chronicled in the press. Having repeatedly rejected offers of evacuation, Shostakovich was ordered out of Leningrad at the end of September, by which time three movements of his symphony were complete; the final one was finished in Kuibyshev at the end of December.

The eagerly awaited première of Shostakovich's Seventh Symphony, the 'Leningrad', was on 5 March 1942 in Kuibyshev in a performance, given by the evacuated orchestra of the Bolshoy Theatre under Samuil

Samosud, that was nationally broadcast. In spite of the length and relative sophistication of the score, Shostakovich's impassioned musical answer to the war – especially vivid in the sinister march of invasion in the first movement – generated a level of emotional identification that made it an instant symbol of heroic resistance, a symbolism that far outstripped its musical merits. The Seventh Symphony was performed and broadcast frequently throughout the war. The day after its première, the microfilmed score was sent by a circuitous route through Iran, Iraq, Egypt, North Africa and South America to London, where on 29 June 1942 it was conducted by Henry Wood. The fierce competition to present the American première was decided in favour of Toscanini, who presented it in a national broadcast on 19 July. The performance of most poignant significance was the première on 9 August 1942 in blockaded Leningrad under conditions of incredible hardship – musicians had to be requisitioned from the frontlines to fill out the meagre, starving ranks of the Leningrad Radio Orchestra, conducted by Karl Eliasberg.

No other work composed during the war came close to equalling the immense impact of Shostakovich's 'Leningrad' Symphony; but other composers were not idle. Soviet composers generated an enormous volume of symphonies, operas, cantatas, chamber music and other works. Conceived in the passion of turbulent times, most did not survive the urgency of the moment.

Prokofiev, however, experienced a burst of creativity which produced memorable scores including his Seventh (1939–42) and Eighth (1939–44) Piano Sonatas and the delightfully escapist ballet score *Cinderella* (1940–44). Already intrigued by Tolstoy's novel as an opera subject, he found the historical parallels with the Napoleonic invasion irresistible and composed his epic *War and Peace* (1941–3, revised 1946–52). The opera experienced a troubled history; although sections were performed in concert in 1944, a revised performing version was not staged until 1957, four years after the composer's death. On the other hand, Prokofiev's Fifth Symphony (1944), his first 'Soviet' symphony, was enthusiastically received at its première in January 1945 and represented a milestone as critical for the composer and Soviet music as had Shostakovich's Fifth Symphony seven years earlier.

As the tide of the war changed and the devastating military reversals of the early years turned to stunning victories, the country's mood became more confident and optimistic. The imminence of victory infected composers too. Shostakovich's powerful Eighth Symphony (1943), an intimate and grim document, had been found disappointing after the inspirational immediacy of the Seventh, and when Shostakovich began work on his Ninth in late 1944 in anticipation of the end of the war, he was planning to write a work for chorus and vocal

Poster advertising a performance (under the direction of Karl Eliasberg) of Shostakovich's Seventh Symphony ('Leningrad') in the Large Hall of the Philharmonia, Leningrad.

soloists as well as orchestra. He urged his countrymen to 'honour with reverence the memory of the brave soldiers who have died and glorify the heroes of our army for all eternity'.[13] Expectations naturally ran high that the composer who had provided the emotional touchstone for the beginning of the war with his 'Leningrad' Symphony would rise to comparable heights to commemorate the war's victorious end.

Thus the festive, frivolous spirit of Shostakovich's brief Ninth Symphony came as an understandable surprise to listeners when it had its première in November 1945. There was no chorus or vocal soloists, no extra-musical programme, no pretensions to the epic grandeur of Beethoven or Mahler, no tribute to heroic sacrifices or glorious victory. Nor did other Soviet composers provide the monumental work which could satisfy expectations. When, before any feeling of postwar euphoria had had time to dissipate, the state-instigated ideological attacks on the arts resumed in 1946 with renewed vigour and harshness, Soviet composers' perceived wartime failures would come to loom far larger than their legitimate triumphs.

Modern Times

NOTES

[1] In 1918 the Soviet government changed observance from the Julian (old style) to the Gregorian (new style) calendar; the anniversary of the 'October' Revolution is now celebrated on 7 November.

[2] The words of Lenin recalled from the reminiscences of Klara Zetkin; cited in *Lenin o kul'ture i iskusstve*, ed. N. I. Kriutikova (Moscow, 1956), 519–20.

[3] During World War I the imperial capital, St Petersburg, was renamed Petrograd. In 1918 the seat of the government was moved to Moscow, and in 1924, after the death of Lenin, Petrograd was renamed Leningrad.

[4] Avraamov was the pseudonym used by Arseny Krasnokutsky (1886–1944).

[5] B. V. Asaf'yev, 'Krizis lichnogo tvorchestva' and 'Kompozitory, pospeshite!'; quoted in *Akademik B. V. Asaf'yev: izbrannïye trudï* [Selected Works], v (Moscow, 1957), 20–24.

[6] V. Lenin, *New Economic Policy* (New York, 1937); quoted in B. Schwarz, *Music and Musical Life in Soviet Russia* (Bloomington, 2/1983 [enlarged edition, covering 1917–81]), 42.

[7] R. Lee, 'Dimitri Szostakovitch: Young Russian Composer Tells of Linking Politics With Creative Work', *New York Times* (20 Dec 1931), section 8, p.8.

[8] 'O perestroike literaturno-khudozhestvennykh organizatsii', *Rabochii i teatr*, no.13 (May 1932), 1.

[9] O. Downes, 'Prokofieff Speaks', *New York Times* (2 Feb 1930), section 8, p.8.

[10] 'Sumbur vmesto muzyki: ob opere "Ledi Makbet Mtsenkogo Uezda" D. Shostakovicha', *Pravda* (28 Jan 1936), 3; the word 'sumbur' in the title is rendered variously in translations as 'chaos', 'mess' or 'muddle'.

[11] 'Baletnaia fal'sh'', *Pravda* (6 Feb 1936), 3.

[12] D. Shostakovich, 'Moi tvorcheskiy otvet', *Vechernyaya Moskva* (25 Jan 1938), 3; the author and source of the quoted review have never been identified.

[13] D. Shostakovich, 'V preddverii velikoi pobedy', *Komsomol'skai pravda* (13 Feb 1945); quoted in S. Khentova, *Shostakovich: zhizn' i tvorchestvo*, ii (Leningrad, 1986), 207.

BIBLIOGRAPHICAL NOTE

History and political culture

The advent of 'glasnost' in Gorbachev's Soviet Union sparked the release of important documents and information about the interwar period. Among recent studies incorporating some of the new perspectives are R. Pipes, *The Russian Revolution 1894–1919* (New York, 1990); R. C. Tucker, *Stalin in Power: the Revolution from Above, 1928–1941* (New York, 1990) and R. Conquest, *Stalin: Breaker of Nations* (New York, 1991). All are provided with up-to-date bibliographies. M. Heller and A. M. Nekrich provide a readable survey of the Soviet period in *Utopia in Power: the History of the Soviet Union from 1917 to the Present* (New York, 1986) and M. Lewin offers stimulating insights in the collection *The Making of the Soviet System: Essays in the Social History of Interwar Russia* (New York, 1985). Articles on a wide range of topics – including creative arts, education and the media – can be found in *Bolshevik Culture: Experiment and Order in the Russian Revolution* ed. A. Gleason, P. Kenez and R. Stites (Bloomington, 1985). Somewhat more subjective – though nonetheless valuable – reflections are represented by R. Medvedev, *Let History Judge: the Origins and Consequences of Stalinism* (rev. New York, 1989) and A. Sinyavsky, *Soviet Civilization: a Cultural History*, trans. J. Turnbull and N. Formozov (New York, 1990).

Literature, the theatre and visual arts

A comprehensive survey of the literary developments, official and dissident, can be found in E. J. Brown, *Russian Literature Since the Revolution* (rev. Cambridge, MA, 1982). M. Hayward's collection of essays on literary topics and individual authors, *Writers in Russia: 1917–1978* (San Diego, 1983), is noteworthy for its intelligence and erudition. An account of the political subjugation of writers by the literary bureaucracy can be found in J. and C. Garrard, *Inside the Soviet Writers' Union* (New York, 1990).

K. Rudnitsky's *Russian & Soviet Theatre: Tradition & the Avant-Garde*, trans. R. Permar (London, 1988) is an impressive survey, lavishly illustrated. The classic study of the artistic development of Soviet film is by J. Leyda, *Kino: a History of the Russian and Soviet Film* (Princeton, 3/1983). In *Soviet Choreographers in the 1920s*, trans. L. Visson, edited by S. Banes (Durham, 1990), E. Souritz presents a fine study of a less-researched creative sphere. D. Elliott, in *New Worlds: Russian Art and Society 1900–1937* (New York, 1986), places developments in the visual arts into cultural and political perspective; his work is complemented by the exhibition catalogue *Soviet Art 1920s–1930s*, ed. V. Leniashin (New York, 1988), a lavish visual panorama of the period. *Pioneers of Soviet Architecture: the Search for New Solutions in the 1920s and 1930s* (New York, 1987) by S. O. Khan-Magomedov is the indispensable study of the subject.

Music

The rehabilitation of historical memory and resulting reassessments of our understanding of the Soviet period have been slow to penetrate musical scholarship. Although written substantially more than 20 years ago, B. Schwarz's *Music and Musical Life in Soviet Russia, 1917–1981* (rev. Bloomington, 1983) remains the standard English-language source on the history of Soviet music. *Soviet Composers and the Development of Soviet Music* (New York, 1970) by S. Dale Krebs, though in many respects outdated, is still useful for its survey of the styles of more obscure Soviet composers. D. Gojowy offers a provocative glimpse into some of the lesser-known experimentalists in *Neue sowjetische Musik der 20er Jahre* (Laaber, 1980). A more tangible introduction to music of the suppressed Soviet avant-garde has begun to surface on disc, including *The Music of Alexander Mosolov* (Olympia OCD 176), Anton Batagov, *Rails, Russian avant-garde piano music of the early 20th century* (MCA Classics AED 10354), Natalia Gerassimova, *Russian Songs of the 1920s* (Saison Russe/CDM LDC 288025) and *Music of the Soviet Composers of the 20s* (Melodiya SUCD 10–00077). S. Frederick Starr provides a fascinating introduction to another little-known subject in *Red & Hot: the Fate of Jazz in the Soviet Union 1917–1980* (New York, 1983).

H. Robinson's *Sergei Prokofiev: a Biography* (New York, 1987) is the most current English-language study of that composer. Shostakovich, the most prominent Soviet composer, has been served poorly by the recent literature. *Testimony: the Memoirs of Dmitri Shostakovich*, ed. S. Volkov, trans. A. W. Bouis (New York, 1979), is sensational in its revelations, but its authenticity has never been established. I. MacDonald's *The New Shostakovich* (London, 1990) is fatally flawed by its singleminded determination to prove the composer a lifelong political dissident, motivated in his music almost exclusively by subversive political concerns. Less pretentious and musically more competent approaches can be found in N. Kay, *Shostakovich* (London, 1971) and K. Meyer, *Dmitri Schostakowitsch* (Leipzig, 1980). J. Jelagin's *Taming of the Arts*, trans. N. Wreden (New York, 1951), remains among the most enlightening memoirs of musical and theatrical life in the USSR in the 1930s.

Chapter VIII

The Nordic Countries, 1918–45

KNUD KETTING

'The symphony is dead – long live music!'. With these words the Danish composer Knudåge Riisager (1897–1974) sought to summarize the state of Nordic music in 1940, immediately before the German occupation of Denmark and Norway disrupted communications and cultural relations:

> I sense an enlightened and courageous release from the conventional scheme which, until now, has been regarded as the only 'correct' one: the all too obvious requirement for a 'symphonic' structure which is really just somnambulism and indecision or perhaps lack of the will to view a problem afresh. But first we must realize that the symphony is dead. Then music will live.[1]

Riisager, who supplemented his Danish training by studying in Paris with Albert Roussel, among others, was an influential contributor to musical debate, a leader not only on a Danish but on a Nordic level. In a newspaper interview for his 40th birthday he stated, 'The Nordic peoples have an important future in store as a major factor in musical evolution – but unfortunately we have been moving ahead far too slowly in the area of music'.

Riisager's views on the symphony are not reflected in the simple statistics: during the first decade of this century 18 symphonies were composed in Denmark, between 1910 and 1919, 27; in the 1920s, 28; in the 1930s 21; and the 1940s as many as 48; the number declined, however, in the very period Riisager was attempting to sum up. In Sweden the corresponding figures are ten, 20, 31, 30 and 53 symphonies: the genre experienced merely a period of stagnation and no decline in the 1930s. Musical developments in Denmark and Sweden have had many similarities, not least stylistically. But there were differences in the scope for symphonic writing in the two countries, and this was connected with the role of the new national radio systems.

Fundamental dislocations took place in the musical life of the Nordic countries in the interwar years and conservative observers can only have thought that the world, in a musical sense, was rapidly coming to an end. Because of its location and low population, Iceland is a special case which will be dealt with separately. The first Danish radio transmissions were in 1922, and in 1926 the government granted itself a monopoly on broadcasting. As early as 1924 the radio employed a permanent piano trio and from 1927 symphonic concerts were broadcast. In 1931 the Danish Radio Symphony Orchestra numbered 60 members. The Finnish broadcasting system was established in 1926; the following year it engaged a nine-member light orchestra which expanded to 24 musicians by the early 1930s and 33 by the outbreak of the war.

Norwegian radio, which became state-owned only in 1934, started with four musicians in 1924 and by 1927 had a 21-strong orchestra. Norway differs from the other Nordic countries in that from 1934 until after World War II it maintained ties with the independent musical world and allowed the Oslo Philharmonic Orchestra to broadcast too.

The Swedes, after initial nervousness at the prospect, arrived at a compromise. In December 1923, just over a year before the state broadcasting system came into being, both the Stockholm Concert Society (now the Stockholm Philharmonic) and the Stockholm Opera agreed to broadcast their performances on an experimental basis; the soloists at the Opera were prohibited from performing exclusively for the radio. In 1925 broadcasting got underway and music transmissions continued: in spring 1925 no fewer than 16 opera performances and 17 concerts were broadcast. At the same time, the radio engaged its own ensemble, comprising ten musicians who were paid out of the income derived from the 40,000 licences already granted. By the 1928–9 season the orchestra consisted of 27 players and was committed to giving 12 concerts a month. The coming of sound film resulted in large-scale redundancy among musicians. In 1932 the musicians' union demanded the engagement of 50 musicians, but achieved only better pay and fewer sessions a month for the existing orchestra. The situation remained precarious for all orchestral musicians other than those of the Stockholm Opera, because they had only seven months' employment a year: for the summer they were left to manage as best they could.

It was therefore a far-sighted and socially responsible step of Swedish Radio when in 1937 it entered into a contract with the Stockholm Concert Society and the Gothenburg Symphony Orchestra: the radio was to pay five monthly wage packets a year, in return for which the orchestras would perform regularly on the radio and make gramophone recordings by agreement between the musicians' union, the radio and the Swedish composers' association. This arrangement benefited the development of both national music and the popular (occasionally serious) repertory that had dominated the Nordic radio stations' 'live' music broadcasting. For instance, the composer Lars-Erik Larsson (1908–86) was engaged that year, not just as assistant conductor but also to compose lyrical-musical suites specifically for radio. One, *Förklädd Gud* ('God in Disguise', 1940) for speaker, soprano, baritone, choir and orchestra, has entered the concert repertory and enjoys considerable popularity in Scandinavia to this day.

In the mid-1930s the Danish composer Jørgen Bentzon (1897–1951) wrote his orchestral *Photomontage* for radio; this piece reflects his research into which sonorities were best suited to gramophones and loudspeakers. The chamber orchestra suite *Ten Pieces* (1930) by Aarre Merikanto (1893–1958) (see p.170) is an example of Finnish music which was prompted by the medium of radio and which proved to be of lasting quality. However, the broadcasting systems of the late 1920s and 30s were not at the forefront of avant-gardism as they were later. Danish State Radio is perhaps an exception because of its proximity to the European continent.

SCANDINAVIA AND THE EUROPEAN AVANT GARDE

In this period it is difficult to find examples of Nordic music that are innovatory rather than drawing on existing styles. The central European attitude to northern Europe is typified in a report from 1918 on Scandinavian music by the French composer and writer Eugène d'Harcourt (1859–1918),[2] part of a series commissioned by the French government. D'Harcourt, who had studied in both Paris and Berlin and who had a broader outlook than most of his French colleagues, devoted 300 pages to Italy, 600 to the German-speaking countries and a total of 150 pages to Denmark, Sweden and Norway. The report was based on visits to Copenhagen and Stockholm (Oslo clearly was deemed not worth the bother) and was concerned principally with the structure of higher musical education and the merits of the local opera companies' productions of French, German and Italian classics. Only in Copenhagen did d'Harcourt attend performances of indigenous music: he was present at the première of Nielsen's *En Sagadrøm*, which he characterized as 'interesting music, pleasing to the ear – moving, but of no originality. It sounds like well-written, modernized Italian music'.

During the interwar period, as previously, Nordic composers supplemented their training with further studies abroad: favoured destinations included Berlin, Leipzig, Vienna and Paris. They also learnt from visits to the Nordic capitals by representatives of the central European avant garde.

During World War I Denmark had suddenly become attractive to leading European soloists. Danish currency was strong in comparison to the belligerents', so for a period it was highly lucrative to perform in this peaceable and solvent little country. But the repertory most visitors brought consisted of Classical or Romantic music. However, not everyone in Danish music was blinkered. As early as 1915 the conductor Frederik Schnedler-Petersen performed Schoenberg's First Chamber Symphony at a summer concert in Tivoli and the following winter season. In the 1920s Copenhagen concert organizers were still in a position to be adventurous, if only occasionally. Schoenberg's *Pierrot lunaire* was first heard in the Danish capital in 1921, whereas music-lovers in Stockholm had to wait until 1937; and in 1923 Schoenberg himself conducted in Copenhagen – his Chamber Symphony, among other works (he never performed in the other Nordic Capitals). Stravinsky did not visit Stockholm until 1935, whereas he appeared at the Tivoli Concert Hall in Copenhagen in July 1924, as the soloist in his newly composed Piano Concerto. He returned in 1925 and on four other occasions before the war to present his own works.

In the 1930s it was Danish radio that took the lead. The Radio Symphony Orchestra season of 1933–4, for instance, featured both Hindemith and Stravinsky as soloists in their own works. But if all the broadcast music programmes are considered together, few would

Stravinsky in front of the main entrance to the Tivoli Concert Hall, Copenhagen, where he performed his Piano Concerto on 18 July 1924.

disagree with Carl Nielsen (1865–1931) who, in the year of his death, wrote on the relative merits of live and reproduced music, in the foreword to a compilation of newspaper articles: 'Never before has the art of music been in such a bad way as it is now. What once was a spiritual rallying-point for all has become a whore who offers herself from open doors and windows, from basement stairways and stinking jazz joints'.[3] Any bitterness in his tone is no doubt because Nielsen was a conductor as well as a composer. For many years, since it was founded in 1836 and particularly under Niels Gade's direction from 1850, the Concert Society had been a cornerstone of the Copenhagen concert season. In 1915 Nielsen took over as its permanent conductor: its membership numbered 900. During Nielsen's first few seasons the membership increased to 1200, enough to provide a capacity audience for one concert (at the height of the Gade era all concerts had to be given twice). Nielsen was at the peak of his creative powers and was able to present a number of important new works. But even so, membership was falling inexorably; when, in 1931, it had declined to just 700 it was disbanded. Nielsen himself had left in 1927. But, ironically, he had been on the platform in 1927 when Danish radio organized its first public orchestral concert. (The Swedish radio orchestra, incidentally, did not start giving public concerts until 1948.)

THE DANISH SHADOW

If anyone was in a position to influence music in Denmark, it was of course Nielsen. All further stylistic developments were to take place in his long shadow, which is what induced Riisager in 1940 to declare the symphonic form dead:

> Any new Danish work is judged in terms of the dichotomy *out of* or *around* Carl Nielsen . . . the grand form which Nielsen introduced to Danish music is set up as a yardstick against which all new works are measured. The very idea of 'carrying on' Nielsen's work is a bad one, because it already has been done better than it possibly could be in the future – by Nielsen himself.[4]

Nielsen gradually achieved international stature. It is significant that the first Nordic symphonic work performed at an ISCM festival was his Fifth; Wilhelm Furtwängler conducted it in Frankfurt in 1927.

The work that had first brought him international attention was his Third Symphony, *Sinfonia espansiva* (1910–11). Only a couple of months after the first performance in Copenhagen (1912) he was conducting it in Amsterdam with the Concertgebouw Orchestra, and here too it was given a cordial reception. The following year saw Nielsen conducting performances in Stuttgart, Stockholm and Helsinki. After the enforced isolation of World War I he was to play it with the Berlin Philharmonic Orchestra, among others. It was published in 1913 by the Leipzig firm of C. F. Kahnt, and Nielsen received considerably more for the rights than his Danish publishers had ever afforded him.

Nielsen's music was characterized by a warm, optimistic outlook. Even the Fourth Symphony, which with its vehement, last-movement timpani duel can leave an impression of having been born of a Europe in flames, ends with an apotheosis that is a celebration of life. Or, in Nielsen's own words, 'With the use of the title "The Inextinguishable" the composer has sought with a single word to suggest what only the music itself has the power to express in full: the basic will to live'.[5]

The Treaty of Versailles brought about the reunion of Denmark with a part of southern Jutland annexed by Germany. When in 1920 it was decided to celebrate the occasion with a gala concert, Nielsen was the natural choice of composer, striking a straightforward, nationalist tone in his music. But thereafter it began to appear as if there were two sides to him: the Fifth Symphony (1921–2) attracted mostly positive comments from the critics even if it did leave audiences somewhat baffled by its stark contrasts between idyll and aggression; the Sixth (and last) Symphony (1924–5) gave rise to confusion with both audience and critics – and, possibly Nielsen himself, who was attempting to break new ground without quite knowing in which direction to go. 'All matters of art are in chaos at the moment, and it appears that it is up to the individual – as in a shipwreck – to save himself as best he can. Even the best musicians of today seem to be stricken with fear of being regarded as "old-fashioned".'[6] The 'other' Nielsen wrote numerous songs that quickly became a vital part of popular culture in Denmark: at his funeral service in 1931 it was claimed that 'the Danish people stands guard of honour at Carl Nielsen's bier'. In combination, these two sides to Nielsen made him the pre-eminent figure in Danish music who was (and perhaps still is) not completely understood but who was unmatched. His only rival was the late Romantic eccentric Rued Langgaard (1893–1952). When, after Nielsen's death, Langgaard was asked for a statement by a Copenhagen newspaper, he said 'Carl Nielsen's importance consists in his having dismantled what Gade had built up. I do not feel I can say any more'. This should not be regarded as an expression of personal animosity: Langgaard wanted to distance himself from Nielsen's stylistic standpoint as well as from what he saw as the Danish music establishment's blind acceptance of everything bearing Nielsen's name. Langgaard had been a prodigy and achieved recognition in his youth, particularly in Germany. But it became increasingly difficult for his work to get a hearing, and not until the 1970s was his large but variable output explored in Denmark. Among his most remarkable works is the *Music of the Spheres* (1916–18) for mezzo-soprano, choir and orchestra, which is one of the earliest pieces to use tone-clusters in the string writing.

Developments in Danish music in the 1930s were a continuation of Nielsen's anti-Romantic ideals. Besides Nielsen, other composers such as Bartók, Hindemith, Stravinsky and Les Six were sources of inspiration although earlier interest in Schoenberg had all but evaporated. Leading composers were Poul Schierbeck (1888–1949), Knudåge Riisager (1897–1951), Ebbe Hamerik (1898–1951), Flemming Weis (1898–1981), Herman D. Koppel (*b* 1908), Finn Høffding (*b* 1899) and Jørgen Bentzon (1897–1951). The last two were particularly interested in teaching, inspired not least by Fritz Jöde in Germany. Høffding characteristically threw himself into the debate that followed Nielsen's 1931 diatribe, pointing out that concert life was not the same as musical life in general and that it was important to remember musical activities in the home and at school.

Of those mentioned above, Schierbeck is little performed today, but his music is still heard occasionally in Denmark. Internationally, however, he and Riisager are best known, Schierbeck for his incidental music to Carl Dreyer's renowned films *The Day of Wrath* (1943) and *The Word* (1948), Riisager for his sparkling, virtuoso reworking of Czerny's *Etudes* for Harald Lander's ballet of the same name. Koppel too composed much film music but he gained real popularity with the simple, jazzy songs he wrote in collaboration with Bernhard Christensen (*b* 1906) for *The Tune that Got Lost*, a play by the socialist playwright and painter Kjell Abell; this satire on the Danish *petite bourgeoisie* became a huge success at a small Copenhagen theatre in 1935.

As Denmark was the nearest Nordic country to Nazi Germany, it might be expected that Danish music in the 1930s would be coloured by events there. But this hardly appears to be the case. The Danish establishment elected – ostensibly at least – to ignore what was going on south of the border. And if there was any nervousness in ruling circles, it was directed at communism as much as at nazism. The German occupation in 1940 changed this attitude overnight. No-one stopped playing Beethoven, but suddenly Danish music found a wider audience than ever before. Evenings of Danish song with the singer Aksel Schiøtz became a national rallying-point and Danes in their thousands attended community singing rallies at which Nielsen's popular songs (with nationalistic words of course) played an important part.

THE FINNISH SHADOW

Not until 1917 was Finland able to declare its independence: from the early Middle Ages until 1809 it had been under first Swedish and later

Russian supremacy. It is therefore not surprising that nationalism was strong, and indeed the interwar years in Finland (as in Norway) were marked by a much more tenacious national-Romantic tradition than in either Denmark or Sweden. It was against this background that the centenary of the first publication of the great epic *Kalevala*, based on medieval ballads, was celebrated in 1935. This publication marked the creation of a standard Finnish language and *Kalevala* has since constituted a central element of Finnish nationalism. All Finland's leading composers contributed to the celebration.

Even though Jean Sibelius (1865–1951) had largely ceased composing by this time, he was still regarded as Finland's foremost composer. He had first made his name with the *Kullervo* symphony (1892) for soloists, choir and orchestra; its text was based on an episode from *Kalevala* and it was also inspired by the ancient tunes that were still to some extent part of the Finnish song tradition. Many of Sibelius's later works, including his last substantial opus, the tone poem *Tapiola* (1926), also have ties to the *Kalevala*. But Sibelius had become a nationalist focus much earlier, particularly with his tone poem *Finlandia* (1899). He became an international figure at an early stage too. His First Symphony (1899) was a success in Paris in 1900 when the Helsinki Philharmonic Orchestra embarked on its first European tour, and Sibelius was soon in demand as a conductor of his own works.

His 50th birthday, in December 1915, was celebrated almost as a national holiday and he had his Fifth Symphony ready for it. He was, however, to regret its conventional, four-movement form and he revised it a couple of times before it found its final shape in 1919. He wrote two further symphonies, in 1923 and in 1924–5; the taut, single-movement Seventh, in particular, counts as a peerless masterpiece of Nordic music of this era. There is a great distance from the Russian-sounding national Romanticism of the First Symphony to the Seventh's subtle seamless progression. But Sibelius, who rejected the early *Kullervo* symphony, remained faithful in his symphonies to his vision of music as an absolute, independent art form:

> My symphonies are meant for and drawn up for musical expression without any literary basis. I am no literary musician – for me, music only starts when the word stops. A painting can reflect a scene, word a drama – a symphony must be music from beginning to end. Naturally it has happened that a soul image has caught hold of me against my will while I have been writing a musical phrase. But the seed and insemination of my symphonies has always been pure music.[7]

Throughout most of his long retirement (over 30 years) Sibelius retained his position as the symphonic master against whom all Finnish composers, whether they liked it or not, were to be measured.

Not until after World War II did reaction set in, and it became imperative to write without a hint of inspiration from the master. Sibelius himself did what he could to encourage and help his younger colleagues, among them Selim Palmgren (1878–1951), Toivo Kuula (1883–1918) and Leevi Madetoja (1887–1947). Palmgren's Second Piano Concerto, *The River* (1913), was performed all over Europe in the 1920s and 30s; it is an excellent demonstration of how his music was rooted in Chopin and Schumann (this was also the case with Langgaard, but his music is tinged with madness unlike Palmgren's).

Uuno Klami (1900–61) was one of very few Finns who turned to France for inspiration. He was given advice by Ravel and Florent Schmitt and immersed himself in jazz, as is evident from his first piano concerto *Une nuit à Montmartre* (1925). Klami's *Kalevala Suite* is the most important score based on the Finnish national epic since Sibelius's compositions. The work took Klami ten years to write and was performed in several versions before it found its final shape in 1943.

In no other Nordic country did late Romanticism hold out for so long as it did in Finland. One Finn who broke the mould was Aarre Merikanto (1893–1958), who composed fairly radical works during the 1920s. His Concerto for violin, clarinet, horn and string sextet (1925), which won an international competition arranged by the publishers Schott, is the only Finnish work of the time to reflect Schoenberg's influence. Apart from Sibelius, Yrjö Kilpinen (1892–1959) was the one Finnish composer to make any international mark. The bulk of his *output* consists of songs – over 700 – a number of which have German texts. From the 1930s Kilpinen's songs were performed by internationally known singers, notably the German baritone Gerhard Hüsch whom Kilpinen accompanied on several extensive recital tours.

THE NORWEGIAN SHADOW

Just as musical developments in Denmark and Finland in the interwar years were in the shadows of Nielsen and Sibelius, so too did Norway have a composer who inevitably left his mark. Edvard Grieg, however, was 20 years older than his two colleagues and had died in 1907, so he never had to take a stance on the stylistic upheavals that marked European music in the years round World War I. Stylistically, then, Grieg's influence in Norway was much less important than, say, Nielsen's in Denmark. But his brand of musical nationalism, with its integration of folk music into art music, never lost its allure.

Norwegian musical nationalism reached a climax at the 1930 celebrations of the 900th anniversary of the death of St Olav. The Norwegian government arranged a major cantata competition, and it was won by Ludvig Irgens Jensen (1894–1969) with his massive oratorio *Heimferd*.

In the period round 1920 there were impressionistic tendencies in Norwegian music; expressionistic features were in evidence, too, in the works of Fartein Valen (1887–1952) and Arvid Kleven (1899–1929), among others. But the leading Norwegian impressionist, Alf Hurum (1882–1972), left Norway in 1924 and spent most of his life in Hawaii, and Kleven, the other principal modernist, died very young. So in the 1930s the field was wide open and nationalism began to gain ground, with Valen and Pauline Hall (1890–1969) the only notable exceptions. This tendency was reinforced further by the German occupation of Norway in World War II.

The most characteristic exponent of musical nationalism was Geirr Tveitt (1908–81) who in 1937 even published a textbook on harmonics based on old Norwegian folk-music scales. But the most important figure – who, like Tveitt, sympathised openly with the Germans during the occupation and who was consequently frozen out by the musical establishment after the war – was David Monrad Johansen (1888–1974); in 1924 he proclaimed his movement's ideals:

> The slogan 'Art is international' has been repeated so many times that it has become tedious. Yes, of course art is international insofar as good art can be adapted to and comprehended in any place where there is culture. But it is a far cry from this to deny that art is peculiar to the locality from which it originates and that it takes its form, colour and character to a large extent from its surroundings. Art is determined by its environment to such a great extent precisely because it is the most sensitive expression of national character.[8]

In 1925 Monrad Johansen was awarded the Norwegian government's artist's stipend. The citation stated that he, more than any other composer, in an era of cultural dissolution and denationalization, had shown that he could 'remain standing on national ground in artistic temperament and musical sentiment'. It was to take another ten years before his contemporary Fartein Valen received similar recognition.

Valen had begun by composing in a late-Romantic style, but he soon found that the musical environment in Norway was too restricting and he spent the period 1911–16 in Berlin. There he started work on his orchestral song *Ave Maria*, which the Norwegian critics denounced as 'blasphemy' and called 'awkward, embarrassing and pathetic' after its first performance in Oslo in 1923. But he was the only composer in Norway at that time writing in a dissonant, contrapuntal style. His grounding included studies of Bach, and he later became involved in 12-note composition, even though he realized it was only partly compatible with the free polyphony that was his ideal. He remained an uncompromising, inquiring spirit and received some recognition only late in life. Today he is recognized as the most important Norwegian composer of his time.

Modern Times

Whereas Helsinki and Copenhagen dominated the centralized musical lives of their respective countries, Norway had another centre apart from its capital Oslo: the west-coast town of Bergen, home of Grieg and of Ole Bull. When the Oslo Philharmonic was established in 1919, the Bergen Harmonien orchestra was granted similar status as a permanent, professional ensemble. During the 1930s, a number of west-coast composers made an impact on Norwegian music (though not formally as a group). Of these, Sparre Olsen (1903–84) is most closely associated with the Grieg tradition. Sverre Jordan (1889–1972) was for many years conductor at Bergen's largest theatre, and theatre music constitutes (with songs) the major part of his output. The most individual force, however, was Harald Sæverud (1897–1992) who, just after the war, dared to challenge Grieg himself with a new score for Ibsen's *Peer Gynt*.

SWEDEN, WITHOUT A SHADOW

Wilhelm Stenhammar (1871–1927) is recognized as the foremost Swedish late Romantic composer. Indeed he is the only one who, internationally, bears comparison with Nielsen and Sibelius (to both of whom he was close musically and personally). Some of his works, the Serenade for orchestra (1913) in particular, require a level of orchestral virtuosity that has only subsequently become the norm in Scandinavia. His last major work was the Cantata *The Song* (1922), to poems by his friend and fellow composer Ture Rangström (1884–1947), who was also a gifted poet and writer on music.

To his contemporaries Stenhammar was well known as a pianist and conductor. He gained early recognition with his First Piano Concerto (1893), which was played under the baton of Richard Strauss, Karl Muck and Hans Richter, among others. Stenhammar was conductor of the Göteburg Symphony Orchestra from 1907 to 1922, and he rapidly transformed this west-coast town into an important musical centre, not just of Sweden but of the entire Nordic region. However, his influence on later Swedish composers was to be at best indirect. One of these was Hilding Rosenberg (1892–1985), for whom Stenhammar was one of many sources of inspiration but who, during and after World War II, became an advocate of a younger generation of composers to a much greater extent than Stenhammar ever did.

Rosenberg's stylistic point of departure had been one of open inquiry but during the 1930s his music was increasingly characterized by gravity and stringency. He became a champion of openness towards the outside world and of workmanship:

> To be able to do something you have to learn it, again and again. So many people forget this. They speak scornfully of the composer as

craftsman. They strive for personality and spontaneity, but they forget that personality all too often comes across as superficiality when it is not underpinned by ability.[9]

Rosenberg composed important works in all common genres. Most substantial are perhaps his string quartets; thanks to Stenhammer's six quartets, the string quartet had a status in Sweden parallel to that held in Denmark by wind chamber music, particularly the wind quintet (the Danish standard being set by Nielsen's masterpiece, op.43).

A parallel to Rosenberg, though more distinctively Romantic, was Gösta Nystroem (1890–1966): 'I am a devotee of absolute music but, strangely enough, at the same time an irredeemable romantic'.[10] Nystroem, who was also a painter, found inspiration primarily in French music and became renowned both as a symphonist and song composer.

The only Swedish composer known in the rest of Europe during the 1920s was Kurt Atterberg (1887–1974). With his Sixth Symphony he won not just the Nordic round but the final of an international competition arranged by the Columbia gramophone company for the Schubert anniversary in 1928. This work, nicknamed *The Dollar Symphony* was recorded by Toscanini. During the 1920s and 30s other world-class conductors, including Furtwängler and Nikisch, performed works by Atterberg, who concentrated on orchestral music. For Les Ballets Suédois he wrote the music for the ballet pantomime *The Wise Virgins* in 1920; it was given no fewer than 375 times, both in Paris where the company was based and on tour. Both its plot and music were based on Swedish folklore, whose primitive quality the somewhat blasé Parisian audience found thrilling – just as they had warmed to Dyagilev's and Stravinsky's treatment of the Russian folk tradition.

In contrast to Rosenberg and his contemporaries, there appeared a new generation of Swedish composers who had received their basic musical training in Stockholm. They included Lars-Erik Larsson, Gunnar de Frumerie (1908–87), Dag Wirén (1905–86) and Erland von Koch (*b* 1910). They cannot be classed as a group, but neo-Baroque and folk music are two of the elements that unite them in a quest for simplicity with lyrical overtones. Lyricism is even more pronounced in the music of Hugo Alfvén (1872–1960) and Wilhelm Peterson-Berger (1867–1942), at least in their smaller-scale works like piano pieces and songs. But these two composers were from an age dominated by Wagner and, in the north at least, Grieg. And though Peterson-Berger won considerable popularity, particularly with his piano pieces, and throughout a long career was a sharply worded newspaper critic and scourge of his younger colleagues, he could not make time stand still. The development of music in Sweden thus continued without the dominance of one pre-eminent figure.

Modern Times

ICELAND AND ISOLATION

To understand the history of Icelandic music and musical life it is necessary to know a little about this North Atlantic island, which lies much closer to Greenland than to Norway. Its population, which in the early 1990s numbered 250,000, consists largely of the descendants of Norwegian migrants who between 874 and 930 left Norway for political and economic reasons. At the end of the nineteenth century, Iceland itself saw an exodus to the USA, and by 1890 the population dropped to about 70,000. Over the next 40 years it grew by 50 per cent, and it was this population growth, in conjunction with urbanization, that provided the basis for the development of a more or less professional musical life. The language spoken in Iceland today is so relatively unchanged from that of the original settlers that modern Icelanders have little difficulty in understanding texts that are more than a thousand years old. The country came under Norwegian control in 1264 and was thus inherited by the Danes in 1380. After World War I it was granted independence 'in union' with Denmark; during World War II the last ties between the two countries were cut and Iceland was declared an independent republic.

For centuries, then, the country had been governed from a distant capital and possessed none of the resources that had formed the basis for the flourishing musical life of the rest of Europe: no noblemen to commission cantatas, no royal court to maintain an opera company. Not until 1876 was the first public concert held in Iceland's capital, Reykjavík; the performers were a wind quintet led by Helgi Helgason (1848–1922), the first Icelander who may properly be termed a composer.

In summer 1867 the 27-year-old Norwegian composer Johan Svendsen visited Iceland after completing his studies in Leipzig. He met Sveinbjörn Sveinbjörnsson (1847–1927), a 20-year-old student of theology who was also musically gifted, and persuaded him to study first in Copenhagen and later in Leipzig. Sveinbjörnsson composed the national anthem of Iceland, heard for the first time in 1874, the millenary of the Norwegian landing and the year the country was granted its first independent constitution by the Danish king.

In 1930 the Icelanders celebrated the millenary of the founding of the Alting, the Icelandic parliament. The celebrations represented the culmination of the nationalism that had swept the country during the 1920s after its partial liberation from Denmark in 1918. The main event was a vast outdoor concert on the site of the old parliament; the composer Páll Isólfsson (1893–1974) conducted the *Alting Cantata* with which he had won equal first prize in a competition arranged by the parliament (Nielsen was a member of the jury). The choir consisted solely of Icelanders, but part of the orchestra had to be imported from

Copenhagen: in Reykjavík there was only a recently established chamber orchestra led by the cathedral organist. Iceland did not get its own symphony orchestra until 1950. That saw the opening of a national theatre, with a commitment to musical drama. The decision to proceed with plans for a theatre had been taken in 1922, with a view to a grand opening in the festival year of 1930, but the economic depression had interrupted this project.

Isólfsson, who had trained in Leipzig, became one of the driving forces behind the expanding Icelandic musical life. He was the first principal of the school of music opened in 1930 and became head of music at Icelandic radio, which started broadcasting the same year. As a composer, Isólfsson made his mark with works that took Brahms and Reger as their points of departure rather than with his folk-inspired pieces. In this respect he represents a stark contrast to Jón Leifs (1899–1968). He too had trained in Leipzig but remained faithful to his Icelandic ideals. He spent a considerable part of his creative period in Germany (where his works were banned under the Nazis) and did not settle permanently in Iceland until 1944. He was also a conductor, and it was under his baton that Icelanders first heard a live symphony orchestra: the Hamburg Philharmonic, which in 1926 gave 13 concerts in Reykjavík. As well as German music, the orchestra played Leifs's *Icelandic Overture*, written the same year.

His list of works demonstrates Leifs's nationalism: the word 'Icelandic' appears in the titles of many of them. His music has not achieved the recognition it deserves, in Iceland or abroad. In Iceland the problem is partly one of resources, for some of his works, among them the great *Saga Symphony* (1942–3), require massive forces. Only latterly has there been evidence in the other Nordic countries of increasing interest in this unusual composer, who considered the south to be degenerate. For him, Icelandic folk music was an inexhaustible source of energy, 'which can be replenished and from which new music can be won'.[11]

NORDIC COOPERATION

The first time the Nordic countries agreed to get together for a collective musical event was in Copenhagen in 1888; Gade arranged it. In 1897 Stockholm organized the second Nordic Music Festival; the third was held in 1919, again in Copenhagen. This was the last occasion at which the pioneers of Nordic music from the 1890s were to appear together, among them some of its foremost representatives of any age: Nielsen, Sibelius and Stenhammar.

Perhaps by virtue of those nationalistic trends which were only expressions of opposition to central European influence, the ground-work was laid for a more systematic collaboration. Nordic Music

Tivoli Music Festival, 10 June 1919; left to right: Frederik Schnedler-Petersen, Robert Kajanus, Jean Sibelius, Georg Høeberg, Erkki Melartin, Wilhelm Stenhammar, Carl Nielsen and Johan Halvorsen.

Festivals were held in Helsinki in 1921, Stockholm in 1927, Helsinki in 1932, Oslo in 1934 and Copenhagen in 1938. In addition, the conductor Tor Mann organized Nordic music fairs in Göteborg in the period 1937–40. World War II rendered all formal cooperation between the Nordic countries impossible. But immediately after the war a new start was made, this time with Iceland as a full partner. Since then the Nordic Music Days, organized every other year by the five Nordic composers' associations, have become one of the most important elements in a collaboration aimed at securing a clear, individual profile for Nordic music.

NOTES

[1] *DMT* [*Danish Music Journal*] (1940), 23.

[2] E. d'Harcourt, *La musique actuelle dans les états scandinaves* (Paris, 1910).

[3] K. Larsen, *Levende Musik – Mekanisk Musik* (Copenhagen, 1931), foreword.

[4] *DMT* (1940), 22.

[5] From Nielsen's note in the printed programme of the first performance on 1 February 1916 in Copenhagen.

[6] From letter of 24 August 1923 to the Danish composer Oluf Ring (1884–1946), who had asked Nielsen for advice on where to go for further studies; quoted from *Carl Nielsens Breve*, ed. I. E. Møller and T. Meyer (Copenhagen, 1954), 227.

[7] Interview from 1934; quoted from *Koncertfører*, ed. H. Lenz and L. Bramsen (Copenhagen, 1962), 192–3.

[8] Lecture in the Kristiania Music Teachers' Association; quoted from N. Grinde, *Contemporary Norwegian Music 1920–1980* (Oslo, 1981), 13.

[9] Interview in *Stockholms-Tidningen* (Dec. 1927); quoted from B. Wallner, *Vår tids musik i Norden* (Stockholm, 1968), 118.

[10] Ibid., 123.
[11] Quoted from G. Bergendal, *New Music in Iceland* (Reykjavík, 1991), 41.

BIBLIOGRAPHICAL NOTE

Unfortunately the main source for the understanding of Nordic music of the interwar period, B. Wallner, *Vår tids musik i Norden* (Stockholm, 1968), exists in Swedish only. Starting its thorough survey in the early 1920s, it covers four of the five Nordic countries extensively, with Iceland as the regrettable exception. Wallner's book contains a multitude of references to useful source material. Wallner also wrote the chapter on modern Scandinavian music in *European Music in the Twentieth Century*, ed. H. Hartog (Harmondsworth, 1961), which – because of its brevity – offers a correct but pale reflection of his expertise. J. H. Yoell, *The Nordic Sound* (Boston, 1974), is based mostly on what has been available to its author by way of recordings – the result is an informative rather than erudite volume. Books covering music from all the Nordic countries have been very sparse: one more is worth mentioning, even though all its articles are in Danish, Norwegian or Swedish: *Modern nordisk musik*, ed. I. Bengtsson (Stockholm, 1957). Out of its fourteen essays, written by the composers themselves, three or four cover works from the interwar period; all are accompanied by worklists.

Denmark

For literature on Nielsen, readers are referred to *Man and Music*, vol. vii and M. Miller, *Carl Nielsen: a Guide to Research* (New York and London, 1987), with English annotations on all available Nielsen research, regardless of the original language. A brief view of the interwar period can be found in J. Jacoby's essay in *Music in Denmark*, ed. K. Ketting (Copenhagen, 1987). More details can be had from V. Kappel, *Danish Composers* (Copenhagen, 3/1967), but a really extensive documentation (though regrettably without source references) can be had only in Danish: N. Schiørring, *Musikkens Historie i Danmark*, iii (Copenhagen, 1978). Only very recently has Rued Langgaard's immense production been properly catalogued, in B. V. Nielsen, *Rued Langgaards Kompositioner* (Odense, 1991). This annotated catalogue with a comprehensive introduction in English is the result of years of diligent work. It will probably be too detailed for most readers, but will still serve as a good starting-point until the publication of the same author's Langgaard biography. Worklists are included in two interesting biographies, both in Danish: O. Mathisen, *Bogen om Poul Schierbeck* (Copenhagen, 1988), and F. Behrendt, *Fra et hjem med klaver: Herman D. Koppels liv og erindringer* (Copenhagen, 1988). Riisager's oeuvre is catalogued in S. Berg and S. Bruhns, *Knudåge Riisagers kompositioner* (Copenhagen, 1967), and Høffding's in S. Bruhns and D. Fog, *Finn Høffdings kompositioner* (Copenhagen, 1969).

Finland

For literature on Sibelius, readers are referred to *Man and Music*, vol. vii. A short, informative survey of the interwar period is by P. Helistö, whose article can be found in two different English translations in *Music of Finland* (pubd. Finnish Music Information Centre, Helsinki, 1983) and *Music in Finland* (pubd. Finnish-American Institute, Helsinki, 1980). The late Walter Legge was not late in discovering the unique songwriter Kilpinen, as can be seen from his *The Songs of Yrjö Kilpinen* (London, 1936). More recent views on Kilpinen can be had from articles on the occasion of his centenary in *Finnish Music Quarterly*, iii (1992), and *Nordic Sounds*, i (1992). For an overview of Kuula, it might be useful to combine T. Elmgreen-Heinonen and E. Roiha, *Toivo*

Modern Times

Kuula: a Finnish Composer of Genius (Helsinki, 1952), with J. Kokkonen, *Toivo Kuula: sävellyshuettelo* [worklist] (Helsinki, 1953). Two catalogues, *Uuno Klami: Works*, ed. T. M. Lehtonen (Helsinki, 1986), and *Leevi Madetoja: Works*, ed. K. Tuukanen and P. Hako (Helsinki, 1982), have introductions in English and discographies.

Norway

Compared to their Nordic colleagues, Norwegian musicologists seem to have been more willing to produce good introductory volumes in international languages on the music history of their country. The most informative is N. Grinde, *Contemporary Norwegian Music 1920–1980* (Oslo, 1981), including a useful bibliography. K. Lange, *Norwegian Music: a Survey* (Oslo, 2/1982), provides a much shorter survey, whereas German-speaking readers will find interesting details in H. Herresthal, *Norwegische Musik von den Anfängen bis zur Gegenwart* (Oslo, 2/1987). Grinde calls Valen 'the most prominent Norwegian composer after 1900', and rightly so, but the only English book on Valen, B. Kortsen, *Fartein Valen: Life and Music* (Oslo, 1965), clearly leaves the field open to more detailed research. A handsomely illustrated introductory article on Saeverud by R. Storaas, written in connection with the memorial service held in Bergen on 6 April 1992, has found its way into *25 Years of Contemporary Norwegian Music* ed. K. Skyllstad and K. Habbestad (Oslo, 1992).

Sweden

Bo Wallner's unique combination of impeccable scholarship and mastery of the Swedish language, mentioned above, can also be found in his *Wilhelm Stenhammar och hans tid* (Stockholm, 3/1991), where the Swedish composer and his oeuvre is put into the perspective of Swedish musical and cultural life. Another important source, also in Swedish, is L. Hedwall, *Den svenska symfonin* (Stockholm, 1983), with fine descriptions of Swedish symphonies, even those forgotten since their first appearance, and a detailed bibliography. Apart from the odd article in music magazines, almost no literature in English is available, Swedish musicologists having used their own language extensively. Nystroem has been treated once by a non-Swedish musicologist: P. K. L. Christensen, *The Orchestral Works of Gösta Nystroem: a Critical Study* (London, 1965) [includes list of works]. Rosenberg's music is catalogued in P. H. Lyne, *Hilding Rosenberg: Catalogue of Works* (Stockholm, 1970). A list of Atterberg's works can be found in *Musikrevy*, xxii (1967), 327, and Alfvén's compositions are catalogued in J. O. Rudén: *Hugo Alfvén: Musical Works* (Stockholm, 1972), which includes an introduction in English and a thematic index. A list of Peterson-Berger's works and writings accompanied the articles in *Wilhelm Peterson-Berger: festskrift den 27. februar 1937* for his 70th anniversary.

Iceland

Hjálmar H. Ragnarsson in his useful *Short History of Icelandic Music to the Beginning of the Twentieth Century* (Reykjavík, 1980) stated that 'scholarly research in the sphere of Icelandic music has lagged far behind the otherwise rapid growth of musical activities'. We are still waiting for Icelandic musicology to produce large-scale studies and are therefore indebted to the Swedish writer G. Bergendal for having compiled a small leaflet in Swedish, *Musiken på Island: om isolering och internationalism* (Stockholm, 1981) and later continued his research, published in various articles and finally, through the initiative of the Iceland Music Information Centre, as a handsome volume in English, *New Music in Iceland* (Reykjavík, 1991). As the title suggests, Bergendal is mainly interested in contemporary music. The first third of the book, however, contains much useful information on the development of Icelandic musical life until the end of World

War II. Catalogues of works by living Icelandic composers are easily available from the Iceland Music Information Centre. Precise information on Icelandic music from the interwar period is much more difficult to obtain, with the notable exception of Jón Leifs, whose compositions are listed in *Jón Leifs: Tónverkaskrá*, edited by his widow, Thorbjörg Leifs (Reykjavík, 1976).

Nordic cooperation

On its centenary, the Royal Swedish Academy of Music, in collaboration with the Society of Swedish Composers, produced a very useful survey, *Nordic Music Days: 100 Years*, ed. S. Hanson (Stockholm, 1988). Its articles are not all relevant to this chapter, but the detailed analysis of the first 50 years of cooperation, by H. Schwab (in German), and the thorough documentation of every concert (during the whole period) should prove interesting.

Chapter IX

England, 1918–45

STEPHEN BANFIELD

THE MUSICAL SPECTRUM

Musical life in Britain between the wars underwent enormous change. The period saw the coming of age of the gramophone and the cinema, and the birth and rapid development of radio broadcasting. (Television also made an early start – Albert Coates's *Pickwick* was the first opera to be televised in Britain, in 1936 – but did not develop broadly until after World War II.) The introduction of electrical recording in 1926 set the gramophone companies on a firm footing, and Elgar's late use of the medium for making recorded performances of his own works and his relation with Fred Gaisberg of the Gramophone Company (HMV) provide a fragment of British musical history to compensate in some measure for the general creative decline of his last decade.[1] The cinema provided employment for thousands of instrumental musicians and organists during its silent heyday in the 1920s and laid them off overnight when the 'talkies' arrived; where they all went to is a mystery.[2] Broadcasting supported sectors of the musical profession almost from the start: the BBC took over the ailing Promenade Concerts in 1927 and enabled Henry Wood not only to provide a summer music festival for Londoners but to make it available to all those elsewhere who possessed wireless sets. The BBC Symphony Orchestra was formed in 1930 with Adrian Boult as conductor (Boult, and later Bliss, were to become music directors of the BBC). Music appreciation was also sponsored and developed by the BBC, and Walford Davies's talks were widely followed (indeed, his open aversion to opera probably exacerbated opera's dismal profile in Britain during this period).

Lord Reith and the BBC's control of the airwaves was also the control of popular music in Britain. The old parlour ballad died out after World War I: broadcasting may have contributed to the fall in sales of sheet music that signalled its demise. Operetta and British musical comedy also declined after the war. Gilbert and Sullivan had bequeathed much to the Edwardian period, when England led the field with Edward German, Lionel Monckton, Howard Talbot and Leslie Stuart; but Jerome Kern, learning his craft among them, took it back to the USA and in the 1920s Britain began to import rather than export musicals. The revival of two period masters, Noel Gay (*Me and My Girl*, 1937/1984) and Vivian Ellis (*Mr Cinders*, 1928/88), has modified this picture, and the return of Noël Coward's *Bitter Sweet* (1929/1988) may alter it further; it must also be borne in mind that amateur productions of such repertory have never died out. Ivor Novello also deserves to be remembered if not professionally revived (his first major musical was *Glamorous Night*, 1935). But in general only native revue could stand up to American musical theatre, flourishing at the hands of C. B. Cochran and André Charlot and providing Coward with a major vehicle for his extraordinary art as performer and songwriter (his first success was *London Calling*, 1924). Nor could such light operas as Thomas Dunhill's *Tantivy Towers* (1931) and Walter Leigh's *Jolly Roger* (1933), admirable if hybrid, turn back the tide of the more commercial forms of musical entertainment geared to the gramophone and the cinema, whose star singers were dubbed 'crooners' and condemned by the BBC, which thus encouraged a polarization of taste (one can only speculate as to how different the history of popular music might have been had it supported them instead).

English bands like those of Jack Hylton and Ray Noble took their cue from the American Paul Whiteman when they purveyed syncopated and Latin American dance styles under the vague term 'jazz'; and if there was an indigenous English popular style at this period to parallel the development of ballroom dancing, it has yet to be identified. As for musical films, staple fare in the 1930s, American imports soon outdistanced their British counterparts, and many British performers were lured to Hollywood. The Hollywood image was escapist. With the decline of music hall, popular music in Britain bore no close relation to the culture of those who imbibed it. A weekend approach to music was adequate for most people during the 'long weekend'[3] of the interwar period. 'The time for social and political commitment to intertwine with mass entertainment had not yet arrived . . . No dance or jazz bands accompanied the Jarrow marchers.'[4] A figurehead on the regional/working-class axis such as the singer Gracie Fields is probably the nearest exception; she was joined, on a broader, more nationalist base, by Vera Lynn during World War II.

The BBC supported light music, and certainly furthered that brand of it (chiefly orchestral) heard at its best in the works of Eric Coates, who in 1919 abandoned a career as principal viola in Henry Wood's Queen's Hall Orchestra to concentrate on composing. In a style owing much to German and Elgar, his march *Knightsbridge* demonstrates how a movement from an unpretentious orchestral suite could become tremendously popular through being taken up as a radio signature-tune (for the BBC programme *In Town Tonight*): the BBC, then as until very recently, had a monopoly over nationwide radio broadcasting.

Like Coates's music, Walton's *Crown Imperial* coronation march

Vera Lynn singing on the 'Girls of the Victory Broadcast' for the troops in 1945.

(1937) and his film scores demonstrate a 'crossover' phenomenon between popular and serious music in which the mediating agent was the more or less classically constituted orchestra. Orchestral life abounded in such crossovers, in the Proms and above all at resorts. The seaside and spa orchestras, of which the Hastings Municipal Orchestra survived until 1939 and the Harrogate one until 1930, played British music of every complexion. Sir Dan Godfrey, founder of the Bournemouth Symphony Orchestra (the only professional and symphonic resort orchestra surviving today), was one of its key champions.[5] So were Boult and Wood. Beecham, recovering from financial embarrassment in 1923, could afford to steer his own course. He organized the Delius Festival of 1929 that set the seal on Delius's reputation as the pre-eminent English pastoral stylist, formed the London Philharmonic Orchestra in 1932, and in a sequence of ventures remained opera's most prominent impresario and exponent in England.

But, though undoubtedly a greater force for good than ill, Beecham's idiosyncratic and autocratic achievements serve to underline the fact that, in spite of the growth of the BBC and the arrival of the first Labour governments in 1923 and 1929, the period was private-spirited and perpetuated Britain's already long reputation for inadequate state sponsorship of the arts;[6] the Arts Council came into existence only after World War II, as a transformation of the wartime Council for the Encouragement of Music and the Arts (1940). At the turn of the century Stanford had called in vain for state subsidies for opera, and British opera remained crippled throughout the interwar period, Covent Garden's occasional forays into native realms notwithstanding, as when it produced Goossens's *Judith* (1929) and *Don Juan de Mañara* (1937). Most serious composers enjoyed at least a small private income – Bax, Bliss, Moeran, Vaughan Williams, Ireland, Gibbs, Quilter and many others (including Bridge under the patronage of the American Elizabeth Sprague Coolidge) – and those who did not, like Howells and Holst, had to teach. In this period there is no obvious correlation between what composers wrote and what they were paid. Most composers attended the Royal College of Music or the Royal Academy of Music (Stanford, teaching composition at the RCM until his death in 1924, produced more famous pupils than anyone else); many also passed through Oxford and Cambridge, though at that time they were unable to study music there as undergraduates. Cathedrals trained choristers and apprentice organists; public schools taught music, though their record was not distinguished. Fewer studied abroad than had done in the late nineteenth century.

Such disparate factors as the rise of the BBC and of American influence on popular music, combined with the *laissez-faire* inadequacy of public funding for the arts, may have precluded any coherent socio-economic musical culture in Britain. Yet a study of the stylistic frames of reference of 'serious' composers – the assessment of their environment on internal rather than external evidence – produces, perhaps surprisingly, a strong sense of national identity.

STYLES AND INFLUENCES: POST-IMPRESSIONISM AND THE FRENCH ALLIANCE

On 29 September 1918, as a leaving present before Gustav Holst embarked for the Balkans as YMCA music educationalist with the troops, his wealthy friend and fellow composer Henry Balfour Gardiner paid for a private rehearsal and performance of his orchestral suite *The Planets*, given in the blacked-out Queen's Hall in London by the young Adrian Boult and the New Queen's Hall Orchestra. With a cosmopolitan assurance that seemed new in British music, it made a powerful impression. Almost a generation later, at the end of another devastating war, Benjamin Britten's first opera *Peter Grimes* was chosen to inaugurate the return on 7 June 1945 of London productions by Sadler's Wells Opera; it was immediately recognized as the herald of a new epoch. These two premières epitomized stylistic *loci* in the reassertion of British music following its lean period in the nineteenth century.

The initial *locus* is best viewed as post-impressionist. The very term is of English coinage; it was applied to Roger Fry's exhibitions in London in 1910 and 1912 of current or recent French art and it can usefully denote one of the constant factors in British music at the end of World War I: the substitution of a Franco-Russian model of influence for the received Austro-German one. The declaration of war with Germany in 1914 boosted this aesthetic realignment, but it had been developing for some while, helped by the visits to London of Dyagilev's Ballets Russes from 1911 and Beecham's opera seasons from 1910, which broadened the public's stylistic horizons. A new generation of music critics was on hand: Edwin Evans wrote on new English and French music, including a series of articles on the former in the *Musical Times* in 1918–20, and the Russian specialist Michel-Dimitri Calvocoressi, born in France, was obliged as a Greek subject to move to London in 1914 to serve in the war; both men were close to Dyagilev. Rosa Newmarch, somewhat older, spoke for Russian and occasionally French music, and the French writer Georges Jean-Aubry, who moved to London in 1915, edited *The Chesterian* from 1919. This was the house journal of J. & W. Chester, whose publishing business, established in London in 1915, linked its English composers with the French and Russian firms for which it acted as agent. Another firm, the Anglo-French Music Company, was active at the same time. And if Russian music had provided the most powerful nationalistic use of indigenous folk melody, the French, both in their painting and in their music, contributed other, ultimately more far-reaching, models.

Colour and texture were no longer perceived as surface applications in a composition but as essences, on a level with – and perhaps determining – form. The equivalent of painting *en plein air* was a discovery of the landscape and the development of ways of depicting or symbolizing it in music (and of purposes for so doing). Above all, the impressionist tradition introduced to the British what is best summarized as the pleasure principle; colour and landscape could contribute, but impressionism also implied the possibility of absorbing elements of popular music and the rediscovery of rhythm, be it of ballet or jazz. Metaphysics no longer held appeal: 'We are tired of music that can only be appreciated by having a knowledge of the philosophic association which envelops it. Must I bring in Nietzsche to save the face of Strauss?', exclaimed Arthur Bliss in a talk, 'What modern composition is aiming at', given to the Society of Women Musicians in London in 1921.[7]

Much of this can be identified in *The Planets*. Rimsky-Korsakov and Musorgsky, Dukas and Debussy, and perhaps Skryabin and the young Stravinsky, are strong stylistic influences. Within the loose concept of a suite, not a symphony, 'Mars' is built on a rhythmic formula, 'Jupiter' joyfully presents a kaleidoscope of balletic gestures, moving abruptly from a Spanish dance to an English procession with no attempt at connecting argument, and 'Saturn' and 'Neptune' equally strikingly suggest the destruction of rhythmic pace. As a study in orchestral technique and colour *The Planets* goes beyond anything previously achieved in Britain, instead begging comparison with Ravel's *Daphnis et Chloé* and Debussy's 'Sirènes' in its use of a wordless female chorus. However, for Holst, as for Stravinsky in his pre-war ballets, this work was a celebration of inclusiveness from which he later retreated into ever more disciplined and sometimes remote aesthetic realms.

Elgar had been the first British composer whose orchestral writing matched continental standards of technique and creativity. By the end of the war he was virtually a spent force, but he occasionally looked over the shoulders of the young and was present when the 1922 Three Choirs Festival at Gloucester brought together as commissioned composers two Francophiles of the new generation, Eugene Goossens (whose ancestry was Belgian) and Bliss. Goossens's work, a choral setting of Walter de la Mare entitled *Silence*, was not a major contribution, unlike Bliss's *A Colour Symphony*. Bliss enjoyed close friendships with visual artists, including Wyndham Lewis, Jacob Epstein and Edward Wadsworth, and his symphony was far from being a vestige of the indulgently sensuous synaesthesia that had enjoyed favour before the war, notwithstanding the presence on the festival programme of Skryabin's *Poème de l'extase*. Bliss's symphony was a study in contrast, using rhythms and textures that related to colour largely by stressing the abstract or the symbolic (Bliss was influenced by his reading on heraldry), though emotional associations were acknowledged too. The implied affinity with décor stood Bliss in good stead when he came to write his ballets. Goossens, meanwhile, as a brilliant young conductor, had helped to rebuild British orchestral life after the war: he founded the Goossens Orchestra to tackle modern virtuoso works and in June 1921 gave two concert performances in the Queen's Hall of Stravinsky's *The Rite of Spring* in a programme that included Ravel's *La valse* and two recent British works, Berners's *Fantaisie espagnole* and Ireland's *The Forgotten Rite*. The public, now in a mood for modernity, provided a large and enthusiastic audience, and Stravinsky, Dyagilev and Massine were present.

The leading orchestral composer among Goossens's contemporaries was Arnold Bax. Claiming never to have had a lesson in orchestration, never conducting his own works and approaching composition at least partly from the perspective of a dextrous pianist, he was nevertheless a superb orchestral craftsman. This is less surprising if we recognize him as a kinsman of Liszt, Musorgsky, Ravel, Debussy and Stravinsky, whose quality of imagination enabled them to conjure up the resources of orchestral colour in virtuoso piano terms and orchestrate the result. Bax's piano works, including four sonatas and many illustrative pieces, are important; but the seven symphonies, composed between the wars, are the peak of his achievement, highly individual stylistically while acknowledging a strong legacy from the Russian school and inviting passing comparisons with Debussy (in the epilogues to nos.3 and 7), Dukas (no.6), Bartók (no.3) and even Gershwin (no.7). The eruptive violence of nos.1 and 2 (1922 and 1926), about whose possible genesis in the trauma of World War I Bax himself was equivocal, and the attempts at extended, cathartic and peaceful epilogues in nos.3, 6 and 7 (no.7, with its sense in the finale's passacaglia of old-world pomp and grandeur passing for ever, was composed for the New York World's Fair in 1939 and dedicated to 'the people of America'), have led commentators to try and provide the cycle of symphonies with an overall critique such as might be appropriate to the multi-volume autobiographical novels of Proust or Powell; Bax's odyssey – if such it be – is so private, though, that few points of contact with society could be suggested, let alone sustained.

True, Bax identified closely with the nationalist struggle in Ireland and was deeply disturbed by the Easter rebellion of 1916 (he had known Padraig Pearse, who was subsequently executed). But the visionary impact on him of Irish and other landscapes – hauntingly encapsulated in his use of folklike (though always original) melodic cells and of orchestral symbols such as the harp in lullaby-like ostinatos, the eerie knocking of the tenor drum in the epilogue to no.6, and the recurring organ climax in no.2 – was surely the result of an overwhelmingly personal struggle, at the forefront of which was the mystery of sexual relations. His unsuccessful marriage, his stormy and protracted relationship with the pianist Harriet Cohen and his affair with Mary Gleave contributed to this and highlighted his inherent spiritual restlessness, which was what had led him to identify with Yeats's poetry and attach himself to Ireland in the first place (even to the extent, early in his career, of living there pseudonymously as a writer).

LANDSCAPE AND THE ENGLISH 'GENIUS LOCI'

The analogue of landscape (or, less pervasively, seascape) became a preoccupation, a legacy of French musical impressionism but one that took English music beyond it. It manifested itself not only in orchestral music but in other genres, especially piano music. John Ireland's piano pieces, if compared with, say, Debussy's, apply their technical vocabulary not to a deliberately vague or ambiguous impression or to a casual vignette but to a specific place or focus of action: *Sarnia* (Guernsey), *London Pieces*, 'The Towing Path', 'Amberley Wild

Brooks', 'The Scarlet Ceremonies' and so on. The same applies to Ireland's orchestral pieces, including *Mai-Dun* (named after the prehistoric Maiden Castle in Dorset). His identification with landscape, with the spirit of place, was intensely personal.

Refulgence of landscape as a concomitant to sexual passion was nothing new (take Debussy's *Prélude à l'après-midi d'un faune*, for example), but the darker side of pagan imagery, the visionary fear of Pan as a psychological symbol and the association of mythological or prehistoric rites with the subconscious, seems to have been a specifically English preoccupation. Ireland learnt it from the writings of Arthur Machen ('How can the critics even begin to understand my music, if they have never read Machen?', he once asked),[8] but he might have identified equally closely with E. M. Forster's pre-war short stories such as *The Story of a Panic* and, above all, *The Curate's Friend*. 'It is uncertain how the Faun came to be in Wiltshire', writes Forster in the latter, adding, 'There is nothing particularly classical about a faun . . . any country which has beech clumps and sloping grass and very clear streams may reasonably produce him'.[9] The mystery of the landscape Forster so pointedly specifies, the English chalk with its prehistoric earthworks, through which the curate in the story finds himself (homo)sexually, was equally germane to Ireland's self-expression. All three of his reflective orchestral tone poems (*Mai-Dun*, *The Forgotten Rite* and the *Legend* for piano and orchestra) relate to it, and he later lived in a Sussex windmill overlooking one of the most famous of those beech clumps on earthworks, Chanctonbury Ring. Such period Englishness tempts parody,[10] but the seriousness of its message has never been adequately fathomed.

Ireland was not the pioneer of the English *genius loci* in music: Vaughan Williams, a key figure in almost all respects during this period, had shown the way. For all Elgar's association with the Malvern Hills, he had rarely tried to convey landscape directly in his music (perhaps the closest he came to doing so was in the opening of the Introduction and Allegro for strings). Vaughan Williams, however, following his non-specific adoption of the romantic figure of the wanderer or vagabond in *Songs of Travel* (1904), spent a few months studying with Ravel in Paris, and not long after his return he wrote two extremely influential works whose musical language is far more specific: the song cycle *On Wenlock Edge* (1908–9) to poems by Housman and the Fantasia on a Theme by Thomas Tallis (1910). The Tallis Fantasia, first performed in Gloucester Cathedral, showed how modal restraint and an intense identification with the Tudor heritage could furnish powerful inspiration, but its use of spatial separation, taking further the string orchestra/quartet contrasts of Elgar's Introduction and Allegro, encourages the listener to hear not just the vast spaces of the cathedral responding but also the hills across the Severn Valley –

Cotswold, Bredon and Malvern. The song 'Bredon Hill' in *On Wenlock Edge* provides separate musical vocabularies for the three participants in the tragic drama: non-functional, super-triadic chords for the heat and haze of the summer landscape, parallel-4th sonorities for the church bells, and free, harmonically unconstrained folklike melody for the human protagonist. All three symbols, with many others, served Vaughan Williams throughout his later works.

Another of his impressionist symbols, the bass ostinato of oscillating steps in 'The Vagabond' from *Songs of Travel* or the oscillating stepwise chords of the end of *A Sea Symphony* (1903–9) and *On Wenlock Edge*, representing the questing tread of the wanderer or spiritual pilgrim, was developed from Elgar (from the end of Part I of *The Dream of Gerontius*). But it was Vaughan Williams's younger contemporary and colleague Herbert Howells who, in the important Piano Quartet of 1916, first put this symbol in context with musical material depicting a specifically English landscape. He and his friend Ivor Gurney had been bowled over as youngsters by the Tallis Fantasia (to the extent, apparently, of tramping the streets of Gloucester all night after its first performance).

Howells probably drew on the sensuous textures of French chamber music with piano as well as the atmospherics of Vaughan Williams when he came to fashion the opening of his Piano Quartet's first movement with its apparent depiction of a misty dawn. The second subject, according to Gurney, represents the Malvern Hills: in a letter to Marion Scott from Gloucester in 1918, Gurney wrote of 'a great sight of Malverns to cheer me sticking up across the miles of plain – enormous enough, and reminding all whom it might concern of [here he quotes the theme]'.[11] It recurs in different guises in all three movements, and in the development (rather, the crux) of the finale it is combined with a near-quotation of the marching motif from Vaughan Williams's 'The Vagabond', suggesting that the hills are the concomitant to the human pilgrimage. Piers Plowman, 'on a morning in May, among the Malvern Hills', is brought to mind, paralleling Vaughan Williams's lifelong identification with Bunyan that underlay his masterly Fifth Symphony (1942) and culminated in his opera *The Pilgrim's Progress* (1950). The Piano Quartet is dedicated 'To The Hill at Chosen and Ivor Gurney who knows it'.[12]

After the death of his young son, Howells was again to see the hills as a powerful emblem. In the 'Sanctus' movement of his masterpiece, *Hymnus paradisi* (1938), with the help of stylistic traits developed from Delius's *A Mass of Life*, bereavement is conquered in an ecstatic vision of heaven viewed in terms of the transformed local landscape: the 'Sanctus' text is counterpointed with that of Psalm 121, 'I will lift up mine eyes unto the hills, from whence cometh my help' as the pliant, smooth but uplifting melodic contours recall the music of the Piano Quartet.

'John Bunyan in Bedford Jail', depicted on a stained-glass window commemorating the tercentenary of the publication of 'The Pilgrim's Progress' in 1978. Bunyan's work inspired Vaughan Williams's stage 'morality' and also influenced his Fifth Symphony.

Reviewing Vaughan Williams's *Pastoral Symphony* (1921), Howells had written: 'None of the themes in this Symphony have exciting lines . . . they will not draw faces or produce crude pictures of craggy heights. But they will often give you a shape akin to such an outline as the Malvern Hills present when viewed from afar'.[13] His and Vaughan Williams's use of such symbols relates easily enough to the English tradition of pastoral Utopianism represented not long previously, for instance, by William Morris or the garden city movement. But to understand the pastoral urge of this post-impressionist period in British music we must bear in mind that Vaughan Williams himself described the symphony as an impression of a desolate, war-torn French landscape rather than of cows looking over gates.[14] The pastoral effusion was not a simple purgative for the horrors of World War I, nor was it pure escapism. That may be the sum of lesser talents' contributions, such as proliferated in songs (for example Michael Head's *Songs of the Countryside*) and piano music (by Percy Fletcher and Walter Carroll), but the relationship of war to landscape goes much deeper. Paul Fussell analysed it as it affects poetry: 'Since war takes place outdoors and always within nature . . . when H. M. Tomlinson asks, "What has the rathe primrose to do with old rags and bones on barbed wire?" we must answer, "Everything" '.[15]

Technique only rarely rose to expressing the confrontation in music. Bax has been discussed above. Bridge's Piano Sonata (1922–4) in memory of a composer who died in the war, Ernest Farrar, consists of violent and apocalyptic outer movements framing a central elegy in which, as in the slow movement of Ireland's Piano Sonata (1918–20), we sense 'bugles calling . . . from sad shires';[16] the work is an eloquent war memorial. Bliss kept war and peace largely separate in his construction of two large-scale choral and orchestral anthologies, the *Pastoral* (1928) and *Morning Heroes* (1930) (the latter containing the first musical setting of Wilfred Owen), but presented them with a compositional technique equal to both. It is difficult, nevertheless, to see anything in English music of this period to equal the poetic achievement of, say, Rosenberg's 'Break of day in the trenches'.

Parallels abound where more modest horizons are concerned. The *Georgian Poetry* anthologies survived the war, and if such war poets as Sassoon and Blunden are generally only pastorally represented in them, the war poet and composer Ivor Gurney is similarly only pastorally represented in his music, many of his songs being settings of the Georgian poets. But even if the pastoral elegy acknowledges its unspeakable corollary, a new musical vocabulary for the depiction of global evil had to await Vaughan Williams's Fourth Symphony (1934), though it is prefigured in his ballet *Job* (1930). Many of the younger generation – for there was still a younger generation in spite of the war – concerned themselves with entirely different issues.

'ENFANTS TERRIBLES' AND THE 1920s

William Walton, as a very young student at Oxford in 1918, tried his wings by writing a Piano Quartet modelled on Howells's. Though stylistically one of several false starts, it was enough to attract the Sitwells' attention, and soon he was living with them in Chelsea and Italy. Their famous – at the time notorious – venture *Façade* (1922), in which nonsense poems by Edith Sitwell were recited through a megaphone, set in a screen painted by Frank Dobson, in rhythmic coordination with music by Walton, was tinged with Italian futurism (Gino Severini painted the screen used for some later performances). But in its later disposition of seven groups of three short numbers, a reference to Schoenberg's *Pierrot lunaire*, and its dance-band instrumentation, similar to that of Stravinsky's *The Soldier's Tale*, it appears more a light-hearted parody intended to amuse as much as to shock. Not that it was alone in this: most of the numbers are based on popular dances or comic-song genres, and through references to the theatre and circus it is very much in line with, for instance, the contemporary paintings of Picasso and the décors of the postwar Ballets Russes, part of a tradition of evoking popular or folk theatre that stretches back at least to Stravinsky's *Petrushka*. The dadaist theatre of the surreal is there too, but largely in the background.

Edith Sitwell and Neil Porter rehearsing for a performance of William Walton's 'Façade' at the Chenil Galleries, London (1926).

Modern Times

Still taking its cue from France (now from figureheads like Satie and *Les Six*), this was Britain's young musical culture of the 1920s: a parade of wit and frivolity intermingled with the acerbic and surreal. Bliss, in the period immediately preceding the *Colour Symphony*, had exploited it; for example, *Rout* for wordless soprano and instrumental ensemble is like a collage or still-life of fairground or other festive images, while the chamber work *Conversations* aims at musical sarcasm in its first movement, 'The Committee Meeting'. Walton's *Façade* might similarly be contrasted with his rebarbative early string quartet, 'full of undigested Bartók and Schoenberg', as the composer later described it.[17] Lord Berners, too, living in Italy at the time of World War I as a diplomatic attaché and on friendly terms with Casella, Stravinsky and others, mingled witty eccentricities in life and art with the more impressively modernistic technique that supports or supplants the wit in such works as *Fragments psychologiques* for piano (1916) (this title and others are reminiscent of Satie). The popular and the surreal came together typically in his ballet *Luna Park* (written for a C. B. Cochran revue in 1930), another fairground piece whose scenario contains such directions as 'In the first niche are merely the two heads. In the second the billiard balls move around in a slot, without the juggler. In the third a leg only. In the fourth four arms, waving wildly'. Likewise the later *A Wedding Bouquet* (Sadler's Wells Ballet, 1936) marries attractive orchestral writing based on dance rhythms with a characteristically unsyntactic libretto by Gertrude Stein, that is chanted chorally.

Dance is the key to the role of the young in the 1920s. The important phenomenon of crossovers with popular music is often identified as the assimilation of jazz, but it has to be questioned whether New Orleans and Mid-West black idioms were much heard by the intelligentsia. It was ragtime, not jazz, that Stravinsky heard, and ragtime syncopation was inescapable (it appears, for instance, in Bliss's 1920s piano pieces 'Bliss' and 'The Rout Trot'). But the main thrust of vernacular assimilation was through white idioms such as the foxtrot and Latin American dances. Yet again, a French composer, Milhaud, provided key examples of the latter in *Le bœuf sur le toit* and other works, while Berners's opera *Le carrosse du Saint Sacrement* (1924) was set – in French – in (admittedly eighteenth-century) Peru, and *A Wedding Bouquet* featured prominent tango rhythms, as did *Façade*.

The composer who most epitomized this impulse was the precocious Constant Lambert. In his early ballet *Romeo and Juliet*, commissioned by Dyagilev for the Ballets Russes, the element of shock resided not in the music itself, which veered towards the neo-classically wan, but in the young and inexperienced Lambert's row with the mighty Dyagilev over what he saw as the inappropriate substitution of décor by Ernst and Miró for that of Lambert's friend Christopher Wood. In spite of such rashness, Lambert soon found his feet and universal public acclaim with *The Rio Grande* (1927) for piano, chorus, strings, brass and percussion; this, it was claimed, heralded the jazz age in classical music, though jazz and blues are in fact nowhere in the score while the later 'novelty' ragtime idiom and Latin American syncopation are everywhere, matched by the escapism of sensuous chromatic harmonies, a witty panoply of percussion effects, and Sacheverell Sitwell's poem:

> Loud is the marimba's note
> Above these half-salt waves,
> And louder still the tympanum,
> The plectrum, and the kettle-drum,
> Sullen and menacing
> Do these brazen voices ring . . .
> Till the ships at anchor there
> Hear this enchantment
> Of the soft Brazilian air.

In other works, however, Lambert was probably the one British composer of the decade to respond to the genuinely ethnic features of black American music. Hearing the singing of Florence Mills was epiphanic; he later wrote his 'Elegiac Blues' (1927) for piano in her memory. Lambert, increasingly unstable as the effects of osteomyelitis aggravated a liking for alcohol which eventually gained the upper hand over his prodigious intelligence, had reason to turn from the frivolity of the 1920s to its darker sequel in the 1930s: his friends Christopher Wood and Philip Heseltine committed suicide (both in 1930), and it was to Heseltine's memory that he dedicated what is probably his most important composition, the Concerto for Piano and Nine Instruments (1931). Like his Piano Sonata, this work inhabits a stylistic world found nowhere else in British music: motoric rhythmic complexity, rough-grained instrumental textures and lacerating blue-note dissonances culminate, in the final, slow movement, in a paralysing melancholy, black as the covers of the score itself, driven onwards by arpeggiated piano chords that could only have been inspired by the blues. Lambert claimed that it gestated as he tramped the streets of Paris nocturnally; they could have been the streets of Chicago or Harlem. In going beyond politeness of sound, conventions of rhetoric and the comfort of flippancy, Lambert, though for different ends and with different means, achieved in England something equal to the Agitprop expression of Weill, Eisler and Blitzstein.

INTO THE 1930s: SERIOUSNESS AND CENTRAL EUROPE

Lambert's talents never found self-sufficient expression in his compositions. His importance in the 1930s lies largely elsewhere, in his work alongside Lilian Baylis and Ninette de Valois as conductor and musical director of the new Vic-Wells Ballet, and in his book *Music Ho!: a Study of Music in Decline* (1934). The former consolidated the work of a decade in which British ballet, following Dyagilev and the French, had come to the forefront of progress in the arts while opera had accomplished little; the latter brought brilliant if ultimately destructive critical focus to bear on the state of music after the trends of the 1920s had run their course.

It was not Lambert but Walton whose music acted as a barometer of taste for the more serious-minded 1930s. Walton's style had matured into an idiom that reflected both the brittle edge of modernism and a strong *rapprochement* with Elgarian romantic melancholy in his Viola Concerto of 1929 (first played by Hindemith) and the virtuoso oratorio *Belshazzar's Feast* (1931, dedicated to Berners). The consolidation of this achievement came, slowly and painfully, with his Symphony no.1, first performed in 1934 without a finale (one had yet to be written). Here again was a mastery of harmony and expressive dissonance that would scarcely have been possible without the example of jazz polyphony, integrated with a reaffirmed symphonic logic inspired by Sibelius (Lambert hailed Sibelius as a saviour in *Music Ho!*).

The première of Walton's symphony attracted a good deal of critical attention, reflected in two literary works. Berners's satirical novel *Count Omega* poked fun at it, at Walton's search for a finale and at his relationship with the Sitwells (with sideswipes at *Façade*) and reputedly led to a threatened lawsuit with the composer. *Casanova's Chinese Restaurant*, the fifth volume of Anthony Powell's *A Dance to the Music of Time*, includes a long scene set at a party following the première of a new British symphony. The composer in the novel is Moreland (modelled largely on Lambert) and the date moved to the weeks after the abdication of Edward VIII, but the mood of international crisis and personal turmoil (an unsatisfactory love-affair was catalyst to Walton's central movements), projected so skilfully in Powell's episode, casts valuable light on the position of Walton's symphony in British interwar musical history, as well as drawing tantalizing portraits of others on the scene (are Cecil Gray, Heseltine and van Dieren compositely recognizable in the music critics Gossage and Maclintick? Is E. J. Moeran's Symphony, marking the highpoint of his career when it was first performed in 1938, a possible further source of inspiration for the episode?). The critical tone also helps pinpoint the 1930s as a period of consolidation, tinged with disillusionment, after the glamour of the

1920s: 'What I said was that the music was "not Moreland's most adventurous" – that the critics had got used to him as an *enfant terrible* and therefore might underestimate the symphony's true value', as Maclintick puts it (in a blazing row with his wife).[18]

Central and southern European affinities in this period are less easy to trace than French ones, but they are significant. The critical rehabilitation of Frank Bridge is a case in point, for until recently his later output was largely written off as the product of one who 'began to uglify his music to keep it up to date'[19] and bring it into line with the central European avant garde with which he was expected to rub shoulders under the aegis of his patron, Mrs Coolidge. Other composers from whom she or her foundation commissioned chamber works included Bartók, Stravinsky, Webern, Schoenberg, Malipiero, Casella, Bloch, Hindemith and Martinů; most came from countries whose political turmoil or threat the English chose to ignore, as they ignored Bridge's music. Not that the isolation was complete: Edward Dent, professor of music at Cambridge, played an important role as president of the London-based International Society for Contemporary Music, and composers like Walton, Bliss and Lambert as well as Bridge participated in ISCM festivals. The ISCM's honorary secretary, Edward Clark, prototype of the contemporary music impresario, also did much to counter parochialism. But Bridge was all too aware of the public's – and not just the British public's – complacency where European new music was concerned, and nobody cared to see him, as we can now, as perhaps the only British composer in the era before 1945 capable of creating a sound-world equal to the far-reaching artistic responsibilities of his time. That sound-world, consolidated after the breakthrough of the Piano Sonata, embraced a metaphysical deepening of the melancholy that seems always to have been part of Bridge's artistic persona, and it reflected the lengthening shadow of World War I in his *Concerto elegiaco: Oration* (1930) for cello and orchestra. The withdrawn mood of the end of the Third Quartet (1926) can only be described as one of existential extremity.

Peter Warlock (the pseudonym of Philip Heseltine) was alone among English composers in being able to match this, in his Yeats song cycle *The Curlew* (1915–22) for tenor, flute, english horn and string quartet; the desolation of its instrumental prelude, haunted by the same 'Curlew' chord as closes the Bridge quartet,[20] is equalled by the tenor's final despairing arc of melody in the last song:

> I wander by the edge
> Of this desolate lake
> Where wind cries in the sedge:
> *Until the axle break*
> *That keeps the stars in their round,*

Modern Times

And hands hurl in the deep
The banners of East and West,
And the girdle of light is unbound,
Your breast will not lie by the breast
Of your beloved in sleep.

This is still romantic, perhaps, in its equation of the personal love-affair with the cosmos, but Bridge's music does not function on such a subjective plane as Warlock's, and indeed it is the very fact that he speaks for his time, not for himself, that caused his critical voice to go unrecognized then and seem so important now. He did this by keeping abreast of central European styles – Berg's in the Third Quartet, Bartók's in the Fourth; conversely, he seemed to grasp like no-one else in English music the threatening decline of Austro-German civilization, and his work is haunted by the ghost of the Viennese waltz – in *Phantasm* (1931) for piano and orchestra, in the Second Piano Trio (1929), perhaps his masterpiece, and even in the English rhapsody *Enter Spring* (1927), where ebullience is almost as close to violence as it is in Ravel's *La valse*.

The emotions and styles of Warlock's songs, ranging from the despair of *The Curlew* to the saucy verve of 'Yarmouth Fair' and 'The Lover's Maze', mirrors the unstable extremes of behaviour characterizing him and his period. It was an era of misfits, in which it was easy to lose touch with one's public or mislead it and, indeed oneself. Such, in their different ways, was the fate of John Foulds, Bernard van Dieren, Kaikhosru Sorabji and Havergal Brian, whom some see as constituting a British avant garde. While it is easier to dismiss such difficult figures than to reassess them, it is probably fair to say that van Dieren, Heseltine's mentor, mistook a post-Wagnerian textural impasse for a Busoni-inspired new polyphony; that Foulds, the first British composer to purvey quarter-tones, was not able to recognize that his *Quartetto intimo* was brilliant gold whereas his *World Requiem* (Royal Albert Hall, Remembrance Day 1922) was base alloy; that Brian never lost the working-class chip on his shoulder and ended by writing anti-social music in his numerous later symphonies; and that Sorabji (who approached his centenary as a sinister recluse in the village of Corfe Castle) became wholly misanthropic, writing phenomenally long and difficult keyboard works which he forbade anyone to play. Both van Dieren and Sorabji tried unsuccessfully to match Lambert's wit as an essayist, the former in *Down Among the Dead Men* (1935), the latter in *Around Music* and *Mi contra fa*.

The figure who drew together the threads of Britain's musical relationship to central European developments, surprisingly, was Vaughan Williams. He alone, as a member of the 'intellectual aristocracy' (he was related to the Darwins, Huxleys, Wedgwoods and other famous families), possessed the social distinction and seniority to act as a spokesman – as 'Uncle Ralph' – for the British composer, through writing to the press, teaching, offering financial help, pulling strings, giving testimony (as when he supported Tippett's conscientious objection in World War II) or venting national prejudice. Some of these roles he had taken over from his teacher Stanford; but his musical reputation stood higher than Stanford's had ever done. His staying-power was extraordinary, helped by longevity, and, in spite of his antipathy towards George Bernard Shaw, he provides an obvious cultural parallel to him. Parallels with other literary figures could be drawn: Vaughan Williams's radical bourgeois humanism, perhaps inspired partly by Parry's, represents a late phase of the English liberal conscience such as we find also in H. G. Wells and J. B. Priestley.

The international side of Vaughan Williams, and a new, contemporary urgency of musical language, came to the fore in *Job*, in the 'alla tedesca' finale of his Piano Concerto (1931) and above all in the Fourth Symphony, not inappropriately dubbed 'Europe 1935' by some at the time of its first performance. If Walton's and Moeran's symphonies learn from Sibelius, Vaughan Williams's show affinities with both the 'New Deal' symphonies of the USA (Harris's Third, for example) and with Shostakovich. In its brutally forthright chromaticism, shrill orchestration, heavily ironic dance rhythms, and mood of totalitarian menace it matches the block colours of a Soviet poster. 'I don't know whether I like it, but it's what I meant', Vaughan Williams said.

This remark suggests a commitment to truth, yet Vaughan Williams, unlike Shaw, stopped short of political or social alignment in his music (though not of social involvement in his life: witness his untiring work with amateur performers), just as, for all its immediacy, the music of the Fourth Symphony 'stopped short of a post-war freedom of rhythm and a post-war harshness of dissonance', as Cardus criticized.[21] It was as far as an English establishment composer of his generation could be expected to go.

THE COMMITTED COMPOSER

A slightly younger friend and contemporary of Vaughan Williams, Rutland Boughton, was almost unique in his political alignment, joining the Communist Party after the General Strike of 1926. Boughton's case is curious – or perhaps typically English. At the beginning of the century he was roughly aligned with William Morris's pastoral socialism; he answered Shaw's call for an English Bayreuth by setting up a homespun opera festival at Glastonbury just before World War I. His operatic study of Celtic yearning, *The Immortal Hour*, following its Glastonbury première, was produced at Birmingham by Barry Jackson after the war and then ran for an extraordinary series of

216 consecutive performances in London in 1922, with revivals in 1923, 1926 and 1932. His later output included a cycle of five Arthurian operas (which, after Wagner, he called music dramas). The problem, as Shaw realized, was not the intention – to establish English music drama on a parochial, socialist basis – but the artistic means; for Boughton's music, mixing Wagnerian preconceptions with a concern for the amateur that too often became amateurism, was dowdy in the extreme. So much a part of his time (for instance, in his use of eurhythmic dance in the stage chorus), Boughton cannot be written off; but he came nowhere near reconciling his vision of the English Utopia with the stringent cosmopolitan demands of music as a professional art. It took Tippett to do that.

A generation younger, Tippett learnt his craft slowly, feeling his way through ventures and teachers throughout the 1920s and 30s. As a socialist yeoman he took part in work camps, and from a modest rural base and resources for several years he ran opera productions at the Barn Theatre, Oxted, ranging from eighteenth-century ballad opera to Stanford's *The Travelling Companion*. Much literature and thought was imbibed slowly and profoundly, perhaps most significantly Shaw, Goethe, Shakespeare and Jung. His breakthrough came in the 1930s when he showed, especially in the First String Quartet (1935), the First Piano Sonata (1938) and the Concerto for Double String Orchestra (1939), that national roots (English folksong, Purcellian jauntiness and madrigalian rhythmic fluidity), social identification (for example, with jazz and blues), a responsible approach to the heritage of one's musical discipline (for Tippett that principally meant Beethoven) and international awareness could be fused into a new style, informed above all by the tonal perspectives and rhythmic life of Stravinsky's neo-classical works. To a certain extent the later Holst belongs here too, and a work like his chamber opera *The Wandering Scholar* (1930) shows points of contact with the nature and spirit of Tippett's early enterprises. But Holst's very private response to lyric poetry, as in his Choral Symphony (1924, to poems by Keats) and the Humbert Wolfe songs (1929), remains closer to the Romantically transcendental than to the new music.

Alan Bush, like Boughton a member of the Communist Party, was Tippett's closest musical comrade in the early days. He set out with a style closer to international modernism than Tippett's (for instance, in his *Dialectic* for string quartet, 1929) and for a while, from 1929, he lived in Berlin in close contact with Brecht's circle. But the main thrust of rising political awareness in the arts in England in the 1930s was to be found elsewhere among those with Berlin connections, in 'the Auden generation',[22] whose musical representative was Britten. Unlike Tippett, Britten was not a slow developer. As a youthful prodigy he became Bridge's pupil and almost an adopted son; Bridge was able to nurture general principles of contemporary expression, but when he suggested that Britten should study in Vienna with Berg, his *alma mater* the Royal College of Music put a stop to the idea (was the censuring voice that of the director, Sir Hugh Allen?): Berg was 'not a good influence'.[23] Neither was Vienna, they probably felt, if it would expose the innocent youngster, like Isherwood's Cliff Bradshaw in Berlin, to dens of iniquity and decadence. Britten was soon consorting with Auden and Isherwood in a circle that was politically radical and homosexual, and he found a musical idiom to match, partly based on cabaret styles and infused with irony. Again Shostakovich's music, particularly his *Lady Macbeth of Mtsensk*, was a reference point, as was Mahler. This set Britten at odds with Bridge, and it is all too symptomatic of British music's (and society's) blinkered approach at this period that Vaughan Williams, Bridge and Britten in the 1930s should all be so close in their awareness of contemporary Europe yet so mutually exclusive in the limits of their outlook and identification.

Britten, for a few years at least, was the musical iconoclast. Working with Auden on a Grub Street basis ensured radicalism, be it in the *Cabaret Songs* (one of which was written for the Group Theatre's production of *The Ascent of F6*) or in the *musique concrète* avant gardism of some of the music for the GPO Film Unit's documentaries. The seal was set on this early period by *Our Hunting Fathers*, 'my op.1 alright' as Britten confided to his diary,[24] a 'symphonic cycle' for soprano and orchestra to texts written and assembled by Auden, performed at the 1936 Norwich Festival. This was the most modernistic score of value yet produced by an Englishman. It was also political, using animals as metaphors for the oppressed (the juxtaposition of the dogs' or hawks' names 'German' and 'Jew' in 'Dance of Death' helped make the point). Yet its raw edge did not entirely suit Britten, and over the next few years he worked (as he was now able partly through the rising reward of commissions) mostly at smaller or more traditionally orientated projects, in which balance, genre, variation, contrast and discipline were paramount arbiters of technique: the Variations on a Theme of Frank Bridge (with which he made his European début, at the Salzburg Festival in 1937), the Piano Concerto (1938), Violin Concerto (1939), *Les illuminations* (1939), the Michelangelo Sonnets (1940), the *Sinfonia da requiem* (1940) and the First Quartet (1941). By this time, still following in Auden's footsteps, he had left Europe and from 1939 was living in the USA.

World War II produced a new set of musical reference-points. Tippett's oratorio *A Child of Our Time* (1939–41) dealt with the pogrom, incorporating not hymns but negro spirituals to represent the music of oppressed people. Vaughan Williams's Fifth Symphony, seen then and now as a radiant and peaceful affirmation of national destiny in the face of Nazi bombardment (and, as we have seen, related to *The Pilgrim's*

Progress), and the slightly postwar Sixth (1947), an 'iron curtain' or post-nuclear work, chilling in its desolation, extended the composer's extraordinary symphonic career. Britten and Tippett trod parallel paths as conscientious objectors, Britten returning from the USA when he could no longer distance himself from his country, Tippett going to prison for violating the terms of his objection. Britten's opera *Peter Grimes* gestated, was composed and went into rehearsal; concern for the role of the unconforming individual in society, relevant to Britten himself both as pacifist and homosexual, became a motivating force in British music of the establishment for the first time in history – the earlier stances of Ethel Smyth the suffragette and Elgar the Roman Catholic notwithstanding.

THE ENGLISH GARDEN

British music did not develop in isolation. We have traced a shift between the 1920s and the late 1930s in viewing Europe and the outside world at first as a source of pleasure, later as a source of pain: Parisian chic gave way to Austro-German agony. There was another shift, from private or elegiac retreat in reaction to World War I to public witness as recognition of the next war. Bridge, Ireland and Bax may be identified more with the former view, Britten and Tippett to the latter, with Bliss somewhere between the two and Vaughan Williams transcending any categories. This might be seen as the musical response to an open society. Yet the nub of central European musical thought, the serial revolution of Schoenberg and the Second Viennese School, failed to make any impact in Britain (except the negative one of something to be resisted at all costs) until long after World War II, in spite of pioneering moves by Humphrey Searle and Elisabeth Lutyens (daughter of the architect Edwin Lutyens and wife of Edward Clark, with Elizabeth Maconchy and Rebecca Clarke one of the few determined women composers of the period) and in spite of Alan Rawsthorne's sophisticated awareness of the properties of chromatic integration. Britain was not alone in this: France, Italy and Russia also failed to respond. But what is uniquely British is the strength and nature of the conservative heritage that countered it.

Vaughan Williams, for all his progressive works discussed above, was nevertheless influential as a conservative figurehead. It is easy to criticize his promotion of a kind of semi-detached, mock-Tudor attitude to music without appreciating what a vital and enduring part of English culture that phenomenon is, in art as in architecture and town planning. The cultivation of a small musical garden was the limited but valuable contribution of many a British composer at this period, seen at its best not in Vaughan Williams himself but in those for whom his appropriation of such traditional symbols as folksong and

Tudor polyphony was a powerful inspiration: Finzi, Howells, Armstrong Gibbs, Dyson and many others who are 'minor' composers in the best sense. Moreover, it was an appropriation not without a sense of the market and a responsibility to the community. It flowered in the continuing climate of British antiquarianism, along with the scholarly revival of the lute-song by Philip Heseltine, the English madrigal and anthem by E. H. Fellowes, English opera by Edward Dent and old instruments by Arnold Dolmetsch. Britain's incalculable role in the early music movement cannot be divorced from conservatism in composition – at least, not in this period. On the other hand, Stravinskian neo-classicism, albeit often only partly assimilated, acted as an invigorating reference-point for conservatism. Howells's Concerto for Strings and Finzi's *Dies natalis* (both 1939) owe much to it. Similarly Bartók's treatment of folk melody and primitive rhythms struck strong resonances in Howells, Vaughan Williams and others who might soften it for their own ends.

Music's utilitarian slant is best seen as part of a continuous process. The rise of the musical amateur in the nineteenth century had been particularly noteworthy in Britain, which led the way with the sight-singing and brass-band movements and with school music. These outlets may already have been shrinking between the wars, but plenty of serviceable music was still being written for competitive festivals; such eminent composers as Howells, Dyson, Gibbs and even Holst sustained contact with amateurs and with the young through adjudicating or conducting. The real watershed between Victorian and modern music-making, as with so many aspects of British life, came after World War II, when competitive festivals and choral singing declined more sharply. Music for children continues to flourish, however: now it is opera and the musical; between the wars it was part-songs, unison songs and arrangements of folk- and traditional tunes for which the foundations of the repertory had been laid early in the century by Somervell, Walford Davies, Cecil Sharp and others. They created a vast body of material of which, as with solo songs, ballads, organ and piano music, the full extent can only be glimpsed through publishers' catalogues and advertising incipits. Composers with a broad commercial or functional base in this period have been neglected, and we are far from reinstating their more enduring works, for example Dyson's large-scale choral and orchestral pieces, especially his brilliant Chaucer setting *The Canterbury Pilgrims* (1931), Gibbs's songs and string quartets and Whitlock's Organ Sonata (1937). A work like Whitlock's sonata may have the quality to endure as a prime testimony to the period's character, for it shows how the legacy of Elgar, Vaughan Williams and Delius was assimilated and transferred to genres other than their own as a national idiom.

Modern Times

Five members of a Yorkshire family practising for the 32nd annual National Band Festival at Alexandra Palace, 1937.

NOTES

[1] J. N. Moore, *Elgar on Record: the Composer and the Gramophone* (London, 1974).

[2] C. Ehrlich, *The Music Profession in Britain Since the Eighteenth Century: a Social History* (Oxford, 1985).

[3] R. Graves and A. Hodge, *The Long Weekend: a Social History of Great Britain 1918–1939* (London, 1940).

[4] I. Whitcomb, *After the Ball: Pop Music from Rag to Rock* (London, 1972), 172.

[5] D. Godfrey, *Memories and Music* (London, 1924); see list of his performances.

[6] J. Minihan, *The Nationalization of Culture: the Development of State Subsidies to the Arts in Great Britain* (London, 1977).

[7] Repr. in A. Bliss, *As I Remember* (London, 1970), 248–55.

[8] J. Longmire, *John Ireland: Portrait of a Friend* (London, 1969), 20.

[9] E. M. Forster, *Collected Short Stories* (Harmondsworth, 1954), 86.

[10] Such parody has been brilliantly done by Peter Ustinov in his sketch of Sir Banbury Cross.

[11] *Ivor Gurney: War Letters*, ed. R. K. R. Thornton (Ashington and Manchester, 1983), 262.

[12] Chosen Hill, now disfigured by a reservoir and a motorway, is on the outskirts of Gloucester and commands panoramic views of the city, the Cotswolds and the Malverns. As a student,

Howells worked his harmony exercises on its summit. The hill and medieval church also inspired Gerald Finzi's *In terra pax*.

[13] H. Howells, 'Vaughan Williams's "Pastoral" Symphony', *ML*, iii (1922), 127.

[14] U. Vaughan Williams, *R. V. W.: a Biography of Ralph Vaughan Williams* (Oxford, 1964), 121.

[15] P. Fussell, 'Arcadian Recourses', in *The Great War and Modern Memory* (New York and London, 1975), 231.

[16] W. Owen, 'Anthem for Doomed Youth', *Collected Poems of Wilfred Owen* (London, 1963).

[17] H. Ottaway, 'Walton, William', *Grove6*.

[18] A. Powell, *Casanova's Chinese Restaurant* (London, 1960), 148.

[19] F. Howes, *The English Musical Renaissance* (London, 1966), 160.

[20] S. Banfield, *Sensibility and English Song: Critical Studies of the Early 20th Century* (Cambridge, 1985), i, 265.

[21] M. Kennedy, *The Works of Ralph Vaughan Williams* (London, 1964, 3/1980), 245.

[22] S. Hynes, *The Auden Generation: Literature and Politics in England in the 1930s* (London, 1976).

[23] M. Kennedy, *Britten* (London, 1981), 13.

[24] D. Mitchell, *Britten and Auden in the Thirties: the Year 1936* (London, 1981), 19.

BIBLIOGRAPHICAL NOTE

General background

The history of Britain in the period is voluminously covered in A. J. P. Taylor, *English History: 1914–1945* (Oxford, 1965; Harmondsworth, 1970), or at shorter length in H. Pelling, *Modern Britain 1885–1955* (London, 1960), and D. Thomson: *England in the Twentieth Century*, The Pelican History of England, ix (Harmondsworth, 1965). None of these books has much to say about culture and the arts. For those topics one might turn first to R. Graves and A. Hodge, *The Long Weekend: a Social History of Great Britain 1918–1939* (London, 1940), for an entertaining account of the social background; then to J. Montgomery, *The Twenties* (London, 1957); D. Goldring, *The Nineteen Twenties* (London, 1945); M. Muggeridge, *The Thirties* (London, 1940) and J. Symon, *The Thirties* (London, 1960).

Further general reading might include C. L. Mowat, *Britain Between the Wars 1918–1940* (London, 1968); L. C. B. Seaman, *Post-Victorian Britain 1902–1951* (London, 1968) and the study text, S. Constantine's *Social Conditions in Britain 1918–1939* (London, 1983).

For the relationship of art and life, P. Fussell's *The Great War and Modern Memory* (New York and London, 1975) cannot be bettered; on a different topic, there is S. Hynes's *The Auden Generation: Literature and Politics in England in the 1930s* (London, 1976). Music's public face is dealt with in J. Minihan, *The Nationalization of Culture: the Development of State Subsidies to the Arts in Great Britain* (London, 1977); C. Ehrlich, *The Music Profession in Britain Since the Eighteenth Century: a Social History* (Oxford, 1985); and A. Briggs, *The History of Broadcasting in the United Kingdom* (1961–), this last a dull, multi-volume affair. D. Russell's recent *Popular Music in England, 1840–1914: a Social History* (Manchester, 1987) awaits its twentieth-century sequel, but I. Whitcomb's *After the Ball: Pop Music from Rag to Rock* (London, 1972) covers much ground entertainingly.

Music

The standard history of British music in the period is still F. Howes's *The English Musical Renaissance* (London, 1966). Its pro-establishment bias is ineffectually countered in P. Pirie's book of the same title (London, 1979). The sixth volume of the Blackwell History of Music in Britain, *The Twentieth Century*, is in preparation. *British*

Modern Times

Music of Our Time (Harmondsworth, 1946), a little book edited by A. L. Bacharach, is still worth reading, while *The Mirror of Music: 1844–1944: a Century of Musical Life in Britain as Reflected in the Pages of the 'Musical Times'*, ed. P. Scholes, 2 vols. (London, 1947) is an encyclopedic reference work. S. Banfield, *Sensibility and English Song: Critical Studies of the Early 20th Century*, 2 vols. (Cambridge, 1985), deals with most of the composers of the period and with much of the background, as does Lewis Foreman, *From Parry to Britten: British Music in Letters 1900–1945* (London, 1987), in its refreshing anthology format.

Foremost among essays is C. Lambert: *Music Ho!: a Study of Music in Decline* (London, 1934, 3/1966); see also R. Vaughan Williams, *National Music and Other Essays* (Oxford, 1963, 2/1987), and the various volumes of Osbert Sitwell's autobiography *Left Hand, Right Hand!*, particularly *Laughter in the Next Room* (London, 1948). Composers who wrote informative autobiographies include Bliss, Lutyens and Goossens, in *As I Remember* (London, 1970), *A Goldfish Bowl* (London, 1972) and *Overture and Beginners* (London, 1951) respectively. Bax's autobiography, *Farewell, My Youth* (London, 1943), is splendid but stops before the First World War.

For coverage of individual composers, *Grove6* is a first recourse; *The New Grove 20th-Century English Masters* (London, 1986) has been published as an updated offprint. *British Composers in Interview* (1963), ed. R. Murray Schafer (London, 1963), is stimulating and sometimes revealing. A. Whittall's *The Music of Britten and Tippett: Studies in Themes and Techniques* (Cambridge, 1982, 2/1990), is a formidable and all-too-rare comparative study. Informative books on individual composers include Lewis Foreman: *Bax: a Composer and his Times* (London, 1983); M. Hurd, *Immortal Hour: the Life and Period of Rutland Boughton* (London, 1962); P. Evans, *The Music of Benjamin Britten* (London, 1979); D. Mitchell, *Britten and Auden in the Thirties: the Year 1936* (London, 1981); J. Longmire, *John Ireland: Portrait of a Friend* (London, 1969); R. Shead, *Constant Lambert: his Life, his Music, and his Friends* (London, 1973); I. Kemp, *Tippett: the Composer and his Music* (London, 1984); M. Kennedy, *The Works of Ralph Vaughan Williams* (London, 1964, 3/1980); and U. Vaughan Williams: *R. V. W.: a Biography of Ralph Vaughan Williams* (Oxford, 1964).

Several books set to become standard sources have recently appeared or made their mark. Some take their place to a greater or lesser extent within established modes of writing and scholarship; such are Tippett's autobiography, *Those Twentieth Century Blues* (London, 1991), *Letters from a Life: the Selected Letters and Diaries of Benjamin Britten: 1913–1976*, ed. D. Mitchell, 2 vols (London, 1991), M. Kennedy, *Portrait of Walton* (Oxford and New York, 1989), M. and S. Harries, *A Pilgrim Soul: the Life and Works of Elisabeth Lutyens* (London, 1989), and C. Palmer, *Herbert Howells: a Centenary Celebration* (London, 1992). Others, however, bear witness to an increasingly contextual or deconstructive approach to artistic creation. Susana Walton's *William Walton: Behind the Façade* (Oxford and New York, 1988) chronicles the dynamics of creativity within a marriage, A. Motion's *The Lamberts: George, Constant & Kit* (London, 1986) those within a family, and H. Carpenter's *Benjamin Britten: a Biography* (London, 1992) epitomizes the 'whole truth' approach. Ehrlich's *Harmonious Allegiance: a History of the Performing Right Society* (Oxford and New York, 1989) furthers his work on the socio-economics of British musical life, and M. Wiener, *English Culture and the Decline of the Industrial Spirit, 1850–1980* (Cambridge, 1981) offers the broadest possible contextual trajectory along which British music may be seen to have travelled throughout the period.

Above all, music as a cultural signifier has moved from the margins to the centre of some historians' agendas. *The Invention of Tradition*, ed. E. Hobsbawm and T. Ranger (Cambridge, 1983) includes an essay by D. Cannadine, 'The Context, Performance and Meaning of Ritual: the British Monarchy and the "Invention of Tradition", *c.* 1820–1977', which highlights music and lies behind J. Crump's chapter on 'The Identity of English Music: the Reception of Elgar 1898–1935' in *Englishness: Politics and Culture 1880–1920*, ed. R. Colls and P. Dodd (London, 1986); the critical stance towards the creation of national identities taken by these authors is furthered in the chapters on Elgar, Delius, and Holst and Vaughan Williams (by M. Hughes, R. Stradling and P. Harrington respectively) in *Music and the Politics of Culture*, ed. C. Norris (London, 1989).

Chapter X

The USA, 1918–45

CAROL J. OJA

In *Exiles Return: a Literary Odyssey of the 1920s*, Malcolm Cowley described his generation of American writers – those born around 1900 – as 'representatives of a new age' with 'a sense of being somehow unique'. Such was also true for their composer contemporaries. The years following World War I did indeed bring a 'new age' in which American creative artists of all sorts gained unprecedented independence and confidence. Aaron Copland, a leading composer of that generation, announced in 1926 that 'The day of the neglected American composer is over', and seven years later Henry Cowell, another such leader, proclaimed, 'Those who follow music recognize that there is an extraordinary development now in process in American composition'.

During the 25 years framed by the two world wars, the fast developments in American music fell into two distinct yet interconnected periods, each defined in part by social, political and economic conditions. The first, from 1918 to around 1931, was a time of flouting old, established institutions and discovering new outlets for performance, publication and criticism. 'Modernism', 'experimentation' and avant gardism were among the rallying cries. Although a few years passed before the 1929 stock-market crash affected the musical community, by the early 1930s American life had changed drastically, and composers responded with their consciences as well as their pens. In the second period, from around 1932 to the end of World War II, the brazen confidence of the previous decade was muted, and composers strove to write music for a broader cut of 'the people', as a new slogan put it. Yet they carried forward many aspects of the musical language from the 1920s and continued devising forums for performance. With government support, especially through the Works Progress Administration, the 1930s witnessed the greatest amount of musical activity ever to take place on American shores.

*

THE EXPERIMENTAL SPIRIT (1918–1931): THE MACHINE AGE

Americans had long been enamoured of inventions, always searching for clever ways to lower costs and heighten productivity. By the 1920s this drive had produced major technological advances, which in turn generated dramatic changes in everyday life. In 1917 approximately 24% of American homes had electricity; by 1940 nearly 90% did. In 1914 eighteen American manufacturers produced some 500,000 phonographs; by 1919 200 of them made two million machines. The fortunes of the phonograph were affected, in turn, by yet another technological advance – the advent of radio. In 1920 the first radio station opened (KDKA of Pittsburgh) and within the next five years it was followed by 570 others. By 1925 there were some 2.75 million receivers across the country. RCA (Radio Corporation of America) was founded in 1919, NBC (National Broadcasting Company) in 1926 and CBS (first known as Columbia Phonograph Broadcasting System) in 1927. For good reason this period has come to be known as the 'machine age'. In 1931 *Modern Music*, the 'little magazine' of the American composer, devoted an issue to 'Music and the Machine'. There the composer Joseph Schillinger wrote: 'It is impossible to predict what will occur within the next ten years, but it is obvious that the development of music will go hand in hand with that of science'.

This fascination with technology was linked to a widespread aesthetic of the day. A 'Machine Age Exposition' had been mounted in the Steinway Hall, New York, in 1927, and there were European musical precedents, especially in the work of the Italian futurist Luigi Russolo and others. Machines inspired many American musical developments. First, new electronic instruments were constructed, like the telharmonium, invented by Thaddeus Cahill in 1895–1900, and the theremin, invented by Lev Termen in 1919. Second, composers wrote pieces that used machines as instruments. Perhaps the most infamous was George Antheil's *Ballet mécanique* of 1923–5, originally conceived for a film by Fernand Léger. When Antheil's score received its Carnegie Hall première in 1927, its battery of xylophones, drums, amplified pianola, three propellers and siren shocked the audience and critics, leaving Antheil with a reputation as an impetuous wild man. Other machine-driven works were composed for electric instruments, including Joseph Schillinger's *First Airphonic Suite for RCA Theremin with Orchestra* (1929) and Henry Cowell's *Rhythmicana* (1931), written for the rhythmicon, an instrument built by Termen to Cowell's design, which could play complex multiple cross-rhythms. Third, imitation of mechanical noises became popular, as in George Gershwin's *An American in Paris* (1928), which simulated the bustle of city traffic, and John Alden Carpenter's *Skyscrapers* (1923–4), where the composer announced in the score's introduction that he aimed to 'reflect some of the many rhythmic movements and sounds of modern American life'. Finally technology had a profound effect on the imagination of certain composers, such as Edgard Varèse, a Frenchman who emigrated to New York in 1915 and saw liberating new possibilities in science. Varèse dreamt of 'a sound-producing machine' in which 'anyone will be able to press a button to release the music exactly as the composer wrote it – exactly like opening a book'.[1] Only after World War II did the means exist for realizing Varèse's vision.

Technology changed the face of American music and music-making in other ways. The increased availability of recordings and radios and the growth of the film industry provided new outlets for composition. At the same time, these factors contributed to a process of homogenization. By the late 1920s a rising country-music star like Jimmie Rodgers, having grown up in Meridian, Mississippi, could count among his influences not only local white musicians but also the African-American blues singers and jazz ensembles he had heard on recordings. This wide-ranging dissemination of musical styles had several results. Insular folk traditions now confronted complex outside forces: many started to change while others died away. Yet, ironically, the growing sophistication of recording equipment made it possible to preserve those local styles – if not to insure their survival in the community. Amateur music-making also underwent a transformation, as performance in the home, which had fuelled America's prolific sheet-music industry in the nineteenth and early twentieth centuries, gave way to passive listening, either over the air-waves or through the grooves. Victrolas and radio receivers replaced pianos in the family parlour, triggering a revolution 'from print to plastic'.[2]

THE MANY VOICES OF MODERNISM

The growth of technology and the continual quest for newness affected aesthetic attitudes during the 1920s. In 1921 a war about modernism was already being waged in the *Musical Quarterly*, the seven-year-old periodical of American musicology that was still under its first editor, Oscar G. T. Sonneck. Three articles appeared that year, 'Against Modern"ism" [sic]' by Constantin von Sternberg of Philadelphia, 'The Rhetoric of Modern Music' by Karl H. Eschman of Granville, Ohio, and 'The Assault on Modernism in Music' by R. D. Welch of Northampton, Massachusetts. Together they showed that the idea of modernism was known outside New York City and that new methods of composition were strong enough to be threatening established traditions. For these authors, modern composers included mostly Debussy and Skryabin, while the Russian-American Leo Ornstein was briefly mentioned. By 1924, when *The League of Composers' Review* was founded

The Woolworth Building, New York City (1913), designed by Cass Gilbert in a distinctly Gothic manner, complete with gargoyles and flying buttresses; it remained the tallest building until 1930.

(soon to be renamed *Modern Music*), the vocabulary of newness and modernism burst forth in its inaugural manifesto: 'We believe that not only is too little modern music played, but that too little is written about it . . . By publishing authoritative and discerning criticism it is our hope to rouse the public out of somnolent tolerance to a live appreciation of the new in music'.

Yet modernism waved many banners, with aural results as different as visual ones in paintings of the period. For every realist like Edward Hopper or abstractionist like Stuart Davis, there was a musical counterpart. The two largest and most influential groups of composers tended to fall under the rubrics of 'neo-classicists' or 'experimentalists', though both labels obscure the individuality of the figures involved. Generally, neo-classicism is seen as a style begun in the late 1910s by Igor Stravinsky and other composers living in France. It drew musical forms, melodies and ideas of past eras into new compositions. Americans affected by neo-classicism tended to spend time in Paris, often to study with the renowned French pedagogue, Nadia Boulanger. Among them were George Antheil, Marc Blitzstein, Theodore Chanler, Israel Citkowitz, Aaron Copland, Roy Harris, Colin McPhee, Walter Piston and Virgil Thomson.

Neo-classicism incorporated cool dispassion, economy, lean linearity, acerbic dissonance (often bi- or polytonality), brittle instrumentation and, at times, brash irreverence. Sentimentality was scorned. American neo-classical works capitalized on these traits, yet personalized them. Some, like Virgil Thomson's *Five Inventions* for piano or his *Sonata da chiesa* for E♭ clarinet, trumpet, viola, horn and trombone (both 1926), evoked Baroque idioms. In the *Inventions* Thomson used the contrapuntal techniques of Bach, doing so again in the last movement of the *Sonata* – a double fugue in which one subject harks back to Bach's 'Wedge' fugue in E minor. But these were no mere imitations of bygone practices. Earlier techniques were twisted into new shapes and often mocked in the process.

Neo-classicism took other forms in America. In the late 1920s, perhaps inspired by Stravinsky's Piano Sonata of 1924, a spate of American ventures in the genre appeared, among them Theodore Chanler's Sonata for violin and piano (1926), Marc Blitzstein's and Carlos Chavez's Piano Sonatas (1927) and Roy Harris's Piano Sonata (1928). Concurrently, the attitude that led neo-classicists to borrow from the past – one that involved a musical counterpart of working with found objects – also freed them to draw on styles of the present, especially popular idioms. Aaron Copland's *Music for the Theatre* (1925), for example, used a small theatre orchestra; it incorporated the tune 'East Side, West Side' in its second movement and exploited 'challenging jazz rhythms', as its composer put it.[3] Another such example was the 'Tango' movement of Thomson's above-mentioned *Sonata da chiesa*.

For many Americans, this neo-classical notion of fragmenting and reusing existing material resulted not only in the transfer of a European aesthetic to the New World but also became one of the prime means by which they sought a national voice. Copland wrote repeatedly that during the 1920s he wanted to create music that was 'identifiably American'. He did not stand alone. Jazz provided the essential material for many (as will be explored later). But another member of this neo-classical group, Thomson, stretched his search for historic material back to American hymnody. By doing so he presaged one of the most important movements of the 1930s. In his *Symphony on a Hymn Tune* (1926–8), Thomson juxtaposed well-known nineteenth-century sacred songs ('How Firm a Foundation', 'Jesus Loves Me') with secular tunes ('For He's a Jolly Good Fellow') and adventurous rhythms. Disjunction reigned, both in fragmentation of melody and in the frequent use of bitonality. In his pioneering analysis of Thomson's work, the composer John Cage likened this symphony to a 'painting that substitutes for brush and pigment scissors, paste, and various ready-made materials'.[4] Thomson used similar techniques in setting the poetry of Gertrude Stein, especially in his opera *Four Saints in Three Acts*, composed in 1928 and first produced in 1934.

Another monument of American neo-classicism is Copland's Piano Variations (1930). Tightly built on a four-note motif, the theme and its subsequent twenty variations are uncompromisingly muscular and hard-hitting; every note emanates from the original four, with consistent angularity and dissonance. Octave displacement and exploitation of register are crucial to the work, and the syncopations of jazz – incorporated so literally in Copland's Piano Concerto of 1926 – have been subtly integrated and personalized, as in the seventeenth variation in which a two-part counterpoint is set up in octaves, grouped in shifting, cross-accented compounds of two and three (such additive rhythms were basic to jazz and, earlier, to ragtime).

Alongside the neo-classicists stood an influential group of experimenters who neither embraced current European idioms nor consciously sought a national style. They simply aimed to re-invent and revolutionize composition. If those experimenters had adopted a motto, it might have been, 'Contemporary music makes almost universal use of materials formerly considered unusable', which in fact is the opening sentence of Henry Cowell's compositional treatise *New Musical Resources*, written in 1916–19 but not published until 1930.

Cowell's early experiments took several forms, challenging conventional notions of timbre, chord formation and rhythm. In *Aeolian Harp* (?1923) and *Banshee* (1925), both for piano, Cowell eschewed keyboard orthodoxy by strumming the instrument's inside strings. In other piano

Henry Cowell's autograph manuscript of 'Aeolian Harp' for piano strings, with a dedication to Armitt Brown.

works, such as *Advertisement* (1917) and *The Tides of Manaunaun* (?1917), he approached the instrument percussively and hammered out tone-clusters – chords built of fists- or forearms-full of 2nds. Similarly he began to incorporate exotic instruments (primarily percussion) in his chamber works, such as the Ensemble for string quintet with Amer-Indian thundersticks (1924). During this period, in the *Quartet Romantic* (1917) and *Quartet Euphometric* (1919), he also developed a mathematical formula for deriving rhythmic patterns from the harmonic ratios of the overtone series.

The other leading experimenter of the 1920s was Edgard Varèse. He was an adventurer in timbre, both in his way of writing for instruments and in his chord structures. *Ionisation* (1930–31), perhaps his most famous work, is scored for percussion, a revolutionary notion to the Western world. *Hyperprism* (1922) and *Intégrales* (1924) not only added large percussion batteries to wind and brass, but used Varèse's obliquely visionary notion of 'sound-masses', an ideal of building intensely concentrated chords in which pitch relationships, tone-colour and range achieved equal importance. Other notable experimenters included John J. Becker, Wallingford Riegger, Dane Rudhyar and Adolph Weiss.

Two important composers of the 1920s who independently mapped out an unclassifiable territory somewhere between the neo-classicists and experimenters were Ruth Crawford and Roger Sessions. Crawford studied with Charles Seeger (whom she married in 1931) and was influenced by his theory of 'dissonant counterpoint'. Perhaps best known is her String Quartet (1931), a highly systematized work in which she organized pitches and dynamics, prefiguring subsequent total serialism in the USA. Sessions also stood outside any school or movement, and spent the latter part of the 1920s living in Europe. After an early work, *Black Maskers* (1923), Sessions's music became increasingly complex. Even his Piano Sonata (1930), which has been linked to the work of Stravinsky, has a particular brand of sombre statement. Sessions was a superb craftsman with a strong commitment to an international rather than an American style.

AN OLDER GENERATION

Charles Ives, who has come to be seen as the father of experimentation in twentieth-century American music, had been discovered by only a few young composers in the 1920s. As Copland later rued, 'Through a curious quirk of musical history the man who was writing such a music – a music that came close to approximating our needs – was entirely unknown to us'.[5] But in spite of his isolation, Ives was gradually receiving recognition. Two movements of his Fourth Symphony were played at a concert by E. Robert Schmitz's Pro Musica in January 1927 and that year he met Cowell, who proved to be his principal conduit to the new-music community. Cowell published the second movement of Ives's Fourth Symphony in *New Music* (January 1929) and introduced him to Nicolas Slonimsky, who conducted the première of his *Three Places in New England* at a Town Hall concert in January 1931. (The main thrust of the Ives revival was to be in the 1930s.) The other principal innovator among the older generation was Carl Ruggles, whose densely difficult works such as *Toys* (1919), *Men and Angels* (1920) and *Portals* (1925) appeared on the concert programmes of Varèse's International Composers' Guild.

Ives remained a musical recluse and Ruggles was known largely to audiences at Varèse's concerts, but more conservative composers of their generation had greater exposure. The 'Second New England School', which included George Chadwick, Frederick Converse, and Daniel Gregory Mason, remained rooted in German Romanticism. Yet another member of this group, Edward Burlingame Hill, some of whose music was as conservative as that of his contemporaries, helped turn Americans away from Germany and towards France. Hill's *Modern French Music* (1924) gave an early endorsement to French clarity and orchestration techniques, and he had considerable influence as a teacher at Harvard on such students as Virgil Thomson and Walter Piston. Other important older figures included John Alden Carpenter and Charles Wakefield Cadman, who both attempted to tie their compositions to American vernacular traditions. For Carpenter, jazz presented intriguing material; Cadman drew upon the music of native Americans.

WIDENING HORIZONS

From early on, the conjunction of America's democratic principles and varied peoples had inspired imaginative artistic results. Such cross-fertilization was probably most stimulated in the 1920s by the music of African- and Asian-Americans. As composers sought new means of expression, as technological advances hastened the distribution of musical styles and as Americans passed through a period of fascination with the exotic, the American concert tradition, until then firmly ensconced in the legacy of Western Europe, began opening up to non-Western sounds and musical concepts.

Jazz was the main instigator of that fusion. Gershwin, whose *Rhapsody in Blue* (1924), *Concerto in F* (1925), *An American in Paris* (1928), Piano Preludes (1923–6) and popular songs were among the most widely embraced pieces of the period, was quoted as saying

> Jazz I regard as an American folk-music; not the only one, but a very powerful one which is probably in the blood and feeling of the American people more than any other style of folk-music. I believe that it can be made the basis of serious symphonic works of lasting value, in the hands of a composer with talent for both jazz and symphonic music.[6]

Many composers agreed and produced a stream of jazz-derived works: Carpenter's *Krazy Kat* (1921), Louis Gruenberg's *The Daniel Jazz*

(1924), Antheil's *Jazz Symphony* (1925), William Grant Still's *Levee Land* (1926) and Copland's Concerto for Piano (1926). But, curiously, some of these figures experienced jazz through the music of white composers such as Gershwin and not through the African-American musicians who originated the style. Segregation imposed potent limitations. For example, in 'Jazz Structure and Influence', a 1927 article in *Modern Music*, Copland puzzled over a definition of jazz. He identified polyrhythm as its principal trait and named only two musicians associated with the genre, Gershwin and the white novelty pianist Zez Confrey. His article showed no awareness of rising, young African-American musicians – Fletcher Henderson, Louis Armstrong, Duke Ellington – and it had a telling conclusion: 'At least one authentic small masterpiece had been inspired in Europe by America, Darius Milhaud's *La création du monde* [1923] – little known, strangely, in this country'. For many composers, Milhaud's interpolations of jazz, like Gershwin's, came to represent the music itself.

Yet in spite of racial barriers, some whites were becoming aware of African-American innovations in jazz. Perhaps most notable was the music critic, novelist and photographer Carl Van Vechten, who invited prominent black intellectuals and musicians – Langston Hughes, James Weldon Johnson, Paul Robeson, Bessie Smith, Ethel Waters – to parties at his New York apartment. Gershwin frequented those gatherings, as did the composer Colin McPhee. Van Vechten also made every effort to hear jazz in Harlem nightclubs.

Other whites chronicled developments in African-American music. The record critic R. D. Darrell started reviewing 'Hot Jazz' in 1926 in the *Phonograph Monthly Review*, the first record magazine in America. His 1932 essay on Duke Ellington, called 'Black Beauty', was the earliest recognition from within the white American concert world of that young composer's genius. *Modern Music* featured occasional articles on jazz, but not until much later did it cover the topic regularly. In 1940 Conlon Nancarrow began including swing recordings in his column 'Over the Air', and in 1943 Colin McPhee undertook 'The Torrid Zone', a jazz column signed with the pseudonym 'Mercure'.

During this period the African-American jazz community gave birth not only to brilliant improvisers but to two leading composers, Ferdinand 'Jelly Roll' Morton and Edward Kennedy 'Duke' Ellington. Both grew out of strong traditions and combined the African-derived notion of collective music-making with the European concept of an individual composer determining a piece's final shape. Morton's roots lay in the rich musical heritage of New Orleans, but his first recordings were made in Chicago in 1923. Like many of his compositions, his *Black Bottom Stomp* (first recorded by Morton's Red Hot Peppers in 1926) uses the strain form of ragtime to build a joyous, polyphonic celebration. For Duke Ellington, raised in the black community in Washington DC, fame came in 1927 when his band started playing at the Cotton Club, New York. Soon his music was broadcast across America and distributed on major record labels. Collaborating closely with members of his band, Ellington shaped works ranging from murky-toned fantasies such as *East Saint Louis Toodle-Oo* (1926) and *Mood Indigo* (1930) to dazzling virtuoso pieces such as *Old Man Blues* (1930).

This cross-cultural fertilization also affected American musical theatre. Eubie Blake and Noble Sissle's *Shuffle Along* (1921) was the first of the period's many black musicals to play before white audiences. As a result, Broadway shows increasingly absorbed African-American traits. But if one work was most responsible for joining black and white traditions and for redirecting Broadway history, it was Jerome Kern's *Show Boat* of 1927. Based on Edna Ferber's novel about life on a Mississippi entertainment steamer, it realistically portrayed a passing tradition in America and unflinchingly dealt with sensitive racial questions. *Show Boat*'s story is a tribute to the seductive power of African-American music. The styles of its tunes ranged from mellifluous operetta-based love songs ('Make Believe') to syncopated, blues-inflected numbers ('Can't Help Lovin' that Man' and 'Ol' Man River'). After hearing the show, the white critic Abbe Niles wrote in *The Bookman* (March 1928),

> As a Negro folksong addict I take disproportionate interest in Kern's experiments – I believe, his first – in jazz and thorough-going ragtime, and a special pleasure in his introduction to 'Can't Help Lovin' that Man,' which is very possibly the first genuine blues written by any white musical-comedy writer.

'Ol' Man River', which Niles praised for so genuinely conveying 'thought and suffering', achieved a kind of folktune status in America. It was principally associated with the renowned black actor and baritone Paul Robeson, who first played the role of Joe in a 1929 London production of *Show Boat* and went on to take up the part in the USA, notably in the 1936 Universal film. In later years, as Robeson mounted his controversial concert crusades for civil rights, 'Ol' Man River' became a staple in his performances.

The music of Asia also lured Americans. Trade with Asian countries, especially China and India, had a long history; the large emigration to the West Coast of Chinese in the 1870s and Japanese in the first decade of the twentieth century allowed a composer like Cowell to grow up more familiar with Asian music than with the Western concert repertory. In 1933 Cowell wrote an article in *Modern Music*, 'Towards Neo-Primitivism', that showed his zeal for non-Western traditions and made a telling prediction of their future importance: 'Now the time has come for a strong new counter-movement, full-blooded and vital; . . .

First section of 'Mood Indigo' (1930) by Duke Ellington, Irving Mills and Albany Bigard (early sheet music publication, 1931).

[Composers need] to draw on those materials common to the music of all the peoples of the world, to build a new music particularly related to our century'.

Americans discovered Asian musics through various means. Charles Tomlinson Griffes, one of the earliest to undertake such explorations, encountered Japanese and Indonesian music through two acquaintances he made in New York around 1916–17 – Michio Ito, a Japanese pantomimist who performed with Adolf Bölm's Ballet-Intime, and Eva Gauthier, a singer who had just returned from several years in Java. These contacts inspired Griffes to write *Sho-Jo* (1917), a pantomime based on Japanese themes, and *Five Poems of Ancient China and Japan* (1917), a song cycle for voice and piano. In the latter he self-consciously displayed each song's authenticity by citing the pentatonic (in one case hexatonic) scale on which it was based. Another composer attuned to Asia was Henry Eichheim who made five trips there beginning in 1915. He interpolated Asian melodies and instruments into his scores, creating atmospheric travelogues. The 'Japanese Nocturne' of *Oriental Impressions* (1918–22) used in one of its movements a *shakuhachi* melody transcribed by Eichheim. Two large orchestral works, *Java* (1929) and *Bali* (1933), included a battery of gamelan instruments.

Cowell and McPhee were probably the two composers of their generation most profoundly involved with Asian repertories. McPhee became fascinated with the sounds of the Balinese gamelan through recordings he heard in New York while struggling to succeed there as a young composer in the late 1920s. In 1931, he journeyed to the island and remained there for most of the decade. His *Tabuh-Tabuhan* (1936) pioneered integration of the sounds and compositional premises of an Asian style into a Western symphonic context. Cowell, on the other hand, did not visit the East until 1956–7. Besides early contact with Asian musics in California, he spent 1931–2 in Berlin studying with the ethnomusicologist Erich von Hornbostel and with musicians from India and Java. His *Ostinato pianissimo* (1934) was written for percussion ensemble and used the delicate layering of ostinatos that is basic to the gamelan repertory.

PERFORMANCE, PUBLICATION AND PATRONAGE

The American concert establishment was slow to recognize new music. Composers responded aggressively, determined that their works would be heard, and they banded together to create new means of disseminating them. Beginning with Varèse's International Composers' Guild (1921–7), a series of societies sprang up, devoted to promoting performances of recent pieces. They included the League of Composers (founded in 1923 and still operating), the Copland–Sessions Concerts

(1928–31), Henry Cowell's New Music Society (1925–58), Howard Hanson's American Composers' Concerts (begun in 1925) and the Pan American Association of Composers (1928–34). Each presented works by the rising young generation of American composers and also introduced the newest compositions of Stravinsky, Schoenberg and other Europeans. Although most American symphony orchestras kept a distance from the 'modernists', some conductors dared to perform the new repertory, especially Serge Koussevitzsky, with the Boston Symphony Orchestra, and Leopold Stokowski, with the Philadelphia Orchestra.

Composers also launched publishing enterprises to get their music into print. Principal among these were *New Music*, edited by Henry Cowell, which was issued quarterly from 1927 and included works by a broad selection of composers. Similarly, the Cos Cob Press was founded in 1929 by Alma Wertheim, a staunch supporter of the League of Composers. It issued scores by Sessions, Thomson, Harris and others, and was Copland's first major publisher. In 1938, it was absorbed by Arrow Music Press, another composer-initiated enterprise.

While the 1920s was a forward-looking era, heralding many major transitions in twentieth-century composition, in the realm of economic support for composers it represented the final stages of an older order. The 1930s would bring money from the federal government and the years after World War II would see the opening of universities as a haven for composers, but in the 1920s private patronage remained the dominant source of sustenance. Its most important figures were women: Mary Senior Churchill (patron of Copland and other League of Composers' figures), Elizabeth Sprague Coolidge (initiator in 1925 of a foundation at the Library of Congress devoted to the commissioning and performing of new works), Blanche Walton (supporter of composers within Cowell's orbit), Alma Morgenthau Wertheim (founder of Cos Cob Press and patron of composers in the League) and Gertrude Vanderbilt Whitney (reigning benefactor of the International Composers' Guild). Yet new forms of subsidy began to appear. The Guggenheim Foundation started giving grants in 1925. And even private industry made itself felt, albeit slightly; Copland won a cash prize in a composers' contest held by RCA Victor in 1929.

MUSIC FOR 'THE PEOPLE' (1932–45)

When Robert Cantwell's *The Land of Plenty* (1934) opened with the words 'The lights went out', it not only set the scene for the story ahead but summed up the state of the American soul in troubled times. Cantwell's novel has since become famous, partly as a chronicle of the workers' struggle but also as an example of the hard-edged realism that

THE FAIRY GODMOTHER
OF CHAMBER MUSIC

ELIZABETH SPRAGUE
COOLIDGE

Plaque in the Library of Congress, Washington, DC, depicting Elizabeth Sprague Coolidge, patron of many English and American composers.

American artists and writers turned to during the Depression. These years were to yield Edmund Wilson's *The American Jitters* (1932), Carl Sandburg's *The People, Yes* (1936), Thornton Wilder's *Our Town* (1938), John Steinbeck's *The Grapes of Wrath* (1939), the muscular factory scenes of Reginald Marsh and the bucolic farm views of Grant Wood – all products of a heightened social consciousness, an awareness that artists bore a responsibility to 'the people' as well as to themselves. In *The Dream of the Golden Mountains*, a sequel to *Exiles Return*, Malcolm Cowley described the aesthetic conversion that overtook his contemporaries as they moved into their thirties and faced grim economic prospects:

> It was as if we had been walking for years in a mist, on what seemed to be level ground, but with nothing visible within a few yards, so that we became preoccupied with the design of things close at hand – friendships, careers, love affairs – and then as if the mist had blown away to reveal that the level ground was only a terrace, that chasms lay on all sides of us, and that beyond them were mountains rising into

the golden sunlight. We could not reach the mountains alone, but perhaps we could merge ourselves in the working class and thereby help to build a bridge for ourselves and for humanity.

Building those bridges became the sustaining mission for American creative artists in the 1930s.

COMPOSERS' SOCIETIES CONTINUE

One of the most important lessons learnt from the 1920s was the advantage of banding together to pursue common goals. Such organizations as the League of Composers, the New Music Society and Hanson's American Composers' Concerts continued to serve composers' needs. They were joined, in turn, by new groups founded in response to changing issues and objectives. First among them was the Young Composers' Group, formed in early 1932 and lasting about a year, which in many respects signalled a transition from the old decade to the new. Its members were of an emerging generation, born around 1910, and included Arthur Berger, Henry Brant, Israel Citkowitz, Lehman Engel, Vivian Fine, Irwin Heilner, Bernard Herrmann, Jerome Moross and Elie Siegmeister; Copland was their informal leader. Although the group gave only one concert (in January 1933) and met sporadically, it fostered a sense of community among struggling young artists. Perhaps its greatest achievements were to challenge the force of French neo-classicism in America and to champion the music of Ives. Similarly, the Yaddo Festivals of American Music, begun during 1932 in Saratoga Springs, New York, galvanized the younger generation while also giving a forum to Copland, Harris and their contemporaries.

During the winter of 1932–3, yet another organization appeared, the Composers' Collective of New York, a group devoted to using composition as a weapon for social revolution. It was a branch of the Workers' Music League, which in turn was an arm of the American Communist Party. Like so many writers and other intellectuals of the period, a number of composers embraced communism as a hopeful ideal – and hope was rare that winter. Christmas sales were down 40% from 1929 and the unemployment rate in March, when Franklin Delano Roosevelt first took office, stood somewhere between 25% and 35%. The Collective was powerless to create jobs, but it could write music tailored for the workers' struggle. Two volumes of the Collective's workers' songs appeared in 1934 and 1935 and the group sponsored concerts at union meetings and participated in the many workers' choruses round New York. Among those active in the Collective were Lan Adomián, Blitzstein, Norman Cazden, Copland, Cowell, Irwin Heilner, Riegger, Earl Robinson, Jacob Schaeffer and

Siegmeister. By 1936, when it disbanded, its members had participated in the painful process of attempting to make their modernist style more palatable to the masses. They did not entirely succeed, but they bequeathed a significant legacy through the subsequent folksong movement and the sustained impact of their worksong style.

The largest group, however, was the Federal Music Project, formed in 1935 as part of Roosevelt's mammoth national job programme, the Works Progress Administration. While its partner organizations, the Federal Arts Project, Federal Writers' Project and Federal Theatre Project, commissioned murals, compiled oral histories and produced plays, the Federal Music Project quickly built up a national network of concert, opera, radio and dance organizations. By July 1936, the FMP had some 15,000 musicians on its payroll, most of them performers. Yet composers were not ignored. Many contributed music to productions by the FTP and in October 1935 the Composers' Forum-Laboratory was formed as part of the FMP in New York City. Soon afterwards, similar groups sprang up in Boston, Chicago, Cleveland, Detroit, Los Angeles, Milwaukee, Oklahoma City and Philadelphia. Ashley Pettis, director of the Forum in New York, declared its purpose:

> Not only are we interested in the composer and his work, *per se*, but in the development of a more definite understanding and relationship between the composer and the public . . . Above all, [the Forums] are designed for the stimulation, in direct contact with an intimate public of disinterested participants, of a strong, indigenous culture – far removed from the vitiated atmosphere which has been the realm of many composers of the day.[7]

Two other large organizations were formed during this period: the American Composers Alliance (founded in 1937) and Broadcast Music, Inc. (1939). Both grew out of the strong unionizing spirit of the day and both guarded the financial rights of composers.

EXPLORING MUSICAL AMERICA

Pettis's 1935 declaration about building links between composer and public shows how attention had turned from experimentation to audience accessibility. With this change, interest surged in discovering a greater musical America, whether through revival of works from the past or acceptance of folk music from the present. The cultural historian Warren Susman has suggested that Americans in the 1930s suddenly realized they possessed a culture distinct from Europe – that colonialism, as a psychological state, ended. He believes that this realization generated a curiosity about the country's history and fuelled a quest for uncovering national myths and heroes.[8]

American tunes and symbols infused much of the music composed from the 1930s to the end of World War II. As the composer and folksong collector Charles Seeger declared in 1939, 'The first thing, it seems to me, is for the professional composer to make up his mind that his place in world music will depend upon finding his place in American music and in American life';[9] and his contemporaries did so with patriotic zeal. Abraham Lincoln was perhaps the most celebrated hero, honoured not only in Carl Sandburg's multi-volume biography (completed in 1939) and the popular Federal Theater Project production of Robert Sherwood's *Abe Lincoln in Illinois* (1938), but in many musical scores, including Siegmeister's *Abraham Lincoln Walks at Midnight* (1937), Robinson's *Ballad for Americans* (1939), Morton Gould's *A Lincoln Legend* (1942), Copland's *A Lincoln Portrait* (1942) and Harris's *Sixth Symphony* (1944; based on excerpts from the Gettysburg Address). Similarly, common American folk were celebrated in works like Gershwin's opera *Porgy and Bess* (1935), Thomson's ballet *Filling Station* (1937) and Rodgers and Hammerstein's musical *Oklahoma!* (1943). Folktunes appeared so frequently in concert literature as to become commonplace.

Concurrently composers, performers and writers unearthed America's musical history, championing several figures, most notably Ives. Copland, Bernard Herrmann and John Kirkpatrick gave historic first performances of his music and articles appeared that mythologized Ives as a quintessential American. In 1932 Herrmann opened an article about Ives with 'The music of Charles Ives is a fundamental expression of America – the America of the transcendental period – of Emerson, Thoreau, and Whittier'.[10] That year Cowell described Ives in similarly idealized terms, writing that he had built 'from the soil up, from the fundamental spirit of the New England American folk'.[11]

Early American music was also being unearthed, especially that of William Billings and other late eighteenth-century New England psalmodists. William Arms Fisher published psalm-tune anthologies in the early 1930s and performing groups took up the music, especially Lehman Engel's Madrigal Singers (formed in 1936 as part of the FMP) and Siegmeister's American Ballad Singers (founded independently in 1939). Both groups presented early American tunes in concert halls, over the radio and on recordings. Nineteenth-century American parlour songs were also enthusiastically embraced (recorded by Siegmeister and Engel and given important attention through S. Foster Damon's *Series of Old American Songs* of 1936), as were African-American folksongs and spirituals. James Weldon Johnson's *The Book of American Negro Spirituals* (arranged by J. Rosamund Johnson) appeared in 1935 and various black singing groups, such as the Hall Johnson Choir and Juanita Hall's Negro Melody Singers, became popular in concert and on the radio.

Yet in spite of intensified interest in America's history during the 1930s, the roots of this movement lay in the previous decade. Composers' fascination with jazz and with writing music that was 'identifiably American' had taken hold then, and by the 1930s grew into a crusading cause. The same was true of folksong. The composer Daniel Gregory Mason and historian John Tasker Howard, in 1918 and 1921 respectively, published articles in the *Musical Quarterly* on American folksong, trying to unravel what it was and what meaning it might have for concert-music composers. Several especially influential folksong anthologies appeared, including John A. Lomax's *Cowboy Songs and Other Frontier Ballads* (1910), Cecil Sharp's *American-English Folk-Songs* (1918) and Carl Sandburg's *American Songbag* (1927) – this last, with piano accompaniments added by local Chicago composers including Leo Sowerby and Ruth Crawford. And in 1928 the Archive of Folksong opened at the Library of Congress.

By the 1930s and early 40s, improvements in equipment made field recordings more easily attainable, and collectors travelled the back roads of America gathering songs. Prominent among them were John Lomax and his son Alan, Sidney Robertson (who was later to marry Henry Cowell) and Charles Seeger. These collectors added vast stores to the Archive of Folksong and published anthologies, among them the Lomaxes' *American Ballads and Folksongs* (1934) and *Folksong U.S.A.* (1947), the latter featuring accompaniments by Charles and Ruth Crawford Seeger. Folk musicians such as Leadbelly and Aunt Molly Jackson became heroes to New York composers eager to make contact with 'the people'. And Woody Guthrie began his career as an itinerant bard, writing tunes that captured both the poverty and pleasures of the working class.

POPULISM AND TECHNOLOGY JOIN FORCES

In late 1933 the American Society of Composers, Authors, and Publishers, a nearly twenty-year-old licensing and protection agency, released a slim volume, *Nothing Can Replace Music*, which showed the degree to which the rapid spread of radio threatened musicians. It included articles with such titles as 'Mechanization Presents Serious Danger to the Musical Art' and 'Starving Composers', and the word 'murder' appeared seven times in the table of contents. Radio and films were overturning the musical status quo.

Radio offered Americans affordable entertainment in the 1930s. Small-town residents in the Midwest, South or Far West, who previously would have heard music through local performers or travelling members of the chautauqua or vaudeville circuits, now had access to all kinds of styles and performers. Country, jazz and folk music shared the air waves with operas and symphonies, and many performers, notably Bing Crosby and Rudy Vallee, advanced their careers through the medium. A number of long-standing radio traditions started during this period. In 1930 CBS began weekly broadcasts of the New York Philharmonic Orchestra; in 1931 the Metropolitan Opera started its weekly broadcasts; in 1937 the NBC Symphony Orchestra was established for America's reigning *maestro*, Arturo Toscanini; and in 1939 NBC began airing the Grand Ole Opry, a weekly show that had begun regionally (in Nashville, Tennessee) in 1925.

Many of these series were geared to historic European classics or contemporary folk and popular idioms, but radio did not ignore the American composer. Cowell and others introduced new-music series on radio and the major networks timidly attempted a few contests and commissions of American compositions. In 1932 an NBC jury chose works by Nicolai Berezowsky, Carl Eppert, Florence Galajikian, Philip James and Max Wald out of a pool of nearly 600 contestants; the prize included cash and a chance to be conducted on radio by Eugene Goossens. And in 1936–7 CBS commissioned works from Copland, Harris, Hanson, Piston and Still. Gruenberg's *Green Mansions* and Blitzstein's *I've Got the Tune* were written for radio in 1937 and Earl Robinson's *Ballad for Americans*, perhaps the best-known composition of the period, received its première on CBS radio in 1939.

For Bernard Herrmann, a graduate of the Young Composers' Group, work in radio led to a career in Hollywood. Herrmann conducted the CBS Symphony Orchestra in important radio premières of new American works and wrote scores for radio drama, most notably productions by Orson Welles. When Herrmann composed the music for Welles's film *Citizen Kane* in 1941, he entered a profession relatively new to the American composer and treated film composition as a subtly sophisticated, yet broadly accessible, art form.

The first sound film had been produced in 1927, and throughout the 1930s and early 40s a number of American composers worked in the medium. For a time there was high hope that film might present composers with a vital new means of income and creative expression. George Antheil, Robert Russell Bennett, David Raksin, Ernst Toch and Franz Waxman moved to Hollywood and Copland wrote scores for film versions of *Our Town* and *Of Mice and Men* (both 1940). Composers also contributed to major documentaries, Thomson to *The Plow That Broke the Plains* and *The River* (directed by Pare Lorentz in 1936 and 1937 respectively), Copland to *The City* (directed by Willard Van Dyke in 1940) and Blitzstein to *Valley Town* (Van Dyke, 1940).

Finally, beginning with *42nd Street* (1933), Hollywood produced films of many musicals, including some of the major shows of Arlen, Berlin, Gershwin, Kern and Porter. Of the many beloved stars involved, perhaps the most mesmerizing was Fred Astaire, whose lithe elegance turned tap and ballroom dancing into artistic enchantment.

Meanwhile, phonograph records, which had showed so much promise in the 1920s, went through rough times in the early 30s. Because of growing interest in radio and general economic malaise, record sales fell from 104 million discs in 1927 to six million in 1932. By the later 1930s, as record companies promoted such popular swing bands as those of Count Basie, Duke Ellington and Benny Goodman, and began to sign on American symphony orchestras, the tide reversed. Record sales for 1938 reached 33 million and by 1941 they were up to 127 million. Partly because of these rocky conditions, contemporary American concert music was slow to be recorded. In 1934 Cowell established the New Music Quarterly Recordings, devoted to recent works, and the previous year Columbia released a recording of Roy Harris's Concerto for Piano, Clarinet and String Quartet, which Irving Kolodin heralded in *Modern Music* as 'the first American work of a serious character to be made available in recorded form'.[12] (By 'American' he seems to have meant 'American concert-music composers born about 1900', since older figures and Gershwin had already been recorded.) Within the next couple of years, recordings of works by Harris, Griffes and Copland were commercially released.

COMPOSERS AND COMPOSITIONS

While leading composers in the 1920s tended to be 'neo-classicists' or 'experimentalists', their work from the early 1930s until the end of World War II did not fall so readily into distinct stylistic schools. Some, such as Sessions and Piston, held tight to their abstract or international goals; others, such as Harry Partch, retained a freewheeling spirit of adventure. Most, however, sought to make their music more accessible. For a few years composers adapted their style to popular taste and took seriously the question of how an artist might serve a democratic society.

Copland's career is a case in point. After his neo-classical Piano Variations (1930), discussed above, he wrote the *Short Symphony* (1932–3) and *Statements* (1932–5) which retained the dissonant, hard edges of his early style. By the mid-1930s those edges started to soften as Copland became a major force behind the 'music for the people' movement. He wrote *El salón México* (1933–6), a tuneful work of wide appeal, then *The Second Hurricane* (1936), which not only communicated to the masses but could be performed by them, in this case by schoolchildren. After scores for radio, film and dance, Copland composed for Martha Graham the ballet *Appalachian Spring* (1943–4), one of his most famous works from the period. Yet in spite of its conservative harmonic idiom and interpolation of the Shaker song 'Simple Gifts', *Appalachian Spring*, like all Copland's music, retained a strong connection with his early style. In seeking accessibility, he did not compromise his personal voice or return to the language of a distant era; rather he reconciled his modernist idiom with the listening potential of an average audience. Throughout *Appalachian Spring* Copland cunningly manipulates register, as in earlier works, and heightens its effect with transparent orchestration in which instruments are exploited in unexpected combinations and ranges. Similarly, rhythmic complexities are presented so as to be inviting rather than intimidating. The score is lean, infectious and remarkably well crafted.

Other compositional landmarks of the 1930s included Still's *Afro-American Symphony* (1930), the first black American work performed by a major orchestra (the Rochester Philharmonic Orchestra gave its première in 1931, followed by a New York Philharmonic performance in 1935); Thomson's *Four Saints in Three Acts* (written in 1928 and first heard in 1934), which made a dada-esque crazy quilt out of American hymnody; Gershwin's 'folk opera' *Porgy and Bess* (1935), which paid homage to the European operatic tradition while reinterpreting American vernacular idioms; Blitzstein's *The Cradle Will Rock* (1936–7), another significant stage achievement in which the language of Tin Pan Alley combined with that of neo-classicism to deliver an angry social outcry; and Roy Harris's Third Symphony (1938), which has an expansive, almost grandiloquent profile, with a shrewd couching of dissonance so that it sounds familiar.

During the 1930s, a new generation also emerged. In addition to members of the Young Composers' Group, it included such conservative figures as Samuel Barber, David Diamond, Gian Carlo Menotti, William Schuman and Robert Ward, and also vanguard leaders like John Cage and Lou Harrison. By the end of World War II, two strains of American composers seemed established: neo-Romantics, writing tonal music of wide popular appeal, and experimenters, reviving and continuing the adventurous spirit of the 1920s.

CANADA, 1918–1945

Although a younger country than the USA, Canada experienced many of the same transitions during the years between the two world wars. The period began with increased urbanization and immigration and felt the depravity of the Depression. Similarly, the growth of technology, especially through radio, was as strong and far-reaching as in the USA. Timothy McGee, one of the chroniclers of music in Canada, credits radio with being 'the first truly nationwide cultural unifying agent in the history of Canadian music'. Broadcasting began there in 1919, and by 1926 the country had 40 stations. Nationwide broadcasts started in 1927 and the Canadian Broadcasting Corporation was founded in 1936. This made it possible for music to be disseminated across the continent, often by native performers like the soprano Eva Gauthier, the Hart House String Quartet and the Toronto Symphony Orchestra.

Many Canadian orchestras were founded, including the Toronto Symphony Orchestra (1923), the Calgary Symphony (1928), the Vancouver Symphony (1931) and the Montreal Symphony Orchestra (1934), and increasing attention was paid to identifying and fostering a national musical idiom. In Quebec City there were two festivals of Canadian folk arts (1927 and 1928), jointly sponsored by the National Museum of Canada and the Canadian Pacific Railway. Included were compositions, based on Canadian folksongs, by Claude Champagne, Ernest MacMillan, Alfred E. Whitehead and Healey Willan.

Two of these figures received the widest recognition, and each had strong ties to the culture of his part of the country. Champagne was born in Montreal, made his career there and studied in France, where he was influenced by composers ranging from Debussy to d'Indy; among his important works are *Suite canadienne* (1927), *Danse villageoise* (1929) and *Berceuse* (1933). By contrast, Willan of Toronto represented the British presence in Canada and was highly regarded as a composer, organist, choral conductor and teacher. Many of his pieces were staples in the Protestant church repertory; his choral works include *Rise Up, my Love, my Fair One* (1929), *Behold the Tabernacle of God* (1933) and *Hodie Christus natus est* (1935).

Another leading composer was Sir Ernest MacMillan, who was born in Ontario and made his career in Toronto. From 1931 he conducted the Toronto Symphony and in 1942 he assumed directorship of the Mendelssohn Choir. A prominent teacher, MacMillan also compiled an anthology of folksongs (*A Canadian Song Book*, 1929).

By the end of World War II both the USA and Canada had made peace with their musical identities. Connection to the European concert tradition remained strong, but artistic autonomy had been achieved and composers' palettes had broadened enormously. This hard-earned cultural self-assurance would serve them well in the years ahead.

NOTES

[1] E. Varèse, 'Freedom for Music', lecture at the University of Southern California in Los Angeles, 1939; repr. in *The American Composer Speaks*, ed. G. Chase (Baton Rouge, 1966), 191.

[2] See R. Sanjek, *From Print to Plastic: Publishing and Promoting America's Popular Music (1900–1980)* (Brooklyn, 1983).

[3] A. Copland and V. Perlis, *Copland: 1900 through 1942* (New York, 1984), 120.

[4] J. Cage, 'Virgil Thomson: his Music', in J. Cage and K. Hoover, *Virgil Thomson: his Life and Music* (New York, 1959), 154–5.

[5] A. Copland, *Music and Imagination* (Cambridge, Mass., 1952), 104.

[6] G. Gershwin, 'The Relation of Jazz to American Music' ('as set down by Henry Cowell'), in

American Composers on American Music: a Symposium, ed. H. Cowell (New York, 1933), 187.

[7] A. Pettis, 'Opening Address', New York City Composers' Forum-Laboratory (30 Oct 1935), WPA Composers' Forum Transcripts, National Archives; quoted in B. A. Zuck, *A History of Musical Americanism* (Ann Arbor, 1980), 171–2.

[8] W. Susman, Introduction to *Culture and Commitment, 1929–1945* (New York, 1973).

[9] C. Seeger, 'Grass Roots for American Composers', *Modern Music*, xvi/3 (1939), 147.

[10] B. Herrmann, 'Charles Ives', *Trend*, i/3 (1932), 99.

[11] H. Cowell, 'American Composers, IX: Charles Ives', *Modern Music*, x/3 (1932), 30.

[12] I. Kolodin, 'American Composers and the Phonograph', *Modern Music*, xi/3 (1934), 128–33.

BIBLIOGRAPHICAL NOTE

Historical-political background

Although the literature on this period is voluminous, the following general histories might be singled out both for their content and their bibliographies: C. C. Alexander, *Nationalism in American Thought, 1930–1945* (Chicago, 1969); R. H. Pells, *Radical Visions and American Dreams* (New York, 1973); G. Perrett, *America in the Twenties: a History* (New York, 1982); and A. M. Schlesinger jr, *The Age of Roosevelt: the Crisis of the Old Order 1919–1933* (Cambridge, Mass., 1957). For an imaginative interpretation of American popular culture during the Depression, see W. I. Susman, *Culture and Commitment: 1929–1945* (New York, 1973).

Literature and the visual arts

Developments in the American literary community, told against a background of cultural and political issues, have been beautifully chronicled in two first-hand accounts by M. Cowley: *Exiles Return: a Literary Odyssey of the 1920s* (New York, 1934, 2/ 1951), and *The Dream of the Golden Mountains: Remembering the 1930s* (New York, 1980). Other important eyewitness accounts include E. Wilson, *The Shores of Light: a Literary Chronicle of the Twenties and Thirties* (New York, 1952), and F. L. Allen, *Only Yesterday: an Informal History of the 1920s* (New York, 1931). Two anthologies of politically inspired literature are *Proletarian Literature in the United States: an Anthology*, ed. G. Hicks (New York, 1935), and *New Masses: an Anthology of the Rebel Thirties*, ed. J. North (New York, 1969). For an excellent survey of literature, with a detailed bibliography, see F. Hoffman's *The Twenties: American Writing in the Postwar Decade* (New York, 1949, 2/ 1962).

For the visual arts, M. Brown's *American Painting from the Armory Show to the Depression* (Princeton, 1955) has become a classic. Two other useful surveys are A. A. Davison, *Early American Modernist Painting 1910–1935* (New York, 1981), and R. G. Wilson, D. H. Pilgrim and D. Tashjian, *The Machine Age in America 1918–1941* (Brooklyn, 1986).

Music

The journal *Modern Music*, published by the League of Composers between 1924 and 1946, provides the most informative view of developments in concert music. Other valuable primary accounts of the period include A. Copland, *The New Music: 1900–1960* (New York, 1968); *American Composers on American Music: a Symposium*, ed. H. Cowell (Palo Alto, 1933); M. Lederman, *The Life and Death of a Small Magazine ('Modern Music', 1924–1946)* (Brooklyn, 1983); P. Rosenfeld, *An Hour with American Music* (London, 1929); V. Thomson, *Virgil Thomson* (New York, 1966); and L. Varèse, *Varèse: a Looking-Glass Diary, i: 1883–1928* (New York, 1972). For historical surveys see especially R. Mead,

Modern Times

Henry Cowell's New Music 1925–1936: the Society, the Music Editions, and the Recordings (Ann Arbor, 1981), and B. Zuck, *A History of Musical Americanism* (Ann Arbor, 1980). Valuable insights and analyses can be found in D. Nicholls, *American Experimental Music, 1890–1940* (Cambridge, MA, 1990). For jazz and popular song, see G. Schuller, *Early Jazz: its Roots and Musical Development* (New York, 1968), and A. Wilder, *American Popular Song: the Great Innovators, 1900–1950* (New York, 1972). The birth of the folk-music movement during the 1930s is discussed in R. S. Denisoff, *Great Day Coming* (Urbana, 1971) and R. Lieberman, *'My Song is My Weapon': People's Songs, American Communism, and the Politics of Culture, 1930–50* (Urbana, 1989).

Chapter XI

The Hispanic World, 1918–45

GERARD BÉHAGUE

The Hispanic world is here understood as comprising primarily Spain and Portugal and the Latin American and Caribbean nations, rather than the entire Spanish- and Portuguese-speaking world. As musical developments in the two areas during the period under consideration were quite independent, they are treated separately. In both, this was a period of experiment and national assertion, with great achievements in art music as well as popular music. In retrospect it was also a period of inward development, with Spain and Portugal relatively isolated from the other western European countries and with little relationship between the musical institutions and personalities in the Latin American and Caribbean countries.

LATIN AMERICA AND THE CARIBBEAN

In Latin American arts the period between the two world wars saw an affirmation of a newly conceived cultural nationalism, experiment with new techniques and aesthetics and a new socio-political consciousness affecting especially the notions of class and race. As in the political and economic arena, this period also represented the era of modernization. Unlike the previous century, in which musical activity continued to reflect European practices and tastes, there was a gradual independence from Europe among some of the most creative composers, resulting in a diversity of trends and styles. Musical nationalism in a Romantic and non-Romantic vein was the motivating force of numerous composers from the 1920s to the 40s. In the 1920s especially, 'national' art tended to mean non-imitative, hence more consequential, art. In spite of the dominance of nationalism, composers turned to other styles, among them post-Romanticism, neo-Romanticism, impressionism, neo-classicism, expressionism, dodecaphony, serialism and experimentalism. In many cases, however, these styles were adopted more for their techniques than their aesthetic approaches, and they did not conflict with a fundamentally nationalist stance. Thus, in their individual search for identity, Latin American composers together represent a wide eclecticism.

THE RISE AND DEVELOPMENT OF NATIONALISM

Mexico, Central America and the Caribbean

It has often been said that the Mexican Revolution was the only truly popular revolution that Latin America witnessed during the twentieth century. Indeed no revolution there had as strong and lasting an impact on a country's socio-cultural outlook as the 1910 revolution had on Mexico. The post-revolutionary period (c1920–34) was not only an era of reconstruction but one of cultural identity on the part of Mexican intellectuals and artists: it saw the emergence of the 'Aztec renaissance' and a consequent Indianist movement in Mexican arts. Besides nationalism and pre-Columbian culture, popular artistic themes were strongly socio-political, such as the recognition of the modern peasant class and its dignity, anti-clericalism, communal effort and the triumph of marxist socialism over capitalism. Visual artists (especially the famous muralists of the 1920s and 30s) and composers symbolized the revolution's aspirations and spirit of change. In an assumed return to pre-conquest Indian musical practices, authenticity mattered less than a subjective evocation of the remote past or of the character and physical setting of ancient (and, indirectly, contemporary) Indian culture.[1]

Among the composers associated with this renaissance, Carlos Chávez (1899–1978) was the most influential from the 1920s to the 50s, being both theorist and the most accomplished practitioner of the nationalist movement. He was not exclusively nationalist: Mexican influence began the ballet *El fuego nuevo* (1921), attained its peak in the 1930s and reappeared only sporadically thereafter. Both in his works of Indianist inspiration and his most abstract compositions (such as the last three symphonies) his highly personal style and Mexican sense are so intimately connected that his music was characterized as 'profoundly non-European' by his lifelong friend Aaron Copland.[2] This non-European character resulted from the exoticism of Chávez's Indianist works. The Aztec ballets *El fuego nuevo* and *Los cuatro soles* (1925) or the later *Xochipilli-Macuilxóchitl* (1940), for example, are not popular works in their appeal or in utilizing indigenous material for local colour. Most such works combine modernistic and 'primitive' elements in an austere but unique style. Chávez studied early pre-Columbian musical instruments and the colonial documentation concerning Aztec music in the sixteenth century and incorporated the results in his music evocative of Aztec culture; but his attempts at reconstructing pre-conquest Indian music ultimately constituted a pretext for writing music of a new character – all of it in line with the prevailing nationalist ideology.

Chávez's attitude towards musical nationalism was resourceful and

Tzeltal [Tzotzil] Indians playing a diatonic marimba in three sections, early 1900s.

sophisticated.[3] His concern was to incorporate the essence of folk elements through the use of melodic, harmonic or rhythmic formulae that could confer a distinctively national flavour. Like many other nationalist composers, he came to believe that art must be national in character but universal in concept and must reach most of the people.[4] The most popular folk tradition in Mexico is that of the mestizos, to which Chávez paid attention in later works; but he never used national mestizo dance music in the type of arrangements such as the well-known *Sones de Mariachi* of Blas Galindo or *Huapango* of José Pablo Moncayo, both students of Chávez at the Mexico City Conservatory. Despite the difficulty of apprehension by the majority of listeners, his modern, abstract style lent itself quite well to his subjective and speculative reconstruction of pre-Columbian Indian music. Chávez also exploited timbre, using replicas of ancient instruments like the *teponaztli* (a slit-drum, a sort of two-key xylophone) or *huehuetl* (upright, cylindrical single-headed drum), as in *Xochipilli* and the *Sinfonía india* (1935). Chávez experimented with new ideas and techniques, numerous later works being neo-classical (see p.243). Some of the most significant are the series of *Soli*, composed mainly in the 1960s; written for various chamber music groups with or without orchestra, they show Chávez's concern with clarity, terseness and timbre, being a 'continuous unfolding of successively new musical ideas, the element of renewal rather than repetition'.[5] This principle results in the unusual impression of the music never reaching a terminal point.

The other Mexican composer with an international reputation was

Silvestre Revueltas (1899–1940), whose music represented a genuinely Mexican musical expression within a modernist style. His approach to nationalism was more spontaneous and of immediate appeal than Chávez's. Most of Revueltas's works date from the last ten years of his life and include orchestral pieces, such as *Cuauhnahuac* (1930), *Janitzio* (1933) and the much-performed *Sensemayá* (1938), in addition to several chamber music works, among them *8 x Radio* (*Ocho por radio*) (1933). *Sensemayá*, especially, reveals the assimilation of the strongly primitivistic and modernistic; based on the verses of the Afro-Cuban poet Nicolás Guillén, it is notable for its rhythmic ostinatos, polyrhythmic, highly dissonant harmony and daring orchestration.[6] In contrast, *Janitzio* (his contribution to 'national tourism', as he called it, with his characteristic humour) typifies Revueltas's melodic style, almost entirely reflective of folk models, which led a number of Mexican scholars to refer to his music as being representative of 'mestizo realism' – the most candid expression of the popular culture of contemporary Mexico.[7]

Under North American tutelage as a protectorate (1901–34), Cuba developed a strong nationalist objection to the American presence, especially in the 1920s. The need to express a national identity was understood by all intellectuals and artists but at first there was no consensus as to how to achieve it. Eduardo Sánchez de Fuentes (1874–1944), for example, turned to subjective evocations of Caribbean Indian music[8] in his operas based on Italian *verismo*, though he was familiar with the most typical popular musical genres, as his *habaneras* bear witness. With the establishment in 1923 of the 'Grupo Minorista' in Havana, however, Afro-Cuban culture came to the fore in Cuban arts. This group included young revolutionary poets, artists and musicians who cultivated in different ways *afrocubanismo*. The studies of Fernando Ortiz, Cuba's foremost ethnologist and ethnomusicologist, were influential in the rediscovery of Afro-Cuban Music, which became the most common source of nationalism in Cuba. In spite of the segregation of black people, the lateness of the abolition of slavery (1886) and the persecution of Afro-Cuban religious groups by local authorities, Afro-Cuban music penetrated Cuban popular music and was essential in the development of the most characteristically national music.

The two most outstanding Cuban nationalists were Amadeo Roldán (1900–39) and Alejandro García Caturla (1906–40), who brought art music to an unprecedented level.[9] In addition to their deep knowledge of Cuban folk and popular music, both were attuned to some of the most contemporary techniques of composition. Roldán's *Obertura sobre temas cubanos*, for example, given its première in 1925, was the first major symphonic work based on Afro-Cuban sources, including instruments, integrated into a modernist style. His most celebrated work, the ballet

La rebambaramba, based on a story by Alejo Carpentier, was inspired by the music of the traditional Afro-Cuban religious groups of the Lucumi and Abakuá integrated within complex and advanced harmonic and orchestral writing. García Caturla was first influenced by the styles and aesthetics of Satie (to whose memory he dedicated his 1927 piano *Preludio corto no.1*), Milhaud and Stravinsky, and also embraced Impressionism and neo-classicism. Dissonant superimpositions appear frequently in his *Tres danzas cubanas* for orchestra (1927) and polytonal passages are a feature of his piano pieces of the late 1920s and early 30s, for example *Comparsa* (1930). García Caturla and Roldán were among the six most performed composers in the concerts organized by the Pan American Association of Composers, which, founded by two of the most eminent avant-garde composers of the period, Edgard Varèse and Henry Cowell, lasted from 1928 to 1934.[10]

The most notable creative personality in Central America was the Panamanian composer and conductor Roque Cordero (*b* 1917). International recognition came later, but his works of the late 1930s and early 1940s reflect nationalist concerns, expressed especially through rhythmic elements of folk dance music. Among these early works is the *Sonatina rítmica* (1943), the first and third movements of which rely on typical accompanimental rhythmic patterns of the *mejorana*, one of Panama's most characteristic folk idioms.

Venezuela and the Andean nations

Just as Venezuela did not come out of the nineteenth century socio-politically until the early 1930s, its musical activities did not fully embrace the twentieth century until musical professionalism became possible with more political and economic stability. Institutions that supported the musical life of Caracas, the capital, included the Orquesta Sinfónica Venezuela (founded in 1930), the choral association Orfeón Lamas and the Escuela Nacional de Música. The strongest force behind these organizations was the composer and conductor Vicente Emilio Sojo (1887–1974), who for almost twenty years conducted the National Symphony Orchestra and taught a large number of composers at the school. He wrote primarily sacred pieces, especially for his choral group, but did not neglect a national style of music in his songs and chamber music. He collected and harmonized over 400 folksongs and dances of Venezuela, the first albums of which were published in the early 1940s.

The composer who gained the most prominent nationalist position, however, was Juan Bautista Plaza (1898–1965), who, as *maestro de capilla* of Caracas Cathedral, wrote much religious music. He was professor of composition and music history at the National School of Caracas and collaborated in the organization of the Venezuelan Association of Concerts, over which he presided for several years. As a composer he cultivated an imaginative national style, as in his *Siete canciones venezolanas* for soprano and piano, clearly related to the popular tradition of songs and dances. Plaza's *Fuga criolla* (1932), for string orchestra, illustrates his skills in combining effectively fugal counterpoint with rhythmic patterns of the *joropo* folkdance.

In spite of regional differences, there was a cultural homogeneity among nationalist composers of the Andean countries because they relied to a great extent on the Amerindian musical traditions in the former Inca area, which have numerous common traits, from Colombia to Chile.[11] Pre-Columbian Indian instruments, such as vertical flutes, clay and reed panpipes, trumpets and drums of various sizes are still used in folk music. Mestizo folk music exhibits considerable diversity in the different countries as a result of ethnic and historical factors. Colombia, for example, is an Andean country, but the music of its Pacific and Atlantic coastal areas is rooted in predominantly black and Caribbean cultures. Black cultural heritage is also evident in Ecuador's and Peru's coastal regions. Mestizo folk music of the entire area is largely Spanish in origin. Thus the nationalistic production of Andean art-music composers reflects in varying degrees the traits of vernacular music.

Composers associated with the Bogotá National Conservatory during the 1920s and early 30s included Guillermo Uribe-Holguín (1880–1971), the most influential musician of his generation in Colombia. He was director of the conservatory for 25 years (1910–35) and organizer and conductor of the concerts of the Sociedad de Conciertos Sinfónicos del Conservatorio. Trained in Paris under Vincent d'Indy, he combined aspects of impressionist styles with elements of folk and popular music. His 300 piano pieces known as *Trozos en el sentimiento popular*, for example, written over a long period, derive their melodic, rhythmic and formal traits from such folkdances as the *pasillo* and the *bambuco*, though none is based on specific folk or popular themes. Also active in the 1930s and 40s was Antonio María Valencia (1902–52), a student of d'Indy and Manuel de Falla in Europe, who cultivated a 'criollo' style in his first compositions.

In Peru, Ecuador and Bolivia, *indigenismo* developed in the 1920s and had lasting influence. *Indigenismo*, the equivalent of the Aztec renaissance in Mexico, was first cultivated by Andean poets, novelists and playwrights who considered the Indian cultural heritage, especially the Incaic past, the most distinctive aspect of their society.[12] Their treatment of that heritage was not meant to be 'authentic' in ethnographic terms; similarly, composers who began to pay serious attention to Indian music did so without regard for accurate sound reproduction. Rather, they intended to express an aesthetic fundamentally alien to them.

In Peru this was well represented by the works of José María Valle

Riestra (1869–1925), whose *Ollanta* was an ambitious attempt to create a national opera at the beginning of the century. The Indianist trend is found in varying degrees in the works of several folklorist-composers, such as Daniel Alomía Robles (1871–1942) and Manuel Aguirre (1863–1951). The most prolific and creative nationalist composer was Teodoro Valcárcel (1900–42), who quickly became interested in treating indigenous folk music in a modern style. His ballet *Suray-Surita* illustrates the idealization of Indian music though Valcárcel had a genuine understanding of Indian ritual songs and dances and mestizo genres. His stylization of Indian music was imaginative and his attempt to express the melancholy of the Indian sentiment was sincere, for example in his 30 *Cantos de alma vernacular* and the *Cuatro canciones incaicas* (published in Paris, 1930). Among the latter the song 'Suray-Surita', with a text in both Quechua and Spanish, is considered the epitome of Indianist expressiveness, in its pentatonic melodies with embellishments reminiscent of *quena* (pre-Colombian vertical flute) performance and cadences.

The most influential teachers and composers of European origin in Peru were Andrés Sas (1900–67) and Rodolfo Holzmann (*b* 1910). Sas settled in Lima in 1924 and founded the Sas-Rosay Academy of Music in 1930. As a composer and musicologist he had a special interest in Peruvian indigenous music and studied colonial cathedral music. Such works as *Tres estampas del Perú* (1936), *Poema indio* (1941) for orchestra and the choral triptych *Ollantai* (1949) attempt a synthesis of impressionist techniques with Indian-like thematic ideas. Holzmann moved to Peru in 1938 and began writing in a 'Peruvian' manner about 1940, though he cannot be considered a typical nationalist composer since he felt great affinity for contemporary European trends (see p.245). Most of the melodic material of the *Suite sobre motivos peruanos* or *Cuarta pequeña suite* for piano, for example, is based on pentatonicism and on harmonies associated with 1930s neo-tonality.[13] It is understandable that these foreign-born composers should turn to the musical culture of their adopted country but their approach to it is arbitrary.

In Bolivia, although the traditional music of both Quechua and Aymara Indians can be found in varying degree of acculturation or *mestizaje*, most composers limited themselves to cultivating a national style that amounted to a Romantic stylization of folk elements. Among these composers are Eduardo Caba (1890–1953), Simeón Roncal (1870–1953) and Humberto Viscarra Monje (*b* 1898). Caba imitated some of the styles of Indian music of the high Bolivian plateau, as in his ballet *Kollana* and his piano pieces *Aires indios*. Roncal and Viscarra Monje, on the other hand, drew from the *criolla* folk tradition, the first especially from the *cueca*, the country's national dance, within a Romantic and academic orientation. Professionalism was enhanced by the activity of José María Velasco Maidana (*b* 1900), the leading national figure in the 1930s and 40s, who wrote many orchestral and chamber works evocative of Aymara-Quechua music.

In Chile few composers felt much affinity with local folk and popular traditions.[14] Pedro Humberto Allende (1885–1949) was the pioneer nationalist, as revealed in his tone poem *La voz de las calles* (1919–20), based on street cries, and in his twelve *Tonadas de carácter popular chileno* (1918–22) for piano. Indianism in Chile was followed most notably by Carlos Lavín (1883–1962) and Carlos Isamitt (1885–1974), who were also ethnomusicologists and whose experience with Indian music was reflected in some of their works from the 1920s to 40s. Indigenous sources, however, were viewed by most Chilean composers as artificial and restrictive. This attitude resulted most probably from the fact that Indians formed a tiny, isolated minority of the population and the mestizo culture was not as pronounced as in the other Andean nations.

Brazil and the River Plate area

The 1920s to 40s in Brazil, Uruguay and Argentina saw the emergence of composers who produced mature works of nationalist content and international significance. Several factors contributed to this, such as the existence of a dynamic and varied popular and folk culture allowing a wide range of national expressions and talented composers who had first-hand exposure to folk and popular music. Concert associations, orchestras and ballet groups, and governmental support, greatly facilitated this development. The strongly nationalist political ideology, especially with the dictatorships of Getulio Vargas in Brazil and Juan Perón in Argentina, also encouraged nationalistic trends in the arts. This was the period of a substantial increase in the leisure class of performers and consumers. Urban growth was very rapid in both Brazil and Argentina, the latter becoming about 60% urban by 1933. With this growth came more poverty, but also more consumers of various types of music, especially middle-class consumers. Sociopolitically and artistically, the main order of the 1940s in Brazil and Argentina was national integration and modernization.

In Brazil, the figure who most represented modernization and nationalism was Heitor Villa-Lobos (1887–1959). By the early 1920s he had already written some of his most adventurous works – the ballets *Amazonas* and *Uirapuru*, several string quartets and symphonies and the nine piano pieces that make up the series *A Prole do Bebê* no.2. He had acquired a reputation as the 'enfant terrible' of Brazilian music, which is partly why he was invited to participate in the 'Week of Modern Art' in 1922. This event, sponsored primarily by leading literary figures from São Paulo, launched the modernist movement, calling for adherence to twentieth-century ideologies and techniques while valuing national subject matter. Villa-Lobos did not write a work for the event but several of his chamber works were performed, an indication that he believed he had already adopted modernist aesthetics and techniques. By 1922 he had repeatedly proclaimed the national basis of his music and had contributed more than any other composer to the establishment of a strongly national creative consciousness.[15]

Under the strong stimulation of his Parisian experiences, the 1920s were a period of experiment, culminating in the series of works known as *Choros*, with which he established an international reputation. Based on an evocation of the popular serenading and dance music (*choro*) of strolling musicians (*chorões* – 'weepers') of Rio de Janeiro, the *choros* include sixteen works for different media, from solo guitar (no.1), solo piano (no.5), to chamber groupings and large orchestra, to two orchestras and band, or orchestra with chorus. Although they are not unified stylistically, they all communicate in a uniquely pictorial way the tropical, exotic nature of Brazilian music. No. 5 is subtitled 'Alma brasileira' ('Brazilian soul') in recognition of the talent and influence of the popular composer and pianist Ernesto Nazareth whose music embodied for Villa-Lobos the very essence of that soul. No.10, subtitled 'Rasga o coração' ('Rend my heart'), for large orchestra and chorus, is a fine example of Villa-Lobos's mature nationalist style. It also consolidates some of Villa-Lobos's typical practices, such as polytonality, tone clusters and complex polyrhythmic passages. It was indeed the prototype of 'modernist' music.

Villa-Lobos's nine compositions bearing the title *Bachianas brasileiras*, written from 1930 to 1945, are, with the *Choros*, the best-known and most significant of his works. Although intended as homage to J. S. Bach, whose music Villa-Lobos considered 'a universal folkloric source, rich and profound . . . intermediary between all peoples',[16] they are not stylized renditions of Bach's music but an attempt to apply certain Baroque procedures to Brazilian music. Villa-Lobos perceived intuitively clear affinities between certain contrapuntal textures and rhythmic procedures in Bach and those of certain genres of Brazilian folk and popular music. The *Bachianas* are suites in the Baroque sense of a sequence of dance movements. Almost all movements bear a dual title, one generic ('prelude', 'introduction', 'aria' etc), the other with a nationalistic reference ('embolada', 'modinha', 'ponteio', etc). These works tend to be strongly tonal, so they are less 'modern' than the *Choros*. The essentially vocal quality of most of Villa-Lobos's melodies is best demonstrated by the long, cantabile theme of the 'Aria' ('Cantilena') of *Bachianas* no.5 for soprano and an ensemble of eight cellos. Its lyricism is at once reminiscent of Puccini and of the nineteenth-century *modinha*. The improvisatory character of this wide phrase, created by its never-ending quality, derives from the popular serenading love song. The *chorões* atmosphere also reappears in the treatment of the cello ensemble accompaniment, with pizzicatos suggesting the picked style of guitar playing known in Brazil as 'ponteio'. Some people have considered the *Bachianas* a reflection of the neo-classicism that had become so fashionable in the 1930s and 40s. Villa-Lobos was not attuned to the ideals of neo-classicism, but it is probably the succesful combination of nationalism and neo-classicism that leant the *Bachianas* universal acceptance. Villa-Lobos's rejection of traditional academic training and his sense of independence were among the most important factors of his legacy to the music of Brazil, particularly its gradual de-colonization in relation to Europe. His example led later generations of Brazilian composers to think and to create for themselves.

Among the many composers who followed the nationalist trend, Francisco Mignone (1897–1987) and Camargo Guarnieri (*b* 1907) are pre-eminent. Mignone was attracted to the ideals of musical national- ism as eloquently set out by Mário de Andrade, and about 1929 he entered a period of intense creativity. This period, extending to about 1960, was characterized by an imaginative exploration of Brazilian folk and popular traditions, cultivating concurrently post-Romantic and neo-classical styles. Typical of Mignone's nationalistic style are the ballets *Maracatu do Chico Rei* (1933), *Batucajé* (1936), *Babaloxá* (1936) and the four *Fantasias brasileiras* for piano and orchestra (1929–36). The ballets draw on Afro-Brazilian subjects and use almost exclusively Afro-Brazilian rhythms and melodic countours. The fantasias epitom- ize Mignone's style: they are rhapsodic, with piano parts reminiscent of the captivating, spontaneous, virtuoso manner of such popular pianist-composers as Ernesto Nazareth, whose music and performances were much admired by Darius Milhaud during his sojourn in Rio during the latter part of World War I. Mignone's solo songs and piano pieces are some of the most successful Brazilian works of the 1930s and 40s. Urban popular music traits appear in many of his piano pieces, particularly *Quatro peças brasileiras* (1930) and *Cucumbizinho* (1931). Two sets of waltzes, *Valsas de esquina* (1938–43) and *Valsas choros* (1946–55), very Romantic in inspiration and tech- nique, attempt to re-create the atmosphere of the popular improvised waltzes of strolling serenaders of the early twentieth century.

Guarnieri's impressive output spans several decades of creative activity, from his first success, the Piano Sonatina (1928), to the Seventh Symphony (1987); most of his works demonstrate a striving for technical refinement. As a modernist, Guarnieri was profoundly influenced by his association with Mário de Andrade, who wrote the libretto for his one-act comic opera *Pedro Malazarte*, produced success- fully in Rio de Janeiro in 1952. His numerous solo songs of the 1930s reveal a basic lyrical quality and an attempt to assimilate Afro- Brazilian and Amerindian folksong characteristics. This lyricism is also present in his 50 piano pieces in five albums entitled *Ponteios*

(1931–59) ('ponteio' implies the melodic plucking of a string instrument).

In Argentina in the latter part of the nineteenth century a nationalist trend in the arts evolved from the 'gauchesco' tradition, on which most Argentine composers of the first half of the twentieth century focussed their attention. The literary masterpiece of the tradition of the gaucho (the cowboy of the pampas) was the epic poem *Martín Fierro* (1872) by José Hernández. The literary historian and critic Ricardo Rojas wrote the bible of the 'gaucheco' tradition in his *History of Argentine Literature* (1917–22), particularly the two volumes called 'Los Gauchescos' in which he paid much attention to the folk music and dances of the pampa.[17] The real thrust towards musical nationalism came with Alberto Williams (1862–1952), who wrote the first works inspired by gaucho folk music (notably his piano pieces *Aires de la pampa*, 1893). Subsequent generations of Argentine composers kept alive the nationalist current in opera, ballet, symphonic and chamber music.

Nationalism has been conspicuous in Argentine operas. The foundation of the new Teatro Colón of Buenos Aires (1908) was a strong incentive for opera composition. Opera composers found in Italian *verismo* a model for their nationalist works. Composers like Pascual de Rogatis, Enrique M. Casella, Arnaldo D'Espósito, Constantino Gaito and Felipe Boero wrote numerous operas based on folk legends from Argentina and other Latin American countries and using folk or popular musical themes. De Rogatis's *Huemac*,[18] on an Aztec myth, had its première at the Colón in 1916; Boero's *El matrero* (1929), based on the folklore of the pampas, won wide popularity in Argentina.

Some composers, instead of using folk material, advocated a more cosmopolitan style through adopting contemporary European compositional techniques while maintaining an Argentine character. This was true of the music of Floro M. Ugarte, the brothers Juan José Castro, José María Castro and Washington Castro, and Luis Gianneo and Honorio Siccardi. Juan José Castro (1895–1968) was the leading figure in the nationalist movement in the 1930s, especially with his *Sinfonía argentina* (1934) in three movements, the first of which explores elements of the tango, and his *Sinfonía de los campos* (1939). The latter, a 'pastoral' symphony, is evocative of the pampa folk traditions and impressionistic in its harmonic language. Castro's contemporary Luis Gianneo cultivated a nationalist style over a longer period and with more regional variety, including Indian elements.

Of the next generation, Alberto Ginastera (1916–83) was one of the leading creative personalities in twentieth-century Latin American music. As early as 1937 he wrote the two works that established his reputation as a 'national' composer: the *Danzas argentinas* for piano and the ballet *Panambi*. His second ballet, *Estancia* (1941), dealt with Argentine rural life and appeared as the most overtly nationalist of the larger works from this time. The inclusion of sung and recited excerpts from *Martín Fierro* connects the work with the pampas. The final section, 'Malambo', derives from the vigorous dance of that name that has long been identified with the gauchos, especially in their competitions called *justa* ('joust'). Now extinct, the *malambo* was characterized by a fast tempo and constant quaver motion in 6/8 metre; it was used by Ginastera in toccata-like final movements of several of his works of the 1930s and 40s. In his *Obertura para el 'Fausto' criollo* (1943), he drew on the humorous *Fausto* by Estanislao del Campo, one of the classics of the gaucho literary tradition, sub-titled 'Impressions of the gaucho Anastasio el Pollo at the representation of this opera'. On a visit to Buenos Aires, Anastasio sees the show at the old Teatro Colón and finds himself confronted with Gounod's *Faust*. On his return home he describes to a friend, in typical gaucho lingo, his impressions of Doctor Faustus's story. Ginastera effectively uses fragments of Gounod's opera, together with rhythmic and melodic elements of Argentine folk music.

In 1947 Ginastera began a series of *Pampeanas*, illustrating his transition to a more subjective treatment of vernacular elements. In his early works he made conspicuous use of the 'natural' chord of the guitar (open strings, *E-A-D-G-B-E*), often presented in chromatically altered form. The supremacy of the guitar as a folk instrument in Argentina made this chord symbolic of the national popular culture. Although Ginastera later almost totally abandoned national sources, he was recognized as leader of the national movement in Argentine music in the 1940s. The fact that during the first half of the century the gaucho became the symbol of *argentinidad* – the very essence of being Argentine – is significant. Cultivators of élite art turned their attention above all to Europe; those in Buenos Aires, especially, were more interested in what happened in the arts in Paris than in the culture of the pampas. Yet when a symbol of nationality was needed, the idealized, somewhat romanticized folk figure of the gaucho seemed the most suitable, perhaps as a revival of a nineteenth-century tradition.

The same tradition served the purposes of some early twentieth-century Uruguayan composers, especially Luis Cluzeau Mortet (1889–1957) who, however, was not exclusively nationalist. The best-known Uruguayan composer of this period, Eduardo Fabini (1882–1950), wrote the tone poem *Campo* (1922), considered the greatest national work in his country.[19] In this and later pieces, he re-created and assimilated elements of the Rioplatense folk music.

ECLECTIC CROSS-CURRENTS

Some composers were indifferent to nationalism; others voiced frank opposition by adhering to advanced techniques and aesthetics. This opposition often resulted from the conviction that musical nationalism was producing works of dubious quality and that it demeaned Latin American music by resorting to a facile, exotic regionalism. Many non-nationalist composers strove to win international approval for the intrinsic quality of their works. Composers who followed the nationalist trend at some point also cultivated different styles which combined national and non-national elements.

Mexico, Central America and the Caribbean

In Mexico the two figures who came to prominence during the 1910s and 20s were Julián Carrillo and Manuel M. Ponce. Ponce (1882–1948) was considered the pioneer of Romantic nationalism in Mexico. He first wrote in a Romantic style, at times reminiscent of nineteenth-century salon music, as his internationally celebrated song *Estrellita* bears witness. Within his nationalist idiom he often used techniques associated with impressionism and neo-classicism. The symphonic sketches *Chapultepec* (1929), for example, are impressionistic in harmony and tone-colour, while his famous guitar pieces, such as the *Sonata clásica* and the *Concierto del sur*, reveal assimilation of neo-classical idioms within a virtuoso guitar style.

With the works of Carrillo (1875–1965), independence from the prevailing nationalist trend was expressed. Although trained at the Mexico City Conservatory, then at the Leipzig and Ghent conservatories, he developed an early interest in experimentation, especially with microtonality. By the 1920s he had refined his theories of microtones, which he called *Sonido 13* and for which he achieved international recognition. Sonido 13 defined the division of the octave beyond the 12 tones of the chromatic scale into units smaller than semitones: microtones of various sizes down to 16ths of a whole tone. One of his first and best-known microtonal works, *Preludio a Colón* (1922), was written for soprano, flute, guitar and violin, all in quarter-tones, octavina (a string instrument designed by the composer) in eighth-tones, and harp in 16th-tones; it successfully created a wailing, incantatory atmosphere which sounded futuristic. Carrillo devised special notation for these sounds, advertised as 'something unique in the entire world! No more special paper to write music!'[20] His method involved an ingenious combination of lines and numbers but was of difficult practical application. He wrote numerous microtonal pieces, including some for microtonal pianos that a German firm undertook to build, as an experiment, in the 1950s. That he was a precursor of ultrachromatic composers is the more remarkable since his outlook and interests in acoustical research were unique in Mexico.[21]

During the period 1920–45, Chávez wrote several non-nationalist works which rely wholly or in part on contemporary European techniques, such as the *Sinfonía de Antígona* (1933), the *Diez preludios para piano* (1937) and the Toccata for percussion instruments (1942). The *Sinfonía de Antígona*, based on Chávez's incidental music for Jean Cocteau's adaptation of Sophocles' tragedy, is one of his orchestral masterpieces. Its archaic modal flavour, sober, austere character, thematic polyphony and wind-dominated orchestration place it at the centre of neo-classicism. The Toccata, written at the suggestion of John Cage, is abstract but not experimental, as one might expect of a percussion piece of the period; in three movements, it appears as a study in rhythm and timbre, the rhythmic organization being predominantly contrapuntal.

The Spanish-born composer Rodolfo Halffter (1900–87) settled in Mexico in 1939. He had a profound influence on Mexican musical life principally as a professor of composition at the National Conservatory, as editor of the journal *Nuestra música* and manager of the *Ediciones mexicanas de música*. Strongly influenced by the neo-classicism of Manuel de Falla of the 1920s, he cultivated a reserved, at times austere, neo-classical style, as seen in his Violin Concerto op.11 (1939–40), his ballet *La madrugada del panadero* (1940) and his *Homenaje a Antonio Machado* (1944) for piano.[22]

Another Spanish-born composer who exerted a lasting influence on the musical life of another country was José Ardévol, who settled in Havana, Cuba, in 1930. His influence was felt especially after the deaths of Roldán and García Caturla. In 1942, with some of his best students, he founded the Grupo de Renovación Musical to create a Cuban school of composers 'which could reach the same degree of universality obtained by other countries'. The group included Harold Gramatges, Edgardo Martín, Julián Orbón, Hilario González, Argeliers León, Serafín Pro and Gisela Hernández. Its philosophy was not dogmatic, but craftsmanship and knowledge of compositional procedures were emphasized. From 1930 to about 1936 Ardévol revealed himself as a radical experimentalist, writing in an atonal style or with the 12-note method. He acknowledged 1936 as marking the beginning of a self-imposed stylistic simplicity in which Spanish and Cuban elements play a certain role.[23] His adherence to neo-classicism in the 1930s and 40s is best seen in such works as the piano Sonatina (1934), the first five of the six *Sonatas a tres* (1937–46), the two Concerti Grossi (1937) and the Concerto for Piano, Winds and Percussion (1944). Many of his students became significant figures in Cuban music.

Venezuela and the Andean nations

The Venezuelan Juan Bautista Plaza was a leading nationalist figure (see p. 235), but in the 1920s he was also productive as a composer of church music, becoming *maestro de capilla* of Caracas Cathedral in 1923. Besides his first four masses, of the mid-1920s, he wrote several tone poems and a choral work with orchestra, *Las horas* (1930), well known in Venezuela. This music reveals the influence of his years of study in Rome, specifically the Romanticism of Puccini with its extreme lyricism.

In Peru, Rodolfo Holzmann, even more than Andrés Sas, initiated a countercurrent to nationalism by exposing his many students to contemporary European styles. Of European training and temperament, he was influenced by Hindemith's new tonal system. Some of his works of the 1940s, such as *Divertimento concertante* (1941) for piano and ten woodwind, the *Cantigas de la Edad de Oro* (1944) for small orchestra and the *Tres madrigales* (1944) for voice and piano, demonstrate the emphasis he placed on craftsmanship and tradition.

Chilean musical life underwent a profound transformation during the 1920s, thanks to the efforts of Domingo Santa Cruz, who founded the Sociedad Bach in 1917. This society, at first merely a small university choir, had much impact on musical development. It was the springboard for numerous activities and its audiences came from the urban middle class, made up of numerous German, Italian and Polish immigrants. A foundation for the establishment of musical institutions was also laid in 1929 with the creation of the Facultad de Bellas Artes within the University of Chile. This had jurisdiction over the conservatory and the various schools of fine and applied arts.

Santa Cruz (1899–1987) was leader of the innovatory movement in Chilean musical life from the 1920s to 60s and was influential as a composer, teacher and administrator. In later years he was Dean of the Faculty of Fine Arts at the National Conservatory (1932–48). As a composer, his most important works were written from the 1930s to 50s. His stylistic orientation tended towards both impressionism and atonality, the latter reflected in the highly chromatic harmony of some of the songs of *Cuatro Poemas* op.9 (1927). Some of the themes of his First String Quartet (1930), however, have a strongly Hispanic flavour, resulting from the type of ornamentation associated with Andalusian folksinging. Later works, such as the Five Pieces for string orchestra op.14 (1937) and the *Sinfonía concertante* op.22 (1945) further expand these early traits. Together with strongly neo-classical elements (linear writing with imitation, fugato, canon and other contrapuntal devices), his style involves extended chromaticism at times generating polytonal harmony. The creation of the Instituto de Extensión Musical at the University of Chile in 1940, with Santa Cruz[24] its first director, resulted in the establishment of a symphony orchestra, a choir, a ballet ensemble and chamber music groups, and annual composition contests. In 1941 the Orquesta Sinfónica de Chile was founded, its first artistic director being the remarkable conductor Armando Carvajal. In 1945 the institute began publication of the important *Revista musical chilena* whose longevity is unprecedented in Latin American music periodical publication.

Modern Times

Other significant Chilean composers of Santa Cruz's generation, among them Enrique Soro (1884–1954) and Alfonso Leng (1894–1974), continued the Romantic and post-Romantic tradition. A notable exception was Acario Cotapos (1889–1969), who belonged to the New York avant garde in the 1920s as one of the founders of the International Composers Guild (with Varèse, Cowell and Milhaud). His *Cuatro preludios sinfónicos* (first performed in Paris in 1930) was well received.

Brazil and the River Plate area

During the first quarter of the twentieth century there was a Europeanized school of composition in Brazil represented mainly by Francisco Braga (1868–1945), Henrique Oswald (1852–1931) and Alberto Nepomuceno (1864–1920), who was also an important figure in the beginnings of musical nationalism. As a professor of composition at the Rio de Janeiro Instituto Nacional de Música for over 35 years, Nepomuceno exerted considerable influence. He had great empathy for Wagner's techniques and aesthetics but drew on post-Romantic models, in many of his non-nationalist works, for example the *Sinfonia* in G minor and String Trio in F minor. Oswald's extensive output reflect a post-Romantic eclecticism, including elements associated with the Schola Cantorum in Paris and with Debussy.

The leading innovators in the 1930s and 40s came from the Música Viva group, which appeared in 1931 under the leadership of the German composer Hans-Joachim Koellreutter. In its manifesto of 1946 the group declared its opposition to folkloristic nationalism.[25] The compositional method that became associated with this anti-national campaign was twelve-note technique, championed by Koellreutter. He lived in Brazil from 1937 to 1963, and again from 1974, and taught many Brazilian composers; in the 1940s they included Cláudio Santoro (1919–89) and César Guerra-Peixe (*b* 1914). Santoro's earlier music, written between 1939 and about 1947, was orientated towards atonality and a pragmatic twelve-note technique, allied to classical structures, Baroque contrapuntal devices and extensive polyphony. Guerra Peixe based many of his early works on serial techniques, for example his *Sonatina 1944* for flute and clarinet. Another composer associated with Música Viva who turned to non-national sources in his last few works was Luiz Cosme (1908–65), a native of Rio Grande do Sul, who freely adopted the twelve-note method in his works of the late 1940s without concealing his interest in national subjects.

In Argentina, contemporary styles appeared only occasionally, in the works of such composers as Juan José Castro and José María Castro, Floro Ugarte and Jacobo Ficher. Juan José Castro's youthful orchestral works of the 1920s reveal his allegiance to his French teacher Vincent d'Indy. Impressionist and Stravinskian influences are found in his *Allegro, Lento e Vivace* (1930) for orchestra. With Juan Carlos Paz and his brother José María, Castro founded the Grupo Renovación (1929), which advocated the involvement of Argentine composers with European modern trends. Twelve-note music, considered in the 1930s the most radical, found its first Latin American supporter in the Argentine composer Juan Carlos Paz (1901–72), the most radical artist of his generation and a unique pioneer of the avant garde in Latin America.[26] Until the mid-1930s he cultivated an essentially neo-classical style characterized in its more mature phase by contrapuntal writing and polytonal and, at times, atonal harmony. After about 1934, he used twelve-note methods in a free, personal way, as in his *Primera composición en los 12 tonos* (1934) and *Diez piezas sobre una serie de los 12 tonos* (1935). Neo-classicism is represented in Argentina by such composers as Roberto García Morillo (*b* 1911), Julián Bautista (1901–61) and Guillermo Graetzer (*b* 1914).

Among the few non-nationalist Uruguayan composers of the period were Carmen Barradas (1888–1963), Carlos Estrada (1909–70) and Héctor Tosar (*b* 1923), who wrote his first works in the 1940s. Estrada had a long association with French culture (hence his numerous settings of French poems and incidental pieces for French plays), generally writing in a sober neo-Classic style.

Until World War II Latin American social and intellectual life reflected a clear dependence on Europe and, to a lesser extent, North America. Only after the 1940s did that cultural dependence lessen considerably. The 1920s saw an adherence to the European 'great tradition' and the discovery of the French impressionist style as well as Stravinsky's works, all epitomizing 'modern' styles in Latin America. During the 1930s and 40s a number of composers became aware of the need to assimilate new methods of composition without concealing their Latin cultural identity. These composers remained in the minority but were able gradually to liberate themselves from the constraint of nationalism. The resulting individualism had its full impact in subsequent decades.

THE DEVELOPMENT OF POPULAR MUSIC

It is perhaps in the realm of urban popular music that Latin America expressed herself most originally. The first characteristic popular styles emerged in the last quarter of the nineteenth century. Urban renditions of folk genres prevailed, together with the cultivation of European salon music. Since the 1920s urban growth in most Latin American countries has resulted in a huge development of urban cultures. In some of the largest cities, this growth and the consequent cultural diversity have been phenomenal and this is reflected in the diversity of urban popular music. Fashionable European and other foreign popular music has always been present in the major cities, where some social groups tend to emulate their European counterparts. Thus the polka, schottische, contredanse and others were readily adopted in cities and towns and suffered the process of 'creolization', or transformation into local or national genres. The waltz, for example, was forerunner of a number of popular Latin American dances, such as *pasillo* or *vals del país* in Colombia, *vals criollo* in Peru, *vals melopeya* in Venezuela and *valsa-choro* in Brazil. The influence of North American Tin Pan Alley and other popular genres had repercussions in the hybrid forms that developed in the 1920s and 30s, such as the *rumba-fox*, the *Inca-fox* and the *samba-fox*. The big jazz band era of the 1930s and 40s also left its imprint on the performing media of many classical Latin American urban popular forms.

Mexico and Spanish Caribbean

The most national popular genres of nineteenth-century Mexico were the *jarabe* and the *danza mexicana*, both of which continued to enjoy popularity in the twentieth century. The late nineteenth-century *jarabe* pieces, though generally published in solo piano versions, were performed by popular bands or ensembles, including the early string ensembles of *mariachis*. The *danza mexicana* grew from the Cuban *contradanza* and *habanera*; it stressed duple metre and the feeling of disjunction between duple and triple divisions of the beat that characterized many Latin American and Caribbean popular dances. Miguel Lerdo de Tejada (1869–1941) was the first major popular composer who used the *danza* as a vocal genre.

There were many types of dance music from the beginning of the century, but the *canción mexicana* and especially the *canción romántica mexicana* came to epitomize Mexican popular music. The history of the *canción* is one of catchy melodies that have remained in the collective memory of the Mexican people. Besides its obvious kinship with Italian opera or operetta, the *canción* has been influenced by song genres, especially the Cuban *bolero*. The type of *canción* known as *ranchera* is more distinctively Mexican in that it originated from folksong and retained performance characteristics of that tradition. It appeared in the 1920s as an urban genre, at first primarily to accompany films, and was popularized in the 1930s. *Canciones* and *boleros* have been written by the hundred since the 1920s. By far the most popular composer of his generation was Agustín Lara (1900–69), whose song *Granada* was an international hit.

In the 1940s, urban composers began to pay attention to the *corrido*, the folk ballad of Mexico. In the process of urbanization, the *corrido* underwent a few changes; it became predominantly duple in metre, structured in quatrain (*copla*) literary form and was performed by vocal duet and trio in harmonized fashion and with *mariachi* and *norteño* ensemble accompaniment. The best example of this phenomenally popular genre is *Juan Charrasqueado*, by Victor Cordero.

Cuba has exerted the widest influence in the development of Latin American popular forms throughout the continent. From the *habanera*, the *son cubano* and the *bolero*, to the *mambo*, *rumba*, *conga* and *chachachá*, Cuban music has either shaped the *criollo* genres in other countries or been adopted wholesale as fashionable dance music. The *habanera* and the *son* first characterized Spanish Caribbean music. The *son* became urbanized during the 1910s and adopted a strongly syncopated rhythmic accompaniment. Since the 1920s the *bolero* has been essentially a highly romantic and sentimental vocal genre. One of the most esteemed composers of *boleros* was Ernesto Lecuona (1896–1963), whose songs *Malagueña*, *María La O* and *Siboney*, among others, immortalized him. Musically and choreographically, the *rumba guaguancó* was the forerunner of the urban *rumba* that developed thanks to the numerous dance bands that appeared in the 1930s; the first to gain popularity was the Havana Casino Orchestra of Don Azpiazu and the most commercialized in the USA was that of Xavier Cugat.

The *merengue*, which originated in the Dominican Republic, has enjoyed popularity throughout the Caribbean and Central and South America. The *méringue* from Haiti developed its own *créole* character but is related to the Dominican genre. Venezuelan popular music shares characteristics with both the Caribbean and the Andean-Colombian areas. The most common genres, however, the *joropo*, the *valse* and the *merengue*, are typical native (*criollo*) expressions. As a music and literary genre, the *joropo* has been cultivated by popular composers since the latter part of the nineteenth century and has remained the most characteristic Venezuelan national popular dance.

The Andean Countries

Since the beginning of the twentieth century, Andean national urban popular music has frequently consisted of transformations of folksongs and dances. In Colombia the most common forms have been the *bambuco*, the *porro*, the *cumbia*, and the *pasillo*. The vocal part of the urban *bambuco* involves a duet of male voices singing in parallel 3rds, though it was originally a serenade for solo voice. The *cumbia* an Afro-Panamanian and Colombian (Atlantic coastal area) folkdance, enjoyed lasting popularity throughout Hispanic America in its urban version as a song-dance genre with heavy percussion and brass accompaniment. The *pasillo* is a moderately slow, waltz-like dance, the rhythm of which does not stress the downbeat as in its European counterpart. Sung by solo voice or duet in parallel 3rds, it is accompanied by piano, *tiple* (treble guitar) and guitar supported by tambourines and 'spoons', or an *estudiantina* (string ensemble).

In Ecuador the most typical popular genres, *sanjuanito*, *pasillo* and *cachullapi*, developed during the 1930s and 40s. The *sanjuanito* is a dance in duple metre, strictly instrumental with syncopated melodies and a regularly and strongly accented accompaniment. In Peru, the popular *huayno*, similar to its folk mestizo counterpart but performed by urban bands with different instrumentation, has maintained its status among highland urban communities. Coastal cities like Trujillo, Chiclayo or Piura in the north and Pisco and Ica in the south developed genres related to *criollo* tradition, for example the *marinera* and the *vals criollo*. The latter has been especially favoured in Lima. The *vals* became the main musical expression of the urban working class throughout the 1920s and 30s, its lyrics reflecting the peoples' cultural personality and the conflicts, attitudes and values resulting from their social and political conditions.

Bolivian popular composers have also cultivated the *huayño popular*, the *cueca*, the *yaraví* and the *taquirari*. The Bolivian *yaraví* is a melancholy love-song; the *taquirari* is a sung dance from the eastern provinces of Beni and Santa Cruz calling for singing in parallel 3rds or 6ths. In the cities and towns of the Bolivian plateau, the *bailecito*, similar to the *cueca*, has been extensively cultivated. The stylized *cuecas* for piano by Simeón Roncal (1870–1953) continue to enjoy great popularity among Bolivian pianists. Chilean urban music includes the *cueca* and urban versions of *tonadas*, *tristes*, *carnaval* and *tiranas*.

Argentina, Uruguay and Brazil

No popular genre in Argentina and Uruguay epitomizes so deeply the socio-cultural history of those countries as the tango. It has therefore remained the most important. In the Río de la Plata area the tango came to symbolize the hopes, successes and failures of the millions of European immigrants who expected to work on farms but who settled instead in the *arrabal*, or ghettos, of Buenos Aires and Montevideo. The *milonga*, a dance of Afro-Argentine and Uruguayan folk tradition, probably contributed to the development of the tango. Choreographic-ally, it is partly a local adaptation of the Andalusian tango, of the Cuban *danzón* and *habanera* and, to a lesser extent, of the European polka and schottische. Essentially three types developed: the strongly rhythmic instrumental *tango-milonga* for popular orchestras; the in-strumental or vocal *tango-romanza*, with a more melodic and romantic character; and the accompanied *tango-canción*, which is lyrical and sentimental. It is in the *tango-canción* that the themes associated with the tango as popular culture appear. Carlos Gardel (1887–1935), an idol who continued to fascinate most Argentines many decades after his death, was important in making the tango fashionable in Europe and the Western hemisphere. Perhaps the most successful tango was *La cumparsita* (1917), written by Gerardo Matos Rodríguez in Montevideo. Other popular pieces included Julio César Sanders's *Adiós muchachos*

(1928), Enrique Santos Discépolo's *Yira, yira* (1930) and Francisco Camaro's *Adiós, pampa mía.*

Brazilian urban popular music acquired its most decisive character during the period under consideration. The *choro* of the 1920s to 40s stressed virtuoso improvisation of instrumental variations. Since the beginning of the century Carnival stimulated the development of popular music, especially in Rio de Janeiro. The most typical Carnival genre, the urban samba, emerged during the second decade of the century. The first to be recorded was *Pelo telefone* by Ernesto dos Santos (nicknamed Donga) in 1917. Several types of Samba appeared from the 1920s to 40s, including the folklike dance known as *partido-alto* and the *samba de morro*, cultivated by the people of the hillside slums (*favelas*) and the first *escolas de samba* (samba schools) of Rio de Janeiro. It was accompanied primarily by percussion instruments. The *samba de carnaval* appealed at first to the lower economic classes, while the ballroom type of samba gradually incorporated elements of middle- and upper-class dance music. Among the best-known composers of urban sambas in the 1920s and 30s were José Luiz de Morais (nicknamed 'Caninha'), Alfredo da Rocha Viana ('Pixinguinha'), Ary Barroso, Noel Rosa and Carlos Ferreira Braga ('João de Barro'). Some of these composers' samba tunes have remained in the collective memory of the Brazilian people.

SPAIN

The most active and recognized composers in Spain about the end of War World I were the Catalans Isaac Albéniz and Enrique Granados, and the Andalucian Manuel de Falla. Spanish music was still searching for its own identity as its affinities with nineteenth-century Romanticism continued to be evident. By 1920, however, the new French aesthetics as defined by Jean Cocteau in *Le coq et l'arlequin* began to have influence, first in Barcelona then in Madrid. The presence of Falla, Turina and Rodrigo in Paris reinforced the French flavour that Spanish music of the period displays.

Gradually, an anti-Romantic and anti-German attitude led to the neo-classical current of the 1920s. By relying on some neo-classical elements while still expressing Spanish themes, Falla associated himself with European thought in such works as *El retablo de Maese Pedro* (1923) and the Harpsichord Concerto (1926). Moreover, Spanish composers generally adopted a more comprehensive humanistic approach to musical life, among them Conrado del Campo, Joaquín Turina, Julio Gómez, Oscar Esplá and the brothers Ernesto and Rodolfo Halffter. Eclecticism continued to dominate musical thinking, with the juxtaposition of neo-Romanticism, avant-garde nationalism, neo-classicism and occasional atonality and twelve-note technique.

Manuel de Falla: portrait by Pablo Picasso, 1920.

Spanish neo-classicism, however, was idiosyncratic in that it referred partly to Spanish eighteenth-century music and partly to Spanish folk music, thus making it appear at times nationalist.

With the advent of the Second Republic in 1931, activities initiated in the 1920s became official Republican musical projects, including the stimulation of musical composition, providing music with a new social purpose, the reform of music instruction, the revitalization of musicological research and the decentralization of music institutions. Official awareness of the social importance of music motivated the creation in 1931 of the Junta Nacional de Música y Teatro Líricos, with Esplá as president, which created a detailed and somewhat utopian programme for the organization of music throughout the country. Many parts of this programme – elaborated primarily by the music critic and composer Adolfo Salazar – could not be implemented under the Second Republic but it revealed a remarkable consciousness of the precarious state of music institutions in the country. The civil war brought a radical change in attitudes towards the more open socio-political use of music but it also provoked a new ideological stance on the part of some of the best-known musicians, who found themselves on the cultural and democratic side in the 1936 conflict. Circumstances also dictated the creation of a socially involved music. Numerous people fought openly for the Republican cause and therefore had to go into exile at the end of the war. Among them were Salvador Bacarisse, Rodolfo Halffter, Gustavo Durán, Adolfo Salazar, Jesús Bal y Gay and Roberto Gerhard. Falla also left his country for Argentina, primarily for economic rather than overt political reasons. The postwar period saw a general lack of incentive for creative innovation. In spite of efforts on the part of Joaquín Turina, in his capacity as director of the Comisaría Nacional de la Música, the little attention paid to music by the new state had to be directed to the expression of its nationalistic ideology. This is why the anachronistic style of Joaquín Rodrigo, particularly that of his acclaimed *Concierto de Aranjuez*, prevailed.

The relative isolationism of Spain during the 1940s also had negative consequences for the development of music education. With precarious facilities, conservatories had little or no interest in new teaching methods. Music was not recognized as an appropriate subject in university curricula. Audiences became smaller and more homogeneous than those of the earlier decades because democratic access to music was reduced. Thus concert-goers in the 1940s were predominantly the conservative aristocracy, segments of the business and bureaucratic community and small groups of true aficionados. The social status of the professional musician had deteriorated, with the economic situation demanding many activities to ensure survival. Only the next decades would bring welcome change.

NOTES

[1] For a detailed explanation of this new era in Mexican culture, see F. Brandenburg, *The Making of Modern Mexico* (Englewood Cliffs, NJ, 1964) and H. F. Cline, *Mexico – Revolution to Evolution, 1940–1960* (London, 1962).

[2] In Copland, *Music and Imagination* (Cambridge, Mass., 1952), 91.

[3] The composer's ideas are articulated in his *Musical Thought* (Cambridge, Mass., 1961).

[4] Expressed in a letter to Roberto García Morillo. See. R. García Morillo, *Carlos Chávez: vida y obra* (Mexico, 1960), 83.

[5] In published score *Soli No. 2 for Wind Quintet* (New York, 1963).

[6] For further explanation, see O. Mayer-Serra, 'Silvestre Revueltas and Musical Nationalism in Mexico', *MQ*, xxvii (1941), 123.

[7] O. Mayer-Serra, *The Present State of Music in Mexico* (Washington, DC, 1946).

[8] E. Sánchez de Fuentes, *El folklor en la música cubana* (Havana, 1923) and *La música aborigen de América* (Havana, 1938).

[9] Recognition of this achievement is mentioned in H. Cowell, 'Roldán and Caturla of Cuba', *Modern Music*, 18/2 (1940), 98.

[10] For a good historical account of the activities of the Association, see D. L. Root, 'The Pan American Association of Composers (1928–1934)', *Yearbook for Inter-American Musical Research*, viii (1972), 49.

[11] For a general discussion of the subject, see G. Béhague, 'Latin American Folk Music', in B. Nettl, *Folk and Traditional Music of the Western Continents* (Englewood Cliffs, NJ, 3/1990), 185.

[12] See J. M. Arguedas, *Formación de una cultura nacional indoamericana* (Lima, 1975), for an excellent discussion of national identity construction in Peru.

[13] R. Holzmann, 'Aporte para la emancipación de la música peruana', *Revista de Estudios Musicales*, i/1 (Aug 1949), 61.

[14] The dean of Chilean composers, Domingo Santa Cruz, expressed this lack of affinity, in 'Trayectoria musical de Chile', *Buenos Aires Musical* 12/197 (Oct 1957), 6.

[15] For a further assessment of this position, see S. Wright, *Villa-Lobos* (Oxford/New York, 1992) and G. Béhague, *Heitor Villa-Lobos: the Search for Brazil's Musical Soul* (forthcoming).

[16] From Villa-Lobos's own notes. *Villa-Lobos, Sua Obra* (Rio de Janeiro, 2/1972), 187.

[17] Ricardo Rojas, *La literatura argentina: ensayo filosófico sobre la evolución de la cultura en el Plata* (Buenos Aires, 1917–22).

[18] For detailed analysis of this work, see M. Kuss, 'Huemac, by Pascual de Rogatis: Native Identity in the Argentine Lyric Theatre', *Yearbook for Inter-American Musical Research*, x (1974), 68.

[19] On this composer's life and work see R. Lagarmilla, *Eduardo Fabini, músical nacional uruguayo* (Montevideo, 1953).

[20] As expressed on the back cover of Carrillo's Six Preludes for Piano published by 'The 13th Sound' in New York in 1928.

[21] That he was considered a figure of paramount importance in the field of sound experiments is confirmed by Vischnegradsky in 'A Letter from Vischnegradsky', *Nouvelles du Mexique*, nos. 43–44 (1965–6), 4.

[22] The analysis of J. Bal y Gay in 'Rodolfo Halffter', *Nuestra Música*, no. 3 (1946), 145.

[23] See J. Ardévol, *Introducción a Cuba: la música* (Havana, 1969).

[24] Santa Cruz's writings illustrate the development of Chilean musical life of the period, see especially his 'Mis recuerdos sobre la Sociedad Bach', *Revista Musical Chilena*, no. 40 (1950–51), 8, and 'Nuestra posición en el mundo contemporáneo de la música', *Revista Musical Chilena*, no. 64 (1959), 46, no. 65 (1959), 31, and no. 67 (1959), 39.

[25] See 'Manifesto 1946', *Música Viva* (Rio de Janeiro), no. 12 (1947), 3.

[26] For a good insight into Paz's ideas see his *Introducción a la música de nuestro tiempo* (Buenos Aires, 1955).

BIBLIOGRAPHICAL NOTE

The period under consideration has been studied extensively by intellectual historians and philosophers. Some of the most informative and engaging sources in English include M. Stabb's *In Quest of Identity: Patterns in the Spanish American Essay of Ideas, 1890–*

1960 (Chapel Hill, NC, 1967), E. J. Williams's chapter on 'Secularization, Integration, and Rationalization: Some Perspectives from Latin American Thought', in *Readings in Latin American History*, ii: *The Modern Experience*, ed. J. J. Johnson, P. J. Bakewell and M. D. Dodge (Durham, NC, 1985). Also thought-provoking and informative is J. Franco's *The Modern Culture of Latin America: Society and the Artist* (New York, 1967). E. Willems provides a useful overview of Latin American culture and its development in his book *Latin American Culture: an Anthropological Synthesis* (New York, 1975).

G. Béhague, *Music in Latin America: an Introduction* (Englewood Cliffs, NJ, 1979), provides a detailed discussion of this period. For the Mesoamerican area, R. Stevenson's *Music in Mexico: a Historical Survey* (New York, 1952) and vol. iv (covering the period 1910–58) by L. A. Estrada, L. Sandi, J. Estrada and A. de los Reyes, of *La música en México*, ed. J. Estrada (Mexico, 1984), should be consulted. Biographical information on C. Chávez and analyses of his works are in R. García Morillo, *Carlos Chávez: vida y obra* (Mexico, 1960) and R. L. Parker, *Carlos Chávez, Mexico's Modern-Day Orpheus* (Boston, 1983), the latter with a catalogue of works and discography. Of historical interest is the section 'Composer from Mexico', in A. Copland, *The New Music: 1900–1960* (New York, 1968). Revueltas's music is studied in O. Mayer-Serra, 'Silvestre Revueltas and Musical Nationalism in Mexico', *MQ*, xxvii (1941), 123. Chávez's autobiographical notes and writings are in *Silvestre Revueltas por él mismo* (Mexico, 1989).

Cuban nationalism and the study of *afrocubanismo* are best treated in A. Carpentier, *La música en Cuba* (Mexico, 1946). H. Cowell wrote sympathetically on Roldán in his '"Motivos de Son": a Series of Eight Songs for Soprano, with a Small Orchestra', *MQ*, xxvi (1950), 270, and A. Salazar on García Caturla in his article, 'La obra musical de Alejandro García Caturla', *Revista Cubana*, xi/31 (1938), 31. More recent data are in E. Martin, *Panorama histórico de la música en Cuba* (Havana, 1971) and R. Cordero's works of the 1940s are reviewed in G. Chase, 'Composed by Cordero', *Inter-American Music Bulletin*, no.7 (1958), l, and R. Sider, 'Roque Cordero, the Composer and his Style seen in Three Representative Works', *Inter-American Music Bulletin*, no.61 (1967), 1. Cordero's piano works are the subject of a special study by P. Filos Gooch, *El piano en las obras de Roque Cordero* (Tibás, Costa Rica, 1985).

Music in Venezuela, especially in Caracas up to the 1950s, is the subject of J. S. Calcaño, *La ciudad y su música* (Caracas, 1958). Sojo's main biographies are Oscar Mago, *Sojo, un hombre y una misión histórica* (Caracas, 1975), E. Lira Espejo, *Vicente Emilio Sojo* (Los Teques, 1987), J. V. Abreu, *Sojo, medio siglo de música* (Caracas, 1987) and G. Acuña, *Maestro Sojo* (Caracas, 1986). M. Castillo Didier has written extensively on Plaza, especially in *Juan Bautista Plaza: una vida por la música y por Venezuela* (Caracas, 1985). Colombian music is treated comprehensively in J. I. P. Escobar, *Historia de la música en Colombia* (Bogotá, 3/1963), and A. P. Tovar, *La Cultura musical en Colombia* (Bogotá, 1966). Uribe-Holguín, *Vida de un músico colombiano* (Bogotá, 1941) is an autobiography; a study of Holguín's piano pieces is E. Duque, *Guillermo Uribe Holguín e sus '300 trozos en el sentimiento popular'* (Bogota, 1980).

Still useful is S. L. Moreno, 'La música en el Ecuador', in *El Ecuador en cien años de independencia*, ed. J. G. Orellana (Quito, 1930). The music of Peru is treated in *La música en el Perú* (Lima, 1985), by several authors, with special attention to the *indigenista* movement in the section 'La música en el siglo XX' by E. Pinilla. R. Holzmann provided an informative article on Valcárcel in 'Ensayo analítico de la obra musical del compositor peruano Theodoro Valcárcel', *Eco Musical*, ii/6 (1943), 22. Bolivian music is surveyed in A. Auza León's *Dinámica musical en Bolivia* (La Paz, 1967). A good survey of Chilean music since 1900 is V. Salas Viu, *La creación musical en Chile, 1900–1951* (Santiago, 1952), considerably updated in S. Claro-Valdés and J. Urrutia Blondel, *Historia de la música en Chile* (Santiago, 1973). Numerous articles on Chilean institutions, composers and compositions are published in the *Revista musical chilena*, whose indexes appear in no.98 (1966), nos.129–130 (1975) and no.163 (1985).

Modern Times

The bibliography on Villa-Lobos is considerable, but only a few items provide truly critical assessment of the composer's works. The main biographers have been V. Mariz, *Heitor Villa-Lobos, compositor brasileiro* (Belo Horizonte, 11/1989) and L. Peppercorn, *Villa-Lobos* (London, 1989). Villa-Lobos's unique qualities both as a nationalist and modern-internationalist composer are the main concerns of J. M. Wisnick, *O Coro dos Contrários: a música em torno da semana de 22* (São Paulo, 1977) and G. Béhague, *Heitor Villa-Lobos: the Search for Brazil's Musical Soul* (forthcoming). A good in-depth introduction to his music is S. Wright, *Villa-Lobos* (Oxford and New York, 1992). The Brazilian art-music scene of the 1920s to 40s is vividly described by L. Heitor (Corrêa de Azevedo), *150 anos de música no Brasil (1800–1950)* (Rio de Janeiro, 1956), especially the works of that period by Camargo Guarnieri and Francisco Mignone, and by V. Mariz in *Figuras da música brasileira contemporânea* (Brasília, 2/1970). A good general coverage of Argentine activities after 1910 is M. García Acevedo, *La música argentina contemporánea* (Buenos Aires, 1963), while opera in Buenos Aires is the subject of R. Caamaño, *La historia del Teatro Colón* (Buenos Aires, 1969).

The life and works of Alberto Ginastera are the subject of G. Chase, 'Alberto Ginastera: Argentine Composer', *MQ*, xliii (1957), 439, and P. Suárez Urtubey, *Alberto Ginastera* (Buenos Aires, 1967) and *Alberto Ginastera en cinco movimientos* (Buenos Aires, 1972). Uruguayan music of the period is thoroughly treated by S. Salgado in her *Breve historia de la música culta en el Uruguay* (Montevideo, 1971).

Julián Carrillo's theoretical concepts and their applications in his works are well explained and assessed in G. Benjamin, 'Julián Carrillo and "Sonido Trece"', *Yearbook*, Inter-American Institute for Musical Research, iii (1967), 33. The major works of Rodolfo Halffter are the subject of J. A. Alcaraz, *La música de Rodolfo Halffter* (Mexico, 1977). On the revolutionary Juan Carlos Paz, the most important sources are J. Romano, 'Juan Carlos Paz, un revitalizador del lenguaje musical', *Revista Musical Chilena*, no. 95 (1966), 22, and by the same author, *Juan Carlos Paz: tribulaciones de un músico* (Buenos Aires, 1970).

An overview of the development of popular music and the available resources for its study is provided in G. Béhague, 'Popular Music', *Handbook of Latin American Popular Culture*, ed. H. E. Hinds jr, and C. M. Tatum (Westport and London, 1985).

The music of Spain has been studied especially by F. Sopeña, *Historia de la música española contemporánea* (Madrid, 1957), M. Valls, *La música española después de Manuel de Falla* (Madrid, 1962) and T. Marco, *Siglo XX: Historia de la música española*, vi, ed. P. López de Osaba (Madrid, 1983).

Chapter XII

Western Europe, 1945–70

ANDREW CLEMENTS

The end of World War II in 1945 left not only the economy and fabric of Europe in ruins but its cultural life fragmented and inchoate. Of the composers who had represented the varied strands of modernism between the two world wars only one, Anton Webern, lived out the upheavals in his native country, Austria. Alban Berg had died in 1935, and in the years preceding the war the rest of the vanguard had joined the cultural diaspora in the New World. Schoenberg and Stravinsky had become part of the burgeoning community of expatriate artists on the west coast of the USA: Stravinsky lived in Hollywood, working as a freelance composer (and relishing some short-lived flirtations with the film industry) and Schoenberg held a professorship in composition at the University of California at Los Angeles. Bartók was living in New York (where he was to die in September 1945), Hindemith was teaching at Yale University, and Weill was busily adapting his language and dramatic skills to the musical theatre of Broadway. After Webern was shot accidentally in Mittersill, Austria, also in September 1945, none of the pioneers of modernism was left in Europe; the postwar reconstruction of musical culture fell to a new generation of composers and theorists.

TOWARDS TOTAL SERIALISM

From 1945 until well into the 1950s, life in Western Europe was dominated by the need to create new systems of economic and political organization. With the capitulation of the National Socialists and the subsequent partition of Germany and Austria between the allied powers, the focus for new artistic activity switched – at least temporarily – away from the German-speaking countries towards those centres in which some semblance of normal cultural activity had been preserved between 1939 and 1945. The Federal Republic of Germany, as it became, was gradually to regain its pre-eminence in the musical avant garde during the early 1950s; but in the immediate postwar period it was Paris, where musical life had continued even during the

Modern Times

Nazi occupation, that offered the most fertile ground for radical movements in all the arts. Musically, the initial centre of interest for young composers became the classes supervised by Olivier Messiaen (1908–92) at the Conservatoire.

After a brief period of internment following the Nazi occupation of Paris, Messiaen returned to the Conservatoire, where he taught harmony from 1942, and five years later he began to give classes in aesthetics, analysis and rhythm. Although it was not until the 1960s that he was sanctioned formally to teach composition, his keenness to break away from the hidebound syllabuses of the Conservatoire system and to direct his students towards a wide range of musical models, including elements of non-Western music, was to prove enticing to the most able and forward-looking of them. In his works composed before World War II Messiaen had revealed the broad-minded eclecticism of his thinking, incorporating Greek metres and the rhythms of the Hindu *deçî-tâlas* into the organ cycle *La nativité du Seigneur* (1935) and establishing his own system of modes.

In 1936 Messiaen had become a member of a group of composers who called themselves La Jeune France;[1] it organized concerts and offered itself as an antidote to the prevailing neo-classicism propagated most obviously in Paris in the 1930s through the teachings of Nadia Boulanger (1887–1979) at the Ecole Normale. By the outbreak of war, however, the group's collective impetus had been lost and Messiaen sought to establish his own theories on a pedagogical basis with the publication in 1939 of the *Vingt leçons d'harmonie*, to be followed in 1944 by *Technique de mon langage musical*.[2] Messiaen's highly individual

Messiaen and students, 1952; Karlheinz Stockhausen is in the back row, fourth from the right.

stylistic mélange was further refined in *Quatuor pour la fin du temps*, the chamber work he composed during his internment; in April 1945 he was to provide Paris with its first artistic scandal since 1939 with the première of his *Trois petites liturgies de la présence divine*, in which the combination of unabashed religious devotion (to texts – 'modern psalms' – by the composer himself) and a highly coloured harmonic palette aroused fierce factionalism.

At that time Pierre Boulez (*b* 1925) was studying with Messiaen. He had arrived at the Conservatoire in 1944[3] after spending a year studying mathematics in Lyons. He swiftly realized that for him and his like-minded contemporaries Messiaen offered the only viable way forward, and he made arrangements to study composition privately with him:

> In the wastes – and wastings – of the Conservatoire a single personality stood out as a clear beacon, teaching only harmony but having a reputation to which more than a hint of sulphur attached. Choosing such a man as master meant, as you can imagine, already isolating oneself from the majority and making onself out as a rebel, because in those days people were very ready to speak of 'the Messiaen class', in inverted commas. Both name and inverted commas were quite justified in fact, because Messiaen's class (harmony was later dropped from its schedule) was the only one that gave its members that conspiratorial feeling beneath all the excitement of technical dicovery for young people devoted to 'l'artisanat furieux'.[4]

Boulez was by far the most radical and gifted of Messiaen's early pupils. Nevertheless, Messiaen's reputation as a teacher of unparalleled open mind spread widely, at the same time as his achievements as a composer were increasingly recognized. Boulanger's absence from Paris during the occupation and the first years of liberation (she taught in the USA from 1940 to 1946) had deprived the neo-classicists temporarily of their pedagogical focus, and though she was to resume her activities in the capital and became director of the American Conservatory at Fontainebleau in 1950, Boulanger's subsequent influence on French-born composers was substantially reduced.

By the time Messiaen's *Turangalîla-Symphonie* received its first performance in 1947, more gifted young composers were being drawn to his classes. Jean-Louis Martinet (*b* 1912) and Serge Nigg (*b* 1924) had been contemporaries of Boulez; Jean Barraqué (1928–73) was to join the classes in 1948. Meanwhile Boulez had discovered the other necessary ingredient for his own radical reappraisal of musical language. After his year of formal studies with Messiaen he had worked with René Leibowitz, a Polish-born pupil of Schoenberg and Webern in

Berlin and Vienna in the early 1930s, who had settled in Paris at the end of World War II. Leibowitz, whose *Schönberg et son école* (1948) was the first book-length study of the Second Viennese School outside the German language, offered Boulez and his contemporaries a rigorous grounding in Schoenbergian twelve-note technique, an aesthetic that pre-war Paris had rejected almost entirely in favour of Stravinskian neo-classicism. Though Schoenberg was soon to be castigated by Boulez for his unwillingness to break away from classical forms, it was that discipline, coupled with the more exotic range of influences encouraged by Messiaen, which formed the basis of Boulez's early style.

Yet Boulez was proving to be much more than a strikingly radical composer. He appeared professionally as a pianist and conductor – since 1946 he had worked for Jean-Louis Barrault and Madeleine Renaud's theatre company based at the Marigny Theatre, and was to remain its music director for the next decade – and established a reputation as a vigorous polemicist. In 1945, with his fellow students from Messiaen's class, Boulez had organized a noisy demonstration after the European première of Stravinsky's *Danses concertantes* in the Salle Gaveau. While he was re-evaluating and reworking musical language to his own requirements, he was also denouncing what he saw as the false historical steps of the previous generation with a forceful-ness in tune with the fervid intellectual climate of postwar Paris, a city at ease with the polemical tradition and with an appetite for radicalism in all the arts unsatisfied after five years of Nazi proscription.

Boulez was quick to reassess recent musical history from the perspective of his own compositional interests, and in a succession of articles, many later reprinted in his *Relevés d'apprenti*,[5] he set down this revised view of the progress of modernism: Webern rather than Schoenberg was saluted as the progressive member of the Second Viennese School, the whole of Stravinsky's neo-classical period (the works after the *Symphonies of Wind Instruments* of 1920) was condemned, and Debussy was restored as the fountain-head of twentieth-century radicalism. A few years later, when Schoenberg died in Los Angeles in 1951, Boulez was able to underscore the new order in the severest possible way; 'Schoenberg is dead', an article published as an obituary the following year in *The Score*, attempted to put straight the historical record as Boulez perceived it:

> It is easy to forget that a certain Webern also laboured; to be sure, one never hears this discussed anymore . . . It has become indispensable to demolish a misunderstanding that is full of ambiguity and contradiction; it is time to neutralize the setback . . . Therefore I do not hesitate to write, not out of any desire to provoke a stupid scandal, but equally without hypocrisy and pointless melancholy: SCHOENBERG IS DEAD.[6]

In the late 1940s, however, in the series of works from the miniature *Notations* for piano (1945, some of which were reworked in the 1980s as orchestral pieces) and the flute Sonatina (1946), through the first two piano sonatas (1946 and 1948), the cantatas *Le visage nuptial* (1947) and *Le soleil des eaux* (1948) to the *Livre pour quatuor* (1949), Boulez established a syntax indebted to Schoenberg or Webern embodying a sensuousness of sound that could not have been derived from the Second Viennese School but traced a lineage, through Messiaen, back to Debussy. By the time the pieces for string quartet appeared Boulez's position at the head of a new Parisian avant garde was unquestioned and his musical language was moving towards a new rigour. Duration, timbre, dynamics and attack, as well as pitch, would be organized using a single numerical series, and the implications of the Schoenbergian twelve-note method could be followed to their logical conclusion.

Impetus for that next theoretical step came, surprisingly perhaps, from Messiaen. In his *Mode de valeurs et d'intensités* for piano, one of the *Quatre études de rythme* composed in 1949, Messiaen used a 'scale' of durations, dynamics and attacks in permutation throughout the piece. It was a line of exploration that Messiaen was to take little further. His music of the 1950s shows a measured retreat from the radical position he had occupied in the late 1940s towards an even more highly personalized musical style; transcribed birdsong, which he had begun to include in his pieces in the 1940s, was to become an increasingly important element. But the first performance of the *Mode de valeurs* served as just the catalyst the younger generation required.

Messiaen had composed the work while attending the Darmstadt summer school in 1949. The school had begun as early as 1946 as a development from the Internationales Musikinstitut, an information centre for composers founded by the young German musicologist Wolfgang Steinecke, who saw the need for a new beginning in German music which had no connection with the Third Reich and which, on the contrary, owed its allegiance to the very music banned by the Nazis. In the first years the school's *éminence grise* was Wolfgang Fortner (*b* 1907), whose music, in spite of his growing fascination with serialism, was rooted in neo-classical sensibilities; so too were the earliest works of Hans Werner Henze (*b* 1926), a pupil of Fortner, and Bernd Alois Zimmermann (1918–70), both of whom attended the summer schools throughout this period.

In 1948 Leibowitz was invited to teach at Darmstadt, and the emphasis of the summer school changed sharply. For the next few years it was firmly wedded to Schoenbergian principles, and the associated technique quickly permeated the music of both Zimmermann and Henze, who, initially at least, attempted to reconcile its precepts with those of neo-classicism. Leibowitz invited some of his French pupils to Darmstadt, but Boulez was not among them; by then he had committed the heresy of rejecting Schoenberg in favour of Webern. The conductor Hermann Scherchen (1891–1966) was a regular contributor and under the Darmstadt aegis gave the first European performances of a number of Schoenberg's scores; he was also responsible for encouraging the Italians Luigi Nono (1924–90) and Bruno Maderna (1920–73) to attend, from 1950. Other young composers were attracted and the radical cadre grew steadily; the following year Karlheinz Stockhausen (*b* 1928) and Karel Goeyvaerts (*b* 1923) enrolled, and their admiration for Messiaen's *Mode de valeurs* led them towards a formulation of total serialism.

The Belgian Goeyvaerts, who had studied with Messiaen in 1947–8, took the first step: his Sonata for Two Pianos, part of which was played (by Stockhausen and the composer) in Theodor Adorno's composition seminar at Darmstadt in 1951, used series of durations, modes of attack and dynamics to organize its central movements. Although the technique was quite primitive, it served to motivate Stockhausen towards his own experiments. Later the same year, Stockhausen completed *Kreuzspiel* for oboe, bass clarinet, piano and percussion, which in the sophistication of its organization went far beyond anything attempted by Messiaen or Goeyvaerts. Until he went to Darmstadt, Stockhausen's scores, and his musical education (his most significant teacher at the Cologne Academy was Frank Martin), appear to have been unremarkable, orientated much more towards Bartók and Stravinsky than the Second Viennese School. His encounter with Goeyvaerts and with the stimulating and cosmopolitan world of the summer school brought about a quantum leap in his development; in 1952 he too became a member of Messiaen's analysis classes in Paris.

Boulez, meanwhile, had sought independently to absorb the significance of *Mode de valeurs*. After the completion of *Livre pour quatuor* in 1949 he wrote no new works for almost two years, in marked contrast to his rush of scores after 1945; the pause for reflection may have been as much the result of his first meeting with John Cage, who visited Paris in 1949 and with whom he kept in close correspondence for several years, as an attempt to find his own way forward in the serialist vanguard.[7] In 1951 he had recruited another young composer to the serialist cause, Henri Pousseur (*b* 1929), and had begun to compose his first totally serial scores – the first book of *Structures* for two pianos and *Polyphonie X* for eighteen instruments.

When Stockhausen arrived in Paris to study with Messiaen at the beginning of 1952 the leaders of the postwar avant garde were, temporarily at least, united in their artistic purpose. 'I recall the first meeting very well', Boulez has said,

I knew no German, Stockhausen knew no French. A friend, Louis
Sauger, translated. We gesticulated wildly. I knew immediately that
here was someone exceptional. I was right. I came to trust his music
more than anything else. We talked about music all the time – in a
way I've never talked about it with anyone else.[8]

From summer 1952 the Second Viennese School's brand of
serialism was supplanted at Darmstadt by the new doctrine promulgated by Boulez, Stockhausen and Pousseur; Stockhausen's
Kreuzspiel and Boulez's Second Piano Sonata received their first
performances that year, and Nono demonstrated that he too had
absorbed the tenets of total serialism in *Polifonica-Monodia-Ritmica*. For
the rest of the decade Darmstadt was the focus of almost all the avant-
garde activity in western Europe: the main forum in which new ideas
were discussed and from which technical innovations were disseminated.

ELECTRONIC MUSIC

In the Darmstadt summer school the newly founded Federal Republic
of Germany had provided an aesthetic home for a generation of
composers who had grown to maturity in the wake of European
fascism. They were empowered to create a new syntax untainted by the
prescriptions and prohibitions of the Third Reich, just as in the 1950s
such writers as Heinrich Böll and Gunther Grass were able to lay the
foundations of a new tradition in postwar German literature that was
outward-looking, left-wing and strongly opposed to its country's
immediate past. In other ways too the federal organization began to
provide further encouragement to new music: the system of regional
radio networks, each with its own orchestra, not only offered composers
increased opportunities for commissions and performances but also the
resources to rehearse technically demanding scores. Where the composers of the Second Viennese School often had to organize their own
concerts to get their music heard (for example Schoenberg's Society for
Private Musical Performance of 1918–21), the total serialists found a
ready supply of performances, and orchestras rapidly gaining the
expertise to unravel the most complex scores.

Such state-funded patronage allowed new musical developments to
be extended in another direction. At the Cologne radio station of
Nordwestdeutscher Rundfunk (NWDR) Herbert Eimert (1897–1972)
founded a studio for electronic music in 1952. It was not Europe's first
such establishment; in Paris in 1948 Pierre Schaeffer (*b* 1910), an
engineer for Radiodiffusion Télévision Française, had produced the
first study in what he called 'musique concrète', using natural sounds
already on disc and transforming them by simple manipulations. (Over

the next few years the increasing availability of the tape recorder, however, was to make more complex transformations of the raw material a practical possibility.) Schaeffer's first results had been broadcast by RTF the same year and in 1951 the radio station had recognized his research by establishing the Groupe de Musique Concrète and opening its facilities to other composers. Some, like Pierre Henry (*b* 1927), one of Schaeffer's early collaborators, were to remain committed to the new medium; others merely sampled its potential. Boulez and Messiaen both produced studies there, the former with increasing disillusionment; so too did Jean Barraqué (1928–73), another member of Messiaen's analysis classes and an adherent of total serialism, though he remained determinedly apart from the Darmstadt orthodoxy.[9] In 1954 Edgard Varèse created the tape part of his *Déserts* using the Paris facilities, revising it some seven years later in the Columbia-Princeton Electronic Music Center in New York.

During his year in Paris, Stockhausen also had produced a preliminary study (since lost) using Schaeffer's facilities, and after his return to West Germany he soon joined Eimert in Cologne. Their interests were different from the explorations of the Paris group; rather than relying on 'found' sound-objects which, as Boulez had discovered, only allowed approximate control of the final product, Eimert and Stockhausen set out to synthesize their raw materials from purely electronic sources, thus maintaining absolute definition over every parameter of each sound. This enabled them to achieve what had become the Grail for the total serialists – the technical means to organize every single aspect of a composition with the precision that only a medium that dispensed with the need for human performers could hope to achieve.

In synthesizing sound complexes from scratch, as it were, Stockhausen and Eimert were applying not only the principles of Fourier analysis and Helmholtz's studies of acoustics, which had been laid down in the second half of the nineteenth century and had demonstrated that any timbre could in theory be constructed from a collection of 'pure' sine tones, but also the more recent research on information theory and phonetics undertaken by Werner Meyer-Eppler of the University of Bonn using the NWDR facilities. In 1950 Meyer-Eppler had delivered a lecture to the Darmstadt summer school on 'The Sound World of Electronic Music' and the following year (the first time Stockhausen was there) he had taken part in a seminar with Eimert on 'Musik und Technik'. Meyer-Eppler's ideas were to influence Stockhausen for several years, and he was later to attend lecture courses in Bonn, but the first compositions to come out of the Cologne studio – Stockhausen's *Studien I* and *II*, resolutely described as 'Electronische Musik' rather than 'musique concrète' – used the theories in a relatively straightforward way. They were only partly successful in producing the sound complexes he sought, in the first study by combining 'pure' sine tones, in the second by filtering specific frequencies and frequency bands out of 'white noise'. But Stockhausen's aesthetic intentions at the time were clear:

> We are all more or less treading on ice, and as long as this is the case, the systems of organization being put forward represent guiderails to prevent the composer from faltering. And one has to face the fact that there are as many systems as there are grains of sand, systems that can be dreamed up and set in motion as easily as clockwork. Their number is probably infinite, but certainly only a very few of them are acceptable systems, compatible with their means of expression, and applicable without self-contradiction to all the dimensions of music. Of these still fewer are so perfectly prefigured that they yield beautiful or interesting music.[10]

In 1953 Stockhausen's activities were by no means confined to the studio, however, and he continued his refinement of serial technique in the instrumental *Kontrapunkte* (1952–3) and the first four of the series Piano Pieces (1952–3), all at least begun during his year in Paris. The première of *Kontrapunkte* established Stockhausen as leader of the total serialists; in that work he had been able to break out from the organizational straightjacket which had been such a restriction in such pieces as Boulez's *Structures*. Emboldened by their ability to put scientific flesh on the musical bones of their electronic experiments, Stockhausen and Eimert began to establish Cologne as a centre for electronic-music research, encouraging other composers to use the studio.

In October 1954 NWDR broadcast a programme of works produced in Cologne; it included Stockhausen's *Studien* as well as pieces by Eimert, Pousseur and Goeyvaerts. Radio stations elsewhere in Europe began to move towards setting up facilities of their own, eager to use the rapidly improving recording techniques and mirroring parallel developments in the USA (there, however, studios were usually funded by universities). In 1955 the Studio di Fonologia opened in Milan under the auspices of Radio Audizioni Italiane; its first directors were Bruno Maderna and Luciano Berio (*b* 1925), another member of the Darmstadt group, from 1954. Further studios opened in Warsaw (1957), London (1958) and Stockholm (1958), all funded by radio stations, and in 1957 the Siemens and Philips electronics companies established facilities in Munich and Eindhoven respectively; it was at Eindhoven that Varèse produced his *Poème électronique*, played through 350 loudspeakers in the Philips Pavilion at the Brussels World Fair in 1958.

It is arguable whether, across Europe as a whole, the lasting artistic results justified this investment in technology. From the outset the

The Philips Pavilion, designed by Le Corbusier, at the Brussels World Fair (1958). Varèse's 'Poème électronique' was staged here.

British Broadcasting Corporation's Radiophonic Workshop in London concentrated on producing incidental music for radio and television rather than on providing resources for composers to pursue their own interests. Perhaps for that reason British composers showed relatively little interest in the medium until the 1980s, when some began to be offered research time on the computer-based hardware at the Institut de Recherche et de Co-ordination Acoustique/Musique (IRCAM) in Paris. In the meantime Stockhausen had gone on to demonstrate the musical potential of the electronic medium in a pair of works hailed as the first masterpieces in the new genre – *Gesang de Jünglinge* (1955–6) and *Kontakte* (1959–60) – in which the techniques of *elektronische Musik* and *musique concrète* were reconciled and which explored the whole continuum of sounds from those naturally produced to electronically synthesized ones. By then, however, Stockhausen's preoccupations had expanded well beyond the horizons of total serialism.

BEYOND SERIALISM

With the initial period of serial experimentation over, the avant garde began to look towards ways of extending its influence and bridging the ever-widening gap between radical composers and their audiences. Institutions like Darmstadt only encouraged such an exclusive approach: there composers were offering their works only to like-minded colleagues. And though radio stations and radio orchestras broadcast new scores, they demonstrated a concern to communicate to a much wider public. At the end of 1953 Boulez conceived the idea of presenting chamber concerts in Paris that would 'serve as a means of communication between the composers of our time and the public that is interested in its time'.[11] In 1954, with the sponsorship of Jean-Louis Barrault and Madeleine Renard, he had started a series of concerts in the Petit-Marigny Theatre; a year later they were transferred to a larger venue, a new sponsor was found (Suzanne Tezenas) and the series relaunched as the Domaine Musical. Though Boulez was always the guiding spirit he did little conducting in the early years, and the direction of most performances was left to Hermann Scherchen. The programmes were designed to present music of the present day in the context of works by those twentieth-century composers who had been influential on the avant garde. The policy that informed the planning of the Domaine Musical would characterize Boulez's career as a conductor and music director for more than two decades:

> Once we had re-established a more accurate picture of the historic period immediately preceding our own, we could perform the works of our own generation in a climate purged of ignorance. Putting the historical record straight was by no means enough: what we wanted

to do was to promote a 'new' music, so that composers would no longer have to wait forty years to hear their works performed . . . We shall not be so bold as to maintain that we have presented a series of masterpieces, should not indeed dream of making such a claim for the very good reason that we consider it quite unnecessary . . . We are not a museum for future generations; we perform what seems most likely to arouse interest.[12]

In the 1970s when Boulez took over orchestras in London and New York (as chief conductor of the BBC Symphony Orchestra), the same mixture of old and new, of works presented in terms of their implications for modernism, informed his programming. Meanwhile the concept of the Domaine Musical concerts was swiftly imitated: the BBC's studio-based Invitation Concerts, begun in 1959 by the new Controller of Music, William Glock, owed much to Boulez's example.

Between 1954 and 1964 the Domaine Musical presented almost 60% of the works of the Second Viennese School, many for the first time in Paris.[13] Concerts were long and elaborately structured. As well as chamber programmes performed by local musicians, visiting orchestras were enlisted for larger projects; in 1957, for instance, under the Domaine's auspices, the orchestra of Sudwestdeutscher Rundfunk conducted by Hans Rosbaud gave the French première of Berg's Three Orchestral Pieces op.6 of 1915. In the first few seasons Domaine programmes included Stockhausen's new *Zeitmasze*, recent scores by Berio, Nono, Pousseur and Barraqué and works by the younger generation of American composers – Cage, Christian Wolff and Feldman. The première of Boulez's own *Le marteau sans maître*, his first completed score since *Structures I*, took place not in Paris but at the festival of the International Society for Contemporary Music in Baden-Baden in 1955; it was conducted by Rosbaud, but Boulez himself introduced it to Paris in a Domaine concert the following year.

Just as Stockhausen had begun to break the bounds of total serialism in *Kontrapunkte*, and was to go further still in his *Zeitmasze* (1955–6), so Boulez had discovered the limitations of such a strict syntax: 'One soon realises', he had written in 1954, 'that composition and organisation cannot be confused for fear of maniac inanity'.[14] He went on to propose that the music of Debussy, especially the late works, offered a better model than the previously sanctified Webern; by further elaborating the serial manipulations (to the point at which, paradoxically, control became less rigorous) a composer could create a wider range of textural and expressive possibilities and, in Boulez's case, invoke Debussy as his model.

The first fruits of this new thinking were presented in *Le marteau*, in which instrumental and vocal movements were linked into a network of allusions and cross-references to create a musical object that offered any number of potential interpretative routes. The fact that Boulez was writing for the voice again shows a reorientation in his attitudes, even though the three texts by René Char, (the surrealist poet whose work had formed the basis of Boulez's earlier *Le visage nuptial* and *Le soleil des eaux*) were embedded in the textures so that their settings became merely the starting-points for instrumental commentaries. The sound-world, with its emphasis on tuned percussion, evoked non-Western musical cultures, especially those of south-east Asia, rather than the hard edges of earlier serialist scores.

Later in his essay of 1954 Boulez formulated an even more radical solution to his structural problems:

> Let us reclaim for music the right to parentheses and italics . . . a notion of discontinuous time achieved, than to structures which will become entangled instead of remaining partitioned and insulated; finally a sort of development in which the closed circle is not the only imaginable solution. We want a musical work to be something other than a succession of compartments which must be visited one after the other; instead let us try to think of it as a domain in which, as it were, one might choose one's own direction.[15]

Le marteau represented the first step towards that 'domain in which . . . one might choose one's own direction', though it would be fully realized only in Boulez's Third Piano Sonata, begun in 1956.

Stockhausen sought to find his own way out of the same impasse by resorting to his statistical studies with Meyer-Eppler. To bolster his theorizing he called on the terminology of quantum mechanics, which, with the growing public perception in the 1950s of the role modern physics (and particularly nuclear theory) would play in the contemporary world, had acquired a fashionable popularity:

> One by one, scores were written in which statistical process became very important. I started doing this in 1954, highly influenced by my teacher Meyer-Eppler, who was teaching communication science at the University of Bonn, where aleatoric processes in statistics, primarily in mathematics, but also in sociology and physics, played a strong role . . . The Hiesenberg Uncertainty Principle is based on this hypothetical behaviour of components of the atom. That was the main thing in the air at the end of the forties and beginning of the fifties. We worked with micro theories in communication science . . .
> I simply transposed everything I learned into the field of music and for the first time composed sounds which have statistical characteristics in the given field with defined limits. The elements could move, and later on this WAS also expressed in the scores. In the beginning I used the deterministic notation for indeterminate textures – I didn't know how to notate it.[16]

Stockhausen's preoccupation in the mid-1950s with the use of statistical processes as a means of musical organization parallels the direction the Greek Iannis Xenakis (*b* 1922) was taking at much the same time. Xenakis had been a member of Messiaen's classes in 1952 but had previously trained as an engineer and worked in the studio of the architect Le Corbusier in Paris. In 1954 he had completed his first orchestral score, *Metastasis*, based on Le Corbusier's designs for the Philips Pavilion at the Brussels World Fair (it received its first performance in 1955, conducted by Rosbaud, at the same ISCM Festival as *Le marteau sans maître*); in *Metastasis* vestiges of serial working are combined with more generalized sound masses controlled by the principles of stochastic processes. In an article published in 1955, Xenakis detailed his dissatisfaction with the serial method as used by the Second Viennese School, enumerating its faults and criticizing the contemporary music being composed in serialism's name:

> Linear polyphony by its present complexity destroys itself. What one hears is in reality no more than a heap of notes in various registers. The enormous complexity prevents the hearer from following the criss-crossing of lines and has as a macroscopic effect an irrational and fortuitous dispersal of notes across the whole range of the sound spectrum. There is consequently a contradiction between the linear polyphonic system and the heard result which is surface, mass.
> This inherent contradiction will disappear as soon as the independence of notes becomes complete. With the linear combinations and their polyphonic superpositions no longer operating, that which counts will be the statistic mean of isolated states of transformation of components in a given moment. The macroscopic effect could then be controlled by the average of movements of the objects chosen by us. There results from it the introduction of the notion of the probability, implied elsewhere in this actual case of the combinatory calculus.[17]

Xenakis went on to set out his stochastic theories of composition in a textbook, *Formalized Music* (1963). The elaborate statistical analyses that lay at the basis of his compositions, used to derive the relationships of large-scale formal structures to the distribution of pitches and durations, in fact permitted him far more choice than the stricter tenets of total serialism. By their very nature the theories were based on approximations and average distributions; by instinct Xenakis was a composer of aural imagination rather than theory, even though in the 1960s he developed his compositional principles to an even higher degree of complexity by using computers to generate his stochastic patterns.

The desire of much of the postwar avant garde to back up its radicalism with pseudo-scientific and quasi-mathematical treatments was characteristic of much writing about contemporary music in the mid-1950s. It centred on two new journals first published in 1955. One was the Swiss-based *Grävesaner Blätter* (the first issue of which contained

Xenakis's article quoted above); the other was *Die Reihe*, an irregular publication begun in 1955 by Universal Edition, the music-publishing house based in Vienna, which had recently begun to publish the scores of many of the Darmstadt-orientated composers, including Boulez, Stockhausen, Pousseur and Berio. Eimert and Stockhausen were the editors of *Die Reihe*, each issue of which concentrated on a single aspect of new music; the first was devoted to electronic music, later numbers (the last appeared in 1962) to Webern, 'musical craftsmanship', young composers, speech and music, and 'form-space'.[18] The articles were a heady mixture of wishful mathematics, minutely detailed analysis, compositional theorizing based on an uneasy mixture of acoustics and physics, and much devotion to what Hans Keller[19] called 'the gospel according to Saint Anton', but they nevertheless included a number of texts that defined much of the avant garde's thinking at the turning-point in total serialism.

Stockhausen was a prolific contributor. In '. . . how time passes . . .'[20] (1957) he presented the results of his studies with Meyer-Eppler and work in the Cologne studios, which had led him to the realization that pitch and duration were but micro- and macro-manifestations of the same physical property – vibration – and that a unified theory of musical organization should be able to encompass both elements within a single system; he illustrated his conclusions by reference to his own recent works, *Gesang der Jünglinge*, *Gruppen* (1955–7) for three orchestras and Piano Piece XI. In 'Music and Speech',[21] first presented as a paper at Darmstadt in 1959, Stockhausen analysed three works of the mid-1950s, his own *Gesang der Jünglinge*, Boulez's *Le marteau sans maître* and Nono's choral *Il canto sospeso*, to demonstrate how words, or more precisely syllables and phonemes, had been integrated into compositional schemes as yet another element to be organized serially.

Boulez was a less conspicuous contributor, but in the first issue of *Die Reihe* he had published 'At the ends of fruitful land . . .'; and a painstaking analysis of his *Structures Ia* by the Hungarian emigré György Ligeti (*b* 1923) became a classic serialist text. After leaving Budapest in December 1956 in the wake of the Hungarian uprising, Ligeti worked in the Cologne electronic studios, absorbing new techniques and coming to terms with total serialism. By the time he completed his first scores in the West, however, the orchestral *Apparitions* (1960) and *Atmosphères* (1961), he had established his own style; it owed as much to the electronic shaping of sound complexes as to serialist constructivism, which he viewed with much suspicion:

> I did not see any necessity for this kind of unified treatment of all the elements. Indeed, I detected in it a discrepancy: quantification applied equally within the various areas produced, from the point of view of our perception and understanding of musical processes,

radically different effects, so that there was no guarantee that a single basic order would produce analogous structures on the various levels of perception and understanding. On the contrary, adherence to a single basic order led to structures that seemed incompatible. Unity remained fixed at the level of commentary, a verbal description of the composition: it was clapped on the musical events from the outside, and had no direct impact on our minds.[22]

INDETERMINACY

'The right to parentheses and italics . . . in a domain in which, as it were, one might choose one's own direction', which Boulez had asserted for music in 'Recherches maintenant' (1954) was claimed first in his own works in the Third Piano Sonata, which he began in 1956. That year, however, Stockhausen had proposed his own radical solution with the completion of Piano Piece XI, the first work in 'mobile form' produced in Europe: the performer is provided with nineteen groups of material and directed to begin with any of them and continue in any order he or she sees fit; a set of instructions at the end of each group determines the levels of attack, dynamics and tempo of the next in the sequence.

Such a concept may have been bolstered by Stockhausen's scientific justification, his invocations of information theory and Markovian chains, but it had been prefigured in developments taking place in the USA, principally by John Cage but also by Earle Brown and Morton Feldman. Boulez had been in contact with Cage since the latter first visited Paris in 1949, when Cage's *Sonatas and Interludes* for prepared piano was performed; he had renewed the acquaintance when he visited New York with the Renaud-Barrault Theatre Company in 1952. Two years later Cage toured Europe with the pianist David Tudor, and for the first time his music was brought to the avant garde's attention. Stockhausen was fascinated by this fresh approach to composing for the piano, and, while it did not produce an immediate relaxation in his methods, his Piano Pieces V–VIII were dedicated to Tudor. But the implications of Cage's thinking were not absorbed fully by Europeans until he was invited to lecture at Darmstadt in 1958.

In the meantime both Stockhausen and Boulez were forced to justify their newly acquired approach to form in terms of their own compositional pasts; Stockhausen, as we have seen, resorted to pseudo-science; Boulez, equally characteristically, appealed to a much wider frame of cultural reference. From the late 1940s he had seen his own development as a radical composer as part of a much broader artistic movement, in which Paris took a leading role:

It was a time of great discovery. For the first time I became acquainted with the work of Klee, Kandinsky and Mondrian. The first time I discovered Schoenberg, Berg and Webern, there was no problem of connection at all. On the contrary everybody was thirsty for something out of the ordinary, different from what we had known before.[23]

In selecting texts from René Char for his first three vocal works Boulez had implicitly placed his music within a wider contemporary cultural context; and for his contribution to the first issue of *Die Reihe* he had borrowed the title from a painting by Paul Klee. Now, to explore beyond the limits of that original 'fruitful land', he had taken over a literary influence from an earlier generation; in connecting his Third Piano Sonata with Mallarmé's concepts of form, Boulez opened up new creative avenues and strengthened his allegiance to the allusive symbolist world, represented by Debussy, which informed many of the processes in *Le marteau sans maître*. The Third Piano Sonata's literary associations are apparent in the titles Boulez allotted to its 'formants'. Five were planned, but only two have been released for performance: *Trope*, which consists of a 'Texte' containing a 'Parenthèse', 'Commentaire' and 'Glose', and *Constellation-Miroir*, in which a number of musical fragments are laid out on the page in a manner influenced by the typography of Mallarmé's poem *Un coup de dès*; the performer is invited to choose one of the routes between them.

From the outset Boulez's concept of mobile form was more circumscribed than Stockhausen's and he criticized openly the loss of control that a work such as Piano Piece XI implied – 'a new sort of automatism, one which, for all its apparent opening of the gates of freedom, has only really let in an element of risk that seems to me absolutely inimical to the integrity of the work'.[24] The choices offered to the performer of his Third Piano Sonata are confined to the order of the formants (eight different sequences are allowed) and, within the two completed sections, to the selections and ordering of specified passages, so that each interpretation becomes a carefully navigated journey through densely detailed territory:

> I have often compared a work with the street-map of a town; you don't change the map, you perceive the town as it is, but there are different ways of going through it, different ways of visiting it. I find this comparison extremely suggestive, the work is like a town or labyrinth. A town is often a labyrinth too: when you visit it you choose your own direction and your own route; but it is obvious that to get to know the town you need an accurate map and knowledge of the traffic regulations.
>
> Personally I have never been in favour of chance. I do not think that chance has much to contribute on its own account. So my idea is not to change the work at every turn nor to make it look like a complete novelty, but rather to change the viewpoints and perspectives from which it is seen while leaving its basic meaning unaltered . . .[25]

Boulez presented his ideas on the use and limitations of chance procedures in 'Aléa',[26] an article published to coincide with the Sonata, and he went on to expand on his ideas of mobile form and the symbiotic relationship between music and text in his 'Portrait de Mallarmé', *Pli selon pli*, composed between 1957 and 1962. In that period, however, Cage's influence on European activities became overwhelming; the last bounds of serialist organization were finally broken and the surrendering of creative control embodied in Piano Piece XI and the Third Piano Sonata was made to seem modest gestures indeed.

Cage's advocacy of the new freedom had gone hand-in-hand with his interest in the possibilities of graphic scores (to the extent of presenting an exhibition of his scores in New York) and in the wake of his 1958 visit to Darmstadt European composers explored many forms of notation, some designed to render more performable complex schemes of durations, others intended to make the final results less prescribed and predictable. In *Zyklus* for solo percussionist and *Refrain* for three players Stockhausen produced some of the most elegant and musically serviceable of all these innovations. *Zyklus* epitomized the openness of its form in the score's construction: spiral-bound, it allowed the performer to begin on any page and play through it forwards or backwards; *Refrain* included a section of music printed on a rotating perspex slide which could be inserted at any point in the otherwise fixed formal scheme.

In more than just a cosmetic sense, however, indeterminacy began to disperse the group of composers who throughout the 1950s had been more or less held together by a shared view of the current state of music. By 1959 Boulez and Stockhausen, the dominating figures in the decade's avant garde, had developed quite different perceptions of what aleatory techniques could offer them. Stockhausen went on to refine his thinking in 'moment form', first in *Kontakte* (conceived in two versions, for tape alone and for tape, piano and percussion) and *Carré* (1959–60) for four choral and instrumental groups, and later in the grand, quasi-theatrical *Momente* (first version, 1964).

Yet the progressive fragmentation of musical language seemed to affect Boulez more profoundly. His output during the 1950s – three published works, one of those only partly completed – had not matched the steady stream of the previous decade, and during the 1960s even that rate of production was not sustained. 'Work in progress' and 'withdrawn' became common qualifications, and even *Pli selon pli*, conceived as a definitive statement of his aesthetics in the wake of total serialism, took many years to reach a final form; Boulez had always been supremely self-critical, withdrawing and leaving scores incomplete, but from the Third Piano Sonata such creative indecision appeared to become almost part of his attitude to composition, and in the 1960s it coincided with his increased celebrity as a conductor. From conducting only the Domaine Musical and his own works, Boulez began to conduct other orchestras in Europe and the USA in the twentieth-century repertory; by the end of the decade his activities in the concert hall appeared to have replaced those of the composer.

INVENTING TRADITIONS

For the composers involved with the remaking of musical language in the 1950s it was easy to discard all vestiges of tradition. World War II had severed so many cultural threads that for the generation of young musicians beginning their careers in the late 1940s, tracing historical links must have seemed more difficult than creating new allegiances; and for central European composers especially it was a process charged with political and emotional resonances. Thus, when Messiaen encouraged his students to look outside the European art-music tradition for technical models, or later when the total serialists found more sustenance in the theories of physics and mathematics than in the music of even the Second Viennese School, the very premises on which composition was based appeared to have been changed utterly; the gap between composer and audience was wider than it had ever been, and communication took second place to the urge to make everything new.

The question of tradition reasserted itself, however, when the tenets of serialism came under threat – from within, because composers began to realize the limitations of the constraints they had imposed on themselves, and from without, as they perceived the implications of the work of Cage and his followers. For some (Boulez being the most obvious example) there could be no retrenchment; the creative consequences of that have been discussed above. Boulez's willingness to pursue an international career as a conductor could be viewed as his attempt to establish links between audiences and twentieth-century music in general and his own compositions in particular. For others, including Stockhausen, highly personalized traditions could be created in which performance played a vital role and which sought out non-Western perceptions. For yet another group, the past could be re-created, filtered and transformed, made viable and made to conform to current compositional requirements.

Stockhausen's direction after the completion of *Momente* was hard to predict. An exercise in symbolic notation, orginally written for a composition class at the Cologne New Music Course in 1963, was published as *Plus-Minus*, '2 × 7 pages for working out', and offered performers a sequence of cells through which they could travel, following the rules and signs contained in each; in doing so they created a piece in which the composer's role had been strictly limited.

For many years I had worked on the idea of writing a piece having such powers of metamorphosis that I might one day come across it and hardly recognise it as my own, until a further encounter assured me of its authenticity . . . When I heard the tape of the [Cornelius] Cardew–[Frederick]Rzewski version of *Plus-Minus* for the first time [in 1964], I was, in a truly unselfish sense, fascinated by it . . . I now find myself listening more adventurously, discovering a music summoned forth from me: feeling myself an instrument in the service of a profound and intangible power, experienciable only in music, in the poetry of sounds.[27]

Plus-Minus began as little more than an experiment in the limits of notation and compositional control, but its techniques came to dominate Stockhausen's music until 1970. In a series of works, beginning with *Mikrophonie I* (1964) for amplified tam-tam, he began to collaborate with a regular ensemble of musicians who became adept at working from his graphic scores and who developed a corporate creative identity which seemed to displace the composer's.

The borderline between this method of working and improvisation came to seem thin, especially when in 1968 Stockhausen produced *Aus den Sieben Tagen*, a sequence of fifteen compositions of unspecified duration and instrumentation, consisting entirely of short texts to which the performers are required to react and collaborate: 'I have called this music, which expresses the spiritual accord among musicians, channelled by means of short texts, *intuitive music*. "Improvisation" no longer seems the right word for what we are playing, since it invariably conjures up an image of underlying structures, formulae, and peculiarities of style'.[28] The text pieces represented the extreme point in Stockhausen's more towards a meditative mode of music in the 1960s. Two years later he would alter course dramatically, returning to fully notated, quasi-tonal composition with *Mantra* (1970) for two pianos. In 1967 he had produced *Stimmung* for six amplified vocalists, an extended exploration of the nuances of vocal technique and harmonic resonance; in many ways it sums up his preoccupations of the period – his interest in the dynamics of group performance and an immersion in Eastern philosophies.

It is tempting to associate Stockhausen's infatuation with the mystical and meditative in the 1960s with the drift of popular culture in Europe and America towards the East, with the West's discovery of transcendental meditation and the growth of communalism. Stockhausen's music chimed with the thinking of a new generation, giving it a popularity to which the postwar avant garde had been quite unaccustomed, and it cannot be an accident that the texts of *Aus den Sieben Tagen* were written in May 1968, the month in which youth culture made its most determined effort to assert itself. But the roots of such musical thinking lay farther in Stockhausen's past, and when in the early 1960s he had visited Japan he had been profoundly interested in many aspects of its culture and perceptions:

I became aware that the Japanese have a completely different *time* [from the European one]. The Japanese have a far larger time scale at the bottom, which means they have much slower and longer events than we would admit; we'd call them boring or wouldn't experience them for any length. We would never conceive of a music that lasts three days, we would never listen to sounds, that, as single sounds, one after another, last longer than ten seconds. And the same is true for the very fast events. There is not very much in the middle region of time. But at the very fast and the very slow regions they have more octaves, so to speak, than we do.[29]

That initial excitement with Japan had crystallized in the exuberant tape piece *Telemusik* (1966), a skilful amalgam of non-European sounds – gagaku instruments, gamelan orchestras and ceremonial cries – which Stockhausen composed in the electronic music studio of NHK in Tokyo. It was his first use of any material other than his own, and in that piece and the much more ambitious electronic work *Hymnen* (also planned in 1966), the raw material of which is a vast array of national anthems, his music came closest to the techniques of collage and quotation that had dominated the work of a number of his European contemporaries in the 1960s.

Luciano Berio had used quotations in relatively few works, but he nevertheless had become associated with the technique; and the third movement of his *Sinfonia* (1968–9) is taken to be the *locus classicus* of this characteristic approach of the 1960s. In it Berio used the Scherzo from Mahler's Second Symphony as the framework on which to assemble an elaborate collection of references – literary as well as musical. The Scherzo becomes, according to Berio,

a generator of harmonic functions and of musical references that are pertinent to them, which appear, disappear, pursue their own courses, return to Mahler, cross paths, transform themselves into Mahler or hide behind it. The references to Bach, Brahms, Boulez, Berlioz, Schoenberg, Stravinsky, Strauss, Stockhausen etc. are therefore *also* signals which indicate which harmonic country we are going through, like bookmarkers, or little flags in different colours struck into a map to indicate salient points during an expedition full of surprises.[30]

Yet from the 1950s Berio had been profoundly affected by James Joyce, setting his poems in *Chamber Music* (1953) and sub-titling his 1958 tape piece *Thema*, 'Omaggio a Joyce'; the structural conceits of both *Ulysses* and *Finnegan's Wake* evidently drew Berio towards a notion of stylistic plurality, towards a lapidary technique in which recognizable musical 'objects' could both retain their identity and acquire new significance from their imposed context. In his preparations for *Thema*, Berio collaborated with the philosopher, semiologist and (much later) novelist Umberto Eco, gaining an insight into 'poetic onomatopeia' that served for a number of subsequent vocal works, including *Circles* (1960), a setting of e e cummings, and *Sequenza III* (1966) for solo soprano, part of a sequence of solo works to which Berio returned regularly since the first, for flute, of 1958. But his other literary associations, with the poet Eduardo Sanguineti and the novelist Italo Calvino, also fostered a sense of common ground between literature and music, and that was unusual in the radical composers of Berio's generation.

In two collaborations for which Sanguineti wrote or assembled the texts, *Epifanie* (1961) and *Laborintus II* (1965), Berio used verbal associations as the points of departure for his musical allusions; the earlier work includes material by Proust, Joyce, Machado, Simon, Brecht and Sanguineti himself, each set by Berio in a different style, divided into twelve sections that constitute a Boulezian mobile form: their order may be changed, though only within limits prescribed by the composer. But in *Laborintus II* Sanguineti's text is more like the anchor than the point of departure, embedded in the textures while Berio constructs round it an array of images, including snatches of jazz, folk- and popular song – what he called 'the (entirely invented) musical catalogue that is *Laborintus II*'.[31]

If Berio's references were essentially outward-looking, designed to create round his music a bundle of connections and to enrich its cultural frame, the quotations that characterized the music of B. A. Zimmermann from the early 1960s until the end of his life were much more consciously intended to restore links with lost culture. In his opera *Die Soldaten*, composed between 1958 and 1964, Zimmermann used quotation as a musical equivalent of the dramatic plurality in which he conceived his setting of Lenz's drama. The action is frequently split on to different stages; similarly the music separates into stylistic strands, some presenting Zimmermann's 'own' style, others quoting freely from a wide assortment of sources ranging from J. S. Bach to the twentieth century. It was an approach he went on to use in other dramatic works (including two 'imaginary ballets') and orchestral and chamber pieces.

In Berio's and Zimmermann's music the use of quotation is overt; just as the emergence of Bach's chorale *Ich habe genug* in the final section of Berg's Violin Concerto was designed to carry a specific emotional charge, so Berio's and Zimmermann's references are meant to be heard as such. A group of British composers, however, who all studied in Manchester in the mid-1950s, used existing material, especially medieval music, as a much more fundamental compositional ingredient, as part of a scheme in which the origins of the borrowing (indeed the fact of the borrowing itself) might or might not be revealed.

Alexander Goehr (*b* 1932), Peter Maxwell Davies (*b* 1934) and Harrison Birtwistle (*b* 1934) received a thorough grounding in serialism and as students remained in touch with developments through Goehr, whose father had been a pupil of Schoenberg and a noted conductor of contemporary music. With the pianist and composer John Ogdon and the trumpeter (later conductor) Elgar Howarth, they formed the New Music Manchester Group which was responsible for introducing many European scores to Britain. None of these composers, however, adopted serial techniques wholeheartedly; rather they had been alerted to the possibilities for controlling and organizing all aspects of a composition. Even from their earliest published works, the procedures were used to manipulate borrowed material, especially plainchant monodies which were combined with medieval devices such as mensuration canon, isorhythm, prolation and verse-and-refrain forms.

Until the mid-1960s Birtwistle's music was heavily indebted to these techniques, though from that point he began to develop a highly personal manner of handling his material; Davies first used such methods in his Trumpet Sonata of 1956 and continued to do so, even if his music from the late 1970s onwards has tended to lose its modernist characteristics. The models changed: the orchestral *Prolation* (1959), as its title indicates, used prolation with a rigour that recalled some of the contemporary serial scores of Nono; the starting-point of the wind sextet *Alma redemptoris mater* was a motet by Dunstable, that of the First String Quartet of 1961 the *Sonata sopra Sancta Maria* from Monteverdi's Vespers of 1610. Davies's music of the late 1950s and early 1960s, however, was dominated by a group of substantial pieces clustered about the evolution of his first opera *Taverner* (1962–8), a project on the life of the Tudor composer John Taverner that he had nurtured since his student days. Much of the material in the opera and in two orchestral *Taverner* fantasias composed as studies for it is derived by transformational processes from Taverner's Mass *Gloria tibi trinitas*.

Davies's interest in early music (as it came to be called) in some respects reflected a growing public awareness of the importance, if not the very existence, of a wealth of material that remained hardly known. In the mid-1960s early-music groups were formed in Europe and the USA and efforts were made to establish 'authentic' performance styles. To young composers in the 1950s, deluged with theory, bombarded with ever more complex rationales and methods, a return to the equally sophisticated (though infinitely less selfconscious) procedures of the fifteenth and sixteenth centuries must have appeared highly seductive as well as providing links with tradition that were less compromising aesthetically than the use of quotation and pastiche.

Modern Times

OPERA, POLITICS AND MUSIC THEATRE

Boulez and his like-minded colleagues had little time for opera in the 1950s; its historical trappings were too overpowering, its associations with outmoded musical grammar too intense to survive the wholesale revision that the new generation required. As a conductor Boulez was tempted into the opera house, but his feelings about the medium have remained, at the very least, ambivalent. In 1976, after he had conducted *Parsifal*, *Pelléas et Mélisande* and *Wozzeck*, and was about to take on the centenary production of the *Ring* at Bayreuth, he reasserted his position:

> I once said that the most elegant solution of the problem of opera was to blow up the opera houses, and I still think this is true. Opera is the area before all others in which things have stood still . . . As I see it, *Wozzeck* is the last 'opera', extending and completing the traditional form.[32]

Boulez was to remain almost the only composer of his generation who did not eventually to make some kind of creative *rapprochement* with the musical theatre. But until the 1960s at least, opera interested only those whose attitude to traditional forms and usages was less uncompromising. From the late 1940s Henze was immersed in the theatre, demonstrating his dramatic abilities in a sequence of operas beginning with the 'lyric drama' *Boulevard Solitude* in 1951, the subject matter and musical language of which were rooted in nineteenth- and early twentieth-century archetypes. The scenario of *Boulevard Solitude*, for instance, adapts the story of Manon Lescaut, as used by Massenet and Puccini, changing the perspective from Manon to that of Des Grieux; its musical language combines neo-classical traits and elements of serialism with references to jazz and to material culled from Puccini's *La bohème*. *Der Prinz von Homburg* (1958) is an adaptation of a story by Kleist. Henze's sequence of operas culminated in 1965 with *The Bassarids*, to a libretto by W. H. Auden and Chester Kallmann (who had provided the text for Henze's *Elegy for Young Lovers* in 1961); Henze imposed a continuous symphonic structure on the action, using Berg's *Lulu* as his prototype.

In Britain the operas of Benjamin Britten (1913–76) paralleled Henze's in their reliance on 'historical' subject matter. But where Henze's attitude to his native country, and in particular to the Nazi period, was profoundly negative (to the extent that he left West Germany in 1953 to live in Italy), the première in London of Britten's *Peter Grimes* in 1945 signalled a renaissance in the fortunes of British opera and the renewal of an operatic tradition that the country had not claimed since the nineteenth century. To a nation immersed in postwar reconstruction, Britten offered works that found a ready audience, in spite of their narrow range of subject and a musical language that was outward-looking (*Wozzeck* and Gershwin's *Porgy and Bess*, for instance, are part of the background of *Peter Grimes*). Britten's operas, though, found few immediate successors.

In his pre-war works, such as *Our Hunting Fathers* (1936, to texts by the poet W. H. Auden), the Variations on a Theme of Frank Bridge (1937) and the Rimbaud settings of *Les illuminations* (1939), Britten had served notice of his precocious talents. He had quickly created a highly personal musical language which, though indebted to a peculiarly English lyricism, also took elements from Mahler, Berg and from the early neo-classicism of Prokofiev and Stravinsky: all were unlikely models for a young British composer in the 1930s. In 1939 Britten emigrated to North America, where he was able to continue his collaboration with Auden. In their ballad opera *Paul Bunyan*, which had its première in New York in 1941, Britten drew on the indigenous style of New Deal populists like Copland.

Britten returned to England in 1942 and was exempted from war service as a conscientious objector. He began work on *Peter Grimes*, which he had conceived in the USA the previous year. Based on an episode in George Crabbe's narrative poem *The Borough*, which portrays a fishing community in Britten's native Suffolk, *Peter Grimes* was an English 'grand opera' par excellence. Its première was an overwhelming success, but economic conditions in postwar England remained inimical to the production of stage works on such an ambitious scale. In *The Rape of Lucretia* (1946) and *Albert Herring* (1947) Britten explored the potential of 'chamber opera', paring down both vocal and orchestral forces.

The première of *Albert Herring* at Glyndebourne marked the debut of the English Opera Group, of which Britten was a co-founder. Formed as a touring company, this group was to remain immensely influential in British operatic life for the next quarter-century. It continued to provide a focus for Britten's own activity – *The Turn of the Screw* (1954), *A Midsummer Night's Dream* (1960) and the three 'parables for church performance', beginning with *Curlew River* (1964), were all composed for the English Opera Group. But the group also introduced works by younger British composers; in 1967 at the Aldeburgh Festival, for instance, it gave the première of Birtwistle's *Punch and Judy*. Britten had made his home at Aldeburgh in 1947, and with his companion, the tenor Peter Pears, initiated a music festival there the following year. Aldeburgh grew steadily in importance, both in Britten's creative career and in British musical life; Britten performed there regularly as pianist and conductor, and increasingly his major works received their first performances under its auspices.

Britten's output continued to be articulated by his operas, right up to his last major work, *Death in Venice* (1972); but he also explored almost every other genre, from ballet (*The Prince of the Pagodas,* 1957) and oratorio (*War Requiem*, 1962) to string quartet and solo instrumental works. Throughout the 1950s and 60s Britten, joined increasingly by Michael Tippett (*b* 1905), provided a core of achievement in British music; their stylistic preoccupations, while far removed from those of the European avant garde, provided a fertile background from which younger composers would eventually be able to make a *rapprochement* with their contemporaries in France, Italy and Germany.

Tippett was slower to find his voice than Britten. He first claimed public attention with the oratorio *A Child of Our Time* (1941). But it was his first opera, *A Midsummer Marriage*, given its première at Covent Garden in 1955, that demonstrated Tippett's dramatic originality and signalled the maturing of his richly lyrical musical language. That expressive world spilt over into the orchestral and instrumental works grouped round *A Midsummer Marriage*. It was to be superseded in his second opera, *King Priam* (1961), which confirmed a new direction, prefigured in his Second Symphony (1957), that was much more rhythmically abrasive, hard-edged and indebted to Stravinskian neo-classicism. Through *The Knot Garden* (1969) and *The Ice Break* (1977) Tippett's operas continued to determine the course of his development and to shape the musical parameters of the works round them. For the generation of British composers born in the 1930s who found the encouragement and resources to write operas in the late 1960s – Goehr (*Arden Must Die*, 1967), Davies (*Taverner*, 1972), Birtwistle (*Punch and Judy*, 1968) and Nicholas Maw (*The Rising of the Moon*, 1970) – it was arguably Tippett's self-renewal and unprejudiced eclecticism rather than Britten's constrained and circumscribed expressive world that proved the more influential and inspirational.

To such operatic events the European avant garde reacted – if it reacted at all – with indifference, and only in 1960 did its opposition to opera begin to disintegrate. In all his works since the early 1950s Luigi Nono had combined his adherence to total serialism with a commitment to Marxism, and it was in an attempt to make political content yet more explicit that he produced the 'scenic action' *Intolleranza 1960*, first staged in Venice in 1961. In its wake Berio wrote *Passaggio* (1962), a '*messa in scena*' for solo soprano, two choruses (one in the pit, one dispersed round the auditorium) and orchestra, which shared many of *Intolleranza*'s social concerns; Sanguineti supplied the text. At the end of the decade came *Opera*, a less convincing synthesis of current theatrical trends and 'happenings' from which Berio went on to abstract self-contained vocal works. Pousseur also turned to opera: *Votre Faust* (1967), in its amalgam of languages, actions and musical quotations (for which the audience is invited to take responsibility by selecting the course of events), offered not only a critique of the history of opera since

Collage of slide and film projections designed by Josef Svoboda for the first production of Nono's 'Intolleranza 1960' in Venice, 1961.

the nineteenth century but also by implication an examination of Pousseur's own development.

Nono's work for the rest of the decade was exclusively concerned with propagating a political message and he moved away from the conventional media of instrumental and orchestral music towards electronic-based composition: in *La fabbrica illuminata* (1964), for soprano and tape, the electronically treated sounds are derived from the noise of a steel foundry; in *Y entonces comprendio* (1970), for female chorus, tape and electronics, the tape contains a recording of Fidel Castro reading a letter from Che Guevara. Nono did not compose another opera until 1974, when *Al gran sole carico d'amore* was staged at La Scala, Milan; only *A floresta è jovem e cheja de vida* (1966), for voices, clarinet, bell plates and tape, contained explicit dramatic elements.

Henze's increasing commitment to left-wing causes in the 1960s led him temporarily to abandon conventional opera after *The Bassarids*, though he was to return to it in 1976 with *We Come to the River*, the 'actions for music' to a text by Edward Bond, staged at Covent Garden. But in a series of works from the late 1960s onwards he used the more fluid conventions of 'music-theatre' to package his politics.

With the increasing expense of opera production and the reluctance of opera houses to commission new works, composers increasingly found the need to explore smaller-scale ways of presenting musico-dramatic ideas. Works as various as Monteverdi's *Il combattimento di Tancredi e Clorinda*, Stravinsky's *The Soldier's Tale*, Schoenberg's *Pierrot lunaire* and Weill's *Mahagonny Songspiel* were cited as precedents. Ligeti's surreal *Aventures* and *Nouvelles aventures* (1962–5) began to suggest a new mode of abstract vocal drama, and many of the works of Mauricio Kagel (*b* 1931) used theatrical devices to question and often to subvert the conventions of musical culture. Kagel arrived in Cologne from his native Argentina in 1957 and in his first European work, *Anagrama* (1958), offered a critique on the avant garde's preciously theoretical attitude to text and music: though his orchestral textures had all the fastidious exactness of a composer who had studied the required scores, his vocal writing, using text simply as a phonetic resource, incorporated a whole range of sounds, from whispering to shrieking, that were to become common among works of the 1960s. In *Sur scène* (1960), however, he turned his attention to performance, and in a series of works in the 1960s, he cast increasingly ironic glances at the activities of musicians and called into question just what constitutes a performance.

The Argentinian composer Mauricio Kagel (centre) in a scene from his 'Staatstheater', performed in the Staatsoper, Hamburg, 1971.

In Britain, Goehr, Maxwell Davies and Birtwistle established their own brand of music theatre that was less subversive and more conventional in its approach to narrative than its European counterparts; Goehr's *Triptych* (1968–70), Davies's *Revelation and Fall* (1966), *Eight Songs for a Mad King* (1969) and *Vesalii Icones* (1969) were all more or less continuous in their dramatic structure, while Birtwistle's *Punch and Judy* (1968) used many of the economies of music theatre in a work with the proportions and forces of conventional opera.

NOTES

[1] The other members of the group were André Jolivet (1905–74), Daniel-Lesur (*b* 1908) and Yves Baudrier (*b* 1906).

[2] O. Messiaen, *Technique de mon langage musical* (Paris, 1944; Eng. trans., 1957).

[3] A fascinating glimpse of Boulez's early years in Paris is offered by P. Heyworth, 'The First Fifty Years', in *Pierre Boulez: a Symposium*, ed. W. Glock (London, 1986).

[4] P. Boulez, 'Une classe et ses chimères', a tribute to Messiaen on his 50th birthday printed in the programme for the Domaine Musical concert on 15 April 1959; repr. in P. Boulez, *Points de repère* (Paris, 1981, rev. 1985); Eng. trans. as *Orientations* (London, 1986), 404.

[5] P. Boulez, *Relevés d'apprenti* (Paris, 1966; Eng. trans., 1968, as *Notes of an Apprenticeship*).

[6] Obituary of Schoenberg, *The Score*, no.6 (1952), 18–22; repr. as 'Schoenberg est mort', in *Relevés d'apprenti*, 265–72.

[7] P. Griffiths, in a programme note for the British première of the revised version of *Le visage nuptial* (BBC SO, Royal Festival Hall, London, 23 Nov 1989).

[8] Quoted in J. Peyser, *Boulez: Composer, Conductor, Enigma* (London, 1977), 76.

[9] A detailed and highy partial account of Barraqué's early development is in A. Hodeir, *La musique depuis Debussy* (Paris, 1961; Eng. trans., 1961 as *Since Debussy*), which also reviews the history of twentieth-century music from the strictest post-Webern perspective.

[10] K. Stockhausen, *Texte I: zur elektronischen und instrumentalen musik* (Cologne, 1963), 47; quoted and translated in R. Maconie, *The Works of Karlheinz Stockhausen* (Oxford, 1976), 73.

[11] Quoted in Peyser, *Boulez*, 109.

[12] P. Boulez, 'Dix ans après', in *Cahiers Renaud-Barrault* no.41 (Dec 1965); Eng. trans. in *Orientations*, 437–8.

[13] See Peyser, *Boulez*, 110.

[14] P. Boulez, 'Recherches maintenant', in *Relevés d'apprenti*, 27–32; quoted and translated in Griffiths, op. cit. p.89.

[15] Quoted and translated in Griffiths, programme note for *Le visage nuptial*, 90.

[16] J. Cott, *Stockhausen: Conversations with the Composer* (London, 1974), 67–8.

[17] I. Xenakis, 'La crise de la musique serielle', *Grävesaner Blätter*, no.1 (1955); quoted and translated in N. Matossian, *Xenakis* (London, 1986), 85–6.

[18] Issues of *Die Reihe* were also published in English translation from 1958 to 1968.

[19] H. Keller, 'Music, 1975', in *1975* (London, 1977), 133–269.

[20] *Die Reihe*, no.3 (1957).

[21] *Die Reihe*, no.6 (1960).

[22] *Ligeti in Conversation* (London, 1983), 129.

[23] Interview with Boulez; quoted in Matossian, *Xenakis*, 44.

[24] A. Goléa, *Rencontres avec Pierre Boulez* (Paris, 1958); quoted and translated in Griffiths, programme note for *Le visage nuptial*, 118.

[25] P. Boulez, *Conversations with Célestin Deliège* (Paris, 1975; Eng. trans., London, 1976), 82–3.

[26] 'Aléa', *Nouvelle revue française*, lix (1957); repr. in *Relevés d'apprenti*, 41–56.

[27] K. Stockhausen, *Texte III: zur Musik 1963–70* (Cologne, 1971); quoted and translated in Maconie, *The Works of Karlheinz Stockhausen*, 181.

[28] Ibid, 251.

[29] Cott, *Stockhausen*, 30.

[30] L. Berio, interview with R. Dalmonte, in *Luciano Berio: Two Interviews*, ed. D. Osmond-Smith (London, 1985), 107.

[31] Ibid, 105.

[32] P. Boulez, 'Libérer la musique', in *Preuves*, 2nd ser. (1972), 133–8; translated in *Orientations*, 485.

BIBLIOGRAPHICAL NOTE

Social history and politics

There is a plethora of studies on the political and social aftermath of World War II and the processes of European reconstruction and realignment. D. W. Urwin, *Western Europe since 1945: a Political History* (Harlow, 1968), A. S. Milward, *The Reconstruction of Western Europe 1945–1951* (London, 1984), and F. R. Willis, *France, Germany and the New Europe 1945–1967* (London, 1969) provide background; C. J. Bartlett, *A History of Post-War Britain 1945–1974* (London, 1977), D. L. Hanley, *Contemporary France: Politics and Society since 1945* (London, 1979), A. Cobban, *A History of Modern France 1871–1962* (London, 1962), are more detailed studies.

Visual arts

Among the varied histories of twentieth-century painting and sculpture, there are few that deal extensively with the period since 1945; those that do inevitably concentrate on American artists. W. Haftmann, *Painting in the Twentieth Century*, 2 vols. (London, 1961), N. Lynton, *The Story of Modern Art* (Oxford, 1989), and R. Hughes, *The Shock of the New* (London, 1980), concern European developments since World War II though they devote much space to the earlier origins of modernism; the essays in *Theories of Modern Art*, ed. H. B. Chipp (Berkeley, 1968), and *Concepts of Modern Art*, ed. N. Stangos (London, 1981), have a similar bias. H. Rosenberg, *The De-Definition of Art: Action Art to Earthworks* (London, 1972), and *Discovering the Present: Three Decades in Art, Culture and Politics* (Chicago, 1973), contain much useful, wide-ranging material; L. Lippard, *Pop Art* (London, 1967), and J. Russell, *Pop Art Redefined* (London, 1969), are studies of what is arguably the one stylistic thread in postwar painting with a significant European component.

Literature

Linguistic barriers have precluded the pan-European studies of postwar literature that the rise of modernism in the first half of the century encouraged; *Modernism*, ed. M. Bradbury and J. McFarlane (Harmondsworth, 1976), and *The Theory of the Modern Stage*, ed. E. Bentley (London, 1968), provide starting-points for an exploration of developments since 1945. M. Hamburger, *The Truth of Poetry* (London, 1969), attempts a wide-ranging synthesis; B. Bergonzi, *The Situation of the Novel* (London, 1970), *The Novel Today*, ed. M. Bradbury (London, 1977), and J. Raban, *The Society of the Poem* (London, 1971), confine themselves to English writing. The most accessible French structuralist writings are those of R. Barthes; *Writing Degree Zero* (1953), *Mythologies* (1957) and *Image-Music-Text*, ed. S. Heath (London, 1977), offer an entrée to the analytical world.

Musical surveys

The period after World War II has provided fertile ground for musical commentators.

The most eccentric and evocative account is A. Hodeir's *Since Debussy* (New York, 1961), fascinating not so much for its judgments but for its illumination of the hard-line serialist aesthetic of the early 1950s. A. Whittall, *Music since the First World War* (London, 1977), P. Griffiths, *Modern Music: the Avant Garde since 1945* (London, 1981), which also covers developments in the USA, and *Contemporary Music in Europe*, ed. P. H. Lang and N. Broder (New York, 1965), offer less partial surveys. The evolution of electronic music is detailed in E. Schwartz, *Electronic Music: a Listener's Guide* (New York, 1973), *The Development and Practice of Electronic Music*, ed. J. Appleton and R. Perera (Englewood Cliffs, 1975), and P. Griffiths, *A Guide to Electronic Music* (London, 1979). M. Nyman's *Experimental Music: Cage and Beyond* (London, 1974) is a guide to the experimental movement in the USA and Europe; C. Cardew's *Treatise Handbook* (London, 1971) and *Stockhausen serves Imperialism* (London, 1974) chart the politicization of the experimental movement in the late 1960s.

Individual composers

Almost all the composers who came to prominence in the 1950s and 60s in western Europe are articulate and often prolific writers. Messiaen's *Technique de mon langage musical* (Paris, 1944) is available in English (1957) but the two books of conversations, A. Goléa, *Rencontres avec Olivier Messiaen* (Paris, 1961), and C. Samuel, *Entretiens avec Olivier Messiaen* (Paris, 1967) await translation. R. S. Johnson, *Messiaen* (London, 1975), R. Nichols, *Messiaen* (Oxford, 1986), and P. Griffiths, *Olivier Messiaen and the Music of Time* (London, 1985), are surveys of his development. Boulez's many articles and polemics have been assembled into collections in English translation – *Notes of an Apprenticeship* (New York, 1968), *Boulez on Music Today* (London, 1971), *Orientations* (London, 1986) and *Conversations with Célestin Deliège* (London, 1976). *Pierre Boulez: a Symposium*, ed. W. Glock (London, 1986), offers the most substantial treatment of his music; P. Griffiths, *Boulez* (London, 1978), is a compact analysis of his compositional methods. The bulk of Stockhausen's writings, as collected in the continuing sequence of *Texte* (Cologne, 1963–), remains unavailable in English, though some early essays are contained in the translations of *Die Reihe* (Pennsylvania, 1958–64) and in K. Wörner, *Stockhausen: Life and Work* (London, 1973). *Stockhausen on Music*, compiled by R. Maconie (London, 1989), contains the texts of lectures delivered in London in 1971; J. Cott, *Stockhausen: Conversations with the Composer* (London, 1974), and M. Tannenbaum, *Conversations with Stockhausen* (Oxford, 1987), are discursive volumes. There are also J. Harvey, *The Music of Stockhausen: an Introduction* (London, 1974), and R. Maconie, *The Works of Karlheinz Stockhausen* (London, 1976). Neither of Pousseur's collections, *Fragments théorique sur la musique experimental* (Brussels, 1970 and 1972) and *Musique/ Sémantique/Société* (Tournai, 1972), has been translated into English, nor has *Luigi Nono: Texte, Studien zu seiner Musik*, ed. J. Stenzl (Zürich, 1975). Both composers remain largely ignored by English-language writers.

Xenakis's *Formalized Music* (Bloomington, IN, 1971) presents the mathematical and statistical bases of his compositional technique; the elements of that, and of *Musique-architecture* (Tournai, 1971), are presented, together with biographical material, in N. Matossian, *Xenakis* (London, 1986). *Luciano Berio: Two Interviews*, ed. D. Osmond-Smith (London, 1985), contains useful reminiscence and Berio's thoughts on music theatre; Osmond-Smith's exhaustive analysis of Berio's *Sinfonia* (London, 1985) remains the most outstanding attempt to discuss any one of Berio's pieces. A selection of Henze's writings has appeared as *Music and Politics* (London, 1982); his substantial output remains in need of detailed treatment. K. Geitel, *Hans Werner Henze* (Berlin, 1968), covers the years discussed here. Kagel, too, remains largely ignored by English-language writers: some early essays are in *Die Reihe*, later ones in *Tamtam: Dialoge und Monologe zur Musik*, ed. F. Schmidt (Munich, 1975). D. Schnebel, *Mauricio Kagel: Musik, Theater, Film* (Cologne, 1970), examines the performance pieces of the 1960s.

Zimmerman's *Intervall und Zeit: Aufsatze und Schriften zum Werk* (Mainz, 1974) is a posthumous collection of his writings.

Among the plethora of books on Britten, the most useful and comprehensive are P. Evans, *The Music of Benjamin Britten* (London, 1979), and *The Britten Companion*, ed. C. Palmer (London, 1984), together with handbooks on *Peter Grimes*, ed. P. Brett (Cambridge, 1983), *The Turn of the Screw*, ed. P. Howard (Cambridge, 1985), and *Death in Venice*, ed. D. Mitchell (Cambridge, 1987). The first volumes of Britten's letters, edited by D. Mitchell, have now been published (London, 1991). Tippett's writings are in *Moving into Aquarius* (St Albans, 1974) and *Music of the Angels*, ed. M. Bowen (London, 1980); his output is best surveyed in I. Kemp, *Tippett: the Composer and his Music* (London, 1984), and M. Bowen, *Michael Tippett* (London, 1982). A. Whittall, *The Music of Britten and Tippett* (Cambridge, 1982), traces the development of both composers. M. Hall, *Harrison Birtwistle* (London, 1984), *The Music of Alexander Goehr*, ed. B. Northcott (London, 1980), P. Griffiths, *Peter Maxwell Davies* (London, 1982), and *Peter Maxwell Davies: Studies from Two Decades*, ed. S. Pruslin (London, 1979), cover by contrasted means the most significant British composers of the post-Britten generation.

Chapter XIII

Russia and Eastern Europe, 1945–70

DETLEF GOJOWY

It seems legitimate to consider together the contemporary music of Russia and the former Soviet-occupied eastern European countries, in spite of differences in their historical backgrounds, since they all suffered from the cultural policies of the Stalin and Zhdanov era, they all adopted and retain the organizations of Soviet musical life, and musical development in them between 1945 and 1970 has entailed opposing Socialist Realism and overcoming their imposed isolation from the rest of the world. That occurred relatively early in Poland, in 1956, but more tentatively and much later in the other countries; from the 1970s the developments resulting from periods of thaw, particularly in the USSR and Czechoslovakia, encountered new set-backs, starting with the invasion of Czechoslovakia in 1968 by the Warsaw Pact countries, an incident that marked the beginning of a new 'Ice Age'.

The resolutions on music passed by the Committee of the Communist Party of the Soviet Union on 20 February 1948 were based on aesthetic principles going back to the conflicts of the 1920s, when the Association of Proletarian Musicians called for intelligibility, a folk element and a sense of the monumental in music; Western modern music, promoted by the Association for Contemporary Music, and jazz were rejected as decadent bourgeois products antipathetic to the working class. After the 1930s rivalry between these two musical associations was ended by the inclusion of both in the Soviet Composers' Union, which thus acquired the authority of a musical guild. A modified version of aesthetic principles was made the criterion of a new Soviet classicism based on folk music; it excluded all that was difficult or experimental and was supposed to radiate optimism. The experimental avant garde of the 1920s (Nikolay Roslavets, Alexander Mosolov, Lev Knipper, Sergey Protopopov) no longer figured in Soviet musical life. Shostakovich had regained favour with his Fifth Symphony after the censure of his opera *Lady Macbeth of the Mtsensk District*; Prokofiev too was able to adapt to the musical climate (see p. 155).

However, the war years had brought a relaxation of cultural pressures and the Allies' opposition to Hitler's Germany had furthered cultural exchange with Western countries. There were in fact similarities between Western New Realism and Eastern Socialist Realism, the result of prevailing circumstances. 'Populist' Russian works were favourably received in the USA, which caused the emigré Russian futurist composer Arthur Lourié to issue a warning against the approaching danger of a new kind of commercialism.[1] Meanwhile, Soviet music was by no means restricted to the required level of superficiality. Shostakovich's Sixth and Eighth Symphonies and Prokofiev' Sixth, with their use of new styles, went far beyond a shallow, optimistic 'realism'. Some of their procedures and idioms almost turn their bombastic element into a caricature of the monumental. Socialist Realism was to some extent becoming socialist surrealism, music that expressed criticism.

Shostakovich's Ninth Symphony, with which he celebrated the end of the war, disappointing expectations of a grand festive ode, also contained elements of caricature, this time of a more playful nature. Such expressions of critical independence and lack of ideological discipline were bound to attract the attention of Stalin's cultural officials; the Cultural Commissar, Andrey Zhdanov, played the leading role in the attacks that followed. In August 1946 literature came under scrutiny; a resolution was passed by the Central Committee of the Communist Party on the journals *Zvezda* and *Leningrad*, condemning the poet Anna Akhmatova and the satirist Mikhail Zoschchenko as ideologically unsound. The same month saw similar resolutions passed on the theatre. In September 1946 the committee turned its attention to the cinema.

Inevitably – if relatively late – music's turn came, in February 1948, when resolutions were passed on Vano Muradeli's opera *The Great Friendship*. They referred to the condemnation in 1936 of *Lady Macbeth*, on the instructions of the Central Committee, and accused Shostakovich, Prokofiev, Khachaturian, Gavriil Popov and Nikolay Myaskovsky of 'maintaining a formalistic trend hostile to the people'. Their work was said to contain 'formalistic distortions and anti-democratic tendencies which are foreign to the Soviet people and its artistic taste . . . This music has surrendered its spirit entirely to the contemporary and over-modern bourgeois music of Europe and America, which reflects the decrepitude of bourgeois culture'. Soviet composers were reprimanded for their 'one-sided enthusiasm for difficult forms of wordless instrumental and symphonic music, and their contemptuous attitude towards such musical genres as opera, choral music, traditional music for small orchestras, for folk instruments, vocal ensembles etc'. Their 'formalistic trend' was condemned as 'alien to the people and leading to the annihilation of music'. A composers' committee was set up, and Tikhon Khrennikov, as newly appointed secretary of the Composers' Union, had to expound the resolution's particularities.

These attacks were attempting to turn the wheel of musical history back 50 years, as it were, in the name of the classical Russian composers – Balakirev, Borodin, Musorgsky, Rimsky-Korsakov, Tchaikovsky and Taneyev.[2] Hardly a contemporary composer of any significance was omitted from the list of those condemned for 'formalism': Hindemith, Krenek, Berg, Schoenberg, Casella, Schreker, Milhaud, Messiaen, Jolivet, Britten, Menotti.[3] Only a few composers on the committee had the courage to object, among them Vissarion Shebalin; it was to cost him his position as director of the Moscow Conservatory. Like Shebalin, Shostakovich lost all his teaching posts, and except for the Fifth and Seventh Symphonies his works were banned. Prokofiev too found himself in economic difficulties.

The measures of 1948 – the banning of performances and pulping of printed music – made a clean sweep of contemporary Soviet music. What was wanted was panegyric 'utility music', optimistic songs for massed choirs and symphonic works in the style of Tchaikovsky or Rakhmaninov, such as Khrennikov wrote; there were even limits to the desirability of folk music if, as in Shostakovich's Jewish *Songs* op.79, it touched on the taboo subject of the Jewish minority and its culture. This and other works by Shostakovich, such as his Violin Concerto op.77, dedicated to David Oistrakh and written at the end of the 1940s, had to wait for their first performances until the mid-1950s, after Stalin's death. Even such classical pieces as the 24 Preludes and Fugues op.87 (written after Shostakovich had been an adjudicator at the Bach Competition in Leipzig) encountered difficulties and were much discussed in the Composers' Union. Shostakovich's Tenth Symphony, which his friend Yevgeny Mravinsky managed to have performed in 1953, provoked three days of debate at the union and a discussion lasting four years in *Sovetskaya muzyka*; such arguments were by no means solely academic but could determine the course of a composer's life.

Even in the atmosphere of Khrushchev's thaw, when the abuses of the Stalinist régime were being put right, those composers who had been forced to conform found that matters improved only slowly. However, they had taken under their wing bolder and more forthright young composers who insisted on the right to go their own way. While he was still teaching at the Leningrad Conservatory, Shostakovich had encouraged and protected such unrestrained talents as Yury Levitin (*b* 1912) and Galina Ustvolskaya (*b* 1919); the latter, shielded from public notice, developed original textures and meditative music, which were properly appreciated only later in the age of minimalism.

Among Shostakovich's composition pupils were Georgy Sviridov (*b*

1915), Orest Yevlakhov (*b* 1912), Moissey Wainberg (*b* 1919), Kara Karayev (*b* 1918), Revol Bunin (*b* 1924), Karen Khachaturian (*b* 1920) and Boris Chaykovsky (*b* 1925). They often adopted his large-scale thinking and also his technique of dissecting tiny musical motifs. It was from one of his pupils, Benjamin Fleishman (who was born in 1913 and killed in 1941 in the first Leningrad tank battles), that Shostakovich derived the interest in Yiddish folk music that was to play such an important part in his middle-period work. Shostakovich completed and orchestrated his dead pupil's unfinished opera *Rothschild's Violin* (from a story by Chekhov); after its studio performance in 1968 in Leningrad, conducted by his son Maxim, Shostakovich was attacked for Zionism.[4]

Among the major events marking the rehabilitation of Shostakovich's earlier works was the first performance of his Fourth Symphony, conducted by Kirill Kondrashin, in 1961 (25 years after he had written it), and the revival of *Lady Macbeth* in 1963 (in its revised version as *Katerina Izmaylova*); a performance of the first version in Düsseldorf in 1959 had paved the way for this revival. However, Shostakovich's experimental chamber opera *The Nose* had to wait until 1974 for another performance, after a revival in East Berlin. In the wake of this gradual reinstatement of banned works, Prokofiev's opera *The Gambler* also had a concert performance in 1963, conducted by Gennady Rozhdestvensky, and his biographer Izrael Nestyev published a revised life of the composer in 1973, removing condemnations of his experimental works. But Prokofiev, who had died on the same day as Stalin in 1953, could not know that his work had been re-evaluated. Other composers who had been attacked in 1948 regained their reputations, for instance, Vissarion Shebalin, whose dramatic symphony *Lenin* was reprinted, along with other works of the 1930s. Myakovsky, Popov and Aram Khachaturian were no longer suspect. On the other hand, avant-garde composers of the 1920s like Roslavetz, Mosolov and Protopopov were still taboo; Western interest in them was considered highly undesirable, and those who had emigrated, such as Arthur Lourié and Joseph Schillinger, were regarded as non-persons and never mentioned. The avant-garde compositions of the 1920s were dismissed by Soviet critics as artistically third-rate until very recently, regardless of the fact that in the West that decade had come to be considered a key period in European cultural history.

In spite of his long-delayed recognition, Shostakovich had to face new criticism over his Thirteenth Symphony (1962), this time not for its musical style but because of the social criticism of the poems by Yevgeny Yevtushenko which he had set. His denunciations of Soviet antisemitism, of problems of supply in the socialist economic system, of the secret service and the opportunist lack of civil courage in Russia, led to a ban on performances of his works for a number of years. But there were areas of Soviet musical life during Krushchev's thaw in which all such quarrels seemed to be long forgotten, and the reunion of Soviet music with that of the rest of the world appeared to be accomplished. The problems Shostakovich and his generation had had with the authorities no longer troubled young Soviet composers; rather, they were concerned with catching up on developments they had hitherto missed. Decades' worth of information that had been withheld suddenly began impinging on Soviet consciousness, in non-chronological confusion: even to know about these musical ideas had once been a punishable offence. As a student, Andrey Volkonsky (*b* 1933) was expelled from the Moscow Conservatory because scores by forbidden bourgeois avant-garde composers were found in a case under his bed in the students' hostel. When the embargo on information was lifted after Stalin's death, he first encountered simultaneously music by Hindemith, Schoenberg and Stravinsky, by Stockhausen, Nono and Boulez: his first works in the modern style, such as his *Mirror Suite*, after texts by Federico García Lorca, and his *Les plaintes de Chtchaza*, setting Daghestani laments for the dead, reflected something of these influences.

This situation in the late 1950s and early 60s helps to explain how those 'polystylistics', now accepted as a concept of Soviet new music, came into being: elements that Russia had been unable to experience flooded in at once, and this voyage of discovery into Western music embraced Classical, pre-Classical and even light music (pre-Classical music had also been ideologically criticized). Interest in the polyphonic linearity and 'objectivity' of Baroque music (particularly reflected in the early works of the neo-polyphonic composer Gavriil Popov) had caused Soviet composers to be condemned for 'formalism' and escaping from the socialist present in the 1948 purges; consequently there were gaps in people's musical knowledge, even though early music was one of the subjects traditionally taught in Russian conservatories. Volkonsky, a member of the Russian princely family of that name, was born in Geneva, where he began his piano studies with Dinu Lipatti among others; he returned to Russia with his parents in 1948 and made his name not only as a composer but as a harpsichordist, playing the music of Frescobaldi and the Fitzwilliam Virginal Book before large and enthusiastic audiences. He founded the instrumental and vocal group Madrigal, giving about a hundred concerts of early music in a season; there was a series of twelve concerts with programmes of music by Dufay, Josquin and Gesualdo, for instance, performed in a Leningrad hall that would hold 2000. Volkonsky, who was in touch with Nono in Venice as well as other composers, left the USSR in 1973 after being forbidden to practice his profession, even as an interpreter. (Since then he has lived in Switzerland.) Like Volkonsky, Rudolf Barshai and his Moscow Chamber Orchestra found an enthusiastic audience in the 1960s, mainly among the young, but he later decided to emigrate to Israel.

Modern Times

The stylistic concept of Socialist Realism had been moulded by nineteenth-century ideas – romantic and emotional, emphatic, inclined to a technical pursuit of 'art for art's sake' – and everything that did not fit into that category, whether old or new, was received with enthusiastic acclaim in the post-Stalinist period. So the rising generation of composers soon looked beyond the example of Shostakovich, Prokofiev and Khachaturian to the generation before them. Webern became more of a model in Russia than in any Western country for the density and complexity of his composition and the concentration of different methods and forms ordered by serial techniques. The composer Alfred Shnitke (*b* 1934) translated Webern's writings into Russian and the musicologists Yuriy and Valentina Kholopov wrote the first Soviet monograph on Webern (though it could not be published until 1984).

A personal link existed between Webern and this Soviet 'Webern school': the composer and theoretician Philipp Moyseyevich Herşcovici (Gershkovich), born in 1906 in Iaşi, had been a pupil of Berg and Webern in Vienna before emigrating first to his native Romania and then to Moscow in 1939 to escape racial persecution. In Moscow he found himself barred from the Composers' Union. But his influence as a private teacher of a generation of young (now middle-aged) Soviet composers was all the more important: they included Shnitke, Volkonsky, Edison Denisov (*b* 1929) and Viktor Suslin (*b* 1942), who may thus be regarded as pupils of Webern at one remove. It was not so much that Herşcovici initiated them into serial procedures as that he taught them by analysing the works of Beethoven, as Webern had with his pupils, and Herşcovici's sarcastic pronouncements went the rounds of Moscow.

To the officials of the Composers' Union, he was one of their most hated opponents, and the mere mention of him in the West aroused shrill protests in the Soviet musical press. (At the age of 82 he was granted an exit visa to Vienna.)

In the Krushchev period there were even short-lived efforts at a Soviet style of electronic music. The record company Melodiya set up an experimental studio in the basement of Alexander Skryabin's house in Moscow, which had been made into a museum; originally this studio was intended only for recording Skryabin's own experimental music with colour and light. Yevgeny Murzin, the engineer, installed a microtonal synthesizer which, by dividing the octave into 72 intervals, allowed any tonal system to be created. (This was not a new idea: in 1924 Arseniy Avraamov had tried out a division of the octave into 48 steps with folk instruments playing in scordatura.) The equipment soon became a playground for Moscow composers who enjoyed experimenting. It was easy to use: lines scratched on a blackened glass plate produced corresponding frequencies and provided a fascinating

Melodiya record sleeve (1967) showing Khachaturian's 'Maskarad'.

means of playing with micro-intervals. The studio became a meeting-place known only to composers hungry for innovation. Among the works in the electronic genre created there were Shnitke's *Potok* ('The River') and Sofiya Gubaydulina's *Vivente – non vivente*, but the composers were not allowed to publish them. All that saw the light of day was a series of pieces of a more illustrative character, reminiscent of film music.[5] The studio was closed in the mid-1970s.

Denisov and Gubaydulina had close contacts with the Shostakovich school. Denisov, born in Tomsk in Siberia in 1929, studied mathematics but in 1949 he decided to become a composer and turned to the revered master. Shostakovich, who was professionally banned, could help him only with advice and suggestions, which Denisov vigorously defended to his colleagues. His peculiarly confident and concise musical language was in fact 'discovered' by Shostakovich, as was Gubaydulina's concern with tonal colour and the way she treated musical forms in conflict, as in a game of chess. Gubaydulina, born in Tchistopol on the Volga in 1931 and of Tartar descent, studied with Shostakovich's assistant Nikolay Peyko from 1959, then with Shostakovich's friend Vissarion Shebalin. When she was criticized at the conservatory for choosing 'the wrong way', Shostakovich encouraged her 'to go on composing in her wrong way'.

Western influences played a part in Shnitke's development. Born in 1934 in Engels (then the capital of the Volga German Soviet Republic), the son of a Volga German mother and a Jewish father in the diplomatic service, he received his musical training in Vienna. Captivated by Webern, he began his career with such studies in sonority as his *Variations on a Chord* (1968), opening up increasingly to a wide variety of influences which he termed 'polystylistics'. After its first performance in Gorki, his First Symphony (1969–72) was banned because it included elements of jazz and light music.

Another remarkable new Moscow composer was Nikolay Karetnikov (*b* 1930); his works include the ballet-opera *Klein Zaches genannt Zinnober*, after the story by E. T. A. Hoffmann, which had its first performance in Hanover in 1970, and an unperformed opera on St Paul, which, because of the unpopularity of religious subjects, has to be described only as an opera about the Emperor Nero. Rodion Shchedrin (*b* 1932) is perhaps the only major talent and acute musical thinker whose early work was not suppressed and who enjoyed official recognition. He has composed a great deal of ballet music – he married the prima ballerina Maya Plissetskaya – including *The Little Hump-Backed Horse*, *Carmen Suite*, *Anna Karenina* (after Tolstoy), *The Gull* (after Chekhov) and an opera, *Dead Souls* (after Gogol). He adopted a liberal stance in cultural, aesthetic and ideological debates, and it was hoped that he would succeed Khrennikov as general secretary of the Soviet Composers' Union; in 1973 he became secretary of the Composers' Union.

Moscow was by no means the only centre of new Soviet music in the 1950s and 60s. Of Leningrad composers, Boris Tischchenko deserves mention. He was a pupil of Galina Ustvolskaya and Orest Yevlakhov, and finally studied with Shostakovich. His compositions show an idiosyncratic tendency towards epic spaciousness and archaic expression. He is interested in seventeenth-century Russian folksong as well as avant-garde music of the 1920s. Also from Leningrad is Sergey Slonimsky (*b* 1932), nephew of the American writer Nicolas Slonimsky and a pupil of Orest Yevlakhov; his work shows some influence from the new Polish school and he has composed a ballet, *Icarus*, and a chamber opera, *The Master and Margarita* (after Bulgakov). He is also author of many writings on musical theory. In Kiev, an individual school of twelve-note composers was formed by the pupils of Boris Lyatoshinskiy (1895–1968).

A prominent figure in the new music of the Baltic republics is Arvo Pärt, born in Paide, Estonia, in 1935. In 1980 he emigrated because of repression and went to live in Berlin (see p.379). Estonia is a focal point of new music, partly because of its connections with Scandinavia. Among the young Moscow composers who were developing during the post-Stalinist thaw are Viktor Yekimovskiy (*b* 1947), whose works include a new 'Brandenburg Concerto' for twelve instruments, Elena Firsova (*b* 1950), whose music pursues a strictly formal classicism, and Viktor Suslin (*b* 1942), who emigrated in 1983.

Russian folklore and Byzantine traditions have often played a part in new Soviet music along with Western influences. Denisov's vocal composition *Sun of the Incas* (1946), to a text by Gabriela Mistral, has some stylistic similarity to French avant-garde music, for instance *Le marteau sans maître* of Boulez, to whom the piece is dedicated; but its significance consists in the way it brings the Russian language and the sound of new music together in an unprecedented way. The archaism of the Old Russian 'long song' has been detected in works by Galina Ustvolskaya and Boris Tishchenko. Byzantine hymns are clearly at the heart of the *Polyphonic Concerto* (1970) by Yuriy Butsko (*b* in Lugny, Poltava, in 1938), although its text, being religious, cannot appear in print. This nineteen-movement work, which lasts for three and a half hours in performance, is for four keyboard instruments (piano, harpsichord, organ and celesta) in all possible combinations of two and three (in the last movement, when all four come together, a choir also performs ad libitum), and in this structural plan it shows parallels with Bach's *Art of Fugue*. Butsko uses a peculiarly eastern European element of 'warped scales', which do not divide the octave in the usual way but have, say, sharps in the upper part and flats in the lower, or vice versa.

The achievements of composers since the 1970s have not gone unchallenged by the controlling Composers' Union. Such composers as Denisov, Shnitke and Gubaydulina have suffered bans on the performance of their works, obstacles put in the way of performances, the refusal of exit visas, attacks in the press (particularly on Denisov when he talked about the Soviet avant garde in interviews); measures have extended beyond the USSR itself, for instance diplomatic manoeuvres were used to ensure that pieces by Denisov, Gubaydulina, Vitaly Ledenyov (*b* 1930) and Vitaly Geviksman (*b* 1924) were not performed at the Warsaw Autumn festival of 1972, and printed music was withheld to prevent the performance of works by Gubaydulina at Düsseldorf in 1982. At such difficult times Shnitke often had to make his living by composing film music, as did Shostakovich. Only with the *glasnost* and *perestroika* policies of Gorbachov were these pressures to some extent relaxed.

POLAND

The first eastern European country to rid itself of Stalinist cultural doctrines in music – and not just in music – as early as 1956 was Poland. Like other Soviet-occupied countries, Poland had gone through a period of Stalinism when it was cut off from the outside world and when not only Western contemporary composers but such established Polish figures as Karol Szymanowski (1882–1937) were dismissed as formal-istic. Szymanowski's work, in a Romantically based vein of neo-classicism founded on French models, had been a formative influence in the 1930s and led the way for Polish music of the Viennese School to follow independent directions. Thus the effect of post-1948 cultural policies was to some extent muted. Art music, forbidden during the German wartime occupation when music could be played only in cafés (Witold Lutosławski and Andrzej Panufnik performed as a piano duo), went through a stormy phase of reconstruction in the postwar period: schools had to be founded, links with France were revived (Nadia Boulanger taught dozens of Polish composition students during her lifetime). Among the key figures of the postwar generation were the composers Kazimierz Sikorski (1895–1986), Bolesław Szabelski (1896–1979), Tadeusz Szeligowski (1896–1963), Bolesłav Woytowicz (1899–1980), who was also famous as an interpreter of Chopin, and Stanisłav Wiechowicz (1893–1963). Szabelski in particular, a pupil of Szymanowski, went his own dodecaphonic way even in the most difficult period.

All of them, and Boulanger's pupil Grażyna Bacewicz (1909–69), who set an example to the increasing number of Polish women composers, had works performed at the Warsaw Autumn, a festival held since 1956, the year of Gomułka's policy of emancipation. Over nine or ten days, the festival offers a concentrated programme of contemporary music from all countries and cultures and thus con-stitutes an excellent international platform for Polish composition:

Artur Malawski, Grażyna Bacewicz, the Minister of Culture (1947–52) Stefan Dybowski, Andrzej Panufnik, and the writer-composer Zygmund Mycielski, Warsaw, 1949.

Poland's new music has made it a leading cultural nation. The idea of the festival came from the composers Tadeusz Baird (1928–81) and Kazimierz Serocki (1922–81). The first year's programme, presenting works by Stravinsky, Honegger, Szymanowski, Bartók and Martinů, was characterized by the need to make up for lost time. Nadia Boulanger was a guest and Messiaen was hailed as a new discovery.

The second Warsaw Autumn, in 1958, showed that it intended to take account of the contemporary Western avant garde, giving performances of Stockhausen's *Gesang der Jünglinge* and Cage's *Music of Changes*. The same line continued to be followed in the festival, held annually, and initially it led to isolation within the socialist camp, where a steady 'freeze' was in progress. For instance, festival events could not be reported in East Germany and performances of undesirable composers' works were repeatedly blocked by the Russians. The Warsaw Autumn, which in more liberal cultural times was a unique platform and an invaluable East–West forum, shrank at times of repression to a mere display of Western innovations; musical Poland took note with interest, but audiences in neighbouring countries remained excluded, and many new musical departures were heard only unofficially and by an invited audience at private concerts or recitals.

The festival has continued in these ambivalent circumstances and in its international range and influence it occupies a unique position among modern music festivals, one frequently recognized and welcomed by Western composers: much new Scandinavian and American music has been heard for the first time in Poland. At the fourth Warsaw Autumn (1960) an experimental electronic studio under Józef Patkowski's direction was set up by Polish Radio, the first in any socialist country; many Polish composers worked there, and composers from East Germany and Scandinavia had their first chance to use the new medium in this studio.

Against this background, what is now known as the 'New Polish School' came into being. The music of its members is marked by the use of modern principles of composition – dodecaphony, serialism, exploration of sound qualities and an encyclopedic use of orchestral colour; but at the same time it reflects its national origins, among them Szymanowski's 'romantic legacy' as well as the strong traditions of Roman Catholic church music and those features of the culture of the Polish nobility derived from the Italian Renaissance. A record of Polish avant-garde music, including pieces by Serocki, Lutosławski and Baird, was brought out in 1958 under the auspices of the International Composers' Tribune of the International Music Council: a sensational event in eastern Europe.[6] Soon a fourth star arose in the Polish avant garde: Krzysztof Penderecki, born in Dębica in 1933, who won all three prizes in the Polish Composers' Union's competition for young composers in 1959. In 1960 he became known throughout Europe with his composition *Threnody* for 52 strings, dedicated to the victims of Hiroshima. At the same time as György Ligeti with his *Atmospheres*, Penderecki had invented a technique of textural tonalities which was to become widespread in Europe, particularly in the New Polish School. Close cooperation with West German institutions helped to disseminate this new style; Penderecki's *St Luke Passion* (1965) and *Utrenia* ('Matins') of 1970–72 were commissioned by West German Radio in Cologne.

Other composers of the New Polish School won international recognition: Andrzej Dobrowolski (*b* 1921), who also works in electronic music; Henryk Mikołaj Górecki (*b* 1933), whose style spans a range from highly expressive experiment with sound to a new archaic simplicity; Wojciech Kilar (*b* 1932), with his monumental orchestral forms; Włodzimierz Kotoński (*b* 1925), with his richly coloured compositions; Zygmunt Krauze (*b* 1939), who uses unconventional collage techniques; Bernadetta Matuszczak (*b* 1937), a composer of music drama; Marta Ptaszyńska (*b* 1943), who is also a virtuoso percussionist; Zbigniew Rudziński (*b* 1935), a composer of enigmatic music dramas; Boguslaw Schäffer (*b* 1929), probably the most radical and consistent avant-garde member of this groups; Witold Szalonek (*b* 1927), who explores sonorities; and Zbigniew Wiszniewski (*b* 1922).

In contrast to the generation of this period of awakening, the composers that followed it, now the 'middle' generation, developed a strong bias towards classical features and forms, among them Augustyn Bloch (*b* 1929), Krzysztof Meyer (*b* 1943), who has composed many symphonies and string quartets (a genre only recently remarkably popular in Poland), and Marek Stachowski (*b* 1936). Penderecki disappointed many of his former admirers in returning to unambiguously late-Romantic forms of expression by the time he wrote his opera *Paradise Lost* (1978, after Milton). The same applied to Górecki. Catholic and traditional sources of Polish music are also prevalent in avant-garde works, and the great surge towards the future may be followed by an equally strong movement back to musical origins. The opera *The Gates of Paradise* (from a text by Jerzy Andrzejewski) by Joanna Bruzdowicz (*b* 1943), a pupil of Messiaen, for instance, is about the thirteenth-century Children's Crusade and includes Latin and medieval elements. Even Polish composers like Bruzdowicz who live in the West (in her case in Brussels) maintain strong contacts with the Polish cultural scene and they are officially regarded as Polish composers: Piotr Moss (*b* 1949), Andrzej Panufnik (1914–91) who settled in England in 1954, Konstanty Regamey (*b* 1907) and Roman Haubenstock-Ramati (*b* 1919), who live in Switzerland and Austria respectively, and Elżbieta Sikora (*b* 1944), who lives in Paris. Many modern Polish composers have also been – or still are –

Nadia Boulanger in discussion with the Polish composer Andrzej Panufnik in his studio, London, 1965. Panufnik fled to England from Poland in 1954.

famous interpreters, among them the conductors Andrzej Markowski (1924–86) and Witold Rowicki (*b* 1914) and the pianist Szabolcs Esztényi (*b* 1939 in Hungary). There is a noticeably high proportion of women among Polish composers compared with other countries: in the Young Composers' section of the Composers' Union, women now make up almost half the members. From the 1970s, Poland's cultural freedom in music has known no restrictions.

CZECHOSLOVAKIA

The musical life of Czechoslovakia after 1945 was determined by a series of incompatible factors. The interwar period, that of the First Republic of 1918–38, had seen the avant garde flourishing in the arts: František Kupka developed his abstract style in painting, Le Corbusier was building for the shoe manufacturer Tomáš Baťa the town of Zlin as a Utopian social model, and the works of Karel Čapek, Jaroslav Hašek, Franz Kafka and Max Brod were prominent in literature. This was the time of Janáček's mature operas, and of Martinů and Hába, whose microtonal ideas attracted a generation of composers from other countries as well as his own. The spirit of this period was never extinguished and became the stimulus for reforms and aspirations to freedom like the Prague Spring: it was remembered as the ideal of a 'democracy which almost alone, among the dictatorial régimes of Central Europe at the time, guaranteed human rights and allowed freedom to all artistic currents'.[7] The policies of the German occupying power in the 'protectorate of Bohemia and Moravia' were carried out less rigorously than in Poland and allowed the national culture of Smetana and Dvořák a certain amount of freedom, apart from such patriotic works as Smetana's *The Brandenburgers in Bohemia*. That freedom was curtailed all the more savagely after the Stalinist seizure of power in 1948, ushering in a reign of terror which passed about 230 death sentences and kept tens of thousands of political prisoners in concentration camps if they opposed the party line, including members of the traditionally left-wing Czech intelligentsia. In 1948 Prague was the scene of a Marxist Second International Congress of Composers and Music Critics, convened to found an International Association of Progressive Composers and Musicologists; it was sanctioned on an international level by the Stalinist and Zhdanovist resolutions on music passed in Russia that February.

Czech musical policies over the next few years were affected. Superficial distinctions were drawn between composers and even styles of interpretation ('a bourgeois vibrato') of a 'progressive and realistic' nature (such composers included Smetana, Fibich and Ostrčil), and 'reactionary' composers like Dvořák and his pupils Josef Suk and Vítězslav Novak. The composer who set the trend for that period was Václav Dobiáš (1909–78), with his cantatas of praise to the Red Army, while men like Hába and Martinů were denounced. (Martinů was prevented from returning to his country from exile in America by the cultural officials, and he died in Liestal in Switzerland in 1959.) These policies also overshadowed the composer Miloslav Kabeláč (1908–79), the first, as a typical Czech intellectual artist, to pave the way for new music on Czech radio; his compositions were honoured more in the West than at home.

However, at a period when simple optimism expressed in major keys was held up as the ideal of realism, the work of Janáček was never attacked for being 'hostile to the people' – something of a tactical success – and when early in the 1960s a series of gramophone records was brought out under the title Musica Nova Bohemica et Slovenica ('Slovenica' to be understood as 'Slovak' rather than 'Slovenian'), the first disc contained Hába's Nonet op.82 and *Ballets for Nonet* by Jan Novák (*b* 1921). These works do not represent new departures in the style of Ligeti and Penderecki but are the last echoes of the neo-classical tradition: craftsmanlike pieces on a chamber-music scale. While Poland began by exploiting the orchestral palette in its exploration of new music, Czechoslovakia remained a kind of 'grammar school' of

'Planes by Colours' (1910–11) by the Czechoslovakian painter František Kupka: an early example of his developing abstract style, initially influenced by Reynard's praxinoscope and Marey's chromophotography. This painting clearly depicts the narrow parallel bands (planes of colour) which Kupka used to express the translation of movement and light.

chamber music, often of a virtuoso nature (the wind quintet, for instance, reached new heights here).

Restrictions on cultural policies disappeared at about the beginning of the 1960s. New music could now develop freely and the Czech Composers' Union became a non-political professional organization. In spring every year, a week of new works by Czechoslavak composers was held in Prague. Among composers featured were Pavel Bořkovec (1894–1972), Petr Eben (*b* 1929, a concentration camp victim in his youth), Jaroslav Doubrava (1909–60), Ilja Hurník (*b* 1922), Jan Kapr (*b* 1914), Viktor Kalabis (*b* 1923) and Marek Kopelent (*b* 1932), whose chamber works were promising. Mention should also be made of Rudolf Komorous (*b* 1931), one of the pioneers of electronic music in Czechoslovakia.

From Slovakia, where art music was composed only from the nineteenth century, Peter Kolman (*b* 1937), Ladislav Kupkovič (*b*

1936) and Ilja Zeljenka (*b* 1932) contributed to new music, although Kupkovič, who started out as a radical experimenter, founding the Hudba Dněska ensemble and holding summer courses in Smolenice on the Darmstadt model, emigrated in 1968 to Germany, where he turned away from experimental concepts towards a new tonality.

The 1960s saw history repeat itself: as in Janáček's time, the Moravian capital of Brno rather than the traditional cultural centres of Prague and Bratislava pioneered innovations. It was here that the composer Alois Piňos (*b* 1925), also a musical theorist who worked out a system of tonal groups, founded the first composers' collective. With Arnošt Parsch (*b* 1936), Miloš Štědroň (*b* 1942), a music historian and writer on the work of Janáček and composer of an opera on Kafka's *In der Strafkolonie*) and Rudolf Ružička (*b* 1941), a pioneer of electronic music, Piňos developed models of collective composition in which a work was created with one composer writing for wind, another for strings and so on; an example is *Divertissement* on themes by the nineteenth-century Brno composer Count Karl Wilhelm Haugwitz. A tradition peculiar to Brno was the genre of the 'mono-opera', arising from the Jesuit drama of Josef Berg (1927–71); in its individual way this genre represented a rediscovery of the monodic principle.

At first these early manifestations of the new music continued after the 1968 invasion, and music festivals and performances were still held. Repression made itself acutely felt only with the fall of Alexander Dubček and the subsequent reorganization of the artists' unions in 1972. The old, non-political Composers' Union was disbanded and not all its members were accepted into the newly founded, ideologically orientated union. While a few composers like Jan Tausinger (*b* 1921) and Václav Kučera (*b* 1929), author of a book about the Soviet avant garde, were able to maintain avant-gardist positions, others like Kopelent, Kabeláč, Hurník and Kapr spent a decade unable to practise their profession. Some, like Piňos, tried writing under another name (his pseudonym was Simandl). Only in the 1980s was there some relaxation of these restrictions: for instance, the work done in the Bratislava Electronic Studio, founded in 1967, was now openly presented to Western audiences. Similar studios have been set up in Prague and Plzeň since the 1960s.

ROMANIA

Romania became an outstandingly progressive musical country in the 1960s, and in the process went its own way, thanks to its Latin and Mediterranean culture, its adherence to Orthodox Christianity and its folklore (which it had preserved to a remarkable extent). Until that time Romania had been represented in international music mainly by George Enescu (1881–1955). Now composers appeared suddenly, and in difficult circumstances, bearing names that would soon become familiar in the new European music: they included Anatol Vieru (*b* 1926), a pupil of Khachaturian at the Moscow Conservatory; Tiberiu Olah (*b* 1928), a pupil of E. R. Golubiev and D. Rogal'-Levitski also at the Moscow Conservatory, Stefan Niculescu (*b* 1927) and Aurel Stroe (*b* 1932), now living in exile in Germany. They were often 'discovered' on Western platforms, for instance at the 'Festival International d'Art Contemporain' at Royan in France or at Darmstadt, where the trail-blazing *Ritual for the Thirst of the Earth* by Myriam Marbé (*b* 1931) was first performed in 1968.

The Romanian avant-garde style owes its compelling originality to its many different points of departure. Less burdened than some other countries by the traditions of central European craftsmanlike composition, Romanian composers see themselves as owing allegiance to laws of beauty and harmony based on Mediterranean antiquity, often mathematically defined: the laws of the Golden Mean and of Fibonnacci's series of prime numbers provided the basis for the kind of 'serial thinking' they accepted. Scepticism towards the idea of the closed work of art, as frequently expressed in phenomena of new Western music in the 1960s, was never shared in Romania, where, as in Russia, art has always been associated with Orthodox thought, appealing earnestly to moral forces, while individualistic ideas or doubts are foreign to its thinking. But Romanian music has drawn colour and striking originality from the traditional folk music of Transylvania (which had already inspired Bartók), with its scales never smoothed out by central European influence, its ability to move freely between sound and language, and its magical implications, close study of which has inspired musical innovation, as in the work of Myriam Marbé and her women pupils.

Women composers became increasingly prominent: they include Violeta Dinescu (*b* 1953), a pupil of Myriam Marbé, Adriana Hölszky (*b* 1953), a pupil of Aurel Stroe, and Carmen Maria Cârneci (*b* 1957), a pupil of Stefan Niculescu, promising talents who continued along the Romanian avant-garde path though living in exile in Germany; meanwhile the curtain of ever bleaker political and economic circumstances came down over the Romanian scene.

HUNGARY

Just as Polish music arose in France in the nineteenth century, with Chopin, so the Hungarian composer who was to be in the vanguard of European developments, György Ligeti, left Hungary in 1956 at the Soviet occupation; he lived in Austria and finally in Hamburg, and for a long time could only be described as Austrian rather than Hungarian. However, if the features of his style as it developed in the late 1950s were influenced by the Cologne avant garde of Stockhausen and Gottfried Michael Koenig, his musical thinking derives from Bartók, to whom he acknowledges his debt and is to some extent a successor. His approach to musical structure and his accessible technique (though informed by an element of metaphysics) is more specifically Hungarian than characteristic of Western culture in general.

Hungary is associated with traditions of central European craftsmanship and perfection which can turn into an ideal. Of his harpsichord piece *Continuum* (1968), which races along at immense speed, using not melodies but tonal clusters, Ligeti said that he had 'intentionally wished to intensify the mechanical element inherent in music written for this instrument'. He followed it with his *Hungarian Rock*; *Aventures*, in the same spirit, is a display of vocal techniques referring to basic types of human behaviour. In the development of orchestral tone-colours and 'sound tapestries', Ligeti in his *Atmospheres* reached solutions similar to those of Penderecki, though they were working independently.

The craftsmanlike element, the ideal of mathematically defined precision, has also left its imprint on the character of the music that has developed in Hungary itself – more slowly than in Poland but more steadily than in Czechoslovakia and without such setbacks. When Ligeti left Hungary, some of Bartók's string quartets were still banned, but now Hungarian composers, among them György Kurtág (*b* 1926), have long since made their own fruitful contacts with Western techniques. Others are Zsolt Durkó (*b* 1934), András Mihály (*b* 1917), Endre Székely (*b* 1912) and Rudolf Maros (b 1927), who has emigrated to Sweden.

Minimalist styles also developed at an early stage in Hungary; minimalist composers include Attila Bozay (*b* 1939), István Láng (*b* 1933), Zoltán Jeney (b 1943), a pupil of Goffredo Petrassi, and László Vidovszky (*b* 1944), a pupil of Pierre Schaeffer and Messiaen. In the preceding generation, tendencies towards classicism were more noticeable among the works of Ferenc Farkas (*b* 1905), Pal Kadosa (*b* 1903), Andras Szöllösy (*b* 1921) and Sándor Szokolay (*b* 1931). Hungarian music reveals a particular kind of transparency, as well as hybrid forms between minimalist and pop music which lend dynamism to the former and a cultural element to the latter.

*

Comparison of the music of eastern and eastern central Europe with Western music is often of doubtful value, particularly where there is no common basis for study and analysis. During a workshop discussion, Soviet composers and interpreters of modern music at the 1989

Lockenhaus chamber music festival in Austria were asked whether Western influences or the eastern European roots of their music were more important to them. Their view was that they were probably equally important, but the two situations were not comparable: in the West information and ideas were freely accessible; in the East information was unavailable and took much longer to become known.

In central European music history, eastern Europe usually assumes the peripheral role of a *quantité négligeable*; its history is regarded, often correctly, as that of the belated reception of Western and central European impulses. Crucial elements in Western music originated in those European areas: polyphony and mensural notation, the triad, major and minor keys, the acceleration of musical experience in the virtuoso tradition of the eighteenth and nineteenth centuries, the advent of musical nationalism. Eastern Europe, its own identity suppressed and damaged by much and various foreign rule, was either late to participate in these developments or found an alleged identity in resisting Italian, French and German influence. At most, central European music history has allowed that this delayed reception could have the advantage of intensity and an individual kind of transformation. Linguistic observations show that languages (like cultures) continue to develop most intensively in their central areas, remaining most conservative in peripheral ones where their original forms are best preserved. Considered in this light, eastern Europe is a fascinating assembly of 'peripheral areas' in the history of music.

NOTES

[1] A. Lourié, 'Approach to the Masses', *Modern Music* (New York, 1944), 203–7.

[2] 'Govoryat klassiki', *Sovetskaya muzyka*, i (1948), 29f.

[3] T. Khrennikov, 'Za tvorchestvo, dostoynoye sovetskogo naroda', *Sovetskaya muzyke*, i (1948), 54–62.

[4] It was not performed publicly until 1984 at Duisburg and the first full stage performance took place in Lucerne in 1986.

[5] The composers of these pieces were Eduard Artemyev, Stanislav Kreychi, Alexander Nyentin and Sandor Kallos (Melodiya D 25631–2).

[6] The record included Serocki's Sinfonietta for two string orchestras, Lutosławski's *Funeral Music* and Baird's *Four Essays* (Polskie Nagrania XL 0072).

[7] V. Karbusický, *Materialen zum Musikleben der Tschechoslowakei*, Gutachten für den Deutscher Musicrat (1972).

BIBLIOGRAPHICAL NOTE

General and Russia

The Seventh International Music Festival, 'The Russian Avantgarde' (Heidelberg, 1991), and the congress of 1992 on musical developments in eastern Europe, 'Die

Musikavantgarde im Osten Europas', are documented in *Russische Avantgarde/ Musikavantgarde im Osten Europas*, ed. R. Sperber and D. Gojowy (Heidelberg, 1992), with contributions from 21 eastern European musicologists. Among the works of G. Abraham, *Essays on Russian and East European Music* (Oxford, 1985), gives a fairly up-to-date picture, while Y. Keldïsh and others, *Istoria russkoy muzïki* (Moscow, 1983–) had by 1991 reached volume vi out of a projected ten. *Sowjetische Musik im Licht der Perestroika* ed. H. Danuser, H. Gerlach and J. Köchel (Laaber, 1990), contains a foreword by Y. Kholopov, articles on contemporary Russian music by 20 Russian, Baltic (including V. Landsbergis) and German writers, 16 'statements and interviews' by and with E. Denisov, S. Gubaydulina, V. Yekimovsky, F. Karayev, B. Kutavičius, A. Pärt, A. Shnitke, R. Shchedrin, V. Shut, V. Silvestrov, D. Smirnov, V. Suslin and A. Terteryan, as well as many composers' biographies and worklists.

Poland

The programme notes of the Warsaw Autumn Festival provide an overview. See also K. Baculewski, *Polska Twórczość Kompozytorska 1945–1984* [Polish Composers' Work 1945–1984] (Kraków, 1987); B. Schaeffer, *Nowa muzyka* (Kraków, 1958); T. Kaczyński and A. Zborski, *Warszawska Jesień* (Kraków, 1983); M. Hanuszewska and B. Schaeffer, *Almanach polskich kompozytorów wspólsczesnych* (Kraków, 1982); G. Michalski, E. Obniska, H. Swolkień and J. Waldorff, *Dzieje muzyki polskiej* [History of Polish Music] (Warsaw, 1983).

Czechoslovakia

Documents of the Czechoslovakian Music Information Centre in Prague provide useful information, as do *Sovyetskaya Musika*, v (1948) and A. Piňos, *Tónové skupiny* [Tone Groups], issued by the Supraphon company (Prague, 1971). See also J. Vysloužil, *Hudobníci 20. Storočia* [Musicians of the 20th Century] (Bratislava, 1981), and V. Karbusický, *Materialien zum Musikleben der Tschechoslowakei*, Gutachten für den Deutschen Musikrat (1972).

Romania and Hungary

Apart from programme notes on Electrecord Records, the main source for Romania is *Compozitori și Musicologi Români*, ed. V. Cosma (Bucharest, 1965). The notes for Warsaw Autumn Festival programmes and those on Hungaroton Records provide information on Hungarian composers; a solid critical biography is H.-K. Metzger and R. Riehn, *György Ligeti* (Munich, 1987).

Chapter XIV

The Americas, 1945–70

WILLIAM BROOKS

At the end of World War II, composers of art music in Western cultures found their craft radically affected in three different but related ways. The first was historical: composers had to face, in their own domain, the shattering consequences (geopolitical, economic, ideological) of the largest and most horrific war in history. The second was technical: the burst of industrial growth which accompanied and followed the war fundamentally altered both the tools of the composer's trade and music's economic and social position. The third was institutional: the postwar conviction that specialization is prerequisite for progress provided composers with a new means of support, while deeply altering their relationship to their audience. These three domains are central to the understanding of all postwar music; in the Americas their impact has been especially keen.

History

Though Americans lost their lives, American countries were in no way devastated by World War II. No battles were fought on American soil; in the New World, schools and industries were stimulated rather than destroyed. The USA, especially, emerged from the war a colossus, dominating world economy during the postwar period. And the war furthered the growth of urban, industrialized societies in several Latin American nations, notably Brazil and Argentina. But though the New World was uninjured by the war, it was not unaffected: the stream of refugees and emigrés became a flood during the 1930s and 40s, and in contrast to previous waves many of the new refugees were highly educated and culturally sophisticated. Some were composers, performers or musicologists, many of whom found homes in orchestras and universities. Similarly, the explosive growth of the postwar music industry in North America was fuelled largely by new recording technologies (tape and long-playing records) developed in part in wartime Germany.

Thus, just as the postwar Western economy became recentred in the

New World, so also, for a time, did Western art music. Characteristic American feelings of cultural inferiority, which had made European art both a symbol of status and an object of ridicule, began to yield to a sense of custodianship. Issues of national identity, national idioms, national music – so important in the 1920s and 30s – were subsumed under more fundamental questions about the nature and purpose of postwar society and art. As the USA, in particular, claimed responsibility for the security and economic well-being of the world, so also it began to influence global culture and art. No longer did its composers necessarily follow European counterparts or imitate European styles; increasingly they claimed to be the vanguard, experimenting, producing, initiating.

But what would be produced, what initiated? Postwar political thought was divided. Moderates argued, in effect, that though the war had been catastrophic, the threads of pre-war culture remained and could be rewoven into a new international fabric, akin to its predecessor but fairer and stronger. In the USA, proponents of this view argued convincingly for the United Nations, the Marshall Plan, the General Agreement on Tariffs and Trade, and the Fulbright exchange programmes. For radicals, however, the war was a watershed; civilization had changed fundamentally and irrevocably. Though certain tools might remain useful, a new world was being constructed; and in it, the central questions concerned control: how much, by whom and of what?[1] During the first postwar decade, the dominant response was conservative, emphasizing the centralization of power; from this sprang NATO, the OAS, the Korean War, the McCarthy hearings and all the concomitants of the Cold War. The next fifteen years saw a more libertarian outlook which stressed limitations on power and the control of control; from this came arms control agreements, the Civil Rights movement, the Cuban revolution and widespread social unrest in the USA. Though the two perspectives and the two periods differ, neither excluded the other; rather, the entire period 1945–70 was, in effect, the working-out of a dialectic centred on control.

Ever the child of its times, postwar art music too had its moderates and radicals, or – less polemically – its progressives and originals. Representing the former were New World composers who continued down paths that had been mapped before the war; together with European colleagues, whom they joined by the 1950s, they formed an 'international avant-garde' which, though often seeming extreme, remained faithful to the European art-music tradition. Other progressives pursued nationalist or regional styles; they too extended a pre-war aesthetic, no matter how highly characterized their idiom. The originals, on the other hand, called into question the most basic purposes and techniques of music. Like their political counterparts, they argued that postwar civilization required a new beginning; and as in politics, the central issue concerned control. But the musical dialectic was articulated earlier than the social one: though the first ten years were dominated by a conservative response, the same period saw the evolution of a libertarian view, fully articulated by 1960. The remaining decade was animated by the interaction between these perspectives, characterized by a restless search for solutions of an experimental, paradoxical and individualistic nature.

Despite this parallel, however, art music during this entire quarter-century remained essentially separate from the social mainstream. Music for mass consumption, dating back at least to the introduction of the player piano, addressed and responded directly to social needs; art music self-consciously stood apart. Since the end of the nineteenth century most art music had been avowedly élitist and defiantly esoteric. Its inherent self-preoccupation was only furthered by the development of academic sanctuaries, and its separatism was highlighted by the great flowering of popular music in the postwar era. Though the internal divisions within the composers' community were structurally like those in the political arena, the two domains did not intersect directly; indeed, like most intellectuals during the postwar years, composers essentially abrogated their responsibilities as citizens in the name of their art.

Technology

Postwar developments in communication technologies furthered the alienation of intellectuals from the citizenry and permanently altered the relationship between information and the individual. In politics the question posed by technology is still being argued: do modern media (television, in particular) encourage creativity and responsibility by promoting the free exchange of information, or do they threaten individuality by imposing a mass culture? Again the question concerns control – do media confine or liberate? – and again the question has been mirrored, but not directly addressed, in the domain of music.

In the postwar period, music technology – indeed, music itself – was transformed by the development of tape recorders and of long-playing records. The two were interconnected: the new 'high fidelity' depended on editing and mixing procedures made possible by tape recorders. But they also came to symbolize the two extreme consequences of the new technology: tape recording seemed to promise access to an extraordinary new creative domain, while the commercial recording industry apparently imposed an unprecedented musical conformism. These dual consequences initially seemed separable, but after 1955 their dialectical relation came to be a central concern to art music.

The creative potential of the new technology evolved in three phases.[2] The invention of practical, reliable, inexpensive tape recorders enabled composers for the first time to work directly with sound. No longer dependent on notation or performers, the making of music could, it seemed, resemble the making of a painting or a poem: composers could make their own sound-objects by manipulating directly the materials they had chosen. Moreover, new devices – mixers, filters, modulators – made possible the transformation of sound; familiar sounds could be rendered unrecognizably abstract, fit material for 'art'. By the mid-1950s such devices had been joined by yet more flexible ones that generated sound directly; it began to seem that any sound that could be imagined could be created.

Most of these devices were relatively inexpensive and hence available to nearly anyone who wished to work with them. But to maximize flexibility, a large number was required; moreover, the desire to optimize fidelity motivated the development of precision equipment which quickly became very expensive. By the mid-1950s composers using this new technology fell into two groups: individuals or small groups who worked with relatively cheap equipment, much of it home-built; and employees of major institutions with access to large, expensive studios.

The second phase was implemented only at large institutions. In the mid-1950s, the first generation of practical, all-purpose computers appeared. Composers quickly realized that these permitted a significant increase in the precision with which sounds could be sculpted. Moreover, computers could be used to answer questions about the very structure of a composition; they could, for example, apply formulae to a field of possibilities or generate musical sequences conforming to a particular algorithm, or list of constraints.[3] By 1960, then, computers were assisting both in composing music and in realizing compositions in studios.

A third phase began in the mid-1960s, when several individuals (notably Robert Moog and Donald Buchla) began marketing compact, small-scale versions of conventional electronic music studios. These synthesizers, as they came to be known, were dependent on the miniaturization and power of transistor technology; for a relatively modest price, they supplied the capabilities previously available only at major institutions. They were, in a sense, a synthesis which joined homebuilt technology and institutional studios.

In the meantime, of course, the recording industry was using tape technology for a different purpose: the production of consumable goods. This fundamentally altered the economics of musical com-merce. Editing made possible the assembly of letter-perfect performances; mixing, the creation of balances inaudible in live performance; and processing, the enhancement or correction of a wide variety of acoustical features. These and other procedures created new realizations of the 'classics', with a new standard: 'fidelity'. The emphasis was shifted from the musical work to the performance, and the art-music repertory became even further standardized to facilitate the comparison of performances.[4]

In popular music, similarly, performers became more important than composers, and small groups, amplified by technology, supplanted large ones. The new economics, together with cheap postwar materials, made possible the production of unprecedented quantities of recordings; national distribution and the growth of 'deejay' radio created a mass audience where previously there had been regions and factions. In all these ways, the postwar recording industry imposed a new uniformity on musical culture, first in the USA and subsequently elsewhere. At the same time, the advent of a universal recording technology made all music potentially available to everyone. Moreover, the development of small, portable recording equipment decentralized the technology; small companies abounded, and it became possible to record any music, anywhere, for release on disc. The new technology empowered listeners to create, in effect, their own concerts, and it encouraged the development of specialized audiences.

In sum, then, postwar technology embodied a kind of dialectic in which was played out the relationship between creativity and consumption, the individual and mass production. It was both a boon and a threat to composers and to the sanctity of their postwar refuges: by enabling composers to produce esoteric sounds in expensive, exclusive studios, it protected their status and furthered their isolation; by providing the public with access to repertory and to new electronic instruments, it threatened to snatch creative initiatives away from academic specialists. By the late 1960s the threat was fully realized. The new technologies were most convincingly used by rock musicians, not academics; and it was rock and pop music, not art music, which most directly expressed its culture's fears, hopes, and anger.[5]

Institutions

Paradoxically, the transference of musical initiative from art music to popular music was furthered, not inhibited, by the great expansion in education. In the USA, the GI bill granted a college education to an unprecedented number; a growing belief that citizens are owed an education up to and including university study accelerated a shift in the purpose of education which had begun in the nineteenth century. Rather than providing a social and economic élite with the general knowledge ('liberal education') appropriate to a ruling class, universities began to teach the skills and techniques necessary for particular trades or specializations.

The effect on art music was significant. First, composition became a speciality like any other, taught and practised primarily at universities and assumed by lay people to occupy a world of its own, no more relevant to day-to-day life than, say, quantum mechanics. Today this assumption pervades even the institutions themselves: although the vast majority of composers in the Americas are employed by universities, their position usually does not directly depend on their compositional work. Rather, they are primarily pedagogues whose purpose is to promote the system which justifies their employment. Second, the entire domain of art music became associated with an outdated ruling class and educational model; art music, by and large, was relegated to history and confined to performance museums like the Lincoln or Kennedy Centers. The values attached to it came to have less to do with its import than with tradition or uniqueness (in a world of recordings, concerts are valued precisely because they are not replicable).[6] Finally, since making music came to imply a specialized university education, since the performance of music occured principally in museums, and since technology permitted music to be heard everywhere, there was little incentive to perform professionally except in the protected environs of academia and the concert hall. It was outside the domain of art music that creative professionals came to flourish.

This situation has been evolving, of course, since the nineteenth century, but the evolution accelerated after World War II. As a result, postwar composers, especially in North America, have confronted profound questions about the relationships between themselves, their craft and their audience. Those we have designated as 'progressives' have attempted to transplant or reinvigorate an older European tradition, while the 'originals' have embraced a spectrum of positions, ranging from defiance (yes, this music is indeed for specialists only) to redefinition (no, music can be reconceived to enable everyone, potentially, to be a composer).

PROGRESSIVES

The academies

From the nineteenth century until the outbreak of World War II, the New World depended largely on the Old for its musical education. In the USA, the obligatory experience was expected to be German until World War I; and some musicians, such as Otto Luening and Wallingford Riegger, were German-trained even after then. However, after that war students from both Americas gravitated to France, where Nadia Boulanger trained several generations of composers. Some of her students pursued careers outside academia – Elliott Carter, Aaron Copland, Alejandro García Caturla, Virgil Thomson – but others returned to found smaller teaching empires of their own: Bernard Rogers at the Eastman School, Walter Piston at Harvard, Ross Lee Finney at the University of Michigan and John Beckwith at the University of Toronto. Boulanger's presence continued to be felt well into the 1960s; her later students included Arthur Berger, Easley Blackwood, Donald Erb and Philip Glass.[7]

Even before Fascism began to infect Europe, a significant group of composers moved to the New World. Some were celebrated teachers; Ernest Bloch, for example, taught Bernard Rogers, Roger Sessions and Quincy Porter, who themselves became important teachers. In the 1930s, when Jews and intellectuals were forced from Europe, several younger immigrant composers proved to be even more influential: Ernst Krenek, who taught Robert Erickson and George Perle: Ernst Toch, who taught Aurelio de la Vega and Richard Wernick; and Stefan Wolpe, who taught Manuel Enriquez, Morton Feldman, Ezra Laderman and Ralph Shapey. All these pupils eventually became leading figures in major academic institutions.[8]

When war came, European music was thus well-ensconced in the USA. Academic departments were staffed largely by European-trained composers, and the wave of refugees made 'Americans' out of some of Europe's most celebrated names, including Bartók, Stravinsky and Schoenberg. Some refugees moved directly into academic positions. Ingolf Dahl joined the faculty at the University of Southern California in 1945; Paul Hindemith joined Yale and Darius Milhaud joined Mills College, both in 1940. It is no wonder that from the 1950s to the present, those wishing to extend the fabric of European music have found friendly homes in American universities.

In the USA and Latin America, indeed, there were few alternatives to university positions. Only in Canada were there national sponsors akin to those established in postwar Europe. The Canadian Broadcasting Corporation, national and provincial arts councils, the Canadian Music Centre and the National Film Board all provided alternative means of support for composers as diverse as Norma Beecroft, Robert Fleming, Pierre Mercure and Harry Somers.[9]

Elsewhere in North America there was only academia. In the USA music departments gained new momentum during the postwar period, both through the general growth of higher education and the increasing influence of academic composers then in their 30s and 40s. Many departments became virtual dynasties, with each generation of students becoming teachers of the next. Thus, at Princeton, Roger Sessions taught Milton Babbitt who taught Peter Westergaard; all three were on the faculty during the 1960s. At Columbia, Otto Luening taught Vladimir Ussachevsky who taught Charles Wuorinen; again, all three later became colleagues. Pupils of both Sessions and Luening became central figures at other institutions: Andrew Imbrie at Berkeley, Leon Kirchner at Harvard, Chou Wen-chung at Columbia and Mario Davidovsky at City College, New York.[10]

Other important teachers fostered the further diffusion of academic music. Pupils of John Weinzweig in Toronto were found throughout

Canada, while Walter Piston at Harvard supplied faculty to many New England Colleges. Students from the Eastman School established themselves in Minnesota, Illinois, Washington, Michigan and elsewhere. By the 1960s the Midwest and West Coast had dynasties of their own, built by composer-teachers like Ross Lee Finney and William Albright at Michigan and Robert Erickson in San Francisco. It is difficult to convey just how explosive and incestuous was the growth of academic music. When the American Society of University Composers was founded in 1966, virtually every art-music composer was a potential recruit.

The development of academic music in Latin America followed a similar course, though it was inevitably constrained by economic and social conditions. By 1900 staid national conservatories existed in Mexico, Chile, Colombia, Ecuador and Argentina, but a significant number of twentieth-century Latin American composers were still trained in Europe. After World War I, however, some institutions were radically reshaped by such composers as Julian Carrillo and Carlos Chávez in Mexico, Domingo Santa Cruz in Chile, Heitor Villa-Lobos in Brazil, and José María Castro and Juan Carlos Paz in Argentina. In the 1930s South American interest in contemporary European music was further augmented by emigrées like Rodolfo Holzmann, who settled in Peru, Hans-Joachim Koellreutter in Brazil and José Ardevol in Cuba. And after World War II came important new institutions: the biannual Chilean Music Festivals (begun in 1947), Koellreutter's Free Music Seminars at Bahia University (1952–62) and the Asociación de Jóvenes Compositores (founded in Argentina in 1957). A late but extremely influential arrival was the Center for Advanced Musical Studies at the Torcuato di Tella Institute, Buenos Aires, organized by Alberto Ginastera in 1964.

The 'international' style

Thus academic institutions in the New World became the *de facto* caretakers of what had been a European tradition of publically supported art music. In the 1950s and 60s, as Europe recovered, New World composers joined the new generation of Europeans to form an international 'avant garde' which endeavoured, in one way or another, to maintain the line of European music that stretched back at least to the late nineteenth century.

The cohesiveness of the avant garde depended heavily on postwar developments in recording and copying technology, which made it possible to exchange scores and recordings with little expense or effort. But it was furthered by the continued exchange of people and performances. Europeans like István Anhalt, Udo Kasemets, Karel Husa and Ernst Widmer made new homes in the Americas, while American composers like Mauricio Kagel, Robert W. Mann and Alvin

Curran moved to Europe. Institutional festivals at Darmstadt, Warsaw and Venice had New World counterparts in places ranging from Santiago, Chile, to Urbana, Illinois. And series of avant-garde concerts were managed by such enterprising individuals as Peter Yates in Los Angeles, Serge Garant in Canada and Max Pollikoff in New York.[11]

With such cross-fertilization, stylistic distinctions between the new 'international' composers ceased to depend on geography; rather, subgroups or schools emerged, characterized by technique, aesthetic or genre. Three can be roughly distinguished: those who continued developing the late Romantic or neo-classical styles prevalent before the war; those who adopted the twelve-note method or some other fully chromatic, expressive technique; and those who adapted the new technology (tape recorders and computers) to traditional aesthetic purposes. Collectively these groups constituted the mainstream of art music. Their members were male, caucasian and self-selecting; most were university-trained and formed the backbone of academic and conservatory faculties in the 1950s and 60s. They sat on committees, awarded prizes, published journals, administered and advised; to them was granted primary responsibility for certifying the legitimate heirs of the European tradition.

In the immediate postwar period the largest group consisted of those faithful to some kind of late Romanticism or neo-classical style. The war had little effect on the tastes and techniques of older composers like Murray Adaskin, Samuel Barber, David Diamond, Carlos Estrada, Ulysses Kay, Jean Papineau-Couture, Vincent Persichetti, Quincy Porter, Domingo Santa Cruz or William Schuman. Several important younger figures – Jack Beeson, William Bergsma, Juan Orrego-Salas, Peter Mennin and others – also adopted a somewhat conservative idiom. Often such composers concentrated on conservative genres like vocal music (Gian Carlo Menotti, Ned Rorem, Hugo Weisgall), band music (Paul Creston, H. Owen Reed) or sacred music (Leo Sowerby, Healey Willan).

By the late 1950s the mainstream had shifted towards fully chromatic, expressive styles, often drawing on twelve-note technique. Highly individualized chromatic idioms had long been used by several individuals, reaching back to Carl Ruggles and forward through Miriam Gideon to Leon Kirchner, Andrew Imbrie and beyond. In addition, twelve-note technique had been used well before 1945 by Ben Weber, John Weinzweig, Adolph Weiss and others; some composers, like Ernst Krenek and George Perle, had developed distinctive uses of the row.[12]

The increasing prominence of systematic chromaticism, however, resulted primarily from its adoption by composers who had previously worked with different techniques. Roger Sessions's first twelve-note piece, the Violin Sonata (1953), was a kind of watershed; Sessions's conversion preceded similar changes by composers like Gustavo Becerra-Schmidt, Arthur Berger, Udo Kasemets, Barbara Pentland, George Rochberg and Cláudio Santoro. Some younger composers adopted serial techniques from the start. For many, like István Anhalt, Roque Cordero, Robert Helps and Ursula Mamlock, they served traditional, expressive ends; others – notably Milton Babbitt and his pupils – applied mathematical properties derived from twelve-note technique to all aspects of a composition. The resulting 'total serialism' precipitated a radical reassessment of music's very purpose, as we shall see later in this chapter.

The pervasiveness of the international style cannot be over-emphasized. In the USA, especially, its institutionalization levelled distinctions and obliterated regional differences; composers moved from one university to another with no effect on their musical idioms.

Regional differences did emerge, however, among academic composers involved with technology. Because the major electronic music studios were designed independently, each had its own character and favoured certain techniques. Studios were conceived as analogous to scientific laboratories, and composers often described themselves as research workers rather than artists.

The earliest studios emphasized the manipulation of pre-recorded sounds; arguably the first was the Columbia Tape Studio, begun in 1953 by Vladimir Ussachevsky and Otto Luening after two years of individual experiments and concerts. The Taller Experimental del Sonido, a similar installation, was built in 1955 at Santiago's Catholic University by José Vincente Asuar and Juan Amenábar. At Canada's National Research Council, Hugh Le Caine began building synthesizing equipment as early as 1952; his work culminated in the establishment of studios at the University of Toronto (1959) and McGill University (1963). These, and installations built at Mills College, Yale and Brandeis at about the same time, were hybrid facilities at which sounds could be both synthesized and manipulated.[13]

The University of Illinois established an electronic music studio in 1958 but was better known for the experiments in computer-assisted composition begun by Lejaren Hiller in 1955. In Hiller's work a computer was used to make a score which was then played by conventional instruments. This approach was complemented by research at Bell Laboratories, where Max Mathews, James Tenney, Gerald Strang and others used computers to generate sounds. In the 1960s software developed at Bell was adapted for university facilities by John Chowning at Stanford and J. K. Randall at Princeton. Princeton and Columbia, with support from the Rockefeller Foundation, sponsored an important hybrid machine, the RCA Mark II synthesizer, which was installed in 1959 and used well into the 1970s.[14]

The Electronic Music Synthesizer RCA MK II, built in 1957, shown here in the Columbia-Princeton Electronic Music Center, where it was installed in 1959.

The design of all these studios differed so much that a listener often could recognize more easily where a piece was made than who had made it. Their development reached a peak between 1958 and 1965, partly because of technical advances but also because of the surge of anxiety created when Sputnik was launched in 1957. Suddenly the USA was convinced that it had 'fallen behind' the Russians and resources were diverted to technical and scientific areas. Academic, 'scientific' music – comprehensible only to a select few – was justified and supported precisely because of its exclusivity; and of all the academic genres, those using technological equipment were the most dramatic and inscrutable.

All this changed when the Buchla and Moog synthesizers were introduced in 1964. These permitted sound synthesis to be stand-ardized in mass-produced units; as prices declined, both private and

institutional studios proliferated (by 1970 an informal census generated a list of over 200 installations). Moreover, since they were easily
used and understood: the composition of electronic music no longer
required a specialized knowledge of engineering or acoustics. Worse,
the new devices were quickly embraced by pop and rock musicians;
suddenly the initiative shifted to non-professionals.[15]

The popularization of electronic music signalled the imminent
collapse of the mainstream 'international' style. Influenced by factors
ranging from tape collage to new European 'sound-mass' compositions
by Xenakis, Penderecki and others, some American composers – Ralph
Shapey, Donald Erb, Alan Stout, Hector Quintanar – began organizing pieces around large blocks of complex sound. Though still
dissonant, even raw, such works were more easily grasped than their
predecessors; built on dynamic and textural contrasts, they had a clear
logic even to unschooled ears.

A more lyrical, traditional chromaticism also evolved, particularly
among writers of vocal music like Dominick Argento, Richard
Felciano, Marlos Nobre and Aurelio de la Vega. This style owed
much to the Italian serial tradition articulated by Dallapiccola and
Berio; in the Americas it was furthered by Berio's residency from
1962 to 1971 and by that of Berio's pupil, Bernard Rands, from 1966.
Music by all these composers was better received than that of the
serialists of the preceding decade, and towards the end of the 1960s
several younger composers – John Corigliano, David Del Tredici, Jacob

*Terry Riley with portable studio equipment, working on his piece 'Poppy Nogood and the Phantom
Band' (1968), which uses the tape loop and electronic keyboard.*

Druckman and John Harbison – began to espouse the more access-ible styles which would reach fruition in the 1970s and 80s as the 'new romanticism'.[16]

The 1950s and 60s were also marked by a greater diversity of genres. Orchestras, opera companies and standard chamber groups became increasingly devoted to music of the past, and composers were less inclined to write for them. They turned to new genres and to performers who specialized in new music, and these contributed further to the fragmentation of the mainstream.

Percussion music, established before the war in seminal works by Varèse, Cage, Harrison, Chávez and others, witnessed a surge of interest, due in part to the work of younger percussionist-composers like Michael Colgrass and William Kraft. Unsuited to conservative or serial techniques, percussion music fostered renewed interest in structuring compositions by rhythm and timbre rather than pitch.[17] Timbre was also a focus for new-music virtuosos, whose 'extended techniques' included playing on the bodies or keys of their instruments, producing multiphonics and other complex sounds or noises, or altering the physical structure of their instruments (playing brass instruments with woodwind mouthpieces, for example). Several of the new virtuosos became composers in their own right, or at least collaborated so closely with composers as to be virtually co-creators: David Tudor (piano), Bert Turetzky (contrabass), Stuart Dempster (trombone), Robert Aitkin and Harvey Sollberger (flute), William O. Smith (clarinet), Cathy Berberian (voice) and others.[18] Many extended techniques were highly unpredictable, and they reinforced a growing interest in improvisation and indeterminacy. Both percussion music and the new techniques were also often intrinsically theatrical, supporting many composers' involvement with music-theatre or mixed-media works. Separately or together, then, timbre, indeter-minacy and theatre became central to the stylistic experiments of a wide range of composers, including George Crumb, Robert Erikson, Eduardo Mata, Bruce Mather and Gilles Tremblay.[19]

New music was also performed by a few conventional chamber groups, such as the Composers, La Salle, Lenox and New Music Quartets, the New York Woodwind Quintet and the American Brass Quintet; but in general the hostility of professional ensembles towards the avant garde increased the isolation of most academic composers. Many institutions responded by sponsoring their own 'Contemporary Chamber Players'; by 1970 such groups could be found at universities from Toronto to Bahia. Most university ensembles consisted of about ten musicians playing a heterogeneous mix of instruments. No two ensembles were alike, and many pieces were scored for odd combina-tions unlikely to be assembled outside the composer's own academy. In the mid-1960s, however, some professional groups emerged for which a larger body of work was generated: Arthur Weisberg's Contemporary Chamber Ensemble, the Aeolian Chamber Players, the Da Capo Chamber Players and others.[20]

By 1965, then, a number of factors had combined to wash out what remained of the channel cut by postwar mainstream composition. In its place there was a kind of new-music delta – complex, fertile and treacherous. The loss of musical norms to some degree paralleled that of cultural norms in the late 1960s, particularly in the USA. The new 'counterculture', new political and ecological paradigms, a new emphasis on individualism – all these lent indirect support to composers who wished to break away from the traditions of their teachers.

In art music such new departures were largely self-indulgent. Academic composers adopted the trappings of socially active rock and popular musicians – they grew beards, wore jeans, 'dropped out' – but their art generally remained hermetic. Commercial success implied artistic failure; academics caught up in the counterculture were more or less obliged to adopt an egocentric, self-absorbed posture. Those who rejected the counterculture had an even more impossible task; though they would endeavour to dredge and channel the waters, to map a mainstream from afar, the 1970s and 80s would turn out to be beyond their control.

Postwar Nationalism and Referentiality

The evolving international style of the postwar years largely supplanted pre-war efforts to define 'national' idioms. Latin American composers were more deeply committed to musical nationalism than most, but even many of these – José Ardevol, Rodolpho Holzmann, Francisco Mignone – turned towards a more abstract style. In addition, major figures on both continents were profoundly affected.

Aaron Copland, in 1945, was the best-known art-music composer in the USA, largely because of his accessible, 'Americanist' works of the 1930s. After the war, however, he began experimenting with serialism, albeit in a highly individual manner. Works like the Piano Quartet (1950), *Connotations* (1961–2) and *Inscape* (1967) are intensely chromatic and tightly controlled, very much a part of the postwar era.[21] A somewhat similar path was traced by the prolific Carlos Chávez, whose penchant for structures based on evolving, non-repetitive material well suited the postwar climate. Chávez was a resolute eclectic, however, and his late works are characterized less by a stylistic shift than by an intensified interest in precision of form and technique. Alberto Ginastera's nationalism lingered past the war, though in the music of his second period (1947–54) national references are increasingly obscured by formal prodecures. By the mid-1950s Ginastera had adopted a fully chromatic expressionist style; over the next 15 years he integrated serialism with other 'international' techniques (microtonality, indeterminacy, timbralism) in a series of powerful music-theatre works.

Not all nationalist styles were abandoned after the war, however. Some North American composers – Claude Champagne, Roy Harris, Eric Stokes and Robert Ward, for example – continued to infuse their work with folk or national references. And a number of Latin composers continued their earlier deep commitment to nationalism: Juan José Castro, Luis Antonio Escobar, Blas Galindo, Camargo Guanieri, Alfonso Letelier. In Cuba the revolution motivated an intense interest in political compositions; these were largely international in style, but Harold Gramatges and Leo Brouwer often borrowed freely from folk and popular music.

Referential music need not be nationalist, of course, and in the postwar period composers made reference to a wide range of musical sources: commercial, popular, ethnic, even historical. References to jazz increased, perhaps because the bebop revolution and the collapse of the big bands brought jazz closer to concert music than to popular music. Musicians attempting to blend the concert and the club ranged from jazz notables (Ornette Coleman, Don Ellis, George Russell, Lalo Schifrin) to essentially conservative composers much influenced by early jazz experiences (Harry Freedman, Billy Jim Layton, Robert McBride, Francis Thorne). In between were composers of what Gunther Schuller called 'third stream' music, in which improvisation and jazz inflections mingled with international techniques.[22] Such composers tended either to gravitate to academia (Schuller, Larry Austin, Howard Brubeck, Donald Erb, Edwin London, Hall Overton, Hale Smith) or to remain jazz professionals (David Amram, Teo Macero, William Russo, Norman Symonds).

Other forms of popular music, both contemporary and historical, began to enter concert music in the 1960s. Marc Blitzstein, Leonard Bernstein and Elie Siegmeister applied concert techniques to popular music and vice versa; Douglas Moore's operas drew heavily on vernacular idioms, as did Virgil Thomson's film scores and his postwar masterpiece, *The Mother of Us All*. With the ragtime revival came composers like William Albright and William Bolcom, who drew on earlier popular styles; and with the maturity of rock in the 1960s appeared a new generation of populists like Michael Sahl and Neely Bruce. All these composers, in their own ways, represented a kind of postmodern nationalism.

In the 1950s and 60s black musicians in the USA developed something akin to a nation of their own, in music as in politics. The early champions of black concert idioms had been active before the war; their music was conservative, often vocal, and drew primarily on black folk and spiritual sources; they included Margaret Bonds,

Ornette Coleman (alto saxophone, trumpet, violin) in rehearsal with Charlie Haden (bass) and Dewey Redman (tenor saxophone, musette), New York, 1971.

William Levi Dawson, Florence Bea Price, William Grant Still, Howard Swanson. After the war they were joined by younger composers who mixed the new international style with references to jazz as well as folksongs: David Baker, Noel Da Costa, Carman Moore, George T. Walker, Olly Wilson.[23]

Stylistic references were also central to the music of a group of composers who, in a sense, were the antithesis of musical nationalists. These globalists sought to infuse Western art music with techniques or aesthetics drawn from elsewhere in the world; their efforts had been anticipated in the 1930s by pioneers like Henry Cowell, Lou Harrison and Colin McPhee. The postwar period saw a steadily increasing interest in non-Western music, which reached a watershed of sorts when the Society for Ethnomusicology was founded in 1955. Of the composers concerned with 'world music', some drew primarily on their own heritage: Chou Wen-Chung, Dai-Keong Lee, Richard Yardumian, Yehudi Wyner. Many had been active before the war. Others followed the lead of Cowell and Harrison, drawing freely from a number of cultures: Gustavo Becerra-Schmidt, Paul Chihara, Philip Corner, Alan Hovhaness, Vincent McDermott, Ron Nelson.[24]

Composers also began making increased reference to Western

historical styles. The models were not necessarily recast or parodied (as had been the case with 'neo-classicism') but used as signs to evoke a particular collection of associations or as raw material in pastiches or collages. Again there was ample precedent in works by Ives, Thomson, Cowell and others; but historical reference became increasingly pertinent after the war, when the proliferation of recordings had the effect of making all music 'contemporary' and hence subject to re-use. Luciano Berio's *Sinfonia* (1968) is commonly taken as a watershed (the third movement is an elaborate gloss on Mahler's Second Symphony); but other composers explored historicism and collage more thoroughly and systematically – John Beckwith, George Crumb, Lucas Foss, Edwin London, George Rochberg and Loren Rush, to name a few.

Globalists and historicists brought about a significant increase in the use of reference as a compositional device, even though nationalism, in the pre-war sense, declined. In some cases, this represented a turning away from the academy, a conscious effort to reach a wider audience, paralleling the rise of pop intellectualism (paperback psychology, science for the layman, continuing education, public broadcasting). In other cases the use of global or historical material was a political gesture not unrelated to the surge of interest in native American culture, spiritualism, oriental religions and alternative 'life-styles'. In still other cases the use of existing material reflected, in musical terms, the collapse of history in society at large; the proliferation of instant detritus (xerox machines, polaroid photography, throwaway utensils) and the appropriation of relics ('granny' glasses, pop art, second-hand shops) compressed history into the recent past or even a constant present from which anything could be selected at any time. In the 1970s and 80s, as 'crossover' styles proliferated and a 'postmodern' aesthetic emerged, referentiality would subvert traditional genres, categories and chronologies even further, raising profound questions about ownership and originality, and would prove to be a vital tool in art music's self-critique and in its analysis of culture at large.

Experimentalists

There remains one other group of New World composers for whom the postwar period represented a continuation rather than a new beginning. Many of the 'experimentalists' of the 1920s and 30s simply picked up the threads of their work after the war. But the continuation was paradoxical, since most of them remained committed to building radically new musics. In this sense most are more properly described as 'originals' rather than 'progressives'.

Of the 'American five', only Henry Cowell broke new paths after the war; and even Cowell's innovations (global music, indeterminate forms) were foreshadowed in his earlier works. John Becker's health declined and he produced little of importance after the remarkable

Violin Concerto (1948). Wallingford Riegger wrote many of his finest pieces after the war, beginning with the celebrated Symphony no.3 (1948), but his pungent, chromatic counterpoint remained unchanged. Carl Ruggles wrote virtually nothing; and Ives nothing at all.

A younger generation closely allied with the radical pioneers came to full maturity. Chief among them was Elliott Carter, whose stylistic evolution reflected the new preoccupation with complexity and control. In his Piano Sonata (1945–6) and Cello Sonata (1948), neo-classicism yielded to new logic, devised for each work, that rested more on structural conflict within time and tonality than on conventional harmony or form. Though Carter never adopted serialism, and though his most basic purposes remained unchanged, his concentrated, disciplined technique was close to the structured chromaticism embraced by other postwar composers. Unlike some, however, Carter adopted few new techniques after the early 1950s. Instead, he created an evolving series of ever more intricate, knotty works (from the Second Quartet through the set of three Concertos) that made him the most uncompromising exponent of atonal expressionism in the USA and, by 1980, the accepted dean of American composers.[25]

For one pioneer, postwar technology made possible what amounted to a second career. Edgard Varèse had completed little since the 1920s and nothing after 1937; then, in 1953, the gift of a tape recorder opened the way to the creation of works he had projected as early as 1933. *Déserts* (1954) was followed by the extraordinary *Poème electronique*, which mixed sounds from both natural and electronic sources, distributing them over 400 loudspeakers in the Philips Pavilion at the 1958 Brussels World Fair. Le Corbusier designed the building and chose projections to fill the space; arguably the first mixed-media environment, the whole was an artistic as well as a technological landmark.[26]

Other composers were preoccupied with the distribution of sound in space. Like Carter, Henry Brant was closely allied with the 'American five', his deepest affinity being with the spatial collages composed by Ives. In a series of works in the 1950s Brant distributed ensembles throughout the performance space, each playing music quite different from the others. Like *Poème electronique*, such compositions as *The Grand Universal Circus* (1956) anticipated many of the mixed-media and environmental works of the 1960s; others following Brant's lead included Larry Austin, Elliott Schwartz and Eric Stokes.[27]

For composers who lacked access to technology or large ensembles experimentation took a highly idiosyncratic course. Conlon Nancarrow left the USA for Mexico City in 1940 and worked there, almost unnoticed, for the next 30 years, composing for two player pianos, inscribing and punching the rolls with a machine he built himself. The rhythmic precision made possible by piano-roll technology led to the exploration of complex metric and tempo proportions, such as 17:18:19:20, or simultaneous accelerandos and ritardandos; in his Studies, Nancarrow also investigated complex harmonies and extremely rapid arpeggiation. It was not until the late 1960s, after nearly three decades of work, that recordings began to make Nancarrow's remarkable compositions more widely available.[28]

The special nature of Nancarrow's music almost guaranteed its isolation, at least initially. A similar problem was encountered by other pioneers who, working with new tunings and scales, had to devise and build instruments on which to realize their music. Julian Carrillo was 70 in 1945, and for nearly 40 years he had been investigating microtones ranging downwards to a sixteenth of a whole tone. In the 1920s his work had attracted international attention; microtonal pianos, harps and other instruments had been constructed to his specification and he had received commissions from such mainstream ensembles as the Philadelphia Orchestra. In the 1930s and 40s, when experimentalism was eclipsed by more utilitarian, conservative styles, Carrillo became a near-forgotten figure; but the late 1950s saw renewed interest in his ideas and music.[29]

Carrillo's equal-tempered microtonalism was explored by composers in the USA, ranging from Lou Harrison through James Tenney to Ezra Sims, but Carrillo's closest counterpart was also his complement: Harry Partch. Carrillo and Partch differed in a fundamental way; whereas Carrillo simply divided the equal-tempered scale into smaller, equal-tempered intervals, Partch discarded equal temperament entirely, replacing it with a complex theory of extended just intonation. In equal temperament all intervals except the octave are acoustically out of tune (that is, the frequency ratios are irrational); in just intonation many more intervals are well tuned (the frequency ratio for a 5th, for example, is truly 3:2; that for a major 3rd is 5:4). The penalty paid is the loss of enharmonic equivalence (B♯ and C, for example, are different pitches), and modulation and chromaticism become extremely problematic; Partch's system, in a certain sense, is mono-tonic in that all the pitches are derived from a single starting-point.

Partch supported his acoustic innovations with an elaborate aesthetic, citing by way of justification such antecedents as Greek drama, Chinese music halls and Yaqui Indian rituals. Music, Partch argued, was 'corporeal', and the physical aspect of performance was as important as the sonorous. Partch's compositions are thus nearly all theatrical to some extent and the instruments he built are sculptures as well as sound-producers.[30] Before the war Partch lived from hand to mouth, but in the 1940s and 50s his work began to be supported by foundations and universities. Because only one complete set of instruments existed, performances were limited primarily to those given under Partch's supervision; nevertheless, by the 1960s his ideas – especially his tuning theories – had become influential. Younger followers, notably Ben Johnston and Joel Mandelbaum, began applying extended just intonation in very different ways; Johnston's music, for example, is conceived primarily for conventional, flexible ensembles (string quartets, in particular), while Mandelbaum has concentrated on retuned keyboards of various sorts.[31]

Although Partch was a rebel and an inventor, and although the basis for his work predates the war, it is no accident that his ideas came to fruition in the postwar decade. In his music problems of control are raised in an especially clear way: on the one hand are the extremely precise constraints imposed by just intonation; on the other are the anarchic, celebratory impulses implied by his 'corporeal' aesthetic. The battle between these two purposes, joined within Partch's music, was fought between other composers of his generation. It is to these 'originals' that we now turn.

ORIGINALS

The dialectic of control: Babbitt and Cage

The legacy of World War II included troubling questions about control, power and government. At the extremes of the possible responses there were idealists of two persuasions. One group argued that everything could be controlled without abuse by applying consistency, clarity and accuracy to all matters. Decisions were to be made by a single, central authority, ensuring that all the components of society work together in a harmonious, mutually supportive fashion. Others felt that nothing should be controlled. Moreover, they argued, steps must be taken to ensure that control does not arise, willy-nilly: control itself must be controlled. This would be achieved by interfering, automatically or individually, with the centralization of power in any single authority; control would rest with each individual, acting responsibly and independently.

These extreme positions could not be implemented socially; political action, it seems, entails compromise. But the arts embody desires, not 'reality', and in the arts – in music, in particular – these two ideals could appear in virtually pure form. In the USA two composers came to symbolize the two positions: Milton Babbitt and John Cage.

Babbitt's life has been tightly circumscribed: his entire career is bounded by the cities of Princeton and New York. He was a student of Roger Sessions, taught composition (and briefly mathematics) at Princeton and became Conant Professor of Music there in 1960; except for the years 1946–8 he has been an academic for all his adult life. Cage has never been one, though he has held important residencies at major universities. He is largely self-taught (he studied privately, but briefly, with Henry Cowell and Arnold Schoenberg). Although a resident of New York, he has spent most of his career travelling, both on his own and as music director of the Merce Cunningham Dance Company.

Both Babbitt and Cage have reconcieved the nature and purpose of music, articulating new beginnings for postwar aesthetics. For Babbitt, music is a manifestation of intellectual mastery, akin to science; composition and audition therefore resemble research, and the domain of qualified composers and listeners is limited to a small group of specialists.[32] For Cage, music is a means for 'changing one's mind', akin to religion; composition and audition resemble contemplation, and everyone is qualified to compose or to listen.[33] Babbitt's position in a sense was an extension of the corporate, scientific ideology of the early Cold War years; Cage's anticipated the anarchic, anti-rationalist movements of the 1960s. Though both composers articulate radical aesthetics, neither stands outside history. Cage's musical ancestry is French (in spite of his studies with Schoenberg); his preoccupation is with sound itself and his aesthetic harks back to the dadaism and surrealism of the 1920s. Babbitt's forebears are German; his work stretches to the limit the implications of the systematic exploration of chromaticism that began in the nineteenth century and reached its crisis in Schoenberg.

Babbitt's music resembles Schoenberg's in that it uses twelve-note rows. For Schoenberg, however, the row served both structural and expressive purposes; it was as much a field of connotations as an abstract collection of pitches. For Babbitt the row is pure structure, and an essential pleasure of composition and audition is found in exploring its structural implications cleanly, consistently and elegantly, much as one might explore the implications of a mathematical theorem. Indeed, mathematics is central to Babbitt's technique. In the 1940s he developed a means of characterizing the twelve-note system numerically so that Schoenberg's classic transformations (transposition, inversion, retrograde) could be formalized as a mathematical group having certain regular properties. Moreover, if the row is interpreted as a set of numbers, these (and the associated mathematical group) could be applied to any element, not merely to pitch. In a series of compositions from the 1950s and 60s, Babbitt developed mechanisms to apply the set to rhythm, dynamics, instrumentation, attacks, even to larger domains like structure and to non-musical ones like phonetics.[34]

Babbitt also conducted exhaustive studies of the properties of rows themselves. He uses rows rich in constructive potential and breaks them into fragments which can be recombined in new configurations that preserve or extend certain properties of the mathematical group established by the original. At its most elaborate, then, Babbitt's work permits a rich and complex system to be defined by a single set which is itself only a particular manifestation of certain well-defined mathematical properties. In this way his music exemplifies an extreme centralist response to questions concerning control.

While Babbitt was devising rigorous methods for linking all aspects of a composition to a single source, Cage was seeking a means of dissolving such links, allowing each sound within a composition to be itself alone, independent of all others. His work began in the late 1930s with the development of structural principles based only on lengths of time. Such structures could be articulated with any sonic material, or even silence; they did not require reliance on pitch, intensity or timbre. Concurrently Cage began investigating the qualities of sound, more as an explorer than a scientist. He wrote extensively for percussion and he devised ways of 'preparing' a piano by inserting small objects between the strings, thus producing a wide range of different timbres. In the works of the 1940s, however, the choice of these timbres and their conjunction – into motifs, patterns and other traditional musical ideas – remained under his control. In the late 1940s, however, Cage began to seek ways of removing this control as well, an objective which led him in 1951 to begin writing music by means of chance techniques. In his subsequent music, Cage's role is simply to ask questions: How long? How many notes? Which ones? For what instrument? How loud? The range of answers is determined by practical circumstances. Within this range, Cage answers each question randomly, asking and answering additional questions as often as necessary to complete the work.[35]

Thus in Cage's music, like Babbitt's, a single method dominates all aspects of a composition; but in Cage's case the effect of that method is to prevent, rather than affirm, the existence of a central starting-point. Only the method is controlled, and that control is directed against the establishment of acoustic controls; control itself is restricted, so that during the act of composition any result is possible at any time. In Babbitt's music, by contrast, an initial choice determines to a large degree all that is to follow.

It is easy to misrepresent the character of both men's work. Cage's music is not self-indulgent; on the contrary, the use of chance techniques requires precision of thought, a great deal of time, and care in execution. Such care and precision are not just a matter of principle; Cage's point, after all, is that sounds should be freed from constraints, including those imposed by personal taste. Cage argues not that a composer can do anything he or she desires but that a composer can do anything once desires are set aside. Similarly, Babbitt's music is not mechanistic. The logic that regulates his compositions is neither self-initiating nor autonomous. Choices are made at every stage; though constrained by and consistent with the central logic, they are choices none the less. The ultimate source of control is Babbitt himself, who selects the structure, sets it in motion and guides it through each juncture.

In the late 1950s and 60s both Babbitt and Cage extended their work into larger domains. In compositions like *All-Set* (1957), *Philomel* (1964) and *Phonemena* (1969–70), Babbitt inflected his system through references to jazz, poetry and phonetics. Cage began making pieces in which chance was applied to performance as well as to composition; many were interpretable in any medium: *Cartridge Music* (1960), *Fontana Mix* (1958) and a series of Variations (1958–66).

In this sense both composers reflected the changing character of the period 1955–70. In the immediate postwar decade, especially in the USA, domains were highly polarized: the Communist world, the free world; scientists, humanists; inner-directed, outer-directed; male, female. So also composers largely believed it necessary to choose between aesthetic antipodes. After 1955, however, they sought to reconcile or challenge such polarities, not only by bridging or integrating extremes, but also by exploring new, unrelated areas. In culture at large, traditional divisions were challenged by the civil rights movement, feminism and gestalt psychology; in drug culture, back-to-the-land movement and alternative education, old debates were declared irrelevant to new initiatives. In both society and art,

'Variations V' (1965), with choreography by Merce Cunningham, music by John Cage, film sequences by Stan VanDerBeek, and distortion of video images by Nam June Paik. The picture shows the dancers Merce Cunningham and Barbara Dilley on stage among the movement-sensitive antennae, and Carolyn Brown offstage; John Cage, David Tudor and Gordon Mumma (foreground) are operating the 'orchestra' of tape recorders, record players and radio receivers which contain the sound materials composed by Cage.

then, a new pluralist vision emerged in which issues of control blended with, and were obscured by, a concern with individuation and interaction.

The dialectic transformed, I: technique

Cage and Babbitt had great influence on other composers. Babbitt's impact was confined primarily to the USA and to academic institutions; Cage's was international and largely outside academia. Babbitt continued the tradition of influential teachers initiated at Princeton by Roger Sessions. His students included, for example, Donald Martino, Peter Westergaard and Henry Weinberg; the music written by these and other pupils is inflected by personality and individual preference yet relies on the sort of set structures devised by Babbitt. The pieces thus resemble each other closely, affirming the virtues of stylistic consistency and continuity rather than those of independence and individuation.

In contrast, the composers most often linked with Cage – Morton Feldman, Earle Brown and Christian Wolff – bear little resemblance to each other. After early experiments with partly indeterminate graphic scores, Feldman settled into a style characterized by fully notated, widely spaced sonorities, very soft dynamics, rhythmic flexibility and intuitive, non-systematic choices. He worked as a dry cleaner in New York until appointed to the faculty at SUNY Buffalo in 1972.

Brown also wrote graphic pieces in the early 1950s, including the celebrated *Folio* (1952); these led to the development of 'open form' compositions, in which the order of fully composed fragments is determined by the performer. Long interested in jazz, Brown infuses his music with a jazzlike affection for dramatic and gestural coherence. He has had tangential connections to several universities (the longest, for ten years, as resident composer at California Institute of the Arts) but has worked free-lance for most of his career, in Europe as well as the Americas.

Christian Wolff was trained as a classicist and has taught at Dartmouth. His earliest works, conventionally notated, were succeeded by compositions in which notational innovations and complex cuing mechanisms permitted performers' choices to reconceive each work for every performance. Since the late 1960s Wolff's music has become increasingly political, promoting responsible, independent action by the performers and referring explicitly to the political music and writings of the American left. Throughout his career, it has been characterized by evenness and consistency, operating within well-defined, wide-ranging fields of events but avoiding a sense of climax or resolution.

Wolff, Brown and Feldman went very different ways after working with Cage in the early 1950s. As a group they manifest individuality

and diversity; stylistic invention, rather than consistency, has characterized their development. In this sense Cage's legacy in the late 1950s
and 60s contrasts clearly with Babbitt's, a contrast – centred on
individuation – that logically reflects the opposed views of control the
two composers typified in the immediate postwar decade.[36]

The same contrasts are evident in the two composers' positions in the
international community. Babbitt's music blended well with the rising
international avant garde in the 1960s. Indeed, his efforts to extend row
techniques to other compositional domains were closely paralleled by
European serialists like Pierre Boulez and Karlheinz Stockhausen, as
well as Americans like Ernst Krenek and Serge Garant. In the 1960s
extended serialism was also adopted by composers whose style had
previously been neo-classical or expressively chromatic: Arthur
Berger, Léon Biriotti, Ross Lee Finney, Léon Schidlowsky and others.
Indeed, many owed more to European serialists than to Babbitt, whose
international impact was quite limited; he was a respected colleague
but not viewed as significantly different from other 'international'
composers.

Cage's viewpoint, on the other hand, was largely unparalleled in
European music. Few were prepared to follow him altogether, but
many adapted and transformed his techniques. Most of the resulting
compositions resembled the graphic notation or 'open form' works of
Earle Brown more than works by Cage himself; Europeans like Berio,
Boulez, Kagel and Stockhausen devised pieces that were indeterminate
in certain limited ways, such as in the order of movements or the
interpretation of brief, graphically notated passages.

Similar techniques were applied by dozens of American composers.
Some, like Sergio Cervetti, Manuel Enriquez, Barbara Pentland and
William Sydeman, found ways of incorporating indeterminacy into
styles that had been chromatic or even fully serial. Others, who had
been eclectics all along, accepted indeterminate techniques as simply
another option; these included Gustavo Beccera-Schmidt, Barney
Childs, Robert Erickson, Sydney Hodkinson, Udo Kassemets and
Pauline Oliveros. These and other composers devised a wide range of
techniques for presenting indeterminate concepts – descriptive texts,
fully-composed modules, graphic notation and so forth.

Cage's ideas, then, unlike Babbitt's, were transformed rather than
absorbed by internationalists on both sides of the Atlantic. Indeterminacy produced a wide range of responses, and Cage's resistance to
control became transformed into a resistance to uniformity. The
argument that sounds should 'be themselves' led to the claim that
composers should also 'be themselves', and this found resonances in the
radical thought of the Vietnam era. At their best, in both politics and
music, anti-establishment positions produced striking critiques of the
status quo and engaging alternatives to traditional structures; at their

worst they led to onanistic, ineffectual posturing. In the short run, in practical terms, all these movements failed; the war continued, Richard Nixon became president, blacks and women remained oppressed, and art was still in the service of an economic and social élite. The long-range outcome remains to be seen; at the very least, it seems, the movements of the 1960s shifted the focus of discourse away from control and towards the nature of responsibility.

The dialectic transformed, II: technology

A similar transformation can be traced in technology. The earliest electronic music studios were assembled by individuals: Louis and Bebe Barron, Edgard Varèse and Vladimir Ussachevsky in the USA, Hugh Le Caine in Canada, José Vicente Asuar and Juan Amenábar in Latin America. For the most part these studios were aesthetically neutral and frankly experimental; the Barrons, Le Caine and Amenábar were as much engineers as composers. From 1953, however, when Ussachevsky's studio became the Columbia Tape Studio, electronic music split into two streams: academic or research installations, increasingly expensive and complex; and privately maintained studios, homebuilt, inexpensive and idiosyncratic. The two streams reflected the aesthetic poles of the 1950s. Again, Babbitt and Cage can serve as paradigms; both were deeply interested in the invention of new sounds, and both pursued their interests in part through technology. Yet their motivations were different.

Babbitt realized that the evolution of sound synthesis techniques would eventually make possible the precise specification of every aspect of every sound in a composition; thus the smallest details could be accurately and completely regulated by a compositional system. Hence Babbitt's interest, from the beginning, was in power and precision. The RCA Mark II Electronic Music Synthesizer, built in 1957 and moved in 1959 to the Columbia-Princeton Electronic Music Center, which Babbitt directed, represented the furthest advance in this field. Complex, cumbersome and expensive, it could only exist in a university.

Cage embraced technology for the opposite reason; it gave him access to new sounds, whose qualities could be predicted by neither the composer nor the user of the equipment. He required neither power nor control; more important were flexible, practical systems in which many simple components could be linked to produce complex, unpredictable results. Hence Cage worked with homebuilt devices, beginning with variable-speed phonographs as early as the 1930s; in the late 1950s and early 60s his compositions and performances often involved intricate circuits jerry-rigged from components like phonograph pickups, throat and contact microphones, simple filters and oscillators and modified tape recorders. Such circuits were cheap, portable and easily modified

– the opposite of the synthesizer housed in the Columbia-Princeton Studio.[37]

Throughout the 1950s, then, the deep split in the application of music technology reflected the underlying aesthetic dispute about control. And just as aesthetics were transformed by developments in the 1960s, so was music technology. The transformation was manifested in three important ways.

First, as technology itself became more flexible, compact and inexpensive, private, homebuilt studios became more complex and sophisticated. At the same time, composers like Gordon Mumma, Alvin Lucier and Richard Teitelbaum began to share and exchange the circuits they built, forming loose associations (the Fluxus group, Sonic Arts Union) or performance ensembles (Musica Elettronica Viva, Canadian Electronic Ensemble).[38] In at least two important cases these associations resulted in the establishment of sophisticated studios with only peripheral connections with academia: the San Francisco Tape Music Center and the Cooperative Studio for Electronic Music in Ann Arbor, Michigan. Most of these groups welcomed a variety of aesthetics, and the increasingly sophisticated technology permitted a wider range of solutions to problems of control and precision. Composers became more preoccupied with discovering distinctive applications, carving out a niche, defining their own identity; at the same time, both practical and ideological forces required that they work towards a common purpose. The resulting tensions and solutions closely resembled those which characterized the utopian communes and radical collectives of the 1960s.

Second, as major institutional installations proliferated, these too began to be more distinctively characterized. The trend accelerated with the introduction of computer composition and sound synthesis in the late 1950s. The RCA Mark II, in a sense, had been computer-controlled; its sound generators were driven by punched paper tape on which a description of each sound had been stored. In the 1960s this technique was extended by Emmanuel Ghent and others, but in the meantime different systems had evolved. The University of Illinois concentrated on computer-assisted composition; equipment and software developed at Bell Labs was reapplied in a number of studios; Max Mathews and Barry Vercoe developed all-purpose, transportable computer languages; at Stanford, Leland Smith and Loren Rush devised distinctive synthesis and notation programs. In many of these systems random numbers played an important role; yet the very nature of computers required precise specification of all compositional parameters. In this sense, computer music bridged the technical gap between Cage and Babbitt; in fact, computers were aesthetically neutral and, as in the independent studios, composers devoted much effort to devising idiosyncratic and highly characterized applications.[39]

Advertisement for a Fluxus Group concert.

Finally, both private studios and university installations were radically altered by the introduction of commercial, integrated synthesizers in 1964. These shared some aspects of both previous prototypes. Like homebuilt technology, they permitted a large number of components to be combined into flexible networks, at their best offering a virtually inexhaustible collection of options. And like large installations, they promised at least a fair degree of precision and control, with stable oscillators, calibrated tunings and designs that permitted established configurations to be reconstructed accurately and efficiently. They even resembled computer synthesis in that certain devices were used to drive or control others; indeed, the next generation of synthesizers, introduced first by Donald Buchla in 1970, replaced many analogue control circuits with digital ones.

Buchla's and Moog's synthesizers were commercially successful, and they made possible both the rapid proliferation of university studios and the private ownership of a powerful technology. A number of composers quickly became associated with the new devices, including Jon Appleton, David Bordon, John C. Eaton, Ron Pellegrino, Terry Riley, Morton Subotnik and John Watts. In addition, synthesizers almost immediately became standard equipment for pop and rock groups; they were further popularized by virtuoso novelties like Walter Carlos's *Switched on Bach* (1968).[40]

The popularity of synthesizers cut two ways, however. They made widely available a technology previously limited to those with access to major studios, but they also quickly created a body of clichés which, in the public mind at least, came to characterize the entire domain of 'electronic music'. To preserve the distinction between art and popular music, many composers devised a new approach to resist the conformity that the new devices seemed to impose. Some (Subotnik, Riley, Bordon and others) responded by making certain clichés the basis of their music; from this came a new emphasis on repetition, which dominated much music of the 1970s. Other composers embedded synthesizers in novel configurations (Richard Teitelbaum, David Rosenboom); still others built new synthesizing instruments with their own characteristics (Sal Martirano, Gustav Ciamaga).

These important developments in music technology raised critical questions about individuation: the degree to which one composer's work could be – should be – distinctively different from another's. Indeed, much technology challenged the very definition of composition: if one person builds circuits structured by a second and activated by a third, who is the composer? Such questions are fundamental to explicitly collaborative work; and it was collaboration, increasingly important throughout the 1960s, that permitted problems of individuation to be addressed most directly.

Modern Times

The dialectic transformed, III: collaboration

The 1960s saw a redefinition of the notion of community within society at large; an explosion in communications technology permitted dialogue regardless of where people were. In the USA the most visible symbols of the new 'networks' were periodicals: the *Whole Earth Catalogue*, *Mother Earth News* and a host of other journals, papers and newsletters. Communities of composers were similarly defined; in the 1960s two important journals helped bind together musicians who were aesthetically linked but geographically dispersed. Composers and theorists like Elaine Barkin, Benjamin Boretz and J. K. Randall, associated with Milton Babbitt and the Columbia–Princeton axis, were prominently represented in the journal *Perspectives of New Music*, which began appearing in 1962. It was not until 1969, when *Source* magazine appeared, that a comparable forum existed for composers more often associated with Cage. In Latin America groups of composers have tended to remain geographically defined; in addition to those associated with institutes like Chávez's Taller de Composicion and Ginastera's Torcuato di Tella Institute, major centres have become established in Buenos Aires, Bahia, Cuba and elsewhere.

Composers in such associations cooperate but do not necessarily collaborate. The 1960s, however, witnessed an unprecedented burst of collaborative activity, both between composers and between contributors from other arts. This was motivated in part by the social thought of the time; utopians and futurists like Marshall McLuhan, Buckminster Fuller and Gregory Bateson projected visions of global cooperation, integration and responsibility, and such visions were enlisted as support for a variety of aesthetic purposes. Whereas traditionalists argued, as they had for centuries, that a 'total art work' involving all the senses is the most complete and powerful form of expression, more radical thinkers contended that art could illuminate present day society only if it permitted a variety of events, in a variety of media, to co-exist regardless of possible conflicts.

Traditional collaborators thus worked much as they always had. Composers continued to supply music for dance, stage, film and television. Some even became known primarily as collaborators: Carlos Surinach (with Martha Graham), Bernard Herrmann (with Alfred Hitchcock), Lucia Dlugoszewski (with Erick Hawkins). The collaborative model developed by Serge Dyagilev, in which a work evolves from the interaction of contributors from diverse arts, was reapplied first in Martha Graham's company and then in Merce Cunningham's. Some retained conceptual control over the entire work, even though large parts might be created by other artists. Composers like Daniel Lentz, Eric Salzman, Michael Sahl and R. Murray Schafer were primarily involved with theatre, while Sal Martirano, Roger Reynolds and

Morton Subotnik designed mixed-media environments which depended heavily on film. Such pieces were often political, especially in Latin America, as seen in works by Juan Blanco, Cesar Bolaños and Leo Brouwer.[41]

Even more authority could be retained by artists who worked in more than one media. Harry Partch's range was almost Wagnerian (he would have hated the comparison), extending to composition, poetry, choreography and instrument design. Alwin Nikolais designs, choreographs and composes many of his works; Meredith Monk performs her own compositions and choreography. Otto Joachim, Ron Pellegrino and others have devised systems which allowed them to compose both sound and visual displays,[42] and several artists associated with the Fluxus group have worked individually in more than one medium: George Brecht, Dick Higgins, Alison Knowles, George Maciunas and Nam June Paik.[43] Kenneth Gaburo based most of his pieces after 1965 on what he called 'compositional linguistics', incorporating text, music, visuals and movement into a totality that is neither theatre nor song.[44] Other composers also became deeply involved with language, producing works with a variety of aesthetic purposes: Charles Amirkhanian, Istvan Anhalt, Robert Ashley, Charles Dodge and Charles Shere.[45]

All these composers, whether trans-media artists or collaborators, attempted to retain control over part or all of the work. Other collaborators sought to relinquish control. Perhaps the most traditional were those who incorporated a high degree of improvisation. The many who were concerned with jazz have already been mentioned. The Improvisation Chamber Ensemble, founded by Lucas Foss in 1957, had more classical antecedents; it directly influenced Foss's own music in such works as *Time Cycle* (1959–60) and *Echoi* (1961–3). Larry Austin, Stanley Lunetta and others formed the New Music Ensemble in 1963; though many of its members had a background in jazz, their improvisations more closely resembled the art-music avant garde.

Improvisation was an important part of many mixed-media works, especially those generated by groups. The ONCE Festivals in Ann Arbor, Michigan, involved the artist Milton Cohen and the film-maker George Manupelli, as well as the composers Gordon Mumma, Roger Reynolds, Robert Ashley and others. Performances by the ONCE group were often credited to individuals, but some of the most remarkable were collective creations.[46] Much the same was true for the Judson Dance Theatre, where improvisations and collective compositions were created by the musicians Robert Dunn and Philip Corner, the dancers Yvonne Rainer, Deborah Hay and Steve Paxton, and the artists Robert Rauschenberg and Alex Hay.[47] Associated with the San Francisco Tape Studio were Pauline Oliveros, Morton Subotnik and Ramon Sender, who, though rarely collaborating directly on a single piece, were interested in improvised, collectively realized performances. In Bahia, Brazil, Ernst Widmer led a lively group of younger composers (Walter Smetak, Rufo Herrera and others) in collaborative and mixed-media projects during the 1960s. And composers in the Grupo Música Nova at São Paulo – Gilberto Mendes, Rogério Duprat, Willy Corrêa de Oliveira – were involved both with visual media and with avant-garde poetry.

In most improvisational or collectively composed works the actions of the contributors are intended to be mutually supportive. But this was not the case for the most important and lasting collaboration of the postwar era, that between John Cage and Merce Cunningham.[48] Cage's music and Cunningham's choreography were conceived and rehearsed independently and sometimes not presented together until a work's first performance. Each contributor repudiated all attempts to shape the totality; rather, two or more components, independently conceived, simply co-existed. This principle was applied by other composers in the 1960s (Udo Kasemets, Jorge Antunes) and was central to the project Experiments in Art and Technology (Cage, Tudor, Lowell Cross and many others). In slightly different form it gave rise to the collective Fluxus performances of the early 1960s and to certain types of happenings and early performance art.[49]

Such collaborations leave little room for composers' preferences; whatever is intended by one contributor may well be contradicted by another. Coherence and control are replaced by quantity and diversity. But it is also possible to yield control to some entity other than co-contributors. Indeed, in an abstract way Cage's chance techniques do just that, producing sequences of sounds determined by factors outside his control.

One of Cage's motivations was simply to 'wake up to the very life we're living'[50] – to learn to appreciate the sounds of daily life as one would appreciate music. Some composers applied this idea directly, devoting themselves to music in and of the environment; their collaborators were, in effect, all those forces, human and otherwise, which generate sounds at a particular place and time. R. Murray Schafer's study of 'soundscapes' evolved into a continuing worldwide project in sound ecology which has generated several reports, two books and uncounted local applications; Schafer asks for no less than a complete re-evaluation of the relationship of humankind to its sonic environment.[51] Maryanne Amacher has built new environments by recording or transmitting sounds from different places; Annea Lockwood has installed sound-making devices (notably pianos) in unexpected locations. From conventional electronic music Ruth Anderson has moved towards psycho-acoustics and the making of holistic environments. Max Neuhaus has designed electronic music installations for public spaces; Stanley Lunetta has built electronic sound sculptures which respond to events in their environment. Robert Moran has conceived an extended series of 'city pieces' which use the sonic resources, and sometimes the entire population, of large urban areas.[52]

Moran's work depends not only on the environment but on the cooperation of large numbers of people, only a few of whom may be musicians. It thus manifests one more way in which composers have relinquished control: by incorporating the participation of amateurs, audiences, even the public. Such works sometimes serve pedagogical or political purposes (Pauline Oliveros, Christian Wolff); sometimes they are presented in conventional concert halls (Udo Kasemets, Mario Lavista, Elliot Schwartz). A wide range of participatory works was first presented in galleries, theatres and similar spaces. David Tudor, David Behrman, Donald Buchla and many others have constructed electronic environments which audiences both 'play' and observe. Alvin Lucier translates waveforms from one medium to another (brainwaves to sound; sound to standing waves, etc), producing a cross between an exhibit and a performance. Gerald Shapiro has designed complex, tightly planned works in which audiences are encouraged to improvise collectively and sensitively by means of interactive circuitry.[53]

BEYOND THE DIALECTIC

Works which come into being only when 'listeners' act on a technological environment call into question not only the role of the composer but that of the audience. Indeed, a preoccupation with audiences – their size, function, responsibilities – was evident in nearly all domains of postwar music. Since the 1920s audiences for contemporary art music had dwindled, as concert halls increasingly became museums in which were re-presented the classics of the past. This situation was not ameliorated during the postwar decade. On the contrary, the paradigmatic responses to the war produced – at least initially – an intensely specialized, hermetic music. Babbitt retreated into the academy, arguing without apology for a music comprehensible only to a few specialists. And Cage's music, though fundamentally egalitarian, was explicitly uncommunicative, at least in traditional musical terms.

The major musical museums (concert halls, symphony orchestras, opera companies) remained largely closed even to more moderate, 'progressive' composers. With the exception of music by a few figures whose vocabulary was unmistakably drawn from the nineteenth century (such as Gian Carlo Menotti or Samuel Barber), new works were usually played once or twice only. Listeners to new music were found either in élitist enclaves such as Ivy League colleges or among the followers of other innovatory arts: dance, theatre, poetry. For a time it seemed that the art-music tradition was dead, or that at best it had entered a mannerist period from which it might – possibly – emerge at some distant date.

The recording industry offered both opportunities and dangers. It was possible to reach specialized audiences by means of recordings, and a number of companies, both commercial (Nonesuch, Folkway, even Columbia) and non-profit-making (CRI, Louisville), released a significant amount of recent music. On the other hand, such recordings did little to widen audiences. Moreover, the increasing commercialization of music tended to reduce all recorded works to fashionable, disposable commodities, a situation many composers found aesthetically and ethically repugnant.

The many works in the 1960s that crossed boundaries – between the arts, between media, between composer, performer and listener – can be viewed, in part, as a response to this situation. In drawing many media together in a single artwork they attempted to overcome music's isolation and to engage followers of other artistic domains. By redefining, or at least challenging, audiences' traditional roles, they invited the public into the act of creation, offering a non-élitist, non-threatening means of encountering new aesthetic thought. And by creating inherently unrecordable works, they disavowed the commercialization inherent in mass reproduction and distribution.

Such works were also implicitly political, and many became explicitly so in the mid- to late 1960s; in the highly charged atmosphere of the Vietnamese War it could hardly be otherwise. To Cage, for example, it became increasingly clear that the change of mind required to accept his music would also entail a change of mind about society, government and personal responsibility.[54] Some composers began to address the latter more directly. Christian Wolff's interactive works, reaching back at least to the two *Duos for Pianists* (1957–8), attempt to put performers in the position of having to act responsibly in an aesthetically difficult or demanding situation; the assumption is that the social discoveries the performers make could be applied in daily life. In the 1970s Wolff, Garrett List, Frederic Rzewski, the composers of the São Paolo group and several others began to make reference to popular or political songs, often simplifying their styles to entice the listener into reconsidering political questions. For the most part, however, such works remained concert-hall pieces and did not significantly alter the relation between art-music composers and their audiences.

There was one other response to the twin dilemmas of comprehensibility and commoditization: minimalism, which eventually generated a new focus for music in the 1970s and 80s. The pivotal work was Terry Riley's *In C* (1964), in which the players choose how and when to proceed through a series of short, repeated musical fragments. The structure of *In C* resembles that of open-form compositions of the 1960s, but its realization is wholly transparent; it can be understood by anyone and the score is so simple that it is reproduced on the jacket of the recording. Moreover, the surface features of *In C*, like those of many commercial releases, are predictable: the unchanging pulse, limited pitch material, repeated fragments and pounded, tonic drone combine to signify not variability but certainty. Such a work is not only a

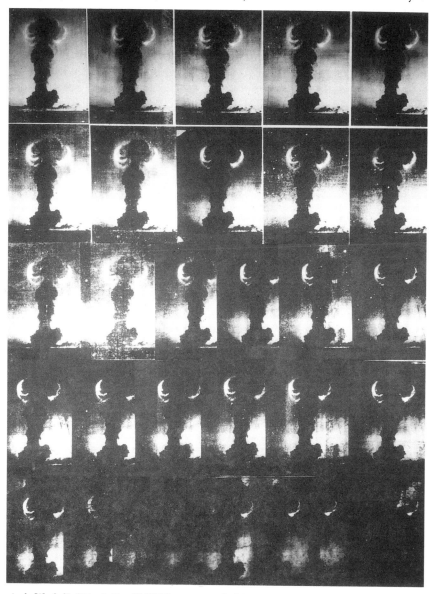

Andy Warhol's 'Atomic Bomb' (1965), a portrayal of desolation and destruction through repetition and over-exposure.

mass-produceable commodity in its totality; its very constituents are commodities. Rather than opposing fashion and disposability, *In C* affirms them; it required an audience not of specialists but of consumers.

In C was roughly contemporaneous with movements in other arts which similarly affirmed mass culture: the pop art of Andy Warhol, Trisha Brown's 'task' and 'accumulation' dances and the new American cinema. All combined many strands from the previous dialectic: they were globalist and referential (like the progressives), anti-academic (like Cage) and highly systematic (like Babbitt). To all these works has been applied the term 'minimalism'. The history of that movement, initiated in music not only by Riley but by Steve Reich, Philip Glass and others, properly belongs to the 1970s and hence is not treated in detail here. But the seeds were planted in the 1960s.[55]

The subsequent history of minimalism made it evident that, if the central issue for the period 1945–55 was control, and that for 1955–70 was individuation, for the 1970s and 80s it was to be production. The argument about music's place in society thereby changed fundamentally. Whereas the entire span between 1945 and 1970 could be said to be centred on the composer and aesthetics, the years after 1970 centred on the audience and commerce. What had been a matter of conscience became a matter of economics; arguments advanced on political grounds in the 1950s and 60s began to rest more heavily on ecological ones in the 1980s.

In the past twenty years music in the Americas, like American culture as a whole, has been searching restlessly for a balance that will enable it to survive past the second millennium. Such a balance, it seems, will be generated not by innovation, as in the pre-war period, nor by dialectic, as in the postwar period. It will instead require integration: musical entities, like social and environmental entities, can no longer stand apart. But the centrepoint for this balance – for all these balances – remains to be found.

NOTES

[1] D. Cope, *New Directions in Music* (Dubuque, 5/1989), 45f.

[2] The content and structure of this discussion of technology draw heavily on H. Davies's 'Electronic Music: History and Development', in *Dictionary of Contemporary Music*, ed. J. Vinton (New York, 1974).

[3] The first, seminal experiments using computers to write music, are described in a pioneering book: L. Hiller and L. Isaacson, *Experimental Music* (New York, 1959).

[4] Good contemporary overviews of 1950s and 60s technology are in E. Schwartz, *Electronic Music: a Listener's Guide* (New York, 1973), and J. A. Appleton and R. C. Perera, *The Development and Practice of Electronic Music* (Englewood Cliffs, 1975).

[5] See S. McLary, 'Terminal Prestige: The Case of Avant-Garde Music Composition', *Cultural Critique*, xii (Spring 1989), 57–81.

[6] W. Benjamin, 'The Work of Art in the Age of Mechanical Reproduction', in *Illuminations* (New York, 1969), 217–51.

[7] There is a reverential account of Boulanger's enormous influence in D. G. Campbell, *Master Teacher: Nadia Boulanger* (Washington, 1984); for Philip Glass's seemingly unlikely tribute, see his interview in C. Cagne and T. Coras, *Soundpieces: Interviews with American Composers* (Metuchen, NJ, 1982), 211f.

[8] In a chapter entitled 'The Rise of American Art Music and the Impact of the Immigrant Wave of the Late 1930's', J. Rockwell examines Krenek as a paradigm at this development; see Rockwell, *All American Music: Composition in the Late Twentieth Century* (New York, 1983).

[9] The importance of the CBC and other Canadian institutions is revealed throughout G. A. Proctor, *Canadian Music of the Twentieth Century* (Toronto, 1980), especially in the preface (pp.ix–xii).

[10] Many of these teacher-pupil relationships are summarized in an appendix to N. Butterworth, *A Dictionary of American Composers* (New York and London, 1964).

[11] Yates is an important figure whose *Twentieth Century Music* (New York, 1967) is neglected.

[12] The central importance of twelve-note technique can be gauged by the fact that by 1961 it alone, among technical procedures, was deemed worthy of an independent bibliography: A. Basart, *Serial Music: a Classified Bibliography of Writings on Twelve-Tone and Electronic Music* (Berkeley, 1961).

[13] H. Davies, 'Electronic Music: History' in *Dictionary of Contemporary Music*; see also G. A. Proctor, *Canadian Music of the Twentieth Century*, 128f.

[14] L. Hiller, 'Music composed with Computers: a Historical Survey', in *The Computer and Music*, ed. H. Lincoln (Ithaca, NY, 1970), 42–96.

[15] E. Schwartz, *Electronic Music*, 67–86.

[16] J. Rockwell provides a good overview of this trend in *All American Music*, 71–83.

[17] A contemporaneous and influential book by R. Smith, *Contemporary Percussion* (London, 1970), helped to focus the wide-ranging experiments in this domain.

[18] The literature on 'extended techniques' began with B. Bartolozzi, *New Sounds for Woodwind* (London, 1967), and continued with numerous articles and a celebrated series of monographs published by the University of California Press (*The Contemporary Contrabass*, *The Avant-Garde Flute*, etc).

[19] Timbre and texture are treated as central compositional tools in R. Erickson, *Sound Structure in Music* (Berkeley, 1975).

[20] Copland gives a cogent summary of the dynamics associated with this development in *The New Music* (New York, 1968), 107f.

[21] Copland also remained a perceptive commentator on musical events, manifested in his addenda to the revised edition of *Our New Music*, repubd as *The New Music* (New York, 1968).

[22] Schuller introduced the term 'third stream' in August 1957, to help identify a body of works already written; see N. Cernovale, *Gunther Schuller: a Bio-Bibliography* (Westport, Conn., 1987), 9.

[23] Information about the former, more conservative composers can be found in A. Tischler's *Fifteen Black American Composers: a Bibliography of their Works* (Detroit, 1981); the latter group is presented in D. Baker, L. M. Belt and H. C. Hudson, *The Black Composer Speaks* (Metuchen, NJ, 1978).

[24] D. Reck, *Music of the Whole Earth* (New York, 1977), though neither about nor for composers, summarizes the emergence of a globalist aesthetic in the 1960s.

[25] Carter's writings are also of great importance, compiled in *The Writings of Elliott Carter: an American Composer Looks at Modern Music*, ed. E. K. Stone (Bloomington, Ind., 1977); his music is well served in D. Schiff, *The Music of Elliott Carter* (London, 1983).

[26] Varèse's late aesthetic was best presented by the composer himself in writings collected as 'The Liberation of Music', in *Contemporary Composers on Contemporary Music*, ed. E. Schwartz and B. Childs (New York, 1967), 196–208.

[27] H. Brant, 'Space as an Essential Aspect of Musical Composition', in *Contemporary Composers on Contemporary Music*, 223–42.

[28] Nancarrow's work has produced a flurry of interest in the past decade; the best single source remains P. Garland, *Conlon Nancarrow: Selected Studies for Player Piano* (Berkeley, 1977).

[29] Carrillo then dropped from view again until the 1970s, when an issue of P. Garland's journal, *Soundings*, no.5 (Jan 1973), included scores, a tribute and a translation of Carrillo's essay 'The Thirteenth Sound'.

[30] In addition to Partch, *Genesis of a Music* (Madison, Wisc., 1949/*R*1977), see B. Johnston, 'The Corporealism of Harry Partch', *PNM*, xiii/2 (1975), 85–97.

[31] Johnston's music is thoroughly discussed in H. V. Gunden, *The Music of Ben Johnston* (Metuchen, NJ, 1986).

[32] M. Babbitt, 'Who Cares if You Listen' [the correct title is 'The Composer as Specialist'] *High Fidelity*, viii/2 (Feb 1958), 38–40, 126f.

[33] See especially two texts in Cage's *Silence* (Middletown, Conn., 1961): 'Experimental Music' (pp. 7–12) and 'Communication' (pp. 41–56).

[34] These developments are traced in four seminal articles by Babbitt: 'Some Aspects of Twelve-Tone Composition', in *The Score and I.M.A. Magazine*, xii (1955), 53–61; 'Twelve-Tone Invariants as Compositional Determinants', *MQ*, xlvi (1960), 246–59; 'Set Structure as a Compositional Determinant', *JMT*, v (1961), 72–94; and 'Twelve-Tone Rhythmic Structure and the Electronic Medium', *PNM*, i/1 (1962), 49–79.

[35] Cage's own summary of his compositional transformation is still the best: 'Changes', in *Silence*, 18–34.

[36] Cage's legacy is discussed in M. Nyman, *Experimental Music: Cage and Beyond* (London, 1974), and T. DeLio, *Circumscribing the Open Universe* (Lanham, 1984).

[37] The instructions that accompany scores, like those for *Cartridge Music* (New York, 1960), give the best indication of Cage's thoughts on technology.

[38] For a creatively constructed overview, see 'Groups', in *Source: Music of the Avant Garde*, ii/1 (Jan 1968), 15–27; the best history of all these activities remains G. Mumma, 'Live Electronic Music', in Appleton and Perera, *The Development and Practice of Electronic Music*, 286–335.

[39] Hiller's contemporaneous overview, 'Music Composed with Computers: a Historical Survey', in *The Computer and Music*, ed. H. Lincoln (Ithaca, NY, 1970), 42–96, has been augmented and extended by C. Ames, 'Automated Composition in Retrospect, 1956–86', *Leonardo* (Oxford, 1987).

[40] Some sense of the excitement generated by the new devices can be gained by browsing in two short-lived journals, *Electronic Music Review* (associated with Robert Moog) and *Synthesis* (containing several articles on Buchla's instruments).

[41] The contemporaneous context for such works is discussed in R. Kostelanetz, *The Theatre of Mixed Means* (New York, 1968).

[42] Pellegrino, *The Electronic Arts of Sound and Light* (New York, 1963), although largely self-serving, includes a compact overview of early experiments.

[43] For the link between Fluxus and music, see M. Nyman, *Experimental Music: Cage and Beyond*, 60–74; also pertinent are parts of D. Higgins, *Postface* (New York, 1964).

[44] Gaburo published 32 of his works in a series entitled *Collection* (San Diego, 1975); his work was the subject of a special issue of *PNM*, xviii (1979).

[45] The interaction of music with language and poetry is well represented in an anthology by R. Kostelanetz, *Text-Sound Texts* (New York, 1980).

[46] R. S. James, 'QNCE: Microcosm of the 1960s Musical and Multimedia Avant-Garde', *American Music*, v/4 (1987), 359–90.

[47] S. Barnes, *Democracy's Body: Judson Dance Theatre, 1962–1964* (Ann Arbor, 1983); see also Barnes, *Terpsichore in Sneakers: Post-modern Dance* (Boston, Mass., 1980).

[48] See M. Cunningham, *Changes: Notes on Choreography* (New York, 1969).

[49] For a superb account of these and other technological collaborations, see G. Mumma, 'Live-Electronic Music', in *The Development and Practice of Electronic Music*, 315–18, 325–35.

[50] Cage, *Silence*, 12.

[51] R. Murray Schafer, *The Tuning of the World* (Philadelphia, 21/1980); and also *Creative Music Education: a Handbook for the Modern Music Teacher* (New York, 1976).

[52] An engaging introduction to such pieces can be had by looking at *Source: Music of the Avant-Garde*.

[53] On participatory works generally, see D. Cope, *New Directions in Music*, 182–210; on electronic systems, see M. Nyman, *Experimental Music*, chapter 5.

[54] In 1965 Cage began a series of texts entitled 'Diary: How to Improve the World (You Will Only Make Matters Worse)'; and the dedication to his second volume of writings, *A Year from Monday* (Middletown, Conn., 1967), reads 'To us and all who hate us, that the U.S.A. may become just another part of the world, no more, no less' (p.[v]).

[55] The link between minimalism and earlier experimentalism is made explicit in M. Nyman', *Experimental Music*.

BIBLIOGRAPHICAL NOTE

For the period 1945–70 the three most essential sources for the USA, Canada and Latin America respectively are all more general references: *The New Grove Dictionary of American Music*, ed. H. W. Hitchcock and S. Sadie (London, 1986); *Contemporary Canadian Composers*, ed. K. MacMillan and J. Beckwith (Toronto, 1975); and G. Béhague, *Music in Latin America: an Introduction* (Englewood Cliffs, 1979). Several other standard texts, though covering a broader domain than that discussed in this chapter, are of considerable use: N. Slonimsky, *Music Since 1900* (New York, 4/1971); J. Machlis, *Introduction to Contemporary Music* (New York, 2/1979); E. Salzman, *Twentieth-Century Music: an Introduction* (Englewood Cliffs, 3/1988); and G. A. Proctor, *Canadian Music of the Twentieth Century* (Toronto, 1980). Especially valuable is D. Cope's *New Directions in Music* (Dubuque, 5/1989); the extensive annotated bibliographies and discographies make this an important research tool as well as an introductory text.

Other research and reference sources are now outdated but remain extremely useful for the contemporaneous insights they offer; prime among them is the *Dictionary of Contemporary Music*, ed. J. Vinton (New York, 1974). Biographical information on particular composers can sometimes be supplemented from sources like E. R. Anderson's *Contemporary American Composers: a Biographical Dictionary* (Boston, Mass., 1976), *Thirty-Four Biographies of Canadian Composers* (Montreal, 1964), and material scattered through the series *Composers of the Americas*, published first by the Pan American Union and later by the Organization of American States. Also outdated but useful are several books on technology: *The Development and Practice of Electronic Music*, ed. J. Appleton and R. C. Perrera (Englewood Cliffs, 1974); E. Schwartz, *Electronic Music: a Listener's Guide* (New York, 1972); *The Computer and Music*, ed. H. Lincoln (Ithaca, NY, 1970); and *Music by Computers*, ed. H. Von Foerster and J. W. Beauchamp (New York, 1969).

Four recent volumes are primarily concerned with later music but contain important discussions of the period 1945–70: J. Rockwell, *All American Music: Composition in the Late Twentieth Century* (New York, 1983); P. Garland, *Americas: Essays on American Music and Culture, 1973–80* (Santa Fe, 1982); J. Schaefer, *New Sounds: a Listener's Guide to New Music* (New York, 1987); and P. Manning, *Electronic and Computer Music* (Oxford, 1985). An important series of Canadian biographies published by the University of Toronto Press includes Barbara Pentland, R. Murray Schafer and others. Three journals occasionally address this period in articles of high quality: *American Music*, the *Yearbook* of the Inter-American Institute for Musical Research and the *Inter-American Music Bulletin*.

Contemporaneous periodicals offer a rich spectrum of opinions and aesthetics. The two best-known are *Source: Music of the Avant-Garde* and *Perspectives of New Music* [*PNM*]; articles from the latter were reprinted in two collections edited by B. Boretz and E. T. Cone: *Perspectives on American Composers* (New York, 1971) and *Perspectives on Contemporary Music Theory* (New York, 1972). For a representative picture, however, these journals should be supplemented with others like *Soundings* (whose editor, P. Garland, also produced important occasional volumes), *The Composer* (California; not to be confused with the British periodical *Composer*), *Numus West*, and the *Proceedings* of the American Society of University Composers. Many other periodicals presented special issues on contemporary music during the 1960s; often overlooked and especially valuable are the November 1968 issue of *Music Educator's Journal*, devoted entirely to electronic music, and the 1970 special issue of *Arts in Society*, edited by G. Chase and called *Sounds and Events of Today's Music*.

Arguably the best sources are the composers themselves. *Contemporary Composers on Contemporary Music*, ed. E. Schwartz and B. Childs (New York, 1976), continued in the tradition of *The American Composer Speaks*, ed. G. Chase (Baton Rouge, 1966). Two important collections of interviews are C. Gagny and T. Caras, *Soundpieces: Interviews with American Composers* (Metuchen, NJ, 1982) and W. Zimmermann, *Desert Plants*

(Vancouver, 1976). Books and articles by composers are far too numerous to be fairly represented here; an interesting sample might include, for entirely different reasons: R. Reynolds, *Mind Models: New Forms of Musical Experience* (New York, 1975); G. Rochberg, *The Aesthetics of Survival: a Composer's View of Twentieth-Century Music* (Ann Arbor, 1984); R. Murray Schafer, *The Tuning of the World* (New York, 1977); J. Tenney, *Meta + Hodos: a Phenomenology of 20th-Century Music and an Approach to the Study of Form* (New Orleans, 1964/*R*1990); B. Johnston, 'On Context', *Proceedings* [of the American Society of University Composers] (1968); and S. Reich, *Writings about Music* (New York, 1974). Babbitt's writings, surprisingly, have not been anthologized; a complete bibliography appears in *PNM*, xv/1 (1976), which is devoted to Babbitt's work, and a recent series of lectures by the composer has been published as *Words about Music*, ed. S. Dembski and J. N. Straus (Madison, 1987). Cage has written, contributed to or been interviewed in hundreds of publications; his first book, *Silence* (Middletown, Conn., 1961), remains a starting-point for (some would say the death of) postwar music in the Americas.

Chapter XV

The Current Musical Scene

KEITH POTTER

These days the only justification I can see for embarking on a new composition is that it must be founded on a radically new idea, and must explore as many of the implications of this idea as possible. By 'new idea' I don't mean writing a fugue with the answer at the tritone instead of the dominant, or using a ten-note row instead of a 12-note one, but something much more fundamental.[1]

The search for originality was a prime motivating force in the work of many composers in the 1950s and it survived until at least the early 1970s, as this quotation from the composer Roger Smalley (*b* 1943) demonstrates. It can be seen in Milton Babbitt's 'total reconsideration of musical relations',[2] in Pierre Boulez's rejection of Schoenberg's twelve-note practice in favour of an all-encompassing serialism, in Karlheinz Stockhausen's insistence that 'Serial music demands serial thought',[3] and in John Cage's espousal of 'non-intention' and 'purposeful purposelessness':[4] these composers were concerned to eliminate not only tonality but melody and repetition and to pursue the opportunities opened up by the new technology of electronic music for avoiding the technical and expressive limitations of human performers.

But the history of music since 1945 cannot be reduced to a handful of neat periods in which there was widespread agreement on how to proceed. For every modernist in the 1950s concerned with rejecting the aesthetics and styles of the past, there were probably at least ten traditionalists working in a personal way within received forms. Yet the 1950s is an important decade of musical revolution in serialism, indeterminacy and electronic music; and the leading avant-garde figures, like Babbitt and Cage, Boulez and Stockhausen, had an impact on musical development far greater than their numbers would suggest. The period since about 1970, however, has increasingly been seen as one of synthesis if not retrenchment. Disillusionment with the avant garde has overwhelmed not only many composers born since about 1950 but also older ones, including several who were previously at the centre of modernism (some will be discussed below). There is also a strong reaction against single-minded and narrow lines of development. So many styles and aesthetics now co-exist.

The term 'pluralism' has been used of music for some time; it is an apt description of current compositional uncertainties and, paradox-ically, of the fragmentation of audiences for music of many kinds as well as the 'crossover' phenomenon that joins styles and aesthetics in unlikely combinations. Compositional uncertainty can be fruitful, as the existence of pluralism within individual outputs and, more interestingly, within individual works, shows. We are reluctant to 'pin down' our own age stylistically, however, partly because we are too close to it to have the necessary perspective.

What follows inevitably leaves out vast areas of the music of our own time and concentrates on a few of the composers, works and issues that illustrate the pluralism of the major 'First World' countries. And though the problems of omitting discussion of what has been termed the 'vernacular' traditions of Western music increase, this chapter concerns itself only with composed music of the 'cultivated' tradition.

*

The development of avant-garde music in the two decades or so after 1945 can be described as part of a larger cyclic pattern from which something about our present situation may be learnt. Postwar musical modernism could be said to have mirrored and, to some degree, to have taken over directly from the pre-war musical modernism of the years *c*1908–14. Many view modernism as a phenomenon beginning in the last years of the nineteenth century and stretching through the twentieth until a point, inevitably disputed, somewhat nearer our own time. Ezra Pound issued the declaration to 'Make it New' in the 1930s.[5] He seems to have meant not just a desire for originality but the idea that 'the modern arts have a special obligation, an advanced or *avant-garde* duty, to go ahead of their own age and transform it, and along with that the very nature of the arts themselves'.[6]

Musically, however, it seems more accurate to speak of two periods of 'high modernism' in this century during which modernist ideas were in the ascendant, challenging received values and causing debate. Dating the close of these periods is harder than establishing their precise beginnings. But there was a retrenchment during the 1930s and early 40s, often labelled 'neo-classicism' (which looks invitingly similar in certain respects to our own time). A concern to make music more accessible to a wider public is discernable in some composers who previously espoused modernism (for example Copland) as well as in others uneasy with the modernist tendencies identified with older figures (for example Samuel Barber).

At least one feature of the second, post-1945, period of modernism was shared by all avant-garde practitioners. The total serialism of Babbitt, Boulez and Stockhausen and the indeterminacy of Cage are highly principled and well-thought-out attempts to start from scratch, to invent new material and organize it along new lines in order to banish all conventions regarding rhetoric and expression. The need to do this after a war waged to end one of the most inhuman political régimes of the last two thousand years is understandable, not least in Germany. In Nazi Germany between 1933 and 1945 right-wing politics forced the abandonment of modernism, the exodus of most leading German and Austrian composers and the promotion of third-rate new compositions. Because of their political affiliations, these folk-influenced works were scorned, and even now the music of an experimental composer like Walter Zimmermann (*b* 1949) drew accusations of Nazi sympathies in the 1970s for using the music of his native Franconia as the basis for works which are far from traditionalist; his large cycle *Lokale Musik* for various ensembles (1977–81) is a good example. It is one of the ironies of the relationship between music and politics that conservative musical tendencies, seen as providing appropriate support to right-wing régimes, are espoused even more enthusiastically by left-wing ones, for example from the 1930s in the USSR.

Both the 1920s and the 1960s saw a mixture of cultural optimism, social unrest and fluctuating economic conditions in different countries which makes it hard to generalize about music; but in both decades radical tendencies permeated everyday life to an unusual extent, and this inevitably had an effect even on the music of the 'cultivated' tradition. The 1930s and 1970s, on the other hand, were times of more clearcut economic and social depression. It is not, of course, impossible for radical art to be fuelled by poverty and cultural neglect; art which has as its main aim the challenging of accepted conventions might even be thought likely to thrive during periods when the social fabric that has helped to foster those conventions is seen to be operating poorly. Nevertheless, there was a strong tendency in both decades for composers to attempt to reach a wider audience. Whether through guilt at the insularity of their pursuits or in the optimistic belief that music can somehow support and even save society, composers felt the need to respond to prevailing economic, and hence social and cultural, conditions. And they did not all have the burning political commitment of the English composer Cornelius Cardew (1936–81), who abandoned his avant-garde approach in about 1972–3.

The boom years of the later 1980s, again with a mixture of problems often disguised, do not have a direct parallel earlier in the century. Here too, though, there are paradoxes. For a culture enlivened by new money and new technology is hardly less resistant to radical art than an impoverished culture that cannot afford it. Some new products of the 'cultivated' tradition during this period – the operas of Philip Glass (*b* 1937), the religious music of Arvo Pärt (*b* 1935), even the performance art of Laurie Anderson (*b* 1947), for instance – have had an impact on a large public. But such successes have been widely seen as affirmations of a 'New Age' mentality which, though it might challenge the materialist preoccupations of an era of proud capitalism and conspicuous consumption, hardly comes with the intellectual substance necessary to satisfy the true modernist, for whom the latest developments in philosophy, psychology and mathematics are essential to the development of a radical music. Though Glass's activities in rock music, such as the album *Songs from Liquid Days* (1986), have helped him become one of the few millionaire 'serious' composers of the century, his achievement in the wider public domain is small beside that of opera and concert superstars like Luciano Pavarotti and Nigel Kennedy. The fact that such performers make their reputations largely with music by dead composers is probably the base from which any serious discussion of our musical life, as opposed to composition, should begin. Even here generalizations are almost impossible, since – as just one example – the countries of what used to be the Eastern bloc experienced a very different history during the 1980s, even if it culminated, in 1989, in revolutions that looked set to bring about the rise of capitalism.

*

Concern with the new has been evaporating since the mid-1950s, first slowly, as the problems inherent in total serialism and radical indeterminacy became apparent, then more quickly as the solidarity of the avant garde gave way to rival careers; a few composers nevertheless still adhere to the essential tenets of modernism. Although the pioneering young revolutionaries of the 1950s have now become senior and influential, some have shown remarkably few signs of the increasing conservatism that generally comes with advancing years. The paradox of an avant-garde generation which has become an important pillar of a new establishment should not be ignored; Babbitt and Boulez provide two good examples.

All Set (1957) for small jazz ensemble by Milton Babbitt is one of the few successful examples of the concern with what is usually called 'Third Stream'. This movement, mixing disparate styles and techniques (here complex serialism and what its composer called 'jazz-like properties'),[7] could be seen as an example of 'crossover', a tendency that has always interested composers and that seemed of particular relevance in the 1980s. That it surfaced, however briefly, in Babbitt's work provides further warning of the dangers of designating periods as 'modernist' or 'reactionary' – as well as being a splendid example of a radical composer letting his hair down. The concern with lyricism and poetic image in *Philomel* (1964) for soprano and tape also seems less 'hard-line' then Babbitt's image would suggest.

There is no evidence that Babbitt underwent any fundamental shift away from the aggressively complicated serial stance he held from the late 1940s, when he abandoned occasional work writing film scores and even an unsuccessful Broadway musical to devote himself to the imperatives of contemporary composition as he saw them. He is anxious that the listener gets some aural idea of the serial building-blocks from which his complex works are constructed. But that has been true at least since the Second String Quartet (1954). Polemically, Babbitt is as caustic as ever and he remains one of the few examples of the unrepentant modernist in the early 1990s. His scorn for the notion that 'music is entering a new era or re-entering an old one' led him a few years ago, on a public occasion, to denounce what he clearly sees as anti-modernist backsliding; or, as he typically put it, the celebration of 'this birth or rebirth . . . by appropriately Dionysian dancing on the tombs of those musics liquidated and interred for the mortal sins and aesthetic transgressions of intellection, academicism, and – even – mathematicization'.[8]

Like Babbitt, Boulez embarked on a 'total reconsideration of musical relations' after 1945; and, with equal determination and arguably greater influence, he remains a staunch defender of the essential tenets of postwar musical modernism, of the broad aesthetic principles that he did so much to create and define. It is possible to interpret at least a few of the characteristically small number of works Boulez has completed since 1970 in terms of a greater relaxation and openness towards material and manners which one associates with traditional rather than modernist concerns. *Rituel* (1974–5) for orchestra is perhaps the most notable example: its unambiguous reliance on one boldly stated melodic line, its severe but clear form involving constant repetitions (the composer describes it as 'verses and refrains'),[9] and its obsessive reliance on regular rhythms combine to make the work a strange and compelling tribute to a fellow avant-garde pioneer, Maderna, who died in 1973. Boulez's concern in the early 1970s to restore Berg, whom he previously compared unfavourably with Webern (the then un-challenged godfather to the new serialism), to full status in the modern pantheon was crowned by his conducting of the première of *Lulu* in its completed version in 1979. With its sumptuous mixture of traditional and radical elements, this opera has been taken to heart by Boulez; his attitude to, for example, harmony and orchestration in the last twenty years has been cautiously revised with a little help from Berg's example, even having a retrospective effect on such early compositions as *Le visage nuptial*, settings of René Char for soloists, chorus and orchestra (originally composed in 1946, revised in 1957 and revised again during the 1980s), to achieve a smoother, simpler surface, from which melodic lines and regular rhythms emerge in surprising ways. This piece is one of several that Boulez has been revising in the course of the almost manic reworking of his early output that has often been a substitute for composition over the last 30 years.

In general, though, Boulez remains a pre-eminent pillar of modernist composition, even though his activities as a conductor have taken him to the heart of traditional music-making during this period. In one respect the last 15 years have seen Boulez's modernist determination re-emphasized and put into effective practice by the setting up of a research institution dedicated, as far as Boulez himself is concerned, to solving the musical problems that remained unsolved in the 1950s. The Institut de Recherche et Co-ordination Acoustique/Musique (IRCAM) is part of the Centre Georges Pompidou in Paris; occupying underground premises close to the main Pompidou building, it commenced regular work in the late 1970s, several years after Boulez was approached to serve as director.

IRCAM brought Boulez back to Paris on his own uncompromisingly avant-garde terms at the point when the principles and precepts of the avant garde were being widely discredited for the first time as anachronistic. The creation of an official, government-sponsored research institution to solve an aesthetic problem provides a good example of the 'establishmentizing' of modernism. While IRCAM represents a typical French approach, it also offers an example of the pleasures and perils to be encountered when notions born out of radical endeavour become constrained by the very institutionalized bonds which that radicalism had sought to break. Unlike much American, campus, old-style modernist composition, that at IRCAM is paid for by public funds.

IRCAM set out to effect a 'comprehensive translation of musical invention', to 'move towards global, generalizable solutions'[10] with musicians and scientists working together. Confrontation with the practical implications of this ambitious stance may have put that rhetoric in a different light. One hesitates to conclude that Boulez wished to impose a single *lingua franca* on all composers, as the total serialism of the early 1950s implied. The urge to establish a philosophical and technological base for composition is, however, detectable; and by bringing together scientific and artistic concerns, IRCAM has had limited but important success.

The clearest advance made by IRCAM in its first decade or so was in the application of computer technology to musical research and composition. The basis for this was laid at Stanford University, California, by the American composer and computer-music pioneer John Chowning (*b* 1934) and others; it is widely held that large computer facilities such as those developed in Paris are dinosaurs in a period that has seen the rise of the slogan 'small is beautiful'. Yet IRCAM took advantage of the fact that its rise coincided with the explosion in 'new technology'; its harnessing of experience in electronic

The Centre Georges Pompidou (1971–9), Paris, designed by Richard Rogers and Renzo Piano, a prime example of late twentieth-century modernism.

music to digital possibilities led to a range of research and creative work that had considerable impact beyond IRCAM itself. The Workstation project has been developed which, with its networking scheme that allows composers to work at home, demonstrates that IRCAM is moving away from the large studio concept; the British Composers' Desktop Project is engaged in similar work.

It is paradoxical that such radical research is being undertaken at precisely the time when many composers have returned to writing music based on conventionally notated pitches and rhythms, using equal temperament, regular metres and, usually, conventional instruments. It should be noted that IRCAM's former director (he retired officially in January 1992) appears to be preoccupied with harmony and duration as the 'fundamental parameters' of organization, rather than the spectro-morphological concerns which originally drove Pierre Schaeffer's *musique concrète* studio, and which still motivate its successors all over the world. The compositional application of these tools has not, of course, been carried out solely by Boulez; indeed, it is arguable that his collaborator rivals at IRCAM have done much more significant creative work with the computer. Xavier Rodet's CHANT program, for instance, has been used for modest but highly popular pieces, such as Jonathan Harvey's *Mortuos plango, vivos voco* (1980), a compelling exercise in composing with simple sound sources (a large cathedral bell, a boy's voice) subtly transformed by computer. In the 1980s Harvey (*b* 1939) was among the most internationally successful composers of computer music, partly through his willingness to integrate the results of his technological investigations with wider concerns. The CHANT program has also been used for large-scale undertakings such as the extensive tape parts of Harrison Birtwistle's opera *The Mask of Orpheus* (1986), realized by Barry Anderson. (These three composers have worked mainly in Britain, including the New Zealander Anderson, who died in 1987.)

The most significant work composed entirely with the resources of IRCAM is Boulez's *Répons* which, typically for its composer, was produced piecemeal between 1981 and 1984 and received its complete première only in summer 1988. For six instrumental soloists, chamber ensemble and live computer facilities, it was designed to make the first full use of what was at the time the most sophisticated of the institute's computer resources. The chamber group, in the centre of the hall, remains unmodified; but the six soloists, in the four corners and halfway down each long side, are subject to live transformation of their sounds by di Giugno's 4X digital sound processor, a kind of combined computer and synthesizer, the advantage of which is that it may be used for both sound generation and modification in 'real time' at the moment of performance.

The audience, surrounded by sound from the instrumentalists and the many loudspeakers, is thus in a position to hear one of the most sophisticated spatial works ever composed. *Répons* reflects its composer's commitment to the avowedly modernist aim of 'breaking the barrier of material' ('The more advanced the technology, the freer the composer', he said in a talk in London in 1985.)[11] Boulez's subsequent concern with electronics and, specifically, with the computer may lead one to conclude that he is even more committedly modernist, since his interest in electronic music in its early years was limited and its products essentially abortive; only now, he argues, can the true potential of electronics for composition be realized.

But other approaches have also emerged from within the avant garde, for example Pousseur's rejection of the serial complexity of postwar New Music made in the mid-1960s. Dissatisfied with the music, first serial and then indeterminate, that he had been writing in the 1950s, he began to argue for the return of expression, which he felt had been forgotten in the avant garde's obsession with the new.[12] In doing so, he was to some extent echoing criticisms of serialism and indeterminacy made by composers as various as Xenakis, Ligeti and Nono;[13] and in fact many of Pousseur's ideas have received their best expression not in his own music but in that of Berio, as we shall see. In the USA, too, composers like Carter had been developing a music of complexity based more on ideas about tempo change and its effect on the perception of large spans of music than on aspects of pitch organization.

The music of these composers sounds quite different; it may seem as though the characteristically teaming surfaces of Carter's music have nothing to do with the rough energies of Xenakis, the fastidious polyphonies of Ligeti or the exquisite detailing of Nono (whose music in the 1980s took on a high degree of refinement very different from his earlier political works; he died in 1990). Yet all shared not only a rejection of 1950s serial practice and Cageian indeterminacy but a concern to find techniques that correspond to acoustic and – even more importantly – psycho-acoustic realities as they understood them. This led them, during the 1960s and 70s, both to greater involvement with audibly evolutionary structures and, eventually, to music of less surface density. Carter, Xenakis and Ligeti may now be the Grand Old Men of modernism, along with such others as Cage, Lutosławski, Stockhausen and Kagel, but each has significantly relaxed his style in the 1970s and 80s. The music of Carter reached a peak of complexity between the Second and Third String Quartets (1959 and 1971, respectively), since when it has reflected his increasing interest in making audible compositional processes, as in his sequence of orchestral pieces *Three Occasions for Orchestra* (completed 1989) where motivic and ultimately melodic material comes to the fore.

Xenakis did not go as far as his early rival, Penderecki, in adopting a tonal/thematic style after using a 'texture composition' method, but he is among those composers who have attempted a synthesis of apparently opposing approaches. Orchestral works from as far back as the early 1970s, such as *Antikhthon* for orchestra (1971), already demonstrate a clearer definition of pitch and rhythm than those of the previous two decades; more recent compositions show an interest in modal counterpoint (*Knephas* for mixed choir, 1990), melody, irony (*Jalons* for ensemble, 1986) and even in extended passages of rhythmic unison (*Echange* for bass clarinet and ensemble, 1989).

There are, however, younger composers who are acknowledged as modernist successors to the 1950s serialists. 'New Complexity' – perhaps a misleading term – is essentially a phenomenon of the 1970s and, more particularly, of the 1980s. The English-born Brian Ferneyhough (*b* 1943) is frequently credited as its father-figure, but older men, notably Xenakis, are also considered important influences by the composers themselves, who include a British group in which Michael Finnissy (*b* 1946), James Dillon (*b* 1950), Chris Dench (*b* 1953) and Richard Barrett (*b* 1959) are the most significant.

In these quarters Xenakis is held in high regard as a rigorous thinker who has nevertheless avoided the cerebral excesses of 1950s composition and invested his work with a strong, even visceral, emotional impact; it might therefore reasonably be concluded that no composer in the domain of 'New Complexity' would have dealings with serialism. Ferneyhough has referred disparagingly to what he calls Boulez's 'Hall of Mad Mirrors',[14] and serialism as represented by Boulez's *Structures Ia* for two pianos (1951) can be ruled out as an influence. But since definitions of serialism are open to such dispute it is hard to estimate the continuing importance of what was regarded by some as the great technical and aesthetic breakthrough of the post-tonal era.

The leading composers of this movement have produced music with a surface complexity and difficulty never equalled by any earlier fully conventionally notated compositions (though it may have been by works using indeterminate notation or free improvisation). Compositions such as Ferneyhough's *Unity Capsule* for solo flute (1976) and Dench's *Tilt* for solo piano (1985) even appear to challenge the capabilities of individual players in order to produce a particular effect and energy unproduceable by other means: what is required of the player (especially rhythmically and in the sheer number of simultaneous actions) is at best at the limits of performability. (Only Ferneyhough, though, has made clear his adherence to such an approach.) Neither freer notation (or no notation, as in free improvisation) nor the use of electronics would, it is argued, have the same effect.

Much of the later work of these composers preserves the same complex surface, though there are signs that the modernist abrasiveness is being tempered, for example in the occasional passages of rhythmic unison in Ferneyhough's Fourth String Quartet (1990); this has a soprano soloist in two of its four movements, like Schoenberg's Second Quartet of 1909. Such grand statements as Ferneyhough's *Carceri d'inventione* cycle (1981–6) and Dillon's evolving cycle of works entitled *Nine Rivers* (1982–), both for a variety of forces, use an impressive array of compositional techniques which, like those of 1950s serialism, can apparently only be elucidated with mathematical terms; Dillon, for instance, speaks of the 'turbulent algorithms'[15] he used to derive the tape part of *Introitus* for 12 strings and electronics (composed at IRCAM in 1989–90), a section of *Nine Rivers*. It is their progress to a goal and their emotional directness that perhaps sets such compositions apart from the more static products of earlier music with a 'complex' surface, whether serial or indeterminate. Finnissy's compositions, with their roots in folk music, Ives, Nancarrow and even Grainger, Gershwin and Verdi as much as the avant garde, have become less turbulent on the surface; works such as the opera *The Undivine Comedy* (to the composer's own libretto after Zygmunt Krasinki's play *Nieboska kommedia*, 1988) and, even more potently, the dark, spare song cycle *Unknown Ground* for baritone and ensemble (settings of texts by AIDS victims, 1990) suggest a revolt against the characteristic flux of the 'New Complexity'.

*

Attitudes to the music of the past, as well as the present, were made more complicated in the late 1960s and early 70s by several new factors. Among them was the introduction into the public domain of medieval and Renaissance music, previously confined to academic circles, and the widening of understanding of Baroque music. Another, ultimately considered of even greater significance, was the arrival of non-Western music from Asia, Africa and elsewhere which now took on a wide appeal and new significance; classical North Indian music is the most obvious example. This, of course, was the result of the rapid expansion of world communications. Musicians were now able to travel vast distances quickly, bringing different music and performing styles to much larger audiences. More significantly, recordings, radio and television brought music of all kinds to increasing numbers.

Initially these changes were widely greeted with great optimism, especially by the younger generation. Marshall McLuhan's concept of the 'global village', espoused by Cage during the 1960s, was perceived as highly desirable. And it was easy to make the leap from increased understanding permeating the world through new telecommunications systems to the breakdown of national, racial, religious and other boundaries; it would surely soon be possible to participate in a pluralistic culture. Such ideas of synthesis were still to prove inspiring when the computer revolution of the new technology broke some ten years later, and everything from mass media to individual acts of communication became subject to new laws and values, both cultural and scientific, of which its users only slowly became aware. However, the drawbacks of an internationalized, homogenized culture that merely encouraged 'sampling', at many levels and in many senses, soon became apparent too.

At its most basic composers now had to compete with the rival claims of a vast body of music, which challenged everything from sources of funding to the extent to which they could impinge on contemporary consciousness. The rise of modernism and the rediscovery of medievalism have often been seen as going hand in hand, particularly in Britain with the pioneering work of Sir William Glock at the BBC in the 1960s. And even a modernist like Boulez had been affected early by non-Western music, notably Asian and African sources in *Le marteau sans maître* (1953–5), a *locus classicus* of 1950s musical modernism.

Composers have been forced to reassess their relationship to the past. It may have been an innate conservatism or cautiousness that prevented many British composers, unlike their continental European and American colleagues, from seeing the avant-garde ideas and music of Boulez or Cage as relevant to their concerns. The most interesting British response to those ideas perhaps came in the work of Peter Maxwell Davies (*b* 1934), Birtwistle (*b* 1934) and others who took some avant-garde elements (for instance, the use of serial matrices by Davies, random numbers by Birtwistle) and combined them with much older concerns (medieval and Renaissance techniques, dramatic and poetic ideas from classical antiquity or English folk traditions). Past and present were thus merged rather than opposed. Nowhere is this seen more clearly than in new works that take music of the past as their basis, materially as well as technically. Davies's use of the sixteenth-century English composer John Taverner, in particular his famous *In nomine*, for a whole series of compositions, culminating in the opera *Taverner* (1972), about the composer's life, is one of the best examples and was widely imitated.

The early and mid-1970s saw the deaths of most of the composers whose works were well known to the general musical public. Stravinsky died in 1971, having stopped composing in the mid-1960s. Shostakovich died in 1975, Britten in 1976. The music which had been 'the present' became 'the past' and could be used in ways quite different from before. It was one thing to be influenced by Stravinsky during his lifetime and to write a kind of pastiche neo-classicism; it is quite another to take, as composers are increasingly doing, Stravinsky rather than Schoenberg as a model in all sorts of other ways, which tell us a lot about composition in the 1970s and 80s. Stravinsky appears especially fascinating, both for his attitudes to notions of originality, style and the role of the composer in society and for his ambiguous and ambivalent answers to questions about tonality and form. The Dutch composer Louis Andriessen (*b* 1939), Kagel, Steve Reich and the Englishmen Dominic Muldowney (*b* 1952) and Christopher Fox (*b* 1955) have drawn on Stravinsky's aesthetic and, in some cases, his musical material.

In the 1960s quotation was seen as the best way of combining the familiar and the unfamiliar. No matter how radical composers felt obliged to be, they could incorporate melody, regular rhythms and even tonality into their work simply by plundering the past. This would achieve a refreshing immediacy of impact arising from the shock of recognition. More important, listeners would be more likely to follow the procedures through which familiar material was put and thus gain a firmer grasp of a work's structure. Stravinsky was by no means the only model. In the 1960s the music of Ives first came into its own; his extensive use of 'vernacular' as well as 'cultivated' sources influenced many composers, particularly those interested in creating the musical equivalent of collage in painting. Stockhausen's *Hymnen* for tape with optional instruments (1966–7), for example, uses banal tunes – national anthems – to allow the transformation of the basic material to be more perceptible than it is in, say, his earlier piece *Gruppen* for three orchestras (1955–7).

The reason so many composers, even formerly radical ones, have tried to re-engage with traditional concerns is that musical modernism has been replaced by something else: postmodernism. This is related to developments in the other arts and in 'culture' generally by the mysterious forces that underlie all social and artistic change.

Possibly the most straightforward definition of 'postmodernism' has come from the architecture critic Charles Jencks, who has a strong claim to be the chief commentator on postmodern architecture and is a leading theorist – his book *The Language of Post-Modern Architecture* has been through many editions.[16] More accessible is his 48-page, lucid *What is Post-Modernism?*, in which he says that 'one must see that [postmodernism's] continual growth and movement mean that no definitive answer is possible – at least not until it stops moving'.[17] A few pages later, however, he reveals an essential core of 'definition' that has stood what, for such contemporary theory, is the test of time: 'To this day I would define Post-Modernism as I did in 1978 as *double coding: the combination of Modern techniques with something else (usually traditional building) in order for architecture to communicate with the public and a concerned minority, usually other architects*'.[18] One must understand what modernism is, and was, therefore, to understand postmodernism. Jencks also answers the vexing question of how exactly the prefix 'post-' is being used: to what extent it indicates acceptance of the phenomenon which, literally, it follows, or rejection of it. According to Jencks it means both:

The Neue Staatsgalerie, Stuttgart (1977–84), designed by James Stirling, Michael Wilford and Associates, a leading example of postmodernist architecture.

'double coding'. By way of explaining this further, postmodernism seeks 'to communicate with the public', to avoid the élitism apparently endemic to modernism by aspiring to be 'more democratic in its appeal',[19] and to this extent to reject modernism. Postmodernism, however, is far from being a simple denial of everything for which modernism has stood, since it accepts 'modern techniques' (either technical methods, like formal ones, material or aspects of style). The simple conclusion is that 'it isn't what you do, it's the way that you do it!'; or rather, it is how the 'codes' in a work are read by those who experience it. Jencks provides us with a framework that we may attempt to apply in evaluating the music of our own time.

*

Two masterpieces – Berio's *Sinfonia* for eight amplified voices and orchestra (completed in 1969) and Stockhausen's *Stimmung* (1968) for six amplified voices – date from a period that has taken on a mythic quality for social and political as well as artistic reasons. Both pieces are richly redolent of their time and are at once summations of mature postwar musical modernism and precursors of the postmodernism that was to undermine it. Berio's *Sinfonia* seems modernist because of its challenging conceptual basis. As the concluding panel in a trilogy stretching back to the beginning of the 1960s, it crowns the settings of texts by the modernist writers Eliot, Joyce and Proust, among others, in *Epiphanie* for soprano and orchestra (1961) and by Eliot, Pound and others in *Laborintus II* for voices, instruments, reciter and tape (1965), with a dense, multi-layered structure that draws on another concluding work from a modernist trilogy, Beckett's *The Unnamable*. *Sinfonia* builds up its musical material too from a bewildering variety of musical and other sources, including previous compositions by Berio himself, in a way that strongly recalls the 'work-in-progress' approach of that arch-modernist Joyce.

The enormous range of treatment, as well as of source material, imposes on *Sinfonia* a multi-faceted surface under which the listener is forced to seek connections and meanings. It is arguably modernist in its strong resistance to easy or singular interpretation (though the temptation to invoke Jencks's 'double coding' as the ultimate cause is already strong), in its refusal to provide any straightforward 'narrative' direction. The most famous illustration is the third movement, in which the scherzo of Mahler's Second Symphony, the *Resurrection*, is used as the structural basis for a switchback ride to and fro over the history of Western music, from Bach to Stockhausen (concentrating on the twentieth century). Berio was at pains to avoid the word 'collage' as a description of what he did with these quotations. As disturbing yet enjoyable as this movement can be, it is far from anarchic. Berio's own comparison is with 'a skeleton that often re-emerges fully fleshed out, then disappears, then comes back again'.[20] Berio's 'creative exploration that was at the same time an analysis, a commentary and an extension of the original' results in something which is formally comprehensible and expressively direct. It is this concern with expression together with extensive use of tonal material that draws Berio's *Sinfonia* into the orbit of postmodernism. In this Berio was drawing on Pousseur's ideas (see p. 357). The work's second movement – a memorial tribute to Martin Luther King, whose name, phonetically dissected, provides the text for what was originally a separate piece written in 1967 – offers an evocative and moving lyricism: whole-tone and even near-triadic consonances belie the use of serial processes, and the simple human message renders the phonetic dislocation of the words (which are assembled rather than dismembered during the work) strangely 'unmodern'. The *Sinfonia*'s postmodernism is reinforced by the work's title (is it in any sense a 'symphony'?) and by the fact that it springs out of the concerns of a 1960s Milanese intelligentsia that included the writer Umberto Eco, who has since become one of the leading scholars in the postmodernist debate.[21]

Stockhausen's *Stimmung*, though capable of a performance duration three times that of Berio's *Sinfonia*, is scored for a more modest complement. Though neither as wide-ranging in its basic material nor as obviously dramatic as, say, *Hymnen*, and not as audaciously reductive or perhaps immediately influential as the text scores collected together as *Aus den sieben Tagen* (also 1968), *Stimmung* was accepted by some as 'a perfect work',[22] and both its material and manner have since made it arguably more influential than *Gruppen* or *Kontakte* (1959–60). The reasons for this have less to do with the work's strongly serial base – it is surprising to learn that *Stimmung* is 'as rigorously serial as any work from the 1950s'[23] – than with the application of Stockhausen's abstruse, earlier serial manipulations to a modest amount of musical and textual material, creating what is, even for him, an unusually original composition. It is harder to separate the modernist and postmodernist aspects of *Stimmung* than those of Berio's *Sinfonia*, possibly simply because *Stimming* is so coherent and unique.

This may be surprising for those who subscribe to the view of *Stimmung* as merely 'Hippy log-fire' music (a phrase used after its Paris première and valid as a reminder of the social and musical context in which the work was created and first received).[24] But it may help to explain its continuing fascination for composers and listeners. One of the few overtly modernist elements of *Stimmung* other than its serialism is its rigorous use of extended vocal techniques. In addition to such textual material as the 'magic names' of gods from both East and West, other single words and four poems by the composer, the basic vocal material consists of overtones produced by shortening the mouth's sound chamber with the tongue and using several lip positions. These methods of vocal production, made audible by amplification, are a natural extension of the developing interest shown in new vocal and instrumental techniques during the 1960s, notable also in the work of Berio. The origin of this method of producing overtones lies, though, not in the phonetic researches of twentieth-century scientists and composers but in techniques developed by Tibetan monks many centuries ago.

More importantly for any postmodernist interpretation of the work, the rooting of all the basic notes in its pitch scheme on the overtones of a low, unsingable B flat leads to *Stimmung*'s most notoriously un-modernist characteristic: the harmonic effect is highly consonant, dealing largely in 3rds, 7ths and 9ths built up into lovingly held chords of a simple beauty quite audacious in the context of avant-garde music of the 1950s and 60s. *Stimmung* represents a vital step towards a reintegration of simple pitch relationships into contemporary music, largely because of increasing interest in oriental music; in its combination of serialism and Tibetan overtones, *Stimmung* seems postmodern. Within a couple of years its influence was clearly felt, and more than any other work it gave young European composers raised on modernist orthodoxies the permission they needed to launch into fresh territory.

*

A good illustration of the declining interest in the avant garde between the late 1960s and the mid-70s is the changing attitude to unconventional musical notation. In the 1950s, and more widely in the 1960s, the way a piece of music was written down assumed an aesthetic importance unknown since the mid-eighteenth century. New methods of notation were invented in abundance, varying in aesthetic purpose and technical detail but all designed to rewrite the contract between composer and performer and, in many cases, encouraging the latter to participate in the creative process. This combined quite naturally with the simultaneous extension of instrumental and vocal techniques, which required new means of notation. Many performers worked in collaboration with composers.

The most fundamental innovations in notation were made in connection with indeterminacy. This term encompasses a wide variety of conflicting aesthetics: from Cage's concern to eradicate 'taste and memory', to Boulez's 'dialectic between order and choice', to the eagerness of many composers simply to facilitate the performance of irregular rhythms through space-time or proportional notation. Few followed up Cage's aesthetic of non-intention with any thoroughness, and the notational innovations of his American pupils Earle Brown (*b* 1926), Morton Feldman (1926–87) and Christian Wolff (*b* 1934) – all of

which allow the performer at least some personal expressive freedom –
have possibly been of more direct importance.

Interest in unconventional notation fell away sharply in the late
1960s and early 70s. Feldman, for example, who had oscillated for years
between conventional and indeterminate notation, made a decisive
return to conventional notation in about 1970 at the start of a period
which saw a new interest in melody and repetition; such works as the
series for solo viola with various accompanying instruments entitled
The Viola in my Life (1970–71) are typical. Groups formed to play
indeterminate scores, live electronic works, improvisations and
'happenings' – whether tight-knit professional composer/performer
groups (like Musica Elettronica Viva in Italy or Intermodulation and
Gentle Fire in Britain) or large, more anarchic organizations open to
amateurs as well as professionals (notably the Scratch Orchestra in
London) – flourished around 1970 but had nearly all disbanded by the
mid-1970s. Even Cage returned to conventional notation with his *Cheap
Imitation* for piano in 1969, though he later used a wide variety of
notations, both fixed and free.

The situation with the related phenomenon of 'extended instrumental techniques' is somewhat similar. Creating new sounds for
standard instruments – especially for the new generation of virtuoso
performers of the 1960s, notably the Slovenian/French trombonist and

The English composer Cornelius Cardew performing with the Scratch Orchestra in London, 1970.

composer Vinko Globokar (*b* 1934) and the Swiss oboist and composer Heinz Holliger – was a natural extension of modernism. After the demise of total serialism and tape music, both of which spelt doom for the player, the creative collaboration of composer and performer was welcomed. The exploration of vocal possibilities, particularly using microphone techniques, was of special interest in the late 1970s and early 80s, for example in the work of such groups as the Extended Vocal Techniques Group from San Diego, California, and Electric Phoenix from London, with composers like the American Kenneth Gaburo (*b* 1926) and the Englishman Trevor Wishart (*b* 1946). The 1970s, however, was a period of consolidation rather than innovation in instrumental techniques; there was a concentration on codification and promotion of existing ideas, for example in a series of books called 'The New Instrumentation'.[25] Organizations such as IRCAM are attempting to prove that harnessing instrumental expertise to the new technology can open up new areas. But since 1970 we have been in a period of refinement and, as far as new research is concerned, increased specialization in a limited area.

Many of those formerly committed to exploration and innovation have now turned back to address the problems of note-to-note melodic and harmonic relationships. The realization that melody was built into all music was expressed as early as the 1950s in Wolff's famous statement that 'No matter what we do it ends by being melodic'.[26] This could express despair or delight: the extent to which melody intrigued those composers, often followers of Cage, who became known in the 1960s as 'experimental' as opposed to 'avant-garde', is an interesting demonstration of how the 'new melody' and even 'new tonality' of the 1970s and 80s grew from earlier concerns.

The acknowledgment of the power of melody is also, of course, in accord with the conservative criticism of 'modern music': that it 'has no tune'. In the early and mid-1970s, however, it became part of a much wider dissatisfaction with the search for the new. Smalley's staunchly modernist declamation quoted at the opening of this chapter was soon countered by such statements as the following by Wolff (1974):

> My feeling in the fifties was that . . . everything was being done from square one . . . Every few months practically you would hear somebody doing something that had never been done before. It seemed inevitable that the situation, as it involves just sound, would exhaust itself – and I think it has. Practically everything's been done now . . . there's a desire now to come back and get reconnected to what most people have been trained for.[27]

Or by Ligeti's more pessimistic view (1978):

I know that dividing periods into decades is vague and does not really fit, but it is rather handy for practical purposes. A typical feature of the '60s was colourfulness: the discovery of *fin de siècle* taste, of ornaments; that was the time of the flower power, of hippies. In music it marked a reaction to serial music or its fine art equivalent, op-art. All this colour brought with it in Western Europe some kind of free and easy mentality in the '60s. Since 1972, or 1973, since the oil crisis, the '70s brought another change in mentality . . . I think 1968 was still essentially part of the hippy movement, whose influence was felt until the early '70s. Music in those years was colourful, whereas today it is grey. Since the mid-'70s conformism has been very much in the air, in any case in Germany, Austria, England and the Scandinavian countries I am more familiar with. The young want security. You could almost say that they want to go on pension as soon as they leave secondary school; well, I am exaggerating. It may be the voice of an adult judging the young harshly and unjustly, but I can sense a desire for security; the new musical trend we have talked about is a manifestation of the same tendency. Back to the nineteenth century, it is safe, let us stop experimenting, you can almost hear them say. Since such a lot happened between 1900 and 1978 I am rather suspicious of such an unthoughtful striving for the past.[28]

Ligeti's interpretation of the difference between the late 1960s and the mid- to late 70s is persuasive, not least because it comes from a composer who, with a work revealingly entitled *Melodien* for strings (1971), made his contribution to the increasing involvement with melody that, on the face of it, was a move in the direction of the neo-Romanticism he was decrying. His development over the next 20 years confirmed this trend in such works as the opera *Le grand macabre* (1978), the Horn Trio (1982), *Etudes* for piano (Book 1 was completed in 1985) and the Piano Concerto (completed in 1987). Ligeti's later music could be interpreted as a postmodernist mixture of the traditional and the radical; he has been influenced by his neo-Romantic pupils of the mid-1970s in Hamburg – the 'brat pack' of young German composers like Wolfgang Rihm (*b* 1952) and Detlev Müller-Siemens (*b* 1957).

Many others made a similar move towards melody in the early 1970s. Stockhausen returned to basing entire compositions on a single melodic statement divided into clearly separate phrases with *Mantra* for two pianos and assorted accessories (1970); the fact that he calls his melodies 'formulae' and his phrases 'limbs' is more indicative of avant-garde unease about composing with a tune than of any fundamental difference between *Mantra* and more familiar types of thematic composition. Wolff's music of the early 1970s became even more overtly based on simple melodic material; *Burdocks* (1971) and *Exercises and Songs* (1973–4), both for any number of performers, are good examples of an individual style, still quirky and extremely flexible, based in the latter case largely on freely counterpointed statements of the same simple lyrical line.

*

Few compositional forms better illustrate the nature and significance of melodic inspiration than the theme and variations. One major composition of the mid-1970s in this form is *The People United Will Never Be Defeated!* for piano (1975) by the American composer and pianist Frederic Rzewski (*b* 1938), an excellent example of the move towards melodic compositions, while Reich's *Music for Eighteen Musicians* (1974–6) illustrates the related move into harmonic-based music; both display a compelling postmodern mix of elements. The traditional aspects of *The People United Will Never Be Defeated!* are the first to strike the listener, especially if the work is played in an 'avant-garde context'. The work divides into a theme, 36 variations and an expanded reprise. The variations are divided into six groups of six, each variation being divided into six sections. The sixth variation of each group functions largely as a summing-up of the previous five, but each also introduces new or transitional material in its last section. The theme is 36 bars long. In the first four groups of variations each variation is 24 bars long. The fifth group expands and loosens this rigid scheme, while the sixth draws the work's elements together in a rigorously schematic but clearly culminating fashion. Listeners can follow something of this scheme, even at first hearing. The work's obsessive rigidity and the way in which macrostructure reflects microstructure are reminiscent of both 1950s serialism and of Cage's proportioning of many of his early works with arithmetical duration schemes.

It is, however, the musical content that is the postmodernist surprise. Rzewski had been known in avant-garde circles from the late 1950s as a formidable pianist, a champion of Stockhausen and Cage and an improvising musician with Musica Elettronica Viva. In the early 1970s he became increasingly concerned with left-wing politics and with finding ways in which his compositions could reflect his concerns and relate to a wider audience. This is part of the move away from modernism and the desire to use music to achieve political change. Many composers were crucially affected by it at this time and radically altered their styles. The most famous British example is Cardew, who abandoned the composition of experimental music and group improvisation to write tonal piano pieces, aimed at influencing the bourgeois concert-goer to consider the left-wing cause, and songs and marches, often in a popular idiom, to aid the working class in their meetings and demonstrations in the pursuit of revolution. *The People United* is based on the song 'El Pueblo Unido Jamás Será Vencido!' by Sergio Ortega and the group Quilapayun which has become a symbol of Chilean

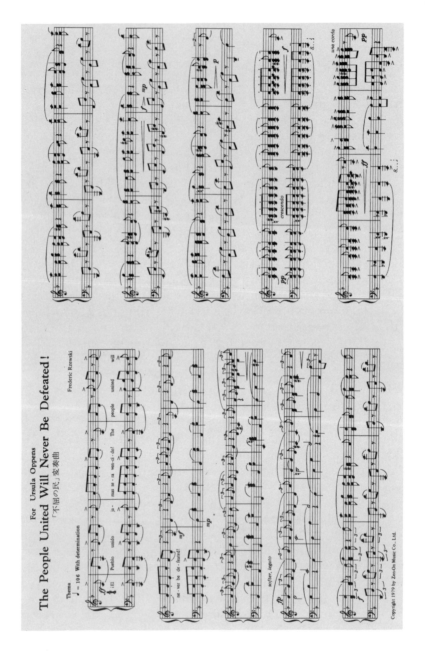

The 36-bar theme of Frederic Rzewski's 'The People United Will Never Be Defeated!' for solo piano, based on a Chilean political song.

resistance. Its moving tune is in a way itself postmodernist, since it arose out of the work of the Unidad Popular, a movement in which folk and classical sources were mixed and simple popular songs were treated to experimental harmonization and sophisticated structural extension.

Rzewski's variations draw on a gamut of styles and techniques, from simple lyric utterance to audacious experiment with keyboard sonorities (and even whistling from the solo pianist), from virtuoso Lisztian pianism to the kind of extensive octave displacement characteristic of serial music. Sometimes the Chilean tune is buried under fresh invention; occasionally it is replaced by references to other songs celebrating working-class struggle (Eisler's 'Solidarity Song' and the Italian socialist song 'Bandiera Rossa'). But the tune remains hauntingly present even when not to the fore and gives the variations an urgency rare in contemporary music. *The People United*'s combination of familiar tune and extended treatment, of 'popular' energy and 'avant-garde' sophistication, makes it a powerful piece of postmodernism.

Rzewski's *Les moutons de Panurge* (1969) represents an individual approach to what has generally been termed 'minimal music'. The most famous composers to be described as 'minimalist' are Reich and Glass. As a description of the music they wrote between the mid-1960s and early 70s, it remains apt; and as a label for the work of their pioneering colleagues La Monte Young and Terry Riley, who did so much to define and establish the territory during the immediately preceding years, it is equally, if not more, appropriate. As the modish tag for a body of work that has latterly become as popular as any 'serious' music can, it is highly misleading. For those inclined to dismiss the compositions of Glass and Reich as merely 'a pop music for intellectuals',[29] the label has a pejorative air that makes its use additionally problematic.

The real musical minimalism of, broadly speaking, the 1960s – where it accords neatly with the image we now have of that decade – was radical, part of 'alternative culture' and thus a branch of modernism. It may have used familiar-sounding material in unfamiliar ways, and thereby appear to qualify as postmodern under Jencks's definition; it is this that helps link it to more recent developments that have attracted the label 'new tonality', again somewhat misleadingly. It may have had important connections with rock music, Indian and African musics and, in Reich's case at least, with medieval compositional methods rather than the heritage of the 'common practice period': again, richly postmodernist perhaps, though borrowing from the exotic and the newly rediscovered rather than the readily accessible. But the original intention of minimalism, especially as practised by Young, was deeply subversive: composers challenged the primacy of note-to-note pitch procedures – whether tonal, serial or whatever – by substituting forms based on rhythm or, in Young's case, long-held sounds that invited listeners to explore acoustic and, more importantly, psycho-acoustic space in ways that have been likened to taking hallucinogenic drugs.

Repetitive music (as one might more accurately call it) since the mid-1970s, however, has increasingly forsaken the art gallery for the concert hall and even, in Glass's case, the opera house. In the process it has become more 'classically' respectable. Melody and harmony have been restored to their position of primacy. Its musical connections are now with Debussy, Bartók and Stravinsky, with classical forms like the chaconne and canon, with regular metre and clear cadences.

Reich's *Music for Eighteen Musicians* exhibits these tendencies in an interesting early state that was both highly prophetic of repetitive music's future and curiously hard for its composer to follow up. It is perhaps no coincidence that all six works examined in this chapter for their postmodern aspects enshrine the paradox of being at once highly influential as breakthrough pieces – for many others besides their own composer – and difficult to develop from. It was only with Reich's discovery, after *Music for Eighteen Musicians* had been toured with enormous success in winter 1976–7, of his Jewish heritage (in the form of Hebrew cantillation techniques) that he found a line of thinking that he could extend over a longer period.

Pitch organization is not the only aspect of *Music for Eighteen Musicians* that connects the repetitive music of the 1970s and 80s to any notion of a 'classical mainstream'. Orchestral instruments (violin, cello, two clarinets doubling bass clarinet) are used for the first time in the newly expanded group of performers who worked regularly with the composer; until then it had consisted of tuned percussion, keyboards and women's voices. Early pieces by Reich and Glass used lean, hard-edged combinations for aesthetic and economic reasons. Latterly Reich has written for chorus and large orchestra and Glass for the full forces of the opera house. In *Music for Eighteen Musicians* the tendency towards a romantic opulence of sound and expressive feeling is enhanced by the dynamic rise and fall of pulsing notes played or sung for the length of a breath, 'gradually washing up like waves against the constant rhythm of the pianos and mallet instruments', according to the composer.[30] But it is the use of a pre-composed harmonic cycle as generator of the entire composition that is of greatest importance. The cycle consists of 11 chords played at the beginning and end of the piece in the 'pulsing' manner just described. As Reich points out, 'There is more harmonic movement in the first 5 minutes of "Music for Eighteen Musicians" than in any other complete work of mine to date'. In between, the bulk of the work consists simply of each chord held in turn for about five minutes while what the composer calls 'a small piece' is constructed on it.

Harmony in *Music for Eighteen Musicians* is a step closer to the 'functional' than in any of Reich's previous works, and the implications of this new concern with tonal direction, as well as the opulence of 7th, 9th and even 11th and 13th chords articulated by a sumptuous ensemble have been followed up, both by him and many others. Yet this is offset by the avoidance of a 'traditionally functional' bass line and the exploration, in ways that Reich enjoys comparing to those of Debussy, of tonal ambiguity. Repeated melodic patterns are now underpinned by rhythmically shifting chord changes, bringing the relationship between melody and harmony closer to traditional models than was the case in minimal music, just as rhythmically they venture far beyond the phasing techniques for which the composer's early music is famous. Later works by Reich chart the move to even greater interest in melody, a kind of functional harmony and the setting of texts, together with the implications of this for rhythm and metre. It is not hard to appreciate the extent to which post-minimal repetitive music is richly postmodernist, or can be made so.

American composers have played a central role in the breaking down of barriers between different types of music and culture that is known as 'crossover'. (This fact diminishes neither American music of the 1950s and 60s nor European developments in the next two decades. But for all the ease with which Berio and Stockhausen can be fitted into a postmodernist scenario, they survived the changing conditions of the 1970s and 80s less well.) One does not have to confine oneself to the twentieth century to find examples of compositional synthesis, particularly of what are sometimes called the 'cultivated' and 'vernacular' traditions. Yet 'crossover' fits neatly into the concept of postmodernism. It may be glib simply to suggest that those who come from a polyglot culture are better placed to explore the 'crossover' phenomenon and its potential; we all live in a cultural confusion of ancient and modern, European and American, African and Asian, highbrow and lowbrow, even if we may legitimately attribute part of the cause to the encroachment of values and manners from the USA. Yet musicians from downtown New York have proved particularly adept at tapping the resources of jazz, rock, folk and other musics to create work that exulted in its very independence from such labels as 'cultivated' and 'vernacular'. Glass and Reich were part of this movement from the early days; indeed, what they did in the late 1960s helped set the scene for the explosion of musical activity in the 1970s that saw the rise of composers like Glenn Branca (*b* 1948) and Rhys Chatham (*b* 1951), whose mixture of repetitive and rock elements characterized this period as much as Glass's music. Later contributors to this 'crossover' – which also crossed between different art forms – include Laurie Anderson; her *United States I-IV* (1979–83), a large-scale, multi-media work with Anderson at the centre (singing, speaking, playing the violin and doing much else) was both critical of American cultural value systems and highly popular. 'Crossover' approaches developed worldwide, as the work of such different composers as the Catalan 'Romantic minimalist' Carles Santos (*b* 1940) and the English 'rock-repetitive' Michael Nyman (*b* 1944) show.

It was probably inevitable that this downtown scene should itself become established and therefore 'establishment', while also moving uptown and outwards; in Glass's case this was via an institution of musical Europe – the opera house. Loft-based and other small-scale music of the kinds that until the mid-1970s and sometimes beyond were called 'experimental' continues to be made both in New York and in every large city in the world, as does music theatre that owes little or nothing to operatic traditions. Yet even the work of such a mainstay of the downtown approach as the American Robert Ashley (*b* 1930) seized the medium of video as the springboard for developing a new kind of opera which, in its use not only of new technologies but of fresh crossovers and innovatory collaborations with other musicians (notably the pianist known as 'Blue' Gene Tyranny) and with video artists, designers and directors, has brought him wide recognition.

Ashley's notion of opera as something that traditionally requires characters who are 'explained to you by what they do musically'[31] allows him to include many of his own works in the genre that might be regarded as having little or nothing to do with opera. *Music with Roots in the Aether* (1975–6), for instance, would be described by most people as a series of seven two-hour documentary television programmes about seven American composers (of whom Ashley is one); *Perfect Lives (Private Parts)* (1978–83), described by Ashley as an 'opera for television in seven 30-minute episodes',[32] comes closer to conventional norms, but is more like a soap opera without a plot (and with some hazily defined characters) than opera as we understand it, and has nothing to do with the opera house. European music theatre as conceived in the early 1960s continued through the 1970s and 80s. Kagel is one of its leading exponents, with his *Staatstheater* for a variety of forces (1971–4) and *Kantrimusik*, described in the score as a 'pastorale for voices and instruments' (1973–5). Many other composers have continued working in this area, for instance Vic Hoyland (*b* 1945), in his triptych *Head and Two Tails* for various forces (1984).

But in the 1980s and 90s the opera house itself became the most sought-after place for composers of every aesthetic and every nationality. Birtwistle, Davies, Finnissy, Harvey, Tippett, John Casken (*b* 1949), Alexander Goehr (*b* 1932), Robin Holloway (*b* 1943), Oliver Knussen (*b* 1952), James MacMillan (*b* 1959), Nigel Osborne (*b* 1948), Robert Saxton (*b* 1953), Mark-Anthony Turnage (*b* 1960) and Judith Weir (*b* 1954) are among the British composers who are working in the genre; Stephen Oliver (1950–92) devoted his whole career to opera. A foreign list of major figures would include everyone from Henze, who has composed operas since the 1950s, to Cage, Messiaen and Stockhausen, who surprised even some of their followers by writing opera. Stockhausen has poured everything he has written since the late 1970s into *Licht*, his seven-evening, late twentieth-century answer to the *Ring*.

It may be argued that the present enthusiasm for opera is no stronger than it was in previous generations. But it does seem that the medium is now widely perceived as a vehicle for new ideas, though chiefly for composers unconcerned with 'making it new' in the conventional sense. Indeed, opera offers every incentive to re-explore aspects of melody, harmony, rhythm and texture in ways that accord closely with Jencks's postmodernist definitions; these sit naturally with both the musical and the dramatic demands of opera. Moreover, in the late 1980s opera became unexpectedly popular with a wide public; as a medium, whether in the established repertory (particularly in radical productions) or new works, it is considered by many to be more innovatory and challenging than 'straight' theatre.

Glass's career as an opera composer began with works which, both dramatically and musically, could not conventionally be called 'operatic'. *Einstein on the Beach* (1976), his collaborative project with the American director-designer Robert Wilson, is better called 'music theatre'. It evolved out of non-narrative theatrical traditions from Antonin Artaud's theatre of pure expression to Wilson's own 'theatre of images'; and when it drew on narrative theatre, it was the kind in which the action is much slower than in 'straight' theatre or Western opera (South Indian Khatikali theatre, for example). The music of *Einstein*, much like Reich's *Music for Eighteen Musicians*, is crucially 'on the edge' between the non-developmental, non-goal-orientated, 'non-narrative' music of his earlier minimalism and the more harmonically and melodically directed approach that was to characterize his later operas. For the progressively greater narrative element, dramatically speaking, in *Satyagraha* (1980), *Akhnaten* (1984), *The Making of the Representative for Planet 8* (1988) and *The Voyage* (1992), finds its musical equivalent in an increasing concern for functional harmony, clear melodic outline and regular metric patterns, even while repetition, in something resembling the minimalist sense, continues to articulate the flow. The parallel development in Glass's output of 'music-theatre' works not designed for the opera house, for instance *1000 Airplanes on the Roof* (1988), frustrates any attempt to fit his development into an anti-modernist or neo-Romantic straitjacket. But the thrust in the direction of a perceived 'mainstream', dramatically and musically, is clear.

John Adams's operas offer further demonstration of how so-called minimalist techniques can be integrated into a personal style. An interesting characteristic of *Nixon in China* (1987) and *The Death of Klinghoffer* (1991) is the extent to which functional tonality, and with it Adams's brand of reference to music of the past, activates and enhances the drama. Both operas are based on real events: *Nixon in China* is concerned with President Nixon's visit to Mao Tse-tung in 1972, *The Death of Klinghoffer* with the hijacking of the *Achille Lauro* cruise ship in 1986. Both were the idea of Peter Sellars, who directed their premières, and their librettist is Alice Goodman. Adams's repetitions are bound to sound close to those of Reich and Glass. But the interest lies in what he does with repetition, which includes allusion to a range of Classical and Romantic composers (among whom Wagner features particularly), both to aid characterization in *Nixon* and in each opera to provide power and depth to the unfolding action.

The two works are, however, quite different, suggesting a change of approach that is reflected in Adams's non-operatic music of the late 1980s. *Nixon*, for the first two acts at least, delights in a swashbuckling array of styles, orchestrated, as always by Adams, with vivid virtuosity. Only in its final act is the music less concerned with stylistic parody, and even less minimalist, as it reflects the move from the public spectacle that dominates the earlier part of the opera to the private emotional world of the characters. *The Death of Klinghoffer* takes this as its point of musical departure, though here the concern is not so much with the characters as individuals but with attempting to build round their story a meditation on politics and morality which, according to the opera's creators, owes more to Bach's Passions than to traditional operatic narratives.

Adams, of course, is far from being the only composer to draw on the music of the past in ways that differ markedly from those of, say, Berio and Davies. One might even assert that in his music Europe is finally dominated and subdued, to an extent that even Cage did not achieve, and ironically at just the time when such dominance is being questioned on many levels. This revolution has been accomplished by harnessing commercial vigour with a kind of postmodernist bravado that even Reich and Glass cannot match. Adams seems 'American' in an almost clichéd way: what he calls his 'Trickster' pieces,[33] such as *Grand Pianola Music* for piano and ensemble (1982), are typical of the up-to-the-minute kleptomania that seems to many to epitomize the 'American way'. But some of Adams's later work, notably *The Death of Klinghoffer*, celebrates too the possibility that from the (largely European-dominated) past and the (partly American-controlled) present can emerge a new synthesis that capitulates to no value systems, whether 'cultivated' or 'vernacular', modernist or commercial. Modernists would continue to deny this possibility; but it is not only hardline modernists who would criticize the wave of orchestral showpiece compositions that swept the USA during the 1980s as merely another kind of 'pop music for intellectuals'.

The move from modernism to postmodernism in the mid-1970s, as we have noted, was perhaps effected most significantly and potently in the USA. This has a great deal to do with that country's economic, political and in many senses cultural dominance. But one might ask how a culture so affected by the mass media and the values associated with television's incursions into everyday lives is able to produce music of more than ephemeral significance unless, like Babbitt, it ignores popular values and the channels by which they are communicated. And even when figures as different as Ashley, the composer and former pianist David Tudor and the 'environmental' composer and former percussionist Max Neuhaus (*b* 1939) find ways of harnessing those media to their own ends, one wonders whether the quantity and quality of American music is simply the result of composers having greater access to technology and funding. Besides, the USA's period of ascendancy is widely perceived to have come to an end, and the implications for musical development are considerable.

*

In the 1990s there is another stage in the cultural shift as we are increasingly exposed to music from eastern Europe and Russia. Soviet music from the 1930s to the 60s was dominated by the tenets of Socialist Realism. A good deal of Russian music from the last 20 years is still beholden to the notions of acceptable art fostered by successive Communist régimes: and Shostakovich's mantle proved extraordinarily hard to shrug off. But the social and political ferment that culminated in eastern Europe in the revolutions of 1989 had been bubbling away in music since about 1960. It is not surprising that composers who are able to acquire only a partial knowledge of avant-garde music, without having had the chance to assimilate its immediate history or development, should view modernism and its aftermath from a different perspective. Russia had no extended period of modernism, unless one counts the heady, confused years immediately after the revolution, when avant-garde ideas were to some degree allowed to flourish; the post-1945 Soviet period saw no real parallels to Western developments. (Poland, most notably, however, developed its own avant garde after 1956.)

It is in the work of some of those composers from the former USSR whose attempts to confront Western modernism date back 20 or 30 years, as well as of their younger contemporaries, that we see the full fruits of that confrontation. Composers like Edison Denisov (*b* 1929), Sofia Gubaydulina (*b* 1931), Alfred Shnitke (*b* 1934) and Pärt have much to say not only about further ways in which modernist ideals may be transmuted rather than abandoned but, significantly, about the search for style in contexts far removed from the one to which Berio responded in *Sinfonia* over 20 years ago. In pre-Soviet Russian music, stylistic identity was bound up with national identity more closely than was the case even in those countries which during the late nineteenth and early twentieth centuries responded more strongly to nationalist trends in politics and culture. Composers, especially those allied with overtly Slavophile tendencies (such as Musorgsky), openly quoted from or imitated Russian church and folk music. Crucially, this identification with the people was undertaken with a complete absence of ironic distance.

Irony, with its potential for affording critiques both of borrowed material and of the new situations in which composers found themselves, was in theory, of course, impossible during the years of Soviet Socialist Realism, especially during the Stalinist era. Yet it was probably solving the problem of how to remain true to himself that made Shostakovich such a great composer. What has been called his 'solution of a higher irony, a hall of stylistic mirrors, a moral maze into which the composer might hope to lure his tormentor but in which, of course, he always risked losing his friends or indeed himself'[34] took many forms; one of the most baffling is the Fifteenth Symphony (1971), his last, with its bizarre quotations of Rossini and Wagner. The most interesting and original Russian composers have learnt from Shostakovich to incorporate stylistic references in music that is deeply ambiguous. Jencks's postmodernist 'double coding' may not synchronize with the intentions and achievements of Shostakovich's music or that of Shnitke or Pärt; it is nevertheless clear that they draw with honesty and feeling on past traditions to evoke pre-Soviet identification with, among other things, religious aspiration, and, perhaps paradoxically, they infuse that identification with the doubt of ironic suggestion.

Shnitke uses borrowed material in ways sufficiently varied to make it hard to determine whether he intends irony. The First Symphony (1969–72), for example, seems a straightforward parody, a kind of collage reaction to his encounters with the Western avant garde, including Cage. The First Concerto Grosso for two violins, harpsichord, piano and strings (1976–7), on the other hand, is at once more straightforward in its stylistic reference (the fifth of its six movements is a sort of tango that draws on Baroque material) and more ambiguous (the fast second movement's clearly Baroque origins quickly move in and out of focus).

The tango has a special fascination for Shnitke: its somewhat sinister undertones of pain as well as pleasure accord with his desire to achieve different levels of meaning in what he calls 'polystylistic' art.[35] (Many other composers have recently been attracted to the tango and other dance genres that combine openness and entertainment with undertones of rage and passion; in the 1970s and 80s there have been 'projects' in which composers of different aesthetic persuasions have been invited to write waltzes, tangos or polkas.)[36] A tango is at the heart of one of Shnitke's major works, *Seid nüchtern und wachet* (1982–3), an extended composition for four solo singers, chorus and orchestra, usually called the *Faust Cantata*. Based on the last chapter of Johann Spies's *History of Dr Johann Fusten, the well-known Magician and Black Magician*, it tells of Faust's last days, culminating with a 'Night Scene' in which Mephistopheles comes to claim him. Its ten sections are cast like a Passion setting, in which the tenor, as narrator, and the bass, as Faust himself, have the lion's share of the music. The role of Mephistopheles is taken by the two remaining solo singers: 'two-faced and two-voiced – hypocritically servile countertenor and triumphant deep female voice', as Shnitke describes them. The orchestration includes saxophones, electric instruments and flexatone. The way Shnitke uses his forces heightens the effect of turning the familiar into the unfamiliar in what the composer calls this 'negative Passion'.[37]

Some of the music of the *Faust Cantata* owes almost as much to Bach as the piece's structure. This, though, is constantly underpinned – almost threatened – by the orchestral commentary and by the ways in which ideas that clearly have origins in, say, Bach recitatives and chorales, are distorted out of all recognition. Most interesting, perhaps, is the tango, in which Mephistopheles (here in mezzo-soprano form) and the choir tell of Faust's end. The starting-point is a simple, rising minor scale, decorated with turns, set against the tango rhythm and culminating in a lurid climax at Faust's demise. The use of such clichéd materials suggests that Shnitke's intention is parody. Yet the effect is rather to make one feel as though the minor scale is being somehow reinvented. This seems less like a process of recycling material from the past than a concern to identify with national roots, with folk and church music and the aspirations they enshrined.

Pärt's music exemplifies this interest in folk and ancient sources as the wellsprings for a new music that in many ways rejects both modernism and the kinds of postmodernism that rely on ironic distancing for their effect and meaning. Pärt, an Estonian, moved to the West in 1980 and settled there. (Shnitke left the USSR and settled in Germany in 1991.) Until 1967 he composed in a style owing much to the Western avant garde though even then he began to use simple tonal gestures and sometimes quotations from earlier music. That year he encountered Gregorian plainsong, and his work soon developed aspects of the mystic simplicity that is now its hallmark. The basic techniques of his mature style were not established until the mid-1970s, notably the elements Pärt calls 'tintinnabuli'. As this suggests, the style is influenced by bells, characterized by stepwise melody, accompanied by an arpeggio-derived lower part and a drone bass. Canonic writing often expands these elements to provide music of rich but essentially simple, haunting beauty; Pärt often draws on Baroque-derived material. *Cantus in Memory of Benjamin Britten* for string orchestra and

Arvo Pärt (b 1935).

bell and *Tabula rasa* for two solo violins, prepared piano and strings (both 1977) are typical of this period.

Pärt's mature style finds expression in the *Passio Domini nostri Jesu Christi secundum Joannem*, composed in West Berlin in 1981–2 shortly after his emigration to the West. Following the practice of Schütz and others, the Evangelist is represented by different combinations formed from a quartet of singers including a countertenor. There are two further solo voices: Pilate (tenor) and Jesus (bass), the latter accompanied by an organ. A chorus, singing only in block chordal, rhythmic unison, and an ensemble of oboe, bassoon, violin and cello complete the forces of what is essentially a 'chamber' Passion, though one suited to performance in a church acoustic. The style of this *St John Passion* is simple and restrained, projecting the Latin text in syllabic fashion, using melodic and harmonic material that sounds to Western ears as though derived from plainchant and medieval music. Occasionally the indulgence of a slightly extended and more dissonant cadence is permitted (recalling Stravinsky). Much of the music is repeated. In spite of its simplicity and the way attention is focussed on the text and its meaning, the listener is not bored. There is a mesmeric quality to

Pärt's work, but his combination of emotion and hieratic rigour ultimately has almost as little to do with American minimalism as Pärt insists it does. Only the final moments of this Passion's ecstatic contemplation, when choir and organ burst into something more Victorian in its harmonic rhetoric (showing how difficult it is successfully to use familiar material in unfamiliar ways), detract from this masterpiece.

Pärt's musical evolution seems to arise from the desire to invent for himself a 'spiritual music' that engages not only with much earlier traditions but with a renewal of spiritual concern, if not a dogmatic adherence to one particular faith. Russian music occupies a special place in this development, coming as it does from a tradition in which art for art's sake was never a meaningful concept. Writing 'spiritual music' for our times has concerned many other composers. John Tavener (*b* 1944) was expressing his Roman Catholic beliefs from the 1960s, culminating in his opera *Thérèse* (1973–6, first performed 1979). But it is in his later music, which reflects a conversion to Orthodox practice, that his kind of 'spiritual music' is best expressed, with a chant-based directness of utterance quite different from his flamboyant early works. Some is for liturgical use and so, following Orthodox practice, it is for voices only. At one point it seemed that Tavener might abandon composing for the concert environment altogether. His major instrumental works, for instance *The Protecting Veil* (1989), a lengthy ecstatic contemplation for cello and orchestra, have nevertheless brought him acclaim. Again, a departure conducted initially at the margin of 'classical' concert life has become integrated with it. Perhaps most astonishing is the sudden rise to prominence of the Polish composer Henryk Górecki (*b* 1933) on account of a new recording of his Third Symphony for soprano and orchestra (1976) entering the British pop charts early in 1993. His brand of what has been dubbed 'holy minimalism' appears voguish and cliché-ridden to some, but the first movement (a setting of the fifteenth-century Polish prayer 'Holy Cross Lament') has an emotional directness and compelling inevitability that is clearly matched by the honesty of utterance of the ensuing two movements.

The Scottish composer James MacMillan, in his orchestral work *The Confession of Isobel Gowdie* (1990), has 'tried to capture the soul of Scotland in music, [using] . . . a multitude of chants, songs and litanies (real and imagined)',[38] to offer a kind of act of contrition for the burning at the stake as a witch of the seventeenth-century Scotswoman of the title. Harvey's work, too, though rooted in avant-garde techniques, is another example of music infused with spiritual impulses; compositions such as *Ritual Melodies* for computer-generated tape (1989) bring together this 'spiritual project', the new technology and the new prominence of melody in a way that seems typical of its time. The

French Tristan Murail (*b* 1947) and the English Diana Burrell (*b* 1948) are also concerned with developing a 'spiritual music'.

*

Much composition of the early 1990s is preoccupied with the search for roots. The Russian composer Dimitri Silvestrov (*b* 1948) feels he is 'just writing down what I hear from the genetic well of culture',[39] an approach that would probably be subscribed to – or at least aspired to – by many composers all over the world. Pärt's use of materials and methods from the past, with their religious connotations, is an example. Shnitke's 'polystylism', however far it may have travelled from the extravagances of the 1970s and early 80s, carries a warning about the health of a culture that could be described as merely parasitic. Adams raises the same issue; Glass's apparent innocence of it is, like Pärt's, something that gives rise to sharply differing opinions: one can regard these composers as anything from holy fools to charlatans. Ashley, meanwhile, makes the 'global village', with its simultaneous promise of a new understanding through new technologies and a threat of fragmentation and isolation, both practical and philosophical, the subject of his discourse.

There is, as we have seen, considerable interest – even on the part of modernist composers like Carter – in re-establishing the sorts of developmental discourse characterized most obviously by sonata form, if in ways that reinterpret it for our own time. It would seem a logical, even postmodernist, step to build symphonic edifices using popular music from the 'genetic well', rather than the modernist material now so widely discredited. In practice, however, composers have produced widely contrasting solutions to the problems of writing what Schoenberg disparagingly called 'folkloristic symphonies'. Some, like David Matthews (*b* 1943), argue for 'the rediscovery of musical archetypes – singable melodies, dance rhythms, tonal harmonies – which can be used in new ways while retaining their traditional resonance';[40] and his four symphonies and five string quartets, like the music of his compatriot Nicholas Maw (*b* 1935), seek a symphonic return to the vernacular. Maw's gigantic *Odyssey* for orchestra (completed in 1987) is rumoured to be the longest continuous instrumental work in existence.

The work of others, like Davies, seems related to this: his symphonies written after 1976 and his many concertos attempt a *rapprochement* with the symphonic ideals of Beethoven and Sibelius, using a harmonic approach which, allowing both the composer himself and his commentators to use words like 'tonic' and 'dominant', is seen as a return to traditional principles. Such 'returns' are, as we have seen, typical in the last 20 years; and though composers may, like Lutosławski, describe their approach to harmony as 'new' (his dates from *c*1979), it is precisely the overlap between such 'new harmony' and the 'functional' one of the eighteenth and nineteenth centuries that presumably allows such composers to write symphonies. (Lutosławski's Third Symphony was composed between 1972 and 1983, demonstrating how hard the process must have been and how the struggle to achieve a new symphonic approach coincides with his seeking 'new harmony'.) Davies's preferred term for development, 'transformation', gives the clue to the differences between his approach and a conventional symphonic one like Matthews's. In fact, Davies's symphonies are built with the same basic material as his early, avant-garde works: plainsong melodies subjected to a wide range of modifications, some extremely abstruse and still in their way serial, and most tending to make the plainsong source largely inaudible.

Many composers who use melodies and harmonies from the past in clearly audible ways have nevertheless denied the validity of any re-engagement with the symphonic principle or with narrative development in, for example, opera. This makes clear how far postmodernism can be from revivalism. Cage, for instance, showed how the heritage of his native America, of opera and of Ireland, to pick three examples, could be used as source material for the invention of music preserving at least some of the modernist aesthetic. *Hymns and Variations* for 12 amplified voices (1979) is based on two psalm settings by the eighteenth-century American William Billings; these are subjected to processes of erasure, whereby notes from the original are removed, and prolongation, whereby some of the remaining notes are extended. The result preserves obvious links with the source, even to the extent of being interpretable in terms that might appear unacceptably 'narrative' to a modernist remaining faithful to the original tenets of Cage's 'purposeful purposelessness'.

Europeras 1–5 for various forces (1987–91) thrives on retaining sufficient sense of operatic convention to turn what could have been a 1960s 'happening' into a 1980s 'opera'. The ways in which Cage harnessed familiar material to unfamiliar ends is sufficiently different from his methods of the 1950s and 60s that we can be tempted to describe them as having postmodern tendencies. *Roaratorio, an Irish Circus on Finnegans Wake*, for reciter, folk musicians and tape (1979), makes extended, clearly audible use of Irish folk music. The work's Joycean basis is but one of *Roaratorio*'s modernist aspects; as Cage said, 'if you go to Dublin and hear those musicians, they all play together in harmony, and in *Roaratorio* they all play separately in circus . . . the result is unpredictable in the case of *Roaratorio*, and to my ear tiresome in the case of the conventional Irish practices. I mean, a little bit of folk music goes a long way'.[41] Here, clearly, is a composer whose use of familiar material was far from nostalgic.

Cage was arguably just the most extreme among many composers who sought a postmodernist direction unlike the *rétro* movement labelled 'neo-Romantic'. Boulez regards all these uses of past material, especially the most obviously 'neo-Romantic' ones, as 'just regurgitation'. One might usefully compare the work of, say, the British Holloway and Colin Matthews (*b* 1946) and the Americans George Rochberg (*b* 1918) and David del Tredici (*b* 1937), as the best means of establishing the range of possibilities for bringing together familiar material with both familiar and unfamiliar forms. The resonances and implications of the material itself and its interaction with the structures composers have devised for it, whether narrative or static, are part of such an investigation. However, there will always be those who write unintentional pastiche through a mixture of technical fluency and love for particular composers' music.

While a return to national, even nationalist, traditions is an important dimension of postmodernism, which seems to set its face firmly against the internationalism of the modernist stance, pluralism will, one hopes, itself be some guard against the return of cultural hegemony – whether American, Russian, German or anything else. It is hard to separate current interest in a particular music from any more durable notions of quality, even if cult figures can to some degree be perceived by their contemporaries as passing fashions. There is now wide interest not only in new Russian music but in work from, for instance, South America, Japan and the whole 'Pacific Rim'. This wider interest manifests itself technically, too, in the diffusion and transmutation of all single-minded compositional systems – serialism, minimalism – until they arguably disappear, if not entirely from the ways in which composers think.

The way in which such modernist techniques have been subsumed, whether by incorporation into a Western classical, narrative, developmental aesthetic or not, seems as good a way as any of defining the music of the 'cultivated' tradition from about 1970. The erosion of boundaries between 'classical' and 'popular', which divide the music discussed here from the music listened to by the majority of world citizens in the late twentieth century, has proved to have limitations. Scepticism over syntheses originally promulgated in the 1960s seems reasonable after all. Though the wrongheadedness of a notion that predicates itself on an 'ethno-centre' (whether European, American or whatever) now appears clear, so does the falseness of any assertion that the borders – geographical, historical, racial, religious – which define these 'centres' have lost all meaning.

Francis Fukuyama's announcement of the triumph of Western liberalism and the 'end of history' is perhaps one more piece of prophecy of the 'death of culture' to be added to those littering the period under scrutiny, if not the entire century; yet it did gain a certain credence and won its author a sizable following. It should also be noted that Fukuyama's notion of 'post-history', tied though it is to the revolutions of 1989, was already a cultural reality in Russian music of the 1980s. Such statements as the observation that 'In the most decisive shift since Pierre Boulez declared 30 years ago that Schoenberg was dead, the Eighties was the decade in which we suddenly realised that the avant-garde had ceased to dominate our musical lives'[42] may be challenged on several grounds: even if we accept the 1980s, rather than the 1970s, as the period in which this realization spread to the observers, as opposed to the practitioners, of composition, the suggestion that the avant garde ever dominated our musical lives must seem suspect.

From the present vantage-point it appears valid to speak of 'the definitive end of the "60s" in the general area of 1972–1974',[43] an end caused in part by economic factors. Whether this will ultimately be viewed as a more important cultural 'break' than any brought about by political developments in eastern Europe and the new technology remains to be seen. It is, however, already evident that twenty-first-century musical historians of the late twentieth century may well consider the 'break' about 1975 to be more significant than the one around 1950; thus the major part of the period reviewed here might constitute the dawn of a new age.

NOTES

[1] 'Roger Smalley writes about his "Beat Music"', *The Listener*, lxxxvi, no. 2211 (12 Aug 1971), 218.

[2] E. Barkin and M. Brody, entry on Babbitt in *The New Grove Dictionary of American Music*, ed. H. Wiley Hitchcock and S. Sadie (London, 1986), i, 102.

[3] K. H. Wörner, *Stockhausen: Life and Work*, trans. and ed. B. Hopkins (London, 1973), 82; the quotation is from Wörner, but the idea is very much Stockhausen's.

[4] J. Cage, 'Experimental Music', in *Silence* (Middletown, CT, 1961), 12.

[5] *Make It New* is the title of a collection of essays by Ezra Pound, published in 1934.

[6] M. Bradbury, *The Modern World: Ten Great Writers* (London, 1988), 3.

[7] Quoted in Barkin and Brody's entry on Babbitt in *The New Grove Dictionary of American Music*, i, 105.

[8] M. Babbitt, 'The More than the Sounds of Music', in the booklet accompanying the New York Philharmonic Orchestra's 'Horizons '84' festival, 10.

[9] Programme note for the world première of the work, Royal Festival Hall, London, 2 April 1975.

[10] From promotional material published by IRCAM from 1977 onwards.

[11] During a pre-concert talk on 12 October 1985, as part of 'IRCAM in London', a series of three concerts presented at St John's, Smith Square.

[12] See, for example, H. Pousseur, trans. D. Behrman, 'The Question of Order in New Music', *Perspectives of New Music*, iv/1 (1966), 93–111.

[13] See, for example, I. Xenakis, 'La crise de la musique sérielle', *Gravesaner Blätter*, i (1955), 2ff.; G. Ligeti, 'Metamorphoses of Musical Form', *Die Reihe*, no. 7 (Eng. trans. 1965), 5–19; L. Nono, 'The Historical Reality of Music Today', *The Score*, no. 27 (July 1960), 41–5.

[14] R. Toop, 'Brian Ferneyhough in Interview', *Contact*, no. 29 (Spring 1985), 5.

[15] Programme note for the world première of the work, Centre Pompidou, Paris, 10 and 11 May 1990.

[16] C. Jencks, *The Language of Post-Modern Architecture* (London, 6/1991).

[17] C. Jencks, *What is Post-Modernism?* (London, 2/1986), 2.

[18] Ibid., 14.

[19] Ibid., 15.

[20] This and the following quotation come from *Luciano Berio: Two Interviews with Rossana Dalmonte and Bálint András Varga*, trans. and ed. D. Osmond-Smith (London, 1985), 107.

[21] See the Bibliographical Note at the end of this chapter.

[22] R. Smalley, review of the world première of *Stimmung*, *The Musical Times*, cx (1969), 184.

[23] R. Toop, in notes for the programme book for the Stockhausen festival 'Music and Machines', Barbican, London, 7–16 January 1985, 40.

[24] Toop refers to this in the programme note referred to above. It is worth drawing attention here to this excellent book, which arguably provides a better, certainly more immediately accessible, introduction to Stockhausen's music up to about 1970 than any other source.

[25] Edited by B. Turetzky and B. Childs, and published by the University of California Press, this series began with Turetzky's *The Contemporary Contrabass* (1974); this was followed by books on the flute (T. Howell, 1975), the clarinet (P. Rehfeldt, 1978) and the trombone (S. Dempster, 1979).

[26] C. Wolff, 'New and Electronic Music', *Audience*, v/3 (1958), 10.

[27] From K. Potter, 'Christian Wolff in Manchester', an interview with the composer in *Music and Musicians*, xxiv (1974–5), 8.

[28] Ligeti, in the interview with Peter Varnai, in *György Ligeti in Conversation*, trans. G. J. Schabert (London, 1983), 73.

[29] S. Lipman, 'From Avant-Garde to Pop', in his collection of articles entitled *The House of Music: Art in an Era of Institutions* (Boston, 1984), 48.

[30] This and the following two quotations are taken from Reich's sleeve notes for the recording of *Music for Eighteen Musicians*, ECM 1129 (1978).

[31] Ashley, quoted in K. Potter, 'Robert Ashley and "Post-Modernist" Opera', *Opera*, xxxviii (1987), 391.

[32] Publicity material from Artservices, New York (1987).

[33] For instance, in Adams's case notes for the recording of *The Wound Dresser* and its 'Trickster' companion *Fearful Symmetries*, Nonesuch 7559–79218–2 (1990).

[34] G. McBurney, 'Schnittke and Stylistic Borrowing', programme book for the 1990 Huddersfield Contemporary Music Festival, p. 38.

[35] For instance, in Shnitke, 'Polystylistic tendencies in modern music', *Music in the USSR* (April/June 1988), 22–4.

[36] See, for example, the *Waltzes by 25 Contemporary Composers*, published by Peters Edition, 17 of which are recorded on Nonesuch D–79011 (1981). The American pianist Yvar Mikhashoff mounted an extensive 'Tango Project' in the mid-1980s.

[37] Quoted in the sleeve notes for the recording of *Seid nüchtern und Wachet* etc., BIS–CD–437 (1989).

[38] Programme note for the world première of the work, Royal Albert Hall, London, 22 August 1990.

[39] Quoted by A. Ivashkin in 'The Paradox of Russian Non-Liberty', a paper delivered at the Royal Musical Association Conference, 7 April 1991.

[40] D. Matthews, 'The Rehabilitation of the Vernacular', *Music and the Politics of Culture*, ed. C. Norris (London, 1989), 246–7.

[41] J. Cage, in *Skladateliske Sinteze Osamdesetih Godina/ Compositional Syntheses in the 1980s*, ed. M. Bozic and E. Sedak (Zagreb, 1986), 157.

[42] N. Kenyon, 'The age of refurbishment and the flop of the new', *The Observer* (24 Dec 1989), 33.

[43] F. Jameson, 'Periodizing the 60s', in *The 60s Without Apology*, ed. S. Sayres, A. Stephanson, S. Aronowitz and F. Jameson (Minneapolis, 1984), 205.

BIBLIOGRAPHICAL NOTE

The only music encyclopedia in English adequately to cover composition in the 'cultivated' tradition during the period with any thoroughness is *Contemporary Composers*, ed. B. Morton and P. Collins (London, 1992). *The New Grove* and some of its specialist successors – notably *The New Grove Dictionary of American Music* (see note 2) – are, however, useful.

Few histories of twentieth-century 'serious' music are sufficiently recent to be able to treat the last 25 years with any thoroughness. Two which do so are E. Salzman, *Twentieth-Century Music: an Introduction* (Englewood Cliffs, NJ, 3/1988) and R. P. Morgan, *Twentieth-Century Music: a History of Musical Style in Modern Europe and America* (New York, 1991); the latter's companion volume, *An Anthology of Twentieth-Century Music* (New York, 1992), contains extracts from five works of the period.

Even surveys of composition since 1945, whether general or specialized, are almost all too old now to be as up-to-date as the above, though P. Griffiths, *Modern Music: the Avant Garde since 1945* (London, 1981) is still useful on the 1970s as well as 1945–70. The revised edition of R. Smith Brindle's *The New Music* (London, 1988) has a final chapter, 'Conclusions – 1986', which ruminates on, rather than covers, developments since the book's first edition was published in 1975, and may interestingly be compared with the original final chapter, 'Conclusions – 1975', republished in the later edition.

More specialist books on the period include M. Nyman, *Experimental Music: Cage and Beyond* (London, 1974), C. Cardew, *Stockhausen Serves Imperialism* (London, 1974), and J. Rockwell, *All American Music: Composition in the Late Twentieth Century* (London, 1985). Collections of interviews include C. Gagne and T. Caras, *Soundpieces: Interviews with American Composers* (Metuchen, NJ, 1982) and P. Griffiths, *New Sounds, New Personalities: British Composers of the 1980s in Conversation* (London, 1985).

Milton Babbitt's own *Words about Music*, ed. S. Dembski and J. N. Straus (Madison, 1987) and Pierre Boulez's *Orientations*, ed. J.-J. Nattiez, trans. M. Cooper (London, 1986) are good. The best book on Boulez is *Pierre Boulez: a Symposium*, ed. W. Glock (London, 1986), though its publication was so long delayed that the core of the volume, S. Bradshaw's chapter on the instrumental and vocal music, written in 1975, had to be given a 1985 update. D. Schiff's *The Music of Elliott Carter* (London, 1983) is solid but already dated. D. Osmond-Smith's *Playing on Words: a Guide to Luciano Berio's 'Sinfonia'* (London, 1985) and *Berio* (Oxford, 1991) are excellent. The 1981 republication of R. Maconie, *The Works of Karlheinz Stockhausen* (London, 1976), is now dated, and the best collections of the composer's own writings and interviews deal with earlier work; this is also true for Carter and Xenakis.

D. Revill's *The Roaring Silence – John Cage: a Life* (London, 1992) is the most up-to-date and complete book on Cage's life and work. Most of the composer's seminal writings date from before the period, but the interviews with Daniel Charles entitled *For the Birds* (London, 1981) are especially relevant. Philip Glass's book on his operas, edited and with supplementary material by R. T. Jones and published in Britain as *Opera on the Beach: Philip Glass on his New World of Music Theatre* (London, 1988) is one of the very few reasonably up-to-date book-length studies in English of any composer under about 65 years old mentioned above. I have not listed here any other books already mentioned in footnotes.

Periodical literature, both specialist and popular, makes up the vast bulk of secondary source material on this area. Specialist journals to look out for in particular are the British *Contact*, *Contemporary Music Review* and *Tempo*, and the American *Perspectives of New Music*.

L.B. Meyer's *Music, the Arts, and Ideas: Patterns and Predictions in Twentieth-Century Culture* (Chicago, 1967) is, though dating from the very beginning of the period, a good way into the wider cultural issues now frequently assessed as 'postmodernist'. The literature on postmodernist music is so far weak, and the extensive literature on postmodernism in literature and philosophy sometimes daunting. M. Sarup's *An Introductory Guide to Post-Structuralism and Postmodernism* (London, 1988) is a useful start. Readers could also do worse than read Umberto Eco's novel *The Name of the Rose*, trans. W. Weaver (London, 1984), and its theoretical follow-up, *Postscript to The Name of the Rose*, also trans. Weaver (San Diego, CA, 1983–4), for some understanding of post-structuralist and post-modernist concerns.

Chapter XVI

Western Music in the Context of World Music

MICHAEL TENZER

Viewed from the West, the topography of late twentieth-century world music presents a teeming array of interlocking traditions and contexts. While the boundaries between musical traditions have never been fixed or impermeable, the political, scientific and social revolutions of this century have catalysed a remarkable process of diffusion and exchange that has fundamentally reshaped the sensibilities of those who make and listen to music everywhere.

The perception of musical cultures as interdependent is relatively new and has come about in the West only with the growing pains associated with a more relativistic view of culture. The universality of the musical language of the great eighteenth- and nineteenth-century Western composers, once held as an unassailable truth, emerges from more recent revisionist scrutiny as a regional dialect – one with far-reaching impact, to be sure, but none the less a product of the aesthetics of the Germanic culture in which it crystallized. Reflecting the relativistic tendencies evident in most areas of contemporary thought, musical cultures are now increasingly seen as interacting and in a constant state of flux, their identities determined by the particular requirements of the social groups from which they derive. The growth of anthropology and other social sciences has persuaded us of the validity of human realities other than our own, and this broadened outlook has enabled us to find meaning in the music of places formerly dismissed as remote and irrelevant.

A few examples will help set the stage for an examination of these developments as they have resounded in the music of performers and composers working in or influenced by the Western tradition, in all types of performance contexts throughout the world.

In the early 1970s, the prominent North Indian *sitarist* Ravi Shankar was riding a wave of popularity in the West (even the Beatles showed a passing interest in Indian music). He released three notable recordings about this time. In one, *East Meets West*, he joined forces with the American violinist Yehudi Menuhin to play traditional North Indian music. A second record, *East Greets East*, featured Shankar performing with traditional Japanese musicians in less conventional music. Finally, Shankar's own *Concerto* for sitar and orchestra was recorded with the London Symphony Orchestra. The accompaniment to Shankar's virtuoso playing was mostly perfunctory, emphasizing the tonic drone that supports all Indian music.

I Ching for solo percussionist (1982), by the Danish composer Per Norgard (*b* 1932), has a first movement that reveals marked similarities with percussion music from Guinea as recorded by the National Percussion ensemble of that country. Both are highly dynamic and polyrhythmic. While the Norgard piece moves from one section and timbre to another at a faster rate than do the African musicians, the difference is merely one of degree, whereas the rhythm-to-rhythm continuities are remarkably alike.

In February 1992 the Kronos Quartet, specialists in the twentieth-century string quartet repertory and commissioners of new music, gave the première of a work by the composer Jin Hi Kim in New York. Kim, a Korean émigré to the USA, performed her music with the quartet on the *komungo*, a traditional Korean zither with nine silk strings. Apart from the unusual timbre of the added instrument, the music sounded much as though it had been written in the 1960s by a composer of the 'cluster' school, typified by Penderecki, though Kim's music was somewhat slower and more delicate.

These vignettes illustrate some of the types of cross-cultural musical encounters that are commonplace in the West. That non-Western music is no longer a fringe element in our culture represents a significant turn, especially when one considers how recently such music was classified simply as exoticism. Still, for all the novelty and excitement that these performances stimulate, it is difficult to assess their ultimate role in our culture. It is more appropriate to note that, taken together as a phenomenon, they raise many fascinating questions. Is this music a harbinger of a new global culture in which the idiosyncratic elements of various musical traditions are subsumed in a new syncretic result? Can listeners adequately assimilate such a hodgepodge of multicultural sounds? In search of answers to these and related questions, this chapter considers the phenomenon of Western music's broadening interface with the rest of world music, arguably the most important and characteristic musical development of the past quarter-century.

CROSS-CULTURAL FACTORS

The familiar elements of mainstream Western music continue to thrive in our time, but they have made room for an array of new styles and contexts. Music's fundamental identity, once characterizable by reference to a discrete group of genres, styles and instruments, has broadened markedly under the impact of these insurgent influences. The presence of so many kinds of music in our cultural milieu is a consequence of the broad technological and social changes of recent decades, which have brought people and ideas of disparate origins into proximity on an unprecedented scale. In response, the tradition has transformed itself rapidly and continually to meet the changing aesthetic needs of Westerners and to reflect their growing diversity.

In previous eras, music developed largely along a single path on which styles and techniques were formed, were explored exhaustively, and were ultimately supplanted by newer ones. Today this unidirectional metaphor is inadequate. Many compositional models now co-exist harmoniously, allowing composers to pick and choose among them, combining them in whatever ways their imaginations suggest. The dozens of current musical genres and subgenres are characterized by their mutability and close interchanges. Composers allying themselves with a particular aesthetic may abandon it for another, shifting from style to style over a short period, or they may remain in a distinctive niche that blends many influences. A figure such as the Estonian Arvo Pärt, whose compositions emulate the austerity of pre-Renaissance sacred music, shares a close affinity with minimalism as it developed in America during the 1960s (see pp. 342, 371). The way the connection between these two tendencies cuts across temporal and cultural boundaries marks it as distinctly of our era. Similarly, the Frenchman Gérard Grisey (*b* 1946), writing in an essentially traditional manner for orchestral and chamber ensembles, explores harmonic series and difference tones, incorporating research on acoustics and sound design from the domain of digital technology; but his music is also dependent on new virtuoso timbral possibilities developed on traditional instruments. Like Pärt's, his music represents a confluence of disparate paths.

Composers may be eclectic in their juxtaposition of the music of past eras, such as George Rochberg or Alfred Shnitke. The overt political content of Frederic Rzewski's music finds expression in a variety of styles ranging from the romantic tonality of *The People United Will Never Be Defeated!*, a set of piano variations based on a Chilean protest song (see p. 369), to the bald minimalism of *Coming Together*, an ensemble piece structured round the repeated recitation of an inspirational letter from a prison inmate. Louis Andreissen and David Lang (*b* 1957) have drawn heavily on popular music and both, in addition to writing concert music, have composed and arranged for rock bands. With the influx of ideas from popular music has come a propensity for mixed-media performance: the composer and performance artist Laurie Anderson is representative, as is the videographer Nam June Paik. Visual arts have also figured in the video operas of Robert Ashley, an alumnus of the 1960s experimental music movement. Other postmodern experimentalists include Alvin Lucier, whose recent works rely in part on the amplification of brain waves.

To these examples would have to be added many others to give an adequate picture of the stylistic pluralism of current Western music. Borrowing from the repertory of tonal music (in some cases quoting from famous works), serialism and 'free' atonality, ultra-complex music, music of reduced means, computer music, collaborations with artists from dance or the plastic arts, aleatoricism, improvised music and jazz, amplified instruments and instrumentations derived from rock music – all are accepted modes of composition viable in the West. And a single composer is likely to write music falling into more than one of these categories.

One of the most prominent components of this diversity is an interest in the sounds, techniques and instruments of non-Western music. Today almost no composer is indifferent to the impact of such music, though responses are as broad and divergent as the variety of the musics themselves. The nature of the contact with non-Western material varies greatly, and may range from the most superficial acquaintance through recordings or performances by non-Western musicians in the West to a deep and abiding interest leading to intensive study. The types of influences are no less multitudinous; anything can be found, from the borrowing of a scale or sonority to the wholesale appropriation of instruments or compositional genres.

Those affected have ranged from figures such as Olivier Messiaen, who used Hindu rhythms in his music after he was introduced to them during his student days at the Paris Conservatoire, to younger composers like the South African Kevin Volans (*b* 1949) or the Spanish-born José Evangelista (*b* 1943), resident in Canada. Volans has set out an elaborate musical response to African music of the Transvaal in a series of compositions entitled *White Man Sleeps*; Evangelista has evinced a strong fascination with the monodic aspects of Burmese and Indonesian music in works such as *Clos de vie*. The trend has been especially marked in the USA, where throughout the twentieth century composers have been more inclined to view European cultural currents as but one stream among many. California, facing east to Asia, has been home to many important figures associated with non-Western traditions, among them Henry Cowell, John Cage, Harry Partch and Lou Harrison, as well as younger composers like Daniel Lentz and Paul Dresher.

Even Messiaen's students Boulez and Stockhausen, both seminal figures in the world of 'pure' music and post-Webernian serialism, have not avoided contact with foreign musics. Boulez's *Le marteau sans maître*, with its attention to sonority and emphasis on percussion (especially the fluid, chime-like timbre of the vibraphone, which hints at a connection with the metallophones of Indonesian gamelan ensembles) betrays at the very least an awareness of non-Western modes of musical organization.[1] Stockhausen has composed a series of works overtly associated with non-Western music, including the extended vocal piece *Stimmung* (1968) and the tape collage *Telemusik* (1974).

In generalizing about the traits of non-Western musics that have appealed to composers, it is important to clarify that there are few, if any, pan-cultural attributes binding all non-Western musics together that set them apart as a group from Western music. All are distinctive and rich on their own terms. None the less, those that have had the most pronounced impact – mostly the more developed traditions of Africa and Asia – share some qualities that, particularly from the standpoint of a Western novice, contrast vividly with Western music. Foremost among these is a non-linear, less directional idea of musical time. Such music generally adheres to a cyclic, repetitive background structure as opposed to the large-scale, organically developed forms of the West. Within such constraints, these musics tend to accentuate other components that are less fully developed in Western music: for instance, the layering of complex rhythmic and melodic patterns heard in shifting relationship to background pulsation, the stratification of simultaneous rhythmic and melodic elements all derived from or related to a single source, and a close attention to sonority and the sculpting of individual notes.

The influence of world music has extended beyond the adoption of technical attributes; the instruments on which music is played and the formats and contexts in which it is heard have also been transformed. As noted, a Korean *komungo* or Indian sitar may be included as a soloist with a Western orchestra or chamber ensemble, but it is equally likely that entire ensembles of non-Western instruments will be used in a composition. Lou Harrison's many compositions for gamelan, Stockhausen's and Takemitsu's music for the Japanese *gagaku* ensemble, and in particular Partch's music for his collection of invented instruments, some based on Asian and African models, are noteworthy examples. For both Harrison and Partch (as well as for Partch's students Ben Johnston and Dean Drummond) an inseparable part of this interest concerns the exploration of new tunings and intonations, based on a belief that Western music embarked on a disastrous course when it adopted the equal-tempered system. Most of the tuning ratios these composers use are variants on the just intonation scales. Although once common in Western music, such scales are now explored partly because of exposure to Indonesian gamelans, which are notable for their invariable tunings and unusual, non-standardized intervals.[2]

Partch found the functional connection between music and ritual, still evident in many non-Western civilizations but largely abandoned in the West, to be particularly compelling. Some of his later works,

Harry Partch with his gourd tree and cone gongs.

notably *Delusion of the Fury* (1967), required the performers to undertake multiple roles as musicians, dancers and actors in a kind of total theatrical experience. The highly stylized action was based on a combination of Asian and African elements. Stockhausen's *Stimmung* (1968) tries to evoke a trance-like mode of concentration with its pure vocal sonorities and the chanting of the names of deities from world religions (see p. 364). La Monte Young's formative influence on the minimalist movement was shaped by his perception that non-Western musical elements are static and could, if listened to long enough, induce altered states of consciousness. These composers and others like them share a yearning for spiritual transformation through music; their assumption that such experiences are embedded in the sound materials of non-Western cultures is indicative of the intensity of the search for musical meaning in pluralistic times.

Taken together, these musical and contextual factors have helped to reshape our musical institutions. Concerts of contemporary music today are often richly multicultural, containing various combinations of non-Western ideas, instruments or performance practice. The cultural life of major cities throughout the Western world also features many concerts devoted exclusively to non-Western music, some performed by Westerners who have studied and become expert in the music themselves, others by touring troupes from around the world (underwritten by presenters confident in the music's appeal to a broad audience). Imaginative cross-cultural fusions abound. The spring 1991 season in New York City featured a concert by the avant-gardist John Zorn entitled 'New Traditions in East Asian Bar Bands', a fanciful combination of Asian popular music with minimalism and performance art; and 'Sunda Swing', the pianist David Lopato's synthesis of postmodern, small-group jazz with elements of West Javanese (Sundanese) gamelan music.

Cultural exchange is no less apparent moving in the other direction. Singapore, Manila and Hong Kong have permanent symphony orchestras that attract international soloists; Kuala Lumpur, Malaysia, supports a fine Baroque ensemble; and a full performance of Mozart's *Così fan tutte* was staged in Jakarta in 1987 using an all-Indonesian cast. In conjunction with such developments, composers anywhere in the world may adopt Western music as their own language. Here Japan has been at the forefront, since Western music education has been a part of musical life there for over a century. Few countries are without composers working in a Western manner, and in some cases they bring a distinctive foreign perspective, derived from their own nation's music, to bear on their work. In Brazil, Marlos Nobre's *Yanomani* for chorus and guitar (1980) was based on the composer's explorations of the Amazon river home of this Indian tribe. The compositions of the Philippino Jose Maceda (*b* 1917) use the instruments of the traditional *kulintang* ensemble in a Western context.

As Western art music's domain expands around the world it engages in cross-fertilization with other cultures, both affecting and being affected by them but in very few cases supplanting them. Yet it is not simply Western music's identity that is changing. Many non-Western traditional musics are undergoing a similar process of expansion, while others are either holding their own, adapting or losing ground to the pressures of modernization. Popular music of all kinds and from all places encircles the globe at a pace that can barely keep up with the appetites of its listeners. Indian film music, one of the most influential kinds of popular music in the world, brims with eclectic borrowings, while Chinese communities living outside Jakarta, in an outrageously inspired mix, incorporate jazz trumpet styles and Hawaiian pedal-steel guitars into their traditional music (already a rich combination of Indonesian and Chinese elements). These are but two examples demonstrating that pluralism is a pan-cultural phenomenon affecting cultures everywhere.

Such multi-directional diffusions of music beyond previously acknowledged boundaries make it difficult to pin down Western music's current identity with any precision. It is no longer limited to the achievements of past Western composers, nor is it exclusively composed and performed by Westerners. It has become part of a global musical culture, developing alongside others in a symbiosis characterized by continual exchange.

THE GROWTH OF PLURALISM

The elements accounting for these cultural interactions are many, but changes in demography and technology are perhaps the most important. The collapse of colonialism scattered indigenous communities. The repressive periods before and after Russia's 1917 revolution, the decline of the British and other European empires, and the often bloody emergence of independent states in Africa and Asia created a massive flow of refugees and émigrés. This trend has not abated but has continued in the aftermath of regional conflicts involving Western powers, and with the rise of poverty and internecine strife in many countries.[3]

With these great new waves of resettlement come the strains of musical cultures transplanted to their new homes. Across the world immigrants practise their own music, be they Cambodians in California, Indians in Great Britain, or Armenians in Canada. Slowly but surely their music becomes part of the cultural life of their adopted communities, changing gradually to meet the cultural needs of succeeding generations as they assimilate. Regional musics now compete for prestige alongside the traditional institutions of Western music, as localities everywhere celebrate the ethnic diversity of their populations.

The importance of technology has been even more dramatic. Today far more music is heard recorded than played by live musicians. Recording technology, in the space of slightly more than a century, has transformed music from an exclusively social, or ritual, performance-orientated event into a hard commodity. A 'music industry' makes music of all times and places available on demand to interested listeners.[4] This has had the effect of expanding the amount and variety of music encountered, as well as irrevocably altering the way listeners relate to it. Music has become a 'thing' more than an experience, emanating ubiquitously from speakers in restaurants and lifts (elevators), in phone-message machines, and so on.

Recording and communications technology, linking remote eras and places, has flattened our perceptions of time and distance. Western musical identities have been thoroughly transformed by the ease of access to music as diverse as Australian Aboriginal songs, Beethoven symphonies and Gregorian chant, all available under the roof of a single shop. For the composer of today, inundated with all music, that of Beethoven is not necessarily more familiar than the isorhythmic motets of the Ars Nova school of fourteenth-century France, or the composer Mutthuswamy Dikshitar's *kritis* from eighteenth-century South India, or the *chimurenga* songs of the contemporary Zimbabwean musician Thomas Mapfumo. Such a composer may have an affinity for the dissonant, multi-part singing of a Bulgarian choir or for the recent works of the American composer Elliott Carter, but he or she is able to know them equally well.

The incipient stages of these processes can be traced to the turn of the century when these technological and demographic revolutions began to gather force. This was indeed a crucial time for musicians in the West, for reasons involving both the extraordinary power and influence of Germanic culture and the inexorable changes overtaking the forms and materials of music. The unshakeable musical hegemony of the Teutonic style as exemplified by Beethoven and Wagner had become objectionable to many by the end of the nineteenth century. Composers in other Western countries often saw themselves as an embattled minority struggling to maintain recognition for the importance of their music. In Italy, Verdi cried out against the oppressiveness of the situation: 'This highly artificial art [German music], often odd by intention, is not suited to our nature . . . we cannot believe in the eccentricities of a foreign art that is lacking in naturalness or simplicity.'[5]

The death knell of traditional tonality was sounded, precipitating a crisis of identity. It was not just functional harmony that had exhausted its usefulness but also the formal and contrapuntal systems that had grown up with it. The atonal and dodecaphonic principles crafted by the Second Viennese School, touted by their creators as the single logical way to preserve the purity of Western music, was one direction taken. But for many other composers the issue of what material and techniques should be used was open. Some continued to write in a more or less traditional manner, some embraced futurism and the machine age, and some continued to promote nationalism. But many were spurred by the stimulus of contact with non-Western musical systems, which by the end of the century were already becoming a significant part of cultural life. These factors set the stage for a race for musical alternatives that characterized the period before World War I.

CROSS-CULTURAL INFLUENCES UNTIL THE MID-TWENTIETH CENTURY

The proliferation of non-Western influences on early twentieth-century Western music forms a continuity with similar tendencies that had been present for hundreds of years on a much smaller and more restricted scale. The earliest significant contact with oriental peoples and ways of life dates to the Age of Discovery; but although non-Western music is occasionally mentioned in the diaries and logs of explorers, it had no impact on European music of the time. The first substantial interaction came in the seventeenth century, when the influence of the Ottoman Empire's reed, drum and cymbal Janissary bands was felt throughout Europe. One of their lasting impacts was to provide European composers with a foreign music to caricature, thereby introducing a model for the 'exotic' in Western music.[6] Lully exploited the potential of Turkish music with derisive comic effect in his incidental music for Molière's *Le bourgeois gentilhomme*, wherein the Turks are mocked as pathetic, ignorant buffoons. Turkish affect, with its easily recognizable pompous marches and minor-mode chromaticism, was an important resource for composers throughout the classical era. Mozart took delight in deploying it, most famously in the A minor Sonata, K331, and in *Die Entführung aus dem Serail*; Beethoven inserted a Turkish march in *Die Ruinen von Athen*. In addition, the influence of Turkish percussion was felt through the adoption of the timpani as a standard orchestral instrument.[7]

Cross-cultural influence later in the nineteenth century was mostly an aspect of musical nationalism. Folksongs were harmonized and given symphonic treatment by composers throughout Europe, Russia and America as regional Western cultures strove to accentuate their differences with German music. Liszt's lifelong interest in the music of the Hungarian gypsies led to the publication of a book on the subject (*Des bohémiens et leur musique en Hongrie*, 1859). The composer's own Hungarian background was a motivating factor, as was a faith in the gypsies' innate, 'pure' musical expression, which corroborated Liszt's belief that the natural power of music was enhanced when freed from the refining influences of civilization. In numerous works, particularly the *Hungarian Rhapsodies*, Liszt mimicked the tremolos of the gypsy cimbalom (hammered dulcimer) with fluttering chords, and used gypsy scales and quotations from popular songs.

Gypsy and other European folk music shared relative proximity to Europe's cultural centres and were readily adaptable to the Romantic musical style and aesthetic. African and oriental music, on the other hand, though more influential in later music, was largely unknown until close to the turn of the century, apart from occasional descriptions in the journals and publications of early ethnographers. Then, in 1889, an Annamite (Vietnamese) theatre group and a Javanese gamelan and dance troupe were brought to the sprawling Exposition Universelle in Paris, creating a stir. Debussy went repeatedly to the exhibition, and for the rest of his life praised the sophistication and elegance of Javanese music.[8] The critics Julien Tiersot and Arthur Pougin also published extensive articles on Javanese music in *Le ménestrel*, and for a time the Javanese were a sensation.

It is difficult to assess precisely what influence the music of the gamelan had on Debussy.[9] There is a certain compatibility between the multi-tiered orchestration in his music and the heterophonic stratification of musical parts in Javanese music. Passages in *Sirènes* (the third of the three *Nocturnes*) or *La mer* feature rippling ornamentation similar to the kind played by the Javanese *gambang* (bamboo xylophone) or *celempung* (zither). There is also some similarity between Debussy's approach to metre and rhythm, which allowed for a new sense of life and detail in the subdivisions of the beat, and the Javanese principles of *irama*, or layers of tempo and density relationships. No doubt the gamelan's unusual tunings resonated for Debussy, who had already used pentatonic, octatonic and whole-tone scales. Pentatonicism had been an element of his style as far back as the songs of the early 1880s. But these are all general characteristics, and none would have required more than a passing familiarity with the gamelan. None the less, Debussy's encounter with Javanese music has for many years been considered a watershed event in the West's growing fascination with Eastern music.

For the Hungarian Bartók, the 'exotic' was in his own backyard. With his colleague Kodály, he saw a way of freeing music from the Germanic stronghold through the investigation and assimilation of the music of eastern European peoples. Although Bartók was sympathetic to Liszt's interest in the gypsies, he realized that his predecessor had been mistaken in claiming that their nomadic, urban culture was the source of authentic Hungarian music, asserting instead that the true folk music of the region was found in villages among peasants.

Bartók's documentation of this music helped establish the fledgling field of ethnomusicology. He recorded and transcribed thousands of songs during the first three decades of the century, writing and lecturing widely about his research. For Bartók, however, the most important aspect of this work was the way it influenced his own style of composition. His contact with the music was considerably more conscious and thorough than had been Debussy's with the gamelan; and from the beginning he set out to create a new style based on a marriage of Western music to the traditions of his folk informants, which he considered to be his own true heritage. Thus, in an important sense, Bartók expanded the Western tradition not by looking outside it for stimulus or perspective, but by widening its perimeter to include what he viewed as his own tradition. In his work the modal scale forms, irregular metres and additive rhythms of his homeland blend with the most modern timbral, formal and tonal gestures of Western art music in a seamless reconciliation, so that it is impossible to separate its components. Bartók's compositions comprise a 'play of overlapping forces, fading gradually into infinity',[10] thereby helping symbolically to open the doors of Western music to outsiders.

Folk music was also important for Stravinsky, particularly before his neo-classical period. From *Petrushka* and *The Rite of Spring* to *Les Noces* and *Mavra*, traditional Russian melodies appear in various stages of assimilation, forming an important component of his primitivist style. Stravinsky rarely revealed the sources of his borrowings, and, unlike his contemporary Bartók, did not engage in collecting.[11] It has been demonstrated that many of his melodies were taken from existing compendiums, which suffered from inaccuracies and adulterations typical of such early 'Westernized' collections. Stravinsky later disavowed his interest in folk music, even going so far as to deride Bartók's attraction to it.[12]

Later European composers, including Jolivet, Messiaen, Milhaud and Britten, continued on the paths forged by Debussy and Bartók. In America, where the sense of being outside the mainstream was even more pronounced, composers felt a greater need to define their separateness from the dominating German traditions of the nineteenth century.[13] Charles Ives, an early exemplar of American musical individualism, blatantly cast off the conservative practices of his teachers and made use of indigenous hymns, folktunes, ragtime and jazz. Edgard Varèse, an immigrant in 1915, used many Latin American percussion instruments, notably in the purely percussive *Ionisation* (1931) and in other works of the 1920s and 30s.

A more conspicuous figure was Henry Cowell (1897–1965), who grew up in San Francisco and considered the Irish folktunes and Chinese music that he heard there in his childhood were more 'his' than European music. He composed with an eclectic mix of material, drawing upon as wide a range of music as he could. In 1931 he spent a year studying in Berlin with the ethnomusicologist Erich von Hornbostel, the South Indian musicologist Sambamoorthy and the Javanese musician Jodjhana, and later he travelled to Asia and the Near East, lecturing and studying the local music. In addition to overseeing the production of a series of Folkways records entitled 'Music of the World's Peoples', he published books and journals, promoted concerts of new music by American composers and presented a weekly radio programme in New York that broadcast non-Western music. He was, in short, a vigorous promulgator of an all-inclusive approach.

With Cowell as their guide, many other American composers turned away from Europe. A few examples will suffice. Colin McPhee (1901–64) went to Bali to study gamelan music, with profound consequences for his own work. Harry Partch, Lou Harrison and John Cage experimented with tuning systems and built instruments reminiscent of Asian and African models. Cage used static, cyclic forms similar to Indian *tālā*, or rhythmic cycles, in his percussion pieces. Later the philosophy of Zen Buddhism, particularly as expressed through the teachings and writings of D. T. Suzuki, influenced his aesthetic of indeterminacy.

By the middle of the century, the situation becomes far too complex to isolate non-Western influences on individual composers. In fact, composers unaffected by cross-cultural change were distinctly in the minority.[14] The social and technological forces discussed earlier began, in the years after World War II, to diminish the predictive effect of national origin. As the boundaries of the tradition widened, the music of composers was no longer shaped exclusively by the central European legacy but increasingly by the particular combination of influences that affected each individual musician.

REPRESENTATIVE WESTERN COMPOSITIONS

Diversity and the process of constant redefinition are qualities that especially apply to the Western music of our era, just as specifically technical or contextual traits defined it in the past. This is not to say that the meaning or relevance of the traditional genres and techniques of the mainstream European tradition have lost their potency; on the contrary, they have broadened their appeal. But the context for Western music has broadened even more, so that traditional art music speaks to a proportionately smaller segment of the total audience.

Most composers who work with non-Western elements nevertheless point out that such influences form only part of the picture. This is reflected in five works ranging in date from 1962 to 1990 which are discussed below, and which, viewed collectively, offer an indication of the diversity of late twentieth-century music and the complexity of its intracultural features. Two are for 'traditional' instruments, two for percussion ensembles and one uses a mixed group designed to imitate specific non-Western instruments. One composer is Hungarian, one American, one French, one Cambodian, while one piece is a collaboration between an American and a Balinese. Such a motley collection would be inconceivable to a late nineteenth-century European musician, as would the social and technological changes that have made possible their classification under the same cultural umbrella. The five are representative, particularly because the various elements conflated in their music derive from separate spheres of musical life. Yet the influences have merged in such a way as to belie their origins, giving rise to a kind of 'meta-style'.

Messiaen: *Sept Haikai* (fourth movement)

The diverse influences assimilated in the later compositions of Olivier Messiaen (1908–92) include birdsong, archaic Greek and Hindu rhythms, kinaesthetic associations of colours with harmonic and orchestrational complexes, and imagery drawn from Christian mysticism. Their combination results in an elaborate, individual sound-world distanced from conventional approaches to form and rhythm. In accordance with his stated religious concerns, Messiaen's compositions move through a seemingly timeless state of suspension, achieved through the superimposition of many layers of additive rhythms. The layering of strata in static relation to one another recalls the cyclic construction of many Asian musical systems, though in Messiaen there is no repeating background structure. The through-composed, large-scale continuity often leaves the impression that the music begins and ends at arbitrary points, as though the listener is offered a segment of a natural musical progression extending beyond the boundaries of the work.

Messiaen's *Sept Haikai* was written in 1962 after he returned from a trip to Japan. The fourth movement, 'Gagaku', convincingly evokes the music of the imperial Japanese court orchestra of that name. A trio consisting of trumpet, english horn and oboe mimics the sound of the *hichiriki*, a Japanese reed instrument that carries the main melody in the original; a pairing of piccolo and E♭ clarinet plays the part of the *ryuteki*, a flute-like instrument that carries a secondary melody; an octet of violins playing sustained chords *sul ponticello* imitates the *sho*, a bamboo mouth organ; and a collection of cymbals, bells and gongs performs the role of Japanese drums. The textures, melodies and stately pace of the music render a superb approximation of the sound of the Japanese ensemble.

While shaped in homage to its model, this movement of *Sept Haikai* nevertheless remains a Western work, inimitably the composer's in conception and execution. The melodies use the full twelve-note chromatic as opposed to the more confined modal scope of Japanese pitch materials, although they do carve out contours like those typical of the *hichiriki* and *ryuteki*. The violin chords are limited in number (an authentic touch, because the *sho* has only eleven chords in its repertory) but are deployed in unpredictable order and according to complex rhythmic calculations. The percussion parts do not set up a distinct metric plan, as would the Japanese drums, but move against the rest of the ensemble, setting up their own layer of sound. What is perhaps most different, however, is the absence in performance of the stately demeanour of the traditional Japanese musicians as they sit in costume in the music building of the Imperial Palace, where for over 1200 years the austere music of the *gagaku* ensemble has filled the air. No doubt it was never Messiaen's idea to write anything other than a personal work; none the less the transformations of the materials and contexts of Japanese music as they passed through the composer's imagination and into the Western concert hall effectively illustrate the compromising effects of cross-cultural process.

Reich: *Drumming*

Steve Reich (*b* 1936) is known as one of the leading members of the 'minimalist' or 'modal pulse' group of composers that came to prominence during the 1970s. In 1970 he realized a longstanding ambition to study music in Ghana, about which he wrote: 'I was overwhelmed by their music, like being in front of a tidal wave, and there I was, just me, with several thousand years of a whole continent's music washing over me. I found myself wondering where, as a composer, my studies were taking me.'[15] After a period studying gamelan music with the Balinese teacher Nyoman Sumandhi at a university summer programme in the USA, he commented: 'I studied Balinese and African music because I love them, and also because I believe that non-Western music is presently the single most important source of new ideas for Western composers and musicians'.[16]

In *Drumming* (1971) we can observe the effects of the peculiar kindred relation between the phase shiftings of tape loops, a process Reich had developed in the late 1960s, and the cyclic structures that underpin Ghanaian drumming. The piece, for a large ensemble of percussionists and singers, uses a repeating 12/8 rhythmic cycle that bears a conspicuous resemblance to the African rhythms Reich absorbed, particularly those of the Ewe tribe's dance 'Agbadza'. In this dance, a polyrhythmic choir of drums and bells plays rhythms in a cycle of 12 pulses that, especially for the novice listener, present a special aural illusion. Depending on what one listens to, the phrase may be variously analysed as four groups of three, three groups of four, or six groups of two. Every time drums in the ensemble change their patterns – which is not often – they do so in response to a command from the lead drummer.

The surface rhythms of Reich's music, strongly African in derivation, produce the same possibilities of multiple perspectives perceptible in a single metric framework. But instead of calling for drastic changes analogous to those imposed by the lead drummer in Ghana, Reich opts for smooth, gradual addition and subtraction of sounds, or for the monitored shifting of phase relationships. This is comparable to his earlier tape pieces, in which two loops of slightly different lengths start up in synchrony and gradually shift out of alignment. In *Drumming* these African and electronic influences are thoroughly blended.

A significant additional non-Western influence on Reich was contextual, not musical. Part of the reason that he abandoned tape music was his dissatisfaction with the performance possibilities it offered. Responding to the group effort and ensemble cohesion of Ghanaian and Balinese music, he formed his own ensemble to emulate these ideals. The great popular success of this group catapulted him to near cult-status in America and Europe. For a time, Reich was one of the best-known Western composers, functioning in a milieu that had previously been largely reserved for pop stars. His appeal blurred cultural and class divisions, as did the content of his music.

Ligeti: *Piano Etude no. 6*

In the mid-1980s, after a brief but conspicuous absence from public life, György Ligeti (*b* 1923) came forward with several new works, among them a set of six *Etudes* for piano. During his self-imposed 'hibernation' Ligeti had made two fascinating discoveries: the polyrhythmic, polytemporal player-piano music of Conlon Nancarrow and the music of the Central African Republic. Of Nancarrow, Ligeti remarked: 'The music is the greatest discovery since Webern and Ives . . . something great and important for all of music history! . . . for me, it's the best music of any composer living today'.[17]

As for the African music, which he encountered through the recordings of the ethnomusicologist Simha Arom, he noted the paradoxical way in which unchanging rhythmic patterns are layered to achieve a whole that is considerably more than the sum of its parts:

> Undoubtedly my interest in the music Arom has recorded stems from the proximity I feel exists between it and my own way of thinking with regards to composition: that is, the creation of structures which are both remarkably simple and highly complex . . . What we can witness in this music is a wonderful combination of order and disorder which in turn merges together to produce a sense of order on a higher level.[18]

Ligeti's earlier styles, like Reich's, were influenced by technology. The orchestral textures in his best-known works of the previous decades evinced a preference for massive sound aggregates not unlike those found in electronic music. At the same time Ligeti exploited more traditional polyphonic techniques, using them to build up, part by part, the dense clouds of texture that characterized his style.

In the sixth *Etude*, 'Autômne à Varsovie' ('Autumn in Warsaw', 1985), Ligeti's concern with polyphony re-emerges in full focus, sharply drawn out by the crisp timbre of the piano. In imitative, stratified succession, gently descending chromatic voices are layered against a relentless semiquaver pulse that recalls the cyclicity of African music. The illusion of multiple tempos is strengthened by associating the lines with unchanging groups of pulses. At a given moment one line may move once every three pulses, another every four, and perhaps still another every seven. This is reminiscent of Nancarrow's technique of juxtaposing canonic voices at different tempos in his player-piano pieces, but Ligeti differs in that the *Etude* is played by a human performer, and in that its tempos are subsumed under the constant background pulse. This result, true to Ligeti's description of African music, is at once 'remarkably simple' in its constituent components, yet 'highly complex' in its superstructure.

It would be rash to give disproportionate attention to the influence of Ligeti's later interests. They are simply new layers added to an already complex stylistic base. Yet it is interesting, as with Reich, to note the strange compatibility between African concepts and those associated with electronic music. The non-Western influence provides another component to Ligeti's musical personality, merging with the others to produce a new 'order on a higher level'. This process mirrors those aspects of African music to which Ligeti was originally drawn.[19]

Chinary Ung: *Khse Buon*

Chinary Ung emigrated to the USA from Cambodia in 1964 to study music and held a series of teaching posts since receiving his DMA from Columbia University. An accomplished performer on native instruments, he directs an ensemble devoted to performing traditional Cambodian music. Ung's earliest pieces situated his music firmly within the conservative American academic style of the 1970s, demonstrating a thorough command of its representative gestural language. A special interest was also the exploration of new timbral possibilities with traditional instruments and a concern for economy of means and materials.

In *Khse Buon* (1980) for solo cello (its Khmer title means 'strings four', referring to the four strings of the cello) those tendencies are developed and combined with a reduced pitch field to create music strongly redolent of many Asian traditions. The cellist is asked to 'bend' pizzicato notes by applying pressure to the strings with the left hand in the manner of the plucked instruments of India and to execute long, slow glissandos to and from non-tempered pitches, thereby suggesting alternative tuning systems. The melodic materials are often limited to a group of pentatonic scales made up of unequal intervals that resemble tunings found throughout south-east Asia. Rhythm is largely unmeasured, frequently swaying in a chant-like manner against a drone provided by an open string, sustained as a double stop.

From another perspective, however, there is nothing explicitly 'Asian' about the music. Extended timbral possibilities were explored by many composers during the 1970s and 80s, and though non-traditional tunings and modes may partly owe their presence to the influence of other cultures, they have been used by many Western composers for some time, so Ung's interest in them does not mark him in any distinct way. Moreover, the success of the composition as a whole lies largely in the deployment of its subtly organic dramatic curve, which is entirely Western in conception.

Khse buon, then, does not necessarily reveal the heritage of its creator; it could well have been written by a composer from anywhere in the world. Even though Ung's Cambodian origins can be said to have had an impact on his compositional voice, there is nothing irreducibly Cambodian about his music. Western music had already absorbed and processed many elements of south-east Asian music long before Ung began composing and was therefore able to provide a hospitable cultural context for his aesthetic concerns. None the less, the very fact of his presence, with his considerable prestige, emphasizes anew the capacity of current Western music to offer a meaningful forum for composers from all places and traditions.

Nyoman Windha and Evan Ziporyn: *Kekembangan*

The unique collaboration of Nyoman Windha (*b* 1956) and Evan Ziporyn (*b* 1959) owes its existence to Sekar Jaya, a California-based organization of Americans that has been active from 1979 performing a virtuoso, modern style of Balinese gamelan music called Gong Kebyar. Windha, a renowned and prolific composer in his native Bali, skilled at all instruments of the ensemble and fluent in a wide repertory, was for a time artistic director-in-residence of the group. Ziporyn, one of the group's most practised members, is an American with a full academic training in Western music. He is an accomplished jazz musician and performs internationally as a composer and clarinettist. For six months in 1981 and a year in 1987 he studied music in Bali, travelling as well through Africa to learn about music there.

Balinese music was a common language for the two collaborators, but for both the contexts were utterly new. As one of the few Balinese to create music for a group of comparatively expert foreigners, Windha belongs to a small but significant côterie of traditional musicians from non-Western cultures who have found a professional role in Western musical contexts. (Others are the Indian drummer Trichy Sankaran, who lives in Toronto and performs with new-music ensembles and computer musicians, and the Korean *komungo* player Jin Hi Kim mentioned at the beginning of the chapter.)

Balinese music is thoroughly worked out by its composer(s) and memorized by the performers note for note; there is no improvisation. In *Kekembangan* ('Flowering'), for Balinese gamelan and saxophone quartet (1990), the challenge for Ziporyn was to take the music that Windha had composed for the gamelan, which was essentially traditional in form and content, and add to it music in a polyphonic style suited to the saxophone quartet. By virtue of their wide dynamic range, the saxophones compete effectively with the intense bronze reverberations of the Balinese ensemble, though the achievement of a blend in tuning and overall character was a challenge requiring innovatory solutions. In many cases the decision was made not to attempt a blend at all, but simply to let the two musics clash.

The finished piece is riveting and devoid of obvious precedent. To a

Performance of 'Kekembangan' (1990) for Balinese gamelan and saxophone quartet by Nyoman Windha (drummer on the right) and Evan Ziporyn (tenor saxophone).

Western audience it may sound like a bizarre jazz *étude* with tuned percussion accompaniment, whereas to a Balinese one it might sound like traditional music with a disconnected, experimental melodic overlay. One wonders for whom such music is intended. Ziporyn offers an explanation:

> After years of study, I finally felt it necessary to stop thinking of Balinese music as *Balinese* music, and to begin thinking of it as *music* – one genre among many, one I happened to know pretty well. By working in this way, it is possible to make a new music which ideally can speak to people in several traditions, saying different but comprehensible things to all of them. In other words, the task as I see it is precisely *not* to achieve cross-cultural understanding, but to make a music that is happy to be different things to different people.

Windha is considerably more laconic: 'It was a good experience working with an American composer. I hope that there will be many opportunities to do so again'.[20]

TOWARDS THE NEW MILLENNIUM

This chapter has generally focussed on the music of Westerners. Yet it is arbitrary to divide the world between 'Western' and 'non-Western', between 'us' and 'them'. We could just as indiscriminately divide music between 'Eastern' and 'non-Eastern' instead. The fact is that a binary framework does not reflect our situation accurately. Eastern-isms infuse the West, and vice versa, making polarized distinctions unsuitable. Although Western music assimilates the music of other cultures at a particularly rapid pace, similar processes also take place independently of the Western tradition. Middle Eastern music influences composers in India; and the rhythms of Cuban popular music, themselves derived from Africa, are resounding once again in the popular music of sub-Saharan Africa.

Once we reconcile the achievements of our Western heritage with the futility of maintaining too exaggerated a notion of separateness from other peoples and cultures, our role in the richly diverse community of world musics is called into focus. Mozart, living and writing music in eighteenth-century Vienna, can then be compared with his Indian contemporary Tyagaraja, inspired poet and composer of devotional songs; and the explosive rhythms of Stravinsky's *Rite of Spring*, first given in Paris in 1913, can be contrasted with the equally mercurial music of the Gamelan Gong Kebyar, which had its beginning in Bali at approximately the same time.

Popular music encompasses a large family of inherently cross-cultural musics that merit much more discussion than has been afforded here. Incredible in its diversity, it touches the lives of most of

407

the world's population. The twentieth century has seen cultures that formerly lived in mutual isolation uprooted and placed in daily contact, producing an array of musical expressions that mirror the experiences of those adjusting to such rapid change. The powerful human dramas of co-existence and transformation embodied in these processes represent a hopeful (if not too idealistic) metaphor for our changing world as we enter the new millennium.

In all, musicians today exhibit a bewildering diversity of means, roles, status, techniques and styles, but they are united in a marriage with the profound abstractions of musical sound which, whatever their function, are continually shifting in meaning. A closing anecdote, related by Lou Harrison, composer and student of Henry Cowell, is apt:

> There was a conference in Tokyo in 1962 at which Henry Cowell got up because everyone was being so 'pure', and the ethnomusicologists didn't want anyone to touch the cultures that they were studying, and so on, and Henry said, 'Look, all the hybrids are healthy. They're the ones that grow new things and make new beauties. So don't put down the hybrids'. I took that on face value because of my admiration for the man, until finally it dawned on me, about a year later. Don't put down the hybrids, *because there isn't anything else.*[21]

NOTES

[1] Boulez does not acknowledge being influenced by specifically musical factors; in 'Traditional Music – a Lost Paradise?', *The World of Music*, ix/2 (1967), 3–10, he remarks that 'The influence is on my spirit and not on my work. The main points are as follows: the conception of time being different, the idea of anonymity; the idea of a work of art not being admired as a masterpiece but as an element of spiritual life'.

[2] Other twentieth-century composers explored non-standard tunings, but most were concerned with expanding the chromatic to 24 tones within the context of equal temperament; among those interested were the American Charles Ives, the Russian Ivan Vïshnegradsky and the Czech Alois Hába.

[3] Perhaps the most astonishing case of musical transplantation is that of the African music diaspora. For centuries the peoples of Africa were uprooted to new lands in the Western hemisphere. In spite of the prolonged hardships of slavery and oppression, the native musics of sub-saharan Africa thrive in transformation, in popular music of all kinds throughout the West and Latin America.

[4] A book on this subject is E. Eisenberg, *The Recording Angel: Explorations in Phonography* (New York, 1987). Eisenberg coins the term 'phonography' to refer to recording technology, an art form he feels deserves special classification; he explores the impact of this technology on our relationship to music in depth.

[5] *Verdi, the Man and his Letters*, ed. F. Werfel and P. Stefan (New York, 1942). For more on Verdi's critique of German music, see J. B. Childs, 'Rethinking the "Classical": Giuseppe Verdi and other European Advocates of Cultural Diversity', *New Observations Journal*, lxxxvi (Dec 1991), 6–10.

[6] See M. R. Obelkevich, 'Turkish Affect in the Land of the Sun King', *MQ*, lxiii (1977), 367–89.

[7] The dramatic solo timpani notes at the beginning of the Scherzo of Beethoven's Ninth Symphony were an innovatory idea and perhaps the first melodic use of percussion in the West. With this gesture, Beethoven had taken an instrument recently borrowed from the non-Western

world and transformed it into something inimitably his own. I am grateful for this insight to William W. Austin, Emeritus Professor of Music at Cornell University.

[8] The romanticism of Debussy's perspective was not far removed from Liszt's. He wrote the following in *Taste* (1913): 'There were, and still are, despite the evils of civilization, some delightful native peoples for whom music is as natural as breathing. Their conservatoire is the eternal rhythm of the sea, the wind among the leaves and the thousand sounds of nature which they understand without consulting an arbitrary treatise. Their traditions reside in old songs, combined with dances, built up throughout the centuries. Yet Javanese music is based on a type of counterpoint by comparison with which that of Palestrina is child's play. And if we listen without European prejudice to the charm of their percussion we must confess that our percussion is like primitive noises at a country fair' (quoted in E. Lockspeiser, *Debussy: his Life and Mind* (London, 1962), i, 115.

[9] Richard Mueller argues for the influence of specific Javanese melodies and tunings on passages of the *Fantaisie* for piano and orchestra, composed by Debussy soon after hearing the gamelan at the Exposition; see 'Javanese Influence on Debussy's *Fantaisie* and Beyond', *Nineteenth-Century Music*, x (1986–7), 157–86.

[10] W. W. Austin, *Music in the Twentieth Century* (New York, 1966), 39.

[11] Richard Taruskin cites an exception in 'Russian Folk Melodies in the Rite of Spring', *JAMS*, xxxiii (1980), 501–43; a photograph (reproduced in the article) shows Stravinsky at work transcribing a song sung by a blind mendicant in 1914.

[12] Ibid, 505–6.

[13] Charles Seeger provides an account of the rise of German musical influence in nineteenth-century America in 'Music and Class Structure in the United States', *Studies in Musicology, 1935–1975* (Berkeley, 1977), 222–37.

[14] Most prominent among these were, of course, the composers of the Second Viennese School. Schoenberg's dream of the continued superiority of German music implicitly asserted the necessity of keeping music pure and free from other cultures' influence. In this light, Theodor Adorno's well-known polemic (in *Philosophy of Modern Music*) admiring Schoenberg and inveighing against Stravinsky can be seen as an effort to keep the gates of culture closed.

[15] S. Reich, *Writings About Music* (New York, 1974), 57.

[16] Ibid, 38.

[17] From Charles Amirkhanian's notes to Conlon Nancarrow's 'Complete Studies for Player Piano, Vol.4' (Arch Records S-1798).

[18] From S. Arom, *African Polyphony and Polyrhythm* (Cambridge, 1991), p.xvii.

[19] Acknowledgment is due to Paul Schick, a graduate student at the Yale Department of Music, for permission to paraphrase this perceptive thought, taken from his unpublished paper 'Ligeti's Sixth Piano *Étude* and the Music of sub-Saharan Africa'.

[20] Ziporyn and Windha's comments were culled from interviews with the author.

[21] Spoken during an interview with Harrison in the 1988 BBC television documentary 'West Coast Story'.

BIBLIOGRAPHICAL NOTE

There is little literature on the subjects discussed in this chapter. W. Wiora's *Four Ages of Music* (New York, 1965) stands alone in its attempt to place the history of music in global perspective. Wiora views post-medieval Western music as one of the special outcomes of a process of development that originated in the pre-civilized ancient world and characterizes our contemporary situation as one in which musical cultures are intermingling again after a long period of independence. L. B. Meyer's *Music, the Arts and Ideas* (Chicago, 1967) offers an excellent framework for conceptualizing cultural plurality and a good model for examining cross-cultural influence in music. Although Meyer's analysis (in Chapter 9) is focussed on the use of styles from past ages of Western music, it is easily applied to the current topic. Bruno Nettl's writings in ethnomusicology encompass Western music in its contextual roles, especially in *The Western Impact on World Music* (New York, 1985) and *The Study of Ethnomusicology: Twenty-Nine Issues and Concepts* (Urbana, 1983). *New Observations Journal* (Nov 1991), contains a group of brief articles showing a common concern for viewing music in multi-cultural perspective.

A concise article proposing a method for dealing with cross-cultural interaction in music is Nettl, 'Some Aspects of the History of World Music in the Twentieth Century: Questions, Problems and Concepts', *Ethnomusicology*, xx/1 (1978), 123–36. Other relevant journal articles include K. Wachsmann, 'Applying Ethnomusicological Methods to Western Art Music', *The World of Music*, xxiii/2 (1981), 74–86; J. Karpati, 'Non-European Influences on Occidental Music', *The World of Music*, xxii/2 (1980), 20–34, and M. J. Kartomi, 'The Processes and Results of Music Culture Contact: a Discussion of Terminology and Concept', *Ethnomusicology*, xxv/2 (1981), 227–50.

New Music in the Orient, ed. H. Ryker (Buren, 1991), is a unique survey of current compositional trends in east Asia, south-east Asia and Australia/New Zealand; it covers a gamut of styles, ranging from the purely Western to those informed by local traditions. F. Feliciano, *Four Contemporary Asian Composers: the Influence of Tradition in their Works* (Quezon City, 1983), is a useful book offering profiles of Chou-Wen Chung, Toru Takemitsu, Isang Yun and Jose Maceda. Two studies documenting specific Asian influences on Western composers are by R. Mueller: 'Javanese Influence on Debussy's *Fantaisie* and Beyond', *Nineteenth-Century Music*, x (1986–7), 157–86, and 'Bali, Tabuh-Tabuhan, and Colin McPhee's Method of Intercultural Composition', *Journal of Musicological Research*, xi (1991), 67–92; see also M. Cooke, 'Britten and Bali', *Journal of Musicological Research*, vii (1987) 307–39. A more general approach is offered in Chou-Wen Chung, 'Asian Concepts and Twentieth Century Western Composers', *MQ*, lvii (1971), 211–29.

Of special interest are a pair of brief articles by two of the best-known composers of our day: Boulez's 'Traditional Music: a Lost Paradise?', *The World of Music*, ix/2 (1967), and Cage's 'The East in the West', *Asian Music Journal*, i/1 (1968–9), 15–22, which, originally written in 1946, stands out as remarkably full of insight for its time.

Among many books on popular music are J. Marre and H. Charlton, *Beats of the Heart* (New York, 1985), which is lively but of dubious scholarly import, and P. Manuel, *Popular Musics of the Non-Western World* (London, 1988), a broad but useful survey. The effects of technology are further examined in E. Eisenberg, *The Recording Angel* (New York, 1987), and in C. Hamm's excellent 'Technology and Music: the Effect of the Phonograph', in *Contemporary Music and Music Cultures*, ed. Hamm and others (Englewood Cliffs, 1975), 253–70.

Chronology

MUSIC AND MUSICIANS	POLITICS, WAR AND RULERS
1914 Alban Berg (1885–1935) composes his Three Orchestral Pieces op.6 and starts *Wozzeck*. Charles Ives (1874–1954) completes his *Three Places in New England*. American Society of Composers, Authors and Publishers (ASCAP) founded, New York, to protect copyright, performance rights and distribute royalties.	**1914** Outbreak of World War I: Germany, Austria-Hungary, Turkey against France, Britain and Russia.
1915 Edgard Varèse (1883–1965) arrives in New York. Richard Strauss (1864–1949) completes his *Alpensinfonie*. *El amor brujo* by Manuel de Falla (1876–1946) given, Madrid. Claude Debussy (1862–1918) composes *En blanc et noir*. Ives completes his *Concord Sonata*. Alexander Skryabin (43) dies, Moscow.	**1915** Italy declares war on Austria-Hungary, Germany and Turkey. Sinking of the *Lusitania* by German U-boats brings America to the verge of war.
1916 Carl Nielsen (1865–1931) completes his Fourth Symphony (The Inextinguishable). Enrique Granados (1867–1916) dies at sea in the English Channel shortly after completing his opera *Goyescas* (amplified from his piano pieces of 1914). Max Reger (43) dies, Leipzig.	**1916** Easter Rebellion in Ireland. Second Battle of Ypres. The Somme campaign causes huge casualties on both sides. Death of Franz Joseph, Emperor of Austria since 1848; succeeded by Karl I. Election of President Wilson.
1917 *Parade* by Erik Satie (1866–1925) given, Paris. Francis Poulenc (1899–1963) composes *Rapsodie nègre*. *Palestrina* by Hans Pfitzner (1869–1949) given, Munich. Salzburg Festival founded. Sergey Rakhmaninov leaves Russia for the USA. Scott Joplin (48) dies, New York.	**1917** Abdication of Tsar Nicholas II. USA declares war on Austria and Germany. Russian Revolution, led by Lenin and Trotsky, followed by armistice with Germany.
1918 *Histoire du soldat* by Igor Stravinsky (1882–1971) given, Lausanne. *Il trittico* by Giacomo Puccini (1858–1924) given, New York. *Duke Bluebeard's Castle*, composed in 1911, by Béla Bartók (1881–1945) given, Budapest. Arnold Schoenberg (1874–1951) founds Society for Private Musical Performance in Vienna, banning critics and applause. Debussy (56) dies, Paris.	**1918** End of First World War on 11 November. Abdication of Karl I and Wilhelm II and disintegration of Austro-Hungarian and German empires. Republics of Czechoslovakia and Yugoslavia created.
1919 Strauss's *Die Frau ohne Schatten* given, Vienna. Edward Elgar (1857–1934) completes his Cello Concerto.	**1919** Treaty of Versailles signed. Civil war in Russia. Weimar Republic set up in Germany. Women over 30 given suffrage in Britain and election of first woman MP.
1920 *Le boeuf sur le toit* by Darius Milhaud (1892–1974) and Stravinsky's ballet *Pulcinella* given, both in Paris. Critic Henri Collet originates the term 'Les Six'.	**1920** Prohibition in USA (until 1933). Foundation of League of Nations, without USA. End of Russian counter-revolution. Government of Ireland Act establishes two Irelands, but war until 1922.

LITERATURE, PHILOSOPHY, RELIGION	SCIENCE, TECHNOLOGY, DISCOVERY	FINE ARTS AND ARCHITECTURE
	1914–17 Ernest Shackleton (1874–1922) leads a second expedition to the Antarctic.	
1915 William Somerset Maugham (1874–1965) publishes *Of Human Bondage*, his best-known, autobiographical novel.	**1915** Hugo Junkers (1859–1935) makes the first all-metal fighter aeroplane, the J.1. Albert Einstein (1879–1955) puts forward his general theory of relativity, his greatest contribution to physics.	**1915–23** Marcel Duchamp (1887–1968) works on *The Bride Stripped Bare by her Bachelors, Even*, a painting and construct on glass with obscure symbolism.
1916 First performance of *La maschero e il volto* by Luigi Chiarelli (1884–1947), which inaugurates the rise of *teatro grottesco*.		
1917 Paul Valéry (1871–1945) makes his reputation with the poem *La Jeune Parque*.	**1916** Robert Millikan (1886–1953) confirms the photo-electric equation of Einstein, evaluating the fundamental physical constant *h*. Gilbert Lewis (1875–1946) and W. Kossel (1888–1919) independently state a new electronic theory of valency. Tanks are first used by the British on the Somme.	**1916** Claude Monet (1840–1926) begins work on a large-scale mural cycle of waterlily paintings, continuing until his death.
1918 Posthumous publication of *Poems* by Gerard Manley Hopkins (1844–85) has a great impact and marks a renewal of poetic energy.		**1917** Pablo Picasso (1881–1973) designs sets and costumes for Dyagilev's ballet *Parade*, described as 'Surrealist' – the first use of the term.
1919 Karl Barth (1886–1968) publishes *Der Romerbrief*, a radical questioning of current theological notions which greatly influences German and Protestant theology. Sherwood Anderson (1876–1941) publishes *Winesburg, Ohio*, which establishes him as a leading naturalistic writer.		**1918** W. J. Polk (1867–1924) designs the Hallidie Building (San Francisco), one of the first buildings with a fully glazed, non-loadbearing outer wall. Kasimir Malevich (1878–1935) paints a series, *White on White*, the ultimate Suprematist paintings.
1920 Sidonie Gabrielle Colette (1873–1954), one of the greatest French writers of the 20th century, publishes *Chéri*. Grazia Deledda (1871–1936) publishes her great novel *La madre*, for which she is the only Italian woman to have been awarded the Nobel Prize for Literature.	**1919** First transatlantic flight by John Alcock (1892–1919) and Arthur Brown (1886–1948) in 16 hours, 27 minutes. Ernest Rutherford (1871–1937), founder of nuclear physics, succeeds in transmuting nitrogen atoms into oxygen atoms, representing an artificial splitting of atoms.	**1919** Amedeo Modigliani (1884–1920) paints *Reclining Nude*, the culmination of his series of graceful and erotic nudes. **1920** Fernand Léger (1881–1955) paints *The Mechanic*, a post-Cubist work inspired by technology.

413

MUSIC AND MUSICIANS	POLITICS, WAR AND RULERS
1921 Fourth Quartet by Alois Hába (1893–1973) given at the first Donaueschingen Festival for contemporary music. *Mörder, Hoffnung der Frauen* by Paul Hindemith (1895–1963) given, Stuttgart. Paul Whiteman (1890–1967) visits Europe with his jazz band. Musicians' Union (GB) formed to improve pay and conditions for professional musicians. Varèse and Carlos Salzedo found the International Composers' Guild, New York. *Kát'a Kabanová* by Leoš Janáček given, Brno.	**1921** Paris conference of Allies fixes heavy German reparations payments, causing economic crisis in Germany. Treaty of Riga ends war between Poland and Russia.
1922 *Façade* by William Walton (1902–83) given privately, London. International Society for Contemporary Music founded in Salzburg by a group of Viennese composers under the presidency of E. J. Dent.	**1922** Mussolini marches on Rome and proclaims a Fascist government. Kemal Ataturk proclaims Turkey a republic. Civil war in China. Official proclamation of the Irish Free State.
1923 Arthur Honegger (1892–1955) composes *Pacific 231*, Zoltán Kodály (1882–1967) his *Psalmus Hungaricus* and Henry Cowell (1897–1965) his *Aeolian Harp*. Stravinsky completes his *Octet* and *Les noces*. Schoenberg completes his first wholly 12-note piece, the Suite op.25 for piano.	**1923** Union of Soviet Socialist Republics established. Independence of Transjordan proclaimed. Palestine mandate begins. Primo de Rivera assumes dictatorship in Spain.
1924 Jean Sibelius (1865–1957) composes his Seventh Symphony. Anton Webern (1883–1945) composes his *Five Canons*, Ottorino Respighi (1879–1936) *The Pines of Rome* and George Gershwin (1898–1937) his *Rhapsody in Blue*. Ferrucio Busoni (58) dies, Berlin. Fauré (79) dies, Paris. Puccini (65) dies, Brussels.	**1924** Death of Lenin. Dissolution of non-Fascist trade unions in Italy. Greece becomes a republic. League of Nations adopts Geneva protocol for settlement of international disputes.
1925 Berg's *Wozzeck* given, Berlin; he composes his Chamber Symphony. *L'enfant et les sortilèges* by Maurice Ravel (1875–1937) given, Monte Carlo. Busoni's *Doktor Faust* given, Dresden; Schoenberg takes over Busoni's masterclass in Berlin. Arnold Dolmetsch (1858–1940), a pioneer in the movement to promote early music, establishes the Haslemere Festival, UK. Erik Satie (59) dies, Paris.	**1925** Locarno conference drafts treaties regarding European boundaries and security. Settlement of Irish boundary.

LITERATURE, PHILOSOPHY, RELIGION	SCIENCE, TECHNOLOGY, DISCOVERY	FINE ARTS AND ARCHITECTURE
1921 J. McTaggart (1866–1925) publishes *the Nature of Existence* (vol. ii, 1927), arguing the Hegelian position. Luigi Pirandello (1867–1936) writes *Sei personaggi in cerca d'autore*, influential in 20th-century drama.	**1921** First medium-wave wireless broadcast in the USA.	**1921** Max Ernst (1891–1976) paints *L'Elephant Célébes*, a Surrealist masterpiece.
1922 Ludwig Wittgenstein (1889–1951) publishes *Tractatus Logico-Philosophicus*, propounding that the only meaningful use of language is as a picture of empirical, scientific fact. T. S. Eliot (1888–1965) publishes *The Waste Land*, seen as a statement of postwar disillusion. James Joyce (1882–1941) publishes *Ulysses* revolutionizing the novel.	**1922** Niels Bohr (1885–1962) publishes *The Theory of Spectra and Atomic Constitution*, revolutionizing atomic theory.	**1922** F. Höger (1877–1949) designs the Chilehaus, Hamburg, one of the masterpieces of North German Expressionism. László Moholy-Nagy (1895–1946) begins his *Light-Space Modulator* (–1930) in metal and plastic, one of the earliest mechanized works.
1923 E. E. Cummings (1894–1962) publishes *Tulips and Chimneys*, the first of 12 volumes of poetry using experimental typography. Martin Buber (1878–1965), Jewish religious thinker, publishes *Ich und Du*, influencing German Protestant theology.	**1923** Arthur Eddington (1882–1944) publishes his *Mathematical Theory of Relativity*, introducing to the public the work of Einstein and Weyl.	**1924** Otto Dix (1891–1969) produces 50 etchings, *The War*, conveying his horror and disgust at the effects of war. Stanley Spencer (1891–1951) begins *The Resurrection: Cookham* (–1926), one of his greatest works, received with critical acclaim.
1924 E. M. Forster (1879–1970) publishes his last novel, *A Passage to India*. Thomas Mann (1875–1955) publishes *Der Zauberberg*, an analysis of the intellectual state of pre-war Europe.	**1924** Edward Victor Appleton (1892–1965) demonstrates experimentally the existence of the electrified reflecting layer in the upper atmosphere postulated by Kennelly and Heaviside. Einstein begins his last great contribution to statistical mechanics, the development of the quantum theory of a monatomic gas.	**1925** Constantin Brancusi (1876–1957) creates *Bird in Space*, a simple expressive form in bronze by one of the most influential 20th-century sculptors. Walter Gropius (1883–1969), one of the outstanding architects of the 20th century, designs the Bauhaus, Dessau, with a glass curtain wall, a major example of the International style.
1925 F. Scott Fitzgerald (1896–1940) publishes *The Great Gatsby*. André Gide (1869–1951) publishes *Les Faux-Monnayeurs*. Franz Kafka (1883–1924) publishes *Der Prozess*; its opening sentence gave rise to 'Kafkaesque' as a description of the combination of the ordinary and the sinister.		

MUSIC AND MUSICIANS	POLITICS, WAR AND RULERS
1926 Puccini's *Turandot* given, Milan. *Ballet méchanique* by George Antheil (1900–59) performed, Paris. *King Roger* by Karol Szymanowski (1882–1937) given, Warsaw.	**1926** Brazil leaves League of Nations; Germany joins. Trotsky and Zinoviev expelled from the Politburo.
1927 Stravinsky's *Oedipus Rex* given as an oratorio, Paris. *Jonny spielt auf* by Ernst Krenek (1900–91) given, Leipzig. Duke Ellington and his band play at the Cotton Club, Harlem. International Musicological Society founded in Basle with Guido Adler as chairman, continuing work of the old International Music Society. Cowell launches the journal *New Music* which publishes music not words; the first issue is devoted to *Men and Mountains* by Carl Ruggles (1876–1971). Wilhelm Stenhammar (56) dies, Stockholm.	**1927** 52 nations attend an economic conference in Geneva. Collapse of Germany's economic system. Socialist riots in Vienna.
1928 *Die Dreigroschenoper* by Kurt Weill (1900–50) given, Berlin. Olivier Messiaen (1908–92) composes *Le banquet céleste* for organ. Schoenberg composes his first serial orchestral work, the Variations op.31. Maurice Martenot demonstrates his 'Ondes musicales' in Paris. Janáček (74) dies, Ostrava.	**1928** Independence of Transjordan recognized by Britain. War between Bolivia and Paraguay. Socialist success in German elections. Chiang-Kai-Shek elected President of China.
1929 Webern's Symphony op.21 performed, New York. Hindemith's *Neues vom Tage* given, Berlin; he gives the first performance, as soloist, of Walton's Viola Concerto, London. Impresario Sergey Dyagilev (57) dies, Venice.	**1929** Trotsky expelled from USSR. Settlement of Arica-Tacua dispute between Chile, Peru and Bolivia. Arabs attack Jews in Palestine. World economic crisis begins with collapse of US stock market.
1930 Stravinsky completes his *Symphony of Psalms*. Schoenberg starts *Moses und Aron* (never completed). Cowell publishes his *New Musical Resources*. Heitor Villa-Lobos (1887–1959) composes the first of his nine *Bachianas Brasileiras*.	**1930** End of Allied occupation of the Rhineland (since 1918). Ras Tafari becomes Emperor Haile Selassie of Abyssinia. Gandhi begins a campaign of civil disobedience in India. Revolutions in Argentina and Brazil.

LITERATURE, PHILOSOPHY, RELIGION	SCIENCE, TECHNOLOGY, DISCOVERY	FINE ARTS AND ARCHITECTURE
	1926 John Logie Baird (1888–1946) first demonstrates television. Stimulated by Einstein, Erwin Schrödinger (1887–1961) publishes a series of papers forming the foundation of wave mechanics.	**1926–7** Robert Mallet-Stevens (1886–1945) designs houses in the Rue Mallet Stevens in Cubist style but with variegated façades and interiors.
1927 Herman Hesse (1877–1962) publishes *Steppenwolf*, a surrealist narrative reflecting his interest in double personalities. François Mauriac (1885–1970) publishes his finest novel, *Thérèse Desqueyroux*. Posthumous publication of *Le Temps retrouvé*, the last part of *À la recherche du temps perdu* by Marcel Proust (1871–1922). Martin Heidegger (1889–1976) publishes *Sein und Zeit*, which focuses on Being in its unity and totality.	**1927** Fritz London (1900–54) and Walter Heitler produce their classic quantum-mechanical treatment of the hydrogen molecule.	**1927–8** G. Terragni (1904–41), a *Gruppo 7* architect opposed to the International style, builds the controversial 'Novocomum' flats in Como.
1928 D. H. Lawrence (1885–1930) completes *Lady Chatterley's Lover*, published in full in Britain only in 1960, after a trial. Bertolt Brecht (1898–1956) writes *Die Dreigroschenoper*, a great success in Weimar Germany.	**1928** Hans Geiger (1882–1945) and W. Müller improve Geiger's counter for *a*-particles to its modern form. Alexander Fleming (1881–1955) discovers penicillin, which is only developed as an antibiotic some 15 years later by Howard Florey and Ernst Chain.	**1929** Henry Moore (1898–1986) creates *Reclining Figure*, his first essay on this theme, in Brown Hornton stone. Piet Mondrian (1872–1944) paints *Composition in Yellow and Blue*, a new geometrical abstract painting – Neo-Plasticism. Oskar Kokoschka (1886–1980) paints *Jerusalem*, an Expressionist 'portrait' picture. Le Corbusier (Charles Edouard Jeanneret, 1887–1965), the dominant figure in modern architecture until 1960, builds the Villa Savoye, Poissy (–1931).
1929 William Faulkner (1897–1962) publishes *The Sound and the Fury*, concerned with the decline of the American South. Virginia Woolf (1882–1941) publishes *A Room of One's Own*, a classic of the feminist movement. Ernest Hemingway (1899–1961) publishes *A Farewell to Arms*, confirming his position as one of the most influential writers of the time.	**1929** The airship *Graf Zeppelin* flies round the world.	
1930 W. H. Auden (1907–73) publishes *Poems*, which establishes him as the most talented poetic voice of his generation.	**1930** Discovery of the planet Pluto, the outermost known major planet, by Clyde Tombaugh at the Lowell observatory. Amy Johnson (1903–41) flies solo to Australia in 19½ days.	**1930** Adolf Loos (1870–1933) designs his last great work, the Müller House in Prague, which has a great influence on the next generation of architects. Raymond Hood (1881–1934) designs the McGraw-Hill Building, New York, introducing the curtain-wall façades of the International style to the USA.

Modern Times

MUSIC AND MUSICIANS	POLITICS, WAR AND RULERS
1931 Hába's *Matka*, the first opera using quarter-tones, given, Munich. Hans Barth (1897–1956) patents the first quarter-tone piano. Ravel completes his Piano Concerto for the Left Hand. The masque *Job* by Ralph Vaughan Williams (1872–1958) is first staged. Varèse composes *Ionisation*. Nielsen (66) dies, Copenhagen.	**1931** Revolution in Spain; Republican constitution drawn up. Japan occupies Manchuria. Britain abandons the gold standard.
1932 Ruggles completes *Suntreader*. Sergey Prokofiev (1891–1953) composes his Fifth Piano Concerto. John Philip Sousa (77) dies, Reading, Penn.	**1932** Growing Nazi success in German elections. Chaco war between Bolivia and Paraguay (until 1935). Election of President Roosevelt.
1933 Weill's ballet *The Seven Deadly Sins* performed, Paris. Schoenberg is dismissed from his post in Berlin; he, Weill and Eisler emigrate to the USA; Prokofiev returns to the USSR. FM radio is developed.	**1933** Bank crisis in USA. Hitler is appointed Chancellor of Germany and forms a Nazi cabinet; he engineers Reichstag fire as an excuse to suspend civil liberties. Persecution of Jews begins in Germany. Japan occupies China north of the Great Wall. Spanish right parties win Cortes elections.
1934 John Christie founds the Glyndebourne Festival. *Four Saints in Three Acts* by Virgil Thomson (1896–1989) given, Hartford, Conn. Elgar (76) dies, Worcester. Frederick Delius (72) dies, Grez-sur-Loing. Franz Schreker (55) dies, Berlin.	**1934** Austrian Chancellor Dollfuss murdered in attempted Nazi coup. Hitler becomes Führer with sole executive power. Assassination of Kirov leads to Stalin's first purge of the Communist Party. Military coup in Bolivia.
1935 Gershwin's *Porgy and Bess* given, New York. Strauss's *Die schweigsame Frau* banned after four performances as the librettist, Stefan Zweig, was a Jew. Berg (50) dies in Vienna, shortly after completing his Violin Concerto. Paul Dukas (69) dies, Paris. Josef Suk (61) dies, Benesov.	**1935** German expansion begins with the restoration of the Saar; Hitler repudiates disarmament clauses of the Versailles Treaty. Stresa conference of Britain, France and Italy to discuss German aggression. Government of India Act separates Burma and Aden from India and reforms governmental system.
1936 Bartók composes his *Music for Strings, Percussion and Celesta*. The newspaper *Pravda* savagely attacks *Lady Macbeth of the Mtsensk District* by Dmitri Shostakovich (1906–75) who subsequently withdraws his Fourth Symphony and starts on his Fifth. La jeune France formed by Messiaen and others. Respighi (56) dies, Rome.	**1936** Germany occupies the Rhineland, violating Treaty of Versailles. Foundation of Arab High Committee against Jewish claims. Outbreak of Spanish Civil War (until 1939). Abdication crisis in Britain; George VI replaces Edward VIII on the throne.
1937 Premières of Berg's *Lulu* in Zürich, *The Cradle will Rock* by Marc Blitzstein (1905–64) in New York and *Carmina Burana* by Carl Orff (1895–1982) in Frankfurt. Bartók writes his Sonata for Two Pianos and Percussion. Ravel (62) dies, Paris. Gershwin (38) dies, Hollywood. Szymanowski (54) dies, Lausanne. First showing on television of a complete opera (Pergolesi's *La serva padrona*), London.	**1937** Japanese capture Peking, Tientsin and Shanghai. Establishment of Arab and Jewish states recommended instead of Palestine mandate. Irish Free State becomes Eire.

LITERATURE, PHILOSOPHY, RELIGION	SCIENCE, TECHNOLOGY, DISCOVERY	FINE ARTS AND ARCHITECTURE
1931 Mikhail Sholokov (1905–84) publishes *Virgin Soil Upturned*, a classic of Socialist Realism.	**1931** Ernest Lawrence (1901–58) devises the cycloron, with which he initiates and studies nuclear reactions of many kinds.	**1931** Salvador Dali (1904–88) paints *The Persistence of Memory*, a disturbing painting of watches by the controversial surrealist.
1932 Karl Jaspers (1883–1969) publishes *Philosophie*, an attempt to interpret the crisis in philosophy and culture in post-1918 Germany. Aldous Huxley (1894–1963) publishes *Brave New World*, a fable where social stability is based on a scientific caste system. Jules Romains (1885–1972) writes *Les hommes de bonne volonté* (–1947), a collection of 27 novels presenting a panorama of French life and thought, 1910–40.	**1932** Sir John Cockcroft (1897–1967) and Ernest Walton perform the classic experiment to split the nucleus.	**1933** Max Beckmann (1884–1950) begins *Departure*, the first of a series of nine great triptychs expressing his philosophy of life and society. The Tecton group of architects design the Highpoint I flats, Highgate, London: the first major building of the modern movement in Britain.
	1933 Wiley Post (1899–1935) flies solo round the world in 7 days, 18 hours and 49 minutes. Jean Frédéric Joliot (1900–58) and Irène Joliot Curie (1897–1956) produce a new unstable isotope in the laboratory and so discover artifical radioactivity.	**1935** Wyndham Lewis (1882–1957), the most original and idiosyncratic artist in Britain, completes his controversial *Portrait of Edith Sitwell*. Eduardo Torroja (1899–1961), an outstanding creator of architectural form, designs the fluted grandstand roofs of the Zarzuela racecourse. Frank Lloyd Wright (1867–1959) builds his masterpiece, the Kaufmann House, Penn. (–1939), in which he realizes a creative synthesis of organic architecture and Cubist and rationalist influences.
1934 Aldo Palazzeschi (1885–1974) publishes his prose masterpiece, *Le sorelle Materassi*. Federico García Lorca (1898–1936) writes the sombre *Llanto por la muerte de Ignacio Sánchez Mejías*. Persecution of Jews in Germany and Austria results in mass exodus to Britain and USA.	**1934** Enrico Fermi (1901–54) works further on artificial radioactivity, which forms the basis for the first atomic pile.	
1936 A. J. Ayer (1910–89) publishes *Language, Truth and Logic*, the first exposition of logical positivism in English.	**1935** Robert Watson-Watt (1892–1973) sets up the first radar detecting equipment for detecting aircraft.	**1936** Mark Tobey (1890–1976) paints *Broadway*, a 'white writing' work inspired by Oriental calligraphy. Julio González (1876–1942), pioneer in the use of iron as a sculptural medium, creates *Montserrat*, commemorating the suffering of the Spanish people in the Civil War.
1937 Criticism of literature, music and works of art is forbidden in Hitler's Germany, with consequent stultification. Georges Bernanos (1888–1948) writes *Les Grandes Cimetières sous la lune*, revealing his spiritual and political disillusionment with the Spanish Civil War.	**1936** The BBC begins the public television service in Britain.	**1937** Picasso paints *Guernica*, probably his most famous work, expressing his horror at the bombing of the city in the Civil War.

Modern Times

MUSIC AND MUSICIANS	POLITICS, WAR AND RULERS
1938 Prokofiev composes his music for Eisenstein's film *Alexander Nevsky*, subsequently developing it into a cantata. Hindemith's *Mathis der Maler* given, Zürich. Webern completes his String Quartet op.28; his *Das Augenlicht* is performed in London. *Billy the Kid* by Aaron Copland (1900–90) performed, Chicago.	**1938** German troops enter Austria which becomes part of the Reich. Japanese set up puppet government in China. Czechoslovakia loses Sudetenland to Germany at Munich conference, from which Chamberlain returns to London believing he has won 'Peace in our time'.
1939 Michael Tippett (*b* 1905) completes his Concerto for Double String Orchestra. John Cage (1912–92) completes the first of his *Imaginary Landscapes*. Roy Harris (1898–1979) composes his Third Symphony. Marian Anderson (1912–93) is barred from singing at Constitution Hill but later (1955) becomes the first black singer to appear at the Metropolitan, New York. Stravinsky settles in the USA.	**1939** Madrid surrenders to Franco, ending Spanish Civil War. Hitler and Mussolini sign a political and military alliance. USSR ratifies non-aggression pact with Germany with secret protocol on Poland, which Hitler invades. Outbreak of World War II (3 September).
1940 Webern composes his Variations op.30 for orchestra. Stravinsky completes his Symphony in C. Cage starts producing works for prepared piano. Hindemith and Bartók emigrate to the USA. Serge Koussevitzky establishes a summer school at the Berkshire Music Center, Tanglewood, Mass., where he later sets up a foundation to commission new works. Carlos Chávez (1899–1978) composes *Xochipilli*.	**1940** Germany invades Norway, Denmark, Belgium, Holland and France; British forces evacuated from Dunkirk. Italy declares war on France and Britain; France (Vichy government) signs armistice with Germany and Italy. De Gaulle starts Free French movement. Battle of Britain.
1941 Messiaen's *Quartet for the End of Time* given, Stalag VIII-A, Görlitz. First complete performance, in Rome, of the *Canti di Prigionia* by Luigi Dallapiccola (1904–75). Copland's *Quiet City* performed as a concert piece (originally incidental music). Frank Bridge (61) dies, Eastbourne.	**1941** Germany invades Yugoslavia, Greece and Crete, and then occupies the rest of the Balkans. British and Free French forces invade Syria to prevent establishment of Axis bases. Germany invades Russia but fails to take Moscow. Japan bombs Pearl Harbor, bringing USA into the war.
1942 Pierre Schaeffer (*b* 1910) founds a studio in Paris for acoustical experiments. *Capriccio*, Strauss's last opera, given, Munich. Messiaen writes his *Technique de mon langage musical*. Chávez composes his Piano Concerto. Alexander von Zemlinsky (70) dies.	**1942** Japanese success in Asia up to the Indian frontier. British convoys to Russia begin. Allied morale boosted by successful battle of El Alamein. Germans move into unoccupied France.
1943 Bartók completes his Concerto for Orchestra, Webern his Second Cantata. Sergey Rakhmaninov (60) dies, Beverly Hills.	**1943** Russians destroy German army besieging Stalingrad. Allies reconquer North Africa and invade Sicily and Italy, who surrenders. Massacre in Warsaw ghetto. USA begins Pacific offensive.

LITERATURE, PHILOSOPHY, RELIGION	SCIENCE, TECHNOLOGY, DISCOVERY	FINE ARTS AND ARCHITECTURE
1938 Frank Buchman (1878–1961) founds Moral Rearmament, a campaign for moral and spiritual regeneration on the principle of the Oxford Group.		**1938** Erik Bryggman (1891–1955) designs the cemetery chapel at Turku (–1941), his ultimate Rationalist work.
1939 John Steinbeck (1902–68) publishes *The Grapes of Wrath*, his epic account of a family emigrating to California. Carl Jung (1875–1961) publishes *Psychologie und Religion*, one of his major works.	**1939** Otto Hahn (1879–1968) and W. Strassmann detect uranium and thorium fission, which proves to be the basis for all methods to tap atomic energy.	**1939** Paul Klee (1879–1940) paints a late masterpiece, *La belle Jardinière*, incorporating mysterious ideograms on a ground of softly merging colours.
1940 George Santayana (1863–1952) completes *Realms of Being*, a modification and supplement to his *Life of Reason* (1905–6). Arthur Koestler (1905–83) publishes *Darkness at Noon*, which did much to draw attention to the nature of Stalin's regime. **1940–41** Eugene O'Neill (1888–1953) writes his masterpiece *Long Day's Journey into Night*, published in 1956. **1940–45** The Holocaust – mass extermination of European Jews by Nazis.	**1940** Edwin McMillan (*b* 1907) and Philip Abelson discover the first transuranium element, neptunium, and open up the whole transuranium field.	**1940** G. Asplund (1885–1940) completes the Stockholm South Cemetery, renowned for its combination of classic Greek architectural sense with the modern.
	1941 Frank Whittle (*b* 1907) first flies the Gloster E28/29 air frame to which had been fitted his jet engine, invented 1937.	**1941–2** Ashile Gorky (1904–48) paints *Mojave*, an influential work on the emerging American school of abstract art.
1941 Louis Aragon (1897–1982) publishes *Le Crève-coeur*, and becomes one of the most popular French Resistance poets.		**1942** Edward Hopper (1882–1967), exponent of the American scene, paints *Nighthawks*, a scene of loneliness and desolation. Alexander Calder (1898–1976) creates *Horizontal Spines*, an example of his developed mobile or 'four-dimensional drawings'.
1942 Albert Camus (1913–60) publishes *L'Étranger*, the first of his novels in which he explores the implications of the 'absurd' nature of the human condition.	**1942** Fermi organizes the first controlled, self-sustaining nuclear reaction in Chicago – the ancestor of all nuclear weapons and nuclear power plants.	**1943** Wassily Kandinsky (1866–1944) paints one of his last abstracts, *Circle and Square No. 716*. Barbara Hepworth (1903–75), an important figure in abstract art in Britain, creates *Wave*, a characteristic sculpture of painted wood and string. Henry Moore creates his *Madonna and Child* for a Northampton church.
1943 Jean-Paul Sartre (1905–80), the principal exponent of Existentialism in France, publishes *L'Être et le néant*.	**1943** Selman Waksman and A. Schatz discover streptomycin, the first important specific agent effective in the treatment of human tuberculosis.	

Modern Times

MUSIC AND MUSICIANS	POLITICS, WAR AND RULERS
1944 Copland composes his *Appalachian Spring*. Tippett's *A Child of our Time* given, Morley College, London.	**1944** Allied invasion of Europe – D-Day. Offensives against Germany on all fronts. Attempted assassination of Hitler fails. Warsaw rising begins. Red Army marches into Hungary.
1945 *Peter Grimes* by Benjamin Britten (1913–76) given, Sadler's Wells, London. Strauss composes his *Metamorphosen*, Stravinsky his Symphony in C. Bartók (64) dies, New York. Webern (61) dies, Mittersill. Mascagni (81) dies, Rome.	**1945** Yalta conference between Roosevelt, Stalin and Churchill. Suicide of Hitler and surrender of Germany, which is divided into four occupation zones. Atomic bombs dropped on Hiroshima and Nagasaki before Japan surrenders. War ends with Russia in control of eastern Europe. Civil war in China. 29 nations form the United Nations.
1946 First staging of Prokofiev's *War and Peace* (begun in 1941); Prokofiev continues to revise it until 1953. Weill's *Street Scene* given, New York. International Summer Courses for New Music established, Darmstadt. Elliott Carter (*b* 1908) composes his Piano Sonata. Manuel de Falla (69) dies, Alta Gracia.	**1946** First meeting of UN General Assembly. Nuremberg Trials – 13 Nazis sentenced to death. Zionists boycott London conference on Palestine.
1947 Vaughan Williams completes his Sixth Symphony. *Dantons Tod* by Gottfried von Einem (*b* 1918) given, Salzburg. Milton Babbitt (*b* 1916) composes his *Three Compositions for Piano*. Edinburgh Festival founded. Reynaldo Hahn (71) dies, Paris.	**1947** Marshall Aid programme outlined for Europe's economic recovery. Indian Independence proclaimed, and partition between India and Pakistan, followed by violence between Muslims and Hindus. USSR demands German reparations.
1948 Britten and Peter Pears found the Aldeburgh Festival. Messiaen completes his *Turangalîla-Symphonie*. Schaeffer coins the term *musique concrète*. Hans Eisler returns to Germany following the McCarthy drive against Communists in the USA. First long-playing records issued in the USA. Umberto Giordano (81) dies, Milan. Franz Léhar (78) dies, Bad Ischl. Ermanno Wolf-Ferrari (72) dies, Venice.	**1948** Brussels treaty between Britain, France, Belgium, Netherlands and Luxembourg. British mandate in Palestine ends and the State of Israel proclaimed. Berlin blockade to September 1949. Apartheid becomes policy in South Africa.
1949 Harry Partch (1901–74) publishes his *Genesis of a Music*. First volumes of *Die Musik in Geschichte und Gegenwart*, edited by Friedrich Blume, published. Theodor Adorno publishes his *Philosophie der neuen Musik*. Messiaen composes his *Modes de valeurs et d'intensités*. Nikos Skalkottas (45) dies, Athens. Hans Pfitzner (80) dies, Salzburg. Strauss (85) dies, Garmisch-Partenkirchen. European Broadcasting Union formed to facilitate the exchange of music broadcasts.	**1949** Statute of Council of Europe signed. Israel admitted to UN. Communists proclaim the People's Republic of China under Mao Tse-Tung and Nationalists withdraw to Taiwan. Foundation of German Federal Republic.
1950 Schaeffer and Pierre Henry compose their *Symphonie pour un homme seul*. Dallapiccola's *Il prigioniero* first staged, Florence. Weill (50) dies, New York. Charles Koechlin (83) dies, Le Canadel.	**1950** Formation of NATO to counteract Russian threat. Korean war begins. USSR announces possession of the atomic bomb. Chinese troops occupy Tibet.

LITERATURE, PHILOSOPHY, RELIGION	SCIENCE, TECHNOLOGY, DISCOVERY	FINE ARTS AND ARCHITECTURE
1944 Alberto Moravia (*b* 1907), one of the greatest Italian writers of the century, publishes *Agostino*, a novel of adolescence.	**1944** Building of second uranium pile in Tennessee, for the manufacture of plutonium for an atomic bomb.	
1945 Karl Popper (*b* 1902) publishes *The Open Society and its Enemies*. Shintoism abolished in Japan. After 1945, Communist regimes in Eastern Europe persecute Christian churches.	**1945** The first atomic bomb is dropped on Hiroshima, revealing to the world the ability of mankind to release and control atomic energy. Developments in radar and other scientific inventions of the war years are made public.	**1945** Francis Bacon (1909–92) exhibits the controversial *Three Studies for Figures at the Base of a Crucifixion*. Mark Chagall (1887–1985) designs sets and costumes for *The Firebird* ballet in New York.
1947 Discovery of the Dead Sea Scrolls: a collection of Hebrew and Aramaic manuscripts belonging to a Jewish library in the early Christian era, and of supreme paleographic importance. Primo Levi (1919–87) writes *Se questo è un uomo*, memoirs of his experience in Auschwitz.	**1946** Discovery by Appleton and Hey that sun spots emit radio waves. First all-electric digital computer built at Pennsylvania University.	**1947** Le Corbusier builds the Unité d'Habitation, Marseilles (–1952), a block with accommodation for some 1800 inhabitants.
	1947 First atomic pile in Britain established at Harwell. Lord Patrick Blackett propounds that 'all massive rotating bodies are magnetic'.	**1948** Jackson Pollock (1912–56) paints *Composition Number One*. Andrew Wyeth (*b* 1917), popular American painter, comes to public attention with *Christina's World*. Pier Luigi Nervi (1891–1979) designs the Exhibition Hall, Turin, an outstanding large-scale prefabrication and inspired design.
1948 Bertrand Russell (1872–1970) publishes his last great work, *Human Knowledge, its Scope and Limits*. Inauguration of the World Council of Churches with representatives from 144 churches in 44 countries.	**1948** P. Goldsmith invents the long-playing record in the USA.	
1949 Simone de Beauvoir (*b* 1908) publishes her feminist essay, *Le Deuxième Sexe*. Gilbert Ryle (1900–76) publishes his best-known work, *The Concept of Mind*. George Orwell (Eric Arthur Blair, 1903–50) publishes his most famous political satire, *Nineteen Eighty-Four*.	**1949** Cortisone (isolated by Edward Kendall in 1935) first used on a human patient.	**1949** Graham Sutherland (1903–80) paints his *Portrait of Somerset Maugham*, a strikingly original realistic painting. Peter (*b* 1923) and Alison (*b* 1928) Smithson build the Hunstanton School, Norfolk (–1954), the first New Brutalist building.
	1950 Plutonium first separated from pitchblende concentrates by US Atomic Energy Commission. Plutonium first produced in UK at Windscale.	**1950** Alberto Giacometti (1901–66) creates *Seven Figures and a Head*. Alvar Aalto (1898–1976) designs the Town Hall, Säynätsalo (–1952).

MUSIC AND MUSICIANS	POLITICS, WAR AND RULERS
1951 French radio establishes a studio for electronic musical research under Schaeffer's direction. Electronic music studio founded at Cologne. Stravinsky's *The Rake's Progress* given, Venice. Britten's *Billy Budd* given, London. Royal Festival Hall opens in London. Karlheinz Stockhausen (*b* 1928) meets Messiaen and Pierre Boulez (*b* 1925) at Darmstadt; he composes *Kreuz-spiel*. Carter composes his First Quartet. Schoenberg (76) dies, Los Angeles.	**1951** Communist forces break through UN lines and take Seoul. Six European countries sign Treaty of Paris, embodying the Schumann plan.
1952 Cage produces *4' 33"* in which the performer makes no sound. Boulez completes *Structures Ia* for two pianos. Jean Barraqué (1928–73) composes his Piano Sonata. *Boulevard Solitude* by Hans Werner Henze (*b* 1926) given, Hanover. Hugo Alfvén (1872–1960) composes the last of his five symphonies. New York Pro Musica, an early music ensemble, founded.	**1952** Arab League Security Pact comes into force. Death of George VI; succeeded by Elizabeth II.
1953 Stockhausen lectures at Darmstadt. Luigi Nono (1924–90) completes his *Epitaffio per García Lorca*. Shostakovich composes his Tenth Symphony. Britten composes *Winter Words*. The Summer School of Music moves to Dartington Hall, Devon. Prokofiev (61) dies, Moscow. Arnold Bax (69) dies, Cork.	**1953** Tito elected President of Yugoslavia. Korean armistice signed, restoring status quo. Death of Stalin; Khrushchev begins his rise to power.
1954 Varèse composes *Déserts* with optional tapes. Witold Lutosławski (*b* 1913) completes his Concerto for Orchestra. Concert performance of Schoenberg's *Moses und Aron* (Acts 1 and 2) given, Hamburg. Iannis Xenakis (*b* 1922) completes *Metastasis*. Ives (79) dies, New York.	**1954** Nasser becomes head of state in Egypt.
1955 Boulez's *Le marteau sans maître* performed at Baden-Baden. Tippett's first major opera *The Midsummer Marriage* given, London. Luciano Berio (*b* 1925) and Bruno Maderna (1920–73) establish an electronic music studio in Milan. International Standards Organization, Stockholm, changes basic tuning pitch 'A' from 435 vibrations per second to 440. Honegger (63) dies, Paris.	**1955** End of three-power occupation of West Germany, who becomes a member of NATO. Austrian independence restored. Warsaw Pact formed in opposition to NATO.
1956 Stockhausen completes *Gesang der Jünglinge* and begins *Gruppen*, for three orchestras. Maderna composes *Notturno* for tape. The ballet *Spartacus* by Aram Khachaturian (1903–78) performed, Leningrad. Autumn festival of contemporary music founded, Warsaw.	**1956** Suez crisis. Israeli troops invade Egypt. Ceasefire with UN peace-keeping force. Hungarian revolution crushed by USSR. Mass treason arrests in South Africa. Pakistan proclaimed an Islamic republic.

LITERATURE, PHILOSOPHY, RELIGION	SCIENCE, TECHNOLOGY, DISCOVERY	FINE ARTS AND ARCHITECTURE
1951 J. D. Salinger (*b* 1919) publishes his best-known novel, *The Catcher in the Rye*. Paul Tillich (1886–1965), German-American theologian, writes his most important work, *Systematic Theology* (–1964), which has great impact.	**1951** First electric power produced from atomic energy at Arcon, Idaho, USA.	**1951** David Smith (1906–65), the most original and influential American sculptor of his time, creates *Hudson River Landscape*. Ossip Zadkine (1890–1967) creates the huge bronze *To a Destroyed City* (–1953), Rotterdam, a masterpiece of 20th-century sculpture.
1952 C. Cassola (*b* 1917) publishes *Fausto e Anna*, giving expression to a widespread belief that the moral and political goals of the Italian Resistance had not been met.	**1952** Britain becomes the chief exporter of radio-isotopes, which are widely used in scientific research, medicine and industry. First contraceptive tablet made from phosphorated hesperidin.	**1952** Marino Marini (1901–80), an outstanding Italian sculptor, creates *Horse and Rider*, one of his many explorations of the theme.
	1953 Edmund Hillary (*b* 1919) and Norgay Tenzing (*b* 1914) are the first to climb Mt Everest, the world's highest mountain. First announcement of the connection between cigarette smoking and lung cancer.	
1954 William Golding (*b* 1911) publishes *Lord of the Flies*, exposing the savagery that underlies man's true nature. Kingsley Amis (*b* 1922) publishes *Lucky Jim*.	**1954** First aircraft constructed with vertical takeoff.	**1954–8** Ludwig Mies van der Rohe (1886–1969) designs the Seagram Building, New York, one of his two classic skyscrapers. Basil Spence (1907–78) designs his best-known work, Coventry Cathedral (–1962), beside the ruins of the medieval foundation.
1955 Vladimir Nabokov (1899–1977), one of the most original prose writers of the 20th century, publishes the successful *Lolita*. Samuel Beckett (1906–90) publishes *Waiting for Godot*, one of the most influential plays of the post-war period. Pierre Teilhard de Chardin (1881–1955) publishes *Le phénomène humain*, an attempt to relate the Christian tradition to the contemporary scientific understanding of nature.	**1955** USA launches the first nuclear-powered submarine, the *Nautilus*, which in 1958 passes under the ice cap at the North Pole. Ultra-High-Frequency waves developed at Massachussetts Institute of Technology. **1956** Inauguration of the transatlantic cable telephone service. Anti-neutrons discovered by scientists at California University.	**1956** Richard Hamilton (*b* 1922) creates the photomontage *Just what is it that makes today's homes so different, so appealing?* considered to be the first Pop art work. Gio Ponti (1891–1979) designs his masterpiece, the Pirelli Skyscraper, Milan (–1958), abandoning the customary rectangular form.

Modern Times

MUSIC AND MUSICIANS	POLITICS, WAR AND RULERS
1957 *Illiac Suite for String Quartet* 'composed' by computer programmed with rules of Fux's counterpoint and modern serial techniques, under the supervision of Lejaren Hiller (*b* 1924). Poulenc's *Dialogues des Carmélites* given, Milan. Stravinsky completes *Agon*. *West Side Story* by Leonard Bernstein (1918–90), lyrics by Stephen Sondheim (*b* 1930), given, New York. Boulez starts his *Pli selon pli*, continuing to revise it over the succeeding years.	**1957** Reopening of the Suez Canal. Israeli–Arab conflict increasingly dominates Middle-Eastern politics.
1958 Berio composes the first of his *Sequenzas*. Messiaen completes his *Catalogues d'oiseaux*. Babbitt publishes his essay 'Who cares if you listen?'. Gian Carlo Menotti (*b* 1911) founds the Festival of Two Worlds at Spoleto, Italy. Vaughan Williams (85) dies, London.	**1958** Khrushchev becomes chairman of the USSR Council of Ministers. De Gaulle comes to power in France. Treaty of Rome establishes the European Economic Community.
1959 Columbia-Princeton Electronic Music Center established. Poulenc's *La voix humaine* given, Paris. Henk Badings (1907–87) composes *Salto mortale*, the first opera with entirely electronic music. Bohuslav Martinů (68) dies, Liestal.	**1959** Castro comes to power in Cuba. Unsuccessful rising in Tibet against China; the Dalai Lama goes into exile. Agreement signed between Turkey, Greece and Britain on Cyprus.
1960 Krzysztof Penderecki (*b* 1933) composes *Anaklasis* and his *Threnody for the Victims of Hiroshima*, Messiaen his *Chronochromie*. Berio composes *Circles* for his wife Cathy Berberian. György Ligeti (*b* 1923) composes *Atmosphères*, Stockhausen *Kontakte*. Mátyas Seiber (55) dies, Krüger National Park, South Africa.	**1960** Massacre of Black South Africans at Sharpeville; South African government bans the African National Congress and Pan-Africanist Congress. Brezhnev becomes President of the USSR. Crisis in the Congo.
1961 Lutosławski completes his *Venetian Games*, Nono his *Intolleranza 1960* and György Kurtag (*b* 1926) *The Sayings of Peter Bornemisza*. Cage publishes his book *Silence*. Percy Grainger (78) dies, New York.	**1961** South Africa leaves the Commonwealth. Overnight construction of the Berlin Wall.
1962 *Sur scène* by Mauricio Kagel (*b* 1931) given, Bremen. Benjamin Boretz founds *Perspectives of New Music*. Jacques Ibert (71) dies, Paris. Eisler (64) dies, Berlin.	**1962** Algeria becomes independent of France and joins the Arab League. Cuban crisis over USSR missile bases there.
1963 Roger Sessions (*b* 1896) completes *Montezuma*. Tippett completes his Concerto for Orchestra. Hindemith (68) dies, Frankfurt. Poulenc (64) dies, Paris.	**1963** De Gaulle vetoes Britain's entry to the EEC. Nuclear Test Ban Treaty between USA, USSR and UK. Overthrow of Vietnamese government in Vietnam. Assassination of President Kennedy (22 November).
1964 Britten's *Curlew River* given, Aldeburgh Festival. Stravinsky completes his *Variations* (in memoriam Aldous Huxley). Edison Denisov (*b* 1929) completes *The Sun of the Incas*. Terry Riley (*b* 1935) composes *In C*.	**1964** Nelson Mandela and seven other Black South Africans sentenced to life imprisonment. USA begins military involvement in Vietnam. Fall of Khrushchev.

LITERATURE, PHILOSOPHY, RELIGION	SCIENCE, TECHNOLOGY, DISCOVERY	FINE ARTS AND ARCHITECTURE
1957 Publication (in Italy) of Boris Pasternak's (1890–1960) *Dr Zhivago*, a witness to the experience of the Russian intelligentsia before, during and after the Revolution.	**1957** USSR launches Sputnik I and II, the first earth satellites. **1958** USA launches Explorer I, rocket Vanguard I and Atlas, and USSR launches Sputnik III.	**1957** H.-G. Adam (1904–67) creates the *Beacon of the Dead* monument at Auschwitz. Oscar Niemeyer (1907–84) designs all the main public buildings of Brasilia (–1979).
1958 Posthumous publication of *Il gattopardo* by Giuseppe di Lampedusa (1896–1957), a masterpiece of modern Italian literature.	**1959** USSR launches Lunik I, Lunik II which reaches the moon (12 September) and Lunik III which photographs it (4 October). USA physicist Luis Walter Alvarez discovers the neutral *xi–particle*.	**1958** Jacob Epstein (1880–1959) creates the enormous bronze group of *St Michael and the Devil* for Coventry Cathedral.
1959 Günter Grass (*b* 1927) publishes his highly original novel *Die Blechtrommel*.	**1960** Don Walsh (USA) and Jacques Piccard (France) dive in the bathyscape *Trieste* to 35,800 feet in the Pacific Ocean. USA launches the first weather satellite, Tiros I, to transmit TV images of cloud cover.	
1960 First visit of an Archbishop of Canterbury (Fisher) to the Vatican since 1397.	**1961** Yuri Gagarin of USSR becomes the first man in space, orbiting the earth in a six-ton satellite.	**1960** Henry Moore creates *Two-Piece Reclining Figure No. 1*, a precursor of the massive bronze groups of the later 1960s and 70s. Antonio Tápies (*b* 1923), the most important postwar Spanish artist, paints *Painting*, a rejection of artificiality.
1962 Second Vatican Council (–1965), convened by Pope John XXIII (*d* 1963) and continued by Paul VI, proposes great changes in the Roman Catholic Church, including the use of vernacular liturgies.	**1962** USA Telstar satellite circles the earth every 157.8 minutes and enables pictures from Maine to be seen in Europe. Side effects of the drug thalidomide cause the malformation of babies. **1963** Anti-di-zeno discovered, a fundamental atomic particle of contra-terrene matter. Rachel Carson's *The Silent Spring* draws attention to the dangers of chemical pest control.	**1962** Mies van der Rohe designs the New National Gallery, West Berlin, the culmination of his series of pavilion buildings.
1964 Philip Larkin (1922–92) publishes *The Whitsun Weddings*, poems including a range of melancholy urban and suburban landscapes.	**1964** Fred Hoyle and J. Narliker postulate a new theory of gravitation, solving the problem of inertia.	**1964** Bridget Riley (*b* 1931) paints *Crest*, the best-known work of the leading British Op artist.

Modern Times

MUSIC AND MUSICIANS	POLITICS, WAR AND RULERS
1965 Voltage-controlled synthesizer developed by Robert Moog. Ligeti completes *Aventures/Nouvelles Aventures*. Varèse (81) and Cowell (68) die, both in New York.	**1965** War between India and Pakistan. Unilateral Declaration of Independence in Rhodesia, declared illegal by Britain.
1966 The new Metropolitan Opera House, New York, opens with *Antony and Cleopatra* by Samuel Barber (1910–81). Henze's *The Bassarids* given, Salzburg. Penderecki's *St Luke Passion* given, Münster Cathedral. Stravinsky composes his *Requiem Canticles*. Ray Dolby introduces his noise reduction system for recordings.	**1966** Launch of the Great Proletarian Cultural Revolution in China. South African apartheid laws extended to south-west Africa.
1967 *Bomarzo* by Alberto Ginastera (1916–83) given, Washington. Steve Reich (*b* 1936) composes his *Piano Phase. Sergeant Pepper's Lonely Hearts Club Band* LP by the Beatles issued. David Munrow founds the Early Music Consort of London. Kodály (84) dies, Budapest.	**1967** Six-Day War between Israel, and Egypt, Syria and Jordan. Israelis occupy the West Bank of the Jordan, including all Jerusalem. Military coup in Greece; monarchy exiled.
1968 Stockhausen composes *Stimmung* and *Aus den sieben Tagen. Punch and Judy* by Harrison Birtwistle (*b* 1934) given, Aldeburgh. Berio's *Sinfonia* performed, New York (later expanded). London Sinfonietta founded.	**1968** Assassination of the US black leader Martin Luther King. Czechoslovakian revolt crushed by Warsaw Pact troops. Student riots in Paris. Election of President Nixon.
1969 Carter composes his Concerto for Orchestra. Cornelius Cardew (1936–81) forms his Scratch Orchestra. Peter Maxwell Davies composes *Eight Songs for a Mad King*, shortly before forming the Fires of London. Adorno (65) dies, Visp.	**1969** IRA violence causes British troops to be sent into Northern Ireland.
1970 Tippett's *The Knot Garden* given, London. Kagel makes his film *Ludwig van*.	**1970** Jordan expels Palestinians who create a base in Lebanon for attacks on Israel. Food riots in Poland.
1971 Shostakovich composes the last of his fifteen symphonies. Boulez publishes his *Boulez on Music Today*. Stravinsky (88) dies, New York. Ruggles (95) dies, Bennington, Vermont.	**1971** Independence of Bangladesh. Treaty banning nuclear weapons on the seabed signed by 40 countries. Mass demonstration in Washington against the Vietnam war.
1972 Maxwell Davies's *Taverner* given, London. Birtwistle composes *The Triumph of Time*. Stockhausen revises his *Momente*. Carter composes his Third Quartet. Duke Ellington (75) dies, New York.	**1972** First World Conference on the Human Environment meets. Britain assumes direct rule in Northern Ireland. End of Cultural Revolution in China.
1973 Britten's *Death in Venice* given, Aldeburgh. Maderna (53) dies, Darmstadt, shortly after completing his *Satyricon*. Barraqué (45) dies, Paris. Gian Francesco Malipiero (91) dies, Treviso.	**1973** Perón re-elected President in Argentina. Bhutto becomes Prime Minister of Pakistan. Arab-Israeli War. Britain joins the EEC.

LITERATURE, PHILOSOPHY, RELIGION	SCIENCE, TECHNOLOGY, DISCOVERY	FINE ARTS AND ARCHITECTURE
	1965 US satellite Mariner IV transmits close-up photos of Mars.	**1965** Jacques Ipoustéguy (*b* 1920) creates *Alexander in Front of Ecbatana*, treating the human figure against an architectural background. Donald Judd (*b* 1928), a leading Minimalist artist, creates *Untitled*, of galvanized iron boxes. J. Kosuth (*b* 1945), a pioneer of Conceptual art, creates his best-known work *One and Three Chairs*.
1966 Tom Stoppard (*b* 1937) publishes *Rosencrantz and Guildenstern are Dead*, making his reputation as a playwright.	**1966** US spacecraft Surveyor I lands on the moon and transmits TV images of the terrain. Soviet Lunik IX also lands.	
1967 Svetlana Alliluyeva, Stalin's daughter, flees to the West and publishes *Twenty Letters to a Friend*.	**1967** Biochemists at Stanford University produce synthetic version of DNA, the substance that controls heredity. Dr Christiaan Barnard performs the first human heart transplant operation, in South Africa.	**1966** Minoru Yamasaki (*b* 1912) designs the World Trade Centre, New York (–1973), with twin towers on delicate arcades.
1968 Pope Paul VI issues the encyclical *Humanae Vitae*, condemning all artifical birth control. Reaffirmed by John Paul II.		**1967** Completion of the Cathedral of Christ the King, Liverpool, designed by F. Gibberd (1908–84), celebrated for its 'Crown of Thorns'.
1969 Isaiah Berlin (*b* 1909) publishes *Four Essays on Liberty*, defending liberalism and moral pluralism.	**1969** Pulsating radio sources (pulsars) discovered by Hewish and Bell in UK. Apollo 11 lands lunar module on the moon's surface; Neil Armstrong is the first man to walk on the moon. Lunar samples brought back to earth by Apollo 11 and 12. Concorde, the Anglo-French supersonic aircraft, makes its first test flight.	**1968** P. Portoghesi (*b* 1931) designs the Church of the Sacra Famiglia, Salerno (–1974), based on complex circular geometrics.
1971 Publication in the West of Jerzy Andrzejewski's *The Appeal*, a Polish political novel.		
1972 Three Roman Catholic workers burn themselves to death in protest against Soviet religious oppression and compulsory inculcation of atheism. Laurens van der Post (*b* 1906) publishes *A Story like the Wind*, an account of traditional African negro life.	**1970** USSR Luna XVII lands a self-propelled eight-wheel vehicle on the moon, and Venera 7, an unmanned Soviet spacecraft, lands on Venus.	**1970** David Hockney (*b* 1937), the best-known British artist of his generation, paints the striking portrait *Mr and Mrs Clark and Percy*.
	1971 USSR soft-lands a space capsule on Mars. US astronomers discover two 'new' galaxies adjacent to the Milky Way.	**1971** Ieoh Ming Pei (*b* 1917) designs the East Wing of the National Gallery of Art in Washington DC (–1978), turning towards a monumentality of simple, stereometric forms.
1973 Australian Patrick White (*b* 1912) wins the Nobel Prize for Literature for *The Eye of the Storm*. M. Dummett (*b* 1925) publishes *Frege: Philosophy of Language*, his first work.	**1973** US spaceprobe Pioneer 10 transmits TV pictures from within 81,000 miles of Jupiter.	**1973** Completion of the daring and original Sydney Opera House by the Danish Jørn Utzon (*b* 1918).

MUSIC AND MUSICIANS	POLITICS, WAR AND RULERS
1974 *Rites of Passage* by Peter Sculthorpe (*b* 1929) given at the newly completed Sydney Opera House. Philip Glass (*b* 1937) composes his *Music in Twelve Parts*. Partch (75) dies, San Diego. Milhaud (81) and Frank Martin (84) die, both in Geneva.	**1974** Deposition of Emperor Haile Selassie of Ethiopa. Resignation of Nixon over Watergate affair. Turkish invasion of Cyprus. Eva Perón succeeds her husband in Argentina.
1975 *Ratsumies* by Aulis Sallinen (*b* 1935) given, Savonlinna. *Einstein on the Beach*, Glass's first opera, given, Avignon. Dallapiccola (71) dies, Florence. Shostakovich (68) dies, Moscow. Arthur Bliss (83) dies, London.	**1975** Latin American Economic system set up by 23 countries. Creation of Economic Community of West African States. Death of Franco; King Juan Carlos becomes a constitutional monarch.
1976 Reich composes his *Music for Eighteen Musicians*, Henryk Górecki (*b* 1933) his Third Symphony. Boulez and Peter Eötvös found the Ensemble InterContemporain. Messiaen composes *Des canyons aux étoiles*. David del Tredici (*b* 1937) composes *Final Alice*.	**1976** Perón regime overthrown; Videla becomes President of Argentina. End of American involvement and reunification of Vietnam under communist regime. Death of Mao Tse-Tung.
1977 Boulez establishes the Institut de recherche et de co-ordination acoustique/musique (IRCAM), Paris. Tippett completes his Fourth Symphony. Toru Takemitsu (*b* 1930) composes *A Flock descends in the Pentagonal Garden*.	**1977** Military coup led by Zia overthows Bhutto in Pakistan. Brezhnev elected President of USSR Supreme Soviet.
1978 Ligeti's *Le grand macabre* given, Stockholm. *Lear* by Aribert Reimann (*b* 1936) given, Munich. Richard Steinitz founds the Huddersfield Contemporary Music Festival. Chávez (79) dies, Mexico City. Khachaturian (74) dies, Moscow.	**1978** Execution of Bhutto. Camp David Summit between President Carter, Sadat and Begin. First sea link since 1949 opened between China and Hong Kong. Vietnamese troops invade Cambodia.
1979 Cage composes his *Roaratorio, an Irish Circus on Finnegans Wake*. Sondheim's *Sweeney Todd* given, New York. John Adams (*b* 1947) composes his *Shaker Loops*. Roy Harris (81) dies, Santa Monica. Paul Dessau (84) dies, Berlin. Nadia Boulanger (92) dies, Paris.	**1979** Overthrow of the Shah of Iran; a fundamentalist Islamic Republic set up under influence of Ayatollah Khomeini. Margaret Thatcher becomes the first woman Prime Minister of Britain. Peace treaty between Israel and Egypt as a result of Camp David Summit. American hostages taken in Iran.

LITERATURE, PHILOSOPHY, RELIGION	SCIENCE, TECHNOLOGY, DISCOVERY	FINE ARTS AND ARCHITECTURE
1974 Aleksandr Solzhenitsyn (*b* 1918) is expelled by the Soviet Government for *The Gulag Archipelago*, published in 1973 in the West.	**1974** US Skylab IV astronauts spend 84 days in space. US Mariner 10 transmits detailed pictures of Venus and Mercury. Discovery of the *psi*-particle independently by Burton Richter and Samuel Ting (both USA).	
1975 Anthony Powell (*b* 1905) publishes the final volume of the series of novels *A Dance to the Music of Time*, which is greeted with more acclaim than any other postwar work.	**1975** USSR Soyuz 19 and US Apollo 15 spacecraft link up for 44 hours in outer space in first ever joint venture, watched by TV viewers all over the world. Theory of the Big Bang in the creation of the universe is vindicated by analysis of background radiation which could only have been given off immediately after the primal explosion.	**1975** Charles Moore (*b* 1925), a leading Post-Modernist, designs the Piazza d'Italia in New Orleans (–1980).
	1976 Dr Har Khorana (USA) announces the successful synthesis of a wholly man-made gene.	**1976** H. Hertzberger (*b* 1932), a leading Post-Structuralist, designs the Vredenburg Music Centre, Utrecht (–1978).
1977 USSR agrees, for the first time since 1917, to allow copies of the Torah to be sent from the USA to the Moscow synagogue.	**1977** Results from the seabed-drilling research ship *Glomar Challenger* prove the repeated emptying and filling of the Mediterranean *c* 5½ million years ago, explaining the interchanging of African and European animals.	**1977** Completion of the Pompidou Centre, Paris, by Renzo Piano (*b* 1937) and Richard Rogers (*b* 1933), a structuralist tour de force.
1978 Election of Pope John Paul II, the first non-Italian pope since 1522.	**1978** Birth of the world's first test-tube baby, Louise Brown. Wrecking of the supertanker *Amoco Cadiz* off Brittany, the world's worst oil-tanker pollution disaster until 1989.	**1978** Completion of the Sainsbury Centre for the Visual Arts at the University of East Anglia by Nigel Foster (*b* 1935), a Post-Modernist building.
1979 After a revival of militant Islam in 1978, the Great Mosque in Mecca is besieged and occupied by Sunni Muslim puritans, with several hundred killed and wounded.	**1979** US Voyager 1 passes close by Jupiter and sends back pictures of the planet and its four giant moons, the so-called Galilean satellites.	

MUSIC AND MUSICIANS	POLITICS, WAR AND RULERS
1980 *Jesu Hochzeit* by Gottfried von Einem (*b* 1918) given, Vienna. Jonathan Harvey (*b* 1939) composes *Mortuos plango, vivos voco*. *The New Grove Dictionary of Music and Musicians*, edited by Stanley Sadie, published.	**1980** Declaration of Zimbabwe Republic (Rhodesia). Soviet invasion of Afghanistan. Polish strikes in Baltic shipyards; recognition of Solidarity as an independent trade union. Trial of Mao's widow Jiang Qing and 9 others on treason charges. Election of President Reagan. Outbreak of Iran-Iraq war.
1981 *Donnerstag aus Licht*, the first of Stockhausen's projected seven-evening cycle *Licht* given, Milan. Boulez's *Répons* performed at Donaueschingen. Arvo Pärt (*b* 1935) completes his *St John Passion*. William Bolcom (*b* 1938) completes his *Songs of Innocence and Experience*. Samuel Barber (70) dies, New York.	**1981** Release of American hostages in Iran. 10 IRA hunger strikers die. Worst street violence in Britain this century. Assassination of President Sadat of Egypt. Imposition of martial law in Poland.
1982 Ligeti composes his Horn Trio, George Benjamin (*b* 1960) his *At First Light*. Carl Orff (86) dies, Munich.	**1982** Britain sends task force to the Falklands after Argentinian invasion. Israeli air attacks against Beirut, Tyre and Sidon. Army assumes control in Argentina. Death of Brezhnev; succeeded by Andropov.
1983 Messiaen's *Saint François d'Assise* given, Paris. Henze's *The English Cat* given, Schwetzingen. The first compact discs issued. George Auric (84) dies, Paris. Werner Egk (82) dies, Inning. Ginastera (67) dies, Geneva. Walton (80) dies, Ischia.	**1983** Famine in Ethiopia. Violence against Tamil community begins in Sri Lanka. Civil war in Lebanon; US warships bombard Druze areas near Beirut. US marines invade Grenada. First Cruise missiles arrive in UK amidst violent demonstrations. USSR walks out of arms limitation talks in Geneva.
1984 Berio's *Un re in ascolto* given, Salzburg. Glass's *Akhnaten* given, Stuttgart. Reich composes his *Desert Music*, Birtwistle his *Secret Theatre*, Maxwell Davies his Third Symphony.	**1984** Shia Muslim and Druze militia overrun West Beirut. Death of Andropov; succeeded by Chernenko. Signing of Anglo-Chinese Agreement on the future of Hong Kong.
1985 Alfred Shnitke (*b* 1934) composes his Viola Concerto. Carter composes his *Penthode*. Celebration of the tercentenaries of Bach and Handel gives added impetus to the Early Music movement. Sessions (88) dies, Princeton.	**1985** Death of Chernenko; succeeded by Gorbachev. Renewal of Warsaw pact for 30 years. President Botha reaffirms apartheid in South Africa. Geneva summit between Gorbachev and Reagan. Zia ends martial law in Pakistan. Heavy fighting in Lebanon.
1986 Birtwistle's *The Mask of Orpheus* given, London. *X* by Anthony Davis (*b* 1951) given, Philadelphia. Maurice Duruflé (84) dies, Paris.	**1986** Communist Party Conference in Moscow approves changes to the membership of the Central Committee and Politburo. US aircraft raid Libya. State of emergency imposed in South Africa and reporting restrictions introduced.

LITERATURE, PHILOSOPHY, RELIGION	SCIENCE, TECHNOLOGY, DISCOVERY	FINE ARTS AND ARCHITECTURE
1980 Evidence of more tolerant attitudes to religion in China; Christian, Islamic and Taoist activities permitted, and Buddhism in Tibet.	**1980** Insulin produced by genetically-engineered bacteria tested in diabetic humans. US Voyager 1 flies past Saturn and sends pictures over 900 million miles to Earth.	**1980–81** The Royal Academy exhibition *A New Spirit in Painting* stimulates contemporary art.
	1981 The first re-usable US space shuttle *Columbia* makes its maiden flight.	**1982** The US architects Skidmore, Owings & Merrill complete the Haj Terminal at King Abdul Aziz Airport, Jeddah, the largest tent-roof construction in the world.
1982 Gabriel García Márquez (*b* 1928), major Colombian novelist, publishes *Chronicle of a Death Foretold*.	**1982** Identification of Acquired Immune Deficiency Syndrome (AIDS). An 8 lb rock, found in the Antarctic, is identified as having come from Mars, having spent some 2 million years en route to Earth.	**1983** Opening of the Burrell Collection, Glasgow, in a building designed by Barry Gasson & Associates.
1983 Ayatollah Khomeini declares that Islam is the 'religion of the sword' which can 'survive only through war'.	**1983** International physicists announce the discoveries of W-boson and Z-boson, fundamental particles, a step towards vindication of the Grand Unification Theory. Publication of a report predicting the warming-up of the Earth ('greenhouse effect'). Also, prediction of the 'nuclear winter' after nuclear war, destroying civilization.	**1984** Reopening of the Museum of Modern Art, New York, with its new extension designed by Cesar Pelli (*b* 1926), and incorporating a tower of exclusive condominiums. The Neue Staatsgalerie extension in Stuttgart by James Stirling (*b* 1926) is described as a major step towards reconciling heroic public architecture with humane and democratic values.
1984 L. Boff, a Franciscan from Brazil, appears before the doctrinal office of the Vatican to answer charges on 'liberation theology'. Siege of the Golden Temple and 37 other Sikh shrines in the Punjab, causing disturbances in India and overseas. Czech exile Milan Kundera (*b* 1929) publishes *The Unbearable Lightness of Being*, to great critical acclaim.	**1984** Particle physicists at Geneva discover the so-called top quark, 6th member of the family, further evidence of an under-lying symmetry in nature.	
1985 Posthumous publication of V. Grossman's *Life and Fate*, a picture of Russia at war unpublished in the USSR.	**1985** The most detailed radio map of the galaxy to date confirms the existence of black holes in the Milky Way and other galaxies.	**1985** Paris commissions a sculpture of clock faces from A. Arman (*b* 1928) and 14 other contemporary artists in a bid to reclaim artistic supremacy lost to New York and London. Completion of Nigel Foster's Hong Kong and Shanghai Bank HQ, a tall sophisticated design and a revolutionary break from the conventional type of office of the last 30 years.
	1986 Disaster at Chernobyl nuclear power station. Voyager 2 flies close to Uranus, revealing a complex world unlike anything previously seen in the solar system.	**1986** Completion of the Lloyds Building, London, by Richard Rogers, a functionalist design that displays structural and service elements on the exterior.

Modern Times

MUSIC AND MUSICIANS	POLITICS, WAR AND RULERS
1987 Adams's *Nixon in China* given, Houston. Dmitry Kabalevsky (82) dies, Moscow. Badings (80) dies, Maarheeze. Morton Feldman (61) dies, Buffalo.	**1987** Shia Amal militia besiege Palestinian refugee camps in Lebanon. Congressional hearings into the Iran–Contra arms scandal in USA. Gorbachev outlines radical reorganization of the Soviet economy. Collapse of world stock markets.
1988 Lutosławski completes *Chain 2*.	**1988** Ethnic minority violence begins in USSR. Anti-Chinese protests in Tibet. Communist Party Conference approves 'perestroika'. End of Iran–Iraq war. Death of President Zia; Benazir Bhutto elected Prime Minister of Pakistan. Flooding in Bangladesh leaves 25 million homeless.
1989 Carter completes his *Three Occasions* for orchestra. Franco Donatoni (*b* 1927) completes *Cloches*. The writer and musicologist Carl Dahlhaus (60) dies, Berlin. Virgil Thomson (92) dies, New York.	**1989** First multi-party elections for Congress of People's Deputies in USSR. Withdrawal of Soviet troops from Afghanistan. Solidarity legalized and political reforms in Poland. Namibian independence. Restoration of full relations between USSR and China. Massacre of peacefully demonstrating students in Peking. Nicolae and Elena Ceausescu shot after overthrow of communist regime in Romania.
1990 Benjamin composes *Upon Silence*. Copland (80) and Bernstein (72) die, both in New York. Nono (66) dies, Venice.	**1990** Release of Nelson Mandela after 27 years in prison; President F. W. De Klerk announces gradual abolition of apartheid. Lithuania becomes first Soviet republic to declare independence. Iraqi forces invade Kuwait. Demolition of the Berlin Wall symbolizes reunification of Germany. Assassination of Rajiv Gandhi.
1991 Adams's *The Death of Klinghoffer* given, Brussels. Jean Langlais (84) dies. Krenek (91) dies, Palm Springs.	**1991** Gulf War. Civil war in Ethiopia following flight of President Mengistu. Presidents Bush and Gorbachev sign Strategic Arms Reduction Treaty. Outbreaks of violence between Croat and Serb communities signal descent of former Yugoslavia into civil war. Soviet Union formally disbanded; republics form Commonwealth of Independent States. Leaders of European Community sign Maastricht Treaty on political and economic union. Boris Yeltsin becomes President of Russia.
1992 Birtwistle's *Gawain* given, Royal Opera House, London. Glass's *The Voyage* given, Metropolitan, New York. Messiaen (83) dies, Paris. Cage (79) dies, New York.	**1992** Independence of Slovenia and Croatia recognized. Increasing terror in Bosnia and imposition of policy of 'ethnic cleansing' against Muslims lead to dispatch of UN forces. Bill Clinton elected President of the USA.

LITERATURE, PHILOSOPHY, RELIGION	SCIENCE, TECHNOLOGY, DISCOVERY	FINE ARTS AND ARCHITECTURE
1987 Nigerian Chinua Achebe publishes *The Anthills of the Savannah*, telling of power struggles in an emergent African nation.	**1987** P. Solomon puts forward evidence to support the theory that the thinning of the ozone layer over Antarctica each autumn is due to chlorinated fluorocarbon (CFC) gases drifting into the stratosphere.	**1987** Renzo Piano completes the ultra-modern De Mencil Museum in Houston, Texas.
1988 Millennium of Orthodox Christianity in Russia celebrated with far greater freedom than anticipated, due to *glasnost*.	**1988** A rash of incidents involving unauthorized tapping into computers ('hacking') raises fears about the security of the world's computer systems. Stephen Hawking's *A Brief History of Time* published, quickly becoming a bestseller.	**1988** *False Start* by Jasper Johns (*b* 1930) is sold at auction for over $17 million, the world record both for contemporary art and for a work by a living artist. Opening of the Tate Gallery, Liverpool, by James Stirling, with a survey of 20th-century British sculpture.
1989 Ayatollah Khomeini calls for the death of Salman Rushdie for his novel *The Satanic Verses*, causing racial tension in Britain. Emperor Akihito ascends throne of Japan; does not claim divinity.	**1989** Wreck of the Exxon II oil tanker off Alaska. Voyager 2 passes 3,000 miles from Neptune's North Pole and takes close-up photographs of its large moon, Triton.	**1989** Controversy in the US Congress over the funding of 'objectionable' art – the supposedly obscene and blasphemous images of Mapplethorpe and Serrano.
1990 Militant Hindus begin construction of temple to Rama at Ayodha (Uttar Pradesh) on the site of a mosque and an ancient Hindu shrine; ensuing disorder claims 380 lives and brings down the government.	**1990** Launch of the Hubble Space Telescope on US shuttle *Discovery*. Completion of service tunnel of Channel Tunnel.	**1990** Controversial restoration of the Sistine Chapel ceiling unveiled. Van Gogh's *Portrait of Dr Gachet* becomes the world's most expensive painting, sold for nearly £50 million in New York.
	1991 Eruption of Mount Pintaubo in the Philippines, the greatest volcanic activity of the century. Discovery of 'Ötze', Bronze Age man preserved in ice in the Tyrol, complete with tools and food supply. Total eclipse of the sun visible from Hawaii for 4 minutes (next not due for 150 years).	**1991** The architect Robert Venturi is awarded the Pritzker Prize.
1992 Synod of the Church of England votes in favour of the ordination of women. Pope John Paul II issues a revised list of 'occasions of sin'; he formally revokes the heresy charge against Galileo.	**1992** Rio de Janeiro 'Earth Summit' convenes. American astronauts recapture a stranded satellite in an unprecedented three-man space walk.	

Index

Page numbers in *italics* refer to captions to illustrations.

Modern Times